Laura Lemay
Rogers Cadenhead

SAMS
Teach Yourself

Java™ 2

in 21 Days

SECOND EDITION

SAMS
A Division of Macmillan USA
201 West 103rd St., Indianapolis, Indiana, 46290 USA

Sams Teach Yourself Java 2 in 21 Days, Second Edition

Copyright © 2000 by Sams Publishing

International Standard Book Number: 0-672-31958-6

Library of Congress Catalog Card Number: 00-105551

Printed in the United States of America

First Printing: September 2000

02   01   4   3

Trademarks

Warning and Disclaimer

ACQUISITIONS EDITOR
Mark Taber

DEVELOPMENT EDITOR
Scott Meyers

MANAGING EDITOR
Charlotte Clapp

PROJECT EDITOR
Carol Bowers

COPY EDITOR
Mike Henry

INDEXER
Sheila Schroeder

PROOFREADER
Jessica McCarty

TECHNICAL EDITOR
Richard Baldwin

INTERIOR DESIGNER
Gary Adair

COVER DESIGNER
Aren Howell

PRODUCTION
Ayanna Lacey

Contents at a Glance

	Introduction	1

WEEK 1 Java's Fundamental Concepts — 7

Day 1	21st Century Java	9
2	Object-Oriented Programming	35
3	The ABCs of Java	59
4	Working with Objects	85
5	Lists, Logic, and Loops	107
6	Creating Classes and Methods	133
7	Writing Java Applets	163

WEEK 2 Swing and Other Visual Java Programming — 193

Day 8	Working with Swing	195
9	Building a Swing Interface	223
10	Arranging Components on a User Interface	243
11	Responding to User Input	269
12	Color, Fonts, and Graphics	297
13	Threads and Animation	329
14	JavaSound	359

WEEK 3 Java's Advanced Features — 379

Day 15	Packages, Interfaces, and Other Class Features	381
16	Error Handling and Security	417
17	Handling Data Through Java Streams	443
18	Object Serialization and Reflection	469
19	Communicating Across the Internet	495
20	Working with JavaBeans	523
21	Java Database Connectivity and Data Structures	543

Appendixes

Appendix A	Configuring the Software Development Kit	571
B	Using a Text Editor with the Software Development Kit	583
C	The Software Development Kit	589
	Index	611

Contents

Introduction   **1**

WEEK 1   **Java's Fundamental Concepts**   **7**

DAY 1   **21st Century Java**   **9**

Exploring Java 2 10
    Java's Past, Present, and Future...11
    Interactive Web Programming 11
    Java Grew from a Little Oak 13
    Versions of the Language 14
    Java's Outlook 15
Why to Choose Java 16
    Java Is Object-Oriented 16
    Java Is Easy to Learn...17
    Java Is Platform Neutral 18
Diving into Java Programming 19
    Selecting a Java Development Tool..19
    Installing the Software Development Kit 20
Your First Java Program 25
    Creating the Source File 26
Summary 32
Q&A 32
Quiz...33
    Questions 33
    Answers 33
Exercises 34

DAY 2   **Object-Oriented Programming**   **35**

Thinking in Terms of Objects...36
Objects and Classes 37
    Object Reuse 38
Attributes and Behavior 40
    Attributes of a Class of Objects 40
    Behavior of a Class of Objects 41
    Creating a Class...42
    Running the Program..44
Organizing Classes and Class Behavior 47
    Inheritance 47
    Creating a Class Hierarchy 49
    Inheritance in Action 51

Single and Multiple Inheritance 53

Interfaces 53

Packages 53

Summary 54

Q&A 55

Quiz...56

Questions 56

Answers 56

Exercises 57

DAY 3 The ABCs of Java   **59**

Statements and Expressions 60

Variables and Data Types 61

Creating Variables 61

Naming Variables..63

Variable Types 64

Assigning Values to Variables 66

Constants 66

Comments 67

Literals 68

Number Literals 68

Boolean Literals..69

Character Literals 70

String Literals 71

Expressions and Operators 72

Arithmetic 72

More About Assignment 74

Incrementing and Decrementing 75

Comparisons 77

Logical Operators 78

Operator Precedence 79

String Arithmetic..80

Summary 81

Q&A 83

Quiz...83

Questions 83

Answers 84

Exercises 84

DAY 4 Working with Objects   **85**

Creating New Objects...85

Using new...86

What new Does 88

A Note on Memory Management 88

Accessing and Setting Class and Instance Variables 89

Getting Values 89

Changing Values 90

Class Variables...91

Calling Methods 92

Nesting Method Calls 93

Class Methods 94

References to Objects 95

Casting and Converting Objects and Primitive Types 97

Casting Primitive Types...98

Casting Objects 99

Converting Primitive Types to Objects and Vice Versa................................100

Comparing Object Values and Classes 101

Comparing Objects 101

Determining the Class of an Object 103

Summary 104

Q&A 104

Quiz..105

Questions 105

Answers 106

Exercises 106

DAY 5 Lists, Logic, and Loops   **107**

Arrays 107

Declaring Array Variables 108

Creating Array Objects 109

Accessing Array Elements...110

Changing Array Elements 111

Multidimensional Arrays...113

Block Statements 114

if Conditionals 115

switch Conditionals 116

for Loops 121

while and do Loops 124

while Loops..124

do…while Loops 126

Breaking Out of Loops 127

Labeled Loops 127

The Conditional Operator 128

Summary 129

Q&A 129

Quiz...130

    Questions 130

    Answers 130

Exercises 131

DAY 6 Creating Classes and Methods   **133**

Defining Classes 134

Creating Instance and Class Variables 134

    Defining Instance Variables..134

    Class Variables 135

Creating Methods 135

    Defining Methods 136

    The this Keyword..138

    Variable Scope and Method Definitions 138

    Passing Arguments to Methods 140

    Class Methods 141

Creating Java Applications 143

    Helper Classes 144

Java Applications and Command-Line Arguments 144

    Passing Arguments to Java Applications..144

    Handling Arguments in Your Java Application 145

Creating Methods with the Same Name, Different Arguments 147

Constructor Methods..150

    Basic Constructors Methods 151

    Calling Another Constructor Method 152

    Overloading Constructors Methods...152

Overriding Methods 154

    Creating Methods That Override Existing Methods 154

    Calling the Original Method 156

    Overriding Constructors 156

Finalizer Methods 158

Summary..159

Q&A 159

Quiz...160

    Questions 160

    Answers 160

Exercises 161

DAY 7 Writing Java Applets   **163**

How Applets and Applications Are Different..164

Applet Security Restrictions 164

    Choosing a Java Version 165

Creating Applets 167
    Major Applet Activities 168
    An Example Applet 171
Including an Applet on a Web Page 174
    The <APPLET> Tag 174
    Testing the Result 175
    Putting Applets on the Web 176
More About the <APPLET> Tag 176
    ALIGN 177
    HSPACE and VSPACE 178
    CODE and CODEBASE 179
    The <OBJECT> Tag 179
Java Archives 180
Passing Parameters to Applets 181
Developing Java 2 Applets 185
    Using the Plug-in on a Web Page 186
    Running the Plug-in..187
Summary 189
Q&A 190
    Questions 190
    Answers 191
Exercises 191

WEEK 2 Swing and Other Visual Java Programming   **193**

DAY 8 Working with Swing   **195**

Creating an Application 196
    Creating an Interface 197
    Developing a Framework 199
    Closing a Window 202
    Creating a Component...204
    Adding Components to a Container 205
    Adding Components to an Applet...207
Working with Components 208
    Image Icons 209
    Labels...210
    Text Fields 211
    Text Areas 212
    Scrolling Panes 214
    Scrollbars...215
    Check Boxes and Radio Buttons..216
    Drop-Down Lists and Combo Boxes 218
Summary 220

Q&A 220
    Questions 221
    Answers 221
Exercises 221

DAY 9 Building a Swing Interface   **223**

Swing Features 224
    Setting the Look and Feel 224
    Standard Dialog Boxes 225
    An Example: The Info Application 229
    Sliders 232
    Scroll Panes 233
    Toolbars 235
    Progress Bars 237
Summary 240
Q&A 240
    Questions 240
    Answers 241
Exercises 241

DAY 10 Arranging Components on a User Interface   **243**

Basic Interface Layout 244
    Laying Out an Interface...244
    Flow Layout..245
    Grid Layout 247
    Border Layout 249
Mixing Layout Managers 250
Card Layout 251
Grid Bag Layout 253
    Designing the Grid 254
    Creating the Grid..255
    Determining the Proportions 258
    Adding and Arranging the Components 260
    Making Adjustments 262
Cell Padding and Insets 264
Summary 265
Q&A 265
    Questions 266
    Answers 266
Exercises 267

DAY 11 Responding to User Input   **269**

Event Listeners 269
  Setting Up Components...270
  Event-Handling Methods...271
Working with Methods 274
  Action Events 274
  Adjustment Events..275
  Focus Events 278
  Item Events 278
  Key Events...280
  Mouse Events 280
  Mouse Motion Events 281
  Window Events 282
  An Example: An RGB-to-HSB Converter 282
  Designing the Layout 283
  Defining the Subpanels 285
  Converting Between sRGB and HSB 287
  Handling User Events 291
Summary 295
Q&A 295
  Questions 295
  Answers 296
Exercises 296

DAY 12 Color, Fonts, and Graphics   **297**

Graphics Classes...298
Creating a Drawing Surface 298
  Casting a `Graphics2D` Object 299
  Creating an Application..299
  The Graphics Coordinate System 301
Drawing and Filling 301
  Lines 302
  Rectangles 302
  Polygons 304
  Ovals 306
  Arcs 306
  Copying and Clearing 310
Text and Fonts..311
  Creating `Font` Objects 311
  Drawing Characters and Strings 312
  Finding Information About a Font 312
Color 314
  Using `Color` Objects 315
  Testing and Setting the Current Colors 316

Advanced Graphics Operations Using Java2D..317
    User and Device Coordinate Spaces 317
    Specifying the Rendering Attributes 318
    Creating Objects to Draw 321
    Drawing Objects 323
Summary 326
Q&A 327
    Questions 327
    Answers 328
Exercises 328

Day 13 Threads and Animation   **329**

Creating Animation in Java 330
    Painting and Repainting 330
    Animating a Component 331
    Controlling Animation Through Threads 335
    Writing a Threaded Program..336
    A Threaded Clock Application 337
    Stopping a Thread 339
Retrieving and Using Images 343
    Getting Images...343
    Drawing Images..344
    A Note About Image Observers 345
Creating Animation Using Images 346
    Pixel Pete Takes a Walk..346
    Tracking Image Loading 355
Summary 356
Q&A 357
    Questions 358
    Answers 358
Exercises 358

Day 14 JavaSound   **359**

Retrieving and Using Sounds 360
JavaSound 363
    MIDI Files...363
    Playing a MIDI File 364
    Manipulating Sound Files 369
Summary 375
Q&A 376
    Questions 376
    Answers 377
Exercises 377

WEEK 3 Java's Advanced Features   379

   DAY 15 Packages, Interfaces, and Other Class Features   381

      Modifiers 382

         Access Control for Methods and Variables 383

      Static Variables and Methods 388

      Final Classes, Methods, and Variables 390

         Variables 391

         Methods 391

         Classes 392

      Abstract Classes and Methods 392

      Packages 393

      Using Packages 394

         Full Package and Class Names 395

         The `import` Declaration 395

         Name Conflicts 396

         A Note About `CLASSPATH` and Where Classes Are Located 397

      Creating Your Own Packages 397

         Picking a Package Name 397

         Creating the Folder Structure 398

         Adding a Class to a Package 398

         Packages and Class Access Control 398

      Interfaces 399

         The Problem of Single Inheritance 400

         Interfaces and Classes 400

         Implementing and Using Interfaces 401

         Implementing Multiple Interfaces 402

         Other Uses of Interfaces 403

      Creating and Extending Interfaces 404

         New Interfaces 404

         Methods Inside Interfaces 405

         Extending Interfaces 406

         Creating an Online Storefront 407

      Inner Classes 413

      Summary 415

      Q&A 415

         Questions 415

         Answers 416

      Exercises 416

   DAY 16 Error Handling and Security   417

      Exceptions, the Old and Confusing Way 418

      Java Exceptions...419

      Managing Exceptions 421

Exception Consistency Checking 421
Protecting Code and Catching Exceptions 422
The `finally` Clause..424
Declaring Methods That Might Throw Exceptions 426
The `throws` Clause..427
Which Exceptions Should You Throw?...428
Passing On Exceptions 428
`throws` and Inheritance 429
Creating and Throwing Your Own Exceptions...430
Throwing Exceptions...430
Creating Your Own Exceptions 431
Combining `throws`, `try`, and `throw`..431
When and When Not to Use Exceptions 432
When to Use Exceptions 432
When Not to Use Exceptions 433
Bad Style Using Exceptions 434
Using Digital Signatures to Identify Applets 434
A Digital Signature Example 436
Browser-Specific Signatures 437
Security Policies 438
Summary 439
Q&A 439
Questions 440
Answers 441
Exercises 441

DAY 17   Handling Data Through Java Streams   443

Introduction to Streams...444
Using a Stream 444
Filtering a Stream 445
Byte Streams 446
File Streams 446
Filtering a Stream 450
Byte Filters 450
Character Streams 458
Reading Text Files..458
Writing Text Files 461
Files and Filename Filters..462
Summary 465
Q&A 465
Questions 466
Answers 466
Exercises 466

DAY 18 Object Serialization and Reflection **469**

Object Serialization..470

Object Output Streams 472

Object Input Streams 475

Transient Variables 477

Inspecting Classes and Methods with Reflection...............................478

Inspecting and Creating Classes 478

Working with Each Part of a Class 480

Inspecting a Class 482

Remote Method Invocation..485

RMI Architecture...485

Creating RMI Applications 487

Summary 492

Q&A 493

Questions 493

Answers 494

Exercises 494

DAY 19 Communicating Across the Internet **495**

Networking in Java 496

Creating Links Inside Applets...496

Opening Web Connections 499

Opening a Stream over the Net 500

Sockets...504

Socket Servers 508

Implementing the Server 510

Testing the Server 518

Summary 520

Q&A 520

Questions 521

Answers 522

Exercises 522

DAY 20 Working with JavaBeans **523**

Reusable Software Components 524

The Goal of JavaBeans 525

How JavaBeans Relates to Java...526

The JavaBeans API 527

Development Tools 528

JavaBeans Development Kit 529

Working with JavaBeans...531

Bean Containers...531

Placing a Bean 532

Adjusting a Bean's Properties 533
Creating Interactions Between Beans 535
Creating a JavaBeans Program 537
Working with Other JavaBeans..538
Summary 539
Q&A 540
Questions 540
Answers 541
Exercises 541

DAY 21 Java Database Connectivity and Data Structures   543

Java Database Connectivity 544
Database Drivers 545
The JDBC-ODBC Bridge 546
Connecting to an ODBC Data Source...547
JDBC Drivers 553
Data Structures 555
Java Data Structures 556
Iterator 557
Bit Sets..558
Vectors 560
Stacks..563
Map 565
Hash Tables 566
Summary 568
Q&A 569
Questions 569
Answers 570
Exercises 570

Appendixes

Appendix A Configuring the Software Development Kit   571

Using a Command-Line Interface 571
Opening Folders in MS-DOS 573
Creating Folders in MS-DOS 574
Running Programs in MS-DOS...575
Configuring the Software Development Kit...577
Setting Up the PATH Command 577
Setting Up the CLASSPATH Command 579
UNIX Configuration 581
Fixing Class Not Found Errors on Other Platforms 581

Appendix B Using a Text Editor with the Software Development Kit   **583**

Choosing a Text Editor 583
Creating a File Association in Windows..585
    Deleting an Existing File Association 586
    Creating a New Association 587
    Associating an Icon with a File Type 587

Appendix C The Software Development Kit   **589**

An Overview of the SDK 590
The java Interpreter 591
The javac Compiler...592
The appletviewer Browser 594
The javadoc Documentation Tool 598
The jdb Debugger...602
    Debugging Applications 603
    Debugging Applets 605
    Advanced Debugging Commands 605
Using System Properties..606
Summary 608
Q&A 609

Index   **611**

About the Authors

ROGERS CADENHEAD is a writer and Web publisher who has written nine books on Internet-related topics, including *Sams Teach Yourself Java 2 in 24 Hours* and *Sams Teach Yourself Microsoft FrontPage 2000 in 24 Hours*, but not *Teach Yourself to Tell Time in 10 Minutes*. Cadenhead is also the author of a question-and-answer column for the *Fort Worth Star-Telegram* and Knight-Ridder News Service and the publisher of Cruel Site of the Day (`http://www.cruel.com`). He maintains this book's official World Wide Web site at `http://www.java21days.com`.

LAURA LEMAY is a technical writer and author. After spending six years writing software documentation for various computer companies in Silicon Valley, she decided that writing books would be much more fun. In her spare time, she collects computers, email addresses, interesting hair colors, and nonrunning motorcycles. She is also the perpetrator of *Sams Teach Yourself Web Publishing with HTML in a Week* and *Sams Teach Yourself Perl in 21 Days*.

Dedication

With much love to the Metcalfes: Aunt Pam, Uncle Kirby, and Cousin Dustin. Pam was like a big sister to me growing up, which makes Dustin like a nephew and Kirby, like, my brother-in-law. (Y'know. Totally.) I still have unresolved issues with Pam for beating me so badly at the Archies boardgame in 1974 that I threw the board across the room instead of making my next move, but as a sign of my personal growth (and improved sportsmanship) 26 years later, I'm ready to agree to a rematch at a neutral site.—Rogers

To Eric, for all the usual reasons (moral support, stupid questions, comfort in dark times, brewing big pots of coffee).—LL

Acknowledgments

From Rogers Cadenhead:

In my eight prior books, I used the acknowledgements to list all the people that I "would like to thank." That phrase makes it sound as if I wanted to thank these people but have been prevented from doing so for some unspecified and possible sinister reason. That isn't the case—in these books, Macmillan gives me free rein to give thanks. So, I thank Macmillan, and I thank the people there who contributed so much to the book, including Mark Taber, Scott Meyers, Amy Patton, Mike Henry, Carol Bowers, Sheila Schroeder, Jessica McCarty, and Richard Baldwin, and I also thank agents David and Sherry Rogelberg. Finally, I thank my wife Mary Moewe and my sons, Max and Eli. I'm so thanking grateful to have you as my family I have trouble putting it into words—which means a lot, because anyone who reads the rest of this 14,000-page book knows I don't normally have trouble putting things into words.

From Laura Lemay:

To the folks on Sun's Java team, for all their hard work on Java, the language, and on the browser, and particularly to Jim Graham, who demonstrated Java and HotJava to me on very short notice in May 1995 and planted the idea for this book.

Special Thanks:

The authors would also like to thank readers who have sent helpful comments about corrections, typos, and suggested improvements regarding prior editions of this book. The list includes, but is not limited to, the following people: Lawrence Chang, Jim DeVries, Ryan Esposto, Bruce Franz, Owen Gailar, Rich Getz, Bob Griesemer, Jenny Guriel, Ben Hensley, Jon Hereng, Drew Huber, Natalie Kehr, Stephen Loscialpo, Brad Kaenel, Chris McGuire, Chip Pursell, Pranay Rajgarhia, Luke Shulenburger, Mike Tomsic, Joseph Walsh, Chen Yan, Kyu Hwang Yeon, and J-F. Zurcher.

Tell Us What You Think!

As the reader of this book, *you* are our most important critic and commentator. We value your opinion and want to know what we're doing right, what we could do better, what areas you'd like to see us publish in, and any other words of wisdom you're willing to pass our way.

You can fax, email, or write me directly to let me know what you did or didn't like about this book—as well as what we can do to make our books stronger.

Please note that I cannot help you with technical problems related to the topic of this book, and that due to the high volume of mail I receive, I might not be able to reply to every message.

When you write, please be sure to include this book's title and author as well as your name and phone or fax number. I will carefully review your comments and share them with the author and editors who worked on the book.

Fax: 317-581-4770

Email: webdev_sams@mcp.com

Mail: Mark Taber
        Associate Publisher
        Sams Publishing
        201 West 103rd Street
        Indianapolis, IN 46290 USA

Introduction

Some revolutions catch the world completely by surprise. The World Wide Web, Linux operating system, and personal digital assistants rose to prominence unexpectedly against conventional wisdom.

The remarkable success of the Java programming language, on the other hand, caught no one by surprise. Java has been the source of great expectations since its introduction more than five years ago. When Sun launched Java by incorporating it into Web browsers, a torrent of publicity welcomed the arrival of the new language. Anyone who passed within eyesight of a World Wide Web page, computer magazine, or newspaper business section knew about Java and how it was expected to change the way software is developed.

Sun Microsystems cofounder Bill Joy didn't hedge his bets at all when describing the company's new language. "This represents the end result of nearly 15 years of trying to come up with a better programming language and environment for building simpler and more reliable software," he proclaimed.

In the years that have passed, Java has lived up to a considerable amount of its hype. The language is becoming as much a part of software development as the liquid of the same name. One kind of Java keeps programmers up nights. The other enables programmers to rest easier after they develop software.

Java was originally considered a technology for enhancing Web sites, and it's still being put to that use today—the AltaVista search engine reports that more than 13 million Web pages contain a Java program.

However, each new release of Java strengthens its capabilities as a general-purpose programming language for environments other than a Web browser. Java is being put to use today in desktop applications, Internet servers, middleware, personal digital assistants, embedded devices, and many other environments.

Now in its fourth major release—Java 2 version 1.3—the Java language is a full-featured competitor to other general-purpose development languages such as C++, Perl, Visual Basic, and Delphi.

You might be familiar with Java programming tools such as Symantec Visual Café, Borland JBuilder, and Sun Forté for Java. These programs make it possible to develop functional Java programs, but the best way to learn the full scope of the language is to work directly with it via Sun's Java Development Kit. The kit, which is available for free on the Web at http://java.sun.com, is a set of command-line tools for writing, compiling, and testing Java programs.

This is where *Sams Teach Yourself Java 2 in 21 Days, Second Edition,* comes in. You'll be introduced to all aspects of Java software development using the most current version of the language and the best available techniques.

By the time you're done, you'll be well acquainted with the reasons Java has become the most talked-about programming language of the past decade, and why it might be the most popular language of the next decade.

How This Book Is Organized

Sams Teach Yourself Java 2 in 21 Days covers the Java language and its class libraries in 21 days, organized as three separate weeks. Each week covers a different, broad area of developing Java applets and applications.

In the first week you learn about the Java language itself:

- Day 1 is the basic introduction: what Java is, why to learn the language, and how to get the software needed to create Java programs. You also create your first Java application.
- On Day 2, you explore basic object-oriented programming concepts as they apply to Java.
- On Day 3, you start getting down to details with the basic Java building blocks: data types, variables, and expressions such as arithmetic and comparisons.
- Day 4 goes into detail about how to deal with objects in Java—how to create them, how to access their variables and call their methods, and how to compare and copy them. You also get your first glance at the Java class libraries.
- On Day 5, you learn more about Java with arrays, conditional statements, loops, and linked lists.
- Day 6 fully explores the creation of classes—the basic building blocks of any Java program.
- Day 7 provides the basics of applets—how they differ from applications, how to create them, and how to use the Java Plug-in to run Java 2 applets in Netscape Navigator, Microsoft Internet Explorer, and other browsers.

Week 2 is dedicated primarily to graphical programming using Swing, which enables you to offer a graphical user interface in your programs:

- Day 8 begins a four-day exploration of visual programming. You learn how to create a graphical user interface using Swing, a set of classes introduced in Java 2 that greatly expands Java's user-interface capabilities.

- Day 9 covers more than a dozen interface components that you can use in a Java program, including buttons, text fields, sliders, scrolling text areas, and icons.
- Day 10 covers how to make a user interface look good using layout managers, a set of classes that determine how components on an interface will be arranged.
- Day 11 concludes the coverage of Swing with event-handling classes, which enable a program to respond to mouse clicks and other user interactions.
- On Day 12, you learn about the drawing shapes and characters on a user interface component such as an applet window—including coverage of the new Java2D classes introduced in Java 2.
- On Day 13, you create multimedia programs that use shapes, graphics files, and animation sequences. You also get your first experience with multithreading—a way to get your programs to handle multiple tasks at the same time.
- Day 14 adds another layer of multimedia with Java's sound capabilities. You add sounds to applets and applications, and work with JavaSound, an extensive new class library for playing, recording, and mixing sound.

Week 3 includes advanced topics such as JavaBeans and Java Database Connectivity:

- On Day 15, you learn more about interfaces and packages, which are useful for grouping classes and organizing a class hierarchy, as well as other advanced aspects of the core language itself.
- Day 16 covers exceptions—errors, warnings, and other abnormal conditions, generated either by the system or by you in your programs; you also learn about Java security.
- Day 17 covers input and output using streams, a set of classes that enable file access, network access, and other sophisticated data handling.
- Day 18 introduces object serialization, a way to make your objects exist even when no program is running. You save them to a storage medium such as a hard disk, read them into a program, and use them again as objects.
- On Day 19, you extend your knowledge of streams to write programs that communicate with the Internet, including socket programming and URL handling.
- Day 20 covers JavaBeans, a way to develop Java programs using the rapid application techniques that are so popular in tools such as Microsoft Visual Basic.
- Day 21 finishes with an in-depth exploration of how data is handled in Java—you connect to databases using Java Database Connectivity (JDBC) and JDBC-ODBC, and then learn about some sophisticated data structures such as vectors, stacks, and maps.

About This Book

This book teaches you all about the Java language and how to use it to create applications for any computing environment and applets that run in Web browsers. By the time you finish *Sams Teach Yourself Java 2 in 21 Days, Second Edition*, you'll have a well-rounded knowledge of Java and the Java class libraries and can develop your own programs for tasks such as data retrieval over the Internet, database connectivity, interactive gaming, and client/server programming.

You learn by doing in this book, creating several programs each day that demonstrate the topics being introduced. The source code for all these programs is available on the book's official Web site at `http://www.java21days.com`, along with other supplemental material such as answers to reader questions.

Who Should Read This Book

This book teaches the Java language to three groups:

- Novices who are relatively new to programming
- People who have been introduced to Java 1.1 or 1.0
- Experienced developers in other languages such as Visual C++, Visual Basic, or Delphi

You learn how to develop applets, which are interactive Java programs that run as part of a World Wide Web page, and applications, which are programs that run anywhere else. When you finish *Sams Teach Yourself Java 2 in 21 Days, Second Edition,* you'll be able to tackle any aspect of the language, and will be comfortable enough with Java to dive into your own ambitious programming projects—on the Web or off.

If you're still reasonably new to programming, or if you have never written a program before, you might be wondering whether this is the right book to tackle. Because all the concepts in this book are illustrated with working programs, you'll be able to work your way through the subject no matter your experience level. If you understand what variables, loops, and functions are, you'll be able to benefit from this book. The sorts of people who might want to read this book include you if any of the following rings true:

- You're a real whiz at HTML, understand CGI programming in Perl, Visual Basic, or some other language and want to move on to the next level in Web page design.
- You had some BASIC or Pascal in school, have a grasp of what programming is, and you've heard Java is easy to learn, powerful, and cool.

- You've programmed C and C++ for a few years, keep hearing accolades in association with Java, and want to see whether it lives up to its hype.
- You've heard that Java is great for Web programming and want to see how well it can be used for other software development.

If you have never been introduced to object-oriented programming, the style of programming embodied by Java, you don't have to worry. This book assumes no background in object-oriented design, and you get a chance to learn this groundbreaking development strategy as you're learning Java.

If you're a complete beginner in programming, this book might move a little fast for you. Java is a good language to start with, though, and if you take it slow and work through all the examples, you can still pick up Java and start creating your own programs.

How This Book Is Structured

This book is intended to be read and absorbed over the course of three weeks. During each week, you read seven chapters that present concepts related to the Java language and the creation of applets and applications.

Conventions

Note

A Note presents interesting, sometimes technical, pieces of information related to the surrounding discussion.

Tip

A Tip offers advice or offers an easier way to do something.

Caution

A Caution advises you of potential problems and helps you steer clear of disaster.

NEW TERM A new term is accompanied by a New Term icon, with the new term in *italics*.

Text that you type and text that should appear on your screen is presented in `monospace` type:

```
It will look like this
```

This font mimics the way text looks on your screen. Placeholders for variables and expressions appear in `monospace italic`.

The end of each lesson offers common questions asked about that day's subject matter with answers from the authors, a chapter-ending quiz to test your knowledge of the material, and two exercises that you can try on your own—with solutions on the book's official Web site at `http://www.java21days.com`.

WEEK 1

Java's Fundamental Concepts

1 21st Century Java

2 Object-Oriented Programming

3 The ABCs of Java

4 Working with Objects

5 Lists, Logic, and Loops

6 Creating Classes and Methods

7 Writing Java Applets

1

2

3

4

5

6

7

DAY 1

21st Century Java

> *Big companies like IBM are embracing Java far more than most people*
> *realize. Half of IBM is busy recoding billions of lines of software to Java. The*
> *other half is working to make Java run well on all platforms, and great on all*
> *future platforms.*
>
> —PBS technology commentator *Robert X. Cringely*

In 1995, when Sun Microsystems first released the Java programming language, it was an inventive toy for the World Wide Web that had the potential to be much more.

The word "potential" is an unusual compliment, because it comes with an expiration date. Sooner or later, potential must be realized or new words such as "letdown," "waste," and "major disappointment to your mother and I" are used in its place.

Now in its fourth major release, Java appears to have lived up to the expectations that accompanied its arrival. More than two million people have learned the language and are using it in places such as NASA, IBM, Kaiser Permanente, ESPN, and New York's Museum of Modern Art. More than 1,700 books have been written about it, according to the most recent *JavaWorld Magazine* count.

First used to create simple programs on World Wide Web pages, Java can be found today in each of the following places and many more:

- Web servers
- Relational databases
- Mainframe computers
- Telephones
- Orbiting telescopes
- Personal digital assistants
- Credit card–sized "smartcards"

Over the next 21 days, you will write Java programs that reflect how the language is being used in the 21st century. In some cases, this is very different than how it was originally envisioned.

Although Java remains useful for Web developers trying to enliven sites, it extends far beyond the Web browser. Java is now a popular general-purpose programming language, and some surveys indicate that there are more professional Java programmers than C++ programmers.

As you develop your skills during the 21 one-day tutorials in *Sams Teach Yourself Java 2 in 21 Days, Second Edition*, you'll be in a good position to judge whether the language has lived up to years of hype.

You'll also become a Java programmer with a lot of potential.

Exploring Java 2

Whenever Sun releases a new version of Java, it makes a free development kit available over the Web to support that version. This book was created using the kit, which is called Java 2 Software Development Kit, Standard Edition, Version 1.3.

Although the authors of a book like this have no business poking fun at long-winded titles, Sun has given its main Java development tool a name that's longer than most celebrity marriages.

For the sake of a few trees, in this book the language will usually be referred to simply as Java and the kit as SDK 1.3. You might see the kit referred to elsewhere as Java Development Kit 1.3 or SDK 1.3.

If you work your way through the 21 days of this book, you'll become well-versed in Java's capabilities, including graphics, file input and output, user-interface design, event handling, JavaBeans, and database connectivity. You will write programs that run on Web pages and others that run on your personal computer, Web servers, and other computing environments.

Today's goals are reasonably modest. You'll learn about the following topics:

- What Java is like today and how it got there
- Why Java is worth learning
- Why Java is being chosen for software projects
- What you need to start writing Java programs
- How to create your first program

Java's Past, Present, and Future

Based on the enormous amount of press Java has received over the past several years and the huge number of books about Java, you might have an inflated impression of what Java is capable of.

Java is a programming language that's well suited to designing software that works in conjunction with the Internet. It's also an object-oriented programming language making use of a methodology that is becoming increasingly useful in the world of software design. Additionally, it's a cross-platform language, which means its programs are designed to run without modification on Microsoft Windows, Apple Macintosh, Linux, Solaris, and other systems. Java extends beyond desktops to run on devices such as televisions, smart cards, and cellular phones.

Java is closer to programming languages such as C, C++, Python, Visual Basic, and Delphi than it is to a page-description language such as HTML, a Web scripting language such as JavaScript, or a data-description language such as XML.

Interactive Web Programming

Java first became popular because of its capability to run on World Wide Web pages. Netscape Navigator, Microsoft Internet Explorer, and other browsers can download a Java program included on a Web page and run it locally on the Web user's system.

These programs, which are called *applets*, appear on a Web page in a similar fashion to images. Unlike images, applets can be interactive—taking user input, responding to it, and presenting ever-changing content.

Applets can be used to create animation, charts, graphs, games, navigational menus, multimedia presentations, and other interactive effects.

Figure 1.1 shows an applet running in the Opera 3.61 Web browser. This applet, Every Icon, is an interactive work of art implemented as a Java program by John F. Simon, Jr., an artist and programmer who has taught at the School of Visual Arts in Manhattan. It has been shown at the 2000 Whitney Biennial art exhibition and purchased by the Guggenheim Museum and the San Francisco Museum of Modern Art.

FIGURE 1.1

A Java applet running on a Web page displayed in the Opera Web browser.

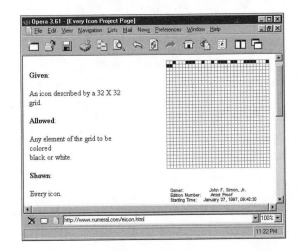

 Note

The Every Icon applet is designed to display every possible icon that can be drawn using black or white squares in a simple 32-by-32 grid. Though the applet displays icons quickly, it takes more than 16 months on a Pentium-equipped computer to display all 4.29 billion variations possible on the top line of the grid alone. Displaying all variations on the top two lines would take around 16 billion years. You can find Every Icon and Simon's other art projects by visiting http://www.numeral.com.

Applets are downloaded over the World Wide Web just like HTML-formatted pages, graphics, and any other element of a Web site. On a Web browser that is equipped to handle Java, the applet will begin running when it finishes downloading.

Applets are written with the Java language, compiled into a form that can be run as a program, and placed on a Web server.

Most applets are written using Java 1.0 or Java 1.1, the first two versions of the language, because the leading browser developers have been slow to add built-in support for subsequent versions.

You can develop applets using Java 2, but the person viewing your applet must be using a browser that supports it. Sun has developed a free browser add-on called the Java Plug-in, and it can be downloaded to add current Java support to most popular browsers.

Note You'll learn more about applets, browsers, and the Java Plug-in during Day 7, "Writing Java Applets."

Like Visual C++, Visual Basic, and Delphi, Java is a robust language that can be used to develop a wide range of software, supporting graphical user interfaces, networking, database connectivity, and other sophisticated functionality.

Java programs that don't run within a Web browser are called *applications*.

Java Grew from a Little Oak

The Java language was developed at Sun Microsystems in December 1990 as part of the Green project, a small research effort into consumer electronics. Researchers were working on a programming language for smart appliances of the future to talk to each other in the tradition of *The Jetsons* TV series—step one in realizing a society in which giant glass bubbles drop down over your body and dress you every morning.

To put its research into action, Green developed a prototype handheld device called the Star 7, a PalmPilot-like gadget that could communicate with others of its own kind.

The original idea was to develop the Star 7 operating system in C++, the hugely popular object-oriented programming language developed by Bjarne Stroustrup. However, Green project member James Gosling became fed up with how C++ was performing on the task, so he barricaded himself in his office and wrote a new language to better handle the Star 7.

The language was named Oak in honor of a tree Gosling could see out his office window. It was later renamed Java in honor of the lawyers who found out about another product called Oak and didn't want to go out on a limb.

Because Java was designed for embedded electronic devices instead of state-of-the-art PCs, it had to be small, efficient, and easily portable to a wide range of hardware devices. It also had to be reliable. People have learned to live with occasional system crashes and lockups in a 30MB software application. However, there aren't many people willing to debug an elevator while its programmers work out the kinks.

Although Java wasn't catching on as an appliance-development tool, just as things were looking grim for the Green project, the World Wide Web started to take off. Many of the things that made Java good for the Star 7 turned out to be good for the Web:

- Java is small—Programs load reasonably quickly on a Web page
- Java is secure—Safeguards protect against programs that cause damage, whether accidental or intentional
- Java is portable—Owners of Windows, Macintosh, Linux, and other operating systems can run the same program in their Web browsers without modification

In order to demonstrate Java's potential, in 1994 project members created HotJava, a Web browser that could run Java applets. The browser demonstrated two things about Java: what it offered the World Wide Web and what kind of program Java could create. Green programmers had used their new language to create the browser, rather than implementing it in C++.

Netscape became the first company to license the Java language in August 1995, incorporating a Java interpreter in its industry-leading Navigator Web browser. Microsoft followed by licensing Java for Internet Explorer, and millions of people could run interactive programs in their browsers for the first time.

Spurred by this huge audience of Web users, more than 300,000 people learned Java programming from 1995 to 1996. Sun added hundreds of employees to its Java effort, believing that the language was ideally suited for a wide variety of desktop, portable, and network computing platforms beyond the Web.

Versions of the Language

Sun has released four major versions of the Java language:

- Java 1.0—A small Web-centered version uniformly available in all popular Web browsers
- Java 1.1—A 1997 release with improvements to the user interface, completely rewritten event handling, and a component technology called JavaBeans
- Java 2 with SDK 1.2—A significantly expanded version released in 1998 with retooled graphical user interface features, database connectivity, and many other improvements
- Java 2 with SDK 1.3—A 2000 release that adds new core features such as improved multimedia, more accessibility, and faster compilation

A Java development kit has always been available at no cost from Sun's Java Web site at http://java.sun.com, and this availability is one of the factors behind the language's rapid growth. It is the first development tool that supports new versions of Java, often six months to a year before other Java development software.

In addition to Java's development kit, there are more than two dozen commercial development tools available for Java programmers. Some of the most popular:

- Symantec Visual Café
- Borland JBuilder
- IBM Visual Age for Java
- Sun Forte for Java

If you are going to use something other than SDK 1.3 to create Java programs as you read this book, you need to make sure that your development tool is up-to-date in its support for Java 2.

Note

> The programs in this book were tested with Java 2 SDK 1.3.0, the most current version of the kit available as the book went to press.

Java's Outlook

Anyone who can accurately predict the future of Java should be going after venture capital instead of writing a book. The technology firm Kleiner, Perkins, Caufield and Byers (KPCB) is investing $100 million in start-up companies on the basis of their future plans involving Java, and has already given millions to Active Software, Marimba, Viant, and a dozen other companies.

With the caveat that neither author of this book is pursuing venture capital, we predict a bright future for Java over the coming decade.

The new version of Java 2 incorporates the following key improvements:

- HotSpot—A new technology that runs Java programs more quickly and takes up less memory
- JavaSound—Greatly enhanced support for 8- and 16-bit playback and recording of WAV, AU, AIFF, and MIDI sound formats
- Swing—More than two dozen added features to components used in the graphical user interface of Java programs
- Performance—In addition to HotSpot, Sun has improved the speed and reliability of several aspects of the language: animation, database connectivity, networking, and multi-threaded programs, which handle multiple tasks at the same time.

You will work with these and other new features in the next three weeks.

> **Note**   You can find out how to apply for KPCB's Java investment fund at the Web
> site http://www.kpcb.com. If your idea is funded and you become an
> overnight Internet millionaire, be aware that Macmillan USA does not forbid
> its authors from receiving a generous finder's fee.

Why to Choose Java

Java applets were a breakthrough in interactive content on the Web, and many top sites used them to deliver news, present information, and attract visitors. Today, ESPN.com uses Java applets for live events in its fantasy sports leagues, which have more than 100,000 subscribers.

Although there are still thousands of applets on the Web today, the most exciting Java-related developments are occurring elsewhere. Sun has extended the language far beyond its roots as an interesting Web technology.

A great example of this is Jini, Sun's Java-based technology for connecting computers and other devices together. The goal of Jini is effortless networking—connect two devices together and they instantly form a network, requiring no installation or configuration.

Jini, which ironically returns Java to the original goals of the Green project, is just one of the new areas where the language is being employed.

Regardless of where you find it running, Java's strengths remain its object-oriented nature, ease of learning, and platform neutrality.

Java Is Object-Oriented

If you're not yet familiar with object-oriented programming, you get plenty of chances to become so during the next week.

Object-oriented programming—also called *OOP*—is a way of conceptualizing a computer program as a set of separate objects that interact with each other. An object contains both information and the means of accessing and changing that information—an efficient way to create computer programs that can be improved easily and used later for other tasks.

Java inherits many of its object-oriented concepts from C++ and borrows concepts from other object-oriented languages as well. You learn more about this beginning on Day 2, "Object-Oriented Programming."

Java Is Easy to Learn

In part, Java was first created at the Green project in rejection of the complexity of C++. C++ is a language with numerous features that are powerful but easy to employ incorrectly.

Java was intended to be easier to write, compile, debug, and learn than other object-oriented languages. It was modeled strongly after C++ and takes much of its syntax from that language.

Note

> The similarity to C++ is so strong that most Java books, including previous editions of this one, make frequent comparisons between the features of the two languages. Today, it's more common for a Java programmer to learn this language either before or in place of C++. For this reason, you won't see many references to C++ in this book after today.

Despite Java's similarities to C++, the most complex and error-prone aspects of that language have been excluded from Java. You won't find pointers or pointer arithmetic because those features are easy to use incorrectly in a program and even harder to fix. Strings and arrays are objects in Java, as is everything else except a few simple data structures such as integers, floating-point numbers, and characters.

Additionally, memory management is handled automatically by Java rather than requiring the programmer to allocate and deallocate memory, and multiple inheritance is not supported.

Experienced C++ programmers will undoubtedly miss these features as they start to use Java, but everyone else will learn Java more quickly because of their absence.

Although Java is easier to learn than many other programming languages, a person with no programming experience at all will find Java challenging. It is more complicated than working in something such as HTML or JavaScript, but definitely something a beginner can accomplish.

Note

> Macmillan USA publishes another line of Java tutorials aimed directly at beginning programmers: *Sams Teach Yourself Java 2 in 24 Hours, Second Edition,* is written by Rogers Cadenhead, one of the coauthors of this book.

Java Is Platform Neutral

Because it was created to run on a wide variety of devices and computing platforms, Java was designed to be platform neutral, working the same no matter where it runs.

This was a huge departure in 1995, when Visual C++, Visual Basic, and other leading programming environments were designed almost exclusively to support Microsoft Windows 95 or Windows NT.

The original goal for Java programs to run without modification on all systems has not been realized. Java developers routinely test their programs on each environment they expect it to be run on, and sometimes are forced into cumbersome workarounds as a result. Even different versions of the same Web browser can require this kind of testing—Java game programmer Karl Hörnell calls it a "hopeless situation."

However, Java's platform-neutral design still makes it much easier to employ Java programs in a diverse range of different computing situations.

As with all high-level programming languages, Java programs are originally written as *source code*, a set of programming statements entered into a text editor and saved as a file.

When you compile a program written in most programming languages, the compiler translates your source file into *machine code*—instructions that are specific to the processor your computer is running. If you compile your code on a Windows system, the resulting program will run on other Windows systems but not on Macs, PalmPilots, and other machines. If you want to use the same program on another platform, you must transfer your source code to the new platform and recompile it to produce machine code specific to that system. In many cases, changes to the source will be required before it will compile on the new machine, because of differences in its processors and other factors.

Java programs are compiled into machine code for a *virtual machine*—a sort of computer-within-a-computer. This machine code is called *bytecode*, and the virtual machine interprets this code by converting it into a specific processor's machine code.

The virtual machine is more commonly known as the *Java interpreter*, and every environment that supports Java must have an interpreter tailored to its own operating system and processor.

Java also is platform neutral at the source level. Java programs are saved as text files before they are compiled, and these files can be created on any platform that supports Java. For example, you could write a Java program on a Windows 98 machine, upload it to a Linux machine over the Internet, and then compile it.

1

Java interpreters can be found in several places. For applets, the interpreter is either built into a Java-enabled browser or installed separately as a browser plug-in.

If you're used to the way other languages create platform-specific code, you might think the Java interpreter adds an unnecessary layer between your source file and the compiled machine code.

The interpreter does cause some significant performance issues—as a rule, Java bytecode executes more slowly than platform-specific machine code produced by a compiled language such as C or C++.

Sun, IBM, Symantec and other Java developers are addressing this with technology such as HotSpot, a new faster virtual machine included with Java 2, and compilers that turn bytecode into platform-specific machine code. Every new generation of processors also increases Java's sometimes laggard performance.

For some Java programs, speed might not be as much of an issue as portability and ease of development. The widespread deployment of Java in large business and government projects shows that the loss in speed is less of an issue than it was for early versions of the language.

Diving into Java Programming

Now that you've been introduced to Java as a spectator, it's time to put some of these concepts into play and create your first Java program.

Before you can get started, you must have SDK 1.3 or a fully compatible development environment on your system.

Selecting a Java Development Tool

If you're using a Microsoft Windows or Apple MacOS system, you probably have a Java interpreter installed that can run Java programs. Usually, this interpreter is part of a Web browser and only can run applets.

To develop Java programs, you need more than an interpreter. You also need a compiler and other tools that are used to create, run, and debug programs.

The programs in this book were tested with SDK 1.3, a set of command-line programs including a compiler, interpreter, appletviewer, file archiver, and several other programs.

A *command-line program* is one that must be run by typing a command at a prompt.

> On a Windows 95 or 98 system, you can get to a command-line prompt by clicking the Start button on the taskbar, choosing Programs, and then clicking MS-DOS Prompt.

Here's an example of a command you could type when using the development kit:

```
javac RetrieveMail.java
```

This command tells the javac program—the Java compiler included with Java 2 SDK 1.3—to read a source code file called RetrieveMail.java and turn it into one or more files of compiled bytecode.

People who are comfortable with MS-DOS, Linux, and other command-line environments will be at home using SDK 1.3. Everyone else will have to become accustomed to the lack of niceties such as a graphical environment and a mouse as they develop programs.

If you have another Java development tool and you're certain it is completely compatible with SDK 1.3, you can use it to create the sample programs in this book.

> If you have any doubts regarding compatibility, or this book is your first experience with the Java language, you should use SDK 1.3. All the examples in the book were prepared using it.

Installing the Software Development Kit

SDK 1.3 is currently available for the following platforms:

- Windows 98
- Windows 95
- Windows 2000
- Windows NT

The kit requires a computer with a Pentium processor that is 166 MHz or faster, 32MB of memory, and 65MB of free disk space. Sun recommends at least 48MB of memory if you're going to work with Java 2 applets.

If you're using another platform, such as the Apple Macintosh, you can check to see whether it has an SDK 1.3–compliant environment by visiting Sun's site at http://java.sun.com:80/cgi-bin/java-ports.cgi.

1

You can download SDK 1.3 from Sun's Java Web site at http://java.sun.com.

The Web site's Products & APIs section offers links to the different Java development kits and related products from Sun. The product you should download is called Java 2 Software Development Kit, Standard Edition, version 1.3.

When you're looking for this product, you might find that the SDK has a third number after 1.3, such as SDK 1.3.1. To fix bugs and security problems, Sun periodically issues new releases of the SDK and numbers them with an extra period and digit after the main version number. Choose the most current version of SDK 1.3 that's offered, whether it's numbered 1.3.0, 1.3.1, 1.3.2, or higher.

Caution

Take care not to download two similarly named products from Sun by mistake—the Java 2 Runtime Environment, Standard Edition, version 1.3 or the Java 2 Software Development Kit, Standard Edition, Source Release.

To go directly to the download page, the current address is http://java.sun.com/j2se/1.3.

To set up SDK 1.3, you must run an installation program that you have either downloaded from Sun or run from a CD.

Sun's Web site contains instructions for several ways to receive SDK 1.3's installation file. After choosing the version of the SDK that's designed for your operating system, you can download it as a single file that's around 25–30MB in size or download a bunch of smaller files. If you choose the latter option, follow Sun's documentation regarding how to combine them together before installing the kit.

After you have a single installation file—either by downloading it or combining a bunch of smaller files—you're ready to set up the development kit.

Windows Installation

Before installing SDK 1.3, you should make sure that no other Java development tools are installed on your system. Having more than one Java programming tool installed is likely to cause configuration problems when you use SDK 1.3.

Also, you should close all other Windows programs before installing SDK 1.3.

To set up the program on a Windows system, double-click the installation file or click Start, Run from the Windows taskbar to find and run the file.

The SDK Setup Wizard will guide you through the process of installing the software. If you accept Sun's terms and conditions for using the software, you'll be asked where to install the program, as shown in Figure 1.2.

FIGURE **1.2**

Choose a destination location for SDK 1.3.

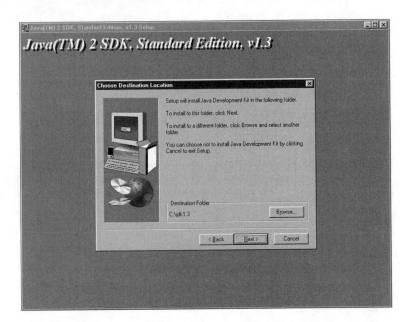

The Setup Wizard will suggest installing the program in a new jdk1.3 folder in the main hard drive on your system. Click the Next button to accept this choice, or Browse if you want to pick a different location.

Tip

> Any configuration problems you might have with the SDK will be easier to fix if you install it in the folder recommended by the Setup Wizard.

The Setup Wizard will place a large number of programs and data files in the folder you have selected. Make a note of the folder, because you'll need to know it later when configuring how SDK 1.3 works on your system.

The next thing you'll be asked is what parts of the kit to install. This dialog box is shown in Figure 1.3.

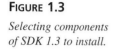

FIGURE 1.3

Selecting components of SDK 1.3 to install.

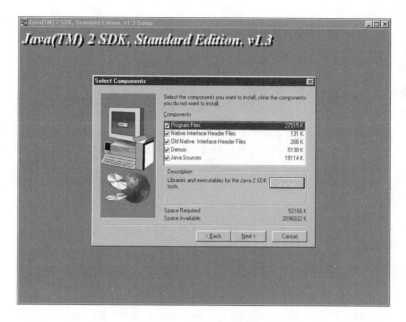

By default, the wizard will install all components of the SDK:

- Program Files—The executable programs needed to create, compile, and test your Java projects.

- Native Interface Header Files and Old Native Interface Header Files—Files used only by programmers who are combining Java code with programs written in other languages. You can omit these for the tutorials in this book.

- Demos—Java 2 programs, with versions you can run and source files you can examine to learn more about the language.

- Java Sources—The source code for the thousands of programs that make up the Java 2 class library.

If you accept the default installation, you need around 50–55MB of free hard disk space. You can save space by omitting everything but the program files, but the demo programs are nice to have around as you're experimenting with the language.

Neither the native header files nor Java source files are needed for any of the material in this book—both are primarily of interest to experienced Java programmers.

After you choose the components to install, click the Next button and the Setup Wizard will install the SDK 1.3 on your system.

Configuring the SDK

After the Setup Wizard installs SDK 1.3, you must adjust your computer's environment variables to include references to the SDK.

Experienced MS-DOS and command-line users can finish setting up the SDK by adjusting two settings, and then rebooting the computer:

- Edit the computer's PATH variable and add a reference to the SDK's bin folder (which is C:\jdk1.3\bin if you installed the SDK into the C:\jdk1.3 folder).
- Remove the CLASSPATH variable if you are not using it for some other Java-related programming. If you are, make sure that it contains a reference to the current folder—a period character ("." without the quotation marks).

These instructions might sound like gobbledygook to people who are used to a graphical, mouse-driven operating system such as Windows.

The following two sections cover how to set the PATH and CLASSPATH correctly on the different Windows systems supported by the SDK.

Users of other operating systems should follow the instructions provided by Sun on its SDK download page.

Windows 95 and 98 Configuration

To set your computer's PATH variable on a Windows 95 or 98 system, use the Windows Notepad text editor to open the AUTOEXEC.BAT file on your computer. It should be located in the root folder of the main hard drive on your computer (usually C:).

Scroll down to the bottom of AUTOEXEC.BAT and add a new line that has the following format:

```
PATH SDKFolder\bin;%PATH%
```

Replace SDKFolder with the name of the folder where you installed the SDK and add the rest without modification. For example, if you installed the SDK into C:\jdk1.3, the line should be the following:

```
PATH C:\jdk1.3\bin;%PATH%
```

After you make this change, keep AUTOEXEC.BAT open and look for any lines that begin with the text SET CLASSPATH=.

If you don't find any, you're done setting up the SDK. Save AUTOEXEC.BAT and reboot your computer.

If you find any CLASSPATH lines, add a new blank line at the bottom of AUTOEXEC.BAT and enter a line with the following format:

```
SET CLASSPATH=.;SDKFolder\lib\tools.jar;%CLASSPATH%
```

As you did with the PATH variable, replace *SDKFolder* with the folder where the SDK was installed. Save AUTOEXEC.BAT and reboot.

Windows NT and 2000 Configuration

To set any environment variables on a Windows NT or Windows 2000 system, choose Start, Control Panel, System, Environment from the taskbar. A dialog box will open where you can view the current values of environmental variables and make changes to them.

The PATH variable might be listed in System Variables or User Variables. PATH contains a list of folders separated by semicolons.

At the beginning of the PATH setting, insert the folder where you installed the SDK followed by the text \bin and a semicolon (";").

For example, if your PATH was c:\windows;c:\command and you installed the SDK into C:\jdk1.3, your new PATH should have the following value:

```
PATH c:\jdk1.3\bin;c:\windows;c:\windows\command
```

After making this change, look for a CLASSPATH variable. If you don't find it, you're done configuring the SDK. Click the Apply button to save your changes, and then reboot your computer.

If you do find CLASSPATH, place your cursor to the left of the existing CLASSPATH value and insert the SDK folder followed by the text \lib\tools.jar;.;.

For example, if you installed the SDK into C:\jdk1.3 and your CLASSPATH had the value c:\javaclasses, your CLASSPATH variable should have the following value:

```
c:\jdk1.3\lib\tools.jar;.;c:\javaclasses
```

After setting your CLASSPATH variable (if necessary), click the Apply button to make your changes permanent, and then reboot the computer.

Your First Java Program

Now that you have learned something about Java and installed development software, you're ready to start working with the language.

Before you do, you might want to take note of the most likely source of problems you'll run into—errors caused by a misconfigured SDK.

Appendix A, "Configuring the Software Development Kit," is a short tutorial for Windows users on how to use MS-DOS and correct errors in how the SDK is set up. See the appendix if you have problems compiling and running the first several examples from Day 1 and Day 2 on a Windows system—especially if you run into "bad command or filename" errors and "NoClassDefFound" errors.

 Tip
You also might want to read the appendix simply to learn a few MS-DOS commands. Windows users will be using the MS-DOS Prompt window throughout the book to compile and run Java programs.

It's a programming tradition to make the first example in a book like this a short program that displays text. Usually the text is simply "Hello world," but this book will break from tradition a bit to display something a little longer—one of the most famous patently untrue predictions in U.S. history:

```
"The advancement of the arts, from year
to year, taxes our credulity, and seems
to presage the arrival of that period
when human improvement must end."
        Henry Ellsworth
        U.S. Commissioner of Patents
        1843 Annual Report of the Patent Office
```

The program that displays Ellsworth's quote will be an *application*, so you'll run it at a command line with the Java interpreter rather than loading it with a Web browser like an applet.

Although a Java program can be designed to be both an applet and an application, almost all programs you encounter will be one or the other.

Creating the Source File

Java programs begin as source code—a series of statements created using a text editor or word processor and saved as a text file. You can use any program you like to create these files, as long as it can save the file as plain unformatted text—a format that's also called ASCII text or DOS text.

Windows users can write Java programs with Notepad or Write, two editors that are included with the operating system. You also can use Microsoft Word, but must save files as text rather than in Word's proprietary format. UNIX and Linux users can author programs with emacs, pico, and vi; Macintosh users have SimpleText for Java source file creation.

The Software Development Kit does not include a text editor, but most other Java development tools include a built-in editor for creating source code files.

Writing the Program

Run your editor of choice and enter the Java program shown in Listing 1.1. Be careful that all the parentheses, braces, and quotation marks in the listing are entered correctly, and capitalize everything in the program exactly as shown. If your editor requires a filename before you start entering anything, use Ellsworth.java.

LISTING 1.1   Source Code of Ellsworth.java

```
 1: public class Ellsworth {
 2:     public static void main(String[] arguments) {
 3:         String line1 = "The advancement of the arts, from year\n";
 4:         String line2 = "to year, taxes our credulity, and seems\n";
 5:         String line3 = "to presage the arrival of that period\n";
 6:         String line4 = "when human improvement must end.";
 7:         String quote = line1 + line2 + line3 + line4;
 8:         String speaker = "Henry Ellsworth";
 9:         String title = "U.S. Commissioner of Patents";
10:         String from = "1843 Annual Report of the Patent Office";
11:         System.out.println('\u0022' + quote + '\u0022');
12:         System.out.println("\t" + speaker);
13:         System.out.println("\t" + title);
14:         System.out.println("\t" + from);
15:     }
16: }
```

The line numbers and colons along the left side of Listing 1.1 are not part of the program—they're included so that the authors of this book can refer to specific lines by number in each program. If you're ever unsure about the source code of a program in this book, you can compare it to a copy on the book's official World Wide Web site at the following address:

http://www.java21days.com

After you finish typing in the program, save the file somewhere on your hard drive with the name Ellsworth.java.

Tip
> If you're a Windows user who is unfamiliar with MS-DOS, open the root folder on your main hard drive and create a new subfolder called J21work. Save Ellsworth.java and all other Java source files from this book into that folder to make it easier to find them within MS-DOS.

If you're using Windows, a text editor such as Notepad might add an extra .txt file extension to the filename of any Java source files you save (which turns a name like Ellsworth.java into Ellsworth.java.txt). To avoid this problem, place quotation marks around the filename when saving a source file. Figure 1.4 shows this technique being used to save the source file Ellsworth.java from Windows Notepad.

FIGURE 1.4

Saving a source file from Windows Notepad.

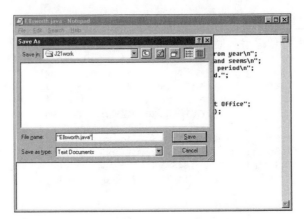

 Tip
> A better solution is to use Windows Explorer to permanently associate .java files with the text editor you'll be using. This enables you to open a source file for editing by double-clicking the file in a Windows folder. To learn how to set this up, see Appendix B, "Using a Text Editor with the Software Development Kit."

Java source files must be saved with the extension .java.

Compiling and Running the Program Under Windows

Now you're ready to compile the source file. If you're using a development tool other than SDK 1.3, you should consult that software's documentation for details on how to compile Java programs.

With the SDK, you need to use the command-line tool javac, the Java compiler. The compiler reads a .java source file and creates one or more .class files that can be run by the Java virtual machine.

The compiler requires a command line. Windows users should open an MS-DOS Prompt window, then change folders to the one that contains Ellsworth.java.

If you saved the file into a newly created J21work folder inside the root folder on your main hard drive, the following MS-DOS command will open that folder:

```
cd \J21work
```

When you are in the correct folder, you can compile Ellsworth.java by entering the following at a command prompt:

```
javac Ellsworth.java
```

Figure 1.5 shows the MS-DOS commands used to switch to the \J21work folder and compile Ellsworth.java.

FIGURE 1.5

Compiling Java programs in an MS-DOS window.

The JDK compiler does not display any message if the program compiles successfully. If there are problems, the compiler lets you know by displaying each error along with a line that triggered the error.

If the program compiled without any errors, a file called Ellsworth.class is created in the same folder that contains Ellsworth.java.

The class file contains the Java bytecode that will be executed by the Java interpreter. If you get any errors, go back to your original source file and make sure that you typed it exactly as it appears in Listing 1.1.

After you have a class file, you can run that file using a Java interpreter. The SDK's interpreter is called java, and it also is run from the command line.

Run the Ellsworth program by switching to the folder containing Ellsworth.class and entering the following:

```
java Ellsworth
```

You should see the Henry Ellsworth quotation displayed along with his name, job, and the place he wrote it.

 Note

> Make sure to leave off the .class extension when running a Java program with the java tool—entering java Ellsworth.class will result in a "NoClassDefFound" error. If you leave off the .class extension and still get this error, you probably need to adjust how the SDK is configured. Help for Windows users with this problem is provided in Appendix A.

Figure 1.6 shows the successful output of the Ellsworth application along with the commands used to get to that point.

FIGURE 1.6

Compiling and running a Java application.

```
Microsoft(R) Windows 98
    (C)Copyright Microsoft Corp 1981-1998.

C:\WINDOWS>cd \J21work

C:\J21work>javac Ellsworth.java

C:\J21work>java Ellsworth
"The advancement of the arts, from year
to year, taxes our credulity, and seems
to presage the arrival of that period
when human improvement must end."
        Henry Ellsworth
        U.S. Commissioner of Patents
        1843 Annual Report of the Patent Office

C:\J21work>_
```

You will begin learning about the syntax and structure of a Java program tomorrow—the purpose of today's tutorial is to compile and run a program successfully.

For now, it can be instructive to simply read source code such as `Ellsworth.java` and make an educated guess about what is happening in each line.

If the `Ellsworth` program were written in English instead of Java, the 16 lines could take the following form:

1. Create a Java class file called `Ellsworth`.
2. Begin the main part of the program.
3. Create a string called `line1` and use it to hold the text "The advancement of the arts, from year" followed by a linefeed character ("\n").
4. Create a string called `line2` and use it to hold "to year, taxes our credulity, and seems" followed by a linefeed.
5. Create the `line3` string and use it to hold "to presage the arrival of that period" followed by a linefeed.
6. Create the `line4` string and use it to hold "when human improvement must end."
7. Create the `quote` string and use it to hold the text contained in `line1`, `line2`, `line3`, and `line4`, in that order.
8. Create the `speaker` string and use it to hold "Henry Ellsworth".
9. Create the `title` string and use it to hold "U.S. Commissioner of Patents".
10. Create the `from` string and use it to hold "1843 Annual Report of the Patent Office".
11. Display a quotation mark (the Unicode character `\u0022`), the text contained in the `quote` string, and another quotation mark.
12. Display a tab character ("\t") followed by the contents of the `speaker` string.
13. Display a tab followed by the contents of `title`.
14. Display a tab followed by the contents of `from`.
15. End the main part of the program.
16. End the program.

Don't worry if you didn't guess right on the function of these lines—everything used in the `Ellsworth` program will be completely introduced this week.

Summary

Java is a different language today than it was in 1995.

This has a good side—a proven market for Java programmers exists at present and the skills are in huge demand. Five years ago you couldn't find "Java" in a classified ad outside of Silicon Valley, and even there the market consisted of Sun, Netscape, and only a few others.

This also has a bad side—Java is at least five times as large today as it was upon its first release, so there's much more to learn.

For this reason, today was the last day for Java to be described in the abstract. The next 20 days will be spent at the command line, creating Java applications and applets, running them with the interpreter or a Web browser, and exploring the fundamental concepts of the language.

Q&A

Q **The license for the SDK is only for 180 days. I thought the kit was free—don't you think you should have mentioned that rather predominately in your book?**

A Sun Microsystems has always made the SDK available for free, and it seems highly doubtful at this point that the company would change the policy. Although Sun has not made any official statements regarding the duration of the license, it appears to be a way to encourage developers to upgrade to new versions when they become available. Sun updates the SDK frequently, by issuing either a bug- and security-fix minor upgrade or a full upgrade such as the move to Java 2.

Q **Java 1.0 programs could be created with JDK 1.0. Java 1.1 programs could be created with JDK 1.1. Why is Java 2 using SDK 1.3? Shouldn't it be either Java 2 SDK 2 or Java 1.3 SDK 1.3?**

A Sun changed its naming scheme after Java 1.1 and JDK 1.1. The language was renamed Java 2 to capitalize on all the different products and technologies available in addition to the Software Development Kit. Although the Java Development Kit (JDK) was renamed as the Software Development Kit after JDK 1.1, it was numbered as version 1.2 instead of 2.

As a result of the changes, Java 1.2 is often used as a synonym for Java 2, JDK 2 is used when referring to SDK 1.2, and now JDK 1.3 is used in place of SDK 1.3. Sun, which received industry praise for the marketing savvy behind the choice of "Java" as a name for the language, has created a lot of confusion with this new numbering.

The current version of the language is called Java 2 and the current software development kit is Software Development Kit 1.3. The best way to figure out whether you're using the right version is to use SDK 1.3 or a tool that is fully compatible with SDK 1.3.

Quiz

Review today's material by taking this three-question quiz.

Questions

1. When Java was first introduced to the public, it was most useful in what computing environment?

   (a) Web servers

   (b) Web browsers

   (c) Personal digital assistants

2. What is the compiled form of a Java program called?

   (a) Machine code

   (b) Espresso

   (c) Bytecode

3. Why did James Gosling create the first version of the Java language?

   (a) He was frustrated with how C++ was performing on a project.

   (b) He was trying to save the Green project from being cancelled by Sun.

   (c) When you put C++ on a resume, personnel directors think it was your average in school.

Answers

1. b. Although Java could run on servers, the main source of interest in the language in 1995 was how it could run in a Web browser as part of a page.

2. c. The Java compiler turns a source code file into bytecode. A Java interpreter translates that bytecode into platform-specific machine code.

3. a. Gosling's inspiration was the difficulty in debugging a large-scale C++ project because of pointer errors, memory allocation problems, and similar issues.

Exercises

To extend your knowledge of the subjects covered today, try the following exercises:

- Take the linefeed characters out of the Ellsworth program, recompile the program, and run it to see how this changes the output.

- Visit Sun's Java applet showcase at http://java.sun.com/applets to see examples of Java programs running on the Web.

Where applicable, exercise solutions are offered on the book's Web site at http://www.java21days.com.

DAY 2

Object-Oriented Programming

The biggest challenge for a new Java programmer is learning object-oriented programming at the same time.

Although this might sound daunting if you are unfamiliar with this style of programming, think of it as a two-for-one discount for your brain. You will learn object-oriented programming by learning Java. There's no other way to make use of the language.

Object-oriented programming, also called *OOP*, is a way of building computer programs that mirrors how objects are assembled in the physical world.

By using this style of development, you will be able to create programs that are more reusable, reliable, and understandable.

To get to that point, you first must explore how Java embodies the principles of object-oriented programming. The following topics are covered:

- Organizing programs into elements called classes, and how these classes are used to create objects
- Defining a class by two aspects of its structure: how it should behave and what its attributes are
- Connecting classes to each other in a way that one class inherits functionality from another class
- Linking classes together through packages and interfaces

If you already are familiar with object-oriented programming, much of today's lesson will be a review for you. Even if you skim over the introductory material, you should create the sample program to get some experience developing, compiling, and running Java programs.

Thinking in Terms of Objects

There are many different ways to conceptualize a computer program. One way is to think of a program as a series of instructions carried out in sequence, and this is commonly called *procedural programming*. Most programmers start by learning a procedural language such as BASIC in its many versions or Pascal.

Procedural languages mimic the way a computer carries out instructions, so the programs you write are tailored to the computer's manner of doing things. One of the first things a procedural programmer must learn is how to break down a problem into a series of simple steps.

Object-oriented programming looks at a computer program from a different angle: focusing on the task you are using the computer for, rather than the way a computer handles tasks.

In object-oriented programming (OOP), a computer program is conceptualized as a set of objects that work together to accomplish a task. Each object is a separate part of the program, interacting with the other parts in specific, highly controlled ways.

For a real-life example of object-oriented design, consider a stereo system. Most systems are built by hooking together a bunch of different objects, which are more commonly called components:

- Speaker components play midrange and high-frequency sounds.
- Subwoofer components play low bass frequency sounds.

- Tuner components receive radio broadcast signals.
- CD player components read audio data from CDs.

These components are designed to interact with each other using standard input and output connectors. Even if you bought the speakers, subwoofer, tuner, and CD player from different companies, you can combine them to form a stereo system as long as they have standard connectors.

Object-oriented programming works under the same principle: You put together a program by combining newly created objects and existing objects in standard ways. Each object serves a specific role in the overall program.

NEW TERM An *object* is a self-contained element of a computer program that represents a related group of features and is designed to accomplish specific tasks. Objects are also called *instances*.

Objects and Classes

Object-oriented programming is modeled on the observation that in the physical world, objects are made up of many kinds of smaller objects.

However, the capability to combine objects is only one aspect of object-oriented programming. Another important feature is the use of classes.

NEW TERM A *class* is a template used to create an object. Every object created from the same class will have similar, if not identical, features.

Classes embody all features of a particular set of objects. When you write a program in an object-oriented language, you don't define individual objects. Instead, you define classes used to create those objects.

For example, you could create a Modem class that describes the features of all computer telephone modems. Some of those common features:

- They connect to a computer's serial port.
- They send and receive information.
- They dial phone numbers.

The Modem class serves as an abstract model for the concept of a modem. To actually have something concrete you can manipulate in a program, you must use the Modem class to create a Modem object. The process of creating an object from a class is called *instantiation*, and created objects are also called *instances*.

A Modem class can be used to create lots of different Modem objects in a program, and each of these objects could have different features:

- Some are internal modems and others are external modems.
- Some use the COM1 port and others use the COM2 port.
- Some have error control and others don't.

Even with these differences, two Modem objects still have enough in common to be recognizable as related objects. Figure 2.1 shows a Modem class and several objects created from that template.

FIGURE 2.1

The Modem *class and several* Modem *objects.*

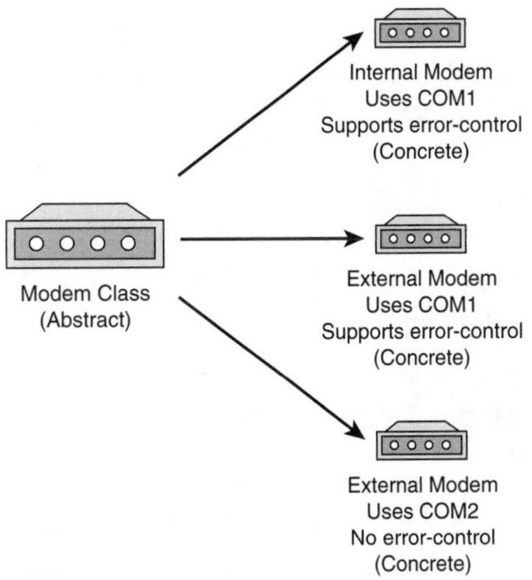

Modem Class
(Abstract)

Internal Modem
Uses COM1
Supports error-control
(Concrete)

External Modem
Uses COM1
Supports error-control
(Concrete)

External Modem
Uses COM2
No error-control
(Concrete)

Object Reuse

Using Java, you could create a class to represent all command buttons—those clickable boxes that show up on windows, dialog boxes, and other parts of a program's graphical user interface.

When the CommandButton class is developed, it could define these features:

- The text that identifies the button's purpose
- The size of the button
- Aspects of its appearance, such as whether it has a 3D shadow

The CommandButton class also could define how a button behaves:

- Whether the button needs a single click or a double-click to use
- Whether it should ignore mouse clicks entirely
- What it does when successfully clicked

After you define the CommandButton class, you can create instances of that button—in other words, CommandButton objects. The objects all take on the basic features of a clickable button as defined by the class, but each one could have a different appearance and slightly different behavior depending on what you need that object to do.

By creating a CommandButton class, you don't have to keep rewriting the code for each command button that you want to use in your programs. In addition, you can reuse the CommandButton class to create different kinds of buttons, as you need them, both in this program and in others.

 Note

> One of Java's standard classes, javax.swing.JButton, encompasses all the functionality of this hypothetical CommandButton example and more. You get a chance to work with it during Day 8, "Working with Swing."

When you write a Java program, you design and construct a set of classes. When your program runs, objects are instantiated from those classes and used as needed. Your task as a Java programmer is to create the right set of classes to accomplish what your program needs to accomplish.

Fortunately, you don't have to start from scratch. The Java language includes hundreds of classes that implement most of the basic functionality you will need. These classes are called the Java 2 class library, and they are installed along with a development kit such as SDK 1.3.

When you're talking about using the Java language, you're actually talking about using this class library and some standard keywords and operators that are recognized by Java compilers.

The class library handles numerous tasks, such as mathematical functions, text handling, graphics, sound, user interaction, and networking. Working with these classes is no different than working with classes you create.

For complicated Java programs, you might create a whole set of new classes with defined interactions between them. These could be used to form your own class library for use in other programs.

Reuse is one of the fundamental benefits of object-oriented programming.

Attributes and Behavior

A Java class consists of two distinct types of information: attributes and behavior.

Both of these are present in `VolcanoRobot`, a project you will implement today as a class. This project, a computer simulation of a volcanic exploration vehicle, is patterned after the Dante II robot used by NASA's Telerobotics Research program to do research inside volcanic craters.

Attributes of a Class of Objects

Attributes are the data that differentiates one object from another. They can be used to determine the appearance, state, and other qualities of objects that belong to that class.

A volcanic exploration vehicle could have the following attributes:

- Status—`exploring`, `moving`, `returning home`
- Speed, in miles per hour
- Temperature, in Fahrenheit degrees

In a class, attributes are defined by variables—places to store information in a computer program. Instance variables are attributes that have values that differ from one object to another.

NEW TERM An *instance variable* defines an attribute of one particular object. The object's class defines what kind of attribute it is, and each instance stores its own value for that attribute. Instance variables also are called *object variables*.

Each class attribute has a single corresponding variable; you change that attribute in an object by changing the value of the variable.

For example, the `VolcanoRobot` class could define a `speed` instance variable. This must be an instance variable because each robot travels at different speeds depending on the circumstances of the environment. The value of a robot's `speed` instance variable could be changed to make the robot move more quickly or slowly.

Instance variables can be given a value when an object is created and stay constant throughout the life of the object. They also can be given different values as the object is used in a running program.

For other variables, it makes more sense to have one value shared by all objects of that class. These attributes are called class variables.

NEW TERM A *class variable* defines an attribute of an entire class. The variable applies to the class itself and to all of its instances, so only one value is stored no matter how many objects of that class have been created.

An example of a class variable for the `VolcanoRobot` class would be a variable that holds the current time. If an instance variable were created to hold the time, each object could have a different value for this variable, which could cause problems if the robots are supposed to perform tasks in conjunction with each other.

Using a class variable prevents this problem, because all objects of that class share the same value automatically. Each `VolcanoRobot` object would have access to that variable.

Behavior of a Class of Objects

Behavior refers to the things that a class of objects can do to themselves and other objects. Behavior can be used to change the attributes of an object, receive information from other objects, and send messages to other objects asking them to perform tasks.

A volcano robot could have the following behavior:

- Check current temperature
- Begin a survey
- Report its current location

Behavior for a class of objects is implemented using methods.

NEW TERM   *Methods* are groups of related statements in a class of objects that handle a task. They are used to accomplish specific tasks on their own objects and others, and are used in the way that functions and subroutines are used in other programming languages.

Objects communicate with each other using methods. A class or an object can call methods in another class or object for many reasons, including the following:

- To report a change to another object
- To tell the other object to change something about itself
- To ask another object to do something

For example, two volcano robots could use methods to report their locations to each other and avoid collisions, and one robot could tell another to stop so it could pass by.

Just as there are instance and class variables, there are also instance and class methods. *Instance methods*, which are so common they're usually just called *methods*, are used when you are working with an object of the class. If a method makes a change to an individual object, it must be an instance method. *Class methods* apply to a class itself.

Creating a Class

To see classes, objects, attributes, and behavior in action, you will develop a
VolcanoRobot class, create objects from that class, and work with them in a running program.

Note

> The main purpose of this project is to explore object-oriented programming.
> You'll learn more about Java programming syntax during Day 3, "The ABCs
> of Java."

To begin creating a class, run the text editor you're using to create Java programs and
open a new file. Enter the text of Listing 2.1 and save the file as VolcanoRobot.java in a
folder you are using to work on programs from this book.

LISTING 2.1   The Full Text of VolcanoRobot.java

```
 1: class VolcanoRobot {
 2:     String status;
 3:     int speed;
 4:     float temperature;
 5:
 6:     void checkTemperature() {
 7:         if (temperature > 660) {
 8:             status = "returning home";
 9:             speed = 5;
10:         }
11:     }
12:
13:     void showAttributes() {
14:         System.out.println("Status: " + status);
15:         System.out.println("Speed: " + speed);
16:         System.out.println("Temperature: " + temperature);
17:     }
18: }
```

The class statement in Line 1 of Listing 2.1 defines and names the VolcanoRobot class.
Everything contained between the bracket on Line 1 and the bracket on Line 18 is part of
this class.

The VolcanoRobot class contains three instance variables and two instance methods.

The instance variables are defined in Lines 2–4:

```
String status;
int speed;
float temperature;
```

The variables are named status, speed, and temperature. Each will be used to store a different type of information:

- status holds a String object, a group of letters, numbers, punctuation, and other characters
- speed holds an int, an integer value
- temperature holds a float, a floating-point number

String objects are created from the String class, which is part of the Java class library and can be used in any Java program.

Tip

As you might have noticed from the use of String in this program, a class can use objects as instance variables.

The first instance method in the VolcanoRobot class is defined in Lines 6–11:

```
void checkTemperature() {
    if (temperature > 660) {
        status = "returning home";
        speed = 5;
    }
}
```

Methods are defined in a manner similar to a class. They begin with a statement that names the method, the kind of information the method produces, and other things.

The checkTemperature() method is contained within the brackets on Line 6 and Line 11 of Listing 2.1. This method can be called on a VolcanoRobot object to find out its temperature.

This method checks to see whether the object's temperature instance variable has a value greater than 660. If it does, two other instance variables are changed:

- The status is changed to the text "returning home", indicating that the temperature is too hot and the robot is heading back to its base.
- The speed is changed to 5. (Presumably, this is as fast as the robot can travel.)

The second instance method, `showAttributes()`, is defined in Lines 13–17:

```
void showAttributes() {
        System.out.println("Status: " + status);
        System.out.println("Speed: " + speed);
        System.out.println("Temperature: " + temperature);
}
```

This method uses `System.out.println()` to display the values of three instance variables along with some text explaining what each value represents.

Running the Program

If you compiled the `VolcanoRobot` class at this point, you couldn't actually use it to simulate the exploratory robots. The class you have created defines what a `VolcanoRobot` object would be like if it were used in a program. It doesn't, however, use one of these objects yet.

There are two ways to put this `VolcanoRobot` class to use:

- Create a separate Java program that uses this class.
- Add a special class method called `main()` to the `VolcanoRobot` class so that it can be run as an application, and then use `VolcanoRobot` objects in that method.

The latter is done for this exercise. Open `VolcanoRobot.java` again in your text editor and insert a blank line directly above the last line of the program (Line 18 in Listing 2.1).

In the space created by this blank line, insert the following class method:

```
public static void main(String[] arguments) {
    VolcanoRobot dante = new VolcanoRobot();
    dante.status = "exploring";
    dante.speed = 2;
    dante.temperature = 510;

    dante.showAttributes();
    System.out.println("Increasing speed to 3.");
    dante.speed = 3;
    dante.showAttributes();
    System.out.println("Changing temperature to 670.");
    dante.temperature = 670;
    dante.showAttributes();
    System.out.println("Checking the temperature.");
    dante.checkTemperature();
    dante.showAttributes();
}
```

With the `main()` method in place, the `VolcanoRobot` class can now be used as an application. Save the file as `VolcanoRobot.java`, and then do the following to compile the program:

1. Go to a command line (in Windows 95 or 98, click Start, Programs, and then MS-DOS Prompt).

2. Open the folder where `VolcanoRobot.java` was saved.

3. Compile the program by typing **javac VolcanoRobot.java** at the command line.

Listing 2.2 shows the final `VolcanoRobot.java` source file.

> **Tip**
>
> If you encounter problems compiling or running any program in this book with SDK 1.3, you can find a copy of the source file and other related files on the book's official Web site at `http://www.java21days.com`.

LISTING 2.2   The Final Text of `VolcanoRobot.java`

```
 1: class VolcanoRobot {
 2:     String status;
 3:     int speed;
 4:     float temperature;
 5:
 6:     void checkTemperature() {
 7:         if (temperature > 660) {
 8:             status = "returning home";
 9:             speed = 5;
10:         }
11:     }
12:
13:     void showAttributes() {
14:         System.out.println("Status: " + status);
15:         System.out.println("Speed: " + speed);
16:         System.out.println("Temperature: " + temperature);
17:     }
18:
19:     public static void main(String[] arguments) {
20:         VolcanoRobot dante = new VolcanoRobot();
21:         dante.status = "exploring";
22:         dante.speed = 2;
23:         dante.temperature = 510;
24:
25:         dante.showAttributes();
26:         System.out.println("Increasing speed to 3.");
27:         dante.speed = 3;
```

LISTING 2.2   continued

```
28:          dante.showAttributes();
29:          System.out.println("Changing temperature to 670.");
30:          dante.temperature = 670;
31:          dante.showAttributes();
32:          System.out.println("Checking the temperature.");
33:          dante.checkTemperature();
34:          dante.showAttributes();
35:      }
36: }
```

To run the VolcanoRobot application, open the folder containing the
VolcanoRobot.class file at a command line, then use the java command:

```
java VolcanoRobot
```

When you run the VolcanoRobot class, the output should be the following:

```
Status: exploring
Speed: 2
Temperature: 510.0
Increasing speed to 3.
Status: exploring
Speed: 3
Temperature: 510.0
Changing temperature to 670.
Status: exploring
Speed: 3
Temperature: 670.0
Checking the temperature.
Status: returning home
Speed: 5
Temperature: 670.0
```

Using Listing 2.2 as a guide, the following things take place in the main() class method:

- Line 19—The main() method is created and named. All main() methods take this
  format, and you'll learn more about them during Day 6, "Creating Classes and
  Methods." For now, the most important thing to note is the static keyword. This
  indicates that the method is a class method.

- Line 20, a new VolcanoRobot object is created using that class as a template. The
  object is given the name dante.

- Lines 21–23—Three instance variables of the dante object are given values:
  status is set to the text "exploring", speed is set to 2, and temperature is set
  to 510.

- Line 25—On this line and several that follow, the `showAttributes()` method of the `dante` object is called. This method displays the current values of the instance variables `status`, `speed`, and `temperature`.
- Line 26—On this line and others that follow, a `System.out.println()` statement is used to display the text within the parentheses.
- Line 27—The `speed` instance variable is set to the value `3`.
- Line 30—The `temperature` instance variable is set to the value `670`.
- Line 33—The `checkTemperature()` method of the `dante` object is called. This method checks to see whether the `temperature` instance variable is greater than 660. If it is, `status` and `speed` are assigned new values.

Organizing Classes and Class Behavior

An introduction to object-oriented programming in Java isn't complete without a first look at three concepts: inheritance, interfaces, and packages.

These three things all are mechanisms for organizing classes and class behavior. The Java class library uses these concepts, and the classes you create for your own programs also need them.

Inheritance

Inheritance is one of the most crucial concepts in object-oriented programming, and it has a direct effect on how you design and write your own Java classes.

 Inheritance is a mechanism that enables one class to inherit all the behavior and attributes of another class.

Through inheritance, a class immediately has all the functionality of an existing class. Because of this, the new class can be created by only indicating how it is different from an existing class.

With inheritance, all classes are arranged in a strict hierarchy—those you create and those from the Java class library and other libraries.

 A class that inherits from another class is called a *subclass*, and the class that gives the inheritance is called a *superclass*.

A class can have only one superclass, but each class can have an unlimited number of subclasses. Subclasses inherit all the attributes and behavior of their superclasses.

In practical terms, this means that if the superclass has behavior and attributes that your class needs, you don't have to redefine it or copy that code to have the same behavior and attributes. Your class automatically receives these things from its superclass, the superclass gets them from its superclass, and so on, all the way up the hierarchy. Your class becomes a combination of all the features of the classes above it in the hierarchy, as well as its own features.

The situation is pretty comparable to the way you inherited all kinds of things from your parents, such as height, hair color, love of ska music, and a reluctance to ask for directions. They inherited some of these things from their parents, who inherited from theirs, and backward through time to the Garden of Eden, Big Bang, or *insert personal cosmological belief here.*

Figure 2.2 shows the way a hierarchy of classes is arranged.

FIGURE 2.2

A class hierarchy.

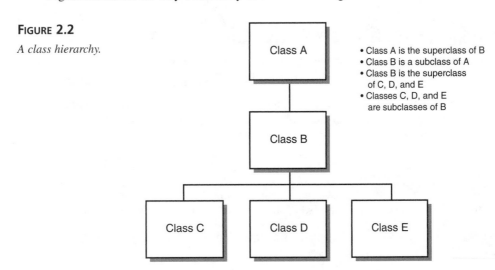

- Class A is the superclass of B
- Class B is a subclass of A
- Class B is the superclass of C, D, and E
- Classes C, D, and E are subclasses of B

At the top of the Java class hierarchy is the class `Object`—all classes inherit from this one superclass. `Object` is the most general class in the hierarchy, and it defines behavior inherited by all the classes in the Java class library. Each class further down the hierarchy becomes more tailored to a specific purpose. A class hierarchy defines abstract concepts at the top of the hierarchy. Those concepts become more concrete further down the line of subclasses.

Often when you create a new class in Java, you will want all the functionality of an existing class with some modifications of your own creation. For example, you might want a version of a `CommandButton` that makes a sound when clicked.

To receive all the `CommandButton` functionality without doing any work to re-create it, you can define your class as a subclass of `CommandButton`. Your class then would automatically inherit behavior and attributes defined in `CommandButton`, and behavior and attributes defined in the superclasses of `CommandButton`. All you have to worry about are the things that make your new class different from `CommandButton` itself. Subclassing is the mechanism for defining new classes as the differences between those classes and their superclass.

NEW TERM *Subclassing* is the creation of a new class that inherits from an existing class. The only task in the subclass is to indicate the differences in behavior and attributes between it and the superclass.

If your class defines entirely new behavior and isn't a subclass of another class, you can inherit directly from the `Object` class. This allows it to fit neatly into the Java class hierarchy. In fact, if you create a class definition that doesn't indicate a superclass, Java assumes that the new class is inheriting directly from `Object`. The `VolcanoRobot` class you created inherited from the `Object` class.

Creating a Class Hierarchy

If you're creating a large set of classes, it makes sense for your classes to inherit from the existing class hierarchy and to make up a hierarchy themselves. Organizing your classes this way takes significant planning, but the advantages include the following:

- Functionality that is common to multiple classes can be put into a superclass, which enables it to be used repeatedly in all classes below it in the hierarchy.

- Changes to a superclass automatically are reflected in all its subclasses, their subclasses, and so on. There is no need to change or recompile any of the lower classes; they receive the new information through inheritance.

For example, imagine that you have created a Java class to implement all the features of a volcanic exploratory robot. (This shouldn't take much imagination.)

The `VolcanoRobot` class is completed, works successfully, and everything is copacetic. Now you want to create a Java class called `MarsRobot`.

These two kinds of robots have similar features—both are research robots that work in hostile environments and conduct research. Your first impulse might be to open up the `VolcanoRobot.java` source file and copy a lot of it into a new source file called `MarsRobot.java`.

A better plan is to figure out the common functionality of `MarsRobot` and `VolcanoRobot` and organize it into a more general class hierarchy. This might be a lot of work just for the classes `VolcanoRobot` and `MarsRobot`, but what if you also want to add `MoonRobot`, `UnderseaRobot`, and `DesertRobot`? Factoring common behavior into one or more reusable superclasses significantly reduces the overall amount of work that must be done.

To design a class hierarchy that might serve this purpose, start at the top with the class Object, the pinnacle of all Java classes. The most general class to which these robots belong might be called Robot. A robot, generally, could be defined as a self-controlled exploration device. In the Robot class, you define only the behavior that qualifies something to be a device, self-controlled, and designed for exploration.

There could be two classes below Robot: WalkingRobot and DrivingRobot. The obvious thing that differentiates these classes is that one travels by foot and the other by wheel. The behavior of walking robots might include bending over to pick something up, ducking, running, and the like. Driving robots would behave differently. Figure 2.3 shows what you have so far.

FIGURE 2.3

The basic Robot *hierarchy.*

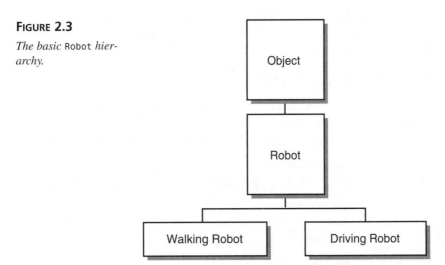

Now, the hierarchy can become even more specific. With WalkingRobot, you might have several classes: ScienceRobot, GuardRobot, SearchRobot, and so on. As an alternative, you could factor out still more functionality and have intermediate classes for TwoLegged and FourLegged robots, with different behaviors for each (see Figure 2.4).

Finally, the hierarchy is done, and you have a place for VolcanoRobot. It can be a subclass of ScienceRobot, which is a subclass of WalkingRobot, which is a subclass of Robot, which is a subclass of Object.

Where do qualities such as status, temperature, or speed come in? They come in at the place they fit into the class hierarchy most naturally. Because all robots have a need to keep track of the temperature of their environment, it makes sense to define temperature as an instance variable in Robot. All subclasses would have that instance variable as well. Remember that you need to define a behavior or attribute only once in the hierarchy, and it automatically is inherited by each subclass.

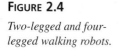

FIGURE 2.4

Two-legged and four-legged walking robots.

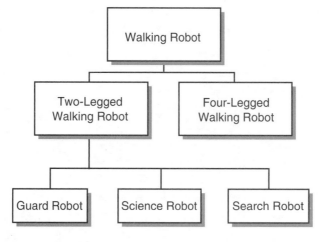

2

> **Note**
>
> Designing an effective class hierarchy involves a lot of planning and revision. As you attempt to put attributes and behavior into a hierarchy, you're likely to find reasons to move some classes to different spots in the hierarchy. The goal is to reduce the number of repetitive features that are needed.

Inheritance in Action

Inheritance in Java works much more simply than it does in the real world. There are no executors, judges, or courts of any kind required in Java.

When you create a new object, Java keeps track of each variable defined for that object and each variable defined for each superclass of the object. In this way, all the classes combine to form a template for the current object, and each object fills in the information appropriate to its situation.

Methods operate similarly: New objects have access to all method names of its class and superclass. This is determined dynamically when a method is used in a running program. If you call a method of a particular object, the Java interpreter first checks the object's class for that method. If the method isn't found, the interpreter looks for it in the superclass of that class, and so on, until the method definition is found. This is illustrated in Figure 2.5.

Things get complicated when a subclass defines a method that has the same name, return type, and arguments that a method defined in a superclass has. In this case, the method definition that is found first (starting at the bottom of the hierarchy and working upward) is the one that is used. Because of this, you can create a method in a subclass that prevents a method in a superclass from being used. To do this, you give the method with the same name, return type, and arguments as the method in the superclass. This procedure is called *overriding* (see Figure 2.6).

FIGURE 2.5

How methods are located in a class hierarchy.

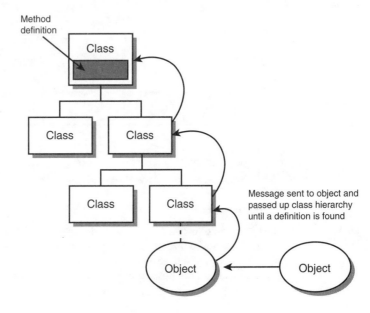

FIGURE 2.6

Overriding methods.

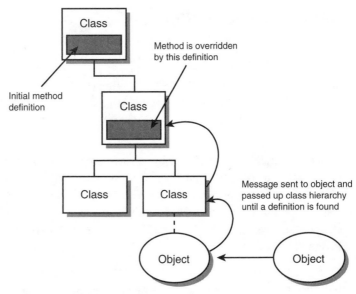

Single and Multiple Inheritance

Java's form of inheritance is called *single inheritance* because each Java class can have only one superclass (although any given superclass can have multiple subclasses).

In other object-oriented programming languages such as C++, classes can have more than one superclass, and they inherit combined variables and methods from all those superclasses. This is called *multiple inheritance*, and it provides the means to create classes that encompass just about any imaginable behavior. However, it significantly complicates class definitions and the code needed to produce them. Java makes inheritance simpler by allowing only single inheritance.

Interfaces

Single inheritance makes the relationship between classes and the functionality those classes implement easier to understand and to design. However, it also can be restrictive—especially when you have similar behavior that needs to be duplicated across different branches of a class hierarchy. Java solves the problem of shared behavior by using interfaces.

NEW TERM　　An *interface* is a collection of methods that indicate a class has some behavior in addition to what it inherits from its superclasses. The methods included in an interface do not define this behavior—that task is left for the classes that implement the interface.

For example, the Comparable interface contains a method that compares two objects of the same class to see which one should appear first in a sorted list. Any class that implements this interface can determine the sorting order for objects of that class. This behavior would not be available to the class without the interface.

You learn more about interfaces during Day 15, "Packages, Interfaces, and Other Class Features."

Packages

Packages in Java are a way of grouping related classes and interfaces. Packages enable groups of classes to be available only if they are needed, and they eliminate potential conflicts between class names in different groups of classes.

For now, there are only a few things you need to know:

- *The class libraries in Java are contained in a package called java.* The classes in the java package are guaranteed to be available in any Java implementation and are the only classes guaranteed to be available across different implementations. The java package contains smaller packages that define specific subsets of the

Java language's functionality, such as standard features, file handling, multimedia, and many other things. Classes in other packages such as sun often are available only in specific implementations.

- *By default, your Java classes have access to only the classes in java.lang (basic language features).* To use classes from any other package, you have to refer to them explicitly by package name or import them in your source file.

- *To refer to a class within a package, you must normally use the full package name.* For example, because the Color class is contained in the java.awt package, you refer to it in your programs with the notation java.awt.Color.

Summary

If today was your first exposure to object-oriented programming, it probably seems theoretical and a bit overwhelming.

Don't be alarmed. You will be using object-oriented techniques for the rest of this book, and it will become familiar as you gain more experience using it.

At this point, you should have a basic understanding of classes, objects, attributes, and behavior. You also should be familiar with instance variables and methods. You'll be using these right away tomorrow.

The other aspects of object-oriented programming, such as inheritance and packages, will be covered in more detail on upcoming days.

To summarize today's material, here's a glossary of terms and concepts that were covered:

Class—A template for an object that contains variables to describe the object and methods to describe how the object behaves. Classes can inherit variables and methods from other classes.

Object—An instance of a class. Multiple objects that are instances of the same class have access to the same methods, but often have different values for their instance variables.

Instance—The same thing as an object. Each object is an instance of some class.

Method—A group of statements in a class that defines how the class's objects will behave. Methods are analogous to functions in other languages, but must always be located inside a class.

Class method—A method that operates on a class itself rather than on specific instances of a class.

Instance method—A method of an object that operates on that object by manipulating the values of its instance variables. Because instance methods are much more common than class methods, they often are just called methods.

Class variable—A variable that describes an attribute of a class instead of specific instances of the class.

Instance variable—A variable that describes an attribute of an instance of a class instead of the class itself.

Interface—A specification of abstract behavior that individual classes can then implement.

Package—A collection of classes and interfaces. Classes from packages other than java.lang must be explicitly imported or referred to by their full package and class name.

Subclass—A class further down the class hierarchy than another class, its superclass. Creating a new class that inherits from an existing one is often called subclassing. A class can have as many subclasses as necessary.

Superclass—A class further up the class hierarchy than another class, its subclass. A class only can have one superclass immediately above it, but that class also can have a superclass, and so on.

Q&A

Q **In effect, methods are functions that are defined inside classes. If they look like functions and act like functions, why aren't they called functions?**

A Some object-oriented programming languages do call them functions. (C++ calls them *member functions.*) Other object-oriented languages differentiate between functions inside and outside a body of a class or object, because in those languages the use of the separate terms is important to understanding how each function works. Because the difference is relevant in other languages, and because the term *method* is now in common use in object-oriented terminology, Java uses the term as well.

Q **What's the distinction between instance variables and methods and their counterparts, class variables and methods?**

A Almost everything you do in a Java program will involve instances (also called objects) rather than classes. However, some behavior and attributes make more sense if stored in the class itself rather than in the object. For example, the Math class in the java.lang package includes a class variable called PI that holds the approximate value of pi. This value does not change, so there's no reason different objects of that class would need their own individual copy of the PI variable. On the other hand, every String object contains a method called length() that reveals the number of characters in that String. This value can be different for each object of that class, so it must be an instance method.

Quiz

Review today's material by taking this three-question quiz.

Questions

1. What is another word for a class?

    (a) Object

    (b) Template

    (c) Instance

2. When you create a subclass, what must you define about that class?

    (a) It already is defined.

    (b) Things that are different from its superclass.

    (c) Everything about the class.

3. What does an instance method of a class represent?

    (a) The attributes of that class.

    (b) The behavior of that class.

    (c) The behavior of an object created from that class.

Answers

1. b. A class is an abstract template used to create objects that are similar to each other.

2. b. You define how the subclass is different from its superclass. The things that are similar are already defined for you because of inheritance. Answer a is technically correct, but if everything in the subclass is identical to the superclass, there's no reason to create the subclass at all.

3. c. Instance methods refer to a specific object's behavior. Class methods refer to the behavior of all objects belonging to that class.

Exercises

To extend your knowledge of the subjects covered today, try the following exercises:

- In the main() method of the VolcanoRobot class, create a second VolcanoRobot robot named virgil, set up its instance variables, and display them.

- Create an inheritance hierarchy for the pieces of a chess set. Decide where the instance variables color, startingPosition, forwardMovement, and sideMovement should be defined in the hierarchy.

Where applicable, exercise solutions are offered on the book's Web site at http://www.java21days.com.

2

DAY 3

The ABCs of Java

A Java program is made up of classes and objects, which in turn are made up of methods and variables. Methods are made up of statements and expressions, which are made up of operators.

At this point, you might be afraid that Java is like the Russian nesting dolls called *matryoshka*. Every one of those dolls seems to have a smaller doll inside it, which is as intricate and detailed as its larger companion.

This chapter clears away the big dolls to reveal the smallest elements of Java programming. You'll leave classes, objects, and methods alone for a day and examine the basic things you can do in a single line of Java code.

The following subjects are covered:

- Java statements and expressions
- Variables and data types
- Constants
- Comments
- Literals
- Arithmetic

- Comparisons
- Logical operators

> **Note**   Because of Java's ties to C and C++, much of the material in this chapter will
> look familiar to programmers who are well versed in those languages.

Statements and Expressions

All tasks that you want to accomplish in a Java program can be broken down into a series of statements.

NEW TERM   A *statement* is a simple command written in a programming language that causes something to happen.

Statements represent a single action that is taken in a Java program. All of the following are simple Java statements:

```
int weight = 295;
```

```
System.out.println("Free the bound periodicals!");
```

```
song.duration = 230;
```

Some statements can convey a value, such as when you add two numbers together in a program or evaluate whether two variables are equal to each other. These kinds of statements are called expressions.

NEW TERM   An *expression* is a statement that results in a value being produced. The value can be stored for later use in the program, used immediately in another statement, or disregarded. The value produced by a statement is called its *return value*.

Some expressions produce a numerical return value, as in the example of adding two numbers together. Others produce a Boolean value—true or false—or can even produce a Java object. They are discussed later today.

Although many Java programs list one statement per line, this is a formatting decision that does not determine where one statement ends and another one begins. Each statement in Java is terminated with a semicolon character (;). A programmer can put more than one statement on a line and it will compile successfully, as in the following example:

```
dante.speed = 2; dante.temperature = 510;
```

Statements in Java are grouped using the opening curly brace ({) and closing curly brace (}). A group of statements organized between these characters is called a *block* or *block statement*, and you learn more about them during Day 5, "Lists, Logic, and Loops."

Variables and Data Types

In the `VolcanoRobot` application you created during Day 2, "Object-Oriented Programming," you used variables to keep track of information.

NEW TERM *Variables* are a place where information can be stored while a program is running. The value can be changed at any point in the program—hence the name.

To create a variable, you must give it a name and identify what type of information it will store. You also can give a variable an initial value at the same time you create it.

There are three kinds of variables in Java: instance variables, class variables, and local variables.

Instance variables, as you learned yesterday, are used to define an object's attributes. *Class variables* define the attributes of an entire class of objects, and apply to all instances of it.

Local variables are used inside method definitions, or even smaller blocks of statements within a method. They can be used only while the method or block is being executed by the Java interpreter, and they cease to exist afterward.

Although all three kinds of variables are created in much the same way, class and instance variables are used in a different manner than local variables. You learn about local variables today and cover instance and class variables during Day 4, "Working with Objects."

Note   Unlike other languages, Java does not have *global variables* (variables that can be used in all parts of a program). Instance and class variables are used to communicate information from one object to another, and these replace the need for global variables.

Creating Variables

Before you can use a variable in a Java program, you must create the variable by declaring its name and the type of information it will store. The type of information is listed first, followed by the name of the variable. The following are all examples of variable declarations:

```
int loanLength;
```

```
String message;
```

```
boolean gameOver;
```

 Note

> You learn about variable types later today, but you might be familiar with the types used in this example. The int type represents integers, boolean is used for true/false values, and String is a special variable type used to store text.

Local variables can be declared at any place inside a method, just like any other Java statement, but they must be declared before they can be used. The normal place for variable declarations is immediately after the statement that names and identifies the method.

In the following example, three variables are declared at the top of a program's main() method:

```
public static void main(String[] arguments ) {
    int total;
    String reportTitle;
    boolean active;
}
```

If you are creating several variables of the same type, you can declare all of them in the same statement by separating the variable names with commas. The following statement creates three String variables named street, city, and state:

```
String street, city, state;
```

Variables can be assigned a value when they are created by using an equal sign (=) followed by the value. The following statements create new variables and give them initial values:

```
int zipCode = 02134;
```

```
int box = 350;
```

```
boolean pbs = true;
```

```
String name = "Zoom", city = "Boston", state = "MA";
```

As the last statement indicates, you can assign values to multiple variables of the same type by using commas to separate them.

Local variables must be given values before they are used in a program, or the program won't compile successfully. For this reason, it is good practice to give initial values to all local variables.

Instance and class variable definitions are given an initial value depending on the type of information they hold:

- Numeric variables `0`
- Characters `'\0'`
- Booleans `false`
- Objects `null`

Naming Variables

Variable names in Java must start with a letter, an underscore character (_), or a dollar sign ($). They cannot start with a number. After the first character, variable names can include any combination of letters or numbers.

Note

> In addition, the Java language uses the Unicode character set, which includes the standard character set plus thousands of others to represent international alphabets. Accented characters and other symbols can be used in variable names as long as they have a Unicode character number.

When naming a variable and using it in a program, it's important to remember that Java is case sensitive—the capitalization of letters must be consistent. Because of this, a program can have a variable named X and another named x—and a `rose` is not a `Rose` is not a `ROSE`.

In programs in this book and elsewhere, Java variables are given meaningful names that include several words joined together. To make it easier to spot the words, the following rule of thumb is used:

- The first letter of the variable name is lowercase.
- Each successive word in the variable name begins with a capital letter.
- All other letters are lowercase.

The following variable declarations follow this rule of naming:

```
Button loadFile;

int areaCode;

boolean quitGame;
```

Variable Types

In addition to a name, a variable declaration must include the type of information being stored. The type can be any of the following:

- One of the basic data types
- The name of a class or interface
- An array

You learn how to declare and use array variables on Day 5. This lesson focuses on the other variable types.

Data Types

There are eight basic variable types for the storage of integers, floating-point numbers, characters, and Boolean values. These often are called *primitive types* because they are built-in parts of the Java language rather than being objects, which makes them more efficient to use. These data types have the same size and characteristics no matter what operating system and platform you're on, unlike some data types in other programming languages.

There are four data types that can be used to store integers. The one to use depends on the size of the integer, as indicated in Table 3.1.

TABLE 3.1   Integer Types

Type	Size	Values That Can Be Stored
byte	8 bits	–128 to 127
short	16 bits	–32,768 to 32,767
int	32 bits	–2,147,483,648 to 2,147,483,647
long	64 bits	–9,223,372,036,854,775,808 to 9,223,372,036,854,775,807

All these types are signed, which means that they can hold either positive or negative numbers. The type used for a variable depends on the range of values it might need to hold. None of these integer variables can reliably store a value that is too large or too small for its designated variable type, so you should take care when designating the type.

Another type of number that can be stored is a floating-point number, which has the type float or double. *Floating-point numbers* represent numbers with a decimal part. The float type should be sufficient for most uses because it can handle any number from 1.4E-45 to 3.4E+38. If not, the double type can be used for more precise numbers ranging from 4.9E-324 to 1.7E+308.

The char type is used for individual characters such as letters, numbers, punctuation, and other symbols.

The last of the eight basic data types is boolean. As you have learned, Boolean values hold either true or false in Java.

All these variable types are listed in lowercase, and you must use them as such in programs. There are classes with the same name as some of these data types but different capitalization—for example, Boolean and Char. These have different functionality in a Java program, so you can't use them interchangeably. You will see how these special classes are used tomorrow.

Class Types

In addition to the eight basic data types, a variable can have a class as its type, as in the following examples:

```
String lastName = "Hopper";

Color hair;

VolcanoRobot vr;
```

When a variable has a class as its type, the variable refers to an object of that class or one of its subclasses.

The last example in the preceding list, VolcanoRobot vr; creates a variable named vr that is reserved for a VolcanoRobot object, although the object itself might not exist yet. You'll learn tomorrow how to associate objects with variables.

Referring to a superclass as a variable type is useful when the variable might be one of several different subclasses. For example, consider a class hierarchy with a CommandButton superclass and three subclasses: RadioButton, CheckboxButton, and ClickButton. If you create a CommandButton variable called widget, it could be used to refer to a RadioButton, CheckboxButton, or ClickButton object.

Declaring a variable of type Object means that it can be associated with any kind of object.

Note

Java does not have anything comparable to the typedef statement from C and C++. To declare new types in Java, a new class is declared and variables can use that class as their type.

Assigning Values to Variables

After a variable has been declared, a value can be assigned to it with the assignment operator, an equal sign (=). The following are examples of assignment statements:

```
idCode = 8675309;
```

```
accountOverdrawn = false;
```

Constants

Variables are useful when you need to store information that can be changed as a program runs. If the value should never change during a program's runtime, you can use a special type of variable called a constant.

 A *constant*, which also is called a *constant variable*, is a variable with a value that never changes. This might seem like a misnomer, given the meaning of the word "variable."

Constants are useful in defining shared values for all methods of an object—in other words, for giving meaningful names to unchanging values that an entire object must have access to. In Java, you can create constants for all kids of variables: instance, class, and local.

> **Note**
>
> Constant local variables were not possible in Java 1.0, but were added to the language for all subsequent versions. This becomes important if you're trying to create an applet that is fully compatible with Java 1.0, as you will learn during Day 7, "Writing Java Applets."

To declare a constant, use the final keyword before the variable declaration and include an initial value for that variable, as in the following:

```
final float PI = 3.141592;
```

```
final boolean DEBUG = false;
```

```
final int PENALTY = 25;
```

In the preceding statements, the names of the constants are capitalized: PI, DEBUG, and PENALTY. This isn't required, but it is a convention used by many Java programmers—Sun uses it in the Java class library. The capitalization makes it clear that you're using a constant.

Constants can be useful for naming various states of an object and then testing for those states. Suppose you have a program that takes directional input from the numeric keypad on the keyboard—push 8 to go up, 4 to go left, and so on. You can define those values as constant integers:

```
final int LEFT = 4;
final int RIGHT = 6;
final int UP = 8;
final int DOWN = 2;
```

Using constants often makes a program easier to understand. To illustrate this point, consider which of the following two statements is more informative of its function:

```
this.direction = 4;
```

```
this.direction = LEFT;
```

Comments

3

One of the most important ways to improve the readability of your program is to use comments.

NEW TERM *Comments* are information included in a program strictly for the benefit of humans trying to figure out what's going on in the program. The Java compiler ignores comments entirely when preparing a runnable version of a Java source file.

There are three different kinds of comments you can use in Java programs, and you can use each of them at your discretion.

The first way to add a comment to a program is to precede it with two slash characters (//). Everything from the slashes to the end of the line is considered a comment, as in the following statement:

```
int creditHours = 3; // set up credit hours for course
```

In this example, everything from the // to the end of the line is a comment and is disregarded by a Java compiler.

If you need to make a comment that takes up more than one line, you can begin it with the text /* and end it with the text */. Everything between these two delimiters is considered as a comment, as in the following:

```
/* This program occasionally deletes all files on
your hard drive and renders it completely unusable
when you spellcheck a document. */
```

The final type of comment is meant to be computer-readable as well as human-readable. If you begin a comment with the text /** (instead of /*) and end it with */, the comment is interpreted to be official documentation on how the class and its public methods work.

This kind of comment then can be read by utilities such as the javadoc tool included with the SDK. The javadoc program uses official comments to create a set of HTML documents that document the program, its class hierarchy, and its methods.

All the official documentation on Java's class library comes from javadoc-style comments. You can view current Java 2 documentation on the Web at the following page:

```
http://java.sun.com/j2se/1.3/docs
```

You also can download all this documentation for faster browsing on your own computer. The documents are more than 23MB in size and are available from the following page:

```
http://java.sun.com/j2se/1.3/docs.html
```

Literals

In addition to variables, you will also use a literal in a Java statement.

New Term A *literal* is any number, text, or other information that directly represents a value.

Literal is a programming term that essentially means that what you type is what you get. The following assignment statement uses a literal:

```
int year = 2000;
```

The literal is 2000, because it directly represents the integer value 2000. Numbers, characters, and strings all are examples of literals.

Although the meaning and usage of literals will seem intuitive most of the time, Java has some special types of literals that represent different kinds of numbers, characters, strings, and Boolean values.

Number Literals

Java has several integer literals. The number 4, for example, is an integer literal of the int variable type. It also can be assigned to byte and short variables because the number is small enough to fit into those integer types. An integer literal larger than an int can hold is automatically considered to be of the type long. You also can indicate that a literal should be a long integer by adding the letter L (L or l) to the number. For example, the following statement treats the value 4 as a long integer:

```
pennyTotal = pennyTotal + 4L;
```

To represent a negative number as a literal, prepend a minus sign (-) to the literal, as in -45.

If you need to use a literal integer with octal numbering, prepend a 0 to the number. For example, the octal number 777 would be the literal 0777. Hexadecimal integers are used as literals by prepending the number with 0x, as in 0x12 or 0xFF.

> **Note**
>
> Octal and hexadecimal numbering systems are convenient for many advanced programming uses, but unlikely to be needed by beginners. *Octal numbers* are a base-8 numbering system, which means they can only represent the values 0 through 7 as a single digit. The eighth number in octal is 10 (or 010 as a Java literal).
>
> Hexadecimal is a base-16 numbering system, and it can represent 16 numbers as a single digit. The letters A through F represent the last six digits, so the first 16 numbers are 0, 1, 2, 3, 4, 5, 6, 7, 8, 9, A, B, C, D, E, F.
>
> The octal and hexadecimal systems are better suited for certain tasks in programming than the normal decimal system is. If you have ever used HTML to set a Web page's background color, you might have used hexadecimal numbers.

3

Floating-point literals use a period character (.) for the decimal point, as you would expect. The following statement uses a literal to set up a double variable:

```
double myGPA = 2.25;
```

All floating-point literals are considered of the double variable type instead of float. To specify a literal of float, add the letter F (F or f) to the literal, as in the following example:

```
float piValue = 3.1415927F;
```

You can use exponents in floating-point literals by using the letter e or E followed by the exponent, which can be a negative number. The following statements use exponential notation:

```
double x = 12e22;
```

```
double y = 19E-95;
```

Boolean Literals

The Boolean values true and false also are literals. These are the only two values you can use when assigning a value to a boolean variable type or using a Boolean in a statement in other ways.

If you have used another language such as C, you might expect that a value of 1 is equivalent to `true` and `0` is equivalent to `false`. This isn't the case in Java—you must use the values `true` or `false` to represent Boolean values. The following statement sets a `boolean` variable:

```
boolean chosen = true;
```

Note that the literal `true` does not have quotation marks around it. If it did, the Java compiler would assume that it was a string of characters.

Character Literals

Character literals are expressed by a single character surrounded by single quotation marks, such as `'a'`, `'#'`, and `'3'`. You might be familiar with the ASCII character set, which includes 128 characters including letters, numerals, punctuation, and other characters useful in computing. Java supports thousands of additional characters through the 16-bit Unicode standard.

Some character literals represent characters that are not readily printable or accessible through a keyboard. Table 3.2 lists the special codes that can represent these special characters as well as characters from the Unicode character set. The letter *d* in the octal, hex, and Unicode escape codes represents a number or a hexadecimal digit (a–f or A–F).

TABLE 3.2   Character Escape Codes

Escape	Meaning
\n	New line
\t	Tab
\b	Backspace
\r	Carriage return
\f	Formfeed
\\	Backslash
\'	Single quotation mark
\"	Double quotation mark
\d	Octal
\xd	Hexadecimal
\ud	Unicode character

Note

C and C++ programmers should note that Java does not include character codes for \a (bell) or \v (vertical tab).

String Literals

The final literal that you can use in a Java program represents strings of characters. A string in Java is an object rather than being a basic data type, and strings are not stored in arrays as they are in languages such as C.

Because string objects are real objects in Java, methods are available to combine strings, modify strings, and determine whether two strings have the same value.

String literals consist of a series of characters inside double quotation marks, as in the following statements:

```
String quitMsg = "Are you sure you want to quit?";

String password = "swordfish";
```

Strings can include the character escape codes listed in Table 3.2 previously, as shown here:

```
String example = "Socrates asked, \"Hemlock is poison?\"";

System.out.println("Sincerely,\nMillard Fillmore\n");

String title = "Sams Teach Yourself Rebol While You Sleep\u2122"
```

In the last example here, the Unicode code sequence \u2122 produces a ™ symbol on systems that have been configured to support Unicode.

Caution

Most users in English-speaking countries aren't likely to see Unicode characters when they run Java programs. Although Java supports the transmission of Unicode characters, the user's system also must support it for the characters to be displayed. Unicode support provides a way to encode its characters for systems that support the standard. Although Java 1.0 supported only the Latin subset of Unicode, Java 1.1 and subsequent versions support the display of any Unicode character that can be represented by a host font.

For more information about Unicode, visit the Unicode Consortium Web site at http://www.unicode.org.

Although string literals are used in a manner similar to other literals in a program, they are handled differently behind the scenes.

When a string literal is used, Java stores that value as a String object. You don't have to explicitly create a new object, as you must do when working with other objects, so they are as easy to work with as basic data types. Strings are unusual in this respect—none of the basic types is stored as an object when used. You learn more about strings and the String class today and tomorrow.

Expressions and Operators

An *expression* is a statement that can convey a value. Some of the most common expressions are mathematical, such as in the following source code example:

```
int x = 3;
int y = x;
int z = x * y;
```

All three of these statements can be considered expressions—they convey values that can be assigned to variables. The first assigns the literal 3 to the variable x. The second assigns the value of the variable x to the variable y. The multiplication operator * is used to multiply the x and y integers, and the expression produces the result of the multiplication. This result is stored in the z integer.

An expression can be any combination of variables, literals, and operators. They also can be method calls, because methods can send back a value to the object or class that called the method.

The value conveyed by an expression is called a *return value*, as you have learned. This value can be assigned to a variable and used in many other ways in your Java programs.

Most of the expressions in Java use operators like *.

 Operators are special symbols used for mathematical functions, some types of assignment statements, and logical comparisons.

Arithmetic

There are five operators used to accomplish basic arithmetic in Java. These are shown in Table 3.3.

TABLE 3.3 Arithmetic Operators

Operator	Meaning	Example
+	Addition	3 + 4
-	Subtraction	5 - 7
*	Multiplication	5 * 5
/	Division	14 / 7
%	Modulus	20 % 7

Each operator takes two operands, one on either side of the operator. The subtraction operator also can be used to negate a single operand—which is equivalent to multiplying that operand by -1.

One thing to be mindful of when using division is the kind of numbers you're dealing with. If you store a division operation into an integer, the result will be truncated to the next lower whole number because the `int` data type can't handle floating-point numbers. As an example, the expression 31 / 9 results in 3 if stored as an integer.

Modulus division, which uses the `%` operator, produces the remainder of a division operation. Using 31 % 9 results in 4 because 31 divided by 9 leaves a remainder of 4.

Note that many arithmetic operations involving integers produce an `int` regardless of the original type of the operands. If you're working with other numbers, such as floating-point numbers or `long` integers, you should make sure that the operands have the same type you're trying to end up with.

Listing 3.1 is an example of simple arithmetic in Java.

3

LISTING 3.1   The Source File `Weather.java`

```
 1: class Weather {
 2:     public static void main(String[] arguments) {
 3:         float fah = 86;
 4:         System.out.println(fah + " degrees Fahrenheit is ...");
 5:         // To convert Fahrenheit into Celsius
 6:         // Begin by subtracting 32
 7:         fah = fah - 32;
 8:         // Divide the answer by 9
 9:         fah = fah / 9;
10:         // Multiply that answer by 5
11:         fah = fah * 5;
12:         System.out.println(fah + " degrees Celsius\n");
13:
14:         float cel = 33;
15:         System.out.println(cel + " degrees Celsius is ...");
16:         // To convert Celsius into Fahrenheit
17:         // Begin by multiplying it by 9
18:         cel = cel * 9;
19:         // Divide the answer by 5
20:         cel = cel / 5;
21:         // add 32 to the answer
22:         cel = cel + 32;
23:         System.out.println(cel + " degrees Fahrenheit");
24:     }
25: }
```

If you run this Java application, it produces the following output:

```
86.0 degrees Fahrenheit is ...
30.0 degrees Celsius

33.0 degrees Celsius is ...
91.4 degrees Fahrenheit
```

In Lines 3–12 of this Java application, a temperature in Fahrenheit is converted to Celsius using the arithmetic operators:

- Line 3: The floating-point variable fah is created with a value of 86.
- Line 4: The current value of fah is displayed.
- Line 5: The first of several comments for the benefit of people trying to figure out what the program is doing. These comments are ignored by the Java compiler.
- Line 7: fah is set to its current value minus 32.
- Line 9: fah is set to its current value divided by 9.
- Line 11: fah is set to its current value multiplied by 5.
- Line 12: Now that fah has been converted to a Celsius value, fah is displayed again.

A similar thing happens in Lines 14–23, but in the reverse direction. A temperature in Celsius is converted to Fahrenheit.

This program also makes use of System.out.println() in several statements. The System.out.println() method is used in an application to display strings and other information to the standard output device, which usually is the screen.

System.out.println() takes a single argument within its parentheses: a string. To present more than one variable or literal as the argument to println(), you can use the + operator to combine these elements into a single string.

You learn more about this use of the + operator later today.

More About Assignment

Assigning a value to a variable is an expression, because it produces a value. Because of this feature, you can string assignment statements together the following way:

```
x = y = z = 7;
```

In this statement, all three variables end up with the value of 7.

The right side of an assignment expression always is calculated before the assignment takes place. This makes it possible to use an expression statement as in the following code example:

```
int x = 5;
x = x + 2;
```

In the expression x = x + 2, the first thing that happens is that x + 2 is calculated. The result of this calculation, 7, is then assigned to x.

Using an expression to change a variable's value is an extremely common task in programming. There are several operators used strictly in these cases.

Table 3.4 shows these assignment operators and the expressions they are functionally equivalent to.

TABLE 3.4 Assignment Operators

Expression	Meaning
x += y	x = x + y
x -= y	x = x - y
x *= y	x = x * y
x /= y	x = x / y

Caution

These shorthand assignment operators are functionally equivalent to the longer assignment statements for which they substitute. However, if either side of your assignment statement is part of a complex expression, there are cases where the operators are not equivalent. For example, if x equals 20 and y equals 5, the following two statements do not produce the same value:

```
x = x / y + 5;
x /= y + 5;
```

When in doubt, simplify an expression by using multiple assignment statements and don't use the shorthand operators.

Incrementing and Decrementing

Another common task is to add or subtract one from an integer variable. There are special operators for these expressions, which are called increment and decrement operations.

NEW TERM   *Incrementing* a variable means to add 1 to its value, and *decrementing* a variable means to subtract 1 from its value.

The increment operator is ++ and the decrement operator is --. These operators are placed immediately after or immediately before a variable name, as in the following code example:

```
int x = 7;
x = x++;
```

In this example, the statement x = x++ increments the x variable from 7 to 8.

These increment and decrement operators can be placed before or after a variable name, and this affects the value of expressions that involve these operators.

NEW TERM   Increment and decrement operators are called *prefix* operators if listed before a variable name, and *postfix* operators if listed after a name.

In a simple expression such as standards--;, using a prefix or postfix operator produces the same result, making the operators interchangeable. When increment and decrement operations are part of a larger expression, however, the choice between prefix and postfix operators is important.

Consider the following two expressions:

```
int x, y, z;
x = 42;
y = x++;
z = ++x;
```

These two expressions yield very different results because of the difference between prefix and postfix operations. When you use postfix operators as in y=x++, y receives the value of x before it is incremented by one. When using prefix operators as in z = ++x, x is incremented by one before the value is assigned to z. The end result of this example is that y equals 42, z equals 44, and x equals 44.

If you're still having some trouble figuring this out, here's the example again with comments describing each step:

```
int x, y, z; // x, y, and z are all declared
x = 42;      // x is given the value of 42
y = x++;     // y is given x's value (42) before it is incremented
             // and x is then incremented to 43
z = ++x;     // x is incremented to 44, and z is given x's value
```

Caution As with shorthand operators, increment and decrement operators can produce results you might not have expected when used in extremely complex expressions. The concept of "assigning x to y before x is incremented" isn't precisely right, because Java evaluates everything on the right side of an expression before assigning its value to the left side. Java stores some values before handling an expression in order to make postfix work the way it has been described in this section. When you're not getting the results you expect from a complex expression that includes prefix and postfix operators, try to break the expression into multiple statements to simplify it.

Comparisons

Java has several operators that are used when making comparisons between variables, variables and literals, or other types of information in a program.

These operators are used in expressions that return Boolean values of `true` or `false`, depending on whether the comparison being made is true or not. Table 3.5 shows the comparison operators.

TABLE 3.5   Comparison Operators

Operator	Meaning	Example
==	Equal	x == 3
!=	Not equal	x != 3
<	Less than	x < 3
>	Greater than	x > 3
<=	Less than or equal to	x <= 3
>=	Greater than or equal to	x >= 3

The following example shows a comparison operator in use:

```
boolean hip;
int age = 33;
hip = age < 25;
```

The expression `age < 25` produces a result of either `true` or `false`, depending on the value of the integer age. Because age is `33` in this example (which is not less than `25`), hip is given the Boolean value `false`.

Logical Operators

Expressions that result in Boolean values such as comparison operations can be combined to form more complex expressions. This is handled through logical operators. These operators are used for the logical combinations AND, OR, XOR, and logical NOT.

For AND combinations, the & or && logical operators are used. When two Boolean expressions are linked by the & or && operators, the combined expression returns a true value only if both Boolean expressions are true.

Consider this example, taken directly from the film *Harold & Maude*:

```
boolean unusual = (age < 21) & (girlfriendAge > 78);
```

This expression combines two comparison expressions: age < 21 and girlfriendAge > 78. If both of these expressions are true, the value true is assigned to the variable unusual. In any other circumstance, the value false is assigned to unusual.

The difference between & and && lies in how much work Java does on the combined expression. If & is used, the expressions on either side of the & are evaluated no matter what. If && is used and the left side of the && is false, the expression on the right side of the && never is evaluated.

For OR combinations, the | or || logical operators are used. These combined expressions return a true value if either Boolean expression is true.

Consider this *Harold & Maude*–inspired example:

```
boolean unusual = (grimThoughts > 10) || (girlfriendAge > 78);
```

This expression combines two comparison expressions: grimThoughts > 10 and girlfriendAge > 78. If either of these expressions is true, the value true is assigned to the variable unusual. Only if both of these expressions are false will the value false be assigned to unusual.

Note the use of || instead of |. Because of this usage, if grimThoughts > 10 is true, unusual is set to true and the second expression is never evaluated.

The XOR combination has one logical operator, ^. This results in a true value only if both Boolean expressions it combines have opposite values. If both are true or both are false, the ^ operator produces a false value.

The NOT combination uses the ! logical operator followed by a single expression. It reverses the value of a Boolean expression the same way that a minus symbol reverses the positive or negative sign on a number.

For example, if age < 30 returns a true value, !(age < 30) returns a false value.

These logical operators can seem completely illogical when encountered for the first time. You get plenty of chances to work with them in subsequent chapters, especially on Day 5.

Operator Precedence

When more than one operator is used in an expression, Java has an established precedence to determine the order in which operators are evaluated. In many cases, this precedence determines the overall value of the expression.

For example, consider the following expression:

```
y = 6 + 4 / 2;
```

The y variable receives the value 5 or the value 8, depending on which arithmetic operation is handled first. If the 6 + 4 expression comes first, y has the value of 5. Otherwise, y equals 8.

In general, the order from first to last is the following:

- Increment and decrement operations
- Arithmetic operations
- Comparisons
- Logical operations
- Assignment expressions

If two operations have the same precedence, the one on the left in the actual expression is handled before the one on the right. Table 3.6 shows the specific precedence of the various operators in Java. Operators farther up the table are evaluated first.

TABLE 3.6 Operator Precedence

Operator	Notes
. [] ()	Parentheses (()) are used to group expressions; period (.) is used for access to methods and variables within objects and classes (discussed tomorrow); square brackets ([]) are used for arrays. (This operator is discussed later in the week.)
++ -- ! ~ instanceof	The instanceof operator returns true or false based on whether the object is an instance of the named class or any of that class's sub-classes (discussed tomorrow).
new (type)expression	The new operator is used for creating new instances of classes; () in this case is for casting a value to another type. (You learn about both of these tomorrow.)

TABLE 3.6 continued

Operator	Notes
* / %	Multiplication, division, modulus.
+ -	Addition, subtraction.
<< >> >>>	Bitwise left and right shift.
< > <= >=	Relational comparison tests.
== !=	Equality.
&	AND
^	XOR
|	OR
&&	Logical AND
||	Logical OR
? :	Shorthand for if...then...else (discussed on Day 5).
= += -= *= /= %= ^=	Various assignments.
&= |= <<= >>= >>>=	More assignments.

Returning to the expression y = 6 + 4 / 2, Table 3.6 shows that division is evaluated before addition, so the value of y will be 8.

To change the order in which expressions are evaluated, place parentheses around the expressions that should be evaluated first. You can nest one set of parentheses inside another to make sure that expressions evaluate in the desired order—the innermost parenthetic expression is evaluated first.

The following expression results in a value of 5:

y = (6 + 4) / 2

The value of 5 is the result because 6 + 4 is calculated before the result, 10, is divided by 2.

Parentheses also can be useful to improve the readability of an expression. If the precedence of an expression isn't immediately clear to you, adding parentheses to impose the desired precedence can make the statement easier to understand.

String Arithmetic

As stated earlier today, the + operator has a double life outside the world of mathematics. It can be used to concatenate two or more strings.

NEW TERM *Concatenate* means to link two things together. For reasons unknown, it is the verb of choice when describing the act of combining two strings—winning out over paste, glue, affix, combine, link, and conjoin.

In several examples, you have seen statements that look something like this:

```
String firstName = "Raymond";
System.out.println("Everybody loves " + firstName);
```

These two lines result in the following text being displayed:

```
Everybody loves Raymond
```

The + operator combines strings, other objects, and variables to form a single string. In the preceding example, the literal Everybody loves is concatenated to the value of the String object firstName.

Working with the concatenation operator is easy in Java because of the way it can handle any variable type and object value as if it were a string. If any part of a concatenation operation is a String or String literal, all elements of the operation will be treated as if they were strings:

```
System.out.println(4 + " score and " + 7 + " years ago.");
```

This produces the output text 4 score and 7 years ago., as if the integer literals 4 and 7 were strings.

There also is a shorthand += operator to add something to the end of a string. For example, consider the following expression:

```
myName += " Jr.";
```

This expression is equivalent to the following:

```
myName = myName + " Jr.";
```

In this example, it changes the value of myName (which might be something like Efrem Zimbalist) by adding Jr. at the end (Efrem Zimbalist Jr.).

Summary

Anyone who pops open a set of matryoska dolls has to be a bit disappointed to reach the smallest doll in the group. Ideally, advances in microengineering should enable Russian artisans to create ever-smaller and smaller dolls, until someone reaches the subatomic threshold and is declared the winner.

You have reached Java's smallest nesting doll today, but it shouldn't be a letdown. Using statements and expressions enables you to begin building effective methods, which make effective objects and classes possible.

Today you learned about creating variables and assigning values to them; using literals to represent numeric, character, and string values; and working with operators. Tomorrow you put these skills to use as you develop objects for Java programs.

To summarize today's material, Table 3.7 lists the operators you learned about. Be a doll and look them over carefully.

TABLE 3.7   Operator Summary

Operator	Meaning
+	Addition
-	Subtraction
*	Multiplication
/	Division
%	Modulus
<	Less than
>	Greater than
<=	Less than or equal to
>=	Greater than or equal to
==	Equal
!=	Not equal
&&	Logical AND
||	Logical OR
!	Logical NOT
&	AND
|	OR
^	XOR
=	Assignment
++	Increment
--	Decrement
+=	Add and assign
-=	Subtract and assign
*=	Multiply and assign
/=	Divide and assign
%=	Modulus and assign

Q&A

Q **What happens if you assign an integer value to a variable that is too large for that variable to hold?**

A Logically, you might think that the variable is converted to the next larger type, but this isn't what happens. Instead, an *overflow* occurs—a situation in which the number wraps around from one size extreme to the other. An example of overflow would be a `byte` variable that goes from 127 (acceptable value) to 128 (unacceptable). It would wrap around to the lowest acceptable value, which is -128, and start counting upward from there. Overflow isn't something you can readily deal with in a program, so you should be sure to give your variables plenty of living space in their chosen data type.

Q **Why does Java have all these shorthand operators for arithmetic and assignment? It's really hard to read that way.**

A Java's syntax is based on C++, which is based on C (more Russian nesting doll behavior). C is an expert language that values programming power over readability, and the shorthand operators are one of the legacies of that design priority. Using them in a program isn't required because effective substitutes are available, so you can avoid them in your own programming if you prefer.

Quiz

Review today's material by taking this three-question quiz.

Questions

1. Which of the following is a valid value for a `boolean` variable?

    (a) `"false"`

    (b) `false`

    (c) `10`

2. Which of these conventions is not used when naming variables in Java?

    (a) Each successive word after the first in the variable name begins with a capital letter.

    (b) The first letter of the variable name is lowercase.

    (c) All letters are capitalized.

3

3. Which of these data types holds numbers from -32,768 to 32,767?

   (a) char

   (b) byte

   (c) short

Answers

1. b. In Java, a boolean can only be true or false. If you put quotation marks around the value, it will be treated like a String rather than one of the two boolean values.

2. c. Constant names are capitalized to make them stand out from other variables.

3. c.

Exercises

To extend your knowledge of the subjects covered today, try the following exercises:

- Create a program that calculates how much a $14,000 investment would be worth if it increased in value by 40% during the first year, lost $1,500 in value the second year, and increased 12% in the third year.

- Write a program that displays two numbers and uses the / and % operators to display the result and remainder after they are divided. Use the \t character escape code to separate the result and remainder in your output.

Where applicable, exercise solutions are offered on the book's Web site at http://www.java21days.com.

WEEK 1

DAY 4

Working with Objects

When you do work in Java, you use objects to get the job done. As you learned two days ago, Java is a heavily object-oriented programming language.

Almost everything you can do using Java is accomplished with objects. You create objects, modify them, move them around, change their variables, call their methods, and combine them with other objects. You develop classes, create objects out of those classes, and use them with other classes and objects.

Today, you work extensively with objects. The following topics are covered:

- Creating objects (also called *instances*)
- Testing and modifying class and instance variables in those objects
- Calling an object's methods
- Converting objects and other types of data from one class to another

Creating New Objects

When you write a Java program, you define a set of classes. As you learned on Day 2, "Object-Oriented Programming," classes are templates that are used to create objects. These objects, which are also called instances, are self-contained elements of a program that contain related features and data. For the most part, you merely use the class to create instances and then work with those instances. In this section, therefore, you learn how to create a new object from any given class.

Remember strings from yesterday? You learned that using a *string literal* (a series of characters enclosed in double quotation marks) creates a new instance of the class `String` with the value of that string.

The `String` class is unusual in that respect. Although it's a class, there's an easy way to create instances of that class using a literal. To create instances of other classes, the `new` operator is used.

Note

> What about the literals for numbers and characters—don't they create objects, too? Actually, they don't. The primitive data types for numbers and characters create numbers and characters, but for efficiency, they actually aren't objects. You can put object wrappers around them if you need to treat them like objects (which you learn to do on Day 6, "Creating Classes and Methods").

Using `new`

To create a new object, you use the `new` operator with the name of the class you want to create an instance of, followed by parentheses:

```
String name = new String();
URL address = new URL("http://www.prefect.com");
VolcanoRobot robbie = new VolcanoRobot();
```

The parentheses are important; don't leave them off. The parentheses can be empty, in which case the most simple, basic object is created, or the parentheses can contain arguments that determine the initial values of instance variables or other initial qualities of that object.

The following examples show objects being created with arguments:

```
Random seed = new Random(6068430714);

Point pt = new Point(0,0);
```

The number and type of arguments you can use inside the parentheses with `new` are defined by the class itself using a special method called a *constructor*. (You learn more about constructors later today.) If you try to create a new instance of a class with the wrong number or type of arguments (or if you give it no arguments and it needs some), you get an error when you try to compile your Java program.

Here's an example of creating different types of objects using different numbers and types of arguments: the StringTokenizer class, part of the java.util package, divides a string into a series of shorter strings called *tokens*.

A string is divided into tokens by using some kind of character or characters as a delimiter. For example, the text "02/20/67" could be divided into three tokens—02, 20, and 67—using the slash character ("/") as a delimiter.

Listing 4.1 is a Java program that creates StringTokenizer objects using new in two different ways and displays each token the objects contain.

LISTING 4.1   The Full Text of ShowTokens.java

```
 1: import java.util.StringTokenizer;
 2:
 3: class ShowTokens {
 4:
 5:     public static void main(String[] arguments) {
 6:         StringTokenizer st1, st2;
 7:
 8:         String quote1 = "VIZY 3 -1/16";
 9:         st1 = new StringTokenizer(quote1);
10:         System.out.println("Token 1: " + st1.nextToken());
11:         System.out.println("Token 2: " + st1.nextToken());
12:         System.out.println("Token 3: " + st1.nextToken());
13:
14:         String quote2 = "NPLI@9 27/32@3/32";
15:         st2 = new StringTokenizer(quote2, "@");
16:         System.out.println("\nToken 1: " + st2.nextToken());
17:         System.out.println("Token 2: " + st2.nextToken());
18:         System.out.println("Token 3: " + st2.nextToken());
19:     }
20: }
```

When you compile and run the program, the output should resemble the following:

```
Token 1: VIZY
Token 2: 3
Token 3: -1/16

Token 1: NPLI
Token 2: 9 27/32
Token 3: 3/32
```

In this example, two different `StringTokenizer` objects are created using different arguments to the constructor listed after `new`.

The first instance (line 9) uses `new StringTokenizer()` with one argument, a `String` object named `quote1`. This creates a `StringTokenizer` object that uses the default delimiters: black spaces, tab, newline, carriage return, or formfeed characters.

If any of these characters is contained in the string, it is used to divide the tokens. Because the `quote1` string contains spaces, these are used as delimiters dividing each token. Lines 10–12 display the values of all three tokens: `VIZY`, `3`, and `-1/16`.

The second `StringTokenizer` object in this example has two arguments when it is constructed in line 14: a `String` object named `quote2` and an at-sign character (`"@"`). This second argument indicates that the `"@"` character should be used as the delimiter between tokens. The `StringTokenizer` object created in line 15 contains three tokens: `NPLI`, `9 27/32`, and `3/32`.

What `new` Does

Several things happen when you use the `new` operator: The new instance of the given class is created, memory is allocated for it, and a special method defined in the given class is called. This special method is called a constructor.

NEW TERM *Constructors* are special methods for creating and initializing new instances of classes. Constructors initialize the new object and its variables, create any other objects that the object needs, and perform any other operations that the object needs to initialize itself.

Multiple constructor definitions in a class each can have a different number or type of arguments. When you use `new`, you can specify different arguments in the argument list, and the correct constructor for those arguments will be called. Multiple constructor definitions are what enabled the `StringTokenizer` class in the previous example to accomplish different things with the different uses of the `new` operator. When you create your own classes, you can define as many constructors as you need to implement the behavior of the class.

A Note on Memory Management

If you are familiar with other object-oriented programming languages, you might wonder whether the `new` statement has an opposite that destroys an object when it is no longer needed.

Memory management in Java is dynamic and automatic. When you create a new object, Java automatically allocates the right amount of memory for that object. You don't have to allocate any memory for objects explicitly. Java does it for you.

Because Java memory management is automatic, you do not need to deallocate the memory that object uses when you're done using the object. Under most circumstances, when you are finished with an object you have created, Java will be able to determine that the object no longer has any live references to it. (In other words, the object won't be assigned to any variables still in use or stored in any arrays.)

As a program runs, Java periodically looks for unused objects and reclaims the memory that those objects are using. This process is called *garbage collection*, and it's entirely automatic. You don't have to explicitly free the memory taken up by an object—you just have to make sure you're not still holding onto an object you want to get rid of.

Accessing and Setting Class and Instance Variables

At this point, you could create your own object with class and instance variables defined in it—but how do you work with those variables? Easy! Class and instance variables are used in largely the same manner as the local variables you learned about yesterday. You can use them in expressions, assign values to them in statements, and the like. You just refer to them slightly differently than you refer to regular variables in your code.

Getting Values

To get to the value of an instance variable, you use dot notation. With dot notation, an instance or class variable name has two parts: a reference to an object or class on the left side of the dot and a variable on the right side of the dot.

 Dot notation is a way to refer to an object's instance variables and methods using a dot (.) operator.

For example, if you have an object assigned to the variable myCustomer and that object has a variable called orderTotal, you refer to that variable's value like this:

```
myCustomer.orderTotal;
```

This form of accessing variables is an expression (that is, it returns a value), and both sides of the dot also are expressions. That means you can nest instance variable access. If the orderTotal instance variable itself holds an object, and that object has its own instance variable called layaway, you could refer to it like this:

```
myCustomer.orderTotal.layaway;
```

Dot expressions are evaluated from left to right, so you start with myCustomer's variable orderTotal, which points to another object with the variable layaway. You end up with the value of that layaway variable.

Changing Values

Assigning a value to that variable is equally easy—just tack on an assignment operator to the right side of the expression:

```
myCustomer.orderTotal.layaway = true;
```

This example sets the value of the `layaway` variable to `true`.

Listing 4.2 is an example of a program that tests and modifies the instance variables in a `Point` object. `Point` is part of the `java.awt` package and refers to a coordinate point with x and y values.

LISTING 4.2   The Full Text of `SetPoints.java`

```
 1: import java.awt.Point;
 2:
 3: class SetPoints {
 4:
 5: public static void main(String[] arguments) {
 6:     Point location = new Point(4, 13);
 7:
 8:     System.out.println("Starting location:");
 9:     System.out.println("X equals " + location.x);
10:     System.out.println("Y equals " + location.y);
11:
12:     System.out.println("\nMoving to (7, 6)");
13:     location.x = 7;
14:     location.y = 6;
15:
16:     System.out.println("\nEnding location:");
17:     System.out.println("X equals " + location.x);
18:     System.out.println("Y equals " + location.y);
19:     }
20: }
```

When you run this application, the output should be the following:

```
Starting location:
X equals 4
Y equals 13

Moving to (7, 6)

Ending location:
X equals 7
Y equals 6
```

In this example, you first create an instance of `Point` where x equals 4 and y equals 13 (line 6). Lines 9 and 10 display these individual values using dot notation. Lines 13 and 14 change the values of x to 7 and y to 6, respectively. Finally, lines 17 and 18 display the values of x and y again to show how they have changed.

Class Variables

Class variables, as you learned, are variables that are defined and stored in the class itself. Their values apply to the class and all its instances.

With instance variables, each new instance of the class gets a new copy of the instance variables that the class defines. Each instance then can change the values of those instance variables without affecting any other instances. With class variables, only one copy of that variable exists. Changing the value of that variable changes it for all instances of that class.

You define class variables by including the `static` keyword before the variable itself. For example, consider the following partial class definition:

```
class FamilyMember {
    static String surname = "Mendoza";
    String name;
    int age;
}
```

Instances of the class `FamilyMember` each have their own values for name and age. But the class variable surname has only one value for all family members: "Mendoza". Change the value of surname and all instances of `FamilyMember` are affected.

 Note

> Calling these `static` variables refers to one of the meanings for the word *static*: fixed in one place. If a class has a `static` variable, every object of that class has the same value for that variable.

To access class variables, you use the same dot notation used with instance variables. To retrieve or change the value of the class variable, you can use either the instance or the name of the class on the left side of the dot. Both lines of output in this example display the same value:

```
FamilyMember dad = new FamilyMember();
System.out.println("Family's surname is: " + dad.surname);
System.out.println("Family's surname is: " + FamilyMember.surname);
```

Because you can use an instance to change the value of a class variable, it's easy to become confused about class variables and where their values are coming from—remember that the value of a class variable affects all its instances. For this reason, it's a good idea to use the name of the class when you refer to a class variable. It makes your code easier to read and makes strange results easier to debug.

Calling Methods

Calling a method in an object is similar to referring to its instance variables: Dot notation is used. The object whose method you're calling is on the left side of the dot, and the name of the method and its arguments are on the right side of the dot:

```
myCustomer.addToOrder(itemNumber, price, quantity);
```

Note that all methods must have parentheses after them, even if the method takes no arguments:

```
myCustomer.cancelAllOrders();
```

Listing 4.3 shows an example of calling some methods defined in the String class. Strings include methods for string tests and modification, similar to what you would expect in a string library in other languages.

LISTING 4.3   The Full Text of CheckString.java

```
 1: class CheckString {
 2:
 3:     public static void main(String[] arguments) {
 4:         String str = "Nobody ever went broke by buying IBM";
 5:         System.out.println("The string is: " + str);
 6:         System.out.println("Length of this string: "
 7:             + str.length());
 8:         System.out.println("The character at position 5: "
 9:             + str.charAt(5));
10:         System.out.println("The substring from 26 to 32: "
11:             + str.substring(26, 32));
12:         System.out.println("The index of the character v: "
13:             + str.indexOf('v'));
14:         System.out.println("The index of the beginning of the "
15:             + "substring \"IBM\": " + str.indexOf("IBM"));
16:         System.out.println("The string in upper case: "
17:             + str.toUpperCase());
18:     }
19: }
```

The following is displayed on your system's standard output device when you run the program:

```
The string is: Nobody ever went broke by buying IBM
Length of this string: 36
The character at position 5: y
The substring from 26 to 32: buying
The index of the character v: 8
The index of the beginning of the substring "IBM": 33
The string in upper case: NOBODY EVER WENT BROKE BY BUYING IBM
```

In line 4, you create a new instance of String by using a string literal. The remainder of the program simply calls different string methods to do different operations on that string:

- Line 5 prints the value of the string you created in line 4: "Nobody ever went broke by buying IBM".

- Line 7 calls the length() method in the new String object. This string has 36 characters.

- Line 9 calls the charAt() method, which returns the character at the given position in the string. Note that string positions start at position 0 rather than 1, so the character at position 5 is y.

- Line 11 calls the substring() method, which takes two integers indicating a range and returns the substring with those starting and ending points. The substring() method also can be called with only one argument, which returns the substring from that position to the end of the string.

- Line 13 calls the indexOf() method, which returns the position of the first instance of the given character (here, 'v'). Character literals are surrounded by single quotation marks—if double quotation marks surrounded the v in line 13, the literal would be considered a String.

- Line 15 shows a different use of the indexOf() method, which takes a string argument and returns the index of the beginning of that string.

- Line 17 uses the toUpperCase() method to return a copy of the string in all uppercase.

Nesting Method Calls

A method can return a reference to an object, a primitive data type, or no value at all. In the CheckString program, all the methods called on the String object str returned values that were displayed—for example, the charAt() method returned a character at a specified position in the string.

The value returned by a method also can be stored in a variable:

```
String label = "From";
String upper = label.toUpperCase();
```

In the preceding example, the `String` object `upper` contains the value returned by calling `label.toUpperCase()`—the text `"From"`, an uppercase version of `"From"` .

If the method returns an object, you can call the methods of that object in the same statement. This makes it possible for you to nest methods as you would variables.

Earlier today, you saw an example of a method called with no arguments:

```
myCustomer.cancelAllOrders();
```

If the `cancelAllOrders()` method returns an object, you can call methods of that object in the same statement:

```
myCustomer.cancelAllOrders().talkToManager();
```

This statement calls the `talkToManager()` method, which is defined in the object returned by the `cancelAllOrders()` method of the `myCustomer` object.

You can combine nested method calls and instance variable references as well. In the next example, the `putOnLayaway()` method is defined in the object stored by the `orderTotal` instance variable, which itself is part of the `myCustomer` object:

```
myCustomer.orderTotal.putOnLayaway(itemNumber, price, quantity);
```

`System.out.println()`, the method you've been using in all program examples to display information, is an example of nesting variables and methods.

The `System` class, part of the `java.lang` package, describes behavior specific to the system on which Java is running. `System.out` is a class variable that contains an instance of the class `PrintStream`. This `PrintStream` object represents the standard output of the system, which is normally the screen, but can be redirected to a monitor or file. `PrintStream` objects have a `println()` method that sends a string to that output stream.

Class Methods

Class methods, like class variables, apply to the class as a whole and not to its instances. Class methods commonly are used for general utility methods that might not operate directly on an instance of that class but fit with that class conceptually. For example, the `String` class contains a class method called `valueOf()` that can take one of many different types of arguments (integers, Booleans, other objects, and so on). The `valueOf()` method then returns a new instance of `String` containing the string value of the argument. This method doesn't operate directly on an existing instance of `String`, but getting a string from another object or data type is definitely a `String`-like operation, and it makes sense to define it in the `String` class.

Class methods also can be useful for gathering general methods together in one place (the class). For example, the `Math` class, defined in the `java.lang` package, contains a large set of mathematical operations as class methods—there are no instances of the class `Math`, but you still can use its methods with numeric or Boolean arguments. For example, the class method `Math.max()` takes two arguments and returns the larger of the two. You don't need to create a new instance of `Math`—it can be called anywhere you need it, as in the following:

```
int maximumPrice = Math.max(firstPrice, secondPrice);
```

Dot notation is used to call a class method. As with class variables, you can use either an instance of the class or the class itself on the left side of the dot. However, for the same reasons noted in the discussion on class variables, using the name of the class makes your code easier to read. The last two lines in this example produce the same result—the string 5:

```
String s, s2;
s = "item";
s2 = s.valueOf(5);
s2 = String.valueOf(5);
```

4

References to Objects

As you work with objects, an important thing to understand is the use of references.

 A *reference* is an address that indicates where an object's variables and methods are stored.

You aren't actually using objects when you assign an object to a variable or pass an object to a method as an argument. You aren't even using copies of the objects. Instead, you're using references to those objects.

To better illustrate the difference, Listing 4.4 shows how references work.

LISTING 4.4 The Full Text of `ReferencesTest.java`

```
1: import java.awt.Point;
2:
3: class ReferencesTest {
4:     public static void main(String[] arguments) {
5:         Point pt1, pt2;
6:         pt1 = new Point(100, 100);
```

LISTING 4.4   continued

```
 7:            pt2 = pt1;
 8:
 9:            pt1.x = 200;
10:            pt1.y = 200;
11:            System.out.println("Point1: " + pt1.x + ", " + pt1.y);
12:            System.out.println("Point2: " + pt2.x + ", " + pt2.y);
13:        }
14: }
```

The following is this program's output:

```
Point1: 200, 200
Point2: 200, 200
```

The following takes place in the first part of this program:

- Line 5   Two Point variables are created.
- Line 6   A new Point object is assigned to pt1.
- Line 7   The value of pt1 is assigned to pt2.

Lines 9–12 are the tricky part. The x and y variables of pt1 are both set to 200, and then all variables of pt1 and pt2 are displayed onscreen.

You might expect pt1 and pt2 to have different values. However, the output shows this is not the case. As you can see, the x and y variables of pt2 also were changed, even though nothing in the program explicitly changes them.

This happens because line 7 creates a reference from pt2 to pt1, instead of creating pt2 as a new object copied from pt1.

pt2 is a reference to the same object as pt1; this is shown in Figure 4.1. Either variable can be used to refer to the object or to change its variables.

If you wanted pt1 and pt2 to refer to separate objects, separate new Point() statements could be used on lines 6 and 7 to create separate objects, as shown in the following:

```
pt1 = new Point(100, 100);
pt2 = new Point(100, 100);
```

The use of references in Java becomes particularly important when arguments are passed to methods. You learn more about this later today.

Note   There are no explicit pointers or pointer arithmetic in Java as there are in C and C++. However, by using references and Java arrays, most pointer capabilities are duplicated without many of their drawbacks.

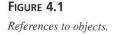
Figure 4.1

References to objects.

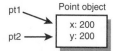

Casting and Converting Objects and Primitive Types

One thing you discover quickly about Java is how finicky it is about the information it will handle. Like Morris, the perpetually dissatisfied cat on the 9-Lives cat food commercials, Java expects things to be a certain way and won't put up with alternatives.

When you are sending arguments to methods or using variables in expressions, you must use variables of the right data types. If a method requires an `int`, the Java compiler responds with an error if you try to send a `float` value to the method. Likewise, if you're setting up one variable with the value of another, they must be of the same type.

Note

> There is one area where Java's compiler is decidedly un-Morrislike: `Strings`. String handling in `println()` methods, assignment statements, and method arguments is simplified with the use of the concatenation operator (+). If any variable in a group of concatenated variables is a string, Java treats the whole thing as a `String`. This makes the following possible:
>
> ```
> float gpa = 2.25F;
> System.out.println("Honest, dad, my GPA is a " + (gpa+1.5));
> ```

4

Sometimes you'll have a value in your Java program that isn't the right type for what you need. It might be the wrong class, or the wrong data type—such as a `float` when you need an `int`.

You use casting to convert a value from one type to another.

NEW TERM *Casting* is the process of producing a new value that has a different type than its source. The meaning is similar to acting, where a character on a TV show can be recast with another actor after a salary dispute or an unfortunate public lewdness arrest.

Although the concept of casting is reasonably simple, the usage is complicated by the fact that Java has both primitive types (such as `int`, `float`, and `boolean`), and object types (`String`, `Point`, `ZipFile`, and the like). There are three forms of casts and conversions to talk about in this section:

- Casting between primitive types, such as `int` to `float` or `float` to `double`
- Casting from an instance of a class to an instance of another class
- Casting primitive types to objects and then extracting primitive values from those objects

When discussing casting, it can be easier to think in terms of sources and destinations. The source is the variable being cast into another type. The destination is the result.

Casting Primitive Types

Casting between primitive types enables you to convert the value of one type to another primitive type. It most commonly occurs with the numeric types, and there's one primitive type that can never be used in a cast. Boolean values must be either `true` or `false` and cannot be used in a casting operation.

In many casts between primitive types, the destination can hold larger values than the source, so the value is converted easily. An example would be casting a `byte` into an `int`. Because a `byte` holds values from –128 to 127 and an `int` holds from –2100000 to 2100000, there's more than enough room to cast a `byte` to an `int`.

You can often automatically use a `byte` or a `char` as an `int`; you can use an `int` as a `long`, an `int` as a `float`, or anything as a `double`. In most cases, because the larger type provides more precision than the smaller, no loss of information occurs as a result. The exception is casting integers to floating-point values—casting an `int` or a `long` to a `float`, or a `long` to a `double` can cause some loss of precision.

 Note
> A character can be used as an `int` because each character has a corresponding numeric code that represents its position in the character set. If the variable `i` has the value 65, the cast `(char)i` produces the character value `'A'`. The numeric code associated with a capital A is 65, according to the ASCII character set, and Java adopted this as part of its character support.

You must use an explicit cast to convert a value in a large type to a smaller type because converting that value might result in a loss of precision. Explicit casts take the following form:

`(typename)value`

In the preceding example, *typename* is the name of the data type you're converting to, such as `short`, `int`, or `float`. *value* is an expression that results in the value of the source type. For example, the value of x is divided by the value of y and the result is cast to an `int` in the following expression:

```
(int)(x / y);
```

Note that because the precedence of casting is higher than that of arithmetic, you have to use parentheses here—otherwise, the value of x would be cast to an `int` first and then divided by y, which could easily produce a different result.

Casting Objects

Instances of classes also can be cast to instances of other classes, with one restriction: The source and destination classes must be related by inheritance—one class must be a subclass of the other.

Analogous to converting a primitive value to a larger type, some objects might not need to be cast explicitly. In particular, because subclasses contain all the same information as their superclass, you can use an instance of a subclass anywhere a superclass is expected.

For example, consider a method that takes two arguments: one of type `Object` and another of type `Window`. You can pass an instance of any class for the `Object` argument because all Java classes are subclasses of `Object`. For the `Window` argument, you can pass in its subclasses such as `Dialog`, `FileDialog`, and `Frame`.

This is true anywhere in a program—not just inside method calls. If you had a variable defined as class `Window`, you could assign objects of that class or any of its subclasses to that variable without casting.

This is true in the reverse, and you can use a superclass when a subclass is expected. There is a catch, however: Because subclasses contain more behavior than their superclasses, there's a loss in precision involved. Those superclass objects might not have all the behavior needed to act in place of a subclass object. For example, if you have an operation that calls methods in objects of the class `Integer`, using an object of class `Number` won't include many methods specified in `Integer`. Errors occur if you try to call methods that the destination object doesn't have.

To use superclass objects where subclass objects are expected, you must cast them explicitly. You won't lose any information in the cast, but you gain all the methods and variables that the subclass defines. To cast an object to another class, you use the same operation that you used for primitive types:

```
(classname)object
```

4

In this case, *classname* is the name of the destination class and *object* is a reference to the source object. Note that casting creates a reference to the old object of the type *classname*; the old object continues to exist as it did before.

The following example casts an instance of the class `VicePresident` to an instance of the class `Employee`; `VicePresident` is a subclass of `Employee` with more information to define that the `VicePresident` has executive washroom privileges:

```
Employee emp = new Employee();
VicePresident veep = new VicePresident();
emp = veep; // no cast needed for upward use
veep = (VicePresident)emp; // must cast explicitly
```

Casting one object is necessary whenever you use Java2D graphics operations. You must cast a `Graphics` object to a `Graphics2D` object before you can draw onscreen. The following example uses a `Graphics` object called `screen` to create a new `Graphics2D` object called `screen2D`:

```
Graphics2D screen2D = (Graphics2D)screen;
```

`Graphics2D` is a subclass of `Graphics`, and both are in the `java.awt` package. You explore the subject fully during Day 12, "Color, Fonts, and Graphics."

In addition to casting objects to classes, you also can cast objects to interfaces—but only if that object's class or one of its superclasses actually implements the interface. Casting an object to an interface means that you can call one of that interface's methods even if that object's class does not actually implement that interface.

Converting Primitive Types to Objects and Vice Versa

One thing you can't do under any circumstance is cast from an object to a primitive data type, or vice versa. Primitive types and objects are very different things in Java and you can't automatically cast between the two or use them interchangeably.

As an alternative, the `java.lang` package includes classes that correspond to each primitive data type: `Float`, `Boolean`, `Byte` and so on. Most of these classes have the same name as the data type, except that the class names begin with a capital letter (`Short` instead of `short`, `Double` instead of `double`, and so on). Also, two classes have names that differ from the corresponding data type—`Character` is used for `char` variables and `Integer` for `int` variables.

Java treats the data types and their class versions very differently, and a program won't compile successfully if you use one when the other is expected.

Using the classes that correspond with each primitive type, you can create an object that holds the same value. The following statement creates an instance of the `Integer` class with the integer value 7801:

```
Integer dataCount = new Integer(7801);
```

After you have an object created in this manner, you can use it as you would any object (although you cannot change its value). When you want to use that value again as a primitive value, there are methods for that as well. For example, if you wanted to get an `int` value from a `dataCount` object, the following statement would be used:

```
int newCount = dataCount.intValue(); // returns 7801
```

A common translation you need in programs is converting a `String` to a numeric type, such as an integer. When you need an `int` as the result, this can be done by using the `parseInt()` class method of the `Integer` class. The `String` to convert is the only argument sent to the method, as in the following example:

```
String pennsylvania = "65000";
int penn = Integer.parseInt(pennsylvania);
```

The Java API documentation includes details on these classes. You can find these HTML pages in the Documentation section of Sun's Java Web site:

```
http://java.sun.com
```

 Note   The following classes can be used to work with objects instead of primitive data types: `Boolean`, `Byte`, `Character`, `Double`, `Float`, `Integer`, `Long`, `Short`, and `Void`.

4

Comparing Object Values and Classes

In addition to casting, there are three other common tasks you will perform often on objects:

- Comparing objects
- Finding out the class of any given object
- Testing to see whether an object is an instance of a given class

Comparing Objects

Yesterday you learned about operators for comparing values: equal, not equal, less than, and so on. Most of these operators work only on primitive types, not on objects. If you try to use other values as operands, the Java compiler produces errors.

The exceptions to this rule are the operators for equality: == (equal) and != (not equal). When used with objects, these operators don't do what you might first expect. Instead of checking whether one object has the same value as the other object, they determine whether both sides of the operator refer to the same object.

To compare instances of a class and have meaningful results, you must implement special methods in your class and call those methods.

A good example of this is the String class. It is possible to have two different String objects that contain the same values. If you used the == operator to compare these objects, however, they would be considered unequal. Although their contents match, they are not the same object.

To see whether two String objects have matching values, a method of the class called equals() is used. The method tests each character in the string and returns true if the two strings have the same values. Listing 4.5 illustrates this.

LISTING 4.5   The Full Text of EqualsTest.java

```
 1: class EqualsTest {
 2:     public static void main(String[] arguments) {
 3:         String str1, str2;
 4:         str1 = "Free the bound periodicals.";
 5:         str2 = str1;
 6:
 7:         System.out.println("String1: " + str1);
 8:         System.out.println("String2: " + str2);
 9:         System.out.println("Same object? " + (str1 == str2));
10:
11:         str2 = new String(str1);
12:
13:         System.out.println("String1: " + str1);
14:         System.out.println("String2: " + str2);
15:         System.out.println("Same object? " + (str1 == str2));
16:         System.out.println("Same value? " + str1.equals(str2));
17:     }
18: }
```

This program's output is as follows:

```
String1: Free the bound periodicals.
String2: Free the bound periodicals.
Same object? true
String1: Free the bound periodicals.
String2: Free the bound periodicals.
Same object? false
Same value? true
```

The first part of this program (lines 3–5) declares two variables (str1 and str2), assigns the literal Free the bound periodicals. to str1, and then assigns that value to str2. As you learned earlier, str1 and str2 now point to the same object, and the equality test at line 9 proves that.

In the second part of this program, you create a new String object with the same value as str1 and assign str2 to that new String object. Now you have two different string objects in str1 and str2, both with the same value. Testing them to see whether they're the same object by using the == operator (line 15) returns the expected answer (false—they are not the same object in memory). Testing them using the equals() method in line 16 also returns the expected answer (true—they have the same values).

Note

Why can't you just use another literal when you change str2, rather than using new? String literals are optimized in Java—if you create a string using a literal and then use another literal with the same characters, Java knows enough to give you the first String object back. Both strings are the same objects—you have to go out of your way to create two separate objects.

Determining the Class of an Object

Want to find out what an object's class is? Here's the way to do it for an object assigned to the variable key:

```
String name = key.getClass().getName();
```

What does this do? The getClass() method is defined in the Object class, and therefore is available for all objects. The result of that method is a Class object (where Class is itself a class), which has a method called getName(). getName() returns a string representing the name of the class.

Another test that might be useful is the instanceof operator. instanceof has two operands: a reference to an object on the left and a class name on the right. The expression returns true or false based on whether the object is an instance of the named class or any of that class's subclasses:

```
"Texas" instanceof String // true
Point pt = new Point(10, 10);
pt instanceof String // false
```

The instanceof operator can also be used for interfaces; if an object implements an interface, the instanceof operator with that interface name on the right side returns true.

Summary

Now that you have spent two days exploring how object-oriented programming is implemented in Java, you're in a better position to decide how useful it can be in your own programming.

If you are a "glass is half empty" person, object-oriented programming is a level of abstraction that gets in the way of what you're trying to use a programming language for. You learn more about why OOP is thoroughly ingrained in Java in the coming chapters.

If you are a "glass is half full" person, object-oriented programming is worth using because of the benefits it offers: improved reliability, reusability, and maintenance.

Today you learned how to deal with objects: creating them, reading their values and changing them, and calling their methods. You also learned how to cast objects from one class to another, or from a data type to a class.

At this point, you possess the skills to handle most simple tasks in the Java language. All that remains are arrays, conditionals, and loops (which are covered tomorrow), and how to define and use classes on Day 6, "Creating Classes and Methods."

Q&A

Q **I'm confused about the differences between objects and the primitive data types, such as `int` and `boolean`.**

A The primitive types (`byte`, `short`, `int`, `long`, `float`, `double`, `boolean`, and `char`) represent the smallest things in the language. They are not objects, although in many ways they can be handled like objects: They can be assigned to variables and passed in and out of methods. Most of the operations that work exclusively on objects, however, will not work with primitive types.

Objects are instances of classes and, as such, are usually much more complex data types than simple numbers and characters, often containing numbers and characters as instance or class variables.

Q **The `length()` and `charAt()` methods in Listing 4.3 don't appear to make sense. If `length()` says that a string is 36 characters long, shouldn't the characters be numbered from 1 to 36 when `charAt()` is used to display characters in the string?**

A The two methods look at strings a little differently. The `length()` method counts the characters in the string, with the first character counting as 1, the second as 2, and so on. The string `"Charlie Brown"` has 13 characters. The `charAt()` method considers the first character in the string to be located at position number 0. This is the same numbering system used with array elements in Java. The string `Charlie Brown` has characters ranging from position 0—the letter `"C"`—to position 12—the letter `"n"`.

Q No pointers in Java? If you don't have pointers, how are you supposed to do something like linked lists, where you have a pointer from one nose to another so you can traverse them?

A It's untrue to say Java has no pointers at all—it has no explicit pointers. Object references are, effectively, pointers. To create something like a linked list, you would create a class called `Node`, which would have an instance variable also of type `Node`. To link together node objects, assign a node object to the instance variable of the object immediately before it in the list. Because object references are pointers, linked lists set up this way behave as you would expect them to.

Quiz

Review today's material by taking this three-question quiz.

Questions

1. What operator is used to call an object's constructor method and create a new object?

    (a) `+`

    (b) `new`

    (c) `instanceof`

2. What kind of methods apply to all objects of a class rather than an individual object?

    (a) Universal methods

    (b) Instance methods

    (c) Class methods

3. If you have a program with objects named `obj1` and `obj2`, what happens when you use the statement `obj2 = obj1`?

    (a) The instance variables in `obj2` are given the same values as `obj1`.

    (b) `obj2` and `obj1` are considered to be the same object.

    (c) Neither (a) nor (b).

Answers

1. b.

2. c.

3. b. The = operator does not copy values from one object to another. Instead, it makes both variables refer to the same objectc

Exercises

To extend your knowledge of the subjects covered today, try the following exercises:

- Create a program that turns a birthday in MM/DD/YYYY format (such as 4/23/2000) into three individual strings.

- Create a class with instance variables for `height`, `weight`, and `depth`, making each an integer. Create a Java application that uses your new class, sets each of these values in an object, and displays the values.

Where applicable, exercise solutions are offered on the book's Web site at `http://www.java21days.com`.

DAY 5

Lists, Logic, and Loops

If you wrote a Java program with what you know so far, it would likely be a little dull. If you wrote a Java program with what you know so far, it would likely be a little dull. That last sentence isn't repeated twice because of an editorial mistake. It is a demonstration of how easy computers make it to repeat the same thing over and over. You learn today how to make part of a Java program repeat itself by using loops.

Additionally, you learn how to make a program decide whether to do something based on logic. (Perhaps a computer would decide it isn't logical to repeat the same sentence twice in a row in a book.)

You also learn how to organize groups of the same class or data type into lists called arrays.

First up on today's list is arrays. First up on today's list is arrays.

Arrays

At this point, you have dealt with only a few variables in each Java program. It's manageable to use individual variables to store information in some cases.

However, what if you had 20 items of related information to keep track of? You could create 20 different variables and set up their initial values, but that becomes progressively more cumbersome as you deal with larger amounts of information. What if there were 100 items, or even 1,000?

Arrays are a way to store a list of items that have the same primitive data type, the same class, or a common parent class. Each item on the list goes into its own slot, which is numbered, so you can access the information easily.

Arrays can contain any type of information that is stored in a variable, but once the array is created, you can use it for that information type only. For example, you can have an array of integers, an array of String objects, or an array of arrays, but you can't have an array that contains both String objects and integers.

Java implements arrays differently than some other languages do—as objects that can be treated just like other objects.

To create an array in Java, you must do the following:

1. Declare a variable to hold the array.
2. Create a new array object and assign it to the array variable.
3. Store information in that array.

Declaring Array Variables

The first step in array creation is to declare a variable that will hold the array. Array variables indicate the object or data type that the array will hold and the name of the array. To differentiate from regular variable declarations, a pair of empty brackets ([ ]) is added to the object or data type, or to the variable name.

The following statements are examples of array variable declarations:

```
String[] requests;
```

```
Point[] targets;
```

```
float[] donations;
```

You also can declare an array by putting the brackets after the variable name instead of the information type, as in the following statements:

```
String requests[];
```

```
Point targets[];
```

```
float donations[];
```

Note

> The choice of which style to use is a matter of personal preference. The sample programs in this book place the brackets after the information type rather than the variable name.

Creating Array Objects

After you declare the array variable, the next step is to create an array object and assign it to that variable. To do this:

- Use the new operator
- Initialize the contents of the array directly

Because arrays are objects in Java, you can use the new operator to create a new instance of an array, as in the following statement:

```
String[] players = new String[10];
```

This statement creates a new array of strings with 10 slots that can contain String objects. When you create an array object by using new, you must indicate how many slots the array will hold. This statement does not put actual String objects in the slots—you must do that later.

Array objects can contain primitive types such as integers or Booleans, just as they can contain objects:

```
int[] temps = new int[99];
```

When you create an array object using new, all its slots automatically are given an initial value (0 for numeric arrays, false for Booleans, '\0' for character arrays, and null for objects).

5

Note

> The Java keyword null refers to a null object (and can be used for any object reference). It is not equivalent to zero or the '\0' character as the NULL constant is in C.

You also can create and initialize an array at the same time by enclosing the elements of the array inside braces, separated by commas:

```
Point[] markup = { new Point(1,5), new Point(3,3), new Point(2,3) };
```

Each of the elements inside the braces must be the same type as the variable that holds the array. When you create an array with initial values in this manner, the array is the same size as the number of elements you have included within the braces. The preceding example creates an array of `Point` objects named `markup` that contains three elements.

Because `String` objects can be created and initialized without the `new` operator, you can do the same when creating an array of strings:

```
String[] titles = { "Mr.", "Mrs.", "Ms.", "Miss", "Dr." };
```

The preceding statement creates a five-element array of `String` objects named `titles`.

Accessing Array Elements

After you have an array with initial values, you can retrieve, change, and test the values in each slot of that array. The value in a slot is accessed with the array name followed by a subscript enclosed within square brackets. This name and subscript can be put into expressions, as in the following:

```
testScore[40] = 920;
```

The preceding statement sets the 40th element of the `testScore` array to a value of `920`. The `testScore` part of this expression is a variable holding an array object, although it also can be an expression that results in an array. The subscript expression specifies the slot to access within the array.

The first element of an array has a subscript of `0` rather than `1`, so an array with 12 elements has array slots that are accessed by using subscripts `0` through `11`.

All array subscripts are checked to make sure that they are inside the array's boundaries, as specified when the array was created. In Java, it is impossible to access or assign a value to an array slot outside the array's boundaries, which avoids problems that result from overrunning the bounds of an array in C-like languages. Note the following two statements:

```
float[] rating = new float[20];

rating[20] = 3.22F;
```

A program with the preceding two lines of code produces a compilation error when `rating[20]` is used. The error occurs because the `rating` array does not have a slot `20`—it has 20 slots that begin at `0` and end at `19`. The Java compiler would make note of this by displaying an `ArrayIndexOutOfBoundsException` error.

The Java interpreter produces an error if the array subscript is calculated when the program is running and the subscript ends up outside the array's boundaries. To be technically correct, the interpreter flags this error by generating an exception. You learn more about exceptions and how to use them on Day 16, "Error Handling and Security."

One way to keep from accidentally overrunning the end of an array in your programs is to use the `length` instance variable, which is part of all array objects, regardless of type. The `length` variable contains the number of elements in the array. The following statement displays the number of elements in the `rating` object:

```
System.out.println("Elements: " + rating.length);
```

Changing Array Elements

As you saw in the previous examples, you can assign a value to a specific slot in an array by putting an assignment statement after the array name and subscript, as in the following:

```
temperature[4] = 85;
```

```
day[0] = "Sunday";
```

```
manager[2] = manager[0];
```

An important thing to note is that an array of objects in Java is an array of references to those objects. When you assign a value to a slot in that kind of array, you are creating a reference to that object. When you move values around inside arrays, you are reassigning the reference rather than copying a value from one slot to another. Arrays of a primitive data type such as `int` or `float` do copy the values from one slot to another, as do elements of a `String` array, even though they are objects.

Arrays are reasonably simple to create and modify, but they provide an enormous amount of functionality for Java. Listing 5.1 shows a simple program that creates, initializes, and displays elements of three arrays.

LISTING 5.1   The Full Text of `HalfDollars.java`

```
 1: class HalfDollars {
 2:     public static void main(String[] arguments) {
 3:         int[] denver = { 15000006, 18810000, 20752110 };
 4:         int[] philadelphia = new int[denver.length];
 5:         int[] total = new int[denver.length];
 6:         int average;
 7:
 8:         philadelphia[0] = 15020000;
 9:         philadelphia[1] = 18708000;
10:         philadelphia[2] = 21348000;
11:
```

LISTING 5.1   continued

```
12:          total[0] = denver[0] + philadelphia[0];
13:          total[1] = denver[1] + philadelphia[1];
14:          total[2] = denver[2] + philadelphia[2];
15:          average = (total[0] + total[1] + total[2]) / 3;
16:
17:          System.out.println("1993 production: " + total[0]);
18:          System.out.println("1994 production: " + total[1]);
19:          System.out.println("1995 production: " + total[2]);
20:          System.out.println("Average production: "+ average);
21:      }
22:
```

The HalfDollars application uses three integer arrays to store production totals for U.S. half-dollar coins produced at the Denver and Philadelphia mints. The output of the program is as follows:

```
1993 production: 30020006
1994 production: 37518000
1995 production: 42100110
Average production: 36546038
```

The class that is created here, HalfDollars, has three instance variables that hold arrays of integers.

The first, which is named denver, is declared and initialized on line 3 to contain three integers: 15000006 in element 0, 18810000 in element 1, and 20752110 in element 2. These figures are the total half-dollar production at the Denver mint for three years.

The second and third instance variables, philadelphia and total, are declared in lines 4–5. The philadelphia array contains the production totals for the Philadelphia mint, and total is used to store the overall production totals.

No initial values are assigned to the slots of the philadelphia and total arrays in lines 4–5. For this reason, each element is given the default value for integers: 0.

The denver.length variable is used to give both of these arrays the same number of slots as the denver array—every array contains a length variable that you can use to keep track of the number of elements it contains.

The rest of the main() method of this application performs the following:

- Line 6 creates an integer variable called average.
- Lines 8–10 assign new values to the three elements of the philadelphia array: 15020000 in element 0, 18708000 in element 1, and 21348000 in element 2.

- Lines 12–14 assign new values to the elements of the `total` array. In line 12, `total` element 0 is given the sum of `denver` element 0 and `philadelphia` element 0. Similar expressions are used in lines 13 and 14.

- Line 15 sets the value of the `average` variable to the average of the three `total` elements. Because `average` and the three `total` elements are integers, the average will be expressed as an integer rather than a floating-point number.

- Lines 17–20 display the values stored in the `total` array and the `average` variable, along with some explanatory text.

One last note to make about Listing 5.1 is that lines 12–14 and lines 17–19 are an inefficient way to use arrays in a program. These statements are almost identical, except for the subscripts that indicate which array element you are referring to. If the `HalfDollars` application was being used to track 100 years of production totals instead of three, your program would contain a lot of repetitive code.

Usually when dealing with arrays, you can use loops to cycle through an array's elements rather than dealing with each individually. This makes the code a lot shorter, and easier to read. When you learn about loops later today, you will see a rewrite of the current example.

Multidimensional Arrays

If you have used arrays in other languages, you might be expecting Java to support *multidimensional arrays*, which are arrays that contain more than one subscript and can store information in multiple dimensions.

A common use of a multidimensional array is to represent the data in an x,y grid of array elements.

Java does not support multidimensional arrays, but you can achieve the same functionality by declaring an array of arrays. Those arrays can also contain arrays, and so on, for as many dimensions as needed.

For example, consider a program that needs to accomplish the following tasks:

- Record an integer value each day for a year
- Organize those values by week

One way to organize this data is to create a 52-element array in which each element contains a 7-element array:

```
int[][] dayValue = new int[52][7];
```

This array of arrays contains a total of 365 integers, one for each day of the year. You could set the value for the first day of the 10th week with the following statement:

5

```
dayValue[10][1] = 14200;
```

You can use the `length` variable with these arrays as you would any other. The following statement contains a three-dimensional array of integers and displays the number of elements in each dimension:

```
int[][][] century = new int[100][52][7];
System.out.println("Elements in the first dimension: " + century.length);
System.out.println("Elements in the second dimension: " + century[0].length);
System.out.println("Elements in the third dimension: " + century[0][0].length);
```

Block Statements

Statements in Java are grouped into blocks. The beginning and ending of a block are noted with brace characters—an opening brace ({) for the beginning and a closing brace (}) for the ending.

You already have used blocks throughout the programs during the first five days. You've used them for both of the following:

- To contain the variables and methods in a class definition
- To define the statements that belong in a method

Blocks also are called *block statements* because an entire block can be used anywhere a single statement could be used (they're called *compound statements* in C and other languages). Each statement inside the block is then executed from top to bottom.

Blocks can be put inside other blocks, as you do when putting a method inside of a class definition.

An important thing to note about a block is that it creates a scope for the local variables that are created inside the block.

NEW TERM   *Scope* is the part of a program in which a variable exists and can be used. If you try to use a variable outside of its scope, an error will occur.

In Java, the scope of a variable is the block in which it was created. When you can declare and use local variables inside a block, those variables cease to exist after the block is finished executing. For example, the following `testBlock()` method contains a block:

```
void testBlock() {
    int x = 10;
    { // start of block
        int y = 40;
        y = y + x;
```

```
    } // end of block
}
```

There are two variables defined in this method: x and y. The scope of the y variable is the block it's in, and it can be used only within that block. An error would result if you tried to use the y variable in another part of the testBlock() method. The x variable was created inside the method but outside of the inner block, so it can be used anywhere in the method. You can modify the value of x anywhere within the method and this value will be retained.

Block statements usually are not used alone in a method definition, as they are in the preceding example. You use them throughout class and method definitions, as well as in the logic and looping structures you learn about next.

if Conditionals

One of the key aspects of programming is a program's capability to decide what it will do. This is handled through a special type of statement called a conditional.

NEW TERM   A *conditional* is a programming statement that is executed only if a specific condition is met.

The most basic conditional is the if keyword. The if conditional uses a Boolean expression to decide whether a statement should be executed. If the expression returns a true value, the statement is executed.

Here's a simple example that displays the message "You call that a haircut?" only on one condition: If the value of the age variable is greater than 39:

```
if (age > 39)
    System.out.println("You call that a haircut?");
```

If you want something else to happen in the case the if expression returns a false value, an optional else keyword can be used. The following example uses both if and else:

```
if (blindDateIsAttractive == true)
    restaurant = "Benihana's";
else
    restaurant = "Burritos-to-Go";
```

The if conditional executes different statements based on the result of a single Boolean test.

Note   A difference between if conditionals in Java and those in C or C++ is that Java requires the test to return a Boolean value (true or false). In C, the test can return an integer.

Using `if`, you only can include a single statement as the code to execute if the test expression is true and another statement if the expression is false.

However, as you learned earlier today, a block can appear anywhere in Java that a single statement can. If you want to do more than just one thing as a result of an `if` statement, you can enclose those statements inside a block. Note the following snippet of code, which was used on Day 2, "Object-Oriented Programming":

```
if (temperature > 660) {
    status = "returning home";
    speed = 5;
}
```

The `if` statement in this example contains the test expression `temperature > 660`. If the `temperature` variable contains a value higher than `660`, the block statement is executed and two things occur:

- The status variable is given the value `returning home`.
- The speed variable is set to `5`.

All `if` and `else` statements use Boolean tests to determine whether statements will be executed. You can use a `boolean` variable itself for this test, as in the following:

```
if (outOfGas)
    status = "inactive";
```

The preceding example uses a `boolean` variable called `outOfGas`. It functions exactly like the following:

```
if (outOfGas == true)
    status = "inactive";
```

`switch` Conditionals

A common programming practice in any language is to test a variable against some value, and if it doesn't match, test it again against a different value, and so on. This process can become unwieldy if you're using only `if` statements, depending on how many different values you have to test. For example, you might end up with a set of `if` statements something like the following:

```
if (operation == '+')
    add(object1, object2);
else if (operation == '-')
    subtract(object1, object2);
else if (operation == '*')
    multiply(object1, object2);
```

```
else if (operation == '/')
    divide(object1, object2);
```

This use of if statements is called a nested if statement, because each else statement contains another if until all possible tests have been made.

A shorthand mechanism for nested if statements that you can use in some programming languages is to group tests and actions together in a single statement. In Java, you can group actions together with the switch statement, which behaves as it does in C. The following is an example of switch usage:

```
switch (grade) {
    case 'A':
        System.out.println("Great job!");
        break;
    case 'B':
        System.out.println("Good job!");
        break;
    case 'C':
        System.out.println("You can do better!");
        break;
    default:
        System.out.println("Consider cheating!");
}
```

The switch statement is built on a test; in the preceding example, the test is on the value of the grade variable, which holds a char value. The test variable, which can be any of the primitive types byte, char, short, or int, is compared in turn with each of the case values. If a match is found, the statement or statements after the test are executed.

If no match is found, the default statement or statements are executed. Providing a default statement is optional—if it is omitted and there is no match for any of the case statements, the switch statement completes without executing anything.

The Java implementation of switch is limited—tests and values can be only simple primitive types that are castable to int. You cannot use larger primitive types such as long or float, strings, or other objects within a switch, nor can you test for any relationship other than equality. These restrictions limit switch to the simplest cases. In contrast, nested if statements can work for any kind of test on any type.

The following is a revision of the nested if example shown previously. It has been rewritten as a switch statement:

```
switch (operation) {
    case '+':
        add(object1, object2);
        break;
```

5

```
    case '*':
        subtract(object1, object2);
        break;
    case '-':
        multiply(object1, object2);
        break;
    case '/':
        divide(object1, object2);
        break;
}
```

There are two things to be aware of in this example: The first is that after each case, you can include a single result statement or more—you can include as many as you need. Unlike with if, you don't need to surround multiple statements with braces for it to work.

The second thing to note about this example is the break statement that is included with each case section. Without a break statement in a case section, after a match is made, the statements for that match and all the statements farther down the switch are executed until a break or the end of the switch is found. In some cases, this might be exactly what you want to do. However, in most cases, you should include the break to ensure that only the right code is executed. break, which you learn about in the section "Breaking Out of Loops," stops execution at the current point and jumps to the code outside of the next closing bracket (}).

One handy use of falling through without a break occurs when multiple values should execute the same statements. To accomplish this task, you can use multiple case lines with no result; the switch will execute the first statement that it finds. For example, in the following switch statement, the string x is an even number. is printed if x has the values of 2, 4, 6, or 8. All other values of x cause the string x is an odd number. to be printed.

```
switch (x) {
    case 2:
    case 4:
    case 6:
    case 8:
        System.out.println("x is an even number.");
        break;
    default: System.out.println("x is an odd number.");
}
```

In Listing 5.2, the DayCounter application takes two arguments, a month and a year, and displays the number of days in that month. A switch statement, if statements, and else statements are used.

LISTING 5.2 The Full Text of `DayCounter.java`

```
 1: class DayCounter {
 2:     public static void main(String[] arguments) {
 3:         int yearIn = 2001;
 4:         int monthIn = 2;
 5:         if (arguments.length > 0)
 6:             monthIn = Integer.parseInt(arguments[0]);
 7:         if (arguments.length > 1)
 8:             yearIn = Integer.parseInt(arguments[1]);
 9:         System.out.println(monthIn + "/" + yearIn + " has "
10:             + countDays(monthIn, yearIn) + " days.");
11:     }
12:
13:     static int countDays(int month, int year) {
14:         int count = -1;
15:         switch (month) {
16:             case 1:
17:             case 3:
18:             case 5:
19:             case 7:
20:             case 8:
21:             case 10:
22:             case 12:
23:                 count = 31;
24:                 break;
25:             case 4:
26:             case 6:
27:             case 9:
28:             case 11:
29:                 count = 30;
30:                 break;
31:             case 2:
32:                 if (year % 4 == 0)
33:                     count = 29;
34:                 else
35:                     count = 28;
36:                 if ((year % 100 == 0) & (year % 400 != 0))
37:                     count = 28;
38:         }
39:         return count;
40:     }
41: }
```

This application uses command-line arguments to specify the month and year to check. The first argument is the month, which should be expressed as a number from 1 to 12. The second argument is the year, which should be expressed a full four-digit year.

After compiling the program, type the following at a command line to see how many days were in February 2000:

```
java DayCounter 2 2000
```

The output will be the following:

```
2/2000 has 29 days.
```

If you run it without arguments, the default month of February 2001 will be used and the output will be the following:

```
2/2001 has 28 days.
```

The `DayCounter` application uses a `switch` statement to count the days in a month. This statement is part of the `countDays()` method in lines 13–40 of Listing 5.2.

The `countDays()` method has two `int` arguments: `month` and `year`. The number of days will be stored in the `count` variable, which is given an initial value of `-1` that will be replaced by the correct count later.

The `switch` statement that begins on line 15 uses `month` as its conditional value.

The number of days in a month is easy to determine for 11 months of the year. January, March, May, July, August, October, and December have 31 days. April, June, September, and November have 30 days.

The count for these 11 months is handled in lines 16–30 of Listing 5.2. Months are numbered from `1` (January) to `12` (December), as you would expect. When one of the `case` statements has the same value as `month`, every statement after that will be executed until `break` or the end of the `switch` statement is reached.

February is a little more complex, and is handled in lines 31–37 of the program. Every leap year has 29 days in February, whereas other years have 28. A leap year must meet either of the following conditions:

- The year must be evenly divisible by 4 and not evenly divisible by 100, or
- The year must be evenly divisible by 400.

As you learned on Day 3, "The ABCs of Java," the modulus operator `%` returns the remainder of a division operation. This is used with several `if-else` statements to determine how many days there are in February, depending on what year it is.

The `if-else` statement in lines 32–35 sets `count` to `29` when the year is evenly divisible by 4, and `28` otherwise.

The `if` statement in lines 36–37 uses the & operator to combine two conditional expressions: `year % 100 == 0` and `year & 400 != 0`. If both of these conditions are true, `count` is set to 28.

The `countDays` method ends by returning the value of `count` in line 39.

When you run the `DayCounter` application, the `main()` method in lines 2–11 is executed.

In all Java applications, command-line arguments are stored in an array of `String` objects. This array is called `arguments` in `DayCounter`. The first command-line argument is stored in `argument[0]`, the second in `argument[1]`, and upwards until all arguments have been stored. If the application was run with no arguments, the array will be created with no elements.

Lines 3–4 create two `yearIn` and `monthIn`, two integer variables to store the year and month that should be checked. They are given the initial values of `2001` and `2`, respectively (February 2001).

The `if` statement in line 5 uses `arguments.length` to make sure the `arguments` array has at least one element. If it does, line 6 is executed.

Line 6 calls `parseInt()`, a class method of the `Integer` class, with `argument[0]` as an argument. This method takes a `String` object as an argument, and if the string could be a valid integer, it returns that value as an `int`. This converted value is stored in `monthIn`. A similar thing happens in line 7—`parseInt()` is called with `argument[1]`, and this is used to set `yearIn`.

The output of the program is displayed in lines 9–11. As part of the output, the `countDays()` method is called with `monthIn` and `yearIn`, and the value returned by this method is displayed.

for Loops

A `for` loop is used to repeat a statement until a condition is met. Although `for` loops frequently are used for simple iteration in which a statement is repeated a certain number of times, `for` loops can be used for just about any kind of loop.

The `for` loop in Java looks roughly like the following:

```
for (initialization; test; increment) {
    statement;
}
```

The start of the `for` loop has three parts:

- *initialization* is an expression that initializes the start of the loop. If you have a loop index, this expression might declare and initialize it, such as `int i = 0`. Variables that you declare in this part of the `for` loop are local to the loop itself; they cease to exist after the loop is finished executing. You can initialize more than one variable in this section by separating each expression with a comma. The statement `int i = 0, int j = 10` in this section would declare the variables `i` and `j`, and both would be local to the loop.

- *test* is the test that occurs before each pass of the loop. The test must be a Boolean expression or a function that returns a `boolean` value, such as `i < 10`. If the test is `true`, the loop executes. Once the test is `false`, the loop stops executing.

- *increment* is any expression or function call. Commonly, the increment is used to change the value of the loop index to bring the state of the loop closer to returning `false` and stopping the loop. The increment takes place after each pass of the loop. Similar to the *initialization* section, you can put more than one expression in this section by separating each expression with a comma.

The *statement* part of the `for` loop is the statement that is executed each time the loop iterates. As with `if`, you can include either a single statement or a block statement; the previous example used a block because that is more common. The following example is a `for` loop that sets all slots of a `String` array to the value `Mr.`:

```
String[] salutation = new String[10];
int i; // the loop index variable

for (i = 0; i < salutation.length; i++)
    salutation[i] = "Mr.";
```

In this example, the variable `i` serves as a loop index—it counts the number of times the loop has been executed. Before each trip through the loop, the index value is compared to `salutation.length`, the number of elements in the `salutation` array. When the index is equal to or greater than `salutation.length`, the loop is exited.

The final element of the `for` statement is `i++`. This causes the loop index to increment by 1 each time the loop is executed. Without this statement, the loop would never stop.

The statement inside the loop sets an element of the `salutation` array equal to `"Mr."`. The loop index is used to determine which element is modified.

Any part of the `for` loop can be an empty statement—that is, you can include a semicolon with no expression or statement and that part of the `for` loop will be ignored. Note that if you do use an empty statement in your `for` loop, you might have to initialize or increment any loop variables or loop indexes yourself elsewhere in the program.

You also can have an empty statement as the body of your for loop if everything you want to do is in the first line of that loop. For example, the following for loop finds the first prime number higher than 4,000. (It calls a method called notPrime(), which returns a Boolean value, presumably to indicate when i is not prime.)

```
for (i = 4001; notPrime(i); i += 2)
    ;
```

A common mistake in for loops is to accidentally put a semicolon at the end of the line that includes the for statement:

```
for (i = 0; i < 10; i++);
    x = x * i; // this line is not inside the loop!
```

In this example, the first semicolon ends the loop without executing x = x * i as part of the loop. The x = x * i line will be executed only once because it is outside the for loop entirely. Be careful not to make this mistake in your Java programs.

To finish up for loops, the HalfDollar application will be rewritten using for loops to remove redundant code. The original example is long and repetitive and works only with an array that is three elements long. This version, shown in Listing 5.3, is shorter and more flexible (but it returns the same output).

LISTING 5.3   The Full Text of HalfLoop.java

```
 1: class HalfLoop {
 2:     public static void main(String[] arguments) {
 3:         int[] denver = { 15000006, 18810000, 20752110 };
 4:         int[] philadelphia = { 15020000, 18708000, 21348000 };
 5:         int[] total = new int[denver.length];
 6:         int sum = 0;
 7:
 8:         for (int i = 0; i < denver.length; i++) {
 9:             total[i] = denver[i] + philadelphia[i];
10:             System.out.println((i + 1993) + " production: "
11:                 + total[i]);
12:             sum += total[i];
13:         }
14:
15:         System.out.println("Average production: "
16:             + (sum / denver.length));
17:     }
18: }
```

The output of the program is as follows:

```
1993 production: 30020006
1994 production: 37518000
```

```
1995 production: 42100110
Average production: 36546038
```

Instead of going through the elements of the three arrays one by one, this example uses a `for` loop. The following things take place in the loop, which is contained in lines 8–13 of Listing 5.3:

- Line 8: The loop is created with an `int` variable called `i` as the index. The index will increment by 1 each pass through the loop, and stop when `i` is equal to or greater than `denver.length`, the total number of elements in the `denver` array.
- Lines 9–11: The value of one of the `total` elements is set using the loop index and then displayed with some text identifying the year.
- Line 12: The value of a `total` element is added to the `sum` variable, which will be used to calculate the average yearly production.

Using a more general-purpose loop to iterate over an array enables you to use the program with arrays of different sizes and still have it assign correct values to the elements of the total array and display those values.

while and do Loops

The remaining types of loop are `while` and `do`. As with `for` loops, `while` and `do` loops enable a block of Java code to be executed repeatedly until a specific condition is met. Whether you use a `for`, `while`, or `do` loop is mostly a matter of your programming style.

while Loops

The `while` loop is used to repeat a statement as long as a particular condition is `true`. The following is an example of a `while` loop:

```
while (i < 10) {
    x = x * i++; // the body of the loop
}
```

The condition that accompanies the `while` keyword is a Boolean expression—`i < 10` in the preceding example. If the expression returns `true`, the `while` loop executes the body of the loop and then tests the condition again. This process repeats until the condition is `false`. Although the preceding loop uses opening and closing braces to form a block statement, the braces are not needed because the loop contains only one statement: `x = x * i++`. Using the braces does not create any problems, though, and the braces will be required if you add another statement inside the loop later on.

Listing 5.4 shows an example of a `while` loop that copies the elements of an array of integers (in `array1`) to an array of `floats` (in `array2`), casting each element to a `float` as it goes. The one catch is that if any of the elements in the first array is 1, the loop will immediately exit at that point.

LISTING 5.4   The Full Text of CopyArrayWhile.java

```
 1: class CopyArrayWhile {
 2:     public static void main(String[] arguments) {
 3:         int[] array1 = { 7, 4, 8, 1, 4, 1, 4 };
 4:         float[] array2 = new float[array1.length];
 5:
 6:         System.out.print("array1: [ ");
 7:         for (int i = 0; i < array1.length; i++) {
 8:             System.out.print(array1[i] + " ");
 9:         }
10:         System.out.println("]");
11:
12:         System.out.print("array2: [ ");
13:         int count = 0;
14:         while ( count < array1.length && array1[count] != 1) {
15:             array2[count] = (float) array1[count];
16:             System.out.print(array2[count++] + " ");
17:         }
18:         System.out.println("]");
19:     }
20: }
```

The output of the program is as follows:

```
array1: [ 7 4 8 1 4 1 4 ]
array2: [ 7.0 4.0 8.0 ]
```

Here's what's going on in the main() method:

- Lines 3–4 declare the arrays; array1 is an array of integers, which are initialized to some suitable numbers. array2 is an array of floating-point numbers that is the same length as array1 but doesn't have any initial values.

- Lines 6–10 are for output purposes; they simply iterate through array1 using a for loop to print out its values.

- Lines 13–17 are where the interesting stuff happens. This bunch of statements both assigns the values of array2 (converting the numbers to floating-point numbers along the array) and prints it out at the same time. You start with a count variable, which keeps track of the array index elements. The test in the while loop keeps track of the two conditions for existing the loop, where those two conditions are running out of elements in array1 or encountering a 1 in array1. (Remember, that was part of the original description of what this program does.)

5

- You can use the logical conditional && to keep track of the test; remember that && makes sure both conditions are true before the entire expression is true. If either one is false, the expression returns false and the loop exits.

The program's output shows that the first four elements in array1 were copied to array2, but that there was a 1 in the middle that stopped the loop from going any further. Without the 1, array2 should end up with all the same elements as array1.

If the while loop's test initially is false the first time it is tested (for example, if the first element in that first array is 1), the body of the while loop will never be executed. If you need to execute the loop at least once, you can do one of two things:

- Duplicate the body of the loop outside the while loop
- Use a do loop (which is described in the following section)

The do loop is considered the better solution of the two.

do...while Loops

The do loop is just like a while loop with one major difference: the place in the loop when the condition is tested. A while loop tests the condition before looping, so if the condition is false the first time it is tested, the body of the loop never will execute. A do loop executes the body of the loop at least once before testing the condition, so if the condition is false the first time it is tested, the body of the loop already will have executed once.

It's the difference between asking Dad to borrow the car and telling him later that you borrowed it. If Dad nixes the idea in the first case, you don't get to borrow it. If he nixes the idea in the second case, you already have borrowed it once.

The following example uses a do loop to keep doubling the value of a long integer until it is larger than 3 trillion:

```
long i = 1;
do {
    i *= 2;
    System.out.print(i + " ");
} while (i < 3000000000000L);
```

The body of the loop is executed once before the test condition, i < 3000000000, is evaluated; then, if the test evaluates as true, the loop runs again. If it is false, the loop exits. Keep in mind that the body of the loop executes at least once with do loops.

Breaking Out of Loops

In all of the loops, the loop ends when a tested condition is met. There might be times when something occurs during execution of a loop and you want to exit the loop early. For that you can use the break and continue keywords.

You already have seen break as part of the switch statement; break stops execution of the switch statement, and the program continues. The break keyword, when used with a loop, does the same thing—it immediately halts execution of the current loop. If you have nested loops within loops, execution picks up with the next outer loop. Otherwise, the program merely continues executing the next statement after the loop.

For example, recall the while loop that copied elements from an integer array into an array of floating-point numbers until the end of the array or a 1 was reached. You can test for that latter case inside the body of the while loop, and then use break to exit the loop:

```
int count = 0;
while (count < array1.length) {
    if (array1[count] == 1)
        break;
    array2[count] = (float) array2[count++];
}
```

The continue keyword starts the loop over at the next iteration. For do and while loops, this means that the execution of the block statement starts over again; with for loops, the increment expression is evaluated and then the block statement is executed. The continue keyword is useful when you want to make a special case out of elements within a loop. With the previous example of copying one array to another, you could test for whether the current element is equal to 1, and use continue to restart the loop after every 1 so that the resulting array never will contain zero. Note that because you're skipping elements in the first array, you now have to keep track of two different array counters:

```
int count = 0;
int count2 = 0;
while (count++ <= array1.length) {
    if (array1[count] == 1)
        continue;

    array2[count2++] = (float)array1[count];
} >
```

Labeled Loops

Both break and continue can have an optional label that tells Java where to resume execution of the program. Without a label, break jumps outside the nearest loop to an enclosing loop or to the next statement outside the loop. The `continue` keyword restarts the loop it is enclosed within. Using `break` and `continue` with a label enables you to use `break` to go to a point outside a nested loop or to use `continue` to go to a loop outside the current loop.

To use a labeled loop, add the label before the initial part of the loop, with a colon between the label and the loop. Then, when you use `break` or `continue`, add the name of the label after the keyword itself, as in the following:

```
out:
    for (int i = 0; i <10; i++) {
        while (x < 50) {
            if (i * x++ > 400)
                break out;
            // inner loop here
        }
        // outer loop here
    }
```

In this snippet of code, the label `out` labels the outer loop. Then, inside both the `for` and `while` loops, when a particular condition is met, a `break` causes the execution to break out of both loops. Without the label `out`, the `break` statement would exit the inner loop and resume execution with the outer loop.

The Conditional Operator

An alternative to using the `if` and `else` keywords in a conditional statement is to use the conditional operator, sometimes called the *ternary operator*. The *conditional operator* is called a ternary operator because it has three operands.

The conditional operator is an expression, meaning that it returns a value—unlike the more general `if`, which can result in only a statement or block being executed. The conditional operator is most useful for short or simple conditionals and looks like the following line:

```
test ? trueresult : falseresult;
```

The `test` is an expression that returns `true` or `false`, just like the test in the `if` statement. If the `test` is `true`, the conditional operator returns the value of `trueresult`. If the `test` is `false`, the conditional operator returns the value of `falseresult`. For example, the following conditional tests the values of `myScore` and `yourScore`, returns the larger of the two as a value, and assigns that value to the variable `ourBestScore`:

```
int ourBestScore = myScore > yourScore ? myScore : yourScore;
```

This use of the conditional operator is equivalent to the following `if-else` code:

```
int ourBestScore;
if (myScore > yourScore)
    ourBestScore = myScore;
else
    ourBestScore = yourScore;
```

The conditional operator has a very low precedence—it usually is evaluated only after all its subexpressions are evaluated. The only operators lower in precedence are the assignment operators. For a refresher on operator precedence, refer to Table 3.7 in Day 3.

Caution

> The ternary operator is of primary benefit to experienced programmers creating complex expressions. Its functionality is duplicated in simpler use of if-else statements, so there's no need to use this operator as you're beginning to learn the language. The main reason it's introduced in this book is because you'll encounter it in the source code of other Java programmers.

Summary

Now that you have been introduced to lists, loops, and logic, you can make a computer decide whether to repeatedly display the contents of an array.

You learned how to declare an array variable, assign an object to it, and access and change elements of the array. With the `if` and `switch` conditional statements, you can branch to different parts of a program based on a Boolean test. You learned about the `for`, `while`, and `do` loops, each enabling a portion of a program to be repeated until a given condition is met.

It bears repeating: You'll use all three of these features frequently in your Java programs.

You'll use all three of these features frequently in your Java programs.

Q&A

Q I declared a variable inside a block statement for an `if`. When the `if` was done, the definition of that variable vanished. Where did it go?

A In technical terms, block statements form a new *lexical scope*. What this means is that if you declare a variable inside a block, it's visible and usable only inside that block. When the block finishes executing, all the variables you declared go away.

It's a good idea to declare most of your variables in the outermost block in which they'll be needed—usually at the top of a block statement. The exception might be

5

very simple variables, such as index counters in `for` loops, where declaring them in the first line of the `for` loop is an easy shortcut.

Q Why can't you use `switch` with strings?

A Strings are objects in Java, and `switch` works only for the primitive types `byte`, `char`, `short`, and `int`. To compare strings, you have to use nested `if` statements, which enable more general expression tests, including string comparison.

Quiz

Review today's material by taking this three-question quiz.

Questions

1. Which loop is used to execute the statements in the loop at least once before the conditional expression is evaluated?

    (a) `do-while`

    (b) `for`

    (c) `while`

2. Which operator returns the remainder of a division operation?

    (a) `/`

    (b) `%`

    (c) `?`

3. Which instance variable of an array is used to find out how big it is?

    (a) `size`

    (b) `length`

    (c) `MAX_VALUE`

Answers

1. a. In a `do-while` loop, the `while` conditional statement appears at the end of the loop. Even if it is initially false, the statements in the loop will be executed once.

2. b. The modulus operator ("`%`").

3. b.

Exercises

To extend your knowledge of the subjects covered today, try the following exercises:

- Using the countDays() method from the DayCounter application, create an application that displays every date in a given year in a single list from January 1 to December 31.

- Create a class that takes words for the first 10 numbers (one up to ten) and converts them into a single long integer. Use a switch statement for the conversion and command-line arguments for the words.

Where applicable, exercise solutions are offered on the book's Web site at http://www.java21days.com.

5

WEEK 1

DAY 6

Creating Classes and Methods

If you're coming to Java from another programming language, you might be struggling with the meaning of the term *class*. It seems synonymous to the term *program*, but you could be uncertain of the relationship between the two.

In Java, a program is made up of a main class and any other classes that are needed to support the main class. These support classes include any of those in Java's class library you might need (such as String, Math, and the like).

Today, the meaning of *class* will be clarified as you create classes and methods, which define the behavior of an object or class. You undertake each of the following:

- The parts of a class definition
- The creation and use of instance variables
- The creation and use of methods
- The main() method used in Java applications

- The creation of overloaded methods that share the same name but have different signatures and definitions
- The creation of constructor methods that are called when an object is created

Defining Classes

Because you have created classes during each of the previous days, you should be familiar with the basics of class definition at this point. A class is defined via the `class` keyword and the name of the class, as in the following example:

```
class Ticker {
    // body of the class
}
```

By default, classes inherit from the `Object` class. It's the superclass of all classes in the Java class hierarchy.

The `extends` keyword is used to indicate the superclass of a class. Look at the following subclass of `Ticker`:

```
class SportsTicker extends Ticker {
    // body of the class
}
```

Creating Instance and Class Variables

Whenever you create a class, you define behavior that makes the new class different from its superclass.

This behavior is defined by specifying the variables and methods of the new class. In this section, you work with three kinds of variables: class variables, instance variables, and local variables. The next section details methods.

Defining Instance Variables

On Day 3, "The ABCs of Java," you learned how to declare and initialize local variables, which are variables inside method definitions. Instance variables are declared and defined in almost the same way local variables are. The main difference is their location in the class definition. Variables are considered instance variables if they are declared outside a method definition and are not modified by the `static` keyword. By programming custom, most instance variables are defined right after the first line of the class definition. Listing 6.1 contains a simple class definition for the class `VolcanoRobot`, which inherits from its superclass, `ScienceRobot`.

LISTING 6.1   The Full Text of `VolcanoRobot.java`

```
1: class VolcanoRobot extends ScienceRobot {
2:
3:     String status;
4:     int speed;
5:     float temperature;
6:     int power;
7: }
```

This class definition contains four variables. Because these variables are not defined inside a method, they are instance variables. The variables are as follows:

- `status`—A string indicating the current activity of the robot (for example, `exploring` or `returning home`)

- `speed`—An integer that indicates the robot's current rate of travel

- `temperature`—A floating-point number that indicates the current temperature of the environment the robot is in

- `power`—An integer indicating the robot's current battery power

Class Variables

As you learned in previous lessons, class variables apply to a class as a whole, rather than being stored individually in objects of the class.

Class variables are good for communicating between different objects of the same class, or for keeping track of classwide information among a set of objects.

The `static` keyword is used in the class declaration to declare a class variable, as in the following:

```
static int sum;
static final int maxObjects = 10;
```

Creating Methods

6

As you learned on Day 4, "Working with Objects," methods define an object's behavior—anything that happens when the object is created and the various tasks the object can perform during its lifetime.

This section introduces method definition and how methods work. Tomorrow's lesson has more detail about advanced things you can do with methods.

Defining Methods

Method definitions have four basic parts:

- The name of the method
- A list of parameters
- The type of object or primitive type returned by the method
- The body of the method

The first two parts of the method definition form what's called the method's *signature*.

Note

> To keep things simpler today, two optional parts of the method definition have been left out: a modifier, such as public or private, and the throws keyword, which indicates the exceptions a method can throw. You learn about these parts of a method definition during Week 3, "Java's Advanced Features."

In other languages, the name of the method—which might be called a function, subroutine, or procedure—is enough to distinguish it from other methods in the program.

In Java, you can have several methods in the same class with the same name but differences in signatures. This practice is called *method overloading*, and you learn more about it tomorrow.

Here's what a basic method definition looks like:

```
returnType methodName(type1 arg1, type2 arg2, type3 arg3 ...) {
    // body of the method
}
```

The *returnType* is the primitive type or class of the value returned by the method. It can be one of the primitive types, a class name, or void if the method does not return a value at all.

Note that if this method returns an array object, the array brackets can either go after the *returnType* or after the parameter list. Because the former way is easier to read, it is used in this book's examples as in the following:

```
int[] makeRange(int lower, int upper) {
    // body of this method
}
```

The method's parameter list is a set of variable declarations, separated by commas, inside parentheses. These parameters become local variables in the body of the method, receiving their values when the method is called.

You can have statements, expressions, method calls on other objects, conditionals, loops, and so on inside the body of the method—everything you've learned about in the previous lessons.

Unless a method has been declared with void as its return type, the method returns some kind of value when it is completed. This value must be explicitly returned at some exit point inside the method, using the return keyword.

Listing 6.2 shows an example of a class that defines a makeRange() method. makeRange() takes two integers—a lower boundary and an upper boundary—and creates an array that contains all the integers between those two boundaries. The boundaries themselves are included in the array of integers.

LISTING 6.2   The Full Text of RangeClass.java

```
 1: class RangeClass {
 2:     int[] makeRange(int lower, int upper) {
 3:         int arr[] = new int[ (upper - lower) + 1 ];
 4:
 5:         for (int i = 0; i < arr.length; i++) {
 6:             arr[i] = lower++;
 7:         }
 8:         return arr;
 9:     }
10:
11:     public static void main(String[] arguments) {
12:         int theArray[];
13:         RangeClass theRange = new RangeClass();
14:
15:         theArray = theRange.makeRange(1, 10);
16:         System.out.print("The array: [ ");
17:         for (int i = 0; i < theArray.length; i++) {
18:             System.out.print(theArray[i] + " ");
19:         }
20:         System.out.println("]");
21:     }
22:
23: }
```

6

The output of the program is the following:

```
The array: [ 1 2 3 4 5 6 7 8 9 10 ]
```

The main() method in this class tests the makeRange() method by creating a range where the lower and upper boundaries of the range are 1 and 10, respectively, and then uses a for loop to print the new array's values in lines 5–7.

The this Keyword

In the body of a method definition, you might want to refer to the current object—the object the method was called on. This can be done to use that object's instance variables or to pass the current object as an argument to another method.

To refer to the current object in these cases, use the this keyword where you normally would refer to an object's name.

The this keyword refers to the current object, and you can use it anywhere a reference to an object might appear: in dot notation, as an argument to a method, as the return value for the current method, and so on. The following are some examples of using this:

```
t = this.x;           // the x instance variable for this object

this.resetData(this); // call the resetData method, defined in
                       // this class, and pass it the current
                       // object

return this;          // return the current object
```

In many cases, you might not need to explicitly use the this keyword because it will be assumed. For instance, you can refer to both instance variables and method calls defined in the current class simply by name because the this is implicit in those references. Therefore, you could write the first two examples as the following:

```
t = x;              // the x instance variable for this object

resetData(this);    // call the resetData method, defined in this
                    // class
```

> **Note**
>
> The viability of omitting the this keyword for instance variables depends on whether variables of the same name are declared in the local scope. You see more on this subject in the next section.

Because this is a reference to the current instance of a class, you should use it only inside the body of an instance method definition. Class methods, methods declared with the static keyword, cannot use this.

Variable Scope and Method Definitions

One of the things you must know in order to use a variable is its scope.

NEW TERM   *Scope* is the part of a program in which a variable or other information can be used. When the part defining the scope has completed execution, the variable ceases to exist.

When you declare a variable in Java, that variable always has a limited scope. A variable with local scope, for example, can be used only inside the block in which it was defined. Instance variables have a scope that extends to the entire class, so they can be used by any of the instance methods within that class.

When you refer to a variable within a method definition, Java checks for a definition of that variable first in the current scope (which might be a block), next in each outer scope, and finally, in the current method definition. If the variable is not a local variable, Java then checks for a definition of that variable as an instance or class variable in the current class. If Java still does not find the variable definition, it searches each superclass in turn.

Because of the way Java checks for the scope of a given variable, it is possible for you to create a variable in a lower scope that hides (or replaces) the original value of that variable and introduces subtle and confusing bugs into your code.

For example, consider the following Java application:

```
class ScopeTest {
    int test = 10;

    void printTest () {
        int test = 20;
        System.out.println("Test: " + test);
    }

    public static void main(String[] arguments) {
        ScopeTest st = new ScopeTest();
        st.printTest();
    }
}
```

In this class, you have two variables with the same name and definition. The first, an instance variable, has the name test and is initialized with the value 10. The second is a local variable with the same name, but with the value 20.

The local variable test within the printTest() method hides the instance variable test. When the printTest() method is called from within the main() method, it displays that test equals 20, even though there's a test instance variable that equals 10. You can avoid this problem by using this.test to refer to the instance variable and using just test to refer to the local variable, but a better solution is to avoid the duplication of variable names and definitions.

A more insidious example occurs when you redefine a variable in a subclass that already occurs in a superclass. This can create subtle bugs in your code; for example, you might call methods that are intended to change the value of an instance variable, but the wrong variable is changed. Another bug might occur when you cast an object from one class to

6

another; the value of your instance variable might mysteriously change because it was getting that value from the superclass instead of your class.

The best way to avoid this behavior is to be aware of the variables defined in all your class's superclasses. This awareness prevents you from duplicating a variable that's used higher in the class hierarchy.

Passing Arguments to Methods

When you call a method with object parameters, the objects you pass into the body of the method are passed by reference. Whatever you do to the objects inside the method affects the original objects. Keep in mind that such objects include arrays and all objects that are contained in arrays. When you pass an array into a method and modify its contents, the original array is affected. Primitive types, on the other hand, are passed by value.

Listing 6.3 demonstrates how this works.

LISTING 6.3   The PassByReference Class

```
 1: class PassByReference {
 2:     int onetoZero(int arg[]) {
 3:         int count = 0;
 4:
 5:         for (int i = 0; i < arg.length; i++) {
 6:             if (arg[i] == 1) {
 7:                 count++;
 8:                 arg[i] = 0;
 9:             }
10:         }
11:         return count;
12:     }
13:
14:     public static void main(String[] arguments) {
15:         int arr[] = { 1, 3, 4, 5, 1, 1, 7 };
16:         PassByReference test = new PassByReference();
17:         int numOnes;
18:
19:         System.out.print("Values of the array: [ ");
20:         for (int i = 0; i < arr.length; i++) {
21:             System.out.print(arr[i] + " ");
22:         }
23:         System.out.println("]");
24:
25:         numOnes = test.onetoZero(arr);
26:         System.out.println("Number of Ones = " + numOnes);
27:         System.out.print("New values of the array: [ ");
```

```
28:          for (int i = 0; i < arr.length; i++) {
29:              System.out.print(arr[i] + " ");
30:          }
31:          System.out.println("]");
32:      }
33: }
```

The following is this program's output:

```
Values of the array: [ 1 3 4 5 1 1 7 ]
Number of Ones = 3
New values of the array: [ 0 3 4 5 0 0 7 ]
```

Note the method definition for the `onetoZero()` method in lines 2–12, which takes a single array as an argument. The `onetoZero()` method does two things:

- It counts the number of 1s in the array and returns that value.
- For every 1 in the array, it substitutes a 0 in its place.

The `main()` method in the `PassByReference` class tests the use of the `onetoZero()` method. Go over the `main()` method line by line so that you can see what is going on and why the output shows what it does.

Lines 15–17 set up the initial variables for this example. The first one is an array of integers; the second one is an instance of the class `PassByReference`, which is stored in the variable `test`. The third is a simple integer to hold the number of 1s in the array.

Lines 19–23 print the initial values of the array; you can see the output of these lines in the first line of the output.

Line 25 is where the real work takes place; this is where you call the `onetoZero()` method defined in the object `test` and pass it the array stored in `arr`. This method returns the number of 1s in the array, which you then assign to the variable `numOnes`. It returns 3, as you would expect.

The last section of lines prints the array values. Because a reference to the array object is passed to the method, changing the array inside that method changes that array's original copy. Printing the values in lines 28–31 proves this—that last line of output shows that all the 1s in the array have been changed to 0s.

Class Methods

The relationship between class and instance variables is directly comparable to how class and instance methods work.

Class methods are available to any instance of the class itself and can be made available to other classes. In addition, unlike an instance method, a class does not require an instance of the class for its methods to be called.

For example, the Java class libraries include a class called Math. The Math class defines a set of math operations that you can use in any program or any of the various number types, as in the following:

```
double root = Math.sqrt(453.0);

System.out.print("The larger of x and y is " + Math.max(x, y));
```

To define class methods, use the static keyword in front of the method definition, just as you would use static in front of a class variable. For example, the class method max() used in the preceding example might have the following signature:

```
static int max(int arg1, int arg2) {
    // body of the method
}
```

Java supplies wrapper classes for each of the base types; for example, Java supplies Integer, Float, and Boolean classes. By using class methods defined in those classes, you can convert objects to primitive types and convert primitive types to objects.

For example, the parseInt() class method in the Integer class can be used with a string. The string is sent to the method as an argument, and this is used to calculate a return value to send back as an int.

The following statement shows how the parseInt() method can be used:

```
int count = Integer.parseInt("42");
```

In the preceding statement, the String value "42" is returned by parseInt() as an integer with a value of 42, and this is stored in the count variable.

The lack of a static keyword in front of a method name makes it an instance method. Instance methods operate in a particular object, rather than a class of objects. On Day 2, "Object-Oriented Programming," you created an instance method called checkTemperature() that checked the temperature in the robot's environment.

Tip

Most methods that operate on or affect a particular object should be defined as instance methods. Methods that provide some general capability, but do not directly affect an instance of the class, should be declared as class methods.

Creating Java Applications

Now that you know how to create classes, objects, class and instance variables, and class and instance methods, you can put it all together into a Java program.

Applications, to refresh your memory, are Java programs that run on their own. Applications are different from applets, which require a Java-enabled browser to view them. The projects you have created up to this point have been Java applications. You get a chance to dive into applets during Day 7, "Writing Java Applets." Applets require a bit more background to get them to interact with the browser, as well as draw and update with the graphics system.

A Java application consists of one or more classes and can be as large or as small as you want it to be. Although all the Java applications you've created up to this point do nothing but output some characters to the screen or to a window, you also can create Java applications that use windows, graphics, and user-interface elements, just as applets do.

The only thing you need in order to make a Java application run, however, is one class that serves as the starting point for the rest of your Java program.

The starting-point class for your application needs only one thing: a `main()` method. When the application is run, the `main()` method is the first thing that is called. None of this should be much of a surprise to you at this point; you've been creating Java applications with `main()` methods all along.

The signature for the `main()` method takes the following form:

```
public static void main(String[] arguments) {
    // body of method
}
```

Here's a rundown of the parts of the `main()` method:

- `public` means that this method is available to other classes and objects. The `main()` method must be declared `public`. You learn more about `public` and `private` methods during Week 3.

- `static` means that `main()` is a class method.

- `void` means that the `main()` method doesn't return a value.

- `main()` takes one parameter, which is an array of strings. This argument is used for program arguments, which you learn about in the next section.

The body of the `main()` method contains any code you need to start your application, such as the initialization of variables or the creation of class instances.

6

When Java executes the main() method, keep in mind that main() is a class method. An instance of the class that holds main() is not created automatically when your program runs. If you want to treat that class as an object, you have to create an instance of it in the main() method.

Helper Classes

Your Java application can have only one class, or in the case of most larger programs, it might be made up of several classes, where different instances of each class are created and used while the application is running. You can create as many classes as you want for your program.

 Note   If you're using the Java 2 SDK, the classes must be accessible from a folder that's listed in your CLASSPATH.

As long as Java can find the class, your program will use it when it runs. Note, however, that only the starting-point class needs a main() method. After it is called, the methods inside the various classes and objects used in your program take over. Although you can include main() methods in helper classes, they will be ignored when the program actually runs.

Java Applications and Command-Line Arguments

Because Java applications are standalone programs, it's useful to pass arguments or options to an application. You did this on Day 5, "Lists, Logic, and Loops," in the DayCounter project.

You can use arguments to determine how an application is going to run or to enable a generic application to operate on different kinds of input. You can use program arguments for many different purposes, such as to turn on debugging input or to indicate a filename to load.

Passing Arguments to Java Applications

How you pass arguments to a Java application varies based on the platform you're running Java on.

To pass arguments to a Java program on Windows or Solaris, the arguments should be appended to the command line when the program is run. For example:

```
java EchoArgs April 450 -10
```

In the preceding example, three arguments were passed to a program: April, 450, and -10. Note that a space separates each of the arguments.

To group arguments that include spaces, the arguments should be surrounded with quotation marks. For example, note the following command line:

```
java EchoArgs Wilhelm Niekro Hough "Tim Wakefield" 49
```

Putting quotation marks around Tim Wakefield causes that text to be treated as a single argument. The EchoArgs program would receive five arguments: Wilhelm, Niekro, Hough, Tim Wakefield, and 49. The quotation marks prevent the spaces from being used to separate one argument from another; they are not included as part of the argument when it is sent to the program and received using the main() method.

 Caution   One thing the quotation marks are not used for is to identify strings. Every argument passed to an application is stored in an array of String objects, even if it has a numeric value (such as 450, -10, and 49 in the preceding examples).

Handling Arguments in Your Java Application

When an application is run with arguments, Java stores the arguments as an array of strings and passes the array to the application's main() method. Take another look at the signature for main():

```
public static void main(String[] arguments) {
    // body of method
}
```

Here, *arguments* is the name of the array of strings that contains the list of arguments. You can call this array anything you like.

Inside the main() method, you then can handle the arguments your program was given by iterating over the array of arguments and handling them in some manner. For example, Listing 6.4 is a simple Java program that takes any number of numeric arguments and returns the sum and the average of those arguments.

6

LISTING 6.4   The Full Text of SumAverage.java

```
1: class SumAverage {
2:     public static void main(String[] arguments) {
```

Listing 6.4   continued

```
 3:            int sum = 0;
 4:
 5:            if (arguments.length > 0) {
 6:                for (int i = 0; i < arguments.length; i++) {
 7:                    sum += Integer.parseInt(arguments[i]);
 8:                }
 9:                System.out.println("Sum is: " + sum);
10:                System.out.println("Average is: " +
11:                    (float)sum / arguments.length);
12:            }
13:        }
14: }
```

The SumAverage application makes sure in line 5 that at least one argument was passed to the program. This is handled through length, the instance variable that contains the number of elements in the arguments array.

You must always do things like this when dealing with command-line arguments. Otherwise, your programs will crash with ArrayIndexOutOfBoundsException errors whenever the user supplies fewer command-line arguments than you were expecting.

If at least one argument was passed, the for loop in lines 6–8 iterates through all the strings stored in the arguments array.

Because all command-line arguments are passed to a Java application as String objects, you must convert them to numeric values before using them in any mathematical expressions. The parseInt() class method of the Integer class is used on line 6. It takes a String object as input and returns an int.

If you can run Java classes on your system with a command line, type the following:

```
java SumAverage 1 4 13
```

You should see the following output:

```
Sum is: 18
Average is: 6.0
```

Note

The array of arguments in Java is not analogous to argv in C and UNIX. In particular, arg[0] or arguments[0], the first element in the array of arguments, is the first command-line argument after the name of the class—not the name of the program, as it would be in C. Be careful of this as you write your Java programs.

Creating Methods with the Same Name, Different Arguments

When you work with Java's class library, you often encounter classes that have numerous methods with the same name.

Methods with the same name are differentiated from each other by two things:

- The number of arguments they take
- The data type or objects of each argument

These two things are part of a method's signature, and using several methods with the same name and different signatures is called *overloading*.

Method overloading can eliminate the need for entirely different methods that do essentially the same thing. Overloading also makes it possible for methods to behave differently based on the arguments they receive.

When you call a method in an object, Java matches the method name and arguments in order to choose which method definition to execute.

To create an overloaded method, you create different method definitions in a class, each with the same name but different argument lists. The difference can be the number, the type of arguments, or both. Java allows method overloading as long as each argument list is unique for the same method name.

Caution
Java does not consider the return type when differentiating between overloaded methods. If you attempt to create two methods with the same signature and different return types, the class won't compile. In addition, the variable names that you choose for each argument to the method are irrelevant—all that matters are the number and the type of arguments.

The next project is creating an overloaded method. It begins with a simple class definition for a class called `MyRect`, which defines a rectangular shape with four instance variables to define the upper-left and lower-right corners of the rectangle, x1, y1, x2, and y2:

```
class MyRect {
    int x1 = 0;
    int y1 = 0;
    int x2 = 0;
    int y2 = 0;
}
```

6

When a new instance of the MyRect class is created, all its instance variables are initialized to 0.

A buildRect() instance method sets the variables to their correct values:

```
MyRect buildRect(int x1, int y1, int x2, int y2) {
    this.x1 = x1;
    this.y1 = y1;
    this.x2 = x2;
    this.y2 = y2;
    return this;
}
```

This method takes four integer arguments and returns a reference to the resulting MyRect object. Because the arguments have the same names as the instance variables, the keyword this is used inside the method when referring to the instance variables.

This method can be used to create rectangles—but what if you wanted to define a rectangle's dimensions in a different way? An alternative would be to use Point objects rather than individual coordinates because Point objects contain both an x and y value as instance variables.

You can overload buildRect() by creating a second version of the method with an argument list that takes two Point objects:

```
MyRect buildRect(Point topLeft, Point bottomRight) {
    x1 = topLeft.x;
    y1 = topLeft.y;
    x2 = bottomRight.x;
    y2 = bottomRight.y;
    return this;
}
```

For the preceding method to work, the java.awt.Point class must be imported so that the Java compiler can find it.

Another possible way to define the rectangle is to use a top corner, a height, and a width:

```
MyRect buildRect(Point topLeft, int w, int h) {
    x1 = topLeft.x;
    y1 = topLeft.y;
    x2 = (x1 + w);
    y2 = (y1 + h);
    return this;
}
```

To finish this example, a printRect() is created to display the rectangle's coordinates and a main() method tries everything out. Listing 6.5 shows the completed class definition.

LISTING 6.5   The Full Text of MyRect.java

```
 1: import java.awt.Point;
 2:
 3: class MyRect {
 4:     int x1 = 0;
 5:     int y1 = 0;
 6:     int x2 = 0;
 7:     int y2 = 0;
 8:
 9:     MyRect buildRect(int x1, int y1, int x2, int y2) {
10:         this.x1 = x1;
11:         this.y1 = y1;
12:         this.x2 = x2;
13:         this.y2 = y2;
14:         return this;
15:     }
16:
17:     MyRect buildRect(Point topLeft, Point bottomRight) {
18:         x1 = topLeft.x;
19:         y1 = topLeft.y;
20:         x2 = bottomRight.x;
21:         y2 = bottomRight.y;
22:         return this;
23:     }
24:
25:     MyRect buildRect(Point topLeft, int w, int h) {
26:         x1 = topLeft.x;
27:         y1 = topLeft.y;
28:         x2 = (x1 + w);
29:         y2 = (y1 + h);
30:         return this;
31:     }
32:
33:     void printRect(){
34:         System.out.print("MyRect: <" + x1 + ", " + y1);
35:         System.out.println(", " + x2 + ", " + y2 + ">");
36:     }
37:
38:     public static void main(String[] arguments) {
39:         MyRect rect = new MyRect();
40:
41:         System.out.println("Calling buildRect with coordinates 25,25,
              ➥50,50:");
42:         rect.buildRect(25, 25, 50, 50);
43:         rect.printRect();
44:         System.out.println("***");
45:
46:         System.out.println("Calling buildRect with points (10,10),
              ➥(20,20):");
```

6

LISTING 6.5   continued

```
47:          rect.buildRect(new Point(10,10), new Point(20,20));
48:          rect.printRect();
49:          System.out.println("***");
50:
51:          System.out.print("Calling buildRect with 1 point (10,10),");
52:          System.out.println(" width (50) and height (50):");
53:
54:          rect.buildRect(new Point(10,10), 50, 50);
55:          rect.printRect();
56:          System.out.println("***");
57:     }
58: }
```

The following is this program's output:

```
Calling buildRect with coordinates 25,25, 50,50:
MyRect: <25, 25, 50, 50>
***
Calling buildRect with points (10,10), (20,20):
MyRect: <10, 10, 20, 20>
***
Calling buildRect with 1 point (10,10), width (50) and height (50):
MyRect: <10, 10, 60, 60>
***
```

You can define as many versions of a method as you need to implement the behavior that is needed for that class.

When you have several methods that do similar things, using one method to call another is a shortcut technique to consider. For example, the buildRect() method in lines 17–23 can be replaced with the following, much shorter method:

```
MyRect buildRect(Point topLeft, Point bottomRight) {
    return buildRect(topLeft.x, topLeft.y,
        bottomRight.x, bottomRight.y);
}
```

The return statement in this method calls the buildRect() method in lines 9–15 with four integer arguments, producing the same result in fewer statements.

Constructor Methods

You also can define constructor methods in your class definition that are called automatically when objects of that class are created.

NEW TERM   A *constructor method* is a method that is called on an object when it is created—in other words, when it is constructed.

Unlike other methods, a constructor cannot be called directly. Java does three things when new is used to create an instance of a class:

- Allocates memory for the object
- Initializes that object's instance variables, either to initial values or to a default (0 for numbers, null for objects, false for Booleans, or '\0' for characters)
- Calls the constructor method of the class, which might be one of several methods

If a class doesn't have any constructor methods defined, an object still is created when the new operator is used in conjunction with the class. However, you might have to set its instance variables or call other methods that the object needs to initialize itself.

By defining constructor methods in your own classes, you can set initial values of instance variables, call methods based on those variables, call methods on other objects, and set the initial properties of an object. You also can overload constructor methods, as you can do with regular methods, to create an object that has specific properties based on the arguments you give to new.

Basic Constructors Methods

Constructors look a lot like regular methods, with three basic differences:

- They always have the same name as the class.
- They don't have a return type.
- They cannot return a value in the method by using the return statement.

For example, the following class uses a constructor method to initialize its instance variables based on arguments for new:

```
class VolcanoRobot {
    String status;
    int speed;
    int power;

    VolcanoRobot(String in1, int in2, int in3) {
        status = in1;
        speed = in2;
        power = in3;
    }
}
```

You could create an object of this class with the following statement:

```
VolcanoRobot vic = new VolcanoRobot("exploring", 5, 200);
```

The status instance variable would be set to exploring, speed to 5, and power to 200.

6

Calling Another Constructor Method

If you have a constructor method that duplicates some of the behavior of an existing constructor method, you can call the first constructor from inside the body of the second constructor. Java provides a special syntax for doing this. Use the following to call a constructor method defined in the current class:

```
this(arg1, arg2, arg3);
```

The use of this with a constructor method is similar to how this can be used to access a current object's variables. In the preceding statement, the arguments with this() are the arguments for the constructor method.

For example, consider a simple class that defines a circle using the (x,y) coordinate of its center and the length of its radius. The class, MyCircle, could have two constructors: one where the radius is defined, and one where the radius is set to a default value of 1:

```
class MyCircle {
    int x, y, radius;

    MyCircle(int xPoint, int yPoint, int radiusLength) {
        this.x = xPoint;
        this.y = yPoint;
        this.radius = radiusLength;
    }

    MyCircle(int xPoint, int yPoint) {
        this(xPoint, yPoint, 1);
    }
}
```

The second constructor in MyCircle takes only the x and y coordinates of the circle's center. Because no radius is defined, the default value of 1 is used. The first constructor is called with xPoint, yPoint, and the integer literal 1, all as arguments.

Overloading Constructors Methods

Like regular methods, constructor methods also can take varying numbers and types of parameters. This capability enables you to create an object with exactly the properties you want it to have, or lets the object calculate properties from different kinds of input.

For example, the buildRect() methods that you defined in the MyRect class earlier today would make excellent constructor methods because they are being used to initialize an object's instance variables to the appropriate values. So, instead of the original buildRect() method you had defined (which took four parameters for the coordinates of the corners), you could create a constructor.

Listing 6.6 shows a new class, MyRect2, that has the same functionality of the original MyRect, except that it uses overloaded constructor methods instead of overloaded buildRect() methods.

LISTING 6.6 The Full Text of MyRect2.java

```
 1: import java.awt.Point;
 2:
 3: class MyRect2 {
 4:     int x1 = 0;
 5:     int y1 = 0;
 6:     int x2 = 0;
 7:     int y2 = 0;
 8:
 9:     MyRect2(int x1, int y1, int x2, int y2) {
10:         this.x1 = x1;
11:         this.y1 = y1;
12:         this.x2 = x2;
13:         this.y2 = y2;
14:     }
15:
16:     MyRect2(Point topLeft, Point bottomRight) {
17:         x1 = topLeft.x;
18:         y1 = topLeft.y;
19:         x2 = bottomRight.x;
20:         y2 = bottomRight.y;
21:     }
22:
23:     MyRect2(Point topLeft, int w, int h) {
24:         x1 = topLeft.x;
25:         y1 = topLeft.y;
26:         x2 = (x1 + w);
27:         y2 = (y1 + h);
28:     }
29:
30:     void printRect() {
31:         System.out.print("MyRect: <" + x1 + ", " + y1);
32:         System.out.println(", " + x2 + ", " + y2 + ">");
33:     }
34:
35:     public static void main(String[] arguments) {
36:         MyRect2 rect;
37:
38:         System.out.println("Calling MyRect2 with coordinates 25,25 50,50:");
39:         rect = new MyRect2(25, 25, 50,50);
40:         rect.printRect();
41:         System.out.println("***");
42:
```

6

LISTING 6.6   continued

```
43:          System.out.println("Calling MyRect2 with points (10,10), (20,20):");
44:          rect= new MyRect2(new Point(10,10), new Point(20,20));
45:          rect.printRect();
46:          System.out.println("***");
47:
48:          System.out.print("Calling MyRect2 with 1 point (10,10)");
49:          System.out.println(" width (50) and height (50):");
50:          rect = new MyRect2(new Point(10,10), 50, 50);
51:          rect.printRect();
52:          System.out.println("***");
53:
54:     }
55: }
```

Overriding Methods

When you call an object's method, Java looks for that method definition in the object's class. If it doesn't find one, it passes the method call up the class hierarchy until a method definition is found. Method inheritance enables you to define and use methods repeatedly in subclasses without having to duplicate the code.

However, there might be times when you want an object to respond to the same methods but have different behavior when that method is called. In that case, you can override the method. To override a method, define a method in a subclass with the same signature as a method in a superclass. Then, when the method is called, the subclass method is found and executed instead of the one in the superclass.

Creating Methods That Override Existing Methods

To override a method, all you have to do is create a method in your subclass that has the same signature (name, return type, and argument list) as a method defined by your class's superclass. Because Java executes the first method definition it finds that matches the signature, the new signature hides the original method definition.

Here's a simple example; Listing 6.7 contains two classes: PrintClass, which contains a method called printMe() that displays information about objects of that class, and PrintSubClass, a subclass that adds a z instance variable to the class.

LISTING 6.7   The Full Text of PrintClass.java

```
1: class PrintClass {
2:     int x = 0;
```

```
 3:     int y = 1;
 4:
 5:     void printMe() {
 6:         System.out.println("x is " + x + ", y is " + y);
 7:         System.out.println("I am an instance of the class " +
 8:             this.getClass().getName());
 9:     }
10: }
11:
12: class PrintSubClass extends PrintClass {
13:     int z = 3;
14:
15:     public static void main(String[] arguments) {
16:         PrintSubClass obj = new PrintSubClass();
17:         obj.printMe();
18:     }
19: }
```

After compiling this file, run PrintSubClass with the Java interpreter to see the following output:

```
x is 0, y is 1
I am an instance of the class PrintSubClass
```

A PrintSubClass object was created and the printMe() method was called in the main() method of PrintSubClass. Because the PrintSubClass does not define this method, Java looks for it in the superclasses of PrintSubClass, starting with PrintClass. PrintClass has a printMe() method, so it is executed. Unfortunately, this method does not display the z instance variable, as you can see from the preceding output.

Note

> There's an important feature of PrintClass to point out: It doesn't have a main() method. It doesn't need one; it isn't an application. PrintClass is simply a utility class for the PrintSubClass class, which is an application and therefore has a main() method. Only the class that you're actually executing with the Java interpreter with needs a main() method.

6

To correct the problem, you could override the printMe() method of PrintClass in PrintSubClass, adding a statement to display the z instance variable:

```
void printMe() {
    System.out.println("x is " + x + ", y is " + y +
        ", z is " + z);
    System.out.println("I am an instance of the class " +
        this.getClass().getName());
}
```

Calling the Original Method

Usually, there are two reasons why you want to override a method that a superclass already has implemented:

- To replace the definition of that original method completely
- To augment the original method with additional behavior

Overriding a method and giving the method a new definition hides the original method definition. There are times, however, when behavior should be added to the original definition instead of replacing it completely, particularly when behavior is duplicated in both the original method and the method that overrides it. By calling the original method in the body of the overriding method, you can add only what you need.

Use the super keyword to call the original method from inside a method definition. This keyword passes the method call up the hierarchy, as shown in the following:

```
void myMethod (String a, String b) {
    // do stuff here
    super.myMethod(a, b);
    // do more stuff here
}
```

The super keyword, somewhat like the this keyword, is a placeholder for the class's superclass. You can use it anywhere that you use this, but super refers to the superclass rather than the current object.

Overriding Constructors

Technically, constructor methods cannot be overridden. Because they always have the same name as the current class, new constructor methods are created instead of being inherited. This system is fine much of the time; when your class's constructor method is called, the constructor method with the same signature for all your superclasses is also called. Therefore, initialization can happen for all parts of a class that you inherit.

However, when you are defining constructor methods for your own class, you might want to change how your object is initialized, not only by initializing new variables added by your class, but also by changing the contents of variables that already are there. To do this, explicitly call the constructor methods of the superclass and subsequently change whatever variables need to be changed.

To call a regular method in a superclass, you use super.*methodname*(*arguments*). Because constructor methods don't have a method name to call, the following form is used:

```
super(arg1, arg2, ...);
```

Note that Java has a specific rule for the use of super(): It must be the very first state-ment in your constructor definition. If you don't call super() explicitly in your construc-tor, Java does it for you—using super() with no arguments. Because a call to a super() method must be the first statement, you can't do something like the following in your overriding constructor:

```
if (condition == true)
    super(1,2,3); // call one superclass constructor
else
    super(1,2); // call a different constructor
```

Similar to using this(...) in a constructor method, super(...) calls the constructor method for the immediate superclass (which might, in turn, call the constructor of its superclass, and so on). Note that a constructor with that signature has to exist in the superclass for the call to super() to work. The Java compiler checks this when you try to compile the source file.

You don't have to call the constructor in your superclass that has the same signature as the constructor in your class; you only have to call the constructor for the values you need initialized. In fact, you can create a class that has constructors with entirely differ-ent signatures from any of the superclass's constructors.

Listing 6.8 shows a class called NamedPoint, which extends the class Point from the java.awt package. The Point class has only one constructor, which takes an x and a y argument and returns a Point object. NamedPoint has an additional instance variable (a string for the name) and defines a constructor to initialize x, y, and the name.

LISTING 6.8 The NamedPoint Class

```
 1: import java.awt.Point;
 2:
 3: class NamedPoint extends Point {
 4:     String name;
 5:
 6:     NamedPoint(int x, int y, String name) {
 7:         super(x,y);
 8:         this.name = name;
 9:     }
10:
11:     public static void main(String[] arguments) {
12:         NamedPoint np = new NamedPoint(5, 5, "SmallPoint");
13:         System.out.println("x is " + np.x);
14:         System.out.println("y is " + np.y);
15:         System.out.println("Name is " + np.name);
16:     }
17: }
```

6

The output of the program is as follows:

```
x is 5
y is 5
Name is SmallPoint
```

The constructor method defined here for NamedPoint calls Point's constructor method to initialize the instance variables of Point (x and y). Although you can just as easily initialize x and y yourself, you might not know what other things Point is doing to initialize itself. Therefore, it is always a good idea to pass constructor methods up the hierarchy to make sure everything is set up correctly.

Finalizer Methods

Finalizer methods are almost the opposite of constructor methods. A *constructor method* is used to initialize an object, and *finalizer methods* are called just before the object is collected for garbage and has its memory reclaimed.

The finalizer method is finalize(). The Object class defines a default finalizer method that does nothing. To create a finalizer method for your own classes, override the finalize() method using this signature:

```
protected void finalize() throws Throwable {
    super.finalize();
}
```

Note

The throws Throwable part of this method definition refers to the errors that might occur when this method is called. Errors in Java are called *exceptions*; you learn more about them on Day 16, "Error Handling and Security." For now, all you need to do is include these keywords in the method definition.

Include any cleaning up that you want to do for that object inside the body of that finalize() method. You also can call super.finalize() to enable your class's superclasses to finalize the object, if necessary.

You can call the finalize() method yourself at any time—it's a method just like any other. However, calling finalize() does not trigger an object to be collected in the garbage. Only removing all references to an object causes it to be marked for deletion.

Finalizer methods are used best for optimizing the removal of an object—for example, by removing references to other objects. In most cases, you don't need to use finalize() at all.

Summary

After finishing today's lesson, you should have a pretty good idea of the relationship between classes in Java and programs you create using the language.

Everything you create in Java involves the use of a main class that interacts with other classes as needed. It's a different programming mindset than you might be used to with other languages.

Today you put together everything you have learned about creating Java classes. Each of the following topics was covered:

- Instance and class variables, which hold the attributes of a class and objects created from it.

- Instance and class methods, which define the behavior of a class. You learned how to define methods—including the parts of a method signature, how to return values from a method, how arguments are passed to methods, and how to use the `this` keyword to refer to the current object.

- The `main()` method of Java applications, and how to pass arguments to it from the command line.

- Overloaded methods, which reuse a method name by giving it different arguments.

- Constructor methods, which define the initial variables and other starting conditions of an object.

Tomorrow, you get some practical experience with subclassing as you create Java applets, programs that run as part of a World Wide Web page.

Q&A

Q In my class, I have an instance variable called `origin`. I also have a local variable called `origin` in a method, which, because of variable scope, gets hidden by the local variable. Is there any way to access the instance variable's value?

A The easiest way is to avoid giving your local variables the same names that your instance variables have. If you feel you must, you can use `this.origin` to refer to the instance variable and `origin` to refer to the local variable.

Q I created two methods with the following signatures:

```
int total(int arg1, int arg2, int arg3) {...}
float total(int arg1, int arg2, int arg3) {...}
```

The Java compiler complains when I try to compile the class with these method definitions, but their signatures are different. What have I done wrong?

6

A Method overloading in Java works only if the parameter lists are different—either in number or type of arguments. Return type is not relevant for method overloading. Think about it—if you had two methods with exactly the same parameter list, how would Java know which one to call?

Q I wrote a program to take four arguments, but if I give it too few arguments, why does it crash with a runtime error?

A Testing for the number and type of arguments your program expects is up to you in your Java program; Java won't do it for you. If your program requires four arguments, test that you have indeed been given four arguments, and return an error message if you haven't.

Quiz

Review today's material by taking this three-question quiz.

Questions

1. If a local variable has the same name as an instance variable, how can you refer to the instance variable in the scope of the local variable?

    (a) You can't; you should rename one of the variables.

    (b) Use the keyword `this` before the instance variable name.

    (c) Use the keyword `super` before the name.

2. Where are instance variables declared in a class?

    (a) Anywhere in the class

    (b) Outside of all methods in the class

    (c) After the class declaration and above the first method

3. How can you send an argument to a program that includes a space character?

    (a) Surround it with quotes

    (b) Separate the arguments with commas

    (c) Separate the arguments with period characters

Answers

1. b. Answer (a) is a good idea, though; variable name conflicts can be a source of subtle errors in your Java programs.

2. b. By custom, instance variables are declared right after the class declaration and before any methods. It's only necessary that they be outside of all methods, however.

3. a. The quotation marks will not be included in the argument when it is passed to the program.

Exercises

To extend your knowledge of the subjects covered today, try the following exercises:

- Modify the VolcanoRobot project from Day 2, "Object-Oriented Programming," so that it includes constructor methods.

- Create a class for four-dimensional points called FourDPoint that is a subclass of Point from the java.awt package.

Where applicable, exercise solutions are offered on the book's Web site at http://www.java21days.com.

6

DAY 7

Writing Java Applets

The first exposure of most people to the Java programming language was in late 1995, when Netscape Navigator began running *applets*—small Java programs that ran within a World Wide Web browser.

At the time, this was a revolutionary development for the Web—the first interactive content that could be delivered as part of a Web page. You can do similar things with Macromedia Flash, Microsoft ActiveX, and other technology today, but Java's still an effective language for Web-based programming.

Today, you start with the basics of applet programming:

- The differences between applets and applications
- How to create a simple applet
- How to put an applet onto a Web page
- How to send information from a Web page to an applet
- How to store an applet in an archive for faster download off a Web page
- How to create applets that are run by the Java Plug-in, a virtual machine that improves a Web browser's Java support

How Applets and Applications Are Different

The difference between Java applets and applications lies in how they are run.

Applications are run by using a Java interpreter to load the application's main class file. This normally is done from a command-line prompt using the java tool from the SDK, as you have done since Day 1, "21st Century Java," of this book.

Applets, on the other hand, are run on any browser that supports Java. At the present time, this includes current versions of Netscape Navigator, Microsoft Internet Explorer, Opera, and Sun's HotJava browser. Applets also can be tested by using the appletviewer tool included with the Java 2 Software Development Kit.

For an applet to run, it must be included on a Web page using HTML tags in the same way images and other elements are included. When a user with a Java-capable browser loads a Web page that includes an applet, the browser downloads the applet from a Web server and runs it on the Web user's own system. A separate Java interpreter is not needed—one is built into the browser. Like an application, a Java applet includes a class file and any other helper classes that are needed to run the applet. Java's standard class library is included automatically.

Because Java applets run inside a Java browser, some of the work of creating a user interface is already done for the applet programmer. There's an existing window for the applet to run in, a place to display graphics and receive information, and the browser's interface.

 Note

> It is possible for a single Java program to function as both an applet and an application. Although different procedures are used to create these types of programs, they do not conflict with each other. The features specific to applets would be ignored when the program runs as an application, and vice versa.

Applet Security Restrictions

Because Java applets are run on a Web user's system, there are some serious restrictions to what an applet is capable of doing. If these restrictions were not in place, a malicious Java programmer could easily write an applet that deletes user files, collects private information from the system, and commits other security breaches.

As a general rule, Java applets run under a "better safe than sorry" security model. Applets cannot do any of the following:

- They cannot read or write files on the user's file system.
- They cannot communicate with an Internet site other than the one that served the Web page that included the applet.
- They cannot run any programs on the reader's system.
- They cannot load programs stored on the user's system, such as executable programs and shared libraries.

All these rules are true for Java applets running under the browsers favored by most Web users today. Other Java-capable browsers and Java development tools might enable you to configure the level of security you want, permitting some file access to specific folders or network connections to selected Internet sites.

As an example, the `appletviewer` tool enables an access control list to be set for the folders to which an applet can read or write files. However, an applet developer can assume that most of the audience will be using a browser that implements the strictest security rules.

Java applications have none of the restrictions in place for applets. They can take full advantage of Java's capabilities.

 Caution

> Although Java's security model makes it extremely difficult for a malicious applet to do harm to a user's system, it will never be 100% secure. Search the Web for "hostile applets," and you'll find discussion of security issues in different versions of Java and how they have been addressed. You might even find examples of applets that cause problems for people using Java browsers. Java is more secure than other Web programming solutions such as ActiveX, but all browser users should acquaint themselves with the issue.

Choosing a Java Version

A Java programmer who writes applets must address this issue: For which Java version should I write?

At the time of this writing, Java 1.1 is the most up-to-date version of the language supported on the current versions of the Navigator, Internet Explorer, and Opera browsers, which comprise more than 90% of the applet-using world.

7

Note

Sun Microsystems offers a Web browser add-on called the Java Plug-in, which enables applet programmers to use Java 2 enhancements in their programs. You'll find out more about it later today.

Because of this split, applet programmers generally choose one of the following three options:

- Write an applet using only Java 1.0 features so that it will run on all Java-capable browsers.
- Write an applet using only Java 1.0 or 1.1 features so that it will run on Navigator 4.0 and higher, Internet Explorer 4 and higher, and Opera 3.6 and higher.
- Write an applet using all Java features and provide a way for users to download and install the Java Plug-in so that they can run the applet.

Java 2 has been designed so that in almost all circumstances, a program using only Java 1.0 features can compile and run successfully on a Java 1.0 interpreter or 1.0-capable browser. Likewise, an applet using Java 1.1 features can run on a browser supporting that language version.

If an applet uses any feature that was introduced with Java 2, the program won't run successfully on a browser that doesn't support that version of the language. The only test environment that always supports the most current version of Java is the latest `appletviewer` from the corresponding SDK.

This is a common source of errors for Java applet programmers. If you write a Java 2 applet and run it on a nonsupporting browser such as Microsoft Internet Explorer 4.0, you get security errors, class-not-found errors, and other problems that prevent it from running.

Note

In this book, Java 2 techniques are used for all programs, even applets. There's a wealth of information available in previous editions of this book for applet programmers who don't want to use Java 2, and Sun also offers full documentation for prior versions at `http://java.sun.com/infodocs`.

The security model described up to this point is the one introduced with Java 1.0. Java's current version includes a way for a Web user to trust an applet, so that applet can run without restriction on the user's system, just as an application can.

Java 2 enables very specific security controls to be put into place or removed from applets and applications. This is covered during Day 16, "Error Handling and Security."

Creating Applets

Most of the Java programs you've created up to this point have been Java applications— simple programs with a `main()` method that is used to create objects, set instance variables, and call other methods.

Applets do not have a `main()` method that automatically is called to begin the program. Instead, there are several methods that are called at different points in the execution of an applet. You learn about these methods today.

All applets are subclasses of either the `JApplet` class in the `javax.swing` package or its superclass, the `Applet` class in the `java.applet` package. The `JApplet` class is a better choice because it supports Swing, the windowing classes you'll be learning about during Week 2.

By inheriting from one of these classes, your applet has the following built-in behavior:

- It works as part of a Web browser and can respond to occurrences such as the browser page being reloaded
- It can present a graphical user interface and take input from users

Although an applet can make use of as many other classes as needed, the `JApplet` class is the main class that triggers the execution of the applet. The subclass of `JApplet` that you create takes the following form:

```
public class yourApplet extends javax.swing.JApplet {
    // Applet code here
}
```

All applets must be declared `public` because the `JApplet` class is a public class. This requirement is true only of your main `JApplet` class, and any helper classes can be public or private. More information on this kind of access control is described on Day 15, "Packages, Interfaces, and Other Class Features."

When a browser's built-in Java interpreter encounters a Java applet on a Web page, that applet's class is loaded along with any other helper classes it uses. The browser automatically creates an instance of the applet's class and calls methods of the `JApplet` class when specific events take place.

Different applets that use the same class use different instances, so you could place more than one copy of the same type of applet on a page, and each could behave differently.

7

Major Applet Activities

Instead of a `main()` method, applets have methods that are called when specific things occur as the applet runs.

An example of these methods is `paint()`, which is called whenever the applet's window needs to be displayed or redisplayed.

By default, these methods do nothing. For example, the `paint()` method that is inherited from `JApplet` is an empty method. For anything to be displayed on the applet window, the `paint()` method must be overridden with behavior to display text, graphics, and other things.

You learn here about `JApplet` class methods that should be overridden as the week progresses. The following sections describe five of the more important methods in an applet's execution: initialization, starting, stopping, destruction, and painting.

Initialization

Initialization occurs when the applet is loaded. *Initialization* might include creating the objects the applet needs, setting up an initial state, loading images or fonts, or setting parameters. To provide behavior for the initialization of an applet, you override the `init()` method as follows:

```
public void init() {
    // Code here
}
```

One useful thing to do when initializing an applet is to set the color of its background window. Colors are represented in Java by the `Color` class, part of the `java.awt` package. Call `setBackground(Color)` in an applet to make the background of the applet window the specified color.

The `Color` class has class variables that represent the most commonly used colors: `black`, `blue`, `cyan`, `darkGray`, `gray`, `green`, `lightGray`, `magenta`, `orange`, `pink`, `red`, `white`, and `yellow`. You can use one of these variables as the argument to the `setBackground()` method, as in the following example:

```
setBackground(Color.green);
```

If used in an applet's `init()` method, the preceding statement makes the entire applet window green.

You also can create your own `Color` objects using integer values for red, green, and blue as three arguments to the constructor:

```
Color avocado = new Color(102, 153, 102);
setBackground(avocado)
```

This code sets the background to avocado green.

Tip

> An applet window is a container—a component in a graphical user interface that can hold other components. You can use `setBackground()` on any container to establish its background color.

You'll learn more about using colors during Day 12, "Color, Fonts, and Graphics."

Starting

An applet is started after it is initialized. *Starting* also can occur if the applet was previously stopped. For example, an applet is stopped if the browser user follows a link to a different page, and it is started again when the user returns to the page containing the applet.

Starting can occur several times during an applet's life cycle, but initialization happens only once. To provide startup behavior for your applet, override the `start()` method as follows:

```
public void start() {
    // Code here
}
```

Functionality that you put in the `start()` method might include starting a thread to control the applet, sending the appropriate messages to helper objects, or in some way telling the applet to begin running.

Stopping

Stopping and starting go hand-in-hand. *Stopping* occurs when the user leaves the page that contains a currently running applet, or when an applet stops itself by calling `stop()` directly. By default, any threads the applet had started continue running even after the user leaves a page. By overriding `stop()`, you can suspend execution of these threads and restart them if the applet is viewed again. The following shows the form of a `stop()` method:

```
public void stop() {
    // Code here
}
```

7

Destruction

Destruction sounds more harsh than it is. The destroy() method enables the applet to clean up after itself just before it is freed from memory or the browser exits. You can use this method to kill any running threads or to release any other running objects. Generally, you won't want to override destroy() unless you have specific resources that need to be released, such as threads that the applet has created. To provide cleanup behavior for your applet, override the destroy() method as follows:

```
public void destroy() {
    // Code here
}
```

Note

You might be wondering how destroy() is different from finalize(), which was described on Day 6, "Creating Classes and Methods." The destroy() method applies only to applets; finalize() is a more general-purpose way for a single object of any type to clean up after itself.

Java has an automatic garbage collector that manages memory for you. The collector reclaims memory from resources after the program is done using them, so you don't normally have to use methods such as destroy().

Painting

Painting is how an applet displays something onscreen, be it text, a line, a colored background, or an image. Painting can occur many hundreds of times during an applet's life cycle: once after the applet is initialized, again if the browser window is brought out from behind another window onscreen, again if the browser window is moved to a different position onscreen, and so on. You must override the paint() method of your Applet subclass to display anything. The paint() method looks like the following: ().

```
public void paint(Graphics g) {
    // Code here
}
```

Note that unlike other methods described in this section, paint() takes an argument: an instance of the class Graphics. This object is created and passed to paint() by the browser, so you don't have to worry about it. However, you always must import the Graphics class (part of the java.awt package) into your applet code, usually through an import statement at the top of your Java source file, as in the following:

```
import java.awt.Graphics;
```

Tip

If you are importing several classes from the same package, such as the Abstract Windowing Toolkit classes, you can use a wildcard character to load them all at the same time. For example, the statement `import java.awt.*;` makes every public class in the `java.awt` package available. The `import` statement does not include subclasses of the package, however, so the `import java.awt.*;` statement does not include the classes of the `java.awt.image` package.

The `paint()` method is called automatically by the environment that contains the applet—normally a Web browser—whenever the applet window must be redrawn.

There are times in an applet when you do something that requires the window to be repainted. For example, if you call `setBackground()` to change the applet's background to a new color, this won't be shown until the applet window is redrawn.

To request that the window be redrawn in an applet, call the applet's `repaint()` method without any arguments:

```
repaint();
```

The `Graphics` object passed to the applet's `paint()` method is required for all text and graphics you will draw in the applet window.

A `Graphics` object represents an area being drawn to; in this case, an applet window. You can use this object to draw text to the window and handle other simple graphical tasks. Many of the Java2D drawing and text-handling techniques you learn about next week are called on a subclass of `Graphics`, `Graphics2D`. To create a new `Graphics2D` object that you can use in an applet's `paint()` method, you must use casting, as in the following `paint()` method:

```
public void paint(Graphics screen) {
    Graphics2D screen2D = (Graphics2D)screen;
}
```

The `screen2D` object in this example was produced via casting. It is the `screen` object converted from the `Graphics` class into the `Graphics2D` class.

All Java2D graphics operations must be called on a `Graphics2D` object. `Graphics2D` is part of the `java.awt` package.

An Example Applet

The `Watch` applet displays the current date and time and updates it roughly once a second.

7

This project uses objects of several different classes:

- GregorianCalendar, a class in the java.util package that represents date/time values in the Gregorian calendar system, which is in use throughout the Western world
- Font, a java.awt class that represents the size, style and family of a display font
- Color and Graphics2D, two java.awt class described in the previous section

Listing 7.1 shows the source code for the applet.

LISTING 7.1   The Full Text of Watch.java

```
 1: import java.awt.*;
 2: import java.util.*;
 3:
 4: public class Watch extends javax.swing.JApplet {
 5:     private Color butterscotch = new Color(255, 204, 102);
 6:     private String lastTime = "";
 7:
 8:     public void init() {
 9:         setBackground(Color.black);
10:     }
11:
12:     public void paint(Graphics screen) {
13:         Graphics2D screen2D = (Graphics2D)screen;
14:         Font type = new Font("Monospaced", Font.BOLD, 20);
15:         screen2D.setFont(type);
16:         GregorianCalendar day = new GregorianCalendar();
17:         String time = day.getTime().toString();
18:         screen2D.setColor(Color.black);
19:         screen2D.drawString(lastTime, 5, 25);
20:         screen2D.setColor(butterscotch);
21:         screen2D.drawString(time, 5, 25);
22:         try {
23:             Thread.sleep(1000);
24:         } catch (InterruptedException e) {
25:             // do nothing
26:         }
27:         lastTime = time;
28:         repaint();
29:     }
30: }
```

After you have created this program, you can compile it but won't be able to try it out yet. The applet overrides the init() method in lines 8–10 to set the background color of the applet window to black.

The paint() method is where this applet's real work occurs. The Graphics object passed into the paint() method holds the graphics state, which keeps track of the current attributes of the drawing surface. The state includes details about the current font and color to use for any drawing operation, for example. By using casting in line 13, a Graphics2D object is created that contains all this information.

Lines 14–15 set up the font for this graphics state. The Font object is held in the type instance variable and set up as a bold, monospaced, 20-point font. The call to setFont() in line 15 establishes this font as the one that will be used for subsequent drawing operations in lines 19 and 21.

Lines 16–17 create a new GregorianCalendar object that holds the current date and time. The getTime() method of this object returns the date and time as a Date object, another class of the java.util package. Calling toString() on this object returns the date and time as a string you can display.

Lines 18–19 set the color for drawing operations to black and then calls drawString() to display the string lastTime in the applet window at the (x,y) position 5, 25. Because the background is black, nothing will appear—you'll see why this is done shortly.

Lines 20–21 set the color using a Color object called butterscotch, and then displays the string time using this color.

Lines 22–26 use a class method of the Thread class to make the program do nothing for 1,000 milliseconds (one second). Because the sleep() method will generate an InterruptedException error if anything occurs that should interrupt this delay, the call to sleep() must be enclosed in a try-catch block. (You'll work more with threads and exceptions on Day 13, "Threads and Animation.")

Line 27–28 make the lastTime variable refer to the same string as the time variable and then call repaint() to request that the applet window be redrawn.

Calling repaint() causes the applet's paint() method to be called again. When this occurs, lastTime is displayed in black text in line 19, overwriting the last time string that was displayed. This clears the screen so that the new value of time can be shown.

Caution   Calling repaint() within an applet's paint() method is not the ideal way to handle animation, as you'll see when you begin working with threads in Day 13. It's suitable here primarily because the applet is a simple one.

7

Note that the 0 point for x, y is at the top left of the applet's drawing surface, with positive y moving downward, so 50 is at the bottom of the applet. Figure 7.1 shows how the applet's bounding box and the string are drawn on the page.

FIGURE 7.1

Drawing the applet.

If you implement the right applet methods in your class (init(), start(), stop(), paint(), and so on), your applet just seamlessly works without needing an explicit jumping-off point.

Including an Applet on a Web Page

After you create the class or classes that compose your applet and compile them into class files, you must create a Web page to place the applet on.

Applets are placed on a page by using the <APPLET> tag, an HTML programming command that works like other HTML elements. There also are numerous Web-page development tools such as Claris Home Page and Macromedia Dreamweaver that can be used to add applets to a page without using HTML.

The purpose of <APPLET> is to place an applet on a Web page and control how it looks in relation to other parts of the page.

Java-capable browsers use the information contained in the tag to find and execute the applet's compiled class files. In this section, you learn how to put Java applets on a Web page and how to serve the executable Java files to the Web at large.

Note

> The following section assumes that you have at least a passing understanding of writing HTML pages or know how to use a Web development tool to approximate HTML. If you need help in this area, one of the coauthors of this book, Laura Lemay, has written *Sams Teach Yourself Web Publishing with HTML 4 in 21 Days* with Denise Tyler.

The <APPLET> Tag

The <APPLET> tag is a special extension to HTML for including Java applets in Web pages; the tag is supported by all browsers that handle Java programs. Listing 7.2 shows a simple example of a Web page with an applet included.

LISTING 7.2   The Full Text of `Watch.html`

```
 1: <html>
 2: <head>
 3: <title>Watch Applet</title>
 4: </head>
 5: <body>
 6: <applet code="Watch.class" height="50" width="345">
 7: This program requires a Java-enabled browser.
 8: </applet>
 9: </body>
10: </html>
```

In Listing 7.2, the <APPLET> tag is contained in lines 6–8. In this example, the <APPLET> tag includes three attributes:

- CODE—Specifies the name of the applet's main class file
- WIDTH—Specifies the width of the applet window on the Web page
- HEIGHT—Specifies the height of the applet window

The class file indicated by the CODE attribute must be in the same folder as the Web page containing the applet, unless you use a CODEBASE attribute to specify a different folder. You learn how to do that later today.

WIDTH and HEIGHT are required attributes because the Web browser needs to know how much space to devote to the applet on the page. It's easy to draw to an area outside the applet window in a program, so you must be sure to provide a window large enough.

Text, images, and other Web page elements can be included between the <APPLET> and </APPLET> tags. These are displayed only on browsers that cannot handle Java programs, and including them is a good way to let people know they're missing out on a Java applet because their browser doesn't offer support for applets. If you don't specify anything between <APPLET> and </APPLET>, browsers that don't support Java display nothing in place of the applet.

Users who have Java browsers see the Watch applet on this page. Users who don't have Java see the alternate text that has been provided—This program requires a Java-enabled browser.

Testing the Result

After you have a main applet class file and an HTML file that uses the applet, you can load the HTML file into a Java-capable browser from your local disk. Using Netscape Navigator 4, local files can be loaded with the File, Open Page, Choose File command. In Internet Explorer, choose File, Open, Browse to find the right file on your system. The browser loads your Web page and the applet contained on it.

7

If you don't have a Java-capable browser, there should be a way to load applets included with your development environment. The SDK includes the `appletviewer` tool for testing your applets. Unlike a browser, `appletviewer` displays only the applets that are included on a Web page. It does not display the Web page itself.

Figure 7.2 shows the `Watch.html` page loaded in `appletviewer`.

FIGURE 7.2

The `Watch.html` *Web page in* `appletviewer`.

You should try to load this Web page with each of the browsers installed on your computer. If it works in `appletviewer` but does not work in others, the most likely cause is that you have tried to load it with a browser that doesn't support Java 2.

Putting Applets on the Web

After you have an applet that works successfully when you test it locally on your own system, you can make the applet available on the World Wide Web.

Java applets are presented by a Web server in the same way that HTML files, images, and other media are. You store the applet in a folder accessible to the Web server—often the same folder that contains the Web page that features the applet. The Web server should be configured to offer Java applets to browsers that support the language.

There are certain files you need to upload to a Web server:

- The HTML page containing the applet
- All `.class` files used by the applet that aren't part of Java's standard class library

If you know how to publish Web pages, image files, and other multimedia files, you don't have to learn any new skills to publish Java applets on your site.

More About the <APPLET> Tag

In its simplest form, the `<APPLET>` tag uses `CODE`, `WIDTH`, and `HEIGHT` attributes to create a space of the appropriate size, and then loads and runs the applet in that space. However, `<APPLET>` includes several other attributes that can help you better integrate an applet into a Web page's overall design.

Note   The attributes available for the `<APPLET>` tag are almost identical to those for the HTML `<IMG>` tag.

ALIGN

The ALIGN attribute defines how the applet will be aligned on a Web page in relation to other parts of the page. This attribute can have one of nine values:

- ALIGN=LEFT aligns the applet to the left of the text that follows the applet on the page.
- ALIGN=RIGHT aligns the applet to the right of the text that follows the applet on the page.
- ALIGN=TEXTTOP aligns the top of the applet with the top of the tallest text in the line.
- ALIGN=TOP aligns the applet with the topmost item in the line (which can be another applet, an image, or the top of the text).
- ALIGN=ABSMIDDLE aligns the middle of the applet with the middle of the largest item in the line.
- ALIGN=MIDDLE aligns the middle of the applet with the middle of the text's baseline.
- ALIGN=BASELINE aligns the bottom of the applet with the text's baseline. ALIGN=BASELINE is the same as ALIGN=BOTTOM, but ALIGN=BASELINE is a more descriptive name.
- ALIGN=ABSBOTTOM aligns the bottom of the applet with the lowest item in the line (which can be the text's baseline or another applet or image).

To end the formatting that is specified with the ALIGN attribute, you can use the HTML line break tag (`<BR>`) with the CLEAR attribute. This takes three values:

- `<BR CLEAR=LEFT>`—Continue displaying the rest of the Web page at the next clear left margin
- `<BR CLEAR=RIGHT>`—Continue displaying at the next clear right margin
- `<BR CLEAR=ALL>`—Continue displaying at the next clear left and right margin

Figure 7.3 shows the various alignment options, in which the smiley face in sunglasses is an applet.

7

FIGURE 7.3

Applet alignment options.

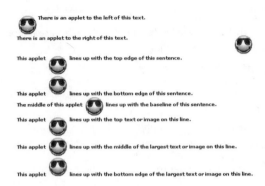

If you are using a Web development tool that enables you to place Java applets on a page, you should be able to set the ALIGN attribute by choosing LEFT, RIGHT, or one of the other values from within the program.

HSPACE and VSPACE

The HSPACE and VSPACE attributes are used to set the amount of space, in pixels, between an applet and its surrounding text. HSPACE controls the horizontal space to the left and right of the applet, and VSPACE controls the vertical space above and below the applet. For example, here's that sample snippet of HTML with vertical space of 50 and horizontal space of 10:

```
<APPLET CODE="ShowSmiley.class" WIDTH=45 HEIGHT=42
ALIGN=LEFT VSPACE=50 HSPACE=10>
Requires Java
</APPLET>
```

Figure 7.4 shows how this applet, which displays a smiley face on a white background, would be displayed with other elements of a Web page. The background of the page is a grid, and each grid is 10×10 pixels in size. You can use the grid to measure the amount of space between the applet and the text on the page.

FIGURE 7.4

Vertical and horizontal space.

CODE and CODEBASE

The CODE and CODEBASE attributes, unlike other parts of the <APPLET> tag, are used to indicate where the applet's main class file and other files can be found. They are used by a Java-capable browser when it attempts to run an applet after downloading it from a Web server.

CODE indicates the filename of the applet's main class file. If CODE is used without an accompanying CODEBASE attribute, the class file will be loaded from the same place as the Web page containing the applet.

You must specify the .class file extension with the CODE attribute. The following is an example of an <APPLET> tag that loads an applet called Bix.class from the same folder as the Web page:

```
<APPLET CODE="Bix.class" HEIGHT=40 WIDTH=400>
</APPLET>
```

The CODEBASE attribute is used to cause the browser to look in a different folder for the applet and any other files it uses. CODEBASE indicates an alternative folder, or even an alternative World Wide Web site, from which to load the class and other files. The following loads a class called Bix.class from a folder called Torshire:

```
<APPLET CODE="Bix.class" CODEBASE="Torshire" HEIGHT=40 WIDTH=400>
</APPLET>
```

Here's an example where the Java class files are loaded from an entirely different Web site than the one containing the page:

```
<APPLET CODE="Bix.class" CODEBASE="http://www.prefect.com/javaclasses"
HEIGHT=40 WIDTH=400>
</APPLET>
```

The <OBJECT> Tag

The <APPLET> tag is an HTML extension introduced specifically to present Java programs on Web pages. Today there are other types of programs that can run interactively on a page, including ActiveX controls, NetRexx applets, and Python programs. In order to deal with all these program types without requiring a different tag for each, the <OBJECT> tag has been added to the HTML specification.

The <OBJECT> tag is used for all objects—interactive programs and other external elements—that can be presented as part of a Web page. It is supported by versions 4.0 and higher of Netscape Navigator and Microsoft Internet Explorer as well as appletviewer. Other browsers such as Opera do not support this new tag, so you might still be using <APPLET> in many cases.

7

The <OBJECT> tag takes the following form:

```
<OBJECT CODE="Bix.class" CODEBASE="http://www.prefect.com/javaclasses"
HEIGHT=40 WIDTH=400">
</OBJECT>
```

Switching from <APPLET> to <OBJECT> requires only that the <OBJECT> tag should be used in place of <APPLET>.

Otherwise, attributes remain the same, including CODEBASE, HEIGHT, WIDTH, and ALIGN. The <OBJECT> tag also can use optional <PARAM> tags, which are described later today.

Java Archives

The standard way of placing a Java applet on a Web page is to use <APPLET> or <OBJECT> to indicate the primary class file of the applet. A Java-enabled browser then downloads and runs the applet. Any other classes and any other files needed by the applet are downloaded from the Web server.

The problem with running applets in this way is that every single file an applet needs—be it another helper class, image, audio file, text file, or anything else—requires a separate connection from a Web browser to the server containing the file. Because a fair amount of time is needed just to make the connection itself, this can increase the amount of time it takes to download an applet and everything it needs to run.

The solution to this problem is a Java archive, or JAR file. A *Java archive* is a collection of Java classes and other files packaged into a single file. By using a Java archive, the browser makes only one connection to the server rather than several. By reducing the number of files the browser has to load from the server, you can download and run your applet more quickly. Java archives also can be compressed, making the overall file size smaller and therefore faster to download—although it will take some time on the browser side for the files to be decompressed before they can run.

Versions 4.0 and higher of the Navigator and Internet Explorer browsers include support for JAR files. To create these archives, the SDK includes a tool called jar that can pack files into Java archives as well as unpack them. JAR files can be compressed using the Zip format or packed without using compression. The following command packs all of a folder's class and GIF image files into a single Java archive called Animate.jar:

```
jar cf Animate.jar *.class *.gif
```

The argument cf specifies two command-line options that can be used when running the jar program. The c option indicates that a Java archive file should be created, andf indicates that the name of the archive file will follow as one of the next arguments.

You also can add specific files to a Java archive with a command such as the following:

```
jar cf AudioLoop.jar AudioLoop.class beep.au loop.au
```

This creates an `AudioLoop.jar` archive containing three files: `AudioLoop.class`, `loop.au`, and `beep.au`.

Run `jar` without any arguments to see a list of options that can be used with the program.

After you create a Java archive, the `ARCHIVE` attribute is used with the `<APPLET>` tag to show where the archive can be found. You can use Java archives with an applet with tags such as the following:

```
<applet code="AudioLoop.class" archive="AudioLoop.jar" width=45 height=42>
</applet>
```

This tag specifies that an archive called `AudioLoop.jar` contains files used by the applet. Browsers and browsing tools that support JAR files will look inside the archive for files that are needed as the applet runs.

Caution   Although a Java archive can contain class files, the `ARCHIVE` attribute does not remove the need for the `CODE` attribute. A browser still needs to know the name of the applet's main class file in order to load it.

Passing Parameters to Applets

With Java applications, you can pass parameters to the `main()` method by using arguments on the command line. You then can parse those arguments inside the body of your class, and the application acts accordingly based on the arguments it is given.

Applets, however, don't have a command line. Applets can get different input from the HTML file that contains the `<APPLET>` or `<OBJECT>` tag through the use of applet parameters. To set up and handle parameters in an applet, you need two things:

- A special parameter tag in the HTML file
- Code in your applet to parse those parameters

Applet parameters come in two parts: a name, which is simply a name you pick, and a value, which determines the value of that particular parameter. For example, you can indicate the color of text in an applet by using a parameter with the name `color` and the value `red`. You can determine an animation's speed using a parameter with the name `speed` and the value `5`.

7

In the HTML file that contains the embedded applet, you indicate each parameter using the <PARAM> tag, which has two attributes for the name and the value called (surprisingly enough) NAME and VALUE. The <PARAM> tag goes inside the opening and closing <APPLET> tags, as in the following:

```
<APPLET CODE="QueenMab.class" WIDTH=100 HEIGHT=100>
<PARAM NAME=font VALUE="TimesRoman">
<PARAM NAME=size VALUE="24">
A Java applet appears here.
</APPLET>
```

This particular example defines two parameters to the QueenMab applet: one named font with a value of TimesRoman, and one named size with a value of 24.

The usage of the <PARAM> tag is the same for applets that use the <OBJECT> tag instead of <APPLET>.

Parameters are passed to your applet when it is loaded. In the init() method for your applet, you can retrieve these parameters by using the getParameter() method. The getParameter() method takes one argument, a string representing the name of the parameter you're looking for, and returns a string containing the corresponding value of that parameter. (As with arguments in Java applications, all parameter values are returned as strings.) To get the value of the font parameter from the HTML file, you might have a line such as the following in your init() method:

```
String theFontName = getParameter("font");
```

 Note

> The names of the parameters as specified in <PARAM> and the names of the parameters in getParameter() must match identically, including the same case. In other words, <PARAM NAME="eecummings"> is different from <PARAM NAME="EECummings">. If your parameters are not being properly passed to your applet, make sure the parameter cases match.

Note that if a parameter you expect has not been specified in the HTML file, getParameter() returns null. Most often, you will want to test for a null parameter and supply a reasonable default, as shown:

```
if (theFontName == null)
    theFontName = "Courier";
```

Keep in mind that getParameter() returns strings; if you want a parameter to be some other object or type, you have to convert it yourself. For example, consider the HTML file for the QueenMab applet. To parse the size parameter and assign it to an integer variable called theSize, you might use the following lines:

```
int theSize;
String s = getParameter("size");
if (s == null)
    theSize = 12;
else theSize = Integer.parseInt(s);
```

Listing 7.3 contains a modified version of the Watch applet that enables the background color to be specified as a parameter called background.

LISTING 7.3   The Full Text of NewWatch.java

```
 1: import java.awt.*;
 2: import java.util.*;
 3:
 4: public class NewWatch extends javax.swing.JApplet {
 5:     private Color butterscotch = new Color(255, 204, 102);
 6:     private String lastTime = "";
 7:     Color back;
 8:
 9: public void init() {
10:         String in = getParameter("background");
11:         back = Color.black;
12:         if (in != null) {
13:             try {
14:                 back = Color.decode(in);
15:             } catch (NumberFormatException e) {
16:                 showStatus("Bad parameter " + in);
17:             }
18:         }
19:         setBackground(back);
20:     }
21:
22:     public void paint(Graphics screen) {
23:         Graphics2D screen2D = (Graphics2D)screen;
24:         Font type = new Font("Monospaced", Font.BOLD, 20);
25:         screen2D.setFont(type);
26:         GregorianCalendar day = new GregorianCalendar();
27:         String time = day.getTime().toString();
28:         screen2D.setColor(back);
29:         screen2D.drawString(lastTime, 5, 25);
30:         screen2D.setColor(butterscotch);
31:         screen2D.drawString(time, 5, 25);
32:         try {
33:             Thread.sleep(1000);
34:         } catch (InterruptedException e) {
35:             // do nothing
36:         }
37:         lastTime = time;
38:         repaint();
39:     }
40: }
```

7

The NewWatch applet contains only a few minor changes outside of the init() method. A Color object is declared in line 7, and line 28 is changed so that it uses this object to set the current color instead of Color.black.

The init() method in lines 9–20 has been rewritten to work with a parameter called background. This parameter should be specified as a hexadecimal string—a pound character ("#") followed by three hexadecimal numbers that represent the red, green, and blue values of a color. Black is #000000, red is #FF0000, green is #00FF00, blue is #0000FF, white is #FFFFFF, and so on. If you are familiar with HTML, you have probably used hexadecimal strings like this before.

The Color class has a decode(*String*) class method that creates a Color object from a hexadecimal string. This occurs in line 14—the try-catch block handles the NumberFormatException error that occurs if in does not contain a valid hexadecimal string.

Line 19 sets the applet window to the color represented by the back object. To try this program, create the HTML document in Listing 7.4.

LISTING 7.4   The Full Text of NewWatch.html

```
 1: <html>
 2: <head>
 3: <title>Watch Applet</title>
 4: </head>
 5: <body bgcolor="#996633">
 6: <p>The current time:
 7: <applet code="NewWatch.class" height="50" width="345">
 8: <param name="background" value="#996633">
 9: This program requires a Java-enabled browser.
10: </applet>
11: </body>
12: </html>
```

Note the <APPLET> tag, which designates the class file for the applet and the appropriate width and height (345 and 50, respectively). Just below it (line 8) is the <PARAM> tag, which is used to pass the parameter to the applet. In this example, the NAME of the parameter is background, and the VALUE is the string #996633, which is a shade of brown. Line 5 sets the background color of the page using the same hexadecimal string.

Loading this HTML file in Opera produces the result shown in Figure 7.5.

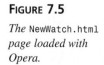

FIGURE 7.5

The NewWatch.html *page loaded with Opera.*

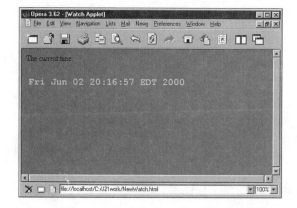

Because the applet window and Web page have the same background color, the edges of the applet are not visible in Figure 7.5. If no background parameter is specified in the HTML code loading the NewWatch applet, the default is black.

Developing Java 2 Applets

When you are planning a Java programming project that includes applets, one of the biggest decisions to make is what version of the language to employ in those applets.

Java 1.0, the first version, is supported in all Web browsers that can run applets. Netscape Navigator and Microsoft Internet Explorer have supported it for more than four years, and it's also offered in Opera and other browsers.

The most recent editions of these browsers also have added support for Java 1.1 in the past year, so you can now take advantage of the improved user interface, event handling, and other features while reaching a wide audience of browser users.

To support Java, browser developers have created their own Java interpreters and integrated them into the software. This has become progressively more difficult with each new version of Java, and it also adds to the size of the browser because the Java class library is more than five times as large today as it was in Java 1.1.

Sun offers the Java Plug-in, an interpreter that can run applets in Web browsers in place of the built-in interpreter. The Plug-in, which was originally called the Java Activator, supports the current version of Java 2, so it's available for applet programmers who want to use the most up-to-date techniques offered in the language.

7

Two things must happen for a Java applet to run using the Java Plug-in:

- The user must have installed the Plug-in.
- The page containing the applet must have HTML code that directs the Plug-in to run the applet.

The Java Plug-in is included with SDK 1.3, so you already should have a copy installed on your system. To download and install it separately, visit Sun's Java Web site at `http://java.sun.com/products/plugin` or visit the main page at `http://java.sun.com` and look in the Products & APIs section of the site.

Using the Plug-in on a Web Page

When you are relying on a browser's built-in Java interpreter, putting an applet on a Web page is simple. You use the `<APPLET>` or `<OBJECT>` tag to put the applet on a page, and use `<PARAM>` to send parameters that customize how the applet runs, as in the following example:

```
<applet code="NewWatch.class" height="50" width="345">
<param name="background" value="#996633">
This program requires a Java-enabled browser.
</applet>
```

Running an applet that uses the Java Plug-in is more complex. You must write HTML code that accounts for the different ways that Internet Explorer and Netscape Navigator handle plug-ins and embedded programs such as applets.

If you modified the preceding example so that it used the Plug-in to execute the applet, here's what the HTML code looks like:

```
<OBJECT classid="clsid:8AD9C840-044E-11D1-B3E9-00805F499D93" WIDTH ="345"
HEIGHT="50" codebase="http://java.sun.com/products/plugin/1.3/jinstall-13-
➥win32.cab#Version=1,3,0,0">
<PARAM NAME=CODE VALUE="NewWatch.class">
<PARAM NAME="type" VALUE="application/x-java-applet;version=1.3">
<PARAM NAME="scriptable" VALUE="false">
<PARAM NAME="background" VALUE="#996633">
<COMMENT>
<EMBED type="application/x-java-applet;version=1.3" CODE="NewWatch.class"
WIDTH="345" HEIGHT="50" background="#996633" scriptable=false
pluginspage="http://java.sun.com/products/plugin/1.3/plugin-install.html">
</COMMENT>
<NOEMBED>
This program requires a Java-enabled browser.
</NOEMBED>
</EMBED>
</OBJECT>
```

```
<!--
<APPLET CODE="NewWatch.class" WIDTH="345" HEIGHT="50">
<PARAM NAME="background" VALUE="#996633">
This program requires a Java-enabled browser.
</APPLET>
-->
```

As you can see, the HTML required by the Java Plug-in is more complex. Different tags are used to make the applet work on as wide a variety of browsers as possible.

Sun has created a Java application called HTMLConverter that converts an existing Web page so that all its applets are run by the Java Plug-in. After you have created a Web page that loads an applet using an <APPLET> tag, HTMLConverter will convert the Web page to use the Plug-in instead.

This program is available from the same page on the Java Web site as the Plug-in. At the time of this writing, the current version of HTMLConverter is offered as a ZIP archive. (Prior versions came with an installation program.)

After downloading the file, extract all the files within the ZIP archive into a folder using a program that handles the ZIP format and make sure that subfolders are created to hold all the files associated with HTMLConverter—your ZIP program should do this automatically. A new converter folder will be created.

If you extracted the files into c:\jdk1.3, the subfolder is c:\jdk1.3\converter. Add this folder to your system's CLASSPATH and reboot the system to make the change take effect.

Once HTMLConverter has been installed, run the program with the Java interpreter, using the name of the HTML document to convert as an argument. For example:

```
java HTMLConverter WatchApplet.html
```

The preceding command will convert all applets contained in WatchApplet.html to run the Java Plug-in.

Caution   The HTMLConverter application overwrites the existing HTML code on the page—if for some reason you also want the non-Plug-in version of the page, you should copy the HTML document and run HTMLConverter on that copy.

7

Running the Plug-in

The Java Plug-in works in conjunction with a browser like other browser plug-ins such as the Macromedia Flash player, Real streaming multimedia player, and PNG graphics viewers.

First, markup code is added to an HTML document to indicate that it contains a file requiring a plug-in. Other information is provided, such as the name of the plug-in and an address from which the plug-in can be downloaded.

When a user loads the document with a Web browser, the browser looks for the plug-in on the user's computer, and if it is found, opens the file with the plug-in.

If the plug-in is not found, a dialog box opens asking for permission to download and install the plug-in. Figure 7.6 shows what this dialog looks like in Internet Explorer 5. By default, Internet Explorer will not install a plug-in, ActiveX control, and other executable programs without the user's approval.

FIGURE 7.6

Deciding whether to install the Java Plug-in.

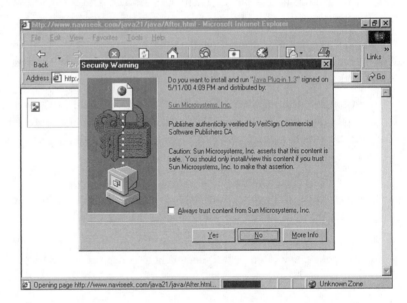

If the user decides to install the Plug-in, it will be downloaded and set up on the user's computer. This can be a time-consuming process—the Java Plug-in is more than 4.5MB at present and takes more than 30 minutes to download over a 28.8Kbps Internet connection.

Note

Because the Java Plug-in is so large, Sun recommends that it should be used only for intranets, large-scale corporate software, and other projects where the audience is well defined. Most applet programmers today whose work is open to all Web users employ Java 1.1 or 1.0 features only and do not require the Java Plug-in.

Once installation is complete, the Plug-in opens the file. All other files that require the plug-in will be run automatically, so that user will be able to use all Java 2 applets as if the browser had a built-in interpreter that supported them.

Summary

Although applets are no longer the focus of Java development, they are still the element of Java technology that reaches the most people. There are applets on thousands of World Wide Web sites—more than 13.6 million Web pages contain an applet, according to the AltaVista search engine at `http://www.altavista.com`.

Because they are executed and displayed within Web pages, applets can use the graphics, user interface, and event structure provided by the Web browser. This capability provides the applet programmer with a lot of functionality without a lot of extra toil.

Today you learned the basics of applet creation, including the following things:

- All applets are subclasses of the `java.applet.Applet` or `javax.swing.JApplet` class, which provide the behavior the program needs to run within a Web browser.
- Applets have five main methods that cover activities an applet performs as it runs: `init()`, `start()`, `stop()`, `destroy()`, and `paint()`. These methods are overridden to provide functionality in an applet.
- Applets are placed on Web pages using the `<APPLET>` or `<OBJECT>` tag in HTML, and the `<PARAM>` tag can be used to specify parameters that customize how the applet functions.
- To reduce the time it takes to download an applet from a Web server, you can use Java archive files.
- Applets can receive information from a Web page by using the `<PARAM>` tag in association with an applet. Inside the body of your applet, you can gain access to those parameters using the `getParameter()` method.
- If you want to use Java 2 features in your applets, you can create HTML documents that use the Java Plug-in rather than a browser's built-in interpreter.

7

Q&A

Q I have an applet that takes parameters and an HTML file that passes it those parameters, but when my applet runs, all I get are `null` values. What's going on here?

A Do the names of your parameters (in the `NAME` attribute) match exactly with the names you're testing for in `getParameter()`? They must be exact, including case, for the match to be made. Make sure also that your `<PARAM>` tags are inside the opening and closing `<APPLET>` tags and that you haven't misspelled anything.

Q Because applets don't have a command line or a standard output stream, how can I do simple debugging output like `System.out.println()` in an applet?

A Depending on your browser or other Java-enabled environment, you might have a console window where debugging output (the result of `System.out.println()`) appears, or it might be saved to a log file. (Netscape has a Java Console under the Options menu; Internet Explorer uses a Java log file that you must enable by choosing Options, Advanced.)

You can continue to print messages using `System.out.println()` in your applets—just remember to remove them after you're done, so that they don't confuse your actual users.

Q I've enabled Java logging on Internet Explorer 4.0. Now where the heck do I view the log?

A Unlike Netscape Navigator, which makes the Java output window available as a pull-down menu command, Microsoft Internet Explorer doesn't appear to have a built-in feature. Under Internet Explorer, you can find the log in the text file `java-log.txt` in your main `\WINDOWS\JAVA` folder (often `C:\WINDOWS\JAVA`).

Questions

1. Which class should an applet inherit from if Swing features will be used in the program?

   (a) `java.applet.Applet`

   (b) `javax.swing.JApplet`

   (c) Either one

2. What method is called whenever an applet window is obscured and must be redrawn?

   (a) `start()`

   (b) `init()`

   (c) `paint()`

3. To reach the widest possible audience, what Java version should your applets employ?

   (a) Java 1.0

   (b) Java 1.1

   (c) Java 2

Answers

1. b. If you're going to use Swing's improved interface and event-handling capabilities, the applet must be a subclass of `JApplet`.

2. c. You also can request that the applet window be redisplayed by calling the applet's `repaint()` method.

3. The answer is a, although it's becoming a toss-up with answer b. More than 85% of the Web audience uses the current Navigator, Internet Explorer, or Opera browsers, which all support Java 1.1.

Exercises

To extend your knowledge of the subjects covered today, try the following exercises:

- Enhance the `NewWatch` applet so that you can set the color of the text with a parameter also.

- Create an applet that does the same thing as `Ellsworth.java` from Day 1, "21st Century Java."

Where applicable, exercise solutions are offered on the book's Web site at `http://www.java21days.com`.

7

WEEK 2

Swing and Other Visual Java Programming

8 Working with Swing

9 Building a Swing Interface

10 Arranging Components on a User Interface

11 Responding to User Input

12 Color, Fonts, and Graphics

13 Threads and Animation

14 JavaSound

8

9

10

11

12

13

14

DAY 8

Working with Swing

During the next four days, you will work with a set of classes called Swing that can implement a user-interface style called Metal. (Sounds like somebody at Sun Microsystems is either a music buff or a frustrated musician.)

Swing, which is part of the Java Foundation Classes library, provides a way to offer a graphical user interface in your Java programs and take user input with the keyboard, mouse, and other input devices.

The Swing library is an extension of the Abstract Windowing Toolkit, the package that offered limited graphical programming support in Java 1.0. Swing offers much-improved functionality over its predecessor—new components, expanded component features, better event handling, and a selectable look and feel.

Today you use Swing to create applications that feature a graphical user interface, using each of these components:

- Frames—windows that can include a title bar and menu bar, as well as maximize, minimize, and close buttons
- Containers—interface elements that can hold other components
- Buttons—clickable regions with text or graphics indicating their purpose

- Labels—text or graphics that provide information
- Text fields and text areas—windows that take keyboard input and allow text to be edited
- Drop-down lists—groups of related items that can be selected from drop-down menus or scrolling windows
- Check boxes and radio buttons—small windows or circles that can be selected or deselected

Creating an Application

The expression "look and feel" is used often when describing interface programming. As you might have guessed, it describes how a graphical user interface looks and feels to a user. Look and feel is something that becomes relevant in Java with the introduction of Swing.

This feature offers the most visually dramatic change from the Abstract Windowing Toolkit (AWT). Swing lets you create a Java program with an interface that uses the style of the native operating system, such as Windows or Solaris, or a new style that has been dubbed Metal, which is unique to Java.

Swing components, unlike their predecessors in previous versions of Java, are implemented entirely in Java. This makes them more compatible across different platforms than the AWT.

All elements of Swing are part of the `javax.swing` package, a standard part of the Java 2 class library. To use a Swing class, you must either use an `import` statement with that class or a catch-all statement such as the following:

```
import javax.swing.*;
```

 Caution

The Swing package had several names before Sun settled on `javax.swing`. If you come across one of the older names in a program's source code—`com.sun.java.swing` or `java.awt.swing`—changing the package name might be all that's required to update the code for Java 2.

Two other packages that are used with graphical user interface programming are `java.awt`, the Abstract Windowing Toolkit, and `java.awt.event`, event-handling classes that handle user input.

When you use a Swing component, you work with objects of that component's class. You create the component by calling its constructor method and then calling methods of the component as needed for proper setup.

All Swing components are subclasses of the abstract class `JComponent`, which includes methods to set the size of a component, change the background color, define the font used for any displayed text, and set up *tooltips*—explanatory text that appears when a user hovers over the component for a few seconds.

> **Caution**
>
> Swing classes inherit from many of the same superclasses as the Abstract Windowing Toolkit, so it is possible to use Swing and AWT components together in the same interface. However, in some cases the two types of components will not be rendered correctly in a container. To avoid these problems, it's best to use Swing components unless you are writing an applet limited to Java 1.0 or 1.1 functionality—there's a Swing version of every AWT component.

Before components can be displayed in a user interface, they must be added to a *container*, a component that can hold other components. Swing containers, which can often be placed in other containers, are subclasses of `java.awt.Container`, a class in the Abstract Windowing Toolkit. This class includes methods to add and remove components from a container, arrange components using an object called a layout manager, and set up empty insets around the inside edges of a container.

Creating an Interface

The first step in creating a Swing application is to create a class that represents the graphical user interface. An object of this class will serve as a container, the component that holds all other components to be displayed.

In many projects, the main interface object will be either a simple window (the `JWindow` class) or a more specialized window called a frame (the `JFrame` class).

A window is a container that can be displayed on a user's desktop. It does not have a title bar; maximize, minimize and close buttons; or other features you see on most windows that open in a graphical user interface operating system. Windows that are enhanced with title bars, those window management buttons, and other features are called frames.

In a graphical environment such as Windows or MacOS, users expect to have the ability to move, resize, and close the windows of programs that they run. The main place a window turns up is when programs are loading—there is sometimes a "title screen" with the program's name, logo, and other information.

One way to create a graphical Swing application is to make the interface a subclass of JFrame, as in the following class declaration:

```
public class Lookup extends JFrame {
    // ...
}
```

This leaves only a few things to do in the constructor method of the class:

- Call a constructor method of the superclass to handle any of its setup procedures.
- Set the size of the frame's window, in pixels.
- Decide what to do if a user closes the window.
- Display the frame.

The JFrame class has two constructors: JFrame() and JFrame(String). One sets the frame's title bar to the specified text, whereas the other leaves this empty. You can also set the title by calling the frame's setTitle(String) method.

The size of a frame can be established by calling the setSize(int, int) with the width and height as arguments. The size of a frame is indicated in pixels, so if you called setSize(600, 600), the frame would take up almost all of a screen at 800×600 resolution once it is displayed.

Note   You also can call the method setSize(Dimension) to set up a frame's size. Dimension, a class in the java.awt package, represents the width and height of a user interface component. Calling the Dimension(int, int) constructor will create a Dimension object representing the width and height specified as arguments.

Frames are invisible when they are created. You can make them visible by calling the frame's show() method with no arguments or setVisible(boolean) with the literal true as an argument.

If you want a frame to be displayed when it is created, call one of these methods in the constructor method. You also can leave the frame invisible, requiring any class that uses the frame to make it visible by calling show() or setVisible(true). (There are also methods of hiding a frame—call either hide() method or setVisible(false).)

When a frame is displayed, the default behavior is for it to be positioned in the upper left corner of the computer's desktop. You can specify a different location by calling the setBounds(*int*, *int*, *int*, *int*) method. The first two arguments to this method are the (x,y) position of the frame's upper left corner on the desktop, and the last two arguments set the width and height of the frame.

The following class represents a 400×100 frame with "Edit Payroll" in the title bar:

```
public class Payroll extends javax.swing.JFrame {
    public Payroll() {
        super("Edit Payroll");
        setSize(300, 100);
        show();
    }
}
```

Every frame has maximize, minimize, and close buttons on the title bar at the user's control—the same controls present in the interface of other software running on your system. In Java, the normal behavior when a frame is closed is for the application to keep running.

To change this, you must call a frame's setDefaultCloseOperation() method with one of four JFrame class variables as an argument:

- EXIT_ON_CLOSE—Exit the program when the frame is closed.
- DISPOSE_ON_CLOSE—Close the frame, dispose of the frame object, and keep running the application.
- DO_NOTHING_ON_CLOSE—Keep the frame open and continue running.
- HIDE_ON_CLOSE—Close the frame and continue running.

To prevent a user from closing a frame at all, add the following statement to the frame's constructor method:

```
setDefaultCloseOperation(JFrame.DO_NOTHING_ON_CLOSE);
```

If you are creating a frame to serve as an application's main user interface, the expected behavior is probably EXIT_ON_CLOSE, which shuts down the application along with the frame.

Developing a Framework

Listing 8.1 contains a simple application that displays a frame 300×100 pixels in size. This class can serve as a framework—pun unavoidable—for any applications you create that use a graphical user interface.

LISTING 8.1   The Full Text of `SimpleFrame.java`

```
 1: import javax.swing.JFrame;
 2:
 3: public class SimpleFrame extends JFrame {
 4:     public SimpleFrame() {
 5:         super("Frame Title");
 6:         setSize(300, 100);
 7:         setDefaultCloseOperation(JFrame.EXIT_ON_CLOSE);
 8:         setVisible(true);
 9:     }
10:
11:     public static void main(String[] arguments) {
12:         SimpleFrame sf = new SimpleFrame();
13:     }
14:
15: }
```

When you compile and run the application, you should see the frame displayed in Figure 8.1.

FIGURE 8.1

Displaying a frame.

The `SimpleFrame` application isn't much to look at—this graphical user interface contains no components a user can actually interface with, aside from the standard maximize, minimize, and close ("X") buttons on the title bar shown in Figure 8.1. You will add components later today.

A `SimpleFrame` object is created in the `main()` method in lines 11–13. If you had not displayed the frame when it was constructed, you could call `sf.setVisible(true)` in the `main()` method to display the frame represented by `sf`.

The work involved in creating the frame's user interface takes place in the `SimpleFrame()` constructor method. If you were adding components to this frame, they could be created and added to the frame within this constructor.

Creating a window using `JWindow` is very similar to working with frames in Swing. The only things you can't do involve features that simple windows don't support—titles, closing a window, and so on.

Listing 8.2 contains an application that creates and opens a window, displays the first 10,000 integers in the command-line window, and then closes the window.

LISTING 8.2   The Full Text of `SimpleWindow.java`

```
1: import javax.swing.JWindow;
2:
3: public class SimpleWindow extends JWindow {
4:     public SimpleWindow() {
5:         super();
6:         setBounds(250, 225, 300, 150);
7: }
8:
9:     public static void main(String[] arguments) {
10:        SimpleWindow sw = new SimpleWindow();
11:        sw.setVisible(true);
12:        for (int i = 0; i < 10000; i++)
13:            System.out.print(i + " ");
14:        sw.setVisible(false);
15:        System.exit(0);
16:    }
17:
18: }
```

Figure 8.2 shows this application running with the `SimpleWindow` container visible over the Java command-line window in Windows.

FIGURE 8.2

Displaying a window.

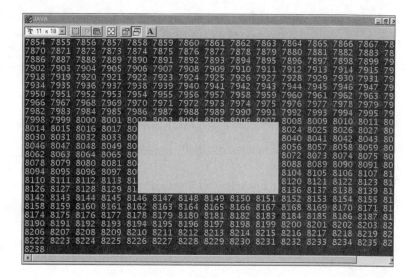

Because of the call to `setBounds(250, 225, 300, 150)` in line 6 of Listing 8.2, the window is 300×150 in size and displayed with its upper left corner at the (x,y) position 250, 225.

The for loop in lines 12–13 is included simply to take up a little time. There are better ways to make time pass in a Java program, as you will see in Day 13, "Threads and Animation."

Closing a Window

Prior to the introduction of the setDefaultCloseOperation() method in Java 2, the only way to close a graphical application after a user closed a window was to explicitly deal with the occurrence.

To do this, the window must be monitored to see if the user has done anything to close it, such as clicking a title bar close button. If so, a program can respond by exiting the program, closing the window, keeping it open, or something else appropriate to the situation.

Monitoring for user interaction requires the use of event-handling classes—features that you explore in great detail on Day 11, "Responding to User Input." The term *event-handling* in Java describes objects that wait for something to occur—such as a button-click or typing text into a field—and then call methods in response to that occurrence.

All of Java's event-handling classes belong to the java.awt.event package.

 Note

> Though this technique isn't necessary in Java 2, it is introduced here because you will see it in many existing Swing applications. It also provides a first look at how Java handles user input in a Swing interface.

To monitor a window in a user interface, your program must do three things:

- Create an object that will monitor the state of the window.
- Implement an interface in the object that handles each way the window can change.
- Associate the window with your user interface.

A window can be monitored by any object that implements the WindowListener interface. As you learned on Day 2, "Object-Oriented Programming," an interface is a set of methods that indicate a class supports more behavior than it has inherited from its superclasses.

In this example, a class that implements the WindowListener interface has behavior to keep track of what a user is doing to a window.

To implement an interface, a class must include all the methods in that interface. Classes that support `WindowListener` must have the following seven methods:

- `windowActivated()`—The window associated with this object is becoming the active window, which means that it will be able to receive keyboard input.

- `windowDeactivated()`—The window is about to become inactive, which means that it won't be able to receive keyboard input.

- `windowClosed()`—The window has been closed.

- `windowClosing()`—The window is being closed.

- `windowOpened()`—The window has been made visible.

- `windowIconified()`—The window has been minimized.

- `windowDeiconified()`—The window has been maximized.

As you can see, each method has something to do with how a user interacts with the window.

Another class in the `java.awt.event` package, `WindowAdapter`, implements this interface with seven empty methods that do nothing. By creating a subclass of `WindowAdapter`, you can override methods pertaining to the user-interaction events that you want to deal with, as shown in Listing 8.3.

LISTING 8.3 The Full Text of `ExitWindow.java`

```
1: import java.awt.event.*;
2:
3: public class ExitWindow extends WindowAdapter {
4:     public void windowClosing(WindowEvent e) {
5:         System.exit(0);
6:     }
7: }
```

The ExitWindow class inherits from `WindowAdapter`, which implements the `WindowListener` interface. As a result, `ExitWindow` objects can be used to monitor frames.

An `ExitWindow` object has only one job: Wait to see if a window is being closed, an event that causes `windowClosing()` method to be called automatically.

Line 5 of Listing 8.3 calls a class method of java.lang.System, exit(), which shuts down the currently running application. The integer argument to exit() should be 0 if the program ended normally or any other value if it ended because of an error of some kind.

Once you have created an object that can monitor a window, you associate it with that window by calling the component's addWindowListener() method, as in the following example:

```
JFrame main = new JFrame("Main Menu");
ExitWindow exit = new ExitWindow();
main.addWindowListener(exit);
```

This example associates the ExitWindow object with a frame called main.

You can use this ExitWindow class with the primary window of any application, provided that the program should shut down and do nothing else after the user closes the window.

Listing 8.4 contains the SimpleFrame application rewritten to use this technique.

LISTING 8.4   The Full Text of ExitFrame.java

```
 1: import javax.swing.JFrame;
 2:
 3: public class ExitFrame extends JFrame {
 4:     public ExitFrame() {
 5:         super("Frame Title");
 6:         setSize(300, 100);
 7:         ExitWindow exit = new ExitWindow();
 8:         addWindowListener(exit);
 9:         setVisible(true);
10:     }
11:
12:     public static void main(String[] arguments) {
13:         ExitFrame sf = new ExitFrame();
14:     }
15:
16: }
```

This application must have access to ExitWindow.class in order to compile and run successfully. The easiest way to do this is to compile both programs in the same folder.

Creating a Component

Creating a graphical user interface is a great way to get experience working with objects in Java because each aspect of the interface is represented by its own class.

8

You have already worked with the containers JFrame and JWindow and the event-handling class WindowAdapter. Yesterday, you used another container, JApplet.

To use an interface component in Java, you create an object of that component's class. One of the simplest to employ is JButton, the class that embodies clickable buttons.

In most programs, buttons trigger an action—click Install to begin installing software, click a Smiley button to begin a new game of Minesweeper, click the Minimize button to prevent your boss from seeing Minesweeper running, and so on.

A Swing button can feature a text label, a graphical icon, or a combination of both.

Constructor methods you can use include

- JButton(*String*)—Creates a button labeled with the specified text.
- JButton(*Icon*)—Creates a button that displays the specified icon.
- JButton(*String, Icon*)—Creates a button with the specified text and icon.

The following statements create the three buttons:

```
JButton play = new JButton("Play");
JButton stop = new JButton("Stop");
JButton rewind = new JButton("Rewind");
```

Adding Components to a Container

Before you can display a user interface component, such as a button in a Java program, you must add it to a container and display that container.

To add a component to a simple container, you call the container's add(*Component*) method with the component as the argument (all user interface components in Swing inherit from java.awt.Component).

The simplest Swing container is the panel (the JPanel class). The following example creates a button and adds it to a panel:

```
JButton quit = new JButton("Quit");
JPanel panel = new JPanel();
panel.add(quit);
```

Most other Swing containers, including frames, windows, applets, and dialog boxes, do not allow components to be added in this manner.

These containers are broken down into *panes*, sort of containers-within-containers. Ordinarily, components are added to the container's *content pane*.

You can add components to a container's content pane using the following steps:

1. Create a panel.
2. Add components to the panel using its add(*Component*) method.
3. Call setContentPane(*Container*) with the panel as an argument.

The program in Listing 8.5 uses the application framework created earlier in this chapter, but adds a button to the frame's content pane.

LISTING 8.5   The Full Text of Buttons.java

```
 1: import javax.swing.*;
 2:
 3: public class Buttons extends JFrame {
 4:     JButton abort = new JButton("Abort");
 5:     JButton retry = new JButton("Retry");
 6:     JButton fail = new JButton("Fail");
 7:
 8:     public Buttons() {
 9:         super("Buttons");
10:         setSize(80, 140);
11:         setDefaultCloseOperation(JFrame.EXIT_ON_CLOSE);
12:         JPanel pane = new JPanel();
13:         pane.add(abort);
14:         pane.add(retry);
15:         pane.add(fail);
16:         setContentPane(pane);
17: }
18:
19:     public static void main(String[] arguments) {
20:         Buttons rb = new Buttons();
21:         rb.show();
22:     }
23: }
```

When you run the application, a small frame will open that contains three buttons (see Figure 8.3).

FIGURE 8.3

The Buttons *application.*

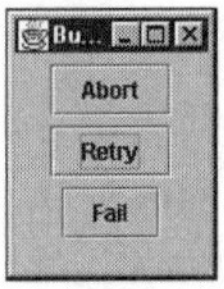

8

The Buttons class has three instance variables: the abort, retry, and fail JButton objects.

In lines 12–15, a new JPanel object is created and the three buttons are added to the panel by calling its add() method. When the panel is complete, the frame's setContentPane() method is called in line 16 with the panel as an argument, making it the frame's content pane.

Note If you click the buttons, absolutely nothing will happen. Doing something in response to a button click is covered in Day 11.

Adding Components to an Applet

Another kind of container you can work with in Swing is the applet window. Because applets are already part of a graphical user interface in a Web browser, they don't require as much initial setup as the windows you create for applications. The window is already open when the applet begins running, and the dimensions are determined by HTML tags on the Web document that contains the applet.

A Swing applet is divided, separating the content pane from other panes. You must add components to the content pane rather than the applet itself.

Note This is a departure from how Java 1.0 and Java 1.1 applets are used as containers. Those applets are subclasses of java.applet.Applet, and you add components directly to the applet using the add() method. They are not subdivided into panes.

Listing 8.6 contains the Buttons application rewritten as an applet.

LISTING 8.6   The Full Text of ButtonApplet.java

```
1: import javax.swing.*;
2:
3: public class ButtonApplet extends JApplet {
4:     JButton abort = new JButton("Abort");
5:     JButton retry = new JButton("Retry");
6:     JButton fail = new JButton("Fail");
7:
8:     public void init() {
9:         JPanel pane = new JPanel();
```

LISTING 8.6   continued

```
10:          pane.add(abort);
11:          pane.add(retry);
12:          pane.add(fail);
13:          setContentPane(pane);
14:      }
15: }
```

The following HTML can be used on a Web document to load the applet shown in Figure 8.4:

```
<applet code="ButtonApplet.class" width="80" height="140">
</applet>
```

FIGURE 8.4

The ButtonApplet *applet loaded by* appletviewer.

Working with Components

Swing offers more than two dozen different user interface components in addition to the buttons and containers you have used thus far. You will work with many of these components for the rest of the day and on Day 9, "Building a Swing Interface."

All Swing components share a common superclass, javax.swing.JComponent, and inherit several methods you will find useful in your own programs.

The setEnabled(*boolean*) method enables a component if the argument is true and disables it if the argument is false. Components are enabled by default, and they must be enabled in order to receive user input. Many disabled components will change in appearance to indicate that they are not presently usable—for instance, a disabled JButton will have light gray borders and gray text. If you want to check whether a component is enabled, you can call the isEnabled() method, which returns a boolean value.

The setVisible(*boolean*) method works for all components the way it does for containers. Use true to display a component and false to hide it. There's also a boolean isVisible() method.

The setSize(*int*, *int*) resizes the component to the width and height specified as arguments, and setSize(*Dimension*) uses a Dimension object to do the same thing. For most components, you do not need to set a size—the default is usually acceptable. To find out the size of a component, call its getSize() method, which returns a Dimension object with the dimensions in height and width instance variables.

As you will see, similar Swing components also have other methods in common, such as setText() and getText() for text components, and setValue() and getValue() for components that store a numeric value.

Image Icons

Earlier today, you created button components that were labeled with text. Swing also supports the use of ImageIcon objects on buttons and other components in which a label can be provided. *Icons* are small graphics, usually in GIF format, that can be placed on a button, label, or other user interface element to identify it. Current operating systems have icons everywhere—garbage cans and recycling bins for deleting files, folder icons for storing files, mailbox icons for email programs, and hundreds of others.

An ImageIcon object can be created by specifying a graphic's filename as the only argument to the constructor. The following example loads an icon from the file zap.gif and creates a JButton with the icon as its label:

```
ImageIcon zap = new ImageIcon("zap.gif");
JButton button = new JButton(zap);
JPanel pane = new JPanel();
pane.add(button);
setContentPane(pane);
```

Listing 8.7 contains a Java application that uses the same ImageIcon to create 24 buttons, add them to a panel, and then designate the panel as a frame's content pane.

LISTING 8.7   The Full Text of Icons.java

```
 1: import javax.swing.*;
 2:
 3: public class Icons extends JFrame {
 4:     JButton[] buttons = new JButton[24];
 5:
 6:     public Icons() {
 7:         super("Icons");
 8:         setSize(335, 318);
 9:         setDefaultCloseOperation(JFrame.EXIT_ON_CLOSE);
10:         JPanel pane = new JPanel();
11:         ImageIcon icon = new ImageIcon("3dman.gif");
12:         for (int i = 0; i < 24; i++) {
```

LISTING 8.7   continued

```
13:             buttons[i] = new JButton(icon);
14:             pane.add(buttons[i]);
15:         }
16:         setContentPane(pane);
17:         show();
18:     }
19:
20:     public static void main(String[] arguments) {
21:         Icons ike = new Icons();
22:     }
23: }
```

Figure 8.5 shows the result.

FIGURE 8.5

An interface contain-ing buttons labeled with icons.

The icon graphic referred to in line 12 can be found on this book's official Web site at `http://www.java21days.com` in the page for Day 8, "Working with Swing," under the filename `3dman.gif`.

Note   The 3D moviegoer icon is from Jeffrey Zeldman's Pardon My Icons! collec-tion, which includes hundreds of icons you can use in your own projects. If you're looking for icons to experiment with in Swing applications, you can find Pardon My Icons at the following address:

`http://www.zeldman.com/icon.html`

Labels

A label is a user component that contains informative text, an icon, or both. Labels, which are created from the JLabel class, are often used to identify the purpose of other components on an interface. They cannot be directly edited by a user.

8

To create a label, you can use the following constructors:

- JLabel(*String*)—A label with the specified text
- JLabel(*String*, *int*)—A label with the specified text and alignment
- JLabel(*String*, *Icon*, *int*)—A label with the specified text, icon, and alignment

The alignment of a label determines how its text or icon are aligned in relation to the area taken up by the window. Three class variables of the SwingConstants interface are used to specify alignment: LEFT, CENTER, or RIGHT.

The contents of a label can be set with setText(*String*) or setIcon(*Icon*) methods. You also can retrieve these things with getText() and getIcon() methods.

The following statements create three labels with left, center, and right alignment, respectively:

```
JLabel tinker = new JLabel("Tinker", SwingConstants.LEFT);
JLabel evers = new JLabel("Evers");
JLabel chance = new JLabel("Chance", SwingConstants.RIGHT);
```

No alignment is specified in the constructor for the evers label, so it is given the default, which is centered alignment.

Text Fields

A *text field* is an area on an interface where a user can enter and modify text with a keyboard. Text fields, which are represented by the JTextField class, can handle one line of input. A similar component, text areas, can handle multiple lines.

Constructor methods include the following:

- JTextField()—An empty text field
- JTextField(*int*)—A text field with the specified width
- JTextField(*String*, *int*)—A text field with the specified text and width

A text field's width attribute only has relevance if the interface is organized in a manner that does not resize components. You get more experience with this when you work with layout managers on Day 10, "Arranging Components on a User Interface."

The following statements create an empty text field that has enough space for roughly 30 characters and a text field of the same size with the starting text "Puddin N. Tane":

```
JTextField name = new JTextField(30);
JTextField name = new JTextField("Puddin N. Tane", 30);
```

Text fields and text areas both inherit from the superclass JTextComponent and share many common methods.

The setEditable(*boolean*) method determines whether a text component can be edited (an argument of true) or not (false). There's also an isEditable() method that returns a corresponding boolean value.

The setText(*String*) method changes the text to the specified string, and the getText() method returns the component's current text as a string. Another method retrieves only the text that a user has highlighted in the getSelectedText() component.

Also, a specialized subclass of text fields, called *password fields*, are used to hide the characters a user is typing into the field.

This class, JPasswordField, has the same constructor methods as its parent class.

Once you have created a password field, call its setEchoChar (*char*) method to obscure input with the specified character.

 Note

> The TextField class in the Abstract Windowing Toolkit supports obscured text with the setEchoCharacter(*char*) method. This method is not supported in the JTextField class—improvements in Java's security necessitated the creation of a new class for obscured text.

The following statements create a password field and set its echo character to #:

```
JPasswordField codePhrase = new JPasswordField(20);
codePhrase.setEchoChar('#');
```

Text Areas

Text areas, editable text fields that can handle more than one line of input, are implemented with the JTextArea class.

JTextArea includes the following constructor methods:

- JTextArea(*int*, *int*)—A text area with the specified number of rows and columns
- JTextArea(*String*, *int*, *int*)—A text area with the specified text, rows, and columns

You can use the getText(), getSelectedText(), and setText(*String*) methods with text areas as you would text fields. Also, an append(*String*) method adds the specified text at the end of the current text and an insert(*String*, *int*) method inserts the specified text at the indicated position.

The setLineWrap(*boolean*) method determines whether text will wrap to the next line when it reaches the far edge of the component. Call setLineWrap(true) to cause line wrapping to occur.

The setWrapStyleWord(*boolean*) method determines what wraps to the next line—either the current word (an argument of true) or the current character (false).

The next project you will create, the Form application in Listing 8.8, uses several Swing components to collect user input: a text field, a password field, and a text area. Labels also are used to indicate the purpose of each text component.

LISTING 8.8   The Full Text of Form.java

```
 1: import javax.swing.*;
 2:
 3: public class Form extends javax.swing.JFrame {
 4:     JTextField username = new JTextField(15);
 5:     JPasswordField password = new JPasswordField(15);
 6:     JTextArea comments = new JTextArea(4, 15);
 7:
 8:     public Form() {
 9:         super("Feedback Form");
10:         setSize(260, 160);
11:         setDefaultCloseOperation(EXIT_ON_CLOSE);
12:
13:         JPanel pane = new JPanel();
14:         JLabel usernameLabel = new JLabel("Username: ");
15:         JLabel passwordLabel = new JLabel("Password: ");
16:         JLabel commentsLabel = new JLabel("Comments:");
17:         comments.setLineWrap(true);
18:         comments.setWrapStyleWord(true);
19:         pane.add(usernameLabel);
20:         pane.add(username);
21:         pane.add(passwordLabel);
22:         pane.add(password);
23:         pane.add(commentsLabel);
24:         pane.add(comments);
25:         setContentPane(pane);
26:
27:         show();
28:     }
29:
```

LISTING 8.8   continued

```
30:     public static void main(String[] arguments) {
31:         Form input = new Form();
32:     }
33: }
```

Figure 8.6 shows the result.

FIGURE 8.6

The Form *application.*

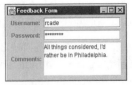

Scrolling Panes

Text areas in Swing do not include horizontal or vertical scroll bars, and there's no way to add them using this component alone. That's a difference between Swing text areas and their counterparts in the Abstract Windowing Toolkit.

The reason for the change is that Swing introduces a new container that can be used to hold any component that can be scrolled: JScrollPane.

A scrolling pane is associated with a component in the pane's constructor method. You can use either of the following:

- JScrollPane(*Component*)—A scrolling pane that contains the specified component
- JScrollPane(*Component*, *int*, *int*)—A scrolling pane with the specified component, vertical scrollbar configuration, and horizontal scrollbar configuration

Scrollbars are configured using class variables of the ScrollPaneConstants interface. You can use each of the following for vertical scrollbars:

- VERTICAL_SCROLLBAR_ALWAYS
- VERTICAL_SCROLLBAR_AS_NEEDED
- VERTICAL_SCROLLBAR_NEVER

There also are three similarly named variables for horizontal scrollbars.

After you create a scrolling pane containing a component, the pane should be added to containers in place of that component.

The following example creates a text area with a vertical scrollbar and no horizontal scrollbar, and then adds it to a content pane:

```
JPanel pane = new JPanel();
JTextArea letter = new JTextArea(5, 15);
JScrollPane scroll = new JScrollPane(letter,
    ScrollPaneConstants.VERTICAL_SCROLLBAR_ALWAYS,
    ScrollPaneConstants.HORIZONTAL_SCROLLBAR_NEVER);
pane.add(scroll);
setContentPane(pane);
```

Scrollbars

Scrollbars are components that enable a value to be selected by sliding a box between two arrows. Several components have built-in scrollbar functionality, including text areas and scrolling lists.

Scrollbars are normally created by specifying the minimum and maximum values that can be set using the component.

You can use the following constructor methods:

- `JScrollBar(int)`—A scrollbar with the specified orientation
- `JScrollBar(int, int, int, int, int)`—A scrollbar with the specified orientation, starting value, scroll box size, minimum value, and maximum value

The orientation is indicated by the `JScrollBar` class variables `HORIZONTAL` and `VERTICAL`.

You also can use `Scrollbar(int, int, int, int, int)`, a third constructor with five integer arguments. The arguments for this method are in order here:

- Orientation is either `JScrollBar.HORIZONTAL` or `JScrollBar.VERTICAL`.
- The initial value of the scrollbar, which should be equal to or between the minimum and maximum values of the bar.
- The overall width or height of the box used to change the scrollbar's value. This can be equal to `0` when using the default size.
- The minimum value of the scrollbar.
- The maximum value.

The following statement creates a vertical scrollbar with a minimum value of `10`, a maximum value of `50`, and an initial value of `33`.

```
JScrollBar bar = new JScrollBar(JScrollBar.HORIZONTAL,
    33, 0, 10, 50);
```

Check Boxes and Radio Buttons

The next two components you learn about are different only in appearance. Check boxes and radio buttons are both components that have only two possible values: selected or not selected. Both also can be grouped together so that only one component in a group can be selected at any time.

Check boxes (the JCheckBox class) are labeled or unlabeled boxes that contain a check mark when they are selected and nothing otherwise. Radio buttons (the JRadioButton class) are circles that contain a dot when selected and are also empty otherwise.

These components are typically used to make a simple yes-no or on-off kind of choice in a program. Both classes have several useful methods inherited from their common super-classes:

- setSelected(*boolean*)—Selects the component if the argument is true and deselects it otherwise.
- isSelected()—Returns a boolean indicating whether the component is currently selected.

The following constructors are available for the JCheckBox class:

- JCheckBox(*String*)—A check box with the specified text label
- JCheckBox(*String, boolean*)—A check box with the specified text label that is selected if the second argument is true
- JCheckBox(*Icon*)—A check box with the specified icon label
- JCheckBox(*Icon, boolean*)—A check box with the specified icon label that is selected if the second argument is true
- JCheckBox(*String, Icon*)—A check box with the specified text label and icon label
- JCheckBox(*String, Icon, boolean*)—A check box with the specified text label and icon label that is selected if the third argument is true

The JRadioButton class has constructors with the same arguments and functionality.

Check boxes and radio buttons are normally *nonexclusive*, meaning that if you have five check boxes in a container, all five can be checked or unchecked at the same time. To make them exclusive, you must organize related components into groups.

To organize several check boxes into a group, allowing only one to be selected at a time, create a ButtonGroup class object, as demonstrated in the following statement:

```
ButtonGroup choice = new ButtonGroup();
```

The `ButtonGroup` object keeps track of all check boxes or radio buttons in its group. Call the group's add(*Component*) method to add the specified component to the group.

The following example creates a group and two radio buttons that belong to it:

```
ButtonGroup betterDarrin = new ButtonGroup();
JRadioButton r1 = new JRadioButton ("Dick York", true);
betterDarrin.add(r1);
JRadioButton r2 = new JRadioButton ("Dick Sargent", false);
betterDarrin.add(r2);
```

The betterDarrin object is used to group together the r1 and r2 radio buttons. The r1 object, which has the label "Dick York", is selected. Only one member of the group can be selected at a time—if one component is selected, the ButtonGroup object will make sure that all others in the group are deselected.

Listing 8.9 contains an application with four radio buttons in a group.

LISTING 8.9   The Full Text of ChooseTeam.java

```
 1: import javax.swing.*;
 2:
 3: public class ChooseTeam extends JFrame {
 4:     JRadioButton[] teams = new JRadioButton[4];
 5:
 6:     public ChooseTeam() {
 7:         super("Choose Team");
 8:         setSize(140, 190);
 9:         setDefaultCloseOperation(JFrame.EXIT_ON_CLOSE);
10:         teams[0] = new JRadioButton("Colorado");
11:         teams[1] = new JRadioButton("Dallas", true);
12:         teams[2] = new JRadioButton("New Jersey");
13:         teams[3] = new JRadioButton("Philadelphia");
14:         JPanel pane = new JPanel();
15:         ButtonGroup group = new ButtonGroup();
16:         for (int i = 0; i < teams.length; i++) {
17:             group.add(teams[i]);
18:             pane.add(teams[i]);
19:         }
20:         setContentPane(pane);
21:         show();
22:     }
23:
24:     public static void main(String[] arguments) {
25:         ChooseTeam ct = new ChooseTeam();
26:     }
27: }
```

Figure 8.7 shows the application running. The four JRadioButton objects are stored in an array, and in the for loop in lines 16–19 each element is first added to a button group, and then added to a panel. After the loop ends, the panel is used for the application's content pane.

FIGURE 8.7

The ChooseTeam *appli-cation.*

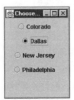

Drop-Down Lists and Combo Boxes

The Swing class JComboBox can be used to create two kinds of user interface components: drop-down lists and combo boxes.

Drop-down lists, also called *choice lists*, are components that enable a single item to be picked from a list. The list can be configured to appear only when a user clicks on the component, taking up less space in a graphical user interface.

Combo boxes are drop-down lists with an extra feature: a text field that also can be used to provide a response.

The following steps show how a drop-down list can be created:

1. The JComboBox() constructor is used with no arguments.
2. The combo box's addItem(*Object*) method adds items to the list.

In a drop-down list, users will only be able to select one of the items in the list. If the component's setEditable() method is called with true as an argument, it becomes a combo box rather than a drop-down list.

In a combo box, the user can enter text into the field instead of using the drop-down list to pick an item. This combination gives combo boxes their name.

The JComboBox class has several methods that can be used to control a drop-down list or combo box:

*   The getItemAt(*int*) method returns the text of the list item at the index position specified by the integer argument. As with arrays, the first item of a choice list is at index position 0, the second at position 1, and so on.
*   The getItemCount() method returns the number of items in the list.

- The getSelectedIndex() method returns the index position of the currently selected item in the list.

- The getSelectedItem() method returns the text of the currently selected item.

- The setSelectedIndex(*int*) method selects the item at the indicated index position.

- The setSelectedIndex(*Object*) method selects the specified object in the list.

- The setMaximumRowCount(*int*) method sets the number of rows in the combo box that are displayed at one time.

The Expiration application in Listing 8.10 contains an application that uses combo boxes to enter an expiration date, something you might use on an interface that conducts a credit-card transaction.

LISTING 8.10   The Full Text of ChooseTeam.java

```
 1: import javax.swing.*;
 2:
 3: public class Expiration extends JFrame {
 4:     JComboBox monthBox = new JComboBox();
 5:     JComboBox yearBox = new JComboBox();
 6:
 7:     public Expiration() {
 8:         super("Expiration Date");
 9:         setSize(220, 90);
10:         setDefaultCloseOperation(JFrame.EXIT_ON_CLOSE);
11:         JPanel pane = new JPanel();
12:         JLabel exp = new JLabel("Expiration Date:");
13:         pane.add(exp);
14:         for (int i = 1; i < 13; i++)
15:             monthBox.addItem("" + i);
16:         for (int i = 2000; i < 2010; i++)
17:             yearBox.addItem("" + i);
18:         pane.add(monthBox);
19:         pane.add(yearBox);
20:         setContentPane(pane);
21:         show();
22:     }
23:
24:     public static void main(String[] arguments) {
25:         Expiration ct = new Expiration();
26:     }
27: }
```

Figure 8.8 shows the application after a date has been selected.

FIGURE 8.8.

The Expiration *application.*

Summary

Today, you began working with Swing, the package of classes that enables you to offer a graphical user interface in your Java programs.

You used more than a dozen classes today, creating interface components such as buttons, labels, and text fields. You put each of these into containers, components that include panels, frames, windows, and applets.

Programming of this kind can be complex, and Swing represents the largest package of classes that a new Java programmer must deal with in learning the language.

However, as you have experienced with components such as text areas and text fields, Sun Microsystems has designed Swing so that components have many superclasses in common. This makes it easier to extend your knowledge into new components and containers, as well as the other aspects of Swing programming you will explore over the next three days.

Q&A

Q Can an application be created without Swing?

A Certainly. Swing is just an expansion of the Abstract Windowing Toolkit, and you can continue to use the AWT for applications with Java 2. However, event handling is different between the AWT and Swing, and there are many things in Swing that have no counterpart in the windowing toolkit. With Swing, you can use many more components and control them in more sophisticated ways.

Q Is there a way to change the font of text that appears on a button and other components?

A The JComponent class includes a setFont(*Font*) method that can be used to set the font for text displayed on that component. You will work with Font objects, color, and more graphics in Day 12, "Color, Fonts, and Graphics."

Q How can I find out what components are available in Swing and how to use them?

A This is the first of two days spent introducing user interface components, so you will learn more about them tomorrow. If you have Web access, you can find out what classes are in the Swing package by visiting Sun's online documentation for Java at the Web address http://java.sun.com/j2se/1.3/docs/api/.

8

Questions

1. Which of the following user interface components is not a container?

    (a) JScrollPane

    (b) JScrollBar

    (c) JWindow

2. Which container does not require the use of a content pane when adding components to it?

    (a) JPanel

    (b) JApplet

    (c) JFrame

3. If you use setSize() on an application's main frame or window, where will it appear on your desktop?

    (a) At the center of the desktop

    (b) At the same spot the last application appeared

    (c) At the upper left corner of the desktop

Answers

1. b.

2. a. JPanel is one of the simple containers that is not subdivided into panes, so you can call its add(*Component*) method to add components directly to the panel.

3. c. You can call setBounds() instead of setSize() to choose where a frame will appear.

Exercises

To extend your knowledge of the subjects covered today, try the following exercises:

- Create an application with a frame that includes all of the VCR controls as individual components: play, stop/eject, rewind, fast-forward, and pause. Choose a size for the window that enables all the components to be displayed on a single row.

- Create a frame that opens a smaller frame with fields asking for a username and password.

Where applicable, exercise solutions are offered on the book's Web site at http://www.java21days.com.

DAY 9

Building a Swing Interface

With the popularity of Apple MacOS and Microsoft Windows, most computer users expect software to feature a graphical user interface and things they can control with a mouse. These software amenities are user friendly but programmer unfriendly in many languages. Writing windowing software can be one of the more challenging tasks for a novice developer.

Java 2 has simplified the process with Swing, a set of classes for the creation and usage of graphical user interfaces.

Swing, an extension of the Abstract Windowing Toolkit introduced in Java 1.0, offers the following features:

- Common user interface components such as buttons, scrollbars, lists, and sliders
- Containers—interface components that can be used to hold other components
- Adjustable look and feel—the ability to change the style of an entire interface to resemble Windows, MacOS, or other distinctive designs

Swing Features

Most of the components and containers you learned about yesterday were Swing versions of classes that were part of the Abstract Windowing Toolkit, the original Java package for graphical user interface programming.

Swing offers many features that are completely new, including a definable look and feel, keyboard mnemonics, ToolTips, and standard dialog boxes.

Setting the Look and Feel

One of the more unusual features in Swing is the ability to define the look and feel of components—the way that the buttons, labels, and other elements of a graphical user interface are rendered onscreen.

Management of look and feel is handled by a user interface manager class in the javax.swing package, UIManager. The choices for look and feel vary depending on the Java development environment you're using. The following are available with Java 2 on a Windows platform:

- A Windows look and feel
- A Motif X Window system look and feel
- Metal, Swing's new cross-platform, look and feel

The UIManager class has a setLookAndFeel(LookAndFeel) method that is used to choose a program's look and feel. To get a LookAndFeel object that you can use with setLookAndFeel(), use one of the following UIManager methods:

- getCrossPlatformLookAndFeelClassName()—This method returns a LookAndFeel object representing Java's cross-platform Metal look and feel.
- getSystemLookAndFeelClassName()—This method returns a LookAndFeel object representing your system's look and feel.

The setLookAndFeel() method throws an UnsupportedLookAndFeelException if it can't set the look and feel.

The following statements can be used in any program to designate Metal as the look and feel:

```
try {
    UIManager.setLookAndFeel(
        UIManager.getCrossPlatformLookAndFeelClassName());
    } catch (Exception e) {
        System.err.println("Can't set look and feel: " + e);
}
```

To select your system's look and feel, use getSystemLookAndFeelClassName(), which is inside the setLookAndFeel() method call in the preceding example. This produces different results on different operating systems. A Windows user would get that platform's look and feel by using getSystemLookAndFeelClassName(). A UNIX user would get the Motif look and feel.

Standard Dialog Boxes

The JOptionPane class offers several methods that can be used to create standard dialog boxes: small windows that ask a question, warn a user, or provide a brief, important message. Figure 9.1 shows a dialog box with the Metal look and feel.

FIGURE 9.1

A standard dialog box.

You have doubtlessly seen dialog boxes of this kind. When your system crashes, a dialog box appears and breaks the bad news. When you delete files, a dialog box might pop up to make sure that you really want to do that. These windows are an effective way to communicate with a user without the overhead of creating a new class to represent the window, adding components to it, and writing event-handling methods to take input. All these things are handled automatically when one of the standard dialog boxes offered by JOptionPane is used.

The four standard dialog boxes are as follows:

- ConfirmDialog—Asks a question, with buttons for Yes, No, and Cancel responses.
- InputDialog—Prompts for text input.
- MessageDialog—Displays a message.
- OptionDialog—Comprises all three of the other dialog box types.

Each of these dialog boxes has its own method in the JOptionPane class.

Confirm Dialog Boxes

The easiest way to create a Yes/No/Cancel dialog box is with the showConfirmDialog(*Component, Object*) method call. The *Component* argument specifies the container that should be considered to be the parent of the dialog box, and this information is used to determine where on the screen the dialog window should be displayed. If null is used instead of a container, or if the container is not a Frame object, the dialog box will be centered onscreen.

The second argument, *Object*, can be a string, a component, or an Icon object. If it's a string, that text will be displayed in the dialog box. If it's a component or an icon, that object will be displayed in place of a text message.

This method returns one of three possible integer values, each a class variable of JOptionPane: YES_OPTION, NO_OPTION, and CANCEL_OPTION.

The following example uses a confirm dialog box with a text message and stores the response in the response variable:

```
int response;
response = JOptionPane.showConfirmDialog(null,
    "Should I delete all of your irreplaceable personal files");
```

Another method offers more options for the confirm dialog: showConfirmDialog(*Component*, *Object*, *String*, *int*, *int*). The first two arguments are the same as those in other showConfirmDialog() methods. The last three arguments are the following:

- A string that will be displayed in the dialog box's title bar.
- An integer that indicates which option buttons will be shown. It should be equal to the class variables YES_NO_CANCEL_OPTION or YES_NO_OPTION.
- An integer that describes the kind of dialog box it is, using the class variables ERROR_MESSAGE, INFORMATION_MESSAGE, PLAIN_MESSAGE, QUESTION_MESSAGE, or WARNING_MESSAGE. This argument is used to determine which icon to draw in the dialog box along with the message.

For example:

```
int response = JOptionPane.showConfirmDialog(null,
    "Error reading file. Want to try again?",
    "File Input Error",
    JOptionPane.YES_NO_OPTION,
    JOptionPane.ERROR_MESSAGE);
```

Figure 9.2 shows the resulting dialog box with the Windows look and feel.

FIGURE 9.2

A confirm dialog box.

Input Dialog Boxes

An input dialog box asks a question and uses a text field to store the response. Figure 9.3 shows an example with the Motif look and feel.

FIGURE 9.3

An input dialog box.

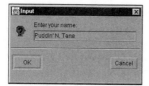

The easiest way to create an input dialog is with a call to the showInputDialog(*Component*, *Object*) method. The arguments are the parent component and the string, component, or icon to display in the box.

The input dialog method call returns a string that represents the user's response. The following statement creates the input dialog box shown in Figure 9.3:

```
String response = JOptionPane.showInputDialog(null,
    "Enter your name:");
```

You also can create an input dialog box with the showInputDialog(*Component*, *Object*, *String*, *int*) method. The first two arguments are the same as the shorter method call, and the last two are the following:

- The title to display in the dialog box title bar
- One of five class variables describing the type of dialog box: ERROR_MESSAGE, INFORMATION_MESSAGE, PLAIN_MESSAGE, QUESTION_MESSAGE, or WARNING_MESSAGE

The following statement uses this method to create an input dialog box:

```
String response = JOptionPane.showInputDialog(null,
    "What is your ZIP code?",
    "Enter ZIP Code",
    JOptionPane.QUESTION_MESSAGE);
```

Message Dialog Boxes

A message dialog box is a simple window that displays information. Figure 9.4 shows an example with the Metal look and feel.

FIGURE 9.4

A message dialog box.

A message dialog box can be created with a call to the showMessageDialog(*Component*, *Object*) method. As with other dialog boxes, the arguments are the parent component and the string, component, or icon to display.

Unlike the other dialog boxes, message dialog boxes do not return any kind of response value. The following statement creates the message dialog shown in Figure 9.4:

```
JOptionPane.showMessageDialog(null,
    "The program has been uninstalled.");
```

You also can create a message input dialog box with the showMessageDialog(*Component*, *Object*, *String*, *int*) method. The use is identical to the showInputDialog() method, with the same arguments, except that showMessageDialog() does not return a value.

The following statement creates a message dialog box using this method:

```
JOptionPane.showMessageDialog(null,
    "An asteroid has destroyed the Earth.",
    "Asteroid Destruction Alert",
    JOptionPane.WARNING_MESSAGE);
```

Option Dialog Boxes

The most complex of the dialog boxes is the option dialog box, which combines the features of all the other dialogs. It can be created with the showOptionDialog(*Component*, *Object*, *String*, *int*, *int*, *Icon*, *Object[]*, *Object*) method.

The arguments to this method are as follows:

- The parent component of the dialog.
- The text, icon, or component to display.
- A string to display in the title bar.
- The type of box, using the class variables YES_NO_OPTION or YES_NO_CANCEL_OPTION, or the literal 0 if other buttons will be used instead.
- The icon to display, using the class variables ERROR_MESSAGE, INFORMATION_MES-SAGE, PLAIN_MESSAGE, QUESTION_MESSAGE, or WARNING_MESSAGE, or the literal 0 if none of these should be used.
- An Icon object to display instead of one of the icons in the preceding argument.
- An array of objects holding the components or other objects that represent the choices in the dialog box, if YES_NO_OPTION and YES_NO_CANCEL_OPTION are not being used.
- The object representing the default selection if YES_NO_OPTION and YES_NO_CANCEL option are not being used.

The last two arguments enable you to create a wide range of choices for the dialog box. You can create an array of buttons, labels, text fields, or even a mixture of different components as an object array. These components are displayed using the flow layout manager—there's no way to specify a different manager within the dialog.

The following example creates an option dialog box that uses an array of JButton objects for the options in the box and the gender[2] element as the default selection:

```
JButton[] gender = new JButton[3];
gender[0] = new JButton("Male");
gender[1] = new JButton("Female");
gender[2] = new JButton("None of Your Business");
int response = JOptionPane.showOptionDialog(null,
    "What is your gender?",
    "Gender",
    0,
    JOptionPane.INFORMATION_MESSAGE,
    null,
    gender,
    gender[2]);
```

Figure 9.5 shows the resulting dialog box with the Motif look and feel.

FIGURE 9.5

An option dialog box.

An Example: The Info Application

The next project shows a series of dialog boxes in a working program. The Info application uses dialogs to get information from the user, which is then placed into text fields on the application's main window.

Enter Listing 9.1 and compile the result.

LISTING 9.1   The Full Text of Info.java

```
1: import java.awt.GridLayout;
2: import java.awt.event.*;
3: import javax.swing.*;
4:
5: public class Info extends JFrame {
6:     private JLabel titleLabel = new JLabel("Title: ",
7:         SwingConstants.RIGHT);
8:     private JTextField title;
9:     private JLabel addressLabel = new JLabel("Address: ",
10:        SwingConstants.RIGHT);
11:    private JTextField address;
12:    private JLabel typeLabel = new JLabel("Type: ",
13:        SwingConstants.RIGHT);
```

LISTING 9.1   continued

```
14:     private JTextField type;
15:
16:     public Info() {
17:         super("Site Information");
18:         setDefaultCloseOperation(JFrame.EXIT_ON_CLOSE);
19:         // Site name
20:         String response1 = JOptionPane.showInputDialog(null,
21:             "Enter the site title:");
22:         title = new JTextField(response1, 20);
23:
24:         // Site address
25:         String response2 = JOptionPane.showInputDialog(null,
26:             "Enter the site address:");
27:         address = new JTextField(response2, 20);
28:
29:         // Site type
30:         String[] choices = { "Personal", "Commercial", "Unknown" };
31:         int response3 = JOptionPane.showOptionDialog(null,
32:             "What type of site is it?",
33:             "Site Type",
34:             0,
35:             JOptionPane.QUESTION_MESSAGE,
36:             null,
37:             choices,
38:             choices[0]);
39:         type = new JTextField(choices[response3], 20);
40:
41:         JPanel pane = new JPanel();
42:         pane.setLayout(new GridLayout(3, 2));
43:         pane.add(titleLabel);
44:         pane.add(title);
45:         pane.add(addressLabel);
46:         pane.add(address);
47:         pane.add(typeLabel);
48:         pane.add(type);
49:
50:         setContentPane(pane);
51:     }
52:
53:     public static void main(String[] arguments) {
54:         try {
55:             UIManager.setLookAndFeel(
56:                 UIManager.getSystemLookAndFeelClassName());
57:         } catch (Exception e) {
58:             System.err.println("Couldn't use the system "
59:                 + "look and feel: " + e);
60:         }
61:
```

```
62:            JFrame frame = new Info();
63:            frame.pack();
64:            frame.setVisible(true);
65:        }
66: }
```

Figure 9.6 shows the first of the three dialog boxes that appears when this application is run. After you fill in the fields in each dialog, you will see the application's main window, which is displayed in Figure 9.7 with the Windows look and feel. Three text fields have values supplied by dialog boxes.

FIGURE 9.6

The site address input dialog box.

FIGURE 9.7

The main window of the Info application.

Much of this application is boilerplate code that can be used with any Swing application. The following lines relate to the dialog boxes:

- Lines 19–22—An input dialog asks the user to enter a site title. This title is used in the constructor for a JTextField object, which puts the title in the text field.

- Lines 24–27—A similar input dialog asks for a site address, which is used in the constructor for another JTextField object. Figure 9.7 shows this option dialog box.

- Line 30—An array of String objects called choices is created, and three elements are given values.

- Lines 31–38—An option dialog box asks for the site type. The choices array is the seventh argument, which sets up three buttons on the dialog with the strings in the array: Personal, Commercial, and Unknown. The last argument, choices[0], designates the first array element as the default selection in the dialog.

- Line 39—The response to the option dialog, an integer identifying the array element that was selected, is stored in a JTextField component called type.

Sliders

Sliders, which are implemented in Swing with the `JSlider` class, enable a number to be set by sliding a control within the range of a minimum and maximum value. In many cases, a slider can be used for numeric input instead of a text field, and it has the advantage of restricting input to a range of acceptable values.

Figure 9.8 shows an example of a `JSlider` component.

FIGURE 9.8

A `JSlider` component.

Sliders are horizontal by default. The orientation can be explicitly set using two class variables of the `SwingConstants` class: `HORIZONTAL` or `VERTICAL`.

You can use the following constructor methods:

- `JSlider(int, int)`—A slider with the specified minimum value and maximum value
- `JSlider(int, int, int)`—A slider with the specified minimum value, maximum value, and starting value
- `JSlider(int, int, int, int)`—A slider with the specified orientation, minimum value, maximum value, and starting value

Slider components have an optional label that can be used to indicate the minimum value, maximum value, and two different sets of tick marks ranging between the values.

The elements of this label are established by calling several methods of `JSlider`:

- `setMajorTickSpacing(int)`—Separates major tick marks by the specified distance. The distance is not in pixels, but in values between the minimum and maximum values represented by the slider.
- `setMinorTickSpacing(int)`—Separates minor tick marks by the specified distance. Minor ticks are displayed as half the height of major ticks.
- `setPaintTicks(boolean)`—Determines whether the tick marks should be displayed (a `true` argument) or not (a `false` argument).
- `setPaintLabels(boolean)`—Determines whether the numeric label of the slider should be displayed (`true`) or not (`false`).

These methods should be called on the slider before it is added to a container.

Listing 9.2 contains the `Slider.java` source code; the application is shown in Figure 9.8.

LISTING 9.2   The Full Text of `Slider.java`

```
 1: import java.awt.event.*;
 2: import javax.swing.*;
 3:
 4: public class Slider extends JFrame {
 5:
 6:     public Slider() {
 7:         super("Slider");
 8:         setDefaultCloseOperation(JFrame.EXIT_ON_CLOSE);
 9:         JSlider pickNum = new JSlider(JSlider.HORIZONTAL, 0, 30, 5);
10:         pickNum.setMajorTickSpacing(10);
11:         pickNum.setMinorTickSpacing(1);
12:         pickNum.setPaintTicks(true);
13:         pickNum.setPaintLabels(true);
14:         JPanel pane = new JPanel();
15:         pane.add(pickNum);
16:
17:         setContentPane(pane);
18:     }
19:
20:     public static void main(String[] args) {
21:         Slider frame = new Slider();
22:         frame.pack();
23:         frame.setVisible(true);
24:     }
25: }
```

Lines 9–17 contain the code that's used to create a `JSlider` component, set up its tick marks to be displayed, and add the component to a container. The rest of the program is a basic framework for an application that consists of a main `JFrame` container with no menus.

Scroll Panes

In versions of Java prior to 1.2, some components (such as text areas) had a built-in scrollbar. The bar could be used when the text in the component took up more space than the component could display. Scrollbars could be used in either the vertical or horizontal direction to scroll through the text.

One of the most common examples of scrolling is in a Web browser, where a scrollbar can be used on any page that is bigger than the browser's display area.

Swing changes the rules for scrollbars to the following:

- For a component to be able to scroll, it must be added to a JScrollPane container.
- This JScrollPane container is added to a container in place of the scrollable component.

Scroll panes can be created using the ScrollPane(*Object*) constructor, where *Object* represents the component that can be scrolled.

The following example creates a text area in a scroll pane and adds it to a container called mainPane:

```
textBox = new JTextArea(7, 30);
JScrollPane scroller = new JScrollPane(textBox);
mainPane.add(scroller);
```

As you're working with scroll panes, it can often be useful to indicate the size you would like it to occupy on the interface. This is done by calling the setPreferredSize(*Dimension*) method of the scroll pane before it is added to a container. The Dimension object represents the width and height of the preferred size represented in pixels.

The following code builds on the previous example by setting the preferred size of the scroller object:

```
Dimension pref = new Dimension(350, 100);
scroller.setPreferredSize(pref);
```

This should be handled before the scroller object is added to a container.

By default, a scroll pane does not display scrollbars unless they are needed. If the component inside the pane is no larger than the pane itself, the bars won't appear. In the case of components such as text areas, where the component size might increase as the program is used, the bars automatically appear when they're needed and disappear when they are not.

To override this behavior, you can set a policy when the JScrollBar component is created by using several ScrollPaneConstants class variables:

- HORIZONTAL_SCROLLBAR_ALWAYS
- HORIZONTAL_SCROLLBAR_AS_NEEDED
- HORIZONTAL_SCROLLBAR_NEVER
- VERTICAL_SCROLLBAR_ALWAYS
- VERTICAL_SCROLLBAR_AS_NEEDED
- VERTICAL_SCROLLBAR_NEVER

These class variables are used with the ScrollPane(*Object*, *int*, *int*) constructor, which specifies the component in the pane, the vertical scrollbar policy, and the horizontal scrollbar policy.

Toolbars

A *toolbar*, created in Swing with the JToolBar class, is a container that groups several components into a row or column. These components are most often buttons.

If you have used software such as Microsoft Word, Netscape Navigator, or Lotus WordPro, you are probably familiar with the concept of toolbars. In these programs and many others, the most commonly used program options are grouped together as a series of buttons. You can click these buttons as an alternative to using pull-down menus or shortcut keys.

Toolbars are horizontal by default, but the orientation is explicitly set with the HORIZONTAL or VERTICAL class variables of the SwingConstants interface.

Constructor methods include the following:

- JToolBar()—Creates a new toolbar.
- JToolBar(*int*)—Creates a new toolbar with the specified orientation.

Once you have created a toolbar, you can add components to it by using the toolbar's add(*Object*) method, where *Object* represents the component to place on the toolbar.

Many programs that use toolbars enable the user to move the bars. These are called *dockable toolbars* because you can dock them along an edge of the screen, similar to docking a boat to a pier. Swing toolbars can also be docked into a new window, separate from the original.

A dockable JToolBar component must be laid out using the BorderLayout manager. As you might recall, a border layout divides a container into five areas: north, south, east, west, and center. Each of the directional components takes up whatever space it needs, and the rest is allocated to the center.

The toolbar should be placed in one of the directional areas of the border layout. The only other area of the layout that can be filled is the center.

Figure 9.9 shows a dockable toolbar occupying the north area of a border layout. A text area has been placed in the center.

FIGURE 9.9

*A dockable toolbar
and a text area.*

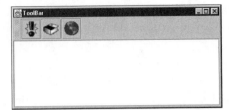

Listing 9.3 contains the source code used to produce this application.

LISTING 9.3   The Full Text of `ToolBar.java`

```
 1: import java.awt.*;
 2: import java.awt.event.*;
 3: import javax.swing.*;
 4:
 5: public class ToolBar extends JFrame {
 6:
 7:     public ToolBar() {
 8:         super("ToolBar");
 9:         setDefaultCloseOperation(JFrame.EXIT_ON_CLOSE);
10:         ImageIcon image1 = new ImageIcon("button1.gif");
11:         JButton button1 = new JButton(image1);
12:         ImageIcon image2 = new ImageIcon("button2.gif");
13:         JButton button2 = new JButton(image2);
14:         ImageIcon image3 = new ImageIcon("button3.gif");
15:         JButton button3 = new JButton(image3);
16:         JToolBar bar = new JToolBar();
17:         bar.add(button1);
18:         bar.add(button2);
19:         bar.add(button3);
20:         JTextArea edit = new JTextArea(8,40);
21:         JScrollPane scroll = new JScrollPane(edit);
22:         JPanel pane = new JPanel();
23:         BorderLayout bord = new BorderLayout();
24:         pane.setLayout(bord);
25:         pane.add("North", bar);
26:         pane.add("Center", scroll);
27:
28:         setContentPane(pane);
29:     }
30:
31:     public static void main(String[] arguments) {
32:         ToolBar frame = new ToolBar();
33:         frame.pack();
34:         frame.setVisible(true);
35:     }
36: }
```

This application uses three images to represent the graphics on the buttons: `button1.gif`, `button2.gif`, and `button3.gif`. You can find these on the book's CD-ROM or the book's official World Wide Web site at `http://www.java21days.com`. You also can use graphics from your own system, although they must be in GIF format and reasonably small.

The toolbar in this application can be grabbed by its handle—the area immediately to the left of the exclamation button in Figure 9.9. If you drag it within the window, you can dock it along different edges of the application window. When you release the toolbar, the application is rearranged using the border layout manager. You also can drag the toolbar out of the application window entirely.

Although toolbars are most commonly used with graphical buttons, they can contain textual buttons, combo boxes, and other components.

Progress Bars

If you have ever installed computer software, you're familiar with *progress bars*. These components are commonly used with long tasks to show the user how much time is left before it is complete.

Progress bars are implemented in Swing through the `JProgressBar` class. A sample Java program that makes use of this component is shown in Figure 9.10.

FIGURE 9.10

A progress bar in a frame.

Progress bars are used to track the progress of a task that can be represented numerically. They are created by specifying a minimum and a maximum value that represent the points at which the task is beginning and ending.

A software installation that consists of 335 different files is an example. The number of files transferred can be used to monitor the progress of the task. The minimum value is `0` and the maximum value `335`.

Constructor methods include the following:

- `JProgressBar()`—Creates a new progress bar.
- `JProgressBar(int, int)`—Creates a new progress bar with the specified minimum value and maximum value.
- `JProgressBar(int, int, int)`—Creates a new progress bar with the specified orientation, minimum value, and maximum value.

The orientation of a progress bar can be established with the SwingConstants.VERTICAL and SwingConstants.HORIZONTAL class variables. Progress bars are horizontal by default.

The minimum and maximum values can also be set up by calling the progress bar's setMinimum(*int*) and setMaximum(*int*) values with the indicated values.

To update a progress bar, you call its setValue(*int*) method with a value indicating how far along the task is at that moment. This value should be somewhere between the minimum and maximum values established for the bar. The following example tells the install progress bar in the previous example of a software installation how many files have been uploaded thus far:

```
int filesDone = getNumberOfFiles();
install.setValue(filesDone);
```

In this example, the getNumberOfFiles() method represents some code that would be used to keep track of how many files have been copied so far during the installation. When this value is passed to the progress bar by the setValue() method, the bar is immediately updated to represent the percentage of the task that has been completed.

Progress bars often include a text label in addition to the graphic of an empty box filling up. This label displays the percentage of the task that has become completed, and you can set it up for a bar by calling the setStringPainted(*boolean*) method with a value of true. A false argument turns this label off.

Listing 9.4 contains Progress, the application shown at the beginning of this section in Figure 9.10.

LISTING 9.4   The Full Text of Progress.java

```
 1: import java.awt.*;
 2: import java.awt.event.*;
 3: import javax.swing.*;
 4:
 5: public class Progress extends JFrame {
 6:
 7:     JProgressBar current;
 8:     JTextArea out;
 9:     JButton find;
10:     Thread runner;
11:     int num = 0;
12:
13:     public Progress() {
14:         super("Progress");
15:
```

```
16:         setDefaultCloseOperation(JFrame.EXIT_ON_CLOSE);
17:         JPanel pane = new JPanel();
18:         pane.setLayout(new FlowLayout());
19:         current = new JProgressBar(0, 2000);
20:         current.setValue(0);
21:         current.setStringPainted(true);
22:         pane.add(current);
23:         setContentPane(pane);
24:     }
25:
26:
27:     public void iterate() {
28:         while (num < 2000) {
29:             current.setValue(num);
30:             try {
31:                 Thread.sleep(1000);
32:             } catch (InterruptedException e) { }
33:             num += 95;
34:         }
35:     }
36:
37:     public static void main(String[] arguments) {
38:         Progress frame = new Progress();
39:         frame.pack();
40:         frame.setVisible(true);
41:         frame.iterate();
42:     }
43: }
```

The Progress application uses a progress bar to track the value of the num variable. The progress bar is created in line 19 with a minimum value of 0 and a maximum value of 2000.

The iterate() method in lines 27–35 loops while num is less than 2000 and increases num by 95 each iteration. The progress bar's setValue() method is called in line 29 of the loop with num as an argument, causing the bar to use that value when charting progress.

Using a progress bar is a way to make the program more user friendly when a computer program is going to be busy for more than a few seconds. Software users like progress bars because they indicate how much more time something's going to take, and this information can be a deciding factor in whether to wait at the computer, launch an expedition for something to drink, or take advantage of the company's lax policy in regard to personal long-distance calls. (If the task is especially time-consuming, a progress bar is essential—artists who create 3D computer scenes have become accustomed to tasks that take 12 hours or more to complete.)

Progress bars also provide another essential piece of information: proof that the program is still running and has not crashed.

Summary

You now know how to paint a user interface onto a Java application window using the components of the Swing package. The same techniques could be applied to applets, a container similar in many ways to a frame.

Swing includes classes for many of the buttons, bars, lists, and fields you would expect to see on a program, along with more advanced components such as sliders, dialog boxes, and progress bars. Interface components are implemented by creating an instance of their class and adding it to a container—such as a frame or an applet window—using the container's add() method.

Today you developed components and added them to a program. During the next two days, you learn more about two things that are needed to make a graphical interface usable: how to arrange components together to form a whole interface and receive input from a user through these components.

Q&A

Q Can an application be created without Swing?

A Certainly. Swing is just an expansion on the Abstract Windowing Toolkit, and if you are developing an applet for Java 1.0, you could only use AWT classes to design your interface and receive input from a user. Whether you should create an application without Swing is another issue. There's no comparison between Swing's capabilities and those offered by the AWT. With Swing, you can use many more components and control them in more sophisticated ways.

Questions

1. What is the default look and feel in a Java application?

    (a) Motif

    (b) Windows

    (c) Metal

2. Which user interface component is commonplace in software installation programs?

(a) Sliders

(b) Progress bars

(c) Dialog boxes

3. Which Java class library includes a class for clickable buttons?

(a) Abstract Windowing Toolkit

(b) Swing

(c) Both

Answers

1. c. If you want to use a look and feel other than Metal, you must explicitly establish that look and feel using a method of the `javax.swing.UIManager` class.

2. b. Progress bars are useful when used to display the progress of a file-copying or file-extracting activity.

3. c. Swing duplicates all the simple user interface components that are included in the Abstract Windowing Toolkit.

Exercises

To extend your knowledge of the subjects covered today, try the following exercises:

- Create an input dialog that can be used to set the title of the frame that loaded the dialog.

- Create a modified version of the `Progress` application that also displays the value of the `num` variable in a text field.

Where applicable, exercise solutions are offered on the book's Web site at `http://www.java21days.com`.

WEEK 2

DAY 10

Arranging Components on a User Interface

If designing a graphical user interface were comparable to painting, you could currently produce only one kind of art: abstract expressionism. You can put components onto an interface, but you don't have much control over where they go.

In order to impose some kind of form on an interface in Java, you must use a set of classes called *layout managers*.

Today you learn how to use five layout managers to arrange components into an interface. You'll take advantage of the flexibility of Swing, which was designed to be presentable on the many different platforms that support the language.

You also learn how to put several different layout managers to work on the same interface when one arrangement doesn't quite suit what you have in mind for a program.

We will start with the basic layout managers.

Basic Interface Layout

As you learned yesterday, a graphical user interface designed with Swing is a very fluid thing. Resizing a window can wreak havoc on your interface, as components move to places on a container that you might not have intended.

This fluidity is by necessity. Java is implemented on many different platforms, and there are subtle differences in the way each platform displays things such as buttons, scroll-bars, and so on.

With programming languages such as Microsoft Visual Basic, a component's location on a window is precisely defined by its x,y coordinates. Some Java development tools allow similar control over an interface through the use of their own windowing classes.

When using Swing, a programmer gains more control over the layout of an interface by using layout managers.

Laying Out an Interface

A layout manager determines how components will be arranged when they are added to a container.

The default layout manager for panels is the FlowLayout class. This class lets components flow from left to right in the order that they are added to a container. When there's no more room, a new row of components begins immediately below the first, and the left-to-right order continues.

Java includes the FlowLayout, GridLayout, BorderLayout, CardLayout, and GridBagLayout layout managers. To create a layout manager for a container, an instance of the container is created using a statement such as the following:

```
FlowLayout flo = new FlowLayout();
```

After you create a layout manager, you make it the layout manager for a container by using the container's setLayout() method. The layout manager must be established before any components are added to the container. If no layout manager is specified, its default layout will be used—FlowLayout for panels and BorderLayout for frames, windows, and applets.

The following statements represent the starting point for an applet that creates a layout manager and uses setLayout() so that it controls the arrangement of all the components that will be added to the applet window:

```
public class Starter extends javax.swing.JApplet {
    FlowLayout lm = new FlowLayout();

    public void init() {
        JPanel pane = new JPanel();
        pane.setLayout(lm);
        setContentPane(pane);
    }
}
```

After the layout manager is set, you can start adding components to the container that it manages. For some of the layout managers such as FlowLayout, the order in which components are added is significant. You learn more in today's subsequent sections as you work with each of the managers.

Flow Layout

The FlowLayout class is the simplest of the layout managers. It lays out components in a manner similar to the way words are laid out on a page—from left to right until there's no more room, and then on to the next row.

By default, the components on each row will be centered when you use the FlowLayout() constructor with no arguments. If you want the components to be aligned along the left or right edge of the container, the FlowLayout.LEFT or FlowLayout.RIGHT class variable should be the constructor's only argument, as in the following statement:

```
FlowLayout righty = new FlowLayout(FlowLayout.RIGHT);
```

The FlowLayout.CENTER class variable is used to specify centered components.

The application in Listing 10.1 displays six buttons arranged by the flow layout manager. Because the FlowLayout.LEFT class variable was used in the FlowLayout() constructor, the components are lined up along the left side of the application window.

LISTING 10.1   The Full Text of Alphabet.java

```
 1: import java.awt.*;
 2: import java.awt.event.*;
 3: import javax.swing.*;
 4:
 5: class Alphabet extends JFrame {
 6:     JButton a = new JButton("Alibi");
 7:     JButton b = new JButton("Burglar");
 8:     JButton c = new JButton("Corpse");
 9:     JButton d = new JButton("Deadbeat");
10:     JButton e = new JButton("Evidence");
```

10

LISTING **10.1**   continued

```
11:        JButton f = new JButton("Fugitive");
12:
13:        Alphabet() {
14:            super("Alphabet");
15:            setSize(360, 120);
16:            JPanel pane = new JPanel();
17:            FlowLayout lm = new FlowLayout(FlowLayout.LEFT);
18:            pane.setLayout(lm);
19:            pane.add(a);
20:            pane.add(b);
21:            pane.add(c);
22:            pane.add(d);
23:            pane.add(e);
24:            pane.add(f);
25:            setContentPane(pane);
26:        }
27:
28:        public static void main(String[] arguments) {
29:            JFrame frame = new Alphabet();
30:            ExitWindow exit = new ExitWindow();
31:            frame.addWindowListener(exit);
32:            frame.show();
33:        }
34: }
35:
36: class ExitWindow extends WindowAdapter {
37:     public void windowClosing(WindowEvent e) {
38:         System.exit(0);
39:     }
40: }
```

Figure 10.1 shows the application running.

FIGURE 10.1

Six buttons arranged in flow layout.

In the Alphabet application, the flow layout manager puts a gap of three pixels between each component on a row and three pixels between each row. You also can change the horizontal and vertical gap between components with some extra arguments to the FlowLayout() constructor.

The FlowLayout(*int*, *int*, *int*) constructor takes the following three arguments, in order:

- The alignment, which must be FlowLayout.CENTER, FlowLayout.LEFT, or FlowLayout.RIGHT
- The horizontal gap between components, in pixels
- The vertical gap, in pixels

The following constructor creates a flow layout manager with centered components, a horizontal gap of 30 pixels, and a vertical gap of 10:

```
FlowLayout flo = new FlowLayout(FlowLayout.CENTER, 30, 10);
```

Grid Layout

The grid layout manager arranges components into a grid of rows and columns. Components are added first to the top row of the grid, beginning with the leftmost grid cell and continuing to the right. When all the cells in the top row are full, the next component is added to the leftmost cell in the second row of the grid—if there is a second row—and so on.

Grid layouts are created with the GridLayout class. Two arguments are sent to the GridLayout constructor—the number of rows in the grid and the number of columns. The following statement creates a grid layout manager with 10 rows and 3 columns:

```
GridLayout gr = new GridLayout(10, 3);
```

As with flow layout, you can specify a vertical and horizontal gap between components with two extra arguments. The following statement creates a grid layout with 10 rows and 3 columns, a horizontal gap of 5 pixels, and a vertical gap of 8 pixels:

```
GridLayout gr2 = new GridLayout(10, 3, 5, 8);
```

The default gap between components under grid layout is 0 pixels in both vertical and horizontal directions.

Listing 10.2 contains an application that creates a grid with 3 rows, 3 columns, and a 10-pixel gap between components in both the vertical and horizontal directions.

LISTING 10.2   The Full Text of Bunch.java

```
1: import java.awt.*;
2: import java.awt.event.*;
3: import javax.swing.*;
4:
```

LISTING 10.2   continued

```
5: class Bunch extends JFrame {
6:     JButton marcia = new JButton("Marcia");
7:     JButton carol = new JButton("Carol");
8:     JButton greg = new JButton("Greg");
9:     JButton jan = new JButton("Jan");
10:     JButton alice = new JButton("Alice");
11:     JButton peter = new JButton("Peter");
12:     JButton cindy = new JButton("Cindy");
13:     JButton mike = new JButton("Mike");
14:     JButton bobby = new JButton("Bobby");
15:
16:     Bunch() {
17:         super("Bunch");
18:         setSize(260, 260);
19:         JPanel pane = new JPanel();
20:         GridLayout family = new GridLayout(3, 3, 10, 10);
21:         pane.setLayout(family);
22:         pane.add(marcia);
23:         pane.add(carol);
24:         pane.add(greg);
25:         pane.add(jan);
26:         pane.add(alice);
27:         pane.add(peter);
28:         pane.add(cindy);
29:         pane.add(mike);
30:         pane.add(bobby);
31:         setContentPane(pane);
32:     }
33:
34:     public static void main(String[] arguments) {
35:         JFrame frame = new Bunch();
36:         ExitWindow exit = new ExitWindow();
37:         frame.addWindowListener(exit);
38:         frame.show();
39:     }
40: }
```

Figure 10.2 shows this application.

FIGURE 10.2

Nine buttons arranged in 3×3 grid layout.

One thing to note about the buttons in Figure 10.2 is that they expanded to fill the space available to them in each cell. This is an important difference between grid layout and some of the other layout managers.

Border Layout

Border layouts, which are created by using the BorderLayout class, divide a container into five sections: north, south, east, west, and center. The five areas of Figure 10.3 show how these sections are arranged.

FIGURE 10.3

*Component arrange-
ment under border
layout.*

Under border layout, the components in the four compass points will take up as much space as they need—the center gets whatever space is left over. Ordinarily, this will result in an arrangement with a large central component and four thin components around it.

A border layout is created with either the BorderLayout() or BorderLayout(*int*, *int*) constructors. The first constructor creates a border layout with no gap between any of the components. The second constructor specifies the horizontal gap and vertical gap, respectively.

After you create a border layout and set it up as a container's layout manager, components are added using a call to the add() method that's different from what you have seen previously:

add(String, component)

The first argument is a string indicating which part of the border layout to assign the component to. There are five possible values: "North", "South", "East", "West", or "Center".

The second argument to this method is the component that should be added to the container.

The following statement adds a button called quitButton to the north portion of a border layout:

```
add("North", quitButton);
```

Listing 10.3 contains the application used to produce Figure 10.3.

LISTING 10.3   The Full Text of Border.java

```
 1: import java.awt.*;
 2: import java.awt.event.*;
 3: import javax.swing.*;
 4:
 5: class Border extends JFrame {
 6:     JButton north = new JButton("North");
 7:     JButton south = new JButton("South");
 8:     JButton east = new JButton("East");
 9:     JButton west = new JButton("West");
10:     JButton center = new JButton("Center");
11:
12:     Border() {
13:         super("Border");
14:         setSize(240, 280);
15:         JPanel pane = new JPanel();
16:         pane.setLayout(new BorderLayout());
17:         pane.add("North", north);
18:         pane.add("South", south);
19:         pane.add("East", east);
20:         pane.add("West", west);
21:         pane.add("Center", center);
22:         setContentPane(pane);
23:     }
24:
25:     public static void main(String[] arguments) {
26:         JFrame frame = new Border();
27:         ExitWindow exit = new ExitWindow();
28:         frame.addWindowListener(exit);
29:         frame.show();
30:     }
31: }
```

Mixing Layout Managers

At this point, you might be wondering how Java's layout managers will work with the kind of graphical user interface you want to design. Choosing a layout manager is an experience akin to Goldilocks checking out the home of the three bears and finding it lacking: "This one is too square! This one is too disorganized! This one is too strange!"

To find the layout that is just right, you often have to combine more than one manager on the same interface.

This is done by adding containers to a main container such as a frame or an applet window, and giving each of these smaller containers their own layout managers.

The container to use for these smaller containers is the panel, which is created from the JPanel class. *Panels* are containers that are used to group components together. There are two things to keep in mind when working with panels:

- The panel is filled with components before it is put into a larger container.
- The panel has its own layout manager.

Panels are created with a simple call to the constructor of the JPanel class, as shown in the following example:

```
JPanel pane = new JPanel();
```

The layout method is set for a panel by calling the setLayout() method on that panel.

The following statements create a layout manager and apply it to a JPanel object called pane:

```
BorderLayout bo = new BorderLayout();
pane.setLayout(bo);
```

Components are added to a panel by calling the panel's add() method, which works the same for panels as it does for other containers, such as applets.

The following statement adds a text area called dialogue to a Panel object called pane:

```
pane.add(dialogue);
```

You'll see several examples of panel use in the rest of today's example programs.

Card Layout

Card layouts differ from the other layouts because they hide some components from view. A *card layout* is a group of containers or components that are displayed one at a time, in the same way that a blackjack dealer reveals one card at a time from a deck. Each container in the group is called a *card*.

If you have used software such as HyperCard on the Macintosh or a tabbed dialog box such as the System Properties portion of the Windows 95 Control Panel, you have worked with a program that uses card layout.

The most common way to use a card layout is to use a panel for each card. Components are added to the panels first, and then the panels are added to the container that is set to use card layout.

A card layout is created from the `CardLayout` class with a simple constructor call:

```
CardLayout cc = new CardLayout();
```

The `setLayout()` method is used to make this the layout manager for the container, as in the following statement:

```
setLayout(cc);
```

After you set a container to use the card layout manager, you must use a slightly different `add()` method call to add cards to the layout.

The method to use is `add(String, container)`. The second argument specifies the container or component that is the card. If it is a container, all components must have been added to it before the card is added.

The first argument to the `add()` method is a string that represents the name of the card. This can be anything you want to call the card. You might want to number the cards in some way and use the number in the name, as in `"Card 1"`, `"Card 2"`, `"Card 3"`, and so on.

The following statement adds a panel called `options` to a container and gives this card the name `"Options Card"`:

```
add("Options Card", options);
```

After you have added a card to the main container for a program, such as an applet window, you can use the `show()` method of your card layout manager to display a card. The `show()` method takes two arguments:

- The container that all the cards have been added to
- The name that was given to the card

The following statement calls the `show()` method of a card layout manager called `cc`:

```
cc.show(this, "Fact Card");
```

The `this` keyword refers to the object that this statement is appearing in, and `"Fact Card"` is the name of the card to reveal. When a card is shown, the previously displayed card will be obscured. Only one card in a card layout can be viewed at a time.

In a program that uses the card layout manager, a card change will usually be triggered by a user's action. For example, in a program that displays mailing addresses on different cards, the user could select a card for display by selecting an item in a scrolling list.

Grid Bag Layout

The last of the layout managers available through Java is grid bag layout, which is an extension of the grid layout manager. A grid bag layout differs from grid layout in the following ways:

- A component can take up more than one cell in the grid.
- The proportions between different rows and columns do not have to be equal.
- Components inside grid cells can be arranged in different ways.

To create a grid bag layout, you use the `GridBagLayout` class and a helper class called `GridBagConstraints`. `GridBagLayout` is the layout manager, and `GridBagConstraints` is used to define the properties of each component to be placed into the cell—its placement, dimensions, alignment, and so on. The relationship between the grid bag, the constraints, and each component defines the overall layout.

In its most general form, creating a grid bag layout involves the following steps:

1. Creating a `GridBagLayout` object and defining it as the current layout manager, as you would for any other layout manager.
2. Creating a new instance of `GridBagConstraints`.
3. Setting up the constraints for a component.
4. Telling the layout manager about the component and its constraints.
5. Adding the component to the container.

The following example adds a single button to a container implementing grid bag layout. (Don't worry about the various values for the constraints; they are covered later in this section.)

```
// set up layout
GridBagLayout gridbag = new GridBagLayout();
GridBagConstraints constraints = new GridBagConstraints();
getContentPane().setLayout(gridbag);

// define constraints for the button
JButton btn = new JButton("Save");
constraints.gridx = 0;
constraints.gridy = 0;
constraints.gridwidth = 1;
constraints.gridheight = 1;
constraints.weightx = 30;
constraints.weighty = 30;
constraints.fill = GridBagConstraints.NONE;
constraints.anchor = GridBagConstraints.CENTER;
```

```
// attach constraints to layout, add button
gridbag.setConstraints(btn, constraints);
getContentPane().add(b);
```

As you can see from this example, you have to set all the constraints for every component you want to add to the panel. Given the numerous constraints, it helps to have a plan and to deal with each kind of constraint one at a time.

Designing the Grid

The first place to start in the grid bag layout is on paper. Sketching out your user interface design beforehand—before you even write a single line of code—will help enormously in the long run with trying to figure out where everything goes. Put your editor aside for a second, pick up a piece of paper and a pencil, and build the grid.

Figure 10.4 shows the panel layout you'll be building for this project's application. Figure 10.5 shows the same layout with a grid imposed on top of it. Your layout will have a grid similar to this one, with rows and columns forming individual cells.

FIGURE 10.4

A grid bag layout.

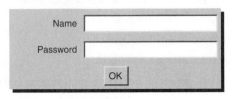

FIGURE 10.5

The grid bag layout from Figure 10.4, with grid imposed.

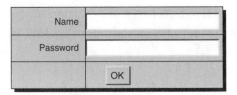

As you draw your grid, keep in mind that each component must have its own cell. You cannot put more than one component into the same cell. The reverse is not true, however; one component can span multiple cells in the x or y directions (as in the OK button in the bottom row, which spans two columns). In Figure 10.5, note that the labels and text fields have their own grids and that the button spans two column cells.

Label the cells with their x and y coordinates while you're still working on paper; this helps you later. They aren't pixel coordinates; rather, they're cell coordinates. The top-left cell is 0,0. The next cell to the right of it in the top row is 1,0. The cell to the right of that one is 2,0. Moving to the next row, the leftmost cell is 1,0, the next cell in the row is 1,1, and so on. Label your cells on the paper with these numbers; you'll need them later when you do the code for this example. Figure 10.6 shows the numbers for each of the cells in this example.

FIGURE 10.6

The grid bag layout from Figure 10.5, with cell coordinates.

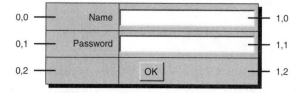

Creating the Grid

Now go back to Java and start implementing the layout you've just drawn on paper. Initially, you're going to focus exclusively on the layout—getting the grid and the proportions right. For that, it might be easier to use buttons as placeholders for the actual elements in the layout. They're easy to create, and they clearly define the space that a component will take up in the layout manager—or managers—that are in use. When everything is set up correctly, the buttons can be replaced with the right elements.

To cut down on the amount of typing you have to do to set up all those constraints, you can start by defining a helper method that takes several values and sets the constraints for those values. The `buildConstraints()` method takes seven arguments: a `GridBagConstraints` object and six integers representing the `GridBagConstraints` instance variables `gridx`, `gridy`, `gridwidth`, `gridheight`, `weightx`, and `weighty`. You'll learn later what these actually do; for now, here's the code to the helper method that you'll use later in this example:

```
void buildConstraints(GridBagConstraints gbc, int gx, int gy,
    int gw, int gh, int wx, int wy) {

    gbc.gridx = gx;
    gbc.gridy = gy;
    gbc.gridwidth = gw;
    gbc.gridheight = gh;
    gbc.weightx = wx;
    gbc.weighty = wy;
}
```

Now move on to the application's constructor method, where all the layout actually occurs. Here's the basic method definition, where you'll define the `GridBagLayout` to be the initial layout manager and create a constraints object (an instance of `GridBagConstraints`):

```
public NamePass() {
    super("Username and Password");
    setSize(290, 110);
```

10

```
GridBagLayout gridbag = new GridBagLayout();
GridBagConstraints constraints = new GridBagConstraints();
JPanel pane = new JPanel();
pane.setLayout(gridbag);

setContentPane(pane);
constraints.fill = GridBagConstraints.BOTH;
}
```

One more small note of explanation: The last line, which sets the value of con-
straints.fill, will be removed (and explained) later. It's there so that the components
will fill the entire cell in which they're contained, which helps you see what's going on.
Add it for now; you'll get a clearer idea of what it's for later.

Now add the button placeholders to the layout. (Remember that you're focusing on basic
grid organization at the moment, so you'll use buttons as placeholders for the actual user
interface elements you'll add later.) Start with a single button so that you can get a feel
for setting its constraints. This code will go into the constructor method just after the
setLayout line:

```
// Name label
 buildConstraints(constraints, 0, 0, 1, 1, 100, 100);
 JButton label1 = new JButton("Name:");
 gridbag.setConstraints(label1, constraints);
 add(label1);
```

These four lines set up the constraints for an object, create a new button, attach the constraints to the button, and then add it to the panel. Note that constraints for a component
are stored in the GridBagConstraints object, so the component doesn't even have to
exist to set up its constraints.

Now you can get down to details: Just what are the values for the constraints that you've
plugged into the helper method buildConstraints()?

The first two integer arguments are the gridx and gridy values of the constraints. They
are the cell coordinates of the cell containing this component. Remember how you wrote
these components down on paper in step one? With the cells neatly numbered on paper,
all you have to do is plug in the right values. Note that if you have a component that
spans multiple cells, the cell coordinates are those of the cell in the top-left corner.

This button is in the top-left corner, so its gridx and gridy (the first two arguments to
buildConstraints()) are 0 and 0, respectively.

The second two integer arguments are the gridwidth and gridheight. They are not the
pixel widths and heights of the cells; rather, they are the number of cells this component
spans: gridwidth for the columns and gridheight for the rows. Here this component
spans only one cell, so the values for both are 1.

The last two integer arguments are for weightx and weighty. They are used to set up the proportions of the rows and columns—that is, how wide or deep they will be. Weights can become very confusing, so for now, set both values to 100. Weights are dealt with in step three.

After the constraints have been built, you can attach them to an object using the setConstraints() method. setConstraints(), which is a method defined in GridBagLayout, takes two arguments: the component (here a button) and the constraints for that component. Finally, you can add the button to the panel.

After you've set and assigned the constraints to one component, you can reuse that GridBagConstraints object to set up the constraints for the next object. You, therefore, duplicate these four lines for each component in the grid, with different values for the buildConstraints() method. To save space, the buildConstraints() methods will only be shown for the last four cells.

The second cell to add is the one to hold the text box for the name. The cell coordinates for this one are 1,0 (second column, first row); it too spans only one cell, and the weights (for now) are both 100:

```
buildConstraints(constraints, 1, 0, 1, 1, 100, 100);
```

The next two components, which will be a label and a text field, are nearly identical to the previous two; the only difference is in their cell coordinates. The password label is at 0,1 (first column, second row), and the password text field is at 1,1 (second column, second row):

```
buildConstraints(constraints, 0, 1, 1, 1, 100, 100);
buildConstraints(constraints, 1, 1, 1, 1, 100, 100);
```

Finally, you need the OK button, which is a component that spans two cells in the bottom row of the panel. Here the cell coordinates are the left and topmost cell, where the span starts (0,2). Here, unlike the previous components, you'll set gridwidth and gridheight to be something other than 1 because this cell spans multiple columns. The gridweight is 2 (it spans two cells) and the gridheight is 1 (it spans only one row):

```
buildConstraints(constraints, 0, 2, 2, 1, 100, 100);
```

You've set the placement constraints for all the components that will be added to the grid layout. You also need to assign each component's constraints to the layout manager and then add each component to the panel. Figure 10.7 shows the result at this point. Note that you're not concerned about exact proportions here, or about making sure everything lines up. What you should keep track of at this point is making sure that the grid is working, that you have the right number of rows and columns, that the spans are correct, and that nothing strange is going on (cells in the wrong place, cells overlapping, that kind of thing).

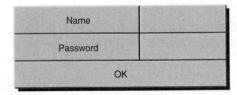

Figure 10.7

Grid bag layout, first pass.

Determining the Proportions

The next step is to determine the proportions of the rows and columns in relation to other rows and columns. For example, in this case you'll want the labels (name and password) to take up less space than the text boxes. You might want the OK button at the bottom to be only half the height of the two text boxes above it. You arrange the proportions of the cells within your layout using the `weightx` and `weighty` constraints.

The easiest way to think of `weightx` and `weighty` is that their values are either percentages of the total width and height of the panel, or 0 if the weight or height has been set by some other cell. The values of `weightx` and `weighty` for all your components, therefore, should add up to 100.

Note

> Actually, the `weightx` and `weighty` values are not percentages; they're simply proportions—they can have any value whatsoever. When the proportions are calculated, all the values in a direction are added up so that each individual value is in proportion to that total. To make this process easier to understand: Look at the weights as percentages and make sure that they add up to 100; that way, you can be sure everything is coming out right.

Which cells get values and which cells get 0? Cells that span multiple rows or columns should always be 0 in the direction they span. Beyond that, deciding is simply a question of picking a cell to have a value, and then all the other cells in that row or columns should be 0.

Look at the five calls to `buildConstraints()` made in the preceding step:

```
buildConstraints(constraints, 0, 0, 1, 1, 100, 100); //name
buildConstraints(constraints, 1, 0, 1, 1, 100, 100); //name text
buildConstraints(constraints, 0, 1, 1, 1, 100, 100); //password
buildConstraints(constraints, 1, 1, 1, 1, 100, 100); //password text
buildConstraints(constraints, 0, 2, 2, 1, 100, 100); //OK button
```

You'll be changing those last two arguments in each call to `buildConstraints` to be either a value or 0. Start with the x direction (the proportions of the columns), which is the second-to-last argument in the preceding list.

If you look back to Figure 10.5 (the picture of the panel with the grid imposed), note that the second column is much larger than the first. If you were going to pick theoretical percentages for those columns, you might say that the first is 10% and the second is 90%. (This is a guess; that's all you need to do as well.) With these two guesses, you can assign them to cells. You don't want to assign any values to the cell with the OK button because that cell spans both columns, and percentages there wouldn't work. Add them to the first two cells, the name label and the name text field:

```
buildConstraints(constraints, 0, 0, 1, 1, 10, 100); //name
buildConstraints(constraints, 1, 0, 1, 1, 90, 100); //name text
```

What about the values of the remaining two cells, the password label and text field? Because the proportions of the columns have already been set up by the name label and field, you don't have to reset them here. Give both of these cells as well as the one for the OK box 0 values:

```
buildConstraints(constraints, 0, 1, 1, 1, 0, 100); //password
buildConstraints(constraints, 1, 1, 1, 1, 0, 100); //password text
buildConstraints(constraints, 0, 2, 2, 1, 0, 100); //OK button
```

Note here that a 0 value does not mean that the cell has 0 width. These values are proportions, not pixel values. A 0 simply means that the proportion has been set somewhere else; all 0 says is "stretch it to fit."

Now that the totals of all the `weightx` constraints are `100`, you can move on to the `weighty` arguments. Here you have three rows. Glancing over the grid you drew, it looks like the button has about 20% and the text fields have the rest (40% each). As with the x values, you have to set the value of only one cell per row (the two labels and the button), with all the other cells having a `weightx` of `0`.

Here are the final five calls to `buildConstraints()` with the weights in place:

```
buildConstraints(constraints, 0, 0, 1, 1, 10, 40); //name
buildConstraints(constraints, 1, 0, 1, 1, 90, 0); //name text
buildConstraints(constraints, 0, 1, 1, 1, 0, 40); //password
buildConstraints(constraints, 1, 1, 1, 1, 0, 0); //password text
buildConstraints(constraints, 0, 2, 2, 1, 0, 20); //OK button
```

Figure 10.8 shows the result with the correct proportions.

FIGURE 10.8

Grid bag layout, second pass.

At this step, the goal is to try to come up with some basic proportions for how the rows and cells will be spaced on the screen. You can make some elementary estimates based on how big you expect the various components to be, but chances are you're going to use a lot of trial and error in this part of the process.

Adding and Arranging the Components

With the layout and the proportions in place, you can now replace the button placeholders with actual labels and text fields. Because you set up everything already, it should all work perfectly, right? Well, almost. Figure 10.9 shows what you get if you use the same constraints as before and replace the buttons with actual components.

FIGURE 10.9

Grid bag layout,
almost there.

This layout is close, but it's weird. The text boxes are too tall, and the OK button stretches across the width of the cell.

What's missing are the constraints that arrange the components inside the cell. There are two of them: fill and anchor.

The fill constraint determines—for components that can stretch in either direction—in which direction to stretch (such as text boxes and buttons). fill can have one of four values, defined as class variables in the GridBagConstraints class:

- GridBagConstraints.BOTH, which stretches the component to fill the cell in both directions
- GridBagConstraints.NONE, which causes the component to be displayed in its smallest size
- GridBagConstraints.HORIZONTAL, which stretches the component in the horizontal direction
- GridBagConstraints.VERTICAL, which stretches the component in the vertical direction

> **Note**
>
> Keep in mind that this layout is dynamic. You're not going to set up the actual pixel dimensions of any components; rather, you're telling these elements in which direction they can grow given a panel that can be of any size.

By default, the `fill` constraint for all components is `NONE`. Why are the text fields and labels filling the cells if this is the case? If you remember way back to the start of the code for this example, this line was added to the `init()` method:

```
constraints.fill = GridBagConstraints.BOTH;
```

Now you know what it does. For the final version of this application, you'll want to remove that line and add `fill` values for each independent component.

The second constraint that affects how a component appears in the cell is `anchor`. This constraint applies only to components that aren't filling the whole cell, and it tells Java where inside the cell to place the component. The possible values for the anchor constraint are `GridBagConstraints.CENTER`, which aligns the component both vertically and horizontally inside the cell, or one of eight direction values:

GridBagConstraints.NORTH	GridBagConstraints.SOUTH
GridBagConstraints.NORTHEAST	GridBagConstraints.SOUTHWEST
GridBagConstraints.EAST	GridBagConstraints.WEST
GridBagConstraints.SOUTHEAST	GridBagConstraints.NORTHWEST

The default value of anchor is `GridBagConstraints.CENTER`.

You set these constraints the same way you did all the other ones: by changing instance variables in the `GridBagConstraints` object. Here you can change the definition of `buildConstraints()` to take two more arguments (they're integers), or you could just set them in the body of the `init()` method. The latter is used on this project.

Be careful with defaults. Keep in mind that because you're reusing the same `GridBagConstraints` object for each component, you might have some values left over when you're done with one component. On the other hand, if a `fill` or `anchor` from one object is the same as the one before it, you don't have to reset that object.

For this example, three changes are going to be made to the `fill` and `anchor` values of the components:

- The labels will have no `fill` and will be aligned `EAST` (so they hug the right side of the cell).

10

- The text fields will be filled horizontally (so they start one line high, but stretch to the width of the cell).
- The button will have no `fill` and will be center-aligned.

This is reflected in the full code at the end of this section.

Making Adjustments

As you work with your own programs and grid bag layouts, you'll notice that the resulting layout often requires some tinkering. You might need to play with various values of the constraints to get an interface to come out right. There's nothing wrong with that—the goal of following the previous steps is to get things fairly close to the final positions, not to come out with a perfect layout every time.

Listing 10.4 shows the complete code for the layout you've been building up in this section. If you had trouble following the discussion up to this point, you might find it useful to go through this code line by line to make sure that you understand the various parts.

LISTING 10.4   The full Text of `NamePass.java`

```
 1: import java.awt.*;
 2: import javax.swing.*;
 3: import java.awt.event.*;
 4:
 5: public class NamePass extends JFrame {
 6:
 7:     void buildConstraints(GridBagConstraints gbc, int gx, int gy,
 8:         int gw, int gh, int wx, int wy) {
 9:
10:         gbc.gridx = gx;
11:         gbc.gridy = gy;
12:         gbc.gridwidth = gw;
13:         gbc.gridheight = gh;
14:         gbc.weightx = wx;
15:         gbc.weighty = wy;
16:     }
17:
18:     public NamePass() {
19:         super("Username and Password");
20:         setSize(290, 110);
21:         GridBagLayout gridbag = new GridBagLayout();
22:         GridBagConstraints constraints = new GridBagConstraints();
23:         JPanel pane = new JPanel();
24:         pane.setLayout(gridbag);
25:
26:         // Name label
27:         buildConstraints(constraints, 0, 0, 1, 1, 10, 40);
28:         constraints.fill = GridBagConstraints.NONE;
29:         constraints.anchor = GridBagConstraints.EAST;
```

```
30:          JLabel label1 = new JLabel("Name:", JLabel.LEFT);
31:          gridbag.setConstraints(label1, constraints);
32:          pane.add(label1);
33:
34:          // Name text field
35:          buildConstraints(constraints, 1, 0, 1, 1, 90, 0);
36:          constraints.fill = GridBagConstraints.HORIZONTAL;
37:          JTextField tfname = new JTextField();
38:          gridbag.setConstraints(tfname, constraints);
39:          pane.add(tfname);
40:
41:          // password label
42:          buildConstraints(constraints, 0, 1, 1, 1, 0, 40);
43:          constraints.fill = GridBagConstraints.NONE;
44:          constraints.anchor = GridBagConstraints.EAST;
45:          JLabel label2 = new JLabel("Password:", JLabel.LEFT);
46:          gridbag.setConstraints(label2, constraints);
47:          pane.add(label2);
48:
49:          // password text field
50:          buildConstraints(constraints, 1, 1, 1, 1, 0, 0);
51:          constraints.fill = GridBagConstraints.HORIZONTAL;
52:          JPasswordField tfpass = new JPasswordField();
53:          tfpass.setEchoChar('*');
54:          gridbag.setConstraints(tfpass, constraints);
55:          pane.add(tfpass);
56:
57:          // OK Button
58:          buildConstraints(constraints, 0, 2, 2, 1, 0, 20);
59:          constraints.fill = GridBagConstraints.NONE;
60:          constraints.anchor = GridBagConstraints.CENTER;
61:          JButton okb = new JButton("OK");
62:          gridbag.setConstraints(okb, constraints);
63:          pane.add(okb);
64:
65:          // Content Pane
66:          setContentPane(pane);
67:      }
68:
69:      public static void main(String[] arguments) {
70:          NamePass frame = new NamePass();
71:          ExitWindow exit = new ExitWindow();
72:          frame.addWindowListener(exit);
73:          frame.show();
74:      }
75: }
76:
77: class ExitWindow extends WindowAdapter {
78:      public void windowClosing(WindowEvent e) {
79:          System.exit(0);
80:      }
81: }
```

10

Cell Padding and Insets

Before you finish up with grid bag layouts, two more constraints deserve mentioning: ipadx and ipady. These two constraints control the *padding* (the extra space around an individual component). By default, no components have extra space around them (which is easiest to see in components that fill their cells).

ipadx adds space to either side of the component, and ipady adds it above and below.

The horizontal and vertical gaps that appear when you create a new layout manager (or use ipadx and ipady in grid bag layouts), are used to determine the amount of space between components in a panel. *Insets*, however, are used to determine the amount of space around the panel itself. The Insets class includes values for the top, bottom, left, and right insets, which are then used when the panel itself is drawn.

Insets determine the amount of space between the edges of a panel and that panel's components.

To include an inset for your layout, you override the insets() method for Java 1.02, or the getInsets() method for Java 2. These methods do the same thing.

Inside the insets() or getInsets() method, create a new Insets object, where the constructor to the Insets class takes four integer values representing the insets on the top, left, bottom, and right of the panel. The insets() method should then return that Insets object. Here's some code to add insets for a grid layout: 10 to the top and bottom and 30 to the left and right. Figure 10.10 shows the inset.

FIGURE **10.10**

A panel with insets of 10 pixels on the top and bottom and 30 pixels to the left and right.

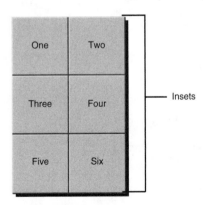

```
public Insets insets() {
    return new Insets(10, 30, 10, 30);
}
```

Summary

Abstract expressionism only goes so far, as you have seen today. Layout managers require some adjustment for people who are used to more precise control over the place that components appear on an interface.

You now know how to use the five different layout managers and panels. As you work with the Abstract Windowing Toolkit, you'll find that it can approximate any kind of interface through the use of nested containers and different layout managers.

Once you master the development of a user interface in Java, your programs can offer something that most other visual programming languages can't: an interface that works on multiple platforms without modification.

To borrow an oft-repeated phrase: I don't know if it's art, but I like it.

Q&A

Q I really dislike working with layout managers; they're either too simplistic or too complicated (the grid bag layout, for example). Even with a whole lot of tinkering, I can never get my applets to look like I want them to. All I want to do is define the sizes of my components and put them at an x,y position on the screen. Can I do this?

A It's possible, but very problematic. Java was designed in such a way that a program's graphical user interface could run equally well on different platforms and with different screen resolutions, fonts, screen sizes, and the like. Relying on pixel coordinates can cause a program that looks good on one platform to be unusable on others, where components overlap each other, are cut off by the edge of a container, and other layout disasters. Layout managers, by dynamically placing elements on the screen, get around these problems. Although there might be some differences between the end result on different platforms, the differences are less likely to be catastrophic.

Still not convinced? Use a `null` layout manager and the `reshape()` method to make a component a specific size and place it at a particular position:

```
setLayout(null);
Button myButton = new Button("OK");
myButton.reshape(10, 10, 30, 15);
```

You can find out more about `reshape()` in the `Component` class.

Q **I was exploring Java classes and I saw this subpackage called `peer`. References to the peer classes are also sprinkled throughout the Java API documentation. What do peers do?**

A *Peers* are responsible for the platform-specific parts of Java. For example, when you create a Java Swing window, you have an instance of the `Window` class that provides generic window behavior, and then you have an instance of a class implementing `WindowPeer` that creates the very specific window for that platform—a motif window under X Window, a Macintosh-style window under the Macintosh, or a Windows 98 window under Windows 98. These peer classes also handle communication between the window system and the Java window itself. By separating the generic component behavior (Java classes) from the actual system implementation and appearance (the peer classes), you can focus on providing behavior in your Java application and let the Java implementation deal with the platform-specific details.

Questions

1. What is the default layout manager for a container in Java?

   (a) None

   (b) `BorderLayout`

   (c) `FlowLayout`

2. Which layout manager requires a compass direction or the word "Center" when adding a component to a container?

   (a) `BorderLayout`

   (b) `MapLayout`

   (c) `FlowLayout`

3. If you want a grid layout in which a component can take up more than one cell of the grid, which layout should you use?

   (a) `GridLayout`

   (b) `GridBagLayout`

   (c) None; it isn't possible to do that.

Answers

1. c.

2. a.

3. b.

Exercises

To extend your knowledge of the subjects covered today, try the following exercises:

- Create a user interface that displays a calendar for a single month, including headings for the seven days of the week and a title of the month across the top.

- Create an interface that incorporates more than one layout manager.

Where applicable, exercise solutions are offered on the book's Web site at
`http://www.java21days.com`.

10

DAY 11

Responding to User Input

In order to turn a working Java interface into a working Java program, you must make the interface receptive to user events.

Swing handles events with a set of interfaces called *event listeners*. You create a listener object and associate it with the user interface component being listened to.

Today you learn how to add listeners of all kinds to your Swing programs, including those that handle action events, mouse events, and other interaction.

When you're done, you'll celebrate the event by completing a full Java application using the Swing set of classes.

Event Listeners

If a class wants to respond to a user event under the Java 2 event-handling system, it must implement the interface that deals with the events. These interfaces are called *event listeners*.

Each listener handles a specific kind of event, and a class can implement as many of them as needed.

The event listeners in Java include each of the following interfaces:

- `ActionListener` —*Action events*, which are generated by a user, taking an action on a component, such as a click on a button
- `AdjustmentListener`—*Adjustment events*, which are generated when a component is adjusted, such as when a scrollbar is moved
- `FocusListener`—*Keyboard focus events*, which are generated when a component such as a text field gains or loses the focus
- `ItemListener`—*Item events*, which are generated when an item such as a check box is changed
- `KeyListener`—*Keyboard events*, which occur when a user enters text on the keyboard
- `MouseListener`—*Mouse events*, which are generated by mouse clicks, a mouse entering a component's area, and a mouse leaving a component's area
- `MouseMotionListener`—*Mouse movement events*, which track all movement by a mouse over a component
- `WindowListener`—*Window events*, which are generated by a window (such as the main application window) being maximized, minimized, moved, or closed

The following class is declared so that it can handle both action and text events:

```
public class Suspense extends JFrame implements ActionListener,
    TextListener {
    // ...
}
```

The `java.awt.event` package contains all the basic event listeners as well as the objects that represent specific events. In order to use these classes in your programs, you can import them individually or use a statement such as the following:

```
import java.awt.event.*;
```

Setting Up Components

When you make a class an event listener, you have set up a specific type of event to be heard by that class. This will never happen if you don't follow up with a second step: A matching listener must be added to the component. That listener generates the events when the component is used.

After a component is created, you can call one of the following methods on the component to associate a listener with it:

- addActionListener()—JButton, JCheckBox, JComboBox, JTextField, and JRadioButton components
- addAdjustmentListener()—JScrollBar components
- addFocusListener()—All Swing components
- addItemListener()—JButton, JCheckBox, JComboBox, and JRadioButton components
- addKeyListener()—All Swing components
- addMouseListener()—All Swing components
- addMouseMotionListener()—All Swing components
- addWindowListener()—All JWindow and JFrame components

> **Caution**
>
> Modifying a component after adding it to a container is an easy mistake to make in a Java program. You must add listeners to a component and handle any other configuration before it is added to any containers; otherwise these settings are disregarded when the program is run.

11

The following example creates a JButton object and associates an action event listener with it:

```
JButton zap = new JButton("Zap");
zap.addActionListener(this);
```

All the different add methods take one argument: the object that is listening for events of that kind. Using this indicates that the current class is the event listener. You could specify a different object, as long as its class implements the right listener interface.

Event-Handling Methods

When you associate an interface with a class, the class must handle all the methods contained in the interface.

In the case of event listeners, each of the methods is called automatically by the windowing system when the corresponding user event takes place.

The ActionListener interface has only one method: actionPerformed(). All classes that implement ActionListener must have a method with a structure similar to the following:

```
public void actionPerformed(ActionEvent evt) {
    // handle event here
}
```

If only one component in your program's graphical user interface has a listener for action events, this `actionPerformed()` method can be used to respond to an event generated by that component.

If more than one component has an action event listener, you must use the method to figure out which component was used and act accordingly in your program.

In the `actionPerformed()` method, you might have noticed that an `ActionEvent` object is sent as an argument when the method is called. This object can be used to discover details about the component that generated the event.

`ActionEvent` and all other event objects are part of the `java.awt.event` package, and they are subclasses of the `EventObject` class.

Every event-handling method is sent an event object of some kind. The object's `getSource()` method can be used to determine the component that sent the event, as in the following example:

```
public void actionPerformed(ActionEvent evt) {
    Object src = evt.getSource();
}
```

The object returned by the `getSource()` method can be compared to components by using the == operator. The following statements can be used inside the preceding `actionPerformed()` example:

```
if (src == quitButton)
    quitProgram();
else if (src == sortRecords)
    sortRecords();
```

This example calls the `quitProgram()` method if the `quitButton` object generated the event; it calls the `sortRecords()` method if the `sortRecords` button generated the event.

Many event-handling methods call a different method for each kind of event or component. This makes the event-handling method easier to read. In addition, if there is more than one event-handling method in a class, each one can call the same methods to get work done.

Using the `instanceof` keyword inside an event-handling method is another useful technique for checking what kind of component generated the event. The following example can be used in a program with one button and one text field, each of which generates an action event:

```
void actionPerformed(ActionEvent evt) {
    Object src = evt.getSource();
    if (src instanceof JTextField)
        calculateScore();
    else if (src instanceof JButton)
        quitProgram();
}
```

The program in Listing 11.1 uses the application framework to create a JFrame and add components to it. The program itself sports two JButton components, which are used to change the text on the frame's title bar.

LISTING 11.1   The Full Text of ChangeTitle.java

```
 1: import java.awt.event.*;
 2: import javax.swing.*;
 3: import java.awt.*;
 4:
 5: public class ChangeTitle extends JFrame implements ActionListener {
 6:     JButton b1 = new JButton("Rosencrantz");
 7:     JButton b2 = new JButton("Guildenstern");
 8:
 9:     public ChangeTitle() {
10:         super("Title Bar");
11:
12:         b1.addActionListener(this);
13:         b2.addActionListener(this);
14:         JPanel pane = new JPanel();
15:         pane.add(b1);
16:         pane.add(b2);
17:
18:         setContentPane(pane);
19:     }
20:
21:     public static void main(String[] arguments) {
22:         JFrame frame = new ChangeTitle();
23:
24:         ExitWindow exit = new ExitWindow();
25:         frame.addWindowListener(exit);
26:
27:         frame.pack();
28:         frame.setVisible(true);
29:     }
30:
31:     public void actionPerformed(ActionEvent evt) {
32:         Object source = evt.getSource();
33:         if (source == b1)
34:             setTitle("Rosencrantz");
35:         else if (source == b2)
36:             setTitle("Guildenstern");
```

11

LISTING 11.1   continued

```
37:          repaint();
38:      }
39: }
40:
41: class ExitWindow extends WindowAdapter {
42:      public void windowClosing(WindowEvent e) {
43:          System.exit(0);
44:      }
45: }
```

After you run this application with the Java interpreter, the program's interface should resemble Figure 11.1.

FIGURE 11.1

The ChangeTitle
application.

Only 11 lines were needed to respond to action events in this application:

- Line 1 imports the java.awt.event package.
- Lines 12 and 13 add action listeners to both JButton objects.
- Lines 31–38 respond to action events that occur from the two JButton objects. The evt object's getSource() method determines the source of the event. If it is equal to the b1 button, the title of the frame is set to Rosencrantz; if it is equal to b2, the title is set to Guildenstern. A call to repaint() is needed so that the frame is redrawn after any title change that might have occurred in the method.

Working with Methods

The following sections detail the structure of each event-handling method and the methods that can be used within them.

In addition to the methods described, the getSource() method can be used on any event object to determine which object generated the event.

Action Events

Action events occur when a user completes an action using one of the following components: JButton, JCheckBox, JComboBox, JTextField, or JRadioButton.

A class must implement the ActionListener interface in order to handle these events. In addition, the addActionListener() method must be called on each component that should generate an action event—unless you want to ignore that component's action events.

The actionPerformed(*Action Event*) method is the only method of the ActionListener interface. It takes the following form:

```
public void actionPerformed(ActionEvent evt) {
    // ...
}
```

In addition to the getSource() method, you can use the getActionCommand() method on the ActionEvent object to discover more information about the event's source.

The action command, by default, is the text associated with the component, such as the label on a JButton. You also can set a different action command for a component by calling its setActionCommand(*String*) method. The string argument should be the action command's desired text.

For example, the following statements create a JButton and a JTextField and give both of them the action command "Sort Files":

```
JButton sort = new JButton("Sort");
JTextField name = new JTextField();
sort.setActionCommand("Sort Files");
name.setActionCommand("Sort Files");
```

11

Note

Action commands become exceptionally useful when you're writing a program in which more than one component should cause the same thing to happen. A program with a Quit button and a Quit option on a pull-down menu is an example of this. By giving both components the same action command, you can handle them with the same code in an event-handling method.

Adjustment Events

Adjustment events occur when a JScrollBar component is moved by using the arrows on the bar or on the box, or by clicking anywhere on the bar. To handle these events, a class must implement the AdjustmentListener interface.

(*AdjustmentEvent*) is the only method in the `AdjustmentListener` interface `adjustmentValueChanged`. It takes the following form:

```
public void adjustmentValueChanged(AdjustmentEvent evt) {
    // ...
}
```

To see what the current value of the `JScrollBar` is within this event-handling method, the `getValue()` method can be called on the `AdjustmentEvent` object. This method returns an integer representing the scrollbar's value.

You can also determine the way the user moved the scrollbar by using the `AdjustmentEvent` object's `getAdjustmentType()` method. This returns one of five values, each of which is a class variable of the `Adjustment` class:

- `UNIT_INCREMENT`—A value increase of 1, which can be caused by clicking a scrollbar arrow or using a cursor key
- `UNIT_DECREMENT`—A value decrease of 1
- `BLOCK_INCREMENT`—A larger value increase, caused by clicking the scrollbar in the area between the box and the arrow
- `BLOCK_DECREMENT`—A larger value decrease
- `TRACK`—A value change caused by moving the box

The program in Listing 11.2 illustrates the use of the `AdjustmentListener` interface. A scrollbar and an uneditable text field are added to a frame, and messages are displayed in the field whenever the scrollbar is moved.

LISTING 11.2   The Full Text of `WellAdjusted.java`

```
 1: import java.awt.event.*;
 2: import javax.swing.*;
 3: import java.awt.*;
 4:
 5: public class WellAdjusted extends JFrame implements AdjustmentListener {
 6:     JTextField value = new JTextField("50", 30);
 7:     JScrollBar bar = new JScrollBar(SwingConstants.HORIZONTAL,
 8:         50, 10, 0, 100);
 9:
10:     public WellAdjusted() {
11:         super("Well Adjusted");
12:         setSize(350, 100);
13:         bar.addAdjustmentListener(this);
14:         value.setHorizontalAlignment(SwingConstants.CENTER);
15:         value.setEditable(false);
16:         JPanel pane = new JPanel();
17:         pane.setLayout(new BorderLayout());
```

```
18:            pane.add(value, "Center");
19:            pane.add(bar, "South");
20:    ▪       setContentPane(pane);
21:        }
22:
23:        public static void main(String[] arguments) {
24:            JFrame frame = new WellAdjusted();
25:
26:            ExitWindow exit = new ExitWindow();
27:            frame.addWindowListener(exit);
28:
29:            frame.show();
30:        }
31:
32:        public void adjustmentValueChanged(AdjustmentEvent evt) {
33:            Object source = evt.getSource();
34:            if (source == bar) {
35:                int newValue = bar.getValue();
36:                value.setText("" + newValue);
37:            }
38:            repaint();
39:        }
40: }
```

11

Compiling this class requires `ExitWindow.class`, the subclass of `WindowAdapter` you have been using, to close applications after the main window closes. If you are creating all of today's programs in the same folder, you should already have `ExitWindow.class` in that folder.

Figure 11.2 shows a screen capture of the application after you run it with the Java interpreter.

FIGURE 11.2

The output of the `WellAdjusted` *application.*

 Tip

> **NEW TERM** You might be wondering why there's an empty set of quotation marks in the call to `setText()` in line 36 of this program. The empty quotation is called a null *string*, and it is concatenated to the `newValue` integer to turn the argument into a string. As you might recall, if a string and nonstring are concatenated, Java always treats the result as a string. The null string is a shortcut when you want to display something that isn't already a string.

Focus Events

Focus events occur when any component gains or loses input focus on a graphical user interface. *Focus* describes the component that is currently active for keyboard input. If one of the fields has the focus (in a user interface with several editable text fields), a cursor will blink in the field. Any text entered goes into this component.

Focus applies to all components that can receive input. In a JButton object, a dotted outline appears on the button that has the focus.

To handle a focus event, a class must implement the FocusListener interface. There are two methods in the interface: focusGained(*FocusEvent*) and focusLost(*FocusEvent*). They take the following forms:

```
public void focusGained(FocusEvent evt) {
    // ...
}

public void focusLost(FocusEvent evt) {
    // ...
}
```

To determine which object gained or lost the focus, the getSource() method can be called on the FocusEvent object sent as an argument to the focusGained() and focusLost() methods.

Item Events

Item events occur when an item is selected or deselected on any of the following components: JButton, JCheckBox, JComboBox, or JRadioButton. A class must implement the ItemListener interface in order to handle these events.

itemStateChanged(*ItemEvent*) is the only method in the ItemListener interface. It takes the following form:

```
void itemStateChanged(ItemEvent evt) {
    // ...
}
```

To determine in which item the event occurred, the getItem() method can be called on the ItemEvent object.

You also can determine whether the item was selected or deselected by using the getStateChange() method. This method returns an integer that will equal either the class variable ItemEvent.DESELECTED or ItemEvent.SELECTED.

The use of item events is illustrated in Listing 11.3. The SelectItem application displays the choice from a combo box in a text field.

LISTING 11.3   The Full Text of SelectItem.java

```
 1: import java.awt.event.*;
 2: import javax.swing.*;
 3: import java.awt.*;
 4:
 5: public class SelectItem extends JFrame implements ItemListener {
 6:     BorderLayout bord = new BorderLayout();
 7:     JTextField result = new JTextField(27);
 8:     JComboBox pick = new JComboBox();
 9:
10:     public SelectItem() {
11:         super("Select Item");
12:
13:         pick.addItemListener(this);
14:         pick.addItem("Navigator");
15:         pick.addItem("Internet Explorer");
16:         pick.addItem("Opera");
17:         pick.setEditable(false);
18:         result.setHorizontalAlignment(SwingConstants.CENTER);
19:         result.setEditable(false);
20:         JPanel pane = new JPanel();
21:         pane.setLayout(bord);
22:         pane.add(result, "South");
23:         pane.add(pick, "Center");
24:
25:         setContentPane(pane);
26:     }
27:
28:     public static void main(String[] arguments) {
29:         JFrame frame = new SelectItem();
30:
31:         ExitWindow exit = new ExitWindow();
32:         frame.addWindowListener(exit);
33:
34:         frame.pack();
35:         frame.setVisible(true);
36:     }
37:
38:     public void itemStateChanged(ItemEvent evt) {
39:         Object source = evt.getSource();
40:         if (source == pick) {
41:             Object newPick = evt.getItem();
42:             result.setText(newPick.toString() + " is the selection.");
43:         }
44:         repaint();
45:     }
46: }
```

11

Figure 11.3 shows this application with the Opera item as the current selection in the combo box. The object's toString() method is used to retrieve the object's text returned by getItem().

FIGURE 11.3

The output of the
SelectItem
application.

Key Events

Key events occur when a key is pressed on the keyboard. Any component can generate these events, and a class must implement the KeyListener interface to support them.

There are three methods in the KeyListener interface. They include keyPressed(*KeyEvent*), keyReleased(*KeyEvent*), and keyTyped(*KeyEvent*). They take the following forms:

```
public void keyPressed(KeyEvent evt) {
    // ...
}

public void keyReleased(KeyEvent evt) {
    // ...
}

public void keyTyped(KeyEvent evt) {
    // ...
}
```

KeyEvent's getKeyChar() method returns the character of the key associated with the event. If there is no Unicode character that can be represented by the key, getKeyChar() returns a character value equal to the class variable KeyEvent.CHAR_UNDEFINED.

Mouse Events

Mouse events are generated by several different types of user interaction:

- A mouse click
- A mouse entering a component's area
- A mouse leaving a component's area

Any component can generate these events, which are implemented by a class through the MouseListener interface. This interface has five methods:

```
mouseClicked(MouseEvent)

mouseEntered(MouseEvent)

mouseExited(MouseEvent)

mousePressed(MouseEvent)

mouseReleased(MouseEvent)
```

Each takes the same basic form as mouseReleased (*MouseEvent*):

```
public void mouseReleased(MouseEvent evt) {
    // ...
}
```

The following methods can be used on MouseEvent objects:

- getClickCount ()—Returns the number of times the mouse was clicked as an integer.
- getPoint () —Returns the x,y coordinates within the component where the mouse was clicked as a Point object.
- getX () —Returns the x position.
- getY ()— Returns the y position.

Mouse Motion Events

Mouse motion events occur when a mouse is moved over a component. As with other mouse events, any component can generate mouse motion events. A class must implement the MouseMotionListener interface in order to support them.

There are two methods in the MouseMotionListener interface: mouseDragged (*MouseEvent*) and mouseMoved (*MouseEvent*). They take the following forms:

```
public void mouseDragged(MouseEvent evt) {
    // ...
}

public void mouseMoved(MouseEvent evt) {
    // ...
}
```

Unlike the other event listener interfaces you have dealt with up to this point, MouseMotionListener does not have its own event type. Instead, MouseEvent objects are used.

Because of this, you can call the same methods you would for mouse events: getClick(), getPoint(), getX(), and getY().

Window Events

Window events occur when a user opens or closes a window object such as a `JFrame` or a `JWindow`. Any component can generate these events, and a class must implement the `WindowListener` interface in order to support them.

There are seven methods in the `WindowListener` interface:

```
windowActivated(WindowEvent)

windowClosed(WindowEvent)

windowClosing(WindowEvent)

windowDeactivated(WindowEvent)

windowDeiconified(WindowEvent)

windowIconified(WindowEvent)

windowOpened(WindowEvent)
```

They all take the same form as the `windowOpened()` method:

```
public void windowOpened(WindowEvent evt) {
    // ...
}
```

The `windowClosing()` and `windowClosed()` methods are similar, but one is called as the window is closing and the other is called after it is closed. In fact, you can take action in a `windowClosing()` method to stop the window from being closed.

There's also an adapter class that implements the `WindowListener` interface called `WindowAdapter`. Throughout the past four days, this class has been subclassed to exit an application when its main window is closed.

An Example: An RGB-to-HSB Converter

As an opportunity to put the past several days' material to more use, the following application demonstrates layout creation, nested panels, interface creation, and event handling.

Figure 11.4 shows the SwingColorTest application, which enables a user to pick colors based on the sRGB or HSB color spaces—systems that describe colors based on their red, green, and blue content or hue, saturation, and brightness values, respectively.

The SwingColorTest application has three main parts: a colored box on the left side and two groups of text fields on the right. The first group indicates RGB values; the second group, HSB. If you change any of the values in any of the text boxes, the colored box is updated to the new color, as are the values in the other group of text boxes.

FIGURE **11.4**

The SwingColorTest application.

This application uses three classes:

- SwingColorTest, which inherits from JFrame and is the main class for the application itself.
- SwingColorControls, which inherits from JPanel. You create this class to represent a group of three text fields and to handle actions from them. Two instances of this class, one for the sRGB values and one for the HSB ones, are created and added to the application.

The code for this application is shown at the end of this section.

Designing the Layout

The first step in a Swing project is to worry about the layout first and the functionality second. When dealing with the layout, you should start with the outermost panel first and work inward.

Making a sketch of your user-interface design can help you figure out how to organize the panels inside your application to best take advantage of layout and space. Paper designs are helpful even when you're not using grid bag layouts, but doubly so when you are. (You'll be using a simple grid layout for this application.)

Figure 11.5 shows the SwingColorTest application with a grid drawn over it so that you can get an idea of how the panels and embedded panels work.

FIGURE **11.5**

SwingColorTest *panels and components.*

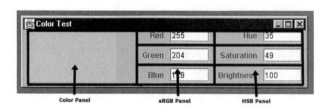

Start with the outermost panel—a JFrame component. This frame has three parts: the color box on the left, the RGB text fields in the middle, and the HSB fields on the right.

Because the outermost panel is the frame itself, the SwingColorTest class will inherit from JFrame. You also import the Swing, AWT, and event-handling classes here. (Note that because you use so many of them in this program, importing the entire package is easiest.)

```
import java.awt.*;
import java.awt.event.*;
import javax.swing.*;

public class SwingColorTest extends JFrame {
    // ...
}
```

This frame has three main elements to keep track of: the color box and the two subpanels. Each of the subpanels refers to different things, but they're extremely similar in how they look and the information they contain. Rather than duplicate a lot of code in this class, you can take this opportunity to create another class strictly for the subpanels, use instances of that class in the frame, and communicate between everything using methods. The new class called SwingColorControls will be defined in a bit.

For now, however, you know you need to keep a handle on all three parts of the application, so you can update them when they change. Create three instance variables: one of type JPanel for the color box and the other two of type SwingColorControls for the control panels:

```
SwingColorControls RGBcontrols, HSBcontrols;
JPanel swatch;
```

Now you can move onto the frame's constructor method, where all the basic initialization and layout of the application take place in the following steps:

1. Set up the class and create the layout for the big parts of the panel. Although a flow layout would work, creating a grid layout with one row and three columns is a better idea.

2. Create and initialize the three components of this application: a panel for the color box and two subpanels for the text fields.

3. Add these components to the application.

The first statement in the constructor method of a subclass should be a call to a constructor of the superclass. The JFrame(*String*) constructor sets the text of the frame's title bar to the indicated String. It will be used here:

```
super("Color Test");
```

Next, a panel is created and its layout is set to a grid layout with a gap of 10 points to separate each of the components:

```
JPanel pane = new JPanel();
pane.setLayout(new GridLayout(1, 3, 5, 15));
```

This panel, pane, will be set up completely and then used to create the frame's content pane—the portion of the frame that can contain other components.

The first component that will be added to pane is the color box, swatch: It is created as a JPanel and given the background color black:

```
swatch = new JPanel();
swatch.setBackground(Color.black);
```

You need also to create two instances of the currently nonexistent SwingColorControls panels here. Because you haven't created the class yet, you don't know what the constructors to that class will look like. In that case, put in some placeholder constructors here; you can fill in the details later.

```
RGBcontrols = new SwingColorControls(...);
HSBcontrols = new SwingColorControls(...);
```

Once all the components have been created, they are added to the panel, which is then used to set up the frame's content pane:

```
pane.add(swatch);
pane.add(RGBcontrols);
pane.add(HSBcontrols);
setContentPane(pane);
```

Because this application's main class is a user interface component, you can override the getInsets() method of the class to establish new inset values:

```
public Insets getInsets() {
    return new Insets(10, 10, 10, 10);
}
```

This gives the application frame 10 points of empty space along all outer edges. At this point your class should contain three instance variables, a constructor method, incomplete constructors for RGBControls and HSBControls, and a getInsets() method. Move on to creating the subpanel layout in the SwingColorControls class, which will enable you to fill in the incomplete constructors and finish up the layout.

Defining the Subpanels

The SwingColorControls class will have behavior for laying out and handling the subpanels that represent the RGB and HSB values for a color. SwingColorControls inherits from JPanel, a simple component that can contain other components:

```
class SwingColorControls extends JPanel {
    // ...
}
```

The SwingColorControls class needs a number of instance variables so that information from the panel can get back to the application. The first of these instance variables is a hook back up to the class that contains this panel. Because the outer application class controls the updating of each panel, this panel needs a way to tell the application that something has changed. To call a method in that application, you need a reference to the object; instance variable number one is a reference to an instance of the class SwingColorTest:

```
SwingColorTest frame;
```

If you figure that the `frame` class is updating everything, that class will be interested in the individual text fields in this subpanel. You create instance variables for these text fields:

```
JTextField[] tfield = new JTextField[3];
```

Now you can move on to the constructor method for this class. You establish the layout for the subpanel, create the text fields, and add them to the panel's content pane inside the constructor.

The goal here is to make the `SwingColorControls` class generic enough so that you can use it for both the panel of RGB fields and the panel of HSB fields. These two panels differ in only one respect: the labels for the text—that's three values to get before you can create the object. You can pass these three values in through the constructors in `SwingColorTest`. You also need one more: the reference to the enclosing application, which you can get from the constructor as well.

You now have two arguments to the basic constructor for the `ColorControls` class—a reference to the parent class and a `String` array containing the text field labels. Here's the signature for the constructor:

```
SwingColorControls(SwingColorTest parent, String[] label) {
    // ..
}
```

Start this constructor by first setting the value of `parent` to the `frame` instance variable:

```
frame = parent;
```

Next, create the layout for this panel. You can also use a grid layout for these subpanels, as you did for the application frame, but this time the grid will have three rows (one for each of the text field and label pairs) and two columns (one for the labels and one for the fields). Also, define a 10-point gap between the components in the grid:

```
setLayout(new GridLayout(3, 2, 10, 10));
```

Now you can create and add the components to the panel. First create a `for` loop named `i` that can iterate three times:

```
for (int i = 0; i < 3; i++) {
    // ...
}
```

Inside this loop, each text field and label will be created and added to a container. First, a text field will be initialized to the string "0" and assigned to the appropriate instance variable:

```
tfield[i] = new JTextField("0");
```

Next, the text field and a label are added to the panel using the String array sent to the SwingColorControls constructor as the text for the labels:

```
add(new JLabel(label[i], JLabel.RIGHT));
add(tfield[i]);
```

This completes the constructor for the subpanel class SwingColorControls, but you will also override getInsets() here to tinker with the panel's layout. Add the inset here as you did in the SwingColorTest class:

```
public Insets getInsets() {
        return new Insets(10, 10, 0, 0);
}
```

Now that a SwingColorControls class has been completed, you can fix the placeholder constructors in SwingColorTest for the subpanel.

The constructor for SwingColorControls that you just created now has two arguments: the SwingColorTest object and an array of strings containing three labels. Replace the RGBcontrols and HSBcontrols placeholder constructors in SwingColorTest so that the array labels are created and used in calls to the SwingColorTest constructor:

```
String[] rgbLabels = { "Red", "Green", "Blue" };
RGBcontrols = new SwingColorControls(this, rgbLabels);
String[] hsbLabels = { "Hue", "Saturation", "Brightness" };
HSBcontrols = new SwingColorControls(this, hsbLabels);
```

The this keyword is used to pass the SwingColorTest object to these constructors.

Note

The number 0 (actually, the string "0") is used for the initial values of all the text fields in this example. For the color black, both the RGB and the HSB values are 0, which is why this assumption can be made. If you want to initialize the application to some other color, you might want to rewrite the SwingColorControls class to use initializer values as well as to initialize labels.

Converting Between sRGB and HSB

At this point, the SwingColorTest application will compile successfully, and you can take a look at the layout. It's common to do this in a programming project, resolving all issues with the interface before spending any time writing code to make the interface function.

This application's main purpose is to convert between sRGB and HSB values, and vice versa. When the value in a text field is changed, the color box updates to the new color, and the value of the fields in the opposite subpanel changes to reflect the new color.

The SwingColorTest class will be made responsible for actually doing the updating when a user has changed a value. A new method will be added to handle this: update().

This update() method takes a single argument: the SwingColorControls instance that contains the changed value. (You will get this argument from event-handling methods in the SwingColorControls object.)

> **Note**
>
> Won't this update() method interfere with the system's update() method? No. Remember, methods can have the same name, but different signatures and definitions. Because this update() has a single argument of type ColorControls, it doesn't interfere with the other version of update().

The update() method is responsible for updating all the panels in the application. To know which panel to update, you need to know which panel changed. You can find out by testing to see whether the argument you got passed from the panel is the same as the subpanels you have stored in the RGBcontrols and HSBcontrols instance variables:

```
void update(SwingColorControls control) {

    if (control == RGBcontrols) {
        // RGB has changed, update HSB
    } else {
        // HSB has changed, update RGB
    }
}
```

This test is the heart of the update() method. Start with the first case—a number has been changed in the RGB text fields. Now, based on these new sRGB values, you have to generate a new Color object and update the values on the HSB panel. You can create a few local variables to hold some basic values in order to reduce the amount of typing you have to do. In particular, the values of the text fields are strings whose values you can get to using the getText() method defined in the JTextField objects of the SwingColorControls object. Because most of the time you'll want to deal with these values as integers in this method, you can get these string values, convert them to integers, and store them in an array of integers, called value. Here's the code to take care of this job:

```
int[] value = new int[3];
for (int i = 0; i < 3; i++) {
    value[i] = Integer.parseInt(control.tfield[i].getText());
    if ((value[i] < 0) || (value[i] > 255)) {
        value[i] = 0;
        control.tfield[i].setText("" + value[i]);
    }
}
```

Each of the values collected from the JTextField objects is checked to see if it is less than 0 or greater than 255 (sRGB and HSB values are represented as integers from 0 to 255). If the value is out of the acceptable range, the text field is set back to its initial value, "0".

While you're defining local variables, you also need one for the new Color object:

```
Color c;
```

Now assume that one of the text fields in the RGB side of the application has changed and add the code to the if part of the update() method. You need to create a new Color object and update the HSB side of the panel. The first part is easy. Given the three sRGB values, you can create a new Color object using these values as arguments to the constructor:

```
c = new Color(value[0], value[1], value[2]);
```

Now you convert the sRGB values to HSB. Standard algorithms can convert an sRGB-based color to an HSB color, but you don't have to look them up. The Color class has a class method called RGBtoHSB() you can use. This method does the work for you—most of it, at least. The RGBtoHSB() method poses two problems, however:

- The RGBtoHSB() method returns an array of the three HSB values, so you have to extract these values from the array.
- The HSB values are measured in floating-point values from 0.0 to 1.0. I prefer to think of HSB values as integers, where the hue is a degree value around a color wheel (0 through 360), and saturation and brightness are percentages from 0 to 100.

Neither of these problems is insurmountable; you just have to add some extra lines of code. Start by calling RGBtoHSB() with the new RGB values you have. The return type of that method is an array of floats, so you create a local variable (HSB) to store the results of the RBGtoHSB() method. (Note that you also need to create and pass in an empty float array as the fourth argument to RGBtoHSB().)

```
float[] HSB = Color.RGBtoHSB(value[0], value[1], value[2],
    (new float[3]));
```

11

Now convert these floating-point values that range from 0.0 to 1.0 to values that range from 0 and 100 (for the saturation and brightness) and 0 to 360 (for the hue) by multiplying the appropriate numbers and reassigning the value back to the array:

```
HSB[0] *= 360;
HSB[1] *= 100;
HSB[2] *= 100;
```

Now you have the numbers you want. The last part of the update puts these values back into the text fields. Of course, these values are still floating-point numbers, so you have to cast them to ints before turning them into strings and storing them:

```
for (int i = 0; i < 3; i++) {
    HSBcontrols.tfield[i].setText(String.valueOf((int)HSB[i]));
```

The next part of the application is the part that updates the sRGB values when a text field on the HSB side has changed. This is the else in the big if-else that defines this method and determines what to update, given a change.

Generating sRGB values from HSB values is actually easier than doing the process the other way around. A class method in the Color class, getHSBColor (), creates a new Color object from three HSB values. After you have a Color object, you can easily pull the RGB values out of there. The catch, of course, is that getHSBColor takes three floating-point arguments, and the values you have are integer values. In the call to getHSBColor, you'll have to cast the integer values from the text fields to floats and divide them by the proper conversion factor. The result of getHSBColor is a Color object. Therefore you can simply assign the object to the c local variable so that you can use it again later:

```
c = Color.getHSBColor((float)value[0] / 360,
    (float)value[1] / 100, (float)value[2] / 100);
```

With the Color object all set, updating the RGB values involves extracting these values from that Color object. The getRed(), getGreen(), and getBlue() methods, defined in the Color class, will do just that job:

```
RGBcontrols.tfield[0].setText(String.valueOf(c.getRed()));
RGBcontrols.tfield[1].setText(String.valueOf(c.getGreen()));
RGBcontrols.tfield[2].setText(String.valueOf(c.getBlue()));
```

Finally, regardless of whether the sRGB or HSB value has changed, you need to update the color box on the left to reflect the new color. Because you have a new Color object stored in the variable c, you can use the setBackground method to change the color. Also note that setBackground doesn't automatically repaint the screen, so fire off a repaint() as well:

```
swatch.setBackground(c);
swatch.repaint();
```

Handling User Events

Three classes are created for this project: SwingColorTest, SwingColorControls, and ExitWindow. SwingColorTest contains the application window and the main() method that is used to set up the window. SwingColorControls, a helper class, is a panel that holds three labels and three text fields used to choose a color. ExitWindow is the helper class used to close down the application when its main window is closed.

All the user input in this program takes place on the color controls—the text fields are used to define sRGB or HSB values.

Because of this, all the event-handling behaviors are added to the SwingColorControls class.

The first thing to do is make the SwingColorControls class handle two kinds of events: action events and focus events. The extends clause should be added to the class declaration statement so that the ActionListener and FocusListener interfaces are implemented. It is shown here:

```
class SwingColorControls extends JPanel
    implements ActionListener, FocusListener {
```

Action and focus listeners must next be added to the three text fields in the class, which are referenced using the tfield array. These listeners must be added after the text fields are created but before they are added to a container. The following statements can be used in a for loop called i that iterates through the tfield array:

```
tfield[i].addFocusListener(this);
tfield[i].addActionListener(this);
```

Finally, you must add all the methods that are defined in the three interfaces this class implements: actionPerformed(ActionEvent), focusLost(FocusEvent), and focusGained(FocusEvent).

The color controls enter a numeric value for a color, and this causes the color to be drawn on a panel. It also causes the other color controls to be updated to reflect the color change.

There are two ways a user can finalize a new color choice—by pressing Enter inside a text field, which generates an action event, or by leaving the field to edit a different field, which generates a focus event.

The following statements compose the actionPerformed() and focusLost() methods that should be added to the class:

```
public void actionPerformed(ActionEvent evt) {
    if (evt.getSource() instanceof JTextField)
        frame.update(this);
}
```

11

```
public void focusLost(FocusEvent evt) {
    frame.update(this);
}
```

One of these, focusGained(), doesn't need to be handled. Because of this, an empty method definition should be added:

```
public void focusGained(FocusEvent evt) { }
```

The event-handling methods added to SwingColorControls call a method in its parent class, update(*SwingColorControls*).

This method doesn't contain any event-handling behavior—it updates the color swatch and all the color controls to reflect a color change.

Listing 11.4 contains the application, including the SwingColorTest, SwingColorControls, and ExitWindow classes.

LISTING 11.4   The Full Text of SwingColorTest.java

```
 1: import java.awt.*;
 2: import java.awt.event.*;
 3: import javax.swing.*;
 4:
 5: public class SwingColorTest extends JFrame {
 6:     SwingColorControls RGBcontrols, HSBcontrols;
 7:     JPanel swatch;
 8:
 9:     public SwingColorTest() {
10:         super("Color Test");
11:
12:         JPanel pane = new JPanel();
13:         pane.setLayout(new GridLayout(1, 3, 5, 15));
14:         swatch = new JPanel();
15:         swatch.setBackground(Color.black);
16:         String[] rgbLabels = { "Red", "Green", "Blue" };
17:         RGBcontrols = new SwingColorControls(this, rgbLabels);
18:         String[] hsbLabels = { "Hue", "Saturation", "Brightness" };
19:         HSBcontrols = new SwingColorControls(this, hsbLabels);
20:         pane.add(swatch);
21:         pane.add(RGBcontrols);
22:         pane.add(HSBcontrols);
23:
24:         setContentPane(pane);
25:     }
26:
27:     public static void main(String[] arguments) {
28:         JFrame frame = new SwingColorTest();
29:
30:         ExitWindow exit = new ExitWindow();
```

```
31:            frame.addWindowListener(exit);
32:
33:            frame.pack();
34:            frame.setVisible(true);
35:        }
36:
37:        public Insets getInsets() {
38:            return new Insets(10, 10, 10, 10);
39:        }
40:
41:        void update(SwingColorControls control) {
42:            Color c;
43:            // get string values from text fields, convert to ints
44:            int[] value = new int[3];
45:            for (int i = 0; i < 3; i++) {
46:                value[i] = Integer.parseInt(control.tfield[i].getText());
47:                if ((value[i] < 0) || (value[i] > 255)) {
48:                    value[i] = 0;
49:                    control.tfield[i].setText("" + value[i]);
50:                }
51:            }
52:            if (control == RGBcontrols) {
53:                // RGB has changed, update HSB
54:                c = new Color(value[0], value[1], value[2]);
55:
56:                // convert RGB values to HSB values
57:                float[] HSB = Color.RGBtoHSB(value[0], value[1], value[2],
58:                    (new float[3]));
59:                HSB[0] *= 360;
60:                HSB[1] *= 100;
61:                HSB[2] *= 100;
62:
63:                // reset HSB fields
64:                for (int i = 0; i < 3; i++) {
65:                    HSBcontrols.tfield[i].setText(String.valueOf((int)HSB[i]));
66:                }
67:            } else {
68:                // HSB has changed, update RGB
69:                c = Color.getHSBColor((float)value[0] / 360,
70:                    (float)value[1] / 100, (float)value[2] / 100);
71:
72:                // reset RGB fields
73:                RGBcontrols.tfield[0].setText(String.valueOf(c.getRed()));
74:                RGBcontrols.tfield[1].setText(String.valueOf(c.getGreen()));
75:                RGBcontrols.tfield[2].setText(String.valueOf(c.getBlue()));
76:            }
77:
78:            // update swatch
79:            swatch.setBackground(c);
80:            swatch.repaint();
81:        }
```

11

LISTING **11.4**   continued

```
 82: }
 83:
 84: class SwingColorControls extends JPanel
 85:     implements ActionListener, FocusListener {
 86:
 87:     SwingColorTest frame;
 88:     JTextField[] tfield = new JTextField[3];
 89:
 90:     SwingColorControls(SwingColorTest parent, String[] label) {
 91:
 92:         frame = parent;
 93:         setLayout(new GridLayout(3, 2, 10, 10));
 94:         for (int i = 0; i < 3; i++) {
 95:             tfield[i] = new JTextField("0");
 96:             tfield[i].addFocusListener(this);
 97:             tfield[i].addActionListener(this);
 98:             add(new JLabel(label[i], JLabel.RIGHT));
 99:             add(tfield[i]);
100:         }
101:     }
102:
103:     public Insets getInsets() {
104:         return new Insets(10, 10, 0, 0);
105:     }
106:
107:     public void actionPerformed(ActionEvent evt) {
108:         if (evt.getSource() instanceof JTextField)
109:             frame.update(this);
110:     }
111:
112:     public void focusLost(FocusEvent evt) {
113:         frame.update(this);
114:     }
115:
116:     public void focusGained(FocusEvent evt) { }
117:
118: }
119:
120: class ExitWindow extends WindowAdapter {
121:     public void windowClosing(WindowEvent e) {
122:         System.exit(0);
123:     }
124: }
```

Summary

Internally, the event-handling system used with Swing is much more sound, and more easily extended to handle new types of user interaction.

Externally, the new system should also make more sense from a programming standpoint. Event handling is added to a program through the same steps:

- A listener interface is added to the class that will contain the event-handling methods.
- A listener is added to each component that will generate the events to handle.
- The methods are added, each with an EventObject class as the only argument to the method.
- Methods of that EventObject class, such as getSource(), are used to learn which component generated the event and what kind of event it was.

Once you know these steps, you can work with each of the different listener interfaces and event classes. You also can learn about new listeners as they are added to Swing with new components.

11

Q&A

Q Can a program's event-handling behavior be put into its own class instead of including it with the code that creates the interface?

A It can, and many programmers will tell you that it's a good way to design your programs. Separating interface design from your event-handling code enables the two to be developed separately—the SwingColorTest application today shows the alternative approach. This makes it easier to maintain the project; related behavior is grouped and isolated from unrelated behavior.

Questions

1. If you use this in a method call such as addActionListener(this), what object is being registered as a listener?

    (a) An adapter class

    (b) The current class

    (c) No class

2. What is the benefit of subclassing an adapter class such as WindowAdapter (which implements the WindowListener interface)?

   (a) You inherit all the behavior of that class.

   (b) The subclass automatically becomes a listener.

   (c) You don't need to implement any WindowListener methods you won't be using.

3. What kind of event is generated when you press Tab to leave a text field?

   (a) FocusEvent

   (b) WindowEvent

   (c) ActionEvent

Answers

1. b. The current class must implement the correct listener interface and the required methods.

2. c. Because most listener interfaces contain more methods than you will need, using an adapter class as a superclass saves the hassle of implementing empty methods just to implement the interface.

3. a. A user interface component loses focus when the user stops editing that component and moves to a different part of the interface.

Exercises

To extend your knowledge of the subjects covered today, try the following exercises:

- Create an application that uses FocusListener to make sure that a text field's value is multiplied by -1 and redisplayed any time a user changes it to a negative value.

- Create a simple calculator that adds the contents of two text fields whenever a button is clicked and displays the result as a label.

Where applicable, exercise solutions are offered on the book's Web site at http://www.java21days.com.

WEEK 2

DAY 12

Color, Fonts, and Graphics

Today you work with Java classes that support graphical features in your programs—color, fonts, and images.

To use graphical features in your programs, you utilize classes of the java.awt and javax.swing packages, which deliver most of Java's visual pizzazz. With these classes you'll draw text and shapes like circles and polygons in an applet. You learn how to use different fonts and colors for the shapes you draw.

Because of the strong support for graphics in the Java class library, you can achieve complex visual effects in relatively few statements. Java2D, a set of classes introduced with Java 2, offers some eye-catching features:

- Anti-aliased objects
- Gradient fill patterns
- Drawing lines of different widths

Graphics Classes

Most of the basic drawing operations are methods defined in the Graphics class, which is part of the java.awt package. Objects of this class represent an environment in which something can be drawn, whether it's an applet window, a section in a graphical user interface, or a printer.

One way to think of an applet is as a canvas for graphical operations. Yesterday, you used the drawString() method to draw text onto an applet. The text's font and color were chosen prior to drawing the characters, the same way an artist would choose a color and a brush before painting.

Text isn't the only thing you can draw using the Graphics class. You can draw lines, ovals, circles, arcs, rectangles, and other polygons.

In an applet, you don't have to create a Graphics object in order to draw something—as you might recall, one of the paint() method's parameters is a Graphics object. This object represents the applet window and its methods are used to draw onto the applet.

The Graphics class is part of the java.awt package, so all applets that draw something must use the import statement to make Graphics available in the program.

Creating a Drawing Surface

Before you can start using the Graphics class, you need something to draw on.

One component that's suitable for this purpose is JPanel in the javax.swing package. This class represents panels in a graphical user interface that can be empty or contain other components.

The following example creates a frame and a panel, and adds the panel to the frame window:

```
JFrame main = new JFrame("Main Menu");
JPanel pane = new JPanel();
main.getContentPane().add(pane);
```

The frame's getContentPane() method returns an object representing the portion of the frame that can contain other components. That object's add() method is called to add the panel to the frame.

Like many other user interface components in Java, JPanel objects have a paintComponent(Graphics) method that is called automatically whenever the component should be redisplayed. The purpose is identical to the paint(Graphics) method in all applets.

By creating a subclass of JPanel, you can override this paintComponent() method and put all of your graphical operations in this method.

Casting a Graphics2D Object

Drawing operations are called on either a Graphics object or a Graphics2D object.

Choosing which class to use depends on whether you'll be using the Java2D graphics features introduced in Java 2. All Java2D graphics operations must be called on a Graphics2D object. Graphics2D is part of the java.awt package.

A Graphics or Graphics2D object represents an area being drawn to—such as an applet window or a frame window. For Java2D, this object must be used to create a new Graphics2D object, as in the following paintComponent() method:

```
public void paintComponent(Graphics comp) {
    Graphics2D comp2D = (Graphics2D)comp;
}
```

The comp2D object in this example was produced via casting.

Creating an Application

Listing 12.1 contains an application that brings all this together and draws the word "Florida" on a panel using the drawString() method to display text.

LISTING 12.1   The Starting Text of Map.java

```
 1: import java.awt.*;
 2: import java.awt.event.*;
 3: import javax.swing.*;
 4:
 5: public class Map extends JFrame {
 6:     public Map() {
 7:         super("Map");
 8:         setSize(350, 350);
 9:         ExitWindow exit = new ExitWindow();
10:         MapPane map = new MapPane();
11:         getContentPane().add(map);
12:         addWindowListener(exit);
13:     }
14:
15:     public static void main(String[] arguments) {
16:         Map frame = new Map();
17:         frame.show();
18:     }
19:
20: }
```

12

LISTING 12.1   continued

```
21:
22: class MapPane extends JPanel {
23:     public void paintComponent(Graphics comp) {
24:         Graphics2D comp2D = (Graphics2D)comp;
25:         comp2D.drawString("Florida", 185, 75);
26:     }
27: }
28:
29: class ExitWindow extends WindowAdapter {
30:     public void windowClosing(WindowEvent e) {
31:         System.exit(0);
32:     }
33: }
```

This application uses the comp2D object's drawString() method to draw the string "Florida" at the coordinates 185,75 (see Figure 12.1).

FIGURE 12.1

Drawing text in an application.

All the basic drawing commands you learn about today will be Graphics methods that are called within a component's paintComponent() method. This is an ideal place for all drawing operations because paintComponent() is automatically called anytime the component needs to be redisplayed. If another program's window overlaps the component, and it needs to be redrawn, putting all the drawing operations in paintComponent() makes sure that no part of the drawing is left out.

> **Tip**
>
> All the drawing operations you use today can be employed in an applet's paint() method. Applets are windows that can contain objects and have many things in common with panels.

Continue to add to the Map application with each of the drawing methods covered in this section.

The Graphics Coordinate System

As in drawString(), all the drawing methods have arguments that indicate x,y coordinates. Some take more than one set of coordinates, such as a line, which has an x,y coordinate to identify its starting point and another x,y coordinate for its endpoint.

Java's coordinate system uses pixels as its unit of measure. The origin coordinate 0,0 is in the upper-left corner of the Applet window. The value of x coordinates increases to the right of 0,0, and y coordinates increase in a downward direction. This differs from other drawing systems in which the 0,0 origin is at the lower left and y values increase in an upward direction.

All pixel values are integers—you can't use decimal numbers to display something between integer values.

Figure 12.2 depicts Java's graphical coordinate system visually with the origin at 0,0. Two of the points of a rectangle are at 20,20 and 60,60.

FIGURE 12.2

The Java graphics coordinate system.

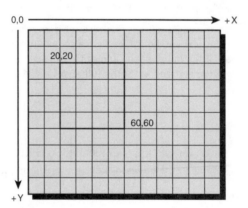

12

Drawing and Filling

Two kinds of drawing methods are available for many of the shapes you can draw onto a component: draw methods, which draw an outline of the object, and fill methods, which fill in the object with the current color. In each type of method, the outline of the object also is drawn with the current color.

Note

You can also draw bitmap graphics files, such as GIF and JPG files, by using the Image class. You learn about this tomorrow.

Lines

The drawLine() method is used to draw a line between two points. The method takes four arguments: the x and y coordinates of the starting point and the x and y coordinates of the ending point, as follows:

```
drawLine(x1, y1, x2, y2);
```

This method draws a line from the point (x1, y1) to the point (x2, y2). The width of the line is fixed at 1 pixel.

Add the following statement to the Map application's paintComponent() method:

```
comp2D..drawLine(185, 80, 222, 80);
```

This draws a line from 185,80 to 222,80—an underline under the text "Florida".

Note

To prevent the whiplash that might result from repeatedly bouncing between this text and your Java source code editor, the final version of Map.java is listed in full at the end of this section. Until then, you can follow along with the text and enter the full Java code at one time.

Rectangles

There are Graphics methods for two kinds of rectangles: normal rectangles and those with rounded corners (similar to the edges of keys on most computer keyboards).

You can draw both types of rectangles in outline form or filled with the current color.

To draw a normal rectangle, use the drawRect() method for outlines and the fillRect() method for filled shapes.

Both of these methods take four arguments:

- The x and y coordinates of the rectangle's top-left corner
- The width of the rectangle
- The height of the rectangle

Add the following statement to the Map application:

```
comp2D.drawRect(2, 2, 335, 320);
```

This adds a rectangle outline just inside the outer edges of the application frame. If the `fillRect()` method had been used instead, a solid rectangle would have filled most of the application's frame and overwritten the underlined text `Florida`.

Rectangles with rounded corners require the `drawRoundRect()` and `fillRoundRect()` methods. They take the same first four arguments that regular rectangles take, with two arguments added at the end.

These last two arguments define the width and height of the area where corners are rounded. The bigger the area, the more round the corners. You can even make a rectangle look like a circle or an oval by making these arguments large enough.

Figure 12.3 shows several examples of rectangles with rounded corners. One rectangle has a width of 30 and a height of 10 for each rounded corner. Another has a width of 20 and a height of 20, and it looks more like a circle than a rectangle.

FIGURE 12.3

Rectangles with rounded corners.

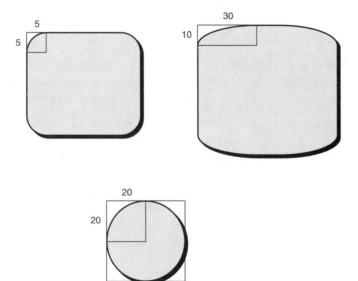

Add the following statement to the Map application's `paintComponent()` method:

```
comp2D.drawRoundRect(182, 61, 43, 24, 10, 8);
```

This draws a rounded rectangle at the coordinates 182,61 with a width of 43 pixels and a height of 24. The rectangular area of each rounded corner is 10 pixels wide and 8 tall. The result is shown in Figure 12.4, a close-up of a portion of the application.

FIGURE 12.4

Adding a rounded
rectangle to the
application.

Polygons

Polygons can be drawn with the `drawPolygon()` and `fillPolygon()` methods.

To draw a polygon, you need x,y coordinates for each point on the polygon. Polygons can be thought of as a series of lines that are connected to each other—one line is drawn from starting point to end point, that end point is used to start a new line, and so on.

You can specify these coordinates two ways:

- As a pair of integer arrays, one holding all the x coordinates and one holding all the y coordinates

- As a `Polygon` object that is created using an integer array of x coordinates and an integer array of y coordinates

The second method listed previously is more flexible because it enables points to be added individually to a polygon before it is drawn.

In addition to the x and y coordinates, you must specify the number of points in the polygon. You cannot specify more x,y coordinates than you have points, or more points than you have x,y coordinates set up for. A compiler error will result in either case.

To create a `Polygon` object, the first step is to create an empty polygon with a `new Polygon()` statement such as the following:

```
Polygon poly = new Polygon();
```

As an alternative, you can create a polygon from a set of points using integer arrays. This requires a call to the `Polygon(int[], int[], int)` constructor, which specifies the array of x points, array of y points, and the number of total points. The following example shows the use of this constructor:

```
int x[] = { 10, 20, 30, 40, 50 };
int y[] = { 15, 25, 35, 45, 55 };
int points = x.length;
Polygon poly = new Polygon(x, y, points);
```

After a `Polygon` object has been created, you can add points to it using the object's `addPoint()` method. This takes x,y coordinates as arguments and adds the point to the polygon. The following is an example:

```
poly.addPoint(60, 65);
```

When you have a Polygon object that has all the points it needs, you can draw it with the drawPolygon() or fillPolygon() methods. These take only one argument—the Polygon object, as shown here:

```
comp2D.drawPolygon(poly);
```

If you use drawPolygon() under Java 1.02, you can close off the polygon by making its last x,y coordinate the same as its first. Otherwise, the polygon will be open on one side.

The fillPolygon() method automatically closes off the polygon without requiring matching points.

Caution

The behavior of drawPolygon() changed after version 1.0 of Java. In version 2, drawPolygon() automatically closes off a polygon the same way fillPolygon() does. If you want to create an open-edged polygon with those versions of the language, you can use the drawPolyline() method. It works just like drawPolygon() worked under Java 1.0.

Add the following statements to the paintComponent() method of the Map application to see polygons in action:

```
int x[] = { 10, 234, 253, 261, 333, 326, 295, 259, 205, 211,
    195, 191, 120, 94, 81, 12, 10 };
int y[] = { 12, 15, 25, 71, 209, 278, 310, 274, 188, 171, 174,
    118, 56, 68, 49, 37, 12 };
int pts = x.length;
Polygon poly = new Polygon(x, y, pts);
comp2D.drawPolygon(poly);
```

12

Figure 12.5 shows what the Map application looks like with the polygon added to everything else already being drawn.

FIGURE 12.5

Adding a polygon to the application.

Ovals

The drawOval() and fillOval() methods are used to draw circles and ovals.

These methods take four arguments:

- The oval's x and y coordinates
- The oval's width and height, which are the same size on circles

Because an oval doesn't have any corners, you might be wondering what the x,y coordinate refers to. Ovals are handled in the same fashion as the corners of rounded rectangles. The x,y coordinate is at the upper-left corner of the area in which the oval is drawn, and will be to the left and above the actual oval itself.

Return to the Map application and add the following statements:

```
comp2D.fillOval(235,140,15,15);
comp2D.fillOval(225,130,15,15);
comp2D.fillOval(245,130,15,15);
```

These are fill methods rather than draw methods, so they create three black circles connected together at a spot in the center of the map of Florida.

Arcs

Of all the drawing operations, arcs are the most complex to construct. An arc is part of an oval, and is implemented in Java as an oval that is partially drawn.

Arcs are drawn with the drawArc() and fillArc() methods, which take six arguments:

- The oval's x,y coordinates
- The oval's width and height
- The angle at which to start the arc
- The number of degrees traveled by the arc

The first four arguments are the same as those for an oval and function in the same manner.

The arc's starting angle ranges from 0 to 359 degrees in a counterclockwise direction. On a circular oval, 0 degrees is the same as the 3 o'clock, 90 degrees is 12 o'clock, 180 degrees is 9 o'clock, and 270 degrees is 6 o'clock.

The number of degrees traveled by an arc ranges from 0 to 359 degrees in a counterclockwise direction, and 0 to –359 degrees in a clockwise direction.

Figure 12.6 shows how the last two arguments are calculated.

FIGURE 12.6

Measuring an arc.

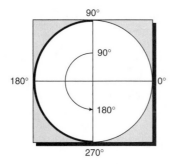

Filled arcs are drawn as if they were sections of a pie; instead of joining the two end-points, both endpoints are joined to the center of the arc's oval.

The following is an example of a drawArc() method call:

```
comp2D.drawArc(20, 25, 315, 150, 5, -190);
```

This statement draws an arc of an oval with the coordinates 20,25, a width of 315 pixels, and a height of 150 pixels. The arc begins at the 5-degree mark and travels 190 degrees in a clockwise direction. The arc is shown in an applet in Figure 12.7.

FIGURE 12.7

An arc.

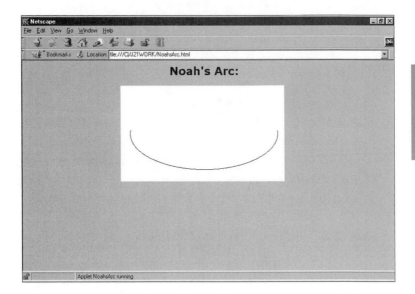

12

To iron out the last wrinkle in the Map application, a bunch of little arcs with four arguments that do not change will be drawn:

- Each arc's oval will have a width and height of 10 pixels, making the ovals circular.
- Each arc will begin at 0 degrees and head clockwise for 180 degrees, making them half circles.

The arc's x,y coordinates will change, and two for loops will cycle through a range of x and y values.

Add the following statements to the Map application's paintComponent() method:

```
for (int ax = 50; ax < 150; ax += 10)
    for (int ay = 120; ay < 320 ; ay += 10)
        comp2D.drawArc(ax, ay, 10, 10, 0, -180);
```

Putting one for loop inside another might appear confusing. Here are the first six x,y coordinates that are created by the loop:

50,120

50,130

50,140

50,150

50,160

50,170

As you can see, the x coordinate—specified by ax—does not change. It won't change until the entire ay loop has run its course. When that happens, ax increases by 10 and the ay loop runs again in full.

Compile the Map application to see what effect these loops produce by drawing a bunch of small half circles. Listing 12.2 shows the full, final source code for Map.java, including all the drawing statements that have been covered during this section.

LISTING 12.2   The Full, Final Text of Map.java

```
1: import java.awt.*;
2: import java.awt.event.*;
3: import javax.swing.*;
4:
5: public class Map extends JFrame {
```

```
 6:     public Map() {
 7:         super("Map");
 8:         setSize(350, 350);
 9:         ExitWindow exit = new ExitWindow();
10:         MapPane map = new MapPane();
11:         getContentPane().add(map);
12:         addWindowListener(exit);
13:     }
14:
15:     public static void main(String[] arguments) {
16:         Map frame = new Map();
17:         frame.show();
18:     }
19:
20: }
21:
22: class MapPane extends JPanel {
23:     public void paintComponent(Graphics comp) {
24:         Graphics2D comp2D = (Graphics2D)comp;
25:         comp2D.drawString("Florida", 185, 75);
26:         comp2D.drawLine(185, 80, 222, 80);
27:         comp2D.drawRect(2, 2, 335, 320);
28:         comp2D.drawRoundRect(182, 61, 43, 24, 10, 8);
29:         int x[] = { 10, 234, 253, 261, 333, 326, 295, 259, 205, 211,
30:             195, 191, 120, 94, 81, 12, 10 };
31:         int y[] = { 12, 15, 25, 71, 209, 278, 310, 274, 188, 171, 174,
32:             118, 56, 68, 49, 37, 12 };
33:         int pts = x.length;
34:         Polygon poly = new Polygon(x, y, pts);
35:         comp2D.drawPolygon(poly);
36:         comp2D.fillOval(235,140,15,15);
37:         comp2D.fillOval(225,130,15,15);
38:         comp2D.fillOval(245,130,15,15);
39:         for (int ax = 50; ax < 150; ax += 10)
40:             for (int ay = 120; ay < 320 ; ay += 10)
41:                 comp2D.drawArc(ax, ay, 10, 10, 0, -180);
42:     }
43: }
44:
45: class ExitWindow extends WindowAdapter {
46:     public void windowClosing(WindowEvent e) {
47:         System.exit(0);
48:     }
49: }
```

12

Figure 12.8 shows the Map application that has been painted with Java's basic drawing methods.

FIGURE 12.8

The Map *application.*

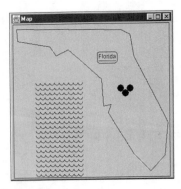

Although no cartographer would fear for his job security at this display of mapmaking, the application combines a sampling of most drawing features that are available through the Graphics class. A program like this could be expanded using Font and Color objects, and the drawing operations could be rearranged to improve the final product.

Copying and Clearing

The Graphics class also includes some cut-and-paste functionality:

- The copyArea() method, which copies a rectangular region of a window onto another region of the window
- The clearRect() method, which clears a rectangular region of a window

The copyArea() method takes six arguments:

- The x,y coordinates of the rectangular region to copy
- The width and the height of that region
- The horizontal and vertical distance, in pixels, to move away from the region before displaying a copy of it

The following statement copies a 100×100 pixel region to an area 50 pixels to the right and 25 pixels down, using a Graphics object called screen:

```
screen.copyArea(0, 0, 100, 100, 50, 25);
```

The clearRect() method takes the same four arguments as the drawRect() and fillRect() methods, and it fills the rectangular region with the current background color of a window. You learn how to set the background color later today.

If you want to clear an entire window, you can determine the window's size via the size() method. This returns a Dimension object, which has width and height variables; they represent the applet's dimensions.

To clear the entire window, you can use the size() method, which returns a Dimension object representing the applet's width and height. You then can get to the actual values for width and height by using the width and height instance variables, as in the following statement:

```
screen.clearRect(0, 0, getSize().width, getSize().height);
```

Note

The getsize() method had a different name in Java 1.0: size(). Both methods return the same thing.

Text and Fonts

java.awt.Font class objects are used in order to use the drawString() method with different fonts. Font objects represent the name, style, and point size of a font. Another class, FontMetrics, provides methods to determine the size of the characters being displayed with a specified font, which can be used for things like formatting and centering text.

Creating Font Objects

A Font object is created by sending three arguments to its constructor:

- The font's name
- The font's style
- The font's point size

The name of the font can be a specific font name such as Arial or Garamond Old Style, and it will be used if the font is present on the system on which the Java program is running.

There also are names that can be used to select Java's built-in fonts: TimesRoman, Helvetica, Courier, Dialog, and DialogInput.

Caution

For Java 2, the font names TimesRoman, Helvetica, and Courier should be replaced with serif, sanserif, and monospaced, respectively. These generic names specify the style of the font without naming a specific font family used to represent it. This is a better choice because some font families might not be present on all implementations of Java, so the best choice for the selected font style (such as serif) can be used.

12

Three Font styles can be selected by using the constants Font.PLAIN, Font.BOLD, and Font.ITALIC. These constants are integers, and you can add them to combine effects.

The last argument of the Font() constructor is the point size of the font.

The following statement creates a 24-point Dialog font that is bold and italicized.

```
Font f = new Font("Dialog", Font.BOLD + Font.ITALIC, 24);
```

Drawing Characters and Strings

To set the current font, the Graphics class' setFont() method is used with a Font object. The following statement uses a Font object named ft:

```
screen.setFont(ft);
```

Text can be displayed in a window using the drawString() methods. This method uses the currently selected font; it uses the default if no font has been selected. A new current font can be set at any time using setFont().

The following paintComponent() method creates a new Font object, sets the current font to that object, and draws the string "I'm very font of you." at the coordinates 10,100.

```
public void paintComponent(Graphics comp) {
    Graphics2D comp2D = (Graphics2D)comp;
    Font f = new Font("TimesRoman", Font.PLAIN, 72);
    comp2D.setFont(f);
    comp2D.drawString("I'm very font of you.", 10, 100);
}
```

The last two arguments to the drawString() method are x and y coordinates. The x value is the start of the leftmost edge of the text, and y is the baseline for the entire string.

Finding Information About a Font

The FontMetrics class can be used for detailed information about the current font, such as the width or height of characters it can display.

To use this class' methods, a FontMetrics object must be created using the getFontMetrics() method. The method takes a single argument: a Font object.

Table 12.1 shows some of the information you can find using font metrics. All these methods should be called on a FontMetrics object.

TABLE 12.1 Font Metrics Methods

Method Name	Action
stringWidth(String)	Given a string, returns the full width of that string in pixels
charWidth(char)	Given a character, returns the width of that character
getHeight()	Returns the total height of the font

Listing 12.3 shows how the Font and FontMetrics classes can be used. The SoLong applet displays a string at the center of the Applet window, using FontMetrics to measure the string's width using the current font.

LISTING 12.3 The Full Text of SoLong.java

```
 1: import java.awt.*;
 2:
 3: public class SoLong extends javax.swing.JApplet {
 4:
 5:     public void paint(Graphics screen) {
 6:         Graphics screen2D = (Graphics2D)screen;
 7:         Font f = new Font("monospaced", Font.BOLD, 18);
 8:         FontMetrics fm = getFontMetrics(f);
 9:         screen2D.setFont(f);
10:         String s = "So long, and thanks for all the fish.";
11:         int x = (getSize().width - fm.stringWidth(s)) / 2;
12:         int y = getSize().height / 2;
13:         screen2D.drawString(s, x, y);
14:     }
15: }
```

Listing 12.4 contains an HTML document that loads two copies of the SoLong applet with different sized windows.

LISTING 12.4 The Full Text of SoLong.html

```
1: <div align="Center">
2: <p>
3: <applet code="SoLong.class" height="150" width="425">
4: </applet>
5: <p>
6: <applet code="SoLong.class" height="150" width="550">
7: </applet>
8: </div>
```

Figure 12.9 shows two copies of the SoLong applet on a Web page, each with windows of different sizes.

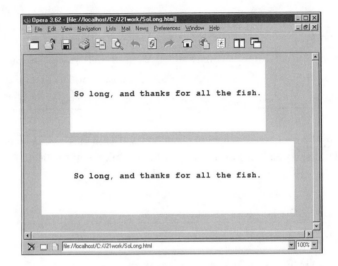

FIGURE **12.9**

Two copies of the
SoLong *applet.*

The getSize() method in lines 11 and 12 should be replaced with size() if you're writing a Java 10 applet. Determining the applet window's size within the applet is preferable to defining an exact size because it's more adaptable. You can change the applet's HTML code on the Web page without changing the program, and it will still work successfully.

Color

The Color and ColorSpace classes of the java.awt package can be used to make your applets and applications more colorful. With these classes you can set the current color for use in drawing operations, as well as the background color of an applet and other windows. You also can translate a color from one color-description system into another.

By default, Java uses colors according to a color-description system called sRGB. In this system, a color is described by the amount of red, green, and blue it contains—that's what the R, G, and B stand for. Each of the three components can be represented as an integer between 0 and 255. Black is 0,0,0—the complete absence of any red, green, or blue. White is 255,255,255—the maximum amount of all three. You also can represent sRGB values using three floating-point numbers ranging from 0 to 1.0. Java can represent millions of colors between the two extremes using sRGB.

A color-description system is called a *color space*, and sRGB is only one such space. There is also CMYK, a system used by printers that describes colors by the amount of cyan, magenta, yellow, and black they contain. Java 1.2 supports the use of any color space desired, as long as a ColorSpace object is used that defines the description system. You also can convert from any color space to sRGB, and vice versa.

Java's internal representation of colors using sRGB is just one color space that's being used in a program. An output device such as a monitor or printer also has its own color space.

When you display or print something of a designated color, the output device might not support the designated color. In this circumstance, a different color will be substituted or a *dithering* pattern will be used to approximate the unavailable color. This happens frequently on the World Wide Web, when an unavailable color is replaced by a dithering pattern of two or more colors that approximate the missing color.

The practical reality of color management is that the color you designated with sRGB will not be available on all output devices. If you need more precise control of the color, you can use ColorSpace and other classes in the java.awt.color package introduced in Java 2.

For most programs, the built-in use of sRGB to define colors will be sufficient.

Using Color Objects

To set the current drawing color, either a Color object must be created that represents it, or you must use one of the standard colors available from the Color class.

There are two ways to call the Color constructor method to create a color:

- Using three integers that represent the sRGB value of the desired color
- Using three floating-point numbers that represent the desired sRGB value

You can specify a color's sRGB value using either three int or float values. The following statements show examples of each:

```
Color c1 = new Color(0.807F,1F,0F);

Color c2 = new Color(255,204,102);
```

The c1 object describes a neon green color and c2 is butterscotch.

12

Note
> It's easy to confuse floating-point literals like 0F and 1F with hexadecimal numbers, which were discussed on Day 3, "The ABCs of Java." Colors are often expressed in hexadecimal, such as when a background color is set up for a Web page using the HTML <BODY> tag. None of the Java classes and methods you work with take hexadecimal arguments, so when you see a literal such as 1F or 0F, you're dealing with floating-point numbers.

Testing and Setting the Current Colors

The current color for drawing is designated by using the Graphics class's setColor() method. This method must be called on the Graphics or Graphics2D object that represents the area you're drawing to.

One way to set the color is to use one of the standard colors available as class variables in the Color class.

These colors use the following Color variables (with sRGB values indicated within parentheses):

black (0,0,0)	magenta (255,0,255)
blue (0,0,255)	orange (255,200,0)
cyan (0,255,255)	pink (255,175,175)
darkGray (64,64,64)	red (255,0,0)
gray (128,128,128)	white (255,255,255)
green (0,255,0)	yellow (255,255,0)
lightGray (192,192,192)	

The following statement sets the current color for the comp2D object using one of the standard class variables:

```
comp2D.setColor(Color.pink);
```

If you have created a Color object, it can be set in a similar fashion:

```
Color brush = new Color(255,204,102);
comp2D.setColor(brush);
```

After you set the current color, all drawing operations will occur in that color.

You can set the background color for a component such as an applet window or frame by calling the component's setBackground() and setForeground() methods.

The setBackground() method sets the component's background color. It takes a single argument, a Color object:

```
setBackground(Color.white);
```

There is also a setForeground() method that is called on user-interface components instead of Graphics objects. It works the same as setColor(), but changes the color of an interface component such as a button or a window.

You can use `setForeground()` in the `init()` method to set the color for drawing operations. This color is used until another color is chosen with either `setForeground()` or `setColor()`.

If you want to find out what the current color is, you can use the `getColor()` method on a `Graphics` object, or the `getForeground()` or `getBackground()` methods of the component.

The following statement sets the current color of `comp2D`—a `Graphics2D` object—to the same color as an component's background:

```
comp2D.setColor(getBackground());
```

Advanced Graphics Operations Using Java2D

One of the enhancements offered with Java 2 is Java2D, a set of classes for offering high-quality 2D graphics, images, and text in your programs. The Java2D classes extend the capabilities of existing `java.awt` classes that handle graphics, such as those you have learned about today. They don't replace the existing classes though—you can continue to use the other classes and programs that implement them.

Java2D features include the following:

- Special fill patterns such as gradients and patterns
- Strokes that define the width and style of a drawing stroke
- Anti-aliasing to smooth edges of drawn objects

User and Device Coordinate Spaces

One of the concepts introduced with Java2D is the difference between an output device's coordinate space and the coordinate space you refer to when drawing an object.

NEW TERM *Coordinate space* is any 2D area that can be described using x,y coordinates.

For all drawing operations up to this point and all operations prior to Java 2, the only coordinate space used was the device coordinate space. You specified the x,y coordinates of an output surface such as an Applet window, and those coordinates were used to draw lines, text, and other elements.

Java2D requires a second coordinate space that you refer to when creating an object and actually drawing it. This is called the *user coordinate space*.

Before any 2D drawing has occurred in a program, the device space and user space have the 0,0 coordinate in the same place—the upper-left corner of the drawing area.

12

The user space's 0,0 coordinate can move as a result of the 2D drawing operations being conducted. The x and y axes even can shift because of a 2D rotation. You learn more about the two different coordinate systems as you work with Java2D.

Specifying the Rendering Attributes

The next step in 2D drawing is to specify how a drawn object will be rendered. Drawings that are not 2D can only select one attribute: color. 2D offers a wide range of attributes for designating color, including line width, fill patterns, transparency, and many other features.

2D Colors

Colors are specified using the setColor() method, which works the same as the Graphics method of the same name. The following is an example:

```
comp2D.setColor(Color.black);
```

> **Caution**
> Although some of the 2D methods work the same as their non-2D counter-parts, they must be called on a Graphics2D object in order to use Java2D's capabilities.

Fill Patterns

Fill patterns control how a drawn object will be filled in. With Java2D, you can use a solid color, gradient fill, texture, or a pattern of your own devising.

A fill pattern is defined by using the setPaint() method of Graphics2D with a Paint object as its only argument. Any class that can be a fill pattern, including GradientPaint, TexturePaint, and Color, can implement the Paint interface. The third might surprise you, but using a Color object with setPaint() is the same thing as filling using a solid color as the pattern.

 A *gradient fill* is a gradual shift from one color at one coordinate point to another color at a different coordinate point. The shift can occur once between the points, which is called an *acyclic gradient*, or it can happen repeatedly, which is a *cyclic gradient*.

Figure 12.10 shows examples of acyclic and cyclic gradients between white and a darker color. The arrows indicate the points that the colors shift between.

FIGURE 12.10

Acyclic and cyclic gradient shifts.

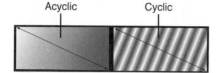

Acyclic   Cyclic

The coordinate points in a gradient do not refer directly to points on the Graphics2D object being drawn onto. Instead, they refer to user space and can even be outside the object being filled with a gradient.

Figure 12.11 illustrates this. Both rectangles on the applet are filled using the same GradientPaint object as a guide. One way to think of a gradient pattern is as a piece of clothing fabric that has been spread out over a flat surface. The shapes being filled with a gradient are the dress patterns cut from the fabric, and more than one pattern can be cut from the same piece of cloth.

FIGURE 12.11

Two rectangles using the same GradientPaint.

A call to the GradientPaint constructor method takes the following format:

```
GradientPaint(x1, y1, color1, x2, y2, color2);
```

The point x1,y1 is where the color represented by color1 begins, and x2,y2 is where the shift ends at color2.

If you want to use a cyclic gradient shift, an extra argument is added at the end:

```
GradientPaint(x1, y1, color1, x2, y2, color2, true);
```

The last argument is a Boolean value that is true for a cyclic shift. A false argument can be used for acyclic shifts, or you can leave this argument off entirely—acyclic shifts are the default behavior.

After you have created a GradientPaint object, you set it as the current paint attribute by using the setPaint() method. The following statements create and select a gradient:

```
GradientPaint pat = new GradientPaint(0f,0f,Color.white,
    100f,45f,Color.blue);
comp2D.setPaint(pat);
```

12

All subsequent drawing operations to the comp2D object will use this fill pattern until another one is chosen.

Setting a Drawing Stroke

As you have learned, the lines drawn in all non-2D graphics operations are 1 pixel wide. Java2D adds the capability to vary the width of the drawing line by using the setStroke() method with a BasicStroke.

A simple BasicStroke constructor takes three arguments:

- A float value representing the line width, with 1.0 as the norm
- An int value determining the style of cap decoration drawn at the end of a line
- An int value determining the style of juncture between two line segments

NEW TERM The endcap- and juncture-style arguments use BasicStroke class variables. *Endcap* styles apply to the end of lines that do not connect to other lines. *Juncture* styles apply to the ends of lines that join other lines.

Possible endcap styles are CAP_BUTT for no endpoints, CAP_ROUND for circles around each endpoint, and CAP_SQUARE for squares. Figure 12.12 shows each endcap style. As you can see, the only visible difference between the CAP_BUTT and CAP_SQUARE styles is that CAP_SQUARE is longer because of the added square endcap.

FIGURE 12.12

Endpoint cap styles.

CAP_BUTT   CAP_ROUND   CAP_SQUARE

Possible juncture styles include JOIN_MITER, which joins segments by extending their outer edges, JOIN_ROUND, which rounds off a corner between two segments, and JOIN_BEVEL, which joins segments with a straight line. Figure 12.13 shows examples of each juncture style.

FIGURE 12.13

Endpoint juncture styles.

JOIN_MITER   JOIN_ROUND   JOIN_BEVEL

The following statements create a BasicStroke object and make it the current stroke:

```
BasicStroke pen = BasicStroke(2.0f,
    BasicStroke.CAP_BUTT,
    BasicStroke.JOIN_ROUND);
comp2D.setStroke(pen);
```

The stroke has a width of 2 pixels, plain endpoints, and rounded segment corners.

Creating Objects to Draw

After you have created a Graphics2D object and specified the rendering attributes, the final two steps are to create the object and draw it.

Drawn objects in Java2D are created by defining them as geometric shapes using the java.awt.geom package classes. You can draw each of the things created earlier today, including lines, rectangles, ellipses, arcs, and polygons.

The Graphics2D class does not have different methods for each of the shapes you can draw. Instead, you define the shape and use it as an argument to draw() or fill() methods.

Lines

Lines are created using the Line2D.Float class. This class takes four arguments: the x,y coordinates of one endpoint followed by the x,y coordinates of the other. Here's an example:

```
Line2D.Float ln = new Line2D.Float(60F,5F,13F,28F);
```

This statement creates a line between 60,5 and 13,28. Note that an F is used with the literals sent as arguments—otherwise, the Java compiler would assume that they are integers.

Rectangles

Rectangles are created by using the Rectangle2D.Float or Rectangle2D.Double classes. The difference between the two is that one takes float arguments and the other takes double arguments.

Rectangle2D.Float takes four arguments: x coordinate, y coordinate, width, and height. The following is an example:

```
Rectangle2D.Float rc = new Rectangle2D.Float(10F,13F,40F,20F);
```

This creates a rectangle at 10,13 that is 40 pixels wide and 20 pixels tall.

Ellipses

NEW TERM Oval objects are called *ellipses* in Java2D, and they can be created with the Ellipse2D.Float class. It takes four arguments: x coordinate, y coordinate, width, and height.

The following statement creates an ellipse at 113,25 with a width of 22 pixels and a height of 40 pixels:

```
Ellipse2D.Float ee = new Ellipse2D.Float(113,25,22,40);
```

12

Arcs

Arcs are created with the `Arc2D.Float` class. They are created in a similar fashion to the non-2D counterpart, but there's an extra feature: You can define how the arc is closed.

`Arc2D.Float` takes seven arguments. The first four apply to the ellipse that the arc is a part of: x coordinate, y coordinate, width, and height. The last three arguments are the starting degree of the arc, the number of degrees it travels, and an integer describing how it is closed.

The number of degrees traveled by the arc is specified in a counterclockwise direction by using positive numbers. This is the opposite of the way a non-2D arc is handled.

The last argument uses one of three class variables: `Arc2D.OPEN` for an unclosed arc, `Arc2D.CHORD` to connect the arc's endpoints with a straight line, and `Arc2D.PIE` to connect the arc to the center of the ellipses like a pie slice. Figure 12.14 shows each of these styles.

FIGURE 12.14

Arc closure styles.

Arc2D.OPEN   Arc2D.CHORD   Arc2D.PIE

> **Note**
>
> The `Arc2D.OPEN` close style does not apply to filled arcs. A filled arc that has `Arc2D.OPEN` as its style will be closed using the same style as `Arc2D.CHORD`.

The following statement creates an `Arc2D.Float` object:

```
Arc2D.Float = new Arc2D.Float(27,22,42,30,33,90,Arc2D.PIE);
```

This creates an arc for an oval at 27,22 that is 42 pixels wide and 30 pixels tall. The arc begins at 33 degrees, extends 90 degrees in a clockwise direction, and will be closed like a pie slice.

Polygons

Polygons are created in Java2D by defining each movement from one point on the polygon to another. A polygon can be formed out of straight lines, quadratic curves, and bezier curves.

The movements to create a polygon are defined as a `GeneralPath` object, which also is part of the `java.awt.geom` package.

A GeneralPath object can be created without any arguments, as shown here:

```
GeneralPath polly = new GeneralPath();
```

The moveTo() method of GeneralPath is used to create the first point on the polygon. The following statement would be used if you wanted to start polly at the coordinates 5,0:

```
polly.moveTo(5f, 0f);
```

After creating the first point, the lineTo() method is used to create lines that end at a new point. This method takes two arguments: the x and y coordinates of the new point.

The following statements add three lines to the polly object:

```
polly.lineTo(205f, 0f);
polly.lineTo(205f, 90f);
polly.lineTo(5f, 90f);
```

The lineTo() and moveTo() methods require float arguments to specify coordinate points.

If you want to close a polygon, the closePath() method is used without any arguments, as shown here:

```
polly.closePath();
```

This method closes a polygon by connecting the current point with the point specified by the most recent moveTo() method. You can close a polygon without this method by using a lineTo() method that connects to the original point.

Once you have created an open or closed polygon, you can draw it like any other shape using the draw() and fill() methods. The polly object is a rectangle with points at 5,0, 205,0, 205,90, and 5,90.

Drawing Objects

After you have defined the rendering attributes, such as color and line width, and have created the object to be drawn, you're ready to draw something in all its 2D glory.

All drawn objects use the same Graphics2D class's methods: draw() for outlines and fill() for filled objects. These take an object as their only argument.

Strings in Java2D are drawn using the drawString() method. This takes three arguments: the String object to draw and its x,y coordinates. As with all coordinates in Java2D, floating-point numbers must be specified instead of integers.

12

A 2D Drawing Example

Earlier today you created a map of Florida using the drawing methods that are available through the Graphics class. The next project you create is a revised version of that map, which uses 2D drawing techniques and implements the program as an applet.

Listing 12.5 contains the Map2D applet. It's a longer program than many in this book because 2D requires more statements to accomplish a drawing operation.

LISTING 12.5   The Full Text of Map2D.java

```
 1: import java.awt.*;
 2: import java.awt.geom.*;
 3:
 4: public class Map2D extends javax.swing.JApplet {
 5:     public void paint(Graphics screen) {
 6:         Graphics2D screen2D = (Graphics2D)screen;
 7:         setBackground(Color.blue);
 8:         // Draw waves
 9:         screen2D.setColor(Color.white);
10:         BasicStroke pen = new BasicStroke(2F,
11:             BasicStroke.CAP_BUTT, BasicStroke.JOIN_ROUND);
12:         screen2D.setStroke(pen);
13:         for (int ax = 10; ax < 340; ax += 10)
14:             for (int ay = 30; ay < 340 ; ay += 10) {
15:                 Arc2D.Float wave = new Arc2D.Float(ax, ay,
16:                     10, 10, 0, -180, Arc2D.OPEN);
17:                 screen2D.draw(wave);
18:             }
19:         // Draw Florida
20:         GradientPaint gp = new GradientPaint(0F,0F,Color.green,
21:             50F,50F,Color.orange,true);
22:         screen2D.setPaint(gp);
23:         GeneralPath fl = new GeneralPath();
24:         fl.moveTo(10F,12F);
25:         fl.lineTo(234F,15F);
26:         fl.lineTo(253F,25F);
27:         fl.lineTo(261F,71F);
28:         fl.lineTo(344F,209F);
29:         fl.lineTo(336F,278F);
30:         fl.lineTo(295F,310F);
31:         fl.lineTo(259F,274F);
32:         fl.lineTo(205F,188F);
33:         fl.lineTo(211F,171F);
34:         fl.lineTo(195F,174F);
35:         fl.lineTo(191F,118F);
36:         fl.lineTo(120F,56F);
37:         fl.lineTo(94F,68F);
38:         fl.lineTo(81F,49F);
```

```
39:        fl.lineTo(12F,37F);
40:        fl.closePath();
41:        screen2D.fill(fl);
42:        // Draw ovals
43:        screen2D.setColor(Color.black);
44:        BasicStroke pen2 = new BasicStroke();
45:        screen2D.setStroke(pen2);
46:        Ellipse2D.Float e1 = new Ellipse2D.Float(235,140,15,15);
47:        Ellipse2D.Float e2 = new Ellipse2D.Float(225,130,15,15);
48:        Ellipse2D.Float e3 = new Ellipse2D.Float(245,130,15,15);
49:        screen2D.fill(e1);
50:        screen2D.fill(e2);
51:        screen2D.fill(e3);
52:    }
53: }
```

In order to view the applet, you need to create a short HTML page that contains it, using Listing 12.6. Because it uses Java 2 classes and methods, the applet can only be viewed with appletviewer or a browser that supports this version of the language (unless you rewrite the HTML so the applet is loaded by the Java Plug-in).

LISTING 12.6   The Full Text of Map2D.html

```
1: <applet code="Map2D.class" height="370" width="350">
2: </applet>
```

Some observations about the Map2D applet:

- Line 2 imports the classes in the java.awt.geom package. This statement is required because import java.awt.*; in Line 1 only handles classes, not packages, available under java.awt.

- Line 6 creates the screen2D object that is used for all 2D drawing operations. It's a cast of the Graphics object that represents the Applet window.

- Lines 10–12 create a BasicStroke object that represents a line width of 2 pixels and then makes this the current stroke with the setStroke() method of Graphics2D.

- Lines 13–17 use two nested for loops to create waves out of individual arcs. This same technique was used for the Map application, but there are more arcs covering the applet window in Map2D.

- Lines 20 and 21 create a gradient fill pattern from the color green at 0,0 to orange at 50,50. The last argument to the constructor, true, causes the fill pattern to repeat itself as many times as needed to fill an object.

12

- Line 22 sets the current gradient fill pattern using the setPaint() method and the gp object that was just created.
- Lines 23–41 create the polygon shaped like the state of Florida and draw it. This polygon will be filled with green-to-orange strips because of the currently selected fill pattern.
- Line 43 sets the current color to black. This replaces the gradient fill pattern for the next drawing operation because colors are also fill patterns.
- Line 44 creates a new BasicStroke() object with no arguments, which defaults to a 1-pixel wide line width.
- Line 45 sets the current line width to the new BasicStroke object pen2.
- Lines 46–51 create three ellipses at 235,140, 225,130, and 245,130. Each is 15 pixels wide and 15 pixels tall, making them circles.

Figure 12.15 shows the output of the Map2D applet in appletviewer.

FIGURE **12.15**

The Map2D *applet.*

Summary

You now have some tools to improve the looks of a Java program. You can draw with lines, rectangles, ellipses, polygons, fonts, colors, and patterns onto a frame, an applet window, and other components using non-2D and 2D classes.

Non-2D drawing operations require the use of methods in the Graphics class, with arguments that describe the object being drawn.

Java2D uses the same two methods for each drawing operation—draw() and fill(). Different objects are created using classes of the java.awt.geom package, and these are used as arguments for the drawing methods of Graphics2D.

You get more chances to work with multimedia in Java in Day 13, "Threads and Animation." Those art lessons include animation, sound, and the display of image files.

Q&A

Q **I want to draw a line of text with a boldface word in the middle. I understand that I need two Font objects—one for the regular font and one for the bold—and that I'll need to reset the current font in between. The problem is that drawString() requires an x and a y position for the start of each string, and I can't find anything that refers to "current point." How can I figure out where to start the boldface word?**

A Java's text display capabilities are fairly primitive. Java has no concept of the current point, so you have to figure out yourself where the end of one string was in order to begin the next string. The stringWidth() methods can help you with this problem, both to find out the width of the string you just drew and to add the space after it.

Q **I am confused by what the lowercase "f" is referring to in source code today. It is added to coordinates, as in the polly method polly.moveTo(5f, 0f). Why is the "f" used for these coordinates and not others, and why is a capital "F" used elsewhere, such as the fl method fl.moveTo(10F, 12F)?**

A The F and f indicate that a number is a floating-point number rather than an integer, and they can be used interchangeably. If you don't use one of them, the Java compiler will assume that the number is an int value. Many methods and constructors in Java require floating-point arguments but can handle integers because an integer can be converted to floating-point without changing its value. For this reason, constructors like Arc2D.Float() can use arguments such as 10 and 180 instead of 10F and 180F.

Questions

1. What object is required before you can draw something in Java?

    (a) Graphics or Graphics2D

    (b) WindowListener

    (c) JFrame

2. Which of the following three fonts should not be used in a Java 2 program?

    (a) `serif`

    (b) `Courier`

    (c) monospaced

3. What does `getSize().width` refer to?

    (a) The width of the applet's window

    (b) The width of the frame's window

    (c) The width of any graphical user interface component in Java

Answers

1. a.

2. b. Choosing specific font names, as opposed to font descriptors like `serif` and `monospaced`, limits the flexibility of Java in selecting which font to use on a specific platform.

3. c. You can call `getSize().width` and `getSize().height` on any component in Java.

Exercises

To extend your knowledge of the subjects covered today, try the following exercises:

- Create an applet that draws a circle with its radius, x,y position, and color all determined by parameters.

- Create a version of `Map2D` that runs as an application instead of an applet.

Where applicable, exercise solutions are offered on the book's Web site at `http://www.java21days.com`.

DAY 13

Threads and Animation

When Java was introduced in 1995, hundreds of programmers put it to use creating animated applets. There was no other way at the time to offer animation on a Web page—animated GIF files were not supported in browsers and Shockwave, Flash, and ActiveX were not yet available—so Java was a great way to create dynamic content for visitors to your site.

Though a lot has changed since then, Java remains one of the easiest ways to create animated content (especially for complex effects) on and off the World Wide Web.

Animation in Java is accomplished by using the Abstract Windowing Toolkit, Swing, and the Thread class in the java.lang package.

Today, you learn how the various parts of Java work together to create moving figures and dynamically updated applications and applets. You explore the following topics:

- How Java animations work—The paint() method in applets and paintComponent() in applications and how to override these methods.

- Threads—How to put animation in its own thread, a task that runs separately from other parts of your programs.

- Using bitmapped images such as GIF, JPEG, and PNG files—Loading them into a program, tracking when they have loaded, and displaying them.

Creating Animation in Java

On previous days, you have drawn graphics and text by using either the paint() method in applets or the paintComponent() method in applications. These methods are used to draw something on a component whenever a program's interface needs to be redrawn. You can call a component's repaint() method to request that it be redrawn.

In most of the programs you have written thus far, these paint methods always draw the same thing—yesterday's Map2D applet always draws Florida in the same way when the applet window is repainted.

When creating animation, you can draw the component in its paint method, as usual. Instead of creating content that never changes, provide a way for the paint method to draw different things each time it is called.

For example, the following paint() method draws the string "Look to the cookie!" in an applet window:

```
public void paint(Graphics screen) {
    Graphics2D screen2D = (Graphics2D)screen;
    screen2D.drawString("Look to the Cookie!", 15, 50);
}
```

The last two arguments to the Graphics2D object's drawString() method are (x,y) coordinates that determine where the string is drawn in the applet window. The following example is rewritten to use variables for these arguments:

```
public void paint(Graphics screen) {
    Graphics2D screen2D = (Graphics2D)screen;
    screen2D.drawString("Look to the Cookie!", xPosition, yPosition);
}
```

The string's drawn location depends on the value of the xPosition and yPosition variables. You can use this paint method to create animation by finding a way to dynamically change the values in these variables and then redrawing the applet window.

This technique can be used for all the animation you create, whether you are drawing text, graphics, image files, or a combination of all three.

Painting and Repainting

As you have learned, a component's paint method automatically is called when its display area must be redrawn. This occurs when the component is first loaded on an interface as well as whenever the component is obscured by something else—such as a dialog box—and then revealed again.

You can ask Java's windowing system to repaint a component by calling its `repaint()` method.

> **Note**
>
> The polite language is used here for a reason—`repaint()` is a request rather than a command. The Java windowing system receives this request and processes it as soon as possible, but if `repaint()` requests stack up faster than Java can handle them, some might be skipped. In most cases, the delay between the call to `repaint()` and the actual window redisplay is negligible.

In an animation program, the following two steps are often repeated:

1. The program makes a change that would affect what a component's paint method draws.
2. The component's `repaint()` method is called.

Step 1 does not usually take place in the component's paint method—if you think of animation as a series of individual frames, `paint()` or `paintComponent()` only handles the current frame.

> **Caution**
>
> Although you can call the `paint()` method yourself, you should make all requests to draw the display area using calls to `repaint()`. The `repaint()` method is easier to use—it doesn't require a `Graphics` object as an argument—unlike `paint()`—and it takes care of all the behavior needed to update the display area. You'll see this later today when you call `repaint()` to create an animated sequence.

13

Animating a Component

Several news- and technology-related Web sites use Java applets to present a scrolling window of current headlines.

The next project you create, the `Headlines` application, will display an animated panel component with several headlines that move from the bottom of the panel upwards.

The following class definition for `HeadlinePanel` creates a string array of news headlines and an integer variable:

```
class HeadlinePanel extends JPanel {
    String[] headlines = {
        "Grandmother of Eight Makes Hole in One",
        "Police Begin Campaign to Run Down Jaywalkers",
        "Dr. Ruth to Talk About Sex with Newspaper Editors",
        "Enraged Cow Injures Farmer with Axe "
    };
    int y = 76;
}
```

> **Note**
>
> These headlines from real newspapers were compiled by Ciarán P. McCarthy of the Salesian English Language Centre in Celbridge, Ireland. You can see the full list on his Web site at `http://indigo.ie/~sdblang/personal/papers/headlines.htm`.

To draw something on a component such as this panel, override its `paintComponent(Graphics)` method, which is analogous to the `paint(Graphics)` method of an applet.

The following method draws every element of the `headlines` array in the component:

```
public void paintComponent(Graphics comp) {
    Graphics2D comp2D = (Graphics2D)comp;
    Font type = new Font("monospaced", Font.BOLD, 14);
    comp2D.setFont(type);
    comp2D.setColor(getBackground());
    comp2D.fillRect(0, 0, getSize().width, getSize().height);
    comp2D.setColor(Color.black);
    for (int i = 0; i < headlines.length; i++)
        comp2D.drawString(headlines[i], 5, y + (20 * i));
}
```

This paint method uses the panel's y instance variable to determine where the headlines are drawn. This variable has the initial value 76, so when the panel is first displayed, the headlines are drawn at the following locations:

- "Grandmother of Eight Makes Hole in One" at (5, 76)
- "Police Begin Campaign to Run Down Jaywalkers" at (5, 96)
- "Dr. Ruth to Talk About Sex with Newspaper Editors" at (5, 116)
- "Enraged Cow Injures Farmer with Axe " at (5, 136)

At this point, you have created a panel with a paint method that is capable of drawing news headlines at different locations. All that remains is to provide a means to change the location of the headlines and to call repaint():

```
void scroll() {
    while (true) {
        y = y - 1;
        if (y < -75)
            y = 76;
        repaint();
        try {
            Thread.sleep(250);
        } catch (InterruptedException e) { }
    }
}
```

The while (true) statement in the scroll() method causes an *infinite loop*, a loop that never ends. In the loop, the value of the y variable is lowered by 1 and the panel is redrawn. If y is less than -75, it is restored to its initial value, 76.

The try-catch block contains a call to Thread.sleep(), a class method that causes Java to pause for the specified number of milliseconds. This method is a convenient way to slow down an animated program.

Note

> The call to sleep() is enclosed within a try-catch block because the sleep() method will generate a type of error called an InterruptedException if something happens in the Java interpreter that interrupts the method. You learn more about exceptions on Day 16, "Error Handling and Security."

You can add the HeadlinePanel component to any application or applet window and call its scroll() method to begin the animation. Listing 13.1 contains a simple Headlines application that incorporates the panel.

13

LISTING 13.1   The Full Text of Headlines.java

```
1: import java.awt.*;
2: import javax.swing.*;
3: import java.util.*;
4:
5: public class Headlines extends JFrame {
6:     HeadlinePanel news = new HeadlinePanel();
7:
8:     public Headlines() {
9:         super("Headlines");
```

LISTING 13.1   continued

```
10:            setSize(420, 100);
11:            setDefaultCloseOperation(JFrame.EXIT_ON_CLOSE);
12:            JPanel pane = new JPanel();
13:            pane.setLayout(new GridLayout(1, 1, 15, 15));
14:            pane.add(news);
15:            setContentPane(pane);
16:            show();
17:            news.scroll();
18:        }
19:
20:        public static void main(String[] arguments) {
21:            Headlines head = new Headlines();
22:        }
23: }
24:
25: class HeadlinePanel extends JPanel {
26:        String[] headlines = {
27:            "Grandmother of Eight Makes Hole in One",
28:            "Police Begin Campaign to Run Down Jaywalkers",
29:            "Dr. Ruth to Talk About Sex with Newspaper Editors",
30:            "Enraged Cow Injures Farmer with Axe "
31:        };
32:        int y = 76;
33:
34:        void scroll() {
35:            while (true) {
36:                y = y - 1;
37:                if (y < -75)
38:                    y = 76;
39:                repaint();
40:                try {
41:                    Thread.sleep(250);
42:                } catch (InterruptedException e) { }
43:            }
44:        }
45:
46:        public void paintComponent(Graphics comp) {
47:            Graphics2D comp2D = (Graphics2D)comp;
48:            Font type = new Font("monospaced", Font.BOLD, 14);
49:            comp2D.setFont(type);
50:            comp2D.setColor(getBackground());
51:            comp2D.fillRect(0, 0, getSize().width, getSize().height);
52:            comp2D.setColor(Color.black);
53:            for (int i = 0; i < headlines.length; i++)
54:                comp2D.drawString(headlines[i], 5, y + (20 * i));
55:        }
56:
57: }
```

Using the `HeadlinePanel` component in another program is fairly straightforward—the panel itself handles everything but starting the animation.

Note that the panel draws headlines to negative coordinates from (5, -1) to (5, -75). Java will draw text and images even if their (x,y) coordinates are outside of a component, displaying only the portion that falls in the component's visible area. The `Headlines` application uses this to make headlines scroll off the top edge of the frame (and also to scroll up from the bottom edge).

Figure 13.1 shows the application running.

FIGURE 13.1

The Headlines *application.*

After the `scroll()` method is called, the infinite loop in that method causes the animation to continue until the application is exited when the frame is closed.

Controlling Animation Through Threads

One of the things to consider in animation programming is how system resources are being used. Moving a lot of graphics around can take up a lot of processor time, especially if you're doing complex things like transforming the graphics or detecting collisions between two moving things.

If you include a sophisticated animated component on a user interface, you might find that the elements of the interface respond slowly—drop-down lists take a second or more to appear, button clicks are recognized slowly, and so on.

Animation, like the other processor-hogging things in a Java program, can be run separately from the rest of a program using a feature of the Java language called threads.

NEW TERM *Threads* are parts of a program that are set up to run on their own while the rest of the program does something else. This also is called *multitasking* because the program can handle more than one task simultaneously.

Threads are ideal for anything that takes up a lot of processing time and runs continuously, such as the repeated drawing operations in the `Headlines` application that drew headlines in an infinite loop.

By putting the workload of the animation into a thread, you free up the rest of the program to handle other things. You also make handling the program easier for the runtime environment because all the intensive work is isolated into its own thread.

13

Writing a Threaded Program

Threads are implemented in Java with the Thread class in the java.lang package. You have already used one of its class methods, sleep(), to pause execution of a program.

One way to make use of threads is to put all the time-consuming behavior into its own class. In the Headlines application, the work involved in the animation is confined to the HeadlinePanel class, so this is already well suited to the use of threads.

To modify a class so that it uses threads, the class must implement the Runnable interface in the java.lang package. To do this, add the keyword implements to the class declaration followed by the name of the interface, as in the following example:

```
public class Cartoon extends JPanel implements Runnable {
    public void run() {
        // ...
    }
}
```

When a class implements an interface, it must include all methods of that interface. The Runnable interface contains only one method, run(), so it's included in the preceding example. You will see how to use this method in a moment.

The first step in creating a thread is to create a reference to an object of the Thread class:

```
Thread runner;
```

This statement creates a reference to a thread, but no Thread object has been assigned to it yet. Threads are created by calling the constructor Thread(*Object*) with the threaded object as an argument. You could create a threaded Cartoon object with the following statement:

```
Cartoon toon = new Cartoon();
Thread toonThread = new Thread(toon);
```

Three good places to create threads are the constructor method for an application, the constructor for a component (such as a panel), or the start() method of an applet.

A thread is begun by calling its start() method, as in the following statement:

```
toonThread.start();
```

 Caution

Applets and threads both have start() methods, which can make things confusing when you are creating an applet that uses threads. The two methods are different and have no connection to each other.

The following statements can be used in a threaded object's class definition to start the thread:

```
Thread runner;
if (runner == null) {
    runner = new Thread(this);
    runner.start();
}
```

The this keyword used in the Thread() constructor refers to the object in which these statements are contained. The runner variable has a value of null before any object is assigned to it, so the if statement is used to make sure that the thread is not started more than once.

To run a thread, its start() method is called, as in this statement from the preceding example:

```
runner.start();
```

Calling a thread's start() method causes another method to be called—the run() method that must be present in the threaded object.

The run() method is the heart of a threaded class. In an animated program, it can be used to make changes that would affect what is drawn in a paint method. (Looking back at the Headlines application, the scroll() method would require few changes to be suitable as a run() method.)

By adding implements Runnable, creating a Thread object associated with the applet, and using the applet's start(), stop(), and run() methods, an applet becomes a threaded program.

A Threaded Clock Application

Threaded programming requires a lot of interaction between different objects, so it should become clearer when you see it in action.

Listing 13.2 contains an application that displays the current time on a panel component. The animation required to update the panel runs in its own thread.

LISTING 13.2   The Full Text of DigitalClock.java

```
1: import java.awt.*;
2: import javax.swing.*;
3: import java.util.*;
4:
5: public class DigitalClock extends JFrame {
6:     WatchPanel watch = new WatchPanel();
```

LISTING 13.2   continued

```
 7:
 8:     public DigitalClock() {
 9:         super("Digital Clock");
10:         setSize(345, 60);
11:         setDefaultCloseOperation(JFrame.EXIT_ON_CLOSE);
12:         JPanel pane = new JPanel();
13:         pane.setLayout(new GridLayout(1, 1, 15, 15));
14:         pane.add(watch);
15:         setContentPane(pane);
16:         show();
17:     }
18:
19:     public static void main(String[] arguments) {
20:         DigitalClock clock = new DigitalClock();
21:     }
22: }
23:
24: class WatchPanel extends JPanel implements Runnable {
25:     Thread runner;
26:
27:     WatchPanel() {
28:         if (runner == null) {
29:             runner = new Thread(this);
30:             runner.start();
31:         }
32:     }
33:
34:     public void run() {
35:         while (true) {
36:             repaint();
37:             try {
38:                 Thread.sleep(1000);
39:             } catch (InterruptedException e) { }
40:         }
41:     }
42:
43:     public void paintComponent(Graphics comp) {
44:         Graphics2D comp2D = (Graphics2D)comp;
45:         Font type = new Font("Serif", Font.BOLD, 24);
46:         comp2D.setFont(type);
47:         comp2D.setColor(getBackground());
48:         comp2D.fillRect(0, 0, getSize().width, getSize().height);
49:         GregorianCalendar day = new GregorianCalendar();
50:         String time = day.getTime().toString();
51:         comp2D.setColor(Color.black);
52:         comp2D.drawString(time, 5, 25);
53:     }
54: }
```

The `DigitalClock` application is shown in Figure 13.2.

FIGURE 13.2

The `DigitalClock`
application.

If you didn't use threads in the `DigitalClock` application, the endless `while()` loop in
lines 35–40 would run in the default Java system thread, which also is responsible for
painting the screen, dealing with user input such as mouse clicks, and keeping everything
internally up-to-date. A loop like this can easily monopolize the main system thread,
slowing down things such as screen repainting to a crawl.

The `DigitalClock` application displays a frame that contains a single interface component, a panel object called `WatchPanel`. In lines 49–50, the `paintComponent()` method
displays the current time by creating a `GregorianCalendar` object, calling the `getTime()`
method of that object, and displaying it as a string.

Every time the panel is redrawn, it shows the current time. You don't have to make any
changes outside of the paint method for this to happen—the `day` object created in line 49
represents the time at the moment of the object's creation.

For this reason, only one task needs to take place outside the paint method for animation
to occur: Something must cause the component to be redrawn frequently. The `run()`
method in lines 34–41 takes care of this. It will be called automatically when a thread
associated with a `WatchPanel` object is started.

The `WatchPanel()` constructor in lines 27–32 creates and starts a `WatchPanel` thread by
calling the thread's `start()` method. This thread will run concurrently with the rest of
the application.

Stopping a Thread

Stopping a thread is a little more complicated than starting one. The `Thread` class
includes a `stop()` method that can be called to stop a thread, but it has been deprecated
in Java 2 because it creates instabilities in Java's runtime environment and can introduce
hard-to-detect errors into a program.

One way to stop a thread is to make a loop in the thread's `run()` method end if a variable
changes in value, as in the following example:

```
public void run() {
    while (okToRun == true) {
        // ...
    }
}
```

13

The okToRun variable could be an instance variable of the thread's class, and if it is changed to false, the loop inside the run() method will end.

Another thing you can do to stop a thread is to only loop in the run() method while the currently running thread has a variable that references it.

In previous examples, a Thread object called runner has been used to hold the current thread.

A class method, Thread.currentThread(), can be called in a thread to return a reference to the current thread.

The following run() method loops as long as runner and currentThread() refer to the same object:

```
public void run() {
    Thread thisThread = Thread.currentThread();
    while (runner == thisThread) {
        // ...
    }
}
```

If you use a loop like this, you can stop the thread anywhere in the class with the following statement:

```
runner = null;
```

This technique is demonstrated in the Checkers application in Listing 13.3, a program that draws a moving checker on a panel that is animated in its own thread. This thread is started and stopped using buttons on the application's interface.

LISTING 13.3   The Full Text of Checkers.java

```
 1: import java.awt.*;
 2: import java.awt.event.*;
 3: import javax.swing.*;
 4:
 5: public class Checkers extends JFrame implements ActionListener {
 6:     CheckersPanel checkers = new CheckersPanel();
 7:     JButton startButton = new JButton("Start");
 8:     JButton stopButton = new JButton("Stop");
 9:
10:     public Checkers() {
11:         super("Checkers");
12:         setSize(210, 170);
13:         setDefaultCloseOperation(JFrame.EXIT_ON_CLOSE);
14:         JPanel pane = new JPanel();
15:         BorderLayout border = new BorderLayout();
16:         pane.setLayout(border);
```

```
17:          pane.add(checkers, "Center");
18:
19:          JPanel buttonPanel = new JPanel();
20:          startButton.addActionListener(this);
21:          buttonPanel.add(startButton);
22:          stopButton.addActionListener(this);
23:          stopButton.setEnabled(false);
24:          buttonPanel.add(stopButton);
25:
26:          pane.add(buttonPanel, "South");
27:          setContentPane(pane);
28:          show();
29:      }
30:
31:      public void actionPerformed(ActionEvent evt) {
32:          if (evt.getSource() == startButton) {
33:              checkers.playAnimation();
34:              startButton.setEnabled(false);
35:              stopButton.setEnabled(true);
36:          } else {
37:              checkers.stopAnimation();
38:              startButton.setEnabled(true);
39:              stopButton.setEnabled(false);
40:          }
41:      }
42:
43:      public static void main(String[] arguments) {
44:          Checkers ck = new Checkers();
45:      }
46:
47: }
48:
49: class CheckersPanel extends JPanel implements Runnable {
50:      private Thread runner;
51:      int xPos = 5;
52:      int xMove = 4;
53:
54:      void playAnimation() {
55:          if (runner == null); {
56:              runner = new Thread(this);
57:              runner.start();
58:          }
59:      }
60:
61:      void stopAnimation() {
62:          if (runner != null); {
63:              runner = null;
64:          }
65:      }
66:
67:      public void run() {
```

13

LISTING **13.3**   continued

```
68:            Thread thisThread = Thread.currentThread();
69:            while (runner == thisThread) {
70:                xPos += xMove;
71:                if ((xPos > 105) | (xPos < 5))
72:                    xMove *= -1;
73:                repaint();
74:                try {
75:                    Thread.sleep(100);
76:                } catch (InterruptedException e) { }
77:            }
78:        }
79:
80:    public void paintComponent(Graphics comp) {
81:            Graphics2D comp2D = (Graphics2D)comp;
82:            comp2D.setColor(Color.black);
83:            comp2D.fillRect(0, 0, 100, 100);
84:            comp2D.setColor(Color.white);
85:            comp2D.fillRect(100, 0, 100, 100);
86:            comp2D.setColor(Color.red);
87:            comp2D.fillOval(xPos, 5, 90, 90);
88:        }
89: }
```

Most of the code in the Checkers application uses techniques that have already been introduced today or during previous days this week. This program demonstrates one way to produce animation using the shapes that can be drawn using Java2D techniques—in a CheckersPanel object, a black square and white square are drawn underneath a red circle representing a checkers piece.

The position of the red checkers piece depends on the value of a CheckersPanel instance variable, xPos. This variable changes in value inside the panel's run() method.

The Checkers class itself is a frame that represents the application's main interface. Two components are added to the frame's content pane: a CheckersPanel component and another panel called buttonPanel. The second panel contains two buttons, startButton and stopButton.

When the application runs (see Figure 13.3), the checker is drawn over the board but is not moving. The animation can be started and stopped by clicking the Start and Stop buttons.

FIGURE 13.3

The Checkers *application.*

The changes to xPos that make the animation move occur in the run() method in lines 67–78. This method contains a while loop that continues as long as runner and thisThread refer to the same thread.

The checkers panel has two methods to start and stop its thread: playAnimation() in lines 54–59 and stopAnimation() in lines 61–65. These methods could easily be reused in any threaded object to start and stop the thread.

Retrieving and Using Images

Basic image handling in Java is conducted through the Image class, which is part of the java.awt package. Image objects can represent graphics in three file formats: GIF, JPEG, and PNG.

You cannot create Image objects directly. Applets have several methods for loading image files using its filename or a URL, an address indicating where the graphics file is available on the Internet. Applications can use class methods of the Toolkit class, part of the java.awt package, to work with images.

After you have an Image object, you can display it in a component using methods of the Graphics or Graphics2D classes.

Getting Images

To associate a graphics file with an Image object in an application, you can call the createImage() method of the Toolkit class.

Toolkit is a behind-the-scenes class used to support the presentation and maintenance of a graphical user interface in Java. You cannot create Toolkit objects, but you can get one by calling the class method getDefaultToolkit().

The Toolkit class can load images using the following methods:

- getImage(*String*)—Creates an Image object from the graphics file with the specified name, which can be a filename (such as fillmore.jpg) or a reference to a folder and filename (such as c:\whigs\fillmore.jpg).

13

- getImage(*URL*)—Creates an Image object from the graphics file at the Internet address specified by the URL object.

Working with URL objects is covered in Day 19, "Communicating Across the Internet."

The following statements create an Image object associated with the file fillmore.jpg:

```
Toolkit kit = Toolkit.getDefaultToolkit();
back = kit.getImage("fillmore.jpg");
```

The JApplet class includes two methods to load images:

- getImage(*URL*)—Creates an Image object from the graphics file at the specified URL.
- getImage(*URL*, *String*)—Creates an Image object at an Internet address that combines the specified URL and filename reference.

By calling getCodeBase() in an applet, you can get a URL object that represents the folder where the applet's class file is stored. If you use this as the first argument to getImage(*URL*, *String*) and store the graphics file in the same folder, you can use the filename as the second argument.

For example, if you have an applet stored at http://www.naviseek.com/java21/java called Fillmore.class and a file called fillmore.jpg in the same folder, you can use the following statement to create an Image object associated with that graphics file:

```
Image millard = getImage(getCodeBase(), "fillmore.jpg");
```

Another applet method, getDocumentBase(), returns a URL associated with the Web page that loaded the applet.

By using getCodeBase() or getDocumentBase() when loading an image in an applet, you make it possible for the applet to work even if you move it (and the associated Web page) to another Web server.

 Note | If you use a Java archive to present your applet, you can include image files and other data files in the archive. These files will be extracted from the archive automatically with any class files in the .JAR file.

Drawing Images

After you have loaded an image into an Image object, you can display it in a paint() or paintComponent() using the drawImage() method of the Graphics2D class.

To display an image, call the drawImage() method with four arguments:

- The Image object to display
- The x coordinate
- The y coordinate
- The keyword this

If a graphics file is stored in the img object, the following paintComponent() method can be used to display it in a user interface component:

```
public void paintComponent(Graphics comp) {
    Graphics2D comp2D = (Graphics2D)comp;
    comp2D.drawImage(img, 0, 0, this);
}
```

The (x,y) coordinates used with drawImage() are comparable to using (x,y) coordinates to display text or graphics such as polygons, circles, and rectangles. The point represents the upper-left corner of the image.

When you are determining the (x,y) coordinate at which to display something in a component, it's often useful to know the dimensions of the component. Use getSize().height and getSize().width to find out the height and width, respectively.

Caution

When using getHeight() and getWidth(), take care not to call these methods before the component has been created and displayed. If you call them in the component's constructor method, you won't get the values you might have been expecting.

A Note About Image Observers

The last argument of the drawImage() method is the keyword this. As you might recall, this can be used inside an object to refer to itself.

The this keyword is used in drawImage() to identify that the applet can keep track of an image as it is downloaded from the World Wide Web. Image loading is tracked through the ImageObserver interface. Classes that implement this interface, such as JApplet, can track the progress of an image. This would be useful to create a program that displays a message such as "Loading images…" while its graphics files are being loaded.

The existing support for ImageObserver should be sufficient for simple uses of images in applets, so the this keyword is used as an argument to drawImage().

13

Creating Animation Using Images

After you have graphics files loaded into Image objects, animating them requires the same techniques you used to move around text, circles, and other graphics. The biggest difference is that you have to devise a way to display the right images in the right places.

The best way to show how to animate images is to work through an example. The next project, one of the longest you will undertake, is an application that draws a cartoon penguin walking across a backdrop of ice blocks and stone barriers.

Pixel Pete Takes a Walk

The Pete application features an animated penguin called Pixel Pete, a character in a Java game applet called Iceblox that was written by Karl Hörnell. Hörnell, who publishes his games on the Web at http://www.javaonthebrain.com, is one of the most accomplished Java game programmers, winning awards from Gamelan and selling programs to Disney and other companies for their own Web sites.

 Tip   Hörnell publishes the source code, graphics files, and development notes for most of his Java applets on his Web site, so it's a great place for an aspiring game programmer to visit.

For this example, you use seven different graphics files of Pixel Pete and his arctic environment. The animation you create in the Pete application will show Pete walking across a panel from left to right, stopping to blink a few times and wave, then walking to the right until he has gone beyond the edge of the panel. The animation loops continuously, so Pete will dutifully continue marching through the application's interface until you close the program down.

Collecting Your Images

The Pete animation uses a large graphics file containing Pete's environment and six smaller files representing the different movements that Pete can accomplish. All these files are in GIF format, which is well suited for small graphics with large amounts of solid color. You also could use PNG graphics for this purpose, if you have graphics software that supports the creation of these files.

The six versions of Pete are shown in Figure 13.4, and the environment is shown in Figure 13.5.

FIGURE 13.4

The six images for Pete's trip across a panel (enlarged).

right1.gif   right2.gif   right3.gif   stop.gif   blink.gif   wave.gif

FIGURE 13.5

The environment that Pete travels across.

You must have these graphic files on your system in order to create this project. The files are available from the book's Web site at http://www.java21days.com. Open the Day 13 page and download the following graphics to the same folder where you will compile the Pete application: backdrop.gif, blink.gif, right1.gif, right2.gif, right3.gif, stop.gif, and wave.gif.

Organizing and Loading the Images

The basic idea in the Pete application is to take the series of images and display them one at a time to create the appearance of movement. The penguin will move from left to right across the area that is free of ice blocks and stone barriers as shown in Figure 13.5.

One way to create an animation from graphics files is to store each image in an array of Image objects and use an integer to keep track of which array element to display.

The Pete application will be organized as a simple frame to hold the application and a PetePanel component in which the animation takes place. The panel will run in its own thread, and is designed so that you can plug it into applets and other graphical user interface programs.

The following instance variables, which will be placed in the PetePanel class, hold the images and an integer to track the image to display:

```
Thread runner;
Image petePics[] = new Image[6];
Image back;
int current = 0;
```

A Thread variable called runner is also declared, though it is not assigned to an object yet. This variable will hold a reference to the thread that animates the program.

13

Because Pete will be drawn in different positions in the panel, the current (x,y) coordinates are also instance variables:

```
int x = -10;
int y = 30;
```

The initial coordinates of (-10, 30) put Pete near the left edge of the component but do not display any part of him (Pete is 30 pixels wide). A common trick of animation programming is to put things "off-screen" as described and move them into the visible area.

The constructor method for `PetePanel` will create `Image` objects for all seven graphics files and start the panel's thread:

```
PetePanel() {
    super();
    setBackground(Color.black);
    String peteSrc[] = { "right1.gif", "right2.gif",
        "right3.gif", "stop.gif", "blink.gif",
        "wave.gif" };
    Toolkit kit = Toolkit.getDefaultToolkit();
    for (int i=0; i < petePics.length; i++) {
        petePics[i] = kit.getImage(peteSrc[i]);
    }
    back = kit.getImage("backdrop.gif");
    if (runner == null) {
        runner = new Thread(this);
        runner.start();
    }
}
```

The panel is a subclass of `JPanel`, like the other panels you have worked with today, and the first two statements call its superclass and set the panel's background color to black.

The filenames for the graphics files are stored in a `String` array, making it possible to use a `for` loop to iterate through that array and create `Image` objects for the `petePicks` array.

The `Toolkit` object created in the constructor is used in the `for` loop. By calling its `getImage(String)` method, you can fill the `petePics` array with the six graphics files of Pete. The `backdrop.gif` image is loaded individually into its own `Image` object, `back`.

The last thing that must be initialized in the constructor is to create the `runner` thread by calling its constructor with `this` as an argument. Using `this` makes the current object—in other words, the `PetePanel` object—the running thread.

Calling the `start()` method of this thread causes the panel's `run()` method to be called. You will create this in the next section.

Animating the Images

With the images loaded, the next step in the application is to begin animating the elements. Because this is a threaded applet, the run() method will be used for this purpose.

Pete takes five successive actions in the program:

- Walks in from the left edge of the panel
- Stops near the middle and blinks three times
- Waves four times
- Walks off the right edge of the panel
- Takes a short rest off-panel, and then repeats the process from the beginning

The run() method of PetePanel will call methods for each of the actions that Pete can accomplish:

```
public void run() {
    while (true) {
        walk(-10, 275);
        look();
        blink(3);
        wave(4);
        walk(x, getSize().width + 10);
        pause(1500);
    }
}
```

The names of these methods tell you what Pete is doing at each step in the animation. The arguments to the walk() method specify the starting and ending x coordinate of Pete's walk, the argument to blink() specifies the number of times Pete blinks, and the wave() argument specifies how often he waves.

The call to getSize() returns a Dimension object with two instance variables, width and height. By adding 10 to width in the second call to the walk() method, the ending coordinate of Pete's walk is set to 10 pixels beyond the right edge of the panel.

The pause() method causes Pete to do nothing for a designated amount of time. Pete will not be visible at the time this takes place, so it's a way to pause before Pete starts his animated journey again.

Each of Pete's activities is contained in its own method. This makes it possible to reuse some of the actions—such as the two calls to walk()—and to rearrange the order of things if desired. You also could expand Pete's repertoire of movements by adding new methods and calling them within the run() method.

13

The first method created is walk(), which takes two integers as arguments: start and end. These determine the x coordinate where Pete begins and ends running. By using arguments, you make the method reusable. Here's the starting code for the method body:

```
void walk(int start, int end) {
  // to do
}
```

There are three images that represent Pete walking: petePics[0], petePics[1], and petePics[2].

To make it appear that Pete is walking across the window, these images are displayed in succession. At the same time, the x coordinate of the image increases, so each image is drawn a little further to the right than its predecessor. A for loop cycles between the start and end values and increases the x coordinate.

The current integer keeps track of the current image to display, so it is changed during each pass through the for loop.

A call to repaint() causes the image tracked by current to display (as you will see when the panel's paintComponent() method is created).

The last thing to do in the walk() method is to pause inside the for loop before each walking image is replaced by a new one.

Several of Pete's movement methods require a pause of some kind, so it will be added as another method:

```
public void pause(int time) {
    try {
        Thread.sleep(time);
    } catch (InterruptedException e) { }
}
```

After the call to pause() is added, the walk() method consists of the following:

```
public void walk(int start, int end) {
    int showpic = 0;
    for (int i = start; i < end; i += 5) {
        x = i;
        // swap images
        current = showpic;
        repaint();
        pause(150);
        showpic++;
        if (showpic > 2)
            showpic = 0;
    }
}
```

The last part of the `for()` statement increments the loop by 5 pixels each time, which kicks the images that distance to the right with each update. This choice, like the 150-millisecond pause in the `pause()` method call, was reached through trial and error to determine what looks best when the animation sequence runs.

You have seen that the `walk()` method stores the value of the current frame in the `current` variable before calling `repaint()`. The `paintComponent()` method of the panel will do the actual work of displaying this image, as shown here:

```
public void paintComponent(Graphics comp) {
    Graphics2D comp2D = (Graphics2D)comp;
    if (back != null)
        comp2D.drawImage(back, 0, 0, this);
    comp2D.setColor(Color.black);
    comp2D.fillRect(0, 30, 450, 30);
    if (petePics[current] != null)
        comp2D.drawImage(petePics[current], x, y, this);
}
```

Three things are drawn in this method:

1. The background image, `back`.

2. A black rectangle 450 pixels wide and 30 pixels high, with its upper left-hand corner at (0, 30).

3. The current Pete image, `petePics[current]`.

These things are drawn from back to front, creating a composite image. The black rectangle is used to wipe out the last image of Pete, which otherwise would still appear on the panel. Before drawing either of the `Image` objects, the paint method makes sure that they exist by testing to confirm they do not equal `null`.

Note

> In early versions of Java, drawing several different things in a paint method caused graphics to flicker. A common solution to this problem was to draw everything to a different `Image` object that was not visible, and then draw only that `Image` in the paint component. This technique is called buffering, and Java 2 supports it automatically within `paintComponent()` and `paint()`.

13

Pete's second activity is to turn and look directly at the user, which is handled in the `look()` method:

```
public void look() {
    current = 3;
    repaint();
    pause(1000);
}
```

By setting current to 3 and calling repaint(), petePics[3] is displayed.

Pete's next activity is to blink, an animation that requires a flip-flop between two images—petePics[4] and petePics[3]:

```
public void blink(int numtimes) {
    for (int i = numtimes; i > 0; i--) {
        current = 4;
        repaint();
        pause(200);
        current = 3;
        repaint();
        pause(1000);
    }
}
```

The for loop uses the numtimes argument to determine how many times to display the two images, making it easy to vary the number of times Pete blinks.

The last new activity for Pete is to wave:

```
public void wave(int numtimes) {
    for (int i = numtimes; i > 0; i--) {
        current = 3;
        repaint();
        pause(600);
        current = 5;
        repaint();
        pause(1100);
    }
}
```

This method has code that's almost identical to the blink() method. It requires a flip-flop between two images, petePics[3] and petePics[5].

Finishing the Application

At this point, you have a PetePanel component that can be added to a container such as a frame or an applet window.

The Pete application creates a frame and adds only one component, PetePanel. Listing 13.4 shows the complete source code for the project.

LISTING 13.4   The Full Text of Pete.java

```
1: import java.awt.*;
2: import javax.swing.*;
3: import java.util.*;
4:
5: public class Pete extends JFrame { ·
```

```
 6:      PetePanel pete = new PetePanel();
 7:
 8:      public Pete() {
 9:          super("Pixel Pete");
10:          setSize(452, 146);
11:          setDefaultCloseOperation(JFrame.EXIT_ON_CLOSE);
12:          JPanel pane = new JPanel();
13:          pane.setLayout(new GridLayout(1, 1, 15, 15));
14:          pane.add(pete);
15:          setContentPane(pane);
16:          show();
17:      }
18:
19:      public static void main(String[] arguments) {
20:          Pete penguin = new Pete();
21:      }
22: }
23:
24: class PetePanel extends JPanel implements Runnable {
25:      Thread runner;
26:      Image petePics[] = new Image[6];
27:      Image back;
28:      int current = 0;
29:      int x = -10;
30:      int y = 30;
31:
32:      PetePanel() {
33:          super();
34:          setBackground(Color.black);
35:          String peteSrc[] = { "right1.gif", "right2.gif",
36:              "right3.gif", "stop.gif", "blink.gif",
37:          "wave.gif" };
38:          Toolkit kit = Toolkit.getDefaultToolkit();
39:          for (int i=0; i < petePics.length; i++) {
40:              petePics[i] = kit.getImage(peteSrc[i]);
41:          }
42:          back = kit.getImage("backdrop.gif");
43:          if (runner == null) {
44:              runner = new Thread(this);
45:              runner.start();
46:          }
47:      }
48:
49:      public void paintComponent(Graphics comp) {
50:          Graphics2D comp2D = (Graphics2D)comp;
51:          if (back != null)
52:              comp2D.drawImage(back, 0, 0, this);
53:          comp2D.setColor(Color.black);
54:          comp2D.fillRect(0, 30, 450, 30);
55:          if (petePics[current] != null)
56:              comp2D.drawImage(petePics[current], x, y, this);
```

13

LISTING 13.4   continued

```
57:        }
58:
59:        public void run() {
60:            while (true) {
61:                walk(-10, 275);
62:                look();
63:                blink(3);
64:                wave(4);
65:                walk(x, getSize().width + 10);
66:                pause(1500);
67:            }
68:        }
69:
70:        public void walk(int start, int end) {
71:            int showpic = 0;
72:            for (int i = start; i < end; i += 5) {
73:                x = i;
74:                // swap images
75:                current = showpic;
76:                repaint();
77:                pause(150);
78:                showpic++;
79:                if (showpic > 2)
80:                    showpic = 0;
81:            }
82:        }
83:
84:        public void blink(int numtimes) {
85:            for (int i = numtimes; i > 0; i--) {
86:                current = 4;
87:                repaint();
88:                pause(200);
89:                current = 3;
90:                repaint();
91:                pause(1000);
92:            }
93:        }
94:
95:        public void wave(int numtimes) {
96:            for (int i = numtimes; i > 0; i--) {
97:                current = 3;
98:                repaint();
99:                pause(600);
100:                current = 5;
101:                repaint();
102:                pause(1100);
103:            }
104:        }
105:
```

```
106:    public void look() {
107:        current = 3;
108:        repaint();
109:        pause(1000);
110:    }
111:
112:    public void pause(int time) {
113:        try {
114:            Thread.sleep(time);
115:        } catch (InterruptedException e) { }
116:    }
117: }
```

Figure 13.6 shows the application running.

FIGURE 13.6

The Pete *application.*

Tracking Image Loading

When the Pete application runs, you might notice an odd effect the first time Pete heads across the panel—he disappears for a moment before he changes from one image to another. This is most noticeable when he stops to look at the user, wave, and blink. On all subsequent trips, Pete displays normally without this glitch.

This disappearing act occurs because of how Java loads images when a method like getImage() is called. Contrary to what you might expect, the call to getImage() returns before the image has actually been loaded. Instead, a thread is begun that will load the image, and the program goes on to other tasks.

If you try to draw an Image object before it has been loaded, a blank image will be drawn. This is what happens whenever Pete disappears—the application tries to draw an image that has not yet been loaded.

You can track whether images have finished loading by using a class in the java.awt package, MediaTracker. A MediaTracker object is created by specifying the component where the image will eventually be drawn.

Inside the PetePanel class, you can create a MediaTracker object associated with the panel as follows:

```
MediaTracker track = new MediaTracker(this);
```

13

To begin tracking an image, call the MediaTracker object's addImage(*Image*, *int*) method. The first argument is the image to track. The second is an index number of your choosing which should be unique to this image.

After you have added an image to the track object, you cause a program (or better, a thread) to wait until it is done loading by calling the tracker's waitForID(*int*) with the index number of the image.

A MediaTracker object can keep track of multiple images. To wait for all of them to finish loading, call the tracker's waitForAll() method.

Both of these images must be enclosed in the same try-catch block that was used earlier today for calls to Thread.sleep().

The following PetePanel() constructor has been modified to wait for all images to load before creating the thread and beginning the animation:

```
PetePanel() {
    super();
    setBackground(Color.black);
    String peteSrc[] = { "right1.gif", "right2.gif",
        "right3.gif", "stop.gif", "blink.gif",
        "wave.gif" };
    MediaTracker track = new MediaTracker(this);
    Toolkit kit = Toolkit.getDefaultToolkit();
    for (int i=0; i < petePics.length; i++) {
        petePics[i] = kit.getImage(peteSrc[i]);
        track.addImage(petePics[i], i);
    }
    back = kit.getImage("backdrop.gif");
    track.addImage(back, petePics.length);
    try {
        track.waitForAll();
    } catch (InterruptedException e) { }
    if (runner == null) {
        runner = new Thread(this);
        runner.start();
    }
}
```

Summary

Animation remains one of the more entertaining things you can undertake with Java though it no longer is one of the main selling features. Animation can be used to convey information, attract attention, and play games.

Today, you learned how to create components that feature animation by writing paint methods that are able to change each time they are called.

Because animation can be a processor-hogging resource, you learned how to put it in a thread that executes separately from the rest of a program.

Java 2 takes care of many animation tasks automatically that required special programming in past versions of the language. One of these is buffering, the technique that enables several things to be drawn in a component without flickering problems.

Tomorrow, you continue the trip through Java's multimedia classes by learning how to add sound to your programs.

Q&A

Q **I compiled and ran the `Pete` application. Something weird is going on; the animation starts in the middle and drops frames. It's as if only some of the images have loaded when the applet is run.**

A That's precisely what's going on. Because image loading doesn't actually load the image right away, your program might be merrily animating blank screens while the images are still being loaded. Depending on how long it takes those images to load, your program might appear to start in the middle, to drop frames, or to not work at all.

There are three possible solutions to this problem. The first is to have the animation loop (that is, start over from the beginning when it stops). Eventually, the images will load and the animation will work correctly. The second solution, and not a very good one, is to sleep for a while before starting the animation, to pause while the images load. The third, and best solution, is to use image observers to make sure that no part of the animation plays before its images have loaded. Check out the documentation for the ImageObserver interface for details.

Q **My applet and graphics files are stored in the same folder as the Web page that displays the applet. Should I use `getCodeBase()` or `getDocumentBase()` when creating images in the applet?**

A The difference between getDocumentBase() and getCodeBase() only matters when an applet's Java class is stored in a different folder than the Web page that contains the applet. For the project you're describing, you can use either method call and get the same result.

13

Questions

1. If a class implements the `Runnable` interface, what methods must the class contain?

   (a) `start()`, `stop()`, and `run()`

   (b) `actionPerformed()`

   (c) `run()`

2. After creating a Thread object, how do you get the thread to begin executing?

   (a) Call the thread's `start()` method

   (b) Do nothing

   (c) Call the thread's `run()` method

3. When a `paint()` or `paintComponent()` method draws something over a background picture, what order will they be drawn in?

   (a) Doesn't matter

   (b) Draw the background first

   (c) Draw the background last

Answers

1. c. The `Runnable` interface is used for objects that can run in their own threads.

2. a. Calling `start()` causes the `run()` method of the threaded object to be called.

3. b. You should draw text, graphics, and images from the back forward.

Exercises

To extend your knowledge of the subjects covered today, try the following exercises:

- Create an applet that displays the Pete animation exactly like the `Pete` application does.
- Create a traffic light animation using circle and rectangle shapes that shift from green to yellow to red like a real light.

Where applicable, exercise solutions are offered on the book's Web site at `http://www.java21days.com`.

DAY 14

JavaSound

Over the past six days, you have taken a sight-seeing tour of the Java language. All the different ways in which a program can be visually interesting—the user interface, graphics, images, and animation—involve the classes of the Swing and Abstract Windowing Toolkit packages.

To finish the week, you will focus on another one of the senses—hearing. Java 2 supports sound using some applet methods that have been available since the introduction of the language and an extensive new class library called JavaSound.

Today you make Java programs audible in two different ways.

First, you use methods of the `Applet` class, the superclass of all Java applets. You can use these methods to retrieve and play sound files in programs using a large number of formats, including WAV, AU, and MIDI.

Next, you begin working with JavaSound, several packages that enable the playback, recording, and manipulation of sound.

Retrieving and Using Sounds

Java supports the playback of sound files through the `Applet` class, and you can play a sound one time only or as a repeating sound loop.

Prior to Java 2, the language could handle only one audio format: 8KHz mono `AU` with mu-law encoding (named for the Greek letter "μ", or mu). If you wanted to use something that was in a format such as `WAV`, you had to translate it to mu-law `AU`, often at a loss of quality.

Java 2 adds much fuller support for audio. You can load and play digitized sound files in the following formats: `AIFF`, `AU`, and `WAV`. Three `MIDI`-based song file formats also are supported: Type 0 `MIDI`, Type 1 `MIDI`, and `RMF`. The greatly improved sound support can handle 8- or 16-bit audio data in mono or stereo, and the sample rates can range from 8KHz to 48KHz.

The simplest way to retrieve and play a sound is through the `play()` method of the `Applet` class. The `play()` method, like the `getImage()` method, takes one of two forms:

- `play()` with one argument—An `URL` object—loads and plays the audio clip stored at that URL.
- `play()` with two arguments—A base URL and a folder pathname—loads and plays that audio file. The first argument often will be a call to `getDocumentBase()` or `getCodeBase()`, as you have seen with `getImage()`.

The following statement retrieves and plays the sound `zap.au`, which is stored in the same place as the applet:

```
play(getCodeBase(), "zap.au");
```

The `play()` method retrieves and plays the given sound as soon as possible after it is called. If the sound file can't be found, the only indication you'll receive of a problem is the silence. No error message will be displayed.

To play a sound repeatedly, start and stop the sound, or play it repeatedly as a loop, you must load it into an `AudioClip` object by using the applet's `getAudioClip` method. `AudioClip` is part of the `java.applet` package, so it must be imported to be used in a program.

The `getAudioClip()` method takes one or two arguments in the same fashion as the `play()` method. The first (or only) argument is a `URL` argument identifying the sound file, and the second is a folder path reference.

The following statement loads a sound file into the clip object:

```
AudioClip clip = getAudioClip(getCodeBase(),
    "audio/marimba.wav");
```

In this example, the filename includes a folder reference, so the file marimba.wav will be loaded from the subfolder audio.

The getAudioClip() method can be called only within an applet. As of Java 2, applications can load sound files by using newAudioClip(), a class method of the java.awt.Applet class. Here's the previous example rewritten for use in an application:

```
AudioClip clip = Applet.newAudioClip("audio/marimba.wav");
```

After you have created an AudioClip object, you can call the play() (plays the sound), stop() (halts playback), and loop()(plays repeatedly) methods.

If the getAudioClip() or newAudioClip() methods can't find the sound file indicated by their arguments, the value of the AudioClip object will be null. Trying to play a null object results in an error, so test for this condition before using an AudioClip object.

More than one sound can play simultaneously—they will be mixed together during playback.

When using a sound loop in an applet, note that it won't stop automatically when the applet's running thread is stopped. If a Web user moves to another page, the sound continues playing, which isn't likely to win you any friends among the Web-surfing public.

You can fix this problem by using the stop() method on the looping sound at the same time the applet's thread is being stopped.

Listing 14.1 is an applet that plays two sounds: a looping sound named train.wav and another sound called whistle.wav that plays every 5 seconds.

LISTING 14.1   The Full Text of Looper.java

```
 1: import java.awt.*;
 2: import java.applet.AudioClip;
 3:
 4: public class Looper extends javax.swing.JApplet implements Runnable {
 5:     AudioClip bgSound;
 6:     AudioClip beep;
 7:     Thread runner;
 8:
 9:     public void init() {
10:         bgSound = getAudioClip(getCodeBase(),"train.wav");
11:         beep = getAudioClip(getCodeBase(), "whistle.wav");
12:     }
13:
```

14

LISTING **14.1**   continued

```
14:     public void start() {
15:         if (runner == null) {
16:             runner = new Thread(this);
17:             runner.start();
18:         }
19:     }
20:
21:     public void stop() {
22:         if (runner != null) {
23:             if (bgSound != null)
24:                 bgSound.stop();
25:             runner = null;
26:         }
27:     }
28:
29:     public void run() {
30:         if (bgSound != null)
31:             bgSound.loop();
32:         Thread thisThread = Thread.currentThread();
33:         while (runner == thisThread) {
34:             try {
35:                 Thread.sleep(9000);
36:                 if (beep != null)
37:                     beep.play();
38:             } catch (InterruptedException e) { }
39:         }
40:     }
41:
42:     public void paint(Graphics screen) {
43:         Graphics2D screen2D = (Graphics2D)screen;
44:         screen2D.drawString("Playing Sounds ...", 10, 10);
45:     }
46: }
```

To test `Looper`, create a Web page with an applet window of any height and width. The audio files `train.wav` and `whistle.wav` can be copied from the book's Web site (`http://www.java21days.com`) into the `\J21work` folder on your system. When you run the applet, the only visual output is a single string, but you should hear two sounds playing as the applet runs.

The `init()` method in lines 9–12 loads the two sound files. No attempt is made in this method to make sure that the files were actually loaded—if they cannot be found, the `bgsound` and `beep` variables would equal `null`. Testing for `null` values in these variables will occur elsewhere before the sound files are used, such as in lines 30 and 36, when the `loop()` and `play()` methods are used on the `AudioClip` objects.

Lines 23–24 turn off the looping sound if the thread is also stopped.

JavaSound

The new version of Java includes several packages that greatly expand the sound playback and creation capabilities of the language.

JavaSound, which was offered separately prior to Java 2 version 1.3, has become an official part of the Java class library as the following packages:

- `javax.sound.midi`—Classes for playing, recording, and synthesizing sound files in `MIDI` format.
- `javax.sound.sampled`—Classes for playing, recording, and mixing recorded audio files.

The JavaSound library supports all the audio formats available for playback in applets and applications: `AIFF`, `AU`, `MIDI`, and `WAV`. It also supports `RMF`, a standard for Rich Media Format music files.

MIDI Files

The `javax.sound.midi` package offers extensive support for `MIDI` music files. `MIDI`, which stands for Musical Instrument Digital Interface, is a format for storing sound as a series of notes and effects to be produced by computer synthesized instruments.

Unlike sampled files representing actual sound recorded and digitized for computer presentation, such as `WAV` and `AU`, `MIDI` is closer to a musical score for a synthesizer than a realized recording. `MIDI` files are stored instructions that tell `MIDI` sequencers how to reproduce sound, which synthesized instruments to use, and other aspects of presentation. The sound of a `MIDI` file depends on the quality and variety of the instruments available on the computer or output device.

`MIDI` files are generally much smaller than recorded audio, and they're not suited to representing voices and some other types of sound. However, because of compactness and effects-capability, `MIDI` is used in many different ways—such as computer game background music, Muzak-style versions of pop songs, or the preliminary presentations of classical composition for composers and students.

`MIDI` files are played back by using a sequencer, which can be a hardware device or software program, to play a data structure called a sequence. A sequence is made up of one or more tracks each containing a series of time-coded `MIDI` note and effect instructions called `MIDI` events.

Each of these elements of MIDI presentation is represented by an interface or class in the `javax.sound.midi` package: the `Sequencer` interface and the `Sequence`, `Track`, and `MidiEvent` classes.

14

There also is a `MidiSystem` class that provides access to the `MIDI` playback and storage resources on a computer system.

Playing a `MIDI` File

To play a `MIDI` file using JavaSound, you must create a `Sequencer` object based on the MIDI handling capability of a particular system.

The `MidiSystem` class method `getSequencer()` returns a `Sequencer` object that represents a system's default sequencer:

```
Sequencer midi = MidiSystem.getSequencer();
```

This class method generates an exception—an object indicating an error—if the sequencer is unavailable for any reason. A `MidiUnavailableException` is generated in this circumstance.

You worked with exceptions briefly yesterday, enclosing calls to `Thread.sleep()` in try-catch blocks because that method generates `InterruptedException` errors if the method is interrupted.

You can handle the exception generated by `getSequencer()` with the following code:

```
try {
    Sequencer.midi = MidiSystem.getSequencer();
    // additional code to play a MIDI sequence ...
} catch (MidiUnavailableException exc) {
    System.out.println("Error: " + exc.getMessage());
}
```

In this example, if a sequencer is available when `getSequencer()` is called, the program continues to the next statement inside the `try` block. If the sequencer can't be accessed because of a `MidiUnavailableException`, the program executes the `catch` block, displaying an error message.

Several methods and constructors involved in playing a MIDI file generate exceptions. Rather than enclosing each one in its own `try-catch` block, it can be easier to handle all possible errors by using `Exception`, the superclass of all exceptions, in the `catch` statement:

```
try {
    Sequencer.midi = MidiSystem.getSequencer();
    // additional code to play a MIDI sequence ...
} catch (Exception exc) {
    System.out.println("Error: " + exc.getMessage());
}
```

This example doesn't just handle `MidiUnavailableException` problems in the `catch` block. When you add additional statements to load and play a MIDI sequence inside the `try` block, any exceptions generated by those statements will cause the `catch` block to be executed. Exceptions are covered fully on Day 16, "Error Handling and Security."

After you have created a `Sequencer` object that can play MIDI files, you call another class method of `MidiSystem` to retrieve a MIDI sequence from a data source:

- `getSequence(File)`—Loads a sequence from the specified file.
- `getSequence(URL)`—Loads a sequence from the specified Internet address.
- `getSequence(InputStream)`—Loads a sequence from the specified data input stream, which can come from a file, input device, or another program.

To load a `MIDI` sequence from a file, you must first create a `File` object using its file-name or a reference to its filename and the folder where it can be found.

If the file is in the same folder as your Java program, you can create it using the `File(String)` constructor with that name. The following statement creates a `File` object for a `MIDI` file called `nevermind.mid`:

```
File sound = new File("nevermind.mid");
```

You can also use relative file references that include subfolders:

```
File sound = new File("tunes/nevermind.mid");
```

The `File` constructor generates a `NullPointerException` if the argument to the constructor has a `null` value.

After you have a `File` object associated with a `MIDI` file, you can call `getSequence(File)` to create a sequence:

```
File sound = new File("aboutagirl.mid");
Sequence seq = MidiSystem.getSequence(sound);
```

If all goes well, the `getSequence()` class method will return a `Sequence` object. If not, two kinds of errors can be generated by the method: `InvalidMidiDataException` if the system can't handle the MIDI data (or it isn't MIDI data at all), and `IOException` if file input was interrupted or failed for some reason.

At this point, if your program has not been derailed by an error, you have a `MIDI` sequencer and a sequence to play. You are ready to play the file—you don't have to deal with tracks or `MIDI` events just to play back an entire `MIDI` file.

14

Playing a sequence involves the following steps:

- Call the sequencer's open() method so the device prepares to play something.
- Call the sequencer's start() method to begin playing the sequence.
- Wait for the sequence to finish playing (or for a user to stop playback in some manner).
- Call the sequencer's close() method to free the device for other things.

The only one of these methods that generates an exception is open(), which produces a MidiUnavailableException if the sequencer can't be readied for playback.

Calling close() stops a sequencer, even if it is currently playing one or more sequences. You can use the sequencer method isRunning(), which returns a boolean value, to check whether it is still playing (or recording) MIDI sequences.

The following example uses this method on a sequencer object called playback that has a sequence loaded:

```
playback.open();
playback.start();
while (playback.isRunning()) {
    try {
        Thread.sleep(1000);
    } catch (InterruptedException e) { }
}
playback.close();
```

The while loop prevents the sequencer from being closed until the sequence has completed playback. The call to Thread.sleep() inside the loop slows it down so that isRunning() is only checked once per second (1000 milliseconds)—otherwise, the program will use a lot of resources by calling isRunning() numerous times per second.

The PlayMidi application in Listing 14.2 plays a MIDI sequence from a file on your system. The application displays a frame that contains a user interface component called MidiPanel, and this panel runs in its own thread and plays the file.

LISTING 14.2   The Full Text of PlayMidi.java

```
1: import javax.swing.*;
2: import javax.sound.midi.*;
3: import java.awt.GridLayout;
4: import java.io.File;
5:
6: public class PlayMidi extends JFrame {
7:
8:     PlayMidi(String song) {
```

```
 9:            super("Play MIDI Files");
10:            setSize(180, 100);
11:            setDefaultCloseOperation(JFrame.EXIT_ON_CLOSE);
12:            MidiPanel midi = new MidiPanel(song);
13:            JPanel pane = new JPanel();
14:            pane.add(midi);
15:            setContentPane(pane);
16:            show();
17:        }
18:
19:        public static void main(String[] arguments) {
20:            if (arguments.length != 1) {
21:                System.out.println("Usage: java PlayMidi filename");
22:            } else {
23:                PlayMidi pm = new PlayMidi(arguments[0]);
24:            }
25:        }
26: }
27:
28: class MidiPanel extends JPanel implements Runnable {
29:        Thread runner;
30:        JProgressBar progress = new JProgressBar();
31:        Sequence currentSound;
32:        Sequencer player;
33:        String songFile;
34:
35:        MidiPanel(String song) {
36:            super();
37:            songFile = song;
38:            JLabel label = new JLabel("Playing file ...");
39:            setLayout(new GridLayout(2, 1));
40:            add(label);
41:            add(progress);
42:            if (runner == null) {
43:                runner = new Thread(this);
44:                runner.start();
45:            }
46:        }
47:
48:        public void run() {
49:            try {
50:                File file = new File(songFile);
51:                currentSound = MidiSystem.getSequence(file);
52:                player = MidiSystem.getSequencer();
53:                player.open();
54:                player.setSequence(currentSound);
55:                progress.setMinimum(0);
56:                progress.setMaximum((int)player.getMicrosecondLength());
57:                player.start();
58:                while (player.isRunning()) {
59:                    progress.setValue((int)player.getMicrosecondPosition());
```

14

LISTING 14.2   continued

```
60:                    try {
61:                        Thread.sleep(1000);
62:                    } catch (InterruptedException e) { }
63:                }
64:                progress.setValue((int)player.getMicrosecondPosition());
65:                player.close();
66:            } catch (Exception ex) {
67:                System.out.println(ex.toString());
68:            }
69:        }
70: }
```

You must specify the name of a MIDI file as a command-line argument when running this application. If you don't have any MIDI files, one is available from the book's Web site—visit http://www.java21days.com and open the Day 14 page.

> Hundreds of MIDI archives are on the World Wide Web. To find some of the most popular archives, visit the search engine Google at http://www.google.com and search for the term MIDI files. Google displays sites in the order of their visitation frequency, so you should be able to find a few great MIDI resources quickly.

The following command runs the application with a MIDI file called betsy.mid (the 19th century folk song "Sweet Betsy from Pike," available from the book's Web site):

```
java PlayMidi betsy.mid
```

Figure 14.1 shows the application in mid-playback.

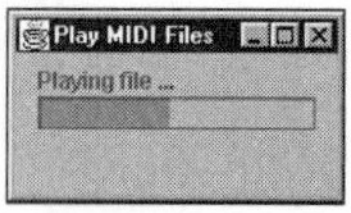

FIGURE 14.1

The PlayMidi application playing a MIDI file.

The application includes a progress bar that displays how much of the sequence has been played. This is handled using the JProgressBar user interface component and two sequencer methods:

- getMicrosecondLength()—The total length of the currently loaded sequence, expressed in microseconds as a long value

- getMicrosecondPosition()—The microsecond that represents the current position in the sequence, also a long value

A microsecond is equal to one-millionth of a second, so you can use these methods to get an astonishingly precise measurement of MIDI playback progress.

The progress bar is created as an instance variable of MidiPanel in line 30. Though you can create a progress bar with a minimum and maximum, there's no way to know the length of a sequence until it has been loaded.

The progress bar's minimum is set to 0 in line 55 and to the sequence's microsecond length in line 56.

> **Caution**
>
> The progress bar's setMinimum() and setMaximum() methods require integer arguments, so this application converts the microsecond values from long to int. Because of this loss of precision, the progress bar won't work correctly for files longer than 2.14 billion microseconds (around 35.6 minutes).

The run() method in lines 48–69 of Listing 14.2 loads the system sequencer and a MIDI file into a sequence, and plays the sequence. The while loop in lines 58–63 uses the sequencer's isRunning() method to wait until the file finishes playing before doing anything else. This loop also updates the progress bar by calling its setValue() method with the current microsecond position of the sequence.

After the file finishes playback and the while loop terminates, the microsecond position of the sequence is reported as 0, which is used in line 64 to set the progress bar back to its minimum value.

Manipulating Sound Files

Up to this point, you have used JavaSound to recreate functionality that's already available in the audio methods of the Applet class, which can play MIDI files in addition to the other supported formats.

JavaSound's strength as an alternative becomes apparent when you manipulate the sound files you are working with. You can change many aspects of the presentation and recording of audio using the JavaSound packages.

One way to change a MIDI file during playback is to alter its tempo, the speed at which the file is played.

To do this on an existing Sequencer object, call its setTempoFactor(float) method.

14

Tempo is represented as a float value from 0.0 upwards. Every MIDI sequence has its own established tempo, which is represented by the value 1.0. A tempo of 0.5 is half as fast, 2.0 twice as fast, and so on.

To retrieve the current tempo, call getTempoFactor(), which returns a float value.

The next project you create, MidiApplet, uses the same technique to load and play a MIDI file as the PlayMidi application—a panel is displayed that plays a MIDI file in its own thread. The MIDI file is loaded using a File object and played using a sequencer's open(), start(), and close() methods.

One difference in this project is that the MIDI file can be played over and over again, rather than just once.

Because this is an applet rather than an application, the MIDI file to play will be specified as a parameter. Listing 14.3 contains an example of an HTML document that can be used to load the applet.

LISTING 14.3   The Full Text of MidiApplet.html

```
1: <applet code="MidiApplet.class" height="100" width="250">
2: <param name="file" value="camptown.mid">
3: </applet>
```

The MIDI file used in this example, a MIDI version of "Camptown Races," is available from the book's Web site at http://www.java21days.com on the Day 14 page. You can, of course, substitute any other MIDI file.

The MidiApplet project has three user interface components you can use to control how the file is played: Play and Stop buttons and a drop-down list for the selection of a tempo.

Figure 14.2 shows what the program looks like when loaded by appletviewer.

FIGURE 14.2

The MidiApplet *program playing "Camptown Races."*

Because applets will continue playing sound in a Web browser even after a user loads a different page, there must be a way to stop playback.

If you are running audio in its own thread, you can stop the audio by using the same thread-stopping techniques introduced for animation yesterday—run the thread in a `Thread` object, loop while that object and `Thread.currentThread()` represent the same object, and set `runner` to `null` when you are ready to stop the thread.

Listing 14.4 contains the `MidiApplet` project. The length of this program is primarily because of the creation of the graphical user interface and the event-handling methods to receive input from the user. The JavaSound-related aspects of the program will be introduced after you have created the applet.

LISTING 14.4   The Full Text of `MidiApplet.java`

```
 1: import javax.swing.*;
 2: import java.awt.event.*;
 3: import javax.sound.midi.*;
 4: import java.awt.GridLayout;
 5: import java.io.File;
 6:
 7: public class MidiApplet extends javax.swing.JApplet {
 8:     public void init() {
 9:         JPanel pane = new JPanel();
10:         MidiPlayer midi = new MidiPlayer(getParameter("file"));
11:         pane.add(midi);
12:         setContentPane(pane);
13:     }
14: }
15:
16: class MidiPlayer extends JPanel implements Runnable, ActionListener {
17:
18:     Thread runner;
19:     JButton play = new JButton("Play");
20:     JButton stop = new JButton("Stop");
21:     JLabel message = new JLabel();
22:     JComboBox tempoBox = new JComboBox();
23:     float tempo = 1.0F;
24:     Sequence currentSound;
25:     Sequencer player;
26:     String songFile;
27:
28:     MidiPlayer(String song) {
29:         super();
30:         songFile = song;
31:         play.addActionListener(this);
32:         stop.setEnabled(false);
33:         stop.addActionListener(this);
34:         for (float i = 0.25F; i < 7F; i += 0.25F)
35:             tempoBox.addItem("" + i);
36:         tempoBox.setSelectedItem("1.0");
```

14

LISTING **14.4**   continued

```
37:             tempoBox.setEnabled(false);
38:             tempoBox.addActionListener(this);
39:             setLayout(new GridLayout(2, 1));
40:             add(message);
41:             JPanel buttons = new JPanel();
42:             JLabel tempoLabel = new JLabel("Tempo: ");
43:             buttons.add(play);
44:             buttons.add(stop);
45:             buttons.add(tempoLabel);
46:             buttons.add(tempoBox);
47:             add(buttons);
48:             if (songFile == null) {
49:                 play.setEnabled(false);
50:             }
51:         }
52:
53:     public void actionPerformed(ActionEvent evt) {
54:         if (evt.getSource() instanceof JButton) {
55:             if (evt.getSource() == play)
56:                 play();
57:             else
58:                 stop();
59:         } else {
60:             String item = (String)tempoBox.getSelectedItem();
61:             try {
62:                 tempo = Float.parseFloat(item);
63:                 player.setTempoFactor(tempo);
64:                 message.setText("Playing " + songFile + " at "
65:                     + tempo + " tempo");
66:             } catch (NumberFormatException ex) {
67:                 message.setText(ex.toString());
68:             }
69:         }
70:     }
71:
72:     void play() {
73:         if (runner == null) {
74:             runner = new Thread(this);
75:             runner.start();
76:             play.setEnabled(false);
77:             stop.setEnabled(true);
78:             tempoBox.setEnabled(true);
79:         }
80:     }
81:
82:     void stop() {
83:         if (runner != null) {
84:             runner = null;
85:             stop.setEnabled(false);
```

```
 86:                    play.setEnabled(true);
 87:                    tempoBox.setEnabled(false);
 88:                }
 89:        }
 90:
 91:        public void run() {
 92:            try {
 93:                File song = new File(songFile);
 94:                currentSound = MidiSystem.getSequence(song);
 95:                player = MidiSystem.getSequencer();
 96:            } catch (Exception ex) {
 97:                message.setText(ex.toString());
 98:            }
 99:            Thread thisThread = Thread.currentThread();
100:            while (runner == thisThread) {
101:                try {
102:                    player.open();
103:                    player.setSequence(currentSound);
104:                    player.setTempoFactor(tempo);
105:                    player.start();
106:                    message.setText("Playing " + songFile + " at "
107:                        + tempo + " tempo");
108:                    while (player.isRunning() && runner != null) {
109:                        try {
110:                            Thread.sleep(1000);
111:                        } catch (InterruptedException e) { }
112:                    }
113:                    message.setText("");
114:                    player.close();
115:                } catch (Exception ex) {
116:                    message.setText(ex.toString());
117:                    break;
118:                }
119:            }
120:        }
121: }
```

Run MidiApplet by loading it on an HTML document using appletviewer or a Web browser that's equipped with the most up-to-date Java 2 plug-in. Internet Explorer 5 and Netscape Navigator 4 cannot run this applet without the plug-in because they do not fully support Java 2.

The tempo of the MIDI file is controlled by a drop-down list component called tempoBox. This component is created with a range of floating-point values from 0.25 to 6.75 in lines 34–35. The list's addItem(Object) method cannot be used with float values, so they are combined with an empty string—quote marks without any text inside—in line 36. This causes the combined argument to be sent to addItem() as a String object.

14

Though the tempo can be set using `tempoBox`, it is stored in its own instance variable, `tempo`. This variable is initialized in line 23 with a value of 1.0, the sequence's default playback speed.

If the drop-down list from which a user selects a value has an `ActionListener` associated with it, the listener's `actionPerformed` method will be called.

The `actionPerformed()` method in lines 53–70 handles all three kinds of possible user input:

- Clicking the Play button causes the `play()` method to be called.
- Clicking the Stop button causes the `stop()` method to be called.
- Choosing a new value from the drop-down list causes that value to become the new tempo.

Because all the items in `tempoBox` are stored as strings, you must convert them into floating-point values before you can use them to set the tempo.

This can be done by calling the class method `Float.parseFloat()`, which is comparable to the method `Integer.parseInt()` that has been used several times to work with integers during the past two weeks.

Like the other parse method, `parseFloat()` generates a `NumberFormatException` error if the string cannot be converted to a `float` value.

> **Note**
>
> When `tempoBox` was created, the only items added to it are strings that convert successfully to floating-point values, so there's no way a `NumberFormatException` can result from using this component to set the tempo. However, Java still requires that the exception be dealt with in a `try-catch` block.

Line 63 calls the sequencer's `setTempoFactor()` method with the tempo selected by the user. This takes effect immediately, so you can modify the tempo of a song to sometimes maniacal results.

After the sequencer and sequence have been created in the `run()` method, the `while` loop in lines 100–119 keeps playing the song until the `Thread` object `runner` has been set to `null`.

Another `while` loop, which is nested inside this one, makes sure that the sequencer is not closed while the song is playing. This loop in lines 108–112 is a little different from the one used in the `PlayMidi` application. Instead of looping while `player.isRunning()` returns the value `true`, it requires two conditions to be met:

```
while (player.isRunning() && runner != null) {
    // statements in loop
}
```

The and operator `&&` causes the `while` loop to continue only if both expressions are `true`. If you did not test for the value of `runner` here, the thread would continue playing the MIDI file until the song ends, rather than stopping when `runner` has been set to `null`, which should signal the end of the thread.

The `MidiApplet` program does not stop the thread when the user goes to a different Web page.

Because `MidiPanel` has a `stop()` method that stops the thread, you can halt MIDI playback when the page is no longer being viewed in two steps:

1. Create an instance variable in `MidiApplet` for the user-interface component `MidiPanel`.

2. Override the applet's `stop()` method and use it to call the panel's `stop()` method.

Summary

During the past two days, you have worked with the dynamic multimedia features of the Java language.

One of the strengths of the Java class library is how complex programming tasks such as user interface programming and sound playback are encapsulated within easy-to-create and workable classes. You can play a MIDI file that can be manipulated in real time using only a few objects and class methods, in spite of the extremely complex behind-the-scenes development work.

Today, you played sound in programs using simple and more sophisticated techniques.

If you are only trying to play an audio file, working with `getAudioClip()` and `newAudioClip()` methods in the `Applet` class is probably sufficient.

If you want to do more complex things with the audio, such as changing its tempo and making other dynamic modifications, JavaSound packages such as `javax.sound.midi` can be used.

14

During the third week of the book, you will explore many of the advanced features of the Java language, including exception handling, file and data input and output, Java database connectivity, and JavaBeans.

Q&A

Q **The method `getSequence(InputStream)` is mentioned in this chapter. What is an input stream, and how are they used with sound files?**

A Input streams are objects that retrieve data as it is being sent from another source. The source can be a wide range of things capable of producing data—files, serial ports, servers, or even objects in the same program. You work with streams extensively on Day 17, "Handling Data Through Java Streams."

Q **What other things are possible in JavaSound, in addition to what's presented here?**

A JavaSound is a set of packages that rival Swing in complexity, and many of the classes involve sophisticated stream- and exception-handling techniques that will be covered next week. You can learn more about JavaSound and the things you can accomplish with the library on Sun's Web site at `http://java.sun.com/products/java-media/sound`. Sun offers a Java application called the Java Sound Demo that collects some of the most impressive features of JavaSound: playback, recording, MIDI synthesis, and programmable MIDI instruments.

Questions

1. Which `Applet` class method can be used to create an `AudioClip` object in an application?

   (a) `newAudioClip()`

   (b) `getAudioClip()`

   (c) `getSequence()`

2. What class represents the MIDI resources that are available on a specific computer system?

   (a) `Sequencer`

   (b) `MIDISystem`

   (c) `MIDIEvent`

3. How many microseconds does it take to cook a 3-minute egg?

(a) 180,000

(b) 180,000,000

(c) 180,000,000,000

Answers

1. a. It's a misnomer for this method to be included in the `Applet` class, but that's a quirk of Java 1.0 that remains in Java 2.0.

2. b. The `MIDISystem` class is used to create objects that represent sequencers, synthesizers, and other devices that handle `MIDI` audio.

3. b. One million microseconds are in a second, so 180 million microseconds is equal to 180 seconds.

Exercises

To extend your knowledge of the subjects covered today, try the following exercises:

- Create an application that uses `newAudioClip()` to play a sound file.
- Convert the `MidiApplet` project so that you can specify more than one `MIDI` file as parameters on a Web page and play each one in succession.

Where applicable, exercise solutions are offered on the book's Web site at `http://www.java21days.com`.

14

WEEK 3

Java's Advanced Features

15 Packages, Interfaces, and Other Class Features

16 Error Handling and Security

17 Handling Data Through Java Streams

18 Object Serialization and Reflection

19 Communicating Across the Internet

20 Working with JavaBeans

21 Java Database Connectivity and Data Structures

DAY 15

Packages, Interfaces, and Other Class Features

The third week of this course extends what you already know. You could quit at this point and develop functional programs, but you would be missing some of the advanced features that express the real strengths of the language.

Today, you extend your knowledge of classes and how they interact with other classes in a Java program. The following subjects will be covered:

- Controlling access to methods and variables from outside a class
- Finalizing classes, methods, and variables so that their values or definitions cannot be subclasses or cannot be overridden
- Creating abstract classes and methods for factoring common behavior into superclasses
- Grouping classes into packages
- Using interfaces to bridge gaps in a class hierarchy

Modifiers

The techniques for programming you learn today involve different strategies and ways of thinking about how a class is organized. But the one thing all these techniques have in common is that they all use special modifier keywords in the Java language.

In Week 1, you learned how to define classes, methods, and variables in Java. Modifiers are keywords that you add to those definitions to change their meaning.

The Java language has a wide variety of modifiers, including

- Modifiers for controlling access to a class, method, or variable: `public`, `protected`, and `private`
- The `static` modifier, for creating class methods and variables
- The `final` modifier, for finalizing the implementations of classes, methods, and variables
- The `abstract` modifier, for creating abstract classes and methods
- The `synchronized` and `volatile` modifiers, which are used for threads

To use a modifier, you include its keyword in the definition of the class, method, or variable that is being modified. The modifier precedes the rest of the statement, as in the following examples:

```
public class MyApplet extends java.applet.Applet { ... }

private boolean offline;

static final double weeks = 9.5;

protected static final int MEANINGOFLIFE = 42;

public static void main(String[] arguments) {
    ...
}
```

If you're using more than one modifier in a statement, you can place them in any order, as long as all modifiers precede the element they are modifying. Make sure to avoid treating a method's return type—such as `void`—as if it were one of the modifiers.

Modifiers are optional—which you should realize, after using very few of them in the preceding two weeks. You can come up with many good reasons to use them, though, as you'll see.

Access Control for Methods and Variables

The modifiersthat you will use the most often in your programs are the ones that control access to methods and variables: `public`, `private`, and `protected`. These modifiers determine which variables and methods of a class are visible to other classes.

By using access control, you control how your class will be used by other classes. Some variables and methods in a class will be of use only within the class itself, and they should be hidden from other classes that might interact with the class. This process is called encapsulation: An object controls what the outside world can know about it and how the outside world can interact with it.

NEW TERM   *Encapsulation* is the process of preventing the variables of a class from being read or modified by other classes. The only way to use these variables is by calling methods of the class, if they are available.

The Java language provides four levels of access control: `public`, `private`, `protected`, and a default level that is specified by using no modifier.

Default Access

For most of the examples in this book, you have not specified any kind of access control. Variables and methods were declared with statements such as the following:

```
String singer = "Phil Harris";
boolean digThatCrazyBeat() {
    return true;
}
```

A variable or method that is declared without any access control modifier is available to any other class in the same package. Previously, you saw how classes in the Java class library are organized into packages. The `java.awt` package is one of them—a set of related classes for behavior related to Java's Abstract Windowing Toolkit.

Any variable declared without a modifier can be read or changed by any other class in the same package. Any method declared the same way can be called by any other class in the same package. No other classes can access these elements in any way.

This level of access control doesn't control much access. When you start thinking more about how your class will be used by other classes, you'll be using one of the three modifiers more often than accepting the default control.

15

Note

> The preceding discussion raises the question about what package your own
> classes have been in up to this point. As you'll see later today, you can make
> your class a member of a package by using the `package` declaration. If you
> don't use this approach, the class is put into a package with all other classes
> that don't belong to any other packages.

Private Access

To completely hide a method or variable from being used by any other classes, you use
the `private` modifier. The only place these methods or variables can be seen is from
within their own class.

A private instance variable, for example, can be used by methods in its own class but not
by objects of any other class. In the same vein, private methods can be called by other
methods in their own class but by no others. This restriction also affects inheritance:
Neither private variables nor private methods are inherited by subclasses.

Private variables are extremely useful in two circumstances:

- When other classes have no reason to use that variable
- When another class could wreak havoc by changing the variable in an inappropri-
  ate way

For example, consider a Java class called `SlotMachine` that generates bingo numbers for
an Internet gambling site. A variable in that class called `winRatio` could control the number of winners and losers that are generated. As you can imagine, this variable has a big
impact on the bottom line at the site. If the variable were changed by other classes, the
performance of `SlotMachine` would change greatly. To guard against this scenario, you
can declare the `winRatio` variable as `private`.

The following class uses private access control:

```
class Writer {
    private boolean writersBlock = true;
    private String mood;
    private int income = 0;

    private void getIdea(Inspiration in) {
        // ...
    }

    Manuscript createManuscript(int numDays, long numPages) {
        // ...
    }
}
```

15

In this code example, the internal data to the class `Writer` (the variables `writersBlock`, `mood`, and `income` and the method `getIdea()`) is all private. The only method accessible from outside the `Writer` class is the `createManuscript()` method. `createManuscript()` is the only task other objects can ask the `Writer` object to perform. `Editor` and `Publisher` objects might prefer a more direct means of extracting a `Manuscript` object from the `Writer`, but they don't have the access to do so.

Using the `private` modifier is the main way that an object encapsulates itself. You can't limit the ways in which a class is used without using `private` in many places to hide variables and methods. Another class is free to change the variables inside a class and call its methods in any way desired if you don't control access.

Public Access

In some cases, you might want a method or variable in a class to be completely available to any other class that wants to use it. Think of the class variable `black` from the `Color` class. This variable is used when a class wants to use the color black, so `black` should have no access control at all.

Class variables often are declared to be `public`. An example would be a set of variables in a `Football` class that represent the number of points used in scoring. The `TOUCHDOWN` variable could equal 7, the `FIELDGOAL` variable could equal 3, and so on. These variables would need to be public so that other classes could use them in statements such as the following:

```
if (position < 0) {
    System.out.println("Touchdown!");
    score = score + Football.TOUCHDOWN;
}
```

The `public` modifier makes a method or variable completely available to all classes. You have used it in every application you have written so far, with a statement such as the following:

```
public static void main(String[] arguments) {
    // ...
}
```

The `main()` method of an application has to be public. Otherwise, it could not be called by the `java` interpreter to run the class.

Because of class inheritance, all public methods and variables of a class are inherited by its subclasses.

Protected Access

The third level of access control is to limit a method and variable to use by the following two groups:

- Subclasses of a class
- Other classes in the same package

You do so by using the protected modifier, as in the following statement:

```
protected boolean outOfData = true;
```

Note

> You might be wondering how these two groups are different. After all, aren't subclasses part of the same package as their superclass? Not always. An example is the Applet class. It is a subclass of java.awt.Panel but is actually in its own package, java.applet. Protected access differs from default access this way; protected variables are available to subclasses, even if they aren't in the same package.

This level of access control is useful if you want to make it easier for a subclass to implement itself. Your class might use a method or variable to help the class do its job. Because a subclass inherits much of the same behavior and attributes, it might have the same job to do. Protected access gives the subclass a chance to use the helper method or variable, while preventing a nonrelated class from trying to use it.

Consider the example of a class called AudioPlayer that plays a digital audio file. AudioPlayer has a method called openSpeaker(), which is an internal method that interacts with the hardware to prepare the speaker for playing. openSpeaker() isn't important to anyone outside the AudioPlayer class, so at first glance you might want to make it private. A snippet of AudioPlayer might look something like this:

```
class AudioPlayer {

    private boolean openSpeaker(Speaker sp) {
        // implementation details
    }
}
```

This code works fine if AudioPlayer isn't going to be subclassed. But what if you were going to create a class called StreamingAudioPlayer that is a subclass of AudioPlayer? That class would want access to the openSpeaker() method so that it can override it and provide streaming audio-specific speaker initialization. You still don't want the method generally available to random objects (and so it shouldn't be public), but you want the subclass to have access to it.

Comparing Levels of Access Control

The differences between the various protection types can become very confusing, particularly in the case of protected methods and variables. Table 15.1, which summarizes exactly what is allowed where, helps clarify the differences from the least restrictive (public) to the most restrictive (private) forms of protection.

TABLE 15.1   The Different Levels of Access Control

Visibility	public	protected	default	private
From the same class	yes	yes	yes	yes
From any class in the same package	yes	yes	yes	no
From any class outside the package	yes	no	no	no
From a subclass in the same package	yes	yes	yes	no
From a subclass outside the same package	yes	yes	no	no

Access Control and Inheritance

One last issue regarding access control for methods involves subclasses. When you create a subclass and override a method, you must consider the access control in place on the original method.

You might recall that Applet methods such as init() and paint() must be public in your own applets.

As a general rule, you cannot override a method in Java and make the new method more controlled than the original. You can, however, make it more public. The following rules for inherited methods are enforced:

- Methods declared public in a superclass must also be public in all subclasses. (For this reason, most of the applet methods are public.)

- Methods declared protected in a superclass must either be protected or public in subclasses; they cannot be private.

- Methods declared without access control (no modifier was used) can be declared more private in subclasses.

Methods declared private are not inherited at all, so the rules don't apply.

Accessor Methods

In many cases, you may have an instance variable in a class that has strict rules for the values it can contain. An example would be a zipCode variable. A ZIP Code in the United States must be a number that is five-digits long.

To prevent an external class from setting the zipCode variable incorrectly, you can declare it private with a statement such as the following:

```
private int zipCode;
```

However, what if other classes must be able to set the zipCode variable for the class to be useful? In that circumstance, you can give other classes access to a private variable by using an accessor method inside the same class as zipCode.

Accessor methods get their name because they provide access to something that otherwise would be off-limits. By using a method to provide access to a private variable, you can control how that variable is used. In the ZIP Code example, the class could prevent anyone else from setting zipCode to an incorrect value.

Often, separate accessor methods to read and write a variable are available. Reading methods have a name beginning with get, and writing methods have a name beginning with set, as in setZipCode(*int*) and getZipCode(*int*).

 Note

> This convention is becoming more standard with each version of Java. You might recall how the size() method of the Dimension class has been changed to getSize() as of Java 2. You might want to use the same naming convention for your own accessor methods, as a means of making the class more understandable.

Using methods to access instance variables is a frequently used technique in object-oriented programming. This approach makes classes more reusable because it guards against a class being used improperly.

Static Variables and Methods

A modifier you already have used in programs is static, which was introduced during Day 6, "Creating Classes and Methods." The static modifier is used to create class methods and variables, as in the following example:

```
public class Circle {
    public static float pi = 3.14159265F;

    public float area(float r) {
        return  pi * r * r;
    }
}
```

Class variables and methods can be accessed using the class name followed by a dot and the name of the variable or method, as in Color.black or Circle.pi. You also can use the name of an object of the class, but for class variables and methods, using the class name is better. This approach makes clearer what kind of variable or method you're working with; instance variables and methods can never be referred to by class name.

The following statements use class variables and methods:

```
float circumference = 2 * Circle.pi * getRadius();
float randomNumber = Math.random();
```

Tip

For the same reason that holds true for instance variables, class variables can benefit from being private and limiting their use to accessor methods only.

Listing 15.1 shows a class called CountInstances that uses class and instance variables to keep track of how many instances of that class have been created.

LISTING 15.1   The Full Text of CountInstances.java

```
 1: public class CountInstances {
 2:     private static int numInstances = 0;
 3:
 4:     protected static int getNumInstances() {
 5:         return numInstances;
 6:     }
 7:
 8:     private static void addInstance() {
 9:         numInstances++;
10:     }
11:
12:     CountInstances() {
13:         CountInstances.addInstance();
14:     }
15:
16:     public static void main(String[] arguments) {
17:         System.out.println("Starting with " +
18:             CountInstances.getNumInstances() + " instances");
19:         for (int  i = 0; i < 10; ++i)
20:             new CountInstances();
21:         System.out.println("Created " +
22:             CountInstances.getNumInstances() + " instances");
23:     }
24: }
```

The output of this program is as follows:

```
Started with 0 instances
Created 10 instances
```

This example has a number of features. In line 2, you declare a `private` class variable to hold the number of instances (called `numInstances`). It is a class variable (declared `static`) because the number of instances is relevant to the class as a whole, not to any one instance. And it's private so that it follows the same rules as instance variables' accessor methods.

Note the initialization of `numInstances` in that same line. Just as an instance variable is initialized when its instance is created, a class variable is initialized when its class is created. This class initialization happens essentially before anything else can happen to that class, or its instances, so the class in the example will work as planned.

In lines 4–6, you create a `get` method for that private instance variable to get its value (`getNumInstances()`). This method is also declared as a class method because it applies directly to the class variable. The `getNumInstances()` method is declared `protected`, as opposed to `public`, because only this class and perhaps subclasses will be interested in that value; other random classes are therefore restricted from seeing it.

Note that you don't have an accessor method to set the value. The reason is that the value of the variable should be incremented only when a new instance is created; it should not be set to any random value. Instead of creating an accessor method, therefore, you create a special private method called `addInstance()` in lines 8–10 that increments the value of `numInstances` by 1.

Lines 12–14 create the constructor method for this class. Remember, constructors are called when a new object is created, which makes this the most logical place to call `addInstance()` and to increment the variable.

Finally, the `main()` method indicates that you can run this as a Java application and test all the other methods. In the `main()` method, you create 10 instances of the `CountInstances` class, reporting after you're done the value of the `numInstances` class variable (which, predictably, prints `10`).

Final Classes, Methods, and Variables

The `final` modifier is used with classes, methods, and variables to indicate that they will not be changed. It has different meanings for each thing that can be made final, as follows:

- A `final` class cannot be subclassed.
- A `final` method cannot be overridden by any subclasses.
- A `final` variable cannot change in value.

Variables

You got a chance to work with final variables during Day 6. They are often called constant variables (or just constants) because they do not change in value at any time.

With variables, the `final` modifier often is used with `static` to make the constant a class variable. If the value never changes, you don't have much reason to give each object in the same class its own copy of the value. They all can use the class variable with the same functionality.

The following statements are examples of declaring constants:

```
public static final int TOUCHDOWN = 7;
static final TITLE = "Captain";
```

As of Java 2, any kind of variable can be a final variable: class, instance, or local variables. A local variable could not be final in Java 1.0, but that was changed as part of the addition of inner classes to the language.

Methods

Final methods are those that can never be overridden by a subclass. You declare them using the `final` modifier in the class declaration, as in the following example:

```
public final void getSignature() {
    // ...
}
```

The most common reason to declare a method `final` is to make the class run more efficiently. Normally, when a Java runtime environment such as the `java` interpreter runs a method, it checks the current class to find the method first, checks its superclass second, and onward up the class hierarchy until the method is found. This process sacrifices some speed in the name of flexibility and ease of development.

If a method is `final`, the Java compiler can put the executable bytecode of the method directly into any program that calls the method. After all, the method won't ever change because of a subclass that overrides it.

When you are first developing a class, you won't have much reason to use `final`. However, if you need to make the class execute more quickly, you can change a few methods into `final` methods to speed up the process. Doing so removes the possibility of the method being overridden in a subclass later on, so consider this change carefully before continuing.

The Java class library declares many of the commonly used methods `final` so that they can be executed more quickly when utilized in programs that call them.

 Note   Private methods are final without being declared that way because they can't be overridden in a subclass under any circumstance.

Classes

You finalize classes by using the `final` modifier in the declaration for the class, as in the following:

```
public final class ChatServer {
    // ....
}
```

A final class cannot be subclassed by another class. As with final methods, this process introduces some speed benefits to the Java language at the expense of flexibility.

If you're wondering what you're losing by using final classes, you must not have tried to subclass something in the Java class library yet. Many of the popular classes are final, such as `java.lang.String`, `java.lang.Math`, and `java.net.InetAddress`. If you want to create a class that behaves like strings but with some new changes, you can't subclass `String` and define only the behavior that is different. You have to start from scratch.

All methods in a final class automatically are final themselves, so you don't have to use a modifier in their declarations.

Because classes that can bequeath their behavior and attributes to subclasses are much more useful, you should strongly consider whether the benefit of using `final` on one of your classes is outweighed by the cost.

Abstract Classes and Methods

In a class hierarchy, the higher the class, the more abstract its definition. A class at the top of a hierarchy of other classes can define only the behavior and attributes that are common to all the classes. More specific behavior and attributes are going to fall somewhere lower down the hierarchy.

When you are factoring out common behavior and attributes during the process of defining a hierarchy of classes, you might sometimes find yourself with a class that doesn't ever need to be instantiated directly. Instead, such a class serves as a place to hold common behavior and attributes shared by their subclasses.

15

These classes are called abstract classes, and they are created using the `abstract` modifier. The following is an example:

```
public abstract class Palette {
    // ...
}
```

An example of an abstract class is `java.awt.Component`, the superclass of all Abstract Windowing Toolkit components. All components inherit from this class, so it contains methods and variables useful to each of them. However, there's no such thing as a generic component that can be added to an interface, so you would never need to create a `Component` object in a program.

Abstract classes can contain anything a normal class can, including constructor methods, because their subclasses might need to inherit the methods. Abstract classes also can contain abstract methods, which are method signatures with no implementation. These methods are implemented in subclasses of the abstract class. Abstract methods are declared with the `abstract` modifier. You cannot declare an abstract method in a nonabstract class. If an abstract class has nothing but abstract methods, you're better off using an interface, as you'll see later today.

Packages

Using packages, as mentioned previously, is a way of organizing groups of classes. A package contains any number of classes that are related in purpose, in scope, or by inheritance.

If your programs are small and use a limited number of classes, you might find that you don't need to explore packages at all. But the more Java programming you create, the more classes you'll find you have. And although those classes might be individually well designed, reusable, encapsulated, and with specific interfaces to other classes, you might find the need for a bigger organizational entity that enables you to group your packages.

Packages are useful for several broad reasons:

- Packages enable you to organize your classes into units. Just as you have folders or directories on your hard disk to organize your files and applications, packages enable you to organize your classes into groups so that you use only what you need for each program.

- Packages reduce problems with conflicts in names. As the number of Java classes grows, so does the likelihood that you'll use the same class name as someone else, opening up the possibility of naming clashes and errors if you try to integrate groups of classes into a single program. Packages enable you to "hide" classes so that conflicts can be avoided.

- Packages enable you to protect classes, variables, and methods in larger ways than on a class-by-class basis, as you learned today. You'll learn more about protections with packages later.

- Packages can be used to identify your classes. For example, if you implement a set of classes to perform some task, you could name a package of those classes with a unique identifier that identifies you or your organization.

Although a package is most typically a collection of classes, packages can also contain other packages, forming yet another level of organization somewhat analogous to the inheritance hierarchy. Each "level" usually represents a smaller, more specific grouping of classes. The Java class library itself is organized along these lines. The top level is called java; the next level includes names such as io, net, util, and awt. The last of them has an even lower level, which includes the package image.

Note

> By convention, the first level of the hierarchy specifies the globally unique name to identify the author or owner of those packages. For example, Sun Microsystems's classes, which are not part of the standard Java environment, all begin with the prefix sun. Classes that Netscape includes with its implementation are contained in the netscape package. The standard package, java, is an exception to this rule because it is so fundamental and because it might someday be implemented by multiple companies.

Using Packages

You've been using packages all along in this book. Every time you use the import command, and every time you refer to a class by its full package name (java.awt.Color, for example), you use packages.

To use a class contained in a package, you can use one of three mechanisms:

- If the class you want to use is in the package java.lang (for example, System or Date), you can simply use the class name to refer to that class. The java.lang classes are automatically available to you in all your programs.

- If the class you want to use is in some other package, you can refer to that class by its full name, including any package names (for example, java.awt.Font).

- For classes that you use frequently from other packages, you can import individual classes or a whole package of classes. After a class or a package has been imported, you can refer to that class by its class name.

15

If you don't declare that your class belongs to a package, it is put into an unnamed default package. You can refer to that class simply by its class name from anywhere in your code.

Full Package and Class Names

To refer to a class in some other package, you can use its full name: the class name preceded by any package names. You do not have to import the class or the package to use it this way:

```
java.awt.Font f = new java.awt.Font()
```

For classes that you use only once or twice in your program, using the full name makes sense. If, however, you use that class multiple times, or if the package name is really long with lots of subpackages, you should import that class instead to save yourself some typing.

The `import` Declaration

To import classes from a package, use the `import` declaration, as you've used throughout the examples in this book. You can either import an individual class, like this:

```
import java.util.Vector;
```

Or you can import an entire package of classes, using an asterisk (*) to replace the individual class names, like this:

```
import java.awt.*
```

Note

> Actually, to be technically correct, this declaration doesn't import all the classes in a package; it imports only the classes that have been declared `public`, and even then imports only those classes that the code itself refers to. You'll learn more about this topic in the section titled "Packages and Class Access Control."

Note that the asterisk (*) in this example is not like the one you might use at a command prompt to specify the contents of a folder or to indicate multiple files. For example, if you ask to list the contents of the directory `classes/java/awt/*`, that list includes all the `.class` files and subdirectories, such as `image` and `peer`. Writing `import java.awt.*` imports all the public classes in that package but does not import subpackages such as `image` and `peer`. To import all the classes in a complex package hierarchy, you must explicitly import each level of the hierarchy by hand. Also, you cannot indicate partial class names (for example, L* to import all the classes that begin with L). The only options when using an import declaration are to load all the classes in a package or just a single class.

The import declarations in your class definition go at the top of the file, before any class definitions (but after the package declaration, as you'll see in the next section).

So, should you take the time to import classes individually or just import them as a group? The answer depends on how specific you want to be. Importing a group of classes does not slow down your program or make it any larger; only the classes you actually use in your code are loaded as they are needed. But importing a package does make it a little more confusing for readers of your code to figure out where your classes are coming from. Using individual import declaration or importing packages is mostly a question of your own coding style.

> **Note**
>
> If you're coming to Java from C or C++, you might expect the import declaration to work like #include, which results in a very large program by including source code from another file. This isn't the case; import indicates only where the Java compiler can find a class. It doesn't do anything to expand the size of a class.

Name Conflicts

After you have imported a class or a package of classes, you can usually refer to a class name simply by its name, without the package identifier. In one case, you might have to be more explicit: when you have multiple classes with the same name from different packages.

Here's an example. Assume that you import the classes from two packages:

```
import com.naviseek.web.*;
import com.prefect.http.*;
```

Inside the com.naviseek.web package is a class called FTP. Unfortunately, inside the com.prefect.http package, you also find a class called FTP that has an entirely different meaning and implementation. You might wonder whose version of FTP is used if you refer to the FTP class in your own program like this:

```
FTP out = new FTP();
```

The answer is neither; the Java compiler will not compile your program because of the naming conflict. In this case, despite the fact that you imported both classes, you still have to refer to the appropriate FTP class by full package name, as follows:

```
com.prefect.http.FTP out = new
    com.prefect.http.FTP();
```

A Note About CLASSPATH and Where Classes Are Located

For Java to be able to use a class, it has to be able to find that class on the file system. Otherwise, you get an error that the class does not exist. Java uses two elements to find classes: the package name itself and the directories listed in your CLASSPATH variable (if you're on a Windows or Solaris system).

First, the package names: Package names map to directory names on the file system, so the class com.naviseek.Mapplet is actually found in the naviseek directory, which in turn is inside the com directory (com\naviseek\Mapplet.class, in other words).

Java looks for those directories, in turn, inside the directories listed in your CLASSPATH variable, if one is provided in your configuration. If you remember back to Day 1, "21st Century Java," when you installed the SDK, you might have used a CLASSPATH variable to point to the various places where your Java classes live. If no CLASSPATH is provided, the SDK looks only in the current folder for classes.

When Java looks for a class you've referenced in your source, it looks for the package and class name in each of those directories and returns an error if it can't find the class file. Most class not found errors result because of misconfigured CLASSPATH variables.

Creating Your Own Packages

Creating a package for some of your classes in Java is not much more complicated than creating a class. You must follow three basic steps, as outlined next.

Picking a Package Name

The first step is to decide on a name. The name you choose for your package depends on how you will be using those classes. Perhaps you will name your package after you or perhaps after the part of the Java system you're working on (such as graphics or messaging). If you intend to distribute your package to the Net at large or as part of a commercial product, you should use a package name that uniquely identifies the author.

A convention for naming packages recommended by Sun is to use your Internet domain name with the elements reversed. If your Internet domain name is naviseek.com, your package name might be com.naviseek. You might want to lengthen the name with something that describes the classes in the package, such as com.naviseek.canasta.

Note

Sun has not followed this recommendation with two of its own Java packages—java, the package that comprises the Java class library, and javax, classes that extend the library.

The idea is to make sure your package name is unique. Although packages can hide conflicting class names, the protection stops there. You cannot make sure your package won't conflict with someone else's package if you both use the same package name.

By convention, package names tend to begin with a lowercase letter to distinguish them from class names. Thus, for example, in the full name of the built-in String class, java.lang.String, you can more easily separate the package name from the class name visually. This convention helps reduce name conflicts.

Creating the Folder Structure

Step two in creating packages is to create a folder structure on your hard drive that matches the package name. If your package has just one name (myPackage), you must create a folder for that one name only. If the package name has several parts, you have to create folders within folders. For the package name com.naviseek.canasta, for example, you need to create a com folder, a naviseek folder inside com, and a canasta folder inside naviseek. Your classes and source files can then go inside the canasta directory.

Adding a Class to a Package

The final step to putting your class inside packages is to add a statement to the class file above any import declarations that are being used. The package declaration is used along with the name of the package, as in the following:

```
package com.naviseek.canasta;
```

The single package declaration, if any, must be the first line of code in your source file, after any comments or blank lines and before any import declarations.

After you start using packages, you should make sure that all your classes belong to some package to reduce the chance of confusion about where your classes belong.

Packages and Class Access Control

Previously, you learned about access control modifiers for methods and variables. You also can control access to classes, as you might have noticed when the public modifier was used in some class declarations on past projects.

15

Classes have the default access control if no modifier is specified, which means that the class is available to all other classes in the same package but is not visible or available outside that package—not even to subpackages. It cannot be imported or referred to by name; classes with package protection are hidden inside the package in which they are contained.

Package protection comes about when you define a class as you have throughout this book, like this:

```
class TheHiddenClass extends AnotherHiddenClass {
    // ...
}
```

To allow a class to be visible and importable outside your package, you can give it public protection by adding the `public` modifier to its definition:

```
public class TheVisibleClass {
    // ...
}
```

Classes declared as `public` can be imported by other classes outside the package.

Note that when you use an `import` statement with an asterisk, you import only the public classes inside that package. Hidden classes remain hidden and can be used only by the other classes in that package.

Why would you want to hide a class inside a package? For the same reason you want to hide variables and methods inside a class: so that you can have utility classes and behavior that are useful only to your implementation, or so that you can limit the interface of your program to minimize the effect of larger changes. As you design your classes, you should take the whole package into consideration and decide which classes you want to declare `public` and which you want to be hidden.

Think of protections not as hiding classes entirely, but more as checking the permissions of a given class to use other classes, variables, and methods.

Creating a good package consists of defining a small, clean set of public classes and methods for other classes to use, and then implementing them by using any number of hidden support classes. You'll see another use for hidden classes later today.

Interfaces

Interfaces, like abstract classes and methods, provide templates of behavior that other classes are expected to implement. Interfaces, however, provide far more functionality to Java and to class and object design than do simple abstract classes and methods.

The Problem of Single Inheritance

After some deeper thought or more complex design experience, however, you might discover that the pure simplicity of the class hierarchy is restrictive, particularly when you have some behavior that needs to be used by classes in different branches of the same tree.

Look at an example that will make the problems clearer. Assume that you have a biological hierarchy with Animal at the top, and the classes Mammal and Bird underneath. Things that define a mammal include bearing live young and having fur. Behavior or features of birds include having a beak and laying eggs. So far, so good, right? So, how do you go about creating a class for the platypus, which has fur and a beak, and lays eggs? You would need to combine behavior from two classes to form the Platypus class. And, because classes can have only one immediate superclass in Java, this sort of problem simply cannot be solved elegantly.

Other OOP languages include the concept of multiple inheritance, which solves this problem. With multiple inheritance, a class can inherit from more than one superclass and get behavior and attributes from all its superclasses at once. A problem with multiple inheritance is that it makes a programming language far more complex to learn, to use, and to implement. Questions of method invocation and how the class hierarchy is organized become far more complicated with multiple inheritance, and more open to confusion and ambiguity. And because one of the goals for Java was that it be simple, multiple inheritance was rejected in favor of the simpler single inheritance.

So, how do you solve the problem of needing common behavior that doesn't fit into the strict class hierarchy? Java has another hierarchy altogether separate from the main class hierarchy, a hierarchy of mixable behavior classes. Then, when you create a new class, that class has only one primary superclass, but it can pick and choose different common behaviors from the other hierarchy. This other hierarchy is the interface hierarchy. A Java interface is a collection of abstract behavior that can be mixed into any class to add to that class's behavior that is not supplied by its superclasses. Specifically, a Java interface contains nothing but abstract method definitions and constants—no instance variables and no method implementations.

Interfaces are implemented and used throughout the Java class library whenever a behavior is expected to be implemented by a number of disparate classes. You'll use one of the interfaces in the Java class hierarchy, java.lang.Comparable, later today.

Interfaces and Classes

Classes and interfaces, despite their different definitions, have a great deal in common. Interfaces, like classes, are declared in source files and are compiled using the Java

15

compiler into .class files. And, in most cases, anywhere you can use a class (as a data type for a variable, as the result of a cast, and so on), you can also use an interface.

Almost everywhere that this book has a class name in any of its examples or discussions, you can substitute an interface name. Java programmers often say "class" when they actually mean "class or interface." Interfaces complement and extend the power of classes, and the two can be treated almost the same. One of the few differences between them is that an interface cannot be instantiated: new can create only an instance of a class.

Implementing and Using Interfaces

You can do two things with interfaces: use them in your own classes and define your own. For now, start with the former.

To use an interface, you include the implements keyword as part of your class definition:

```
public class AnimatedSign extends javax.swing.JApplet
    implements Runnable {
    //...
}
```

In this example, javax.swing.JApplet is the superclass, but the Runnable interface extends the behavior that it implements.

Because interfaces provide nothing but abstract method definitions, you then have to implement those methods in your own classes, using the same method signatures from the interface. Note that after you include an interface, you have to implement all the methods in that interface; you can't pick and choose the methods you need. By implementing an interface, you're telling users of your class that you support all of that interface.

After your class implements an interface, subclasses of your class inherit those new methods (and can override or overload them) just as if your superclass had actually defined them. If your class inherits from a superclass that implements a given interface, you don't have to include the implements keyword in your own class definition.

Examine one simple example now—creating the new class Orange. Suppose that you already have a good implementation of the class Fruit and an interface, Fruitlike, that represents what a Fruit is expected to be able to do. You want an orange to be a fruit, but you also want it to be a spherical object that can be tossed, rotated, and so on. Here's how to express it all. (Don't worry about the definitions of these interfaces for now; you'll learn more about them later today.)

```
interface  Fruitlike {
    void  decay();
    void  squish();
```

```
    // ...
}

class  Fruit implements Fruitlike {
    private Color myColor;
    private int daysTilIRot;
    // ...
}

interface  Spherelike {
    void  toss();
    void  rotate();
    // ...
}

class  Orange extends Fruit implements Spherelike {
    // toss()ing may squish() me (unique to me)
}
```

Note that the class Orange doesn't have to say implements Fruitlike because, by
extending Fruit, it already has! One of the nice things about this structure is that you
can change your mind about what class Orange extends (if a really great Sphere class is
suddenly implemented, for example), yet class Orange still understands the same two
interfaces:

```
class  Sphere implements Spherelike {    // extends Object
    private float  radius;
    // ...
}

class  Orange extends Sphere implements Fruitlike {
    // ... users of Orange never need know about the change!
}
```

Implementing Multiple Interfaces

Unlike with the singly inherited class hierarchy, you can include as many interfaces as
you need in your own classes, and your class will implement the combined behavior of
all the included interfaces. To include multiple interfaces in a class, just separate their
names with commas:

```
public class AnimatedSign extends javax.swing.JApplet
    implements Runnable, Observable {

    // ...
}
```

Note that complications might arise from implementing multiple interfaces. What happens if two different interfaces both define the same method? You can solve this problem
in three ways:

15

- If the methods in each of the interfaces have identical signatures, you implement one method in your class and that definition satisfies both interfaces.
- If the methods have different parameter lists, it is a simple case of method overloading; you implement both method signatures, and each definition satisfies its respective interface definition.
- If the methods have the same parameter lists but differ in return type, you cannot create a method that satisfies both. (Remember that method overloading is triggered by parameter lists, not by return type.) In this case, trying to compile a class that implements both interfaces produces a compiler error. Running across this problem suggests that your interfaces have some design flaws that you might need to reexamine.

Other Uses of Interfaces

Remember that almost everywhere that you can use a class, you can use an interface instead. So, for example, you can declare a variable to be of an interface type:

```
Runnable aRunnableObject = new MyAnimationClass()
```

When a variable is declared to be of an interface type, it simply means that any object the variable refers to is expected to have implemented that interface; that is, it is expected to understand all the methods that interface specifies. It assumes that a promise made between the designer of the interface and its eventual implementors has been kept. In this case, because aRunnableObject contains an object of the type Runnable, the assumption is that you can call aRunnableObject.run().

The important point to realize here is that although aRunnableObject is expected to be able to have the run() method, you could write this code long before any classes that qualify are actually implemented (or even created!). In traditional object-oriented programming, you are forced to create a class with "stub" implementations (empty methods, or methods that print silly messages) to get the same effect. You can also cast objects to an interface, just as you can cast objects to other classes. So, for example, go back to that definition of the Orange class, which implemented both the Fruitlike interface (through its superclass, Fruit) and the Spherelike interface. Here you can cast instances of Orange to both classes and interfaces:

```
Orange anOrange = new Orange();
Fruit aFruit = (Fruit)anOrange;
Fruitlike aFruitlike = (Fruitlike)anOrange;
Spherelike aSpherelike = (Spherelike)anOrange;


aFruit.decay(); // fruits decay
```

```
aFruitlike.squish(); //  and squish

aFruitlike.toss(); // things that are fruitlike do not toss
aSpherelike.toss(); // but things that are spherelike do

anOrange.decay(); // oranges can do it all
anOrange.squish();
anOrange.toss();
anOrange.rotate();
```

Declarations and casts are used in this example to restrict an orange's behavior to acting more like a mere fruit or sphere.

Finally, note that although interfaces are usually used to mix in behavior to other classes (method signatures), interfaces can also be used to mix in generally useful constants. So, for example, if an interface defines a set of constants, and then multiple classes use those constants, the values of those constants could be globally changed without having to modify multiple classes. This is yet another example of a case in which the use of interfaces to separate design from implementation can make your code more general and more easily maintainable.

Creating and Extending Interfaces

After you use interfaces for a while, the next step is to define your own interfaces. Interfaces look a lot like classes; they are declared in much the same way and can be arranged into a hierarchy. However, you must follow certain rules for declaring interfaces.

New Interfaces

To create a new interface, you declare it like this:

```
interface Growable {
    // ...
}
```

This declaration is, effectively, the same as a class definition, with the word `interface` replacing the word `class`. Inside the interface definition, you have methods and constants. The method definitions inside the interface are `public` and `abstract` methods; you can either declare them explicitly as such, or they are turned into `public` and `abstract` methods if you do not include those modifiers. You cannot declare a method inside an interface to be either `private` or `protected`. So, for example, here's a `Growable` interface with one method explicitly declared `public` and `abstract` (`growIt()`) and one implicitly declared as such (`growItBigger()`):

15

```
public interface Growable {
    public abstract void growIt(); // explicitly public and abstract
    void growItBigger(); // effectively public and abstract
}
```

Note that, as with abstract methods in classes, methods inside interfaces do not have bodies. Remember, an interface is pure design; no implementation is involved.

In addition to methods, interfaces can also have variables, but those variables must be declared `public`, `static`, and `final` (making them constant). As with methods, you can explicitly define a variable to be `public`, `static`, and `final`, or it is implicitly defined as such if you don't use those modifiers. Here's that same `Growable` definition with two new variables:

```
public interface Growable {
    public static final int increment = 10;
    long maxnum = 1000000; // becomes public static and final

    public abstract void growIt(); //explicitly public and abstract
    void growItBigger(); // effectively public and abstract
}
```

Interfaces must have either public or package protection, just like classes. Note, however, that interfaces without the `public` modifier do not automatically convert their methods to `public` and `abstract` nor their constants to `public`. A non-public interface also has non-public methods and constants that can be used only by classes and other interfaces in the same package.

Interfaces, like classes, can belong to a package. Interfaces can also import other interfaces and classes from other packages, just as classes can.

Methods Inside Interfaces

Here's one trick to note about methods inside interfaces: Those methods are supposed to be abstract and apply to any kind of class, but how can you define parameters to those methods? You don't know what class will be using them! The answer lies in the fact that you use an interface name anywhere a class name can be used, as you learned earlier. By defining your method parameters to be interface types, you can create generic parameters that apply to any class that might use this interface.

So, for example, consider the interface `Fruitlike`, which defines methods (with no arguments) for `decay()` and `squish()`. You might also have a method for `germinateSeeds()`, which has one argument: the fruit itself. Of what type is that argument going to be? It can't be simply `Fruit` because you may have a class that's `Fruitlike` (that is, one that implements the `Fruitlike` interface) without actually being a fruit. The solution is to declare the argument as simply `Fruitlike` in the interface:

```
public interface Fruitlike {
    public abstract germinate(Fruitlike self) {
        // ...
    }
}
```

Then, in an actual implementation for this method in a class, you can take the generic `Fruitlike` argument and cast it to the appropriate object:

```
public class Orange extends Fruit {

public germinate(Fruitlike self) {
    Orange theOrange = (Orange)self;
    // ...
    }
}
```

Extending Interfaces

As you can do with classes, you can organize interfaces into a hierarchy. When one interface inherits from another interface, that "subinterface" acquires all the method definitions and constants that its "superinterface" declared. To extend an interface, you use the extends keyword just as you do in a class definition:

```
interface Fruitlike extends Foodlike {
    // ...
}
```

Note that, unlike classes, the interface hierarchy has no equivalent of the `Object` class; this hierarchy is not rooted at any one point. Interfaces can either exist entirely on their own or inherit from another interface.

Note also that, unlike the class hierarchy, the inheritance hierarchy is multiply inherited. So, for example, a single interface can extend as many classes as it needs to (separated by commas in the extends part of the definition), and the new interface will contain a combination of all its parent's methods and constants. Here's an interface definition for an interface called `BusyInterface` that inherits from a whole lot of other interfaces:

```
public interface BusyInterface extends Runnable, Growable, Fruitlike,
    Observable {

    // ...
}
```

In multiply inherited interfaces, the rules for managing method name conflicts are the same as for classes that use multiple interfaces; methods that differ only in return type result in a compiler error.

15

Creating an Online Storefront

To explore all the topics covered up to this point today, the Storefront application uses packages, access control, interfaces, and encapsulation. This application manages the items in an online storefront, handling two main tasks:

- Calculating the sale price of each item depending on how much of it is presently in stock
- Sorting items according to sale price

The Storefront application consists of two classes, Storefront and Item. These classes will be organized as a new package called com.prefect.ecommerce, so the first task is to define a directory structure on your system where this package's classes will be stored.

SDK 1.3 and other Java development tools look for packages in the folders listed in the system's CLASSPATH. The package name is also taken into account, so if c:\jdk1.3 is in your CLASSPATH, Storefront.class and Item.class could be stored in c:\jdk1.3\com\prefect\ecommerce.

One way to manage your own packages is to create a new folder that will contain packages, and then add a reference to this folder when setting your CLASSPATH.

Tip

> On a Windows 95 or 98 system, CLASSPATH can be set at a command line or by editing AUTOEXEC.BAT in the system's root folder. For help setting your CLASSPATH, read Appendix A, "Configuring the Software Development Kit."

After you have created a folder where this package's files will be stored, create Item.java from Listing 15.2.

LISTING 15.2 The Full Text of Item.java

```
 1: package com.prefect.ecommerce;
 2:
 3: import java.util.*;
 4:
 5: public class Item implements Comparable {
 6:     private String id;
 7:     private String name;
 8:     private double retail;
 9:     private int quantity;
10:     private double price;
11:
```

LISTING 15.2 continued

```
12:        Item(String idIn, String nameIn, String retailIn, String quanIn) {
13:            id = idIn;
14:            name = nameIn;
15:            retail = Double.parseDouble(retailIn);
16:            quantity = Integer.parseInt(quanIn);
17:
18:            if (quantity > 400)
19:                price = retail * .5D;
20:            else if (quantity > 200)
21:                price = retail * .6D;
22:            else
23:                price = retail * .7D;
24:            price = Math.floor( price * 100 + .5 ) / 100;
25:        }
26:
27:        public int compareTo(Object obj) {
28:            Item temp = (Item)obj;
29:            if (this.price < temp.price)
30:                return 1;
31:            else if (this.price > temp.price)
32:                return -1;
33:            return 0;
34:        }
35:
36:        public String getId() {
37:            return id;
38:        }
39:
40:        public String getName() {
41:            return name;
42:        }
43:
44:        public double getRetail() {
45:            return retail;
46:        }
47:
48:        public int getQuantity() {
49:            return quantity;
50:        }
51:
52:        public double getPrice() {
53:            return price;
54:        }
55: }
```

The Item class is a support class that represents a product sold by an online store. There are private instance variables for the product ID code, name, how many are in stock (quantity), and the retail and sale prices.

15

Because all the instance variables of this class are private, no other class can set or retrieve their values. Simple accessor methods are created in lines 36–54 of Listing 15.2 to provide a way for other programs to retrieve these values. Each method begins with get followed by the capitalized name of the variable, which is standard in the Java class library. For example, getPrice() returns a double containing the value of price. No methods are provided for setting any of these instance variables—that will be handled in the constructor method for this class.

Line 1 establishes that the Item class is part of the com.prefect.ecommerce package.

Note

Prefect.com is the personal domain of this book's co-author, so this project follows Sun's package-naming convention by beginning with a top-level domain (com), following it with the developer's domain name (prefect), and then by a name that describes the purpose of the package (ecommerce).

The Item class implements the Comparable interface (line 5), which makes it easy to sort objects of a class. This interface has only one method, compareTo(Object), which returns an integer.

The compareTo() method compares two objects of a class: the current object and another object passed as an argument to the method. The value returned by the method defines the natural sorting order for objects of this class:

- If the current object should be sorted above the other object, return -1.
- If the current object should be sorted below the other object, return 1.
- If the two objects are equal, return 0.

You determine in the compareTo() method which of an object's instance variables to consider when sorting. Lines 27–34 override the compareTo() method for the Item class, sorting on the basis of the price variable. Items are sorted by price from highest to lowest.

After you have implemented the Comparable interface for an object, there are two class methods that can be called to sort an array, linked list, or other collection of those objects. You will see this when Storefront.class is created.

The Item() constructor in lines 12–25 takes four String objects as arguments and uses them to set up the id, name, retail, and quantity instance variables. The last two must be converted from strings to numeric values using the Double.parseDouble() and Integer.parseInt() class methods, respectively.

The value of the `price` instance variable depends on how much of that item is presently in stock:

- If there are more than 400 in stock, `price` is 50 percent of `retail` (lines 18–19).
- If there are between 201 and 400, `price` is 60 percent of `retail` (lines 20–21).
- For everything else, `price` is 70 percent of `retail` (lines 22–23).

Line 24 rounds off `price` so that it contains two or fewer decimal points, turning a price such as $6.92999999999999 to $6.99. The `Math.floor()` method rounds off decimal numbers to the next lowest mathematical integer, returning them as a double values.

After you have compiled `Item.class`, you're ready to create a class that represents a storefront of these products. Create `Storefront.java` from Listing 15.3.

LISTING 15.3   The Full Text of `Storefront.java`

```
 1: package com.prefect.ecommerce;
 2:
 3: import java.util.*;
 4:
 5: public class Storefront {
 6:     private LinkedList catalog = new LinkedList();
 7:
 8:     public void addItem(String id, String name, String price,
 9:         String quant) {
10:
11:         Item it = new Item(id, name, price, quant);
12:         catalog.add(it);
13:     }
14:
15:     public Item getItem(int i) {
16:         return (Item)catalog.get(i);
17:     }
18:
19:     public int getSize() {
20:         return catalog.size();
21:     }
22:
23:     public void sort() {
24:         Collections.sort(catalog);
25:     }
26: }
```

The `Storefront.class` is used to manage a collection of products in an online store. Each product is an `Item` object, and they are stored together in a `LinkedList` instance variable named `catalog` (line 6).

The addItem() method in lines 8–13 creates a new Item object based on four arguments sent to the method: the ID, name, price, and quantity in stock of the item. After the item is created, it is added to the catalog linked list by calling its add() method with the Item object as an argument.

The getItem() and getSize() methods provide an interface to the information stored in the private catalog variable. The getSize() method in lines 19–21 calls the catalog.size() method, which returns the number of objects contained in catalog.

Because objects in a linked list are numbered like arrays and other data structures, you can retrieve them using an index number. The getItem() method in lines 15–17 calls catalog.get() with an index number as an argument, returning the object stored at that location in the linked list.

The sort() method in lines 23–25 is where you benefit from the implementation of the Comparable interface in the Item class. The class method Collections.sort() will sort a linked list and other data structures based on the natural sort order of the objects they contain, calling the object's compareTo() method to determine this order.

After you have created the Storefront class, you're ready to develop a program that actually makes use of the com.prefect.ecommerce package. Open the folder on your system where you've been creating the programs of this book (such as \J21work) and create GiftShop.java from Listing 15.4.

LISTING 15.4   The Full Text of Giftshop.java

```
 1: import com.prefect.ecommerce.*;
 2:
 3: public class GiftShop {
 4:     public static void main(String[] arguments) {
 5:         Storefront store = new Storefront();
 6:         store.addItem("C01", "MUG", "9.99", "150");
 7:         store.addItem("C02", "LG MUG", "12.99", "82");
 8:         store.addItem("C03", "MOUSEPAD", "10.49", "800");
 9:         store.addItem("D01", "T SHIRT", "16.99", "90");
10:         store.sort();
11:
12:         for (int i = 0; i < store.getSize(); i++) {
13:             Item show = (Item)store.getItem(i);
14:             System.out.println("\nItem ID: " + show.getId() +
15:                 "\nName: " + show.getName() +
16:                 "\nRetail Price: $" + show.getRetail() +
17:                 "\nPrice: $" + show.getPrice() +
18:                 "\nQuantity: " + show.getQuantity());
19:         }
20:     }
21: }
```

The GiftShop class demonstrates each part of the public interface that the Storefront and Item classes make available. You can do each of the following:

- Create an online store
- Add items to it
- Sort the items by sale price
- Loop through a list of items to display information about each one

Note

If you have created the Item.class and Storefront.class files in the same folder as Giftshop.java, you might not be able to compile the program because the Java compiler expects to find those files in their package folder. Move those files to the com\prefect\ecommerce folder and compile Giftshop.java in another folder, such as \J21work.

The output of this program is the following:

```
Item ID: D01
Name: T SHIRT
Retail Price: $16.99
Price: $11.89
Quantity: 90

Item ID: C02
Name: LG MUG
Retail Price: $12.99
Price: $9.09
Quantity: 82

Item ID: C01
Name: MUG
Retail Price: $9.99
Price: $6.99
Quantity: 150

Item ID: C03
Name: MOUSEPAD
Retail Price: $10.49
Price: $5.25
Quantity: 800
```

Many of the implementation details of these classes are hidden from GiftShop and other classes that would make use of the package.

For instance, the programmer who developed GiftShop doesn't need to know that

Storefront uses a linked list to hold all the store's product data. If the developer of Storefront decided later to use a different data structure, as long as getSize() and getItem() returned the expected values, GiftShop would continue to work correctly.

Inner Classes

The classes you have worked with thus far are all members of a package, either because you specified a package name with the package declaration or because the default package was used. Classes that belong to a package are known as *top-level* classes. When Java was introduced, they were the only classes supported by the language.

Beginning with Java 1.1, you could define a class inside a class, as if it were a method or a variable. These types of classes are called *inner* classes. Listing 15.5 contains the Inner applet, which uses an inner class called BlueButton to represent clickable buttons that have a default background color of blue.

LISTING 15.5 The Full Text of Inner.java

```
 1: import java.awt.*;
 2: import javax.swing.*;
 3:
 4: public class Inner extends javax.swing.JApplet {
 5:     JButton b1 = new JButton("One");
 6:     BlueButton b2 = new BlueButton("Two");
 7:
 8:     public void init() {
 9:         Container pane = getContentPane();
10:         pane.setLayout(new FlowLayout());
11:         pane.add(b1);
12:         pane.add(b2);
13:     }
14:
15:     class BlueButton extends JButton {
16:         BlueButton(String label) {
17:             super(label);
18:             this.setBackground(Color.blue);
19:         }
20:     }
21: }
```

Figure 15.1 was produced on appletviewer using the following HTML tag:

```
<applet code="Inner.class" width="200" height="100">
</applet>
```

Figure 15.1

The Inner *applet.*

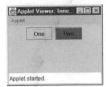

In this example, the BlueButton class isn't any different from a helper class that is included in the same source file as a program's main class file. The only difference is that the helper is defined inside the class file, which has several advantages:

- Inner classes are invisible to all other classes, which means that you don't have to worry about name conflicts between it and other classes.
- Inner classes can have access to variables and methods within the scope of a top-level class that they would not have as a separate class.

In many cases, an inner class is a short class file that exists only for a limited purpose. In the Inner applet, because BlueButton doesn't contain a lot of complex behavior and attributes, it is well suited for implementation as an inner class.

The name of an inner class is associated with the name of the class in which it is contained, and it is assigned automatically when the program is compiled. In the example of the BlueButton class, it is given the name Inner$BlueButton.class by the JDK.

Caution

> When you're using inner classes, you must be more careful to include all .class files when making a program available. Each inner class has its own class file, and these class files must be included along with any top-level classes. If you publish the Inner applet on the World Wide Web, for example, you must publish both the Inner.class and Inner$BlueButton.class files together.

Inner classes, although seemingly a minor enhancement, actually represent a significant modification to the language.

Rules governing the scope of an inner class closely match those governing variables. An inner class's name is not visible outside its scope, except in a fully qualified name, which helps in structuring classes within a package. The code for an inner class can use simple names from enclosing scopes, including class and member variables of enclosing classes, as well as local variables of enclosing blocks.

15

In addition, you can define a top-level class as a static member of another top-level class. Unlike an inner class, a top-level class cannot directly use the instance variables of any other class. The ability to nest classes in this way allows any top-level class to provide a package-style organization for a logically related group of secondary top-level classes.

Summary

Today, you learned how to encapsulate an object by using access control modifiers for its variables and methods. You also learned how to use other modifiers such as static, final, and abstract in the development of Java classes and class hierarchies.

To further the effort of developing a set of classes and using them, you learned how classes can be grouped into packages. These groupings better organize your programs and enable the sharing of classes with the many other Java programmers who are making their code publicly available.

Finally, you learned how to implement interfaces and inner classes, two structures that are helpful when designing a class hierarchy.

Q&A

Q Won't using accessor methods everywhere slow down my Java code?

A Not always. As Java compilers improve and can create more optimizations, they will be able to make accessor methods fast automatically, but if you're concerned about speed, you can always declare accessor methods to be final, and they'll be comparable in speed to direct instance variable accesses under most circumstances.

Q Based on what I've learned, private abstract methods and final abstract methods or classes don't seem to make sense. Are they legal?

A Nope, they're compile-time errors, as you have guessed. To be useful, abstract methods must be overridden, and abstract classes must be subclassed, but neither of those two operations would be legal if they were also private or final.

Questions

1. What packages are automatically imported into your Java classes?

   (a) None

   (b) The classes stored in the folders of your CLASSPATH

   (c) The classes in the java.lang package

2. According to the convention for naming packages, what should be the first part of the name of a package you create?

   (a) Your name followed by a period

   (b) Your top-level Internet domain followed by a period

   (c) The text java followed by a period

3. If you create a subclass and override a `public` method, what access modifiers can you use with that method?

   (a) `public` only

   (b) `public` or `protected`

   (c) `public`, `protected`, or default access

Answers

1. c. All other packages must be imported if you want to use short class names such as `LinkedList` instead of full package and class names such as `java.util.LinkedList`.

2. b. This convention assumes that all Java package developers will own an Internet domain or have access to one so that the package can be made available for download.

3. a. All `public` methods must remain `public` in subclasses.

Exercises

To extend your knowledge of the subjects covered today, try the following exercises:

- Create a modified version of the `Storefront` project that includes a `noDiscount` variable for each item. When this variable is `true`, sell the item at the retail price.

- Create a `ZipCode` class that uses access control to ensure that its `zipCode` instance variable always has a five-digit value.

Where applicable, exercise solutions are offered on the book's Web site at `http://www.java21days.com`.

DAY 16

Error Handling and Security

Programmers in any language endeavor to write bug-free programs, programs that never crash, programs that can handle any situation with grace and that can recover from unusual situations without causing the user any undue stress. Good intentions aside, programs like this don't exist.

In real programs, errors occur either because the programmer didn't anticipate every situation the code would get into (or didn't have the time to test the program enough), or because of situations out of the programmer's control—bad data from users, corrupt files that don't have the right data in them, network connections that don't connect, hardware devices that don't respond, sun spots, gremlins, whatever.

In Java, these sorts of strange events that might cause a program to fail are called *exceptions*. Java defines a number of language features that deal with exceptions, including the following:

- How to handle them in your code and recover gracefully from potential problems

- How to tell Java and your methods' users that you're expecting a potential exception
- How to create an exception if you detect one
- How your code is limited, yet made more robust by exceptions

In addition to exceptions, you learn the system being established for Java 2 that enables applets to do things in a program that normally would cause security exceptions.

Exceptions, the Old and Confusing Way

Handling error conditions with most programming languages requires much more work than handling a program that is running properly. It can require a very confusing structure of statements, similar in functionality to Java's if...else and switch blocks, to deal with errors that might occur.

As an example, consider the following statements, which show the structure of how a file might be loaded from disk. Loading a file is something that can be problematic because of a number of different circumstances—disk errors, file-not-found errors, and the like. If the program must have the data from the file in order to operate properly, it must deal with any of these circumstances before continuing.

Here's the structure of one possible solution:

```
int status = loadTextfile();
if (status != 1) {
    // something unusual happened, describe it
    switch (status) {
        case 2:
            // file not found
            break;
        case 3:
            // disk error
            break;
        case 4:
            // file corrupted
            break;
        default:
            // other error
    }
} else {
    // file loaded OK, continue with program
}
```

This code tries to load a file with a method call to loadTextfile(), which has been defined elsewhere in the program. This method returns an integer that indicates whether the file loaded properly (`status == 1`) or an error occurred (`status` equals anything other than 1).

Depending on the error that occurs, the program uses a `switch` statement to try to work around it. The end result is an elaborate block of code in which the most common circumstance—a successful file load—can be lost amid the error-handling code. This is just to handle one possible error. If other errors might take place later in the program, you might end up with more nested `if...else` and `switch-case` blocks.

Error management can become a major problem after you start creating larger systems. Different programmers use different special values for handling errors, and might not document them well, if at all. You might inconsistently use errors in your own programs. Code to manage these kinds of errors can often obscure the program's original intent, making that code difficult to read and maintain. Finally, if you try dealing with errors in this way, there's no easy way for the compiler to check for consistency the way it can check to make sure you called a method with the right arguments.

Although the previous example uses Java syntax, you don't have to deal with errors that way in your programs. The language introduces a better way to deal with exceptional circumstances in a program: through the use of a group of classes called exceptions.

Exceptions include errors that could be fatal to your program, but also include other unusual situations. By managing exceptions, you can manage errors and possibly work around them.

Through a combination of special language features, consistency checking at compile time, and a set of extensible exception classes, errors and other unusual conditions in Java programs can be much more easily managed.

Given these features, you can now add a whole new dimension to the behavior and design of your classes, of your class hierarchy, and of your overall system. Your class and interface definitions describe how your program is supposed to behave given the best circumstances. By integrating exception handling into your program design, you can consistently describe how the program will behave when circumstances are not quite as good, and allow people who use your classes to know what to expect in those cases.

Java Exceptions

At this point in the book, it's likely that you've run into at least one Java exception—perhaps you mistyped a method name or made a mistake in your code that caused a problem. Maybe you tried to run a Java applet written using version 2 of the language in a browser that doesn't support it yet, and saw a `Security Exception` message on the browser's status line.

Chances are, a program quit and spewed a bunch of mysterious errors to the screen. Those errors are exceptions. When your program quits, it's because an exception was *thrown*. Exceptions can be thrown by the system, thrown by classes you use, or intentionally thrown in your own programs.

The term *thrown* is fitting because exceptions also can be caught. Catching an exception involves dealing with the exceptional circumstance so that your program doesn't crash—you learn more about this later. *An exception was thrown* is the proper Java terminology for *an error happened*.

The heart of the Java exception system is the exception itself. Exceptions in Java are actual objects—instances of classes that inherit from the class `Throwable`. An instance of a `Throwable` class is created when an exception is thrown.

`Throwable` has two subclasses: `Error` and `Exception`. Instances of `Error` are internal errors in the Java runtime environment (the virtual machine). These errors are rare and usually fatal; there's not much you can do about them (either to catch them or to throw them yourself), but they exist so that Java can use them if it needs to.

The class `Exception` is more interesting. Subclasses of `Exception` fall into two general groups:

- Runtime exceptions (subclasses of the class `RuntimeException`) such as `ArrayIndexOutofBounds`, `SecurityException`, and `NullPointerException`
- Other exceptions such as `EOFException` and `MalformedURLException`

Runtime exceptions usually occur because of code that isn't very robust. An `ArrayIndexOutofBounds` exception, for example, should never be thrown if you're properly checking to make sure your code stays within the bounds of an array. `NullPointerException` exceptions won't happen unless you try to use a variable before it has been set up to hold an object.

> **Caution**   If your program is causing runtime exceptions under any circumstances whatsoever, you should fix those problems before you even begin dealing with exception management.

The final group of exceptions is the most interesting because these are the exceptions that indicate something very strange and out of control is happening. `EOFException`s, for example, happen when you're reading from a file and the file ends before you expect it to. A MalformedURLException happens when an URL isn't in the right format (perhaps your user typed it wrong). This group includes exceptions that you create to signal unusual cases that might occur in your own programs.

Exceptions are arranged in a hierarchy just as other classes are, where the Exception superclasses are more general errors and subclasses are more specific errors. This organization becomes more important to you as you deal with exceptions in your own code.

Most of the exception classes are part of the java.lang package (including Throwable, Exception, and RuntimeException). Many of the other packages define other exceptions, and those exceptions are used throughout the class library. For example, the java.io package defines a general exception class called IOException, which is subclassed not only in the java.io package for input and output exceptions (EOFException and FileNotFoundException), but also in the java.net classes for networking exceptions such as MalformedURLException.

Managing Exceptions

Now that you know what an exception is, how do you deal with one in your own code? In many cases, the Java compiler enforces exception management when you try to use methods that use exceptions; you need to deal with those exceptions in your own code or it simply won't compile. In this section, you learn about consistency checking and how to use the try, catch, and finally language keywords to deal with exceptions that might occur.

Exception Consistency Checking

The more you work with the Java class libraries, the more likely it is that you'll run into a compiler error (an exception!) similar to this one:

```
XMLParser.java:32: Exception java.lang.InterruptedException
must be caught or it must be declared in the throws clause
of this method.
```

What on earth does that mean? In Java, a method can indicate the kinds of errors it might possibly throw. For example, methods that read from files might potentially throw IOException errors, so those methods are declared with a special modifier that indicates potential errors. When you use those methods in your own Java programs, you have to protect your code against those exceptions. This rule is enforced by the compiler itself, in the same way the compiler checks to make sure that you're using methods with the right number of arguments and that all your variable types match the thing you're assigning to them.

Why is this check in place? It makes your programs less likely to crash with fatal errors because you know, up front, the kind of exceptions that can be thrown by the methods a program uses. You no longer have to carefully read the documentation or the code of an object you're going to use to ensure that you've dealt with all the potential problems—Java does the checking for you. On the other side, if you define your methods so that they indicate the exceptions they can throw, Java can tell your objects' users to handle those errors.

Protecting Code and Catching Exceptions

Assume that you've been happily coding and you ran into that exception message during a test compile. According to the message, you have to either catch the error or declare that your method throws it. Deal with the first case: catching potential exceptions.

You do two things to catch an exception:

- You protect the code that contains the method that might throw an exception inside a try block.
- You deal with an exception inside a catch block.

What try and catch effectively mean is, "Try this bit of code that might cause an exception. If it executes okay, go on with the program. If the code doesn't execute, catch the exception and deal with it."

You've seen try and catch before, when you first dealt with threads. On Day 13, "Threads and Animation," you used code to pause between each frame in an animation sequence:

```
try {
    Thread.sleep(1000);
} catch (InterruptedException e) { }
```

Although this example uses try and catch, it's not a very good use of it. Here's what's happening in these statements: The Thread.sleep() class method could potentially throw an exception of type InterruptedException, which signifies that the thread has been interrupted for some reason.

To handle this exception, the call to sleep() is placed inside a try block and an associated catch block has been set up. This catch block receives any InterruptedException objects that are thrown within the try block.

The reason this isn't a good example of exception handling is that there isn't anything inside the catch clause—in other words, you'll catch the exception if it happens, but then you'll do nothing to respond to its occurrence. In all but the simplest cases (such as this one, where the exception really doesn't matter), you need something inside the catch block that does something to clean up after the exception happens.

The part of the catch clause inside the parentheses is similar to a method definition's argument list. It contains the class of exception to be caught and a variable name (e is commonly used). You can refer to that exception object inside the catch block.

One common use for this object is to call its getMessage() method. This method is present in all exceptions, and it displays a detailed error message describing what happened.

16

The following example is a revised version of the try...catch statement used on Day 9:

```
try {
    Thread.sleep(1000);
} catch (InterruptedException e) {
    System.out.println("Error: " + e.getMessage());
}
```

For another example, revisit the subject of file handling in Java. If you have a program that reads from a file, it's likely to use one of the input/output stream classes you'll learn about on Day 17, "Handling Data Through Java Streams." The basic idea is that you open a connection to a file and use the read() method to get data from that file. This can cause several exceptions, such as a disk error or an attempt to read more data than the file contains. In either of these cases, the read() method would throw an IOException, which would either cause the program to stop executing if you didn't catch the exception or cause the program to crash.

By putting your read() method inside a try block, you can deal gracefully with that error inside a catch block. You could clean up after the error and return to some safe state, patch things up enough for the program to proceed, or if all else fails, save as much of the current program's state as possible and exit.

The following example tries to read from a file and catches exceptions if they happen:

```
try {
    while (numBytes <= mybuffer.length) {
        myInputStream.read(myBuffer);
        numBytes++;
    }
} catch (IOException e) {
    System.out.println("Oops! IO Exception -- only read " + numBytes);
    // other cleanup code
}
```

Here, the "other cleanup code" can be anything you want it to be; you can go on with the program using the partial information you got from the file, or perhaps you want to display a dialog box enabling the user to select a different file.

The examples you have seen thus far catch a specific type of exception. Because exception classes are organized into a hierarchy and you can use a subclass anywhere a superclass is expected, you can catch groups of exceptions within the same catch statement.

As an example, there are several different types of IOException exceptions, such as EOFException and FileNotFoundException. By catching IOException, you also catch instances of any IOException subclass.

What if you do want to catch very different kinds of exceptions, even if they aren't related by inheritance? You can use multiple catch blocks for a single try, like this:

```
try {
    // code that might generate exceptions
} catch (IOException e) {
    // handle IO exceptions
} catch (ClassNotFoundException e) {
    // handle class not found exceptions
} catch (InterruptedException e) {
    // handle interrupted exceptions
}
```

In a multiple catch block, the first catch block that matches will be executed and the rest ignored.

Caution

You can run into unexpected problems by using an Exception superclass in a catch block followed by one or more of its subclasses in their own catch blocks. For example, the input-output exception IOException is the superclass of the end-of-file exception EOFException. If you put an IOException block above an EOFException block, the subclass will never catch any exceptions.

The finally Clause

Suppose that there is some action in your code that you absolutely must do, no matter what happens, whether an exception is thrown or not. This is usually to free some external resource after acquiring it, to close a file after opening it, or something similar. Although you could put that action both inside a catch block and outside it, that would be duplicating the same code in two different places. Instead, put one copy of that code inside a special optional part of the try...catch block called finally. The following example shows how a try...catch...finally block is structured:

```
try {
    readTextfile();
} catch (IOException e) {
```

```
   // deal with IO errors
} finally {
   closeTextfile();
}
```

The `finally` statement is actually useful outside exceptions; you can also use it to execute cleanup code after a `return`, a `break`, or a `continue` inside loops. For the latter cases, you can use a `try` statement with a `finally` but without a `catch` statement.

Listing 16.1 shows how a `finally` statement can be used inside a method.

16

LISTING 16.1 The Full Text of HexRead.java

```
 1: class HexRead {
 2:     String[] input = { "000A110D1D260219 ",
 3:         "78700F1318141E0C ",
 4:         "6A197D45B0FFFFFF " };
 5:
 6:     public static void main(String[] arguments) {
 7:         HexRead hex = new HexRead();
 8:         for (int i = 0; i < hex.input.length; i++)
 9:             hex.readLine(hex.input[i]);
10:     }
11:
12:     void readLine(String code) {
13:         try {
14:             for (int j = 0; j + 1 < code.length(); j += 2) {
15:                 String sub = code.substring(j, j+2);
16:                 int num = Integer.parseInt(sub, 16);
17:                 if (num == 255)
18:                     return;
19:                 System.out.print(num + " ");
20:             }
21:         } finally {
22:             System.out.println("**");
23:         }
24:         return;
25:     }
26: }
```

The output of this program is as follows:

```
0 10 17 13 29 38 2 25 **
120 112 15 19 24 20 30 12 **
106 25 125 69 176 **
```

The HexRead application reads sequences of two-digit hexadecimal numbers and displays their decimal values. There are three sequences to read:

- `000A110D1D260219`

- `78700F1318141E0C`

- `6A197D45B0FFFFFF`

As you learned on Day 3, "The ABCs of Java," hexadecimal is a base-16 numbering system where the single-digit numbers range from `00` (decimal 0) to `0F` (decimal 15) and double-digit numbers range from `10` (decimal 16) to `FF` (decimal 255).

Line 15 of the program reads two characters from `code`, the string that was sent to the `readLine()` method, by calling the string's `substring(int, int)` method.

> **Note**
>
> In the `substring()` method of the String class, you select a substring in a somewhat counterintuitive way. The first argument specifies the index of the first character to include in the substring, but the second argument does not specify the last character. Instead, the second argument indicates the index of the last character plus 1. A call to `substring(2, 5)` for a string would return the characters from index position 2 to index position 4.

The two-character substring contains a hexadecimal number stored as a `String`. The `Integer` class method `parseInt` can be used with a second argument to convert this number into an integer. Use `16` as the argument for a hexadecimal (base 16) conversion, `8` for an octal (base 8) conversion, and so on.

In the `HexRead` application, the hexadecimal `FF` is used to fill out the end of a sequence and should not be displayed as a decimal value. This is accomplished by using a `try-finally` block in lines 13–23 of Listing 16.1.

The `try...finally` block causes an unusual thing to happen when the `return` statement is encountered at line 18. You would expect `return` to cause the `readLine()` method to be exited immediately.

Because it is within a `try...finally` block, the statement within the `finally` block is executed no matter how the `try` block is exited. The text `"**"` is displayed at the end of a line of decimal values.

Declaring Methods That Might Throw Exceptions

In previous examples, you learned how to deal with methods (by protecting code and catching any exceptions that occur) that might throw exceptions. The Java compiler checks to make sure that you've somehow dealt with a method's exceptions—but how did it know which exceptions to tell you about in the first place?

The answer is that the original method indicated in its signature contains the exceptions that it might possibly throw. You can use this mechanism in your own methods—in fact, it's good style to do so to make sure your classes' other users are alerted to the errors your methods may come across.

To indicate that a method may possibly throw an exception, you use a special clause in the method definition called `throws`.

The `throws` Clause

To indicate that some code in your method's body may throw an exception, simply add the `throws` keyword after the signature for the method (before the opening brace) with the name or names of the exception that your method throws:

```
public boolean myMethod (int x, int y) throws AnException {
    // ...
}
```

If your method may throw multiple kinds of exceptions, you can put them all in the `throws` clause, separated by commas:

```
public boolean myOtherMethod (int x, int y)
    throws AnException, AnotherException, AThirdException {
        // ...
}
```

Note that, as with `catch`, you can use a superclass of an exceptions group to indicate that your method may throw any subclass of that exception:

```
public void YetAnotherMethod() throws IOException {
    // ...
}
```

Keep in mind that adding a `throws` method to your method definition simply means that the method might throw an exception if something goes wrong, not that it actually will. The `throws` clause simply provides extra information to your method definition about potential exceptions and allows Java to make sure that your method is being used correctly by other people.

Think of a method's overall description as a contract between the designer of that method (or class) and the caller of the method. (You can be on either side of that contract, of course.) Usually the description indicates the types of a method's arguments, what it returns, and the general semantics of what it normally does. By using `throws`, you also add information about the abnormal things the method can do. This new part of

16

the contract helps separate and make explicit all the places where exceptional conditions should be handled in your program, and that makes large-scale design easier.

Which Exceptions Should You Throw?

After you decide to declare that your method might throw an exception, you must decide which exceptions it might throw (and actually throw them or call a method that will throw them—you'll learn about throwing your own exceptions in the next section). In many instances, this is apparent from the operation of the method itself. Perhaps you're creating and throwing your own exceptions, in which case, you'll know exactly which exceptions to throw.

You don't really have to list all the possible exceptions that your method could throw; some exceptions are handled by the runtime itself and are so common (not common per se, but ubiquitous) that you don't have to deal with them. In particular, exceptions of either class Error or RuntimeException (or any of their subclasses) do not have to be listed in your throws clause. They get special treatment because they can occur any-where within a Java program and are usually conditions that you, as the programmer, did not directly cause. One good example is OutOfMemoryError, which can happen any-where, at any time, and for any number of reasons. These two kinds of exceptions are called *implicit exceptions*, and you don't have to worry about them.

Implicit exceptions are exceptions that are RuntimeException and Error subclasses. Implicit exceptions are usually thrown by the Java runtime itself. You do not have to declare that your method throws them.

 Note

> You can, of course, choose to list these errors and runtime exceptions in your throws clause if you like, but your method's callers will not be forced to handle them; only non-runtime exceptions must be handled.

All other exceptions are called *explicit exceptions* and are potential candidates for a throws clause in your method.

Passing On Exceptions

In addition to declaring methods that throw exceptions, there's one other instance in which your method definition may include a throws clause. In this case, you want to use a method that throws an exception, but you don't want to catch or deal with that excep-tion. In many cases, it might make more sense for the method that calls your method to deal with that exception rather than for you to deal with it. There's nothing wrong with this; it's a fairly common occurrence that you won't actually deal with an exception, but will pass it back to the method that calls yours. At any rate, it's a better idea to pass on exceptions to calling methods than to catch them and ignore them.

Rather than using the `try` and `catch` clauses in your method's body, you can declare your method with a `throws` clause such that it, too, might possibly throw the appropriate exception. It's then the responsibility of the method that calls your method to deal with that exception. This is the other case that satisfies the Java compiler that you have done something with a given method. Here's another way of implementing an example that reads characters from a stream:

```
public void readFile(String filename) throws IOException {
    // open the file, initialize the stream here
    while (numBytes <= myBuffer.length) {
        myInputStream.read(myBuffer);
    numBytes;++
}
```

This example is similar to an example used previously today; remember that the `read()` method was declared to throw an `IOException`, so you had to use `try` and `catch` to use it. After you declare your method to throw an exception, however, you can use other methods that also throw those exceptions inside the body of this method, without needing to protect the code or catch the exception.

Note

> You can, of course, deal with other exceptions using `try` and `catch` in the body of your method in addition to passing on the exceptions you listed in the `throws` clause. You also can both deal with the exception in some way and then rethrow it so that your method's calling method has to deal with it anyhow. You learn how to throw methods in the next section.

throws and Inheritance

If your method definition overrides a method in a superclass that includes a `throws` clause, there are special rules for how your overridden method deals with `throws`. Unlike other parts of the method signature that must mimic those of the method it is overriding, your new method does not require the same set of exceptions listed in the `throws` clause.

Because there's a possibility that your new method might deal better with exceptions rather than just throwing them, your method can potentially throw fewer types of exceptions. It could even throw no exceptions at all. That means that you can have the following two class definitions and things will work just fine:

```
public class RadioPlay {
    public void startPlaying() throws SoundException {
        // ...
    }
}
public class StereoPlay extends RadioPlay {
    public void startPlaying() {
        // ...
    }
}
```

The converse of this rule is not true: A subclass method cannot throw more exceptions (either exceptions of different types or more general exception classes) than its superclass method.

Creating and Throwing Your Own Exceptions

There are two sides to every exception: the side that throws the exception and the side that catches it. An exception can be tossed around a number of times to a number of methods before it's caught, but eventually it will be caught and dealt with.

Who does the actual throwing? Where do exceptions come from? Many exceptions are thrown by the Java runtime or by methods inside the Java classes themselves. You can also throw any of the standard exceptions that the Java class libraries define, or you can create and throw your own exceptions. This section describes all these things.

Throwing Exceptions

Declaring that your method throws an exception is useful only to your method's users and to the Java compiler, which checks to make sure that all your exceptions are being dealt with—but the declaration itself doesn't do anything to actually throw that exception should it occur; you have to do that yourself in the body of the method.

Remember that exceptions are all instances of some exception class, of which there are many defined in the standard Java class library. You need to create a new instance of an exception class to throw an exception. After you have that instance, use the throw statement to throw it. The simplest way to throw an exception is like this:

```
NotInServiceException() nis = new NotInServiceException();
throw nis;
```

Note   You can throw only objects that are subclasses of Throwable. This is different from C++'s exceptions, which enable you to throw objects of any type.

Depending on the exception class you're using, the exception also may have arguments to its constructor that you can use. The most common of these is a string argument, which enables you to describe the actual problem in greater detail (which can be very useful for debugging purposes). Here's an example:

```
NotInServiceException() nis = new
    NotInServiceException("Exception: Database Not in Service");
throw nis;
```

After an exception is thrown, the method exits immediately, without executing any other code (other than the code inside `finally`, if that block exists) and without returning a value. If the calling method does not have a `try` or `catch` surrounding the call to your method, the program might very well exit based on the exception you threw.

Creating Your Own Exceptions

Although there are a fair number of exceptions in the Java class library that you can use in your own methods, you might need to create your own exceptions to handle different kinds of errors your programs run into. Fortunately, creating new exceptions is easy.

Your new exception should inherit from some other exception in the Java hierarchy. All user-created exceptions should be part of the `Exception` hierarchy rather than the `Error` hierarchy, which is reserved for errors involving the Java virtual machine. Look for an exception that's close to the one you're creating; for example, an exception for a bad file format would logically be an `IOException`. If you can't find a closely related exception for your new exception, consider inheriting from `Exception`, which forms the "top" of the exception hierarchy for explicit exceptions. (Remember that implicit exceptions, which include subclasses of `Error` and `RuntimeException`, inherit from `Throwable`.)

Exception classes typically have two constructors: The first takes no arguments and the second takes a single string as an argument. In the latter case, you should call `super()` in that constructor to make sure that the string is applied to the right place in the exception.

Beyond those three rules, exception classes look just like other classes. You can put them in their own source files and compile them just as you would other classes:

```
public class SunSpotException extends Exception {
    public SunSpotException() {}
    public SunSpotException(String msg) {
        super(msg);
    }
}
```

Combining throws, try, and throw

What if you want to combine all the approaches shown so far? You'd like to handle incoming exceptions yourself in your method, but also you'd like to pass the exception up to your caller. Simply using `try` and `catch` doesn't pass on the exception, and simply adding a `throws` clause doesn't give you a chance to deal with the exception. If you want to both manage the exception and pass it on to the caller, use all three mechanisms: the `throws` clause, the `try` statement, and a `throw` statement to explicitly rethrow the exception.

```
public void responsibleExceptionalMethod() throws IOException {
    MessageReader mr = new MessageReader();

    try {
        mr.loadHeader();
    } catch (IOException e) {
        // do something to handle the
        // IO exception
        throw e; // rethrow the exception
    }
}
```

This works because exception handlers can be nested. You handle the exception by doing something responsible with it, but decide that it is too important to not give an exception handler that might be in your caller a chance to handle it as well. Exceptions float all the way up the chain of method callers this way (usually not being handled by most of them) until, at last, the system itself handles any uncaught exceptions by aborting your program and printing an error message. This is not such a bad idea in a standalone program, but it can cause the browser to crash in an applet. Most browsers protect themselves from this disaster by catching all exceptions themselves whenever they run an applet, but you can never tell. If it's possible for you to catch an exception and do something intelligent with it, you should.

When and When Not to Use Exceptions

Because throwing, catching, and declaring exceptions are related concepts and can be very confusing, here's a quick summary of when to do what.

When to Use Exceptions

You can do one of three things if your method calls another method that has a `throws` clause:

- Deal with the exception by using `try` and `catch` statements
- Pass the exception up the calling chain by adding your own `throws` clause to your method definition
- Perform both of the preceding methods by catching the exception using `catch` and then explicitly rethrowing it using `throw`

In cases where a method throws more than one exception, you can handle each of those exceptions differently. For example, you might catch some of those exceptions while allowing others to pass up the calling chain.

If your method throws its own exceptions, you should declare that it throws those methods using the `throws` statement. If your method overrides a superclass method that has a `throws` statement, you can throw the same types of exceptions or subclasses of those exceptions; you cannot throw any different types of exceptions.

Finally, if your method has been declared with a `throws` clause, don't forget to actually throw the exception in the body of your method using the `throw` statement.

When Not to Use Exceptions

There are several cases in which you should not use exceptions, even though they might seem appropriate at the time.

First, you should not use exceptions if the exception is something that you expect and could avoid easily with a simple expression. For example, although you can rely on an `ArrayIndexOutofBounds` exception to indicate when you've gone past the end of the array, it's easy to use the array's `length` variable to prevent you from going out of bounds.

In addition, if your users will enter data that must be an integer, testing to make sure that the data is an integer is a much better idea than throwing an exception and dealing with it somewhere else.

Exceptions take up a lot of processing time for your Java program. A simple test or series of tests will run much faster than exception handling and make your program more efficient. Exceptions should be used only for truly exceptional cases that are out of your control.

It's also easy to get carried away with exceptions and to try to make sure that all your methods have been declared to throw all the possible exceptions that they can possibly throw. This makes your code more complex in general; in addition, if other people will be using your code, they'll have to deal with handling all the exceptions that your methods might throw.

You're making more work for everyone involved when you get carried away with exceptions. Declaring a method to throw either few or lots of exceptions is a trade-off; the more exceptions your method can throw, the more complex that method is to use. Declare only the exceptions that have a reasonably fair chance of happening and that make sense for the overall design of your classes.

Bad Style Using Exceptions

When you first start using exceptions, it might be appealing to work around the compiler errors that result when you use a method that declared a throws statement. Although it is legal to add an empty catch clause or to add a throws statement to your own method (and there are appropriate reasons for doing both these things), intentionally dropping exceptions without dealing with them subverts the checks that the Java compiler does for you.

The Java exception system was designed so that if an error can occur, you're warned about it. Ignoring those warnings and working around them makes it possible for fatal errors to occur in your program—errors that you could have avoided with a few lines of code. Even worse, adding throws statements to your methods to avoid exceptions means that the users of your methods (objects further up in the calling chain) will have to deal with them. You've just made your methods more difficult to use.

Compiler errors regarding exceptions are there to remind you to reflect on these issues. Take the time to deal with the exceptions that might affect your code. This extra care will richly reward you as you reuse your classes in later projects and in larger and larger programs. Of course, the Java class library has been written with exactly this degree of care, and that's one of the reasons it's robust enough to be used in constructing all your Java projects.

Using Digital Signatures to Identify Applets

One of the fundamental assumptions of Java's applet security strategy is that you can't trust anyone on the World Wide Web. Such thinking might sound cynical, but what it means in practice is this: Java security assumes that someone might try to write malicious applets, so it prevents anything malicious from being attempted. As a result, any language feature that has potential for abuse has been blocked from use in applets. The prohibited features include the following:

- Reading files from the system on which the applet is running
- Writing files to the system on which the applet is running
- Getting information about a file on the system
- Deleting a file on the system
- Making a network connection to any machine other than the one that delivered the Web page containing the applet
- Displaying a window that does not include the standard "Java applet window" warning

Java 2 makes it possible for applets to do everything that a Java application can do—but only if they come from a trusted applet provider and are digitally signed to verify their authenticity. A digital signature is an encrypted file or files that accompany a program indicating exactly from whom the file(s) came. The document that represents this digital signature is called a *certificate*.

In order to establish trust, an applet provider must verify its identity using a group called a *certificate authority*. Ideally, these groups are not affiliated with the applet developer in any way, and they should have an established reputation as a reliable company. At present, the following companies are offering certificate authentication services in some form:

- VeriSign—The first and most widely established certificate authority, offering both Microsoft- and Netscape-specific authorization. `http://www.verisign.com`
- Thawte Certification—A newer authority for Microsoft, Netscape, and test certificates. `http://www.thawte.com`

Other companies offer certification for clients in specific geographic areas. Netscape lists the certificate authorities it works with at the following Web address:

`https://certs.netscape.com/`

Users, armed with the knowledge of who produced a program, can decide whether that group or individual should be trusted. People who are familiar with ActiveX controls will recognize this system—it's similar to how ActiveX programs are made available on World Wide Web pages.

Note

> The general security model described here is the official one created by Sun for use in its own HotJava browser and any browsers that fully support Java 2. Netscape and Microsoft have introduced their own security models for use in their browsers, so an applet must implement a different system for each browser in which it should run. Fortunately, the systems are similar, so mastering one makes it much easier to learn the others.

You also can establish levels of security other than complete trust (an applet can do anything) or no trust (an applet can't do anything that might be damaging). Java 2 enables this with a set of classes called *permissions*.

For now, all applets will be fully restricted unless the developer takes steps to digitally sign the applet and a user goes through the process of establishing that the developer is trustworthy.

A Digital Signature Example

You might find understanding the applet-trusting process easier if you use these three fictional entities: an applet developer called Fishhead Software, a Java industry group called J-Signer, and a Web user named Gilbert.

Fishhead Software offers a game applet on its Web site that saves high scores and other information on the user's hard drive. This capability isn't normally possible with an applet—disk access is a definite no-no. For the game to be playable, Fishhead must digitally sign the applet and enable users to establish Fishhead as a trusted programmer.

This process has five steps:

1. Fishhead Software uses keytool, a tool that comes with the SDK, to create two encrypted files called *a public key* and *a private key*. Together, these keys are an electronic ID card that fully identifies the company. Fishhead makes sure that its private key is hidden from anyone else. It can—and should—make its public key available to anyone as a partial form of ID.

2. Fishhead Software needs an entity that can verify who it is. It sends its public key and a descriptive file about Fishhead Software to an independent group that Java users are likely to trust—J-Signer.

3. J-Signer checks out Fishhead Software to see that it's a legitimate group with the same public key that was sent to J-Signer. When Fishhead passes muster, J-Signer creates a new encrypted file called a certificate. It is sent back to Fishhead.

4. Fishhead creates a Java archive file that contains its game applet and all related files. With a public key, private key, and a certificate, Fishhead Software can now use the jar tool to digitally sign the archive file.

5. Fishhead puts the signed archive on the Web site along with a way to download its public key.

Following this process is all that Fishhead Software needs to do to make the applet available to anyone who trusts the company enough to run it over the Web. One of the people who decides to trust Fishhead is a Web user named Gilbert, who has a Java 2–enabled browser.

His process is simpler:

1. Gilbert realizes that he can't run Fishhead's new game applet without establishing the company as a trustworthy programmer. He downloads Fishhead's public key.

2. Deciding that Fishhead is an organization he can trust, Gilbert uses another SDK security tool, jarsigner, in conjunction with Fishhead's public key to add the company to his system's list of trusted programmers.

Now Gilbert can play Fishhead's game applet to his heart's content. Depending on how the security permissions are established within the applet, it could possibly read and write files and open other network connections, as well as other insecure things. This means that malicious or unintentionally damaging code can be executed on Gilbert's system, but this is also true of any software that he could install and run on his computer. The advantage of a digital signature is that the programmers are clearly identified. Ask yourself how many virus writers would distribute their work under any kind of system that provided a trail of digital crumbs leading straight to their house.

One aspect of the new Java security model you might be unclear about is why you have a public key and a private key. If they can be used together to identify someone, how can the public key alone be used as an ID for Fishhead?

A public key and a private key are a matched set. Because they fully identify Fishhead Software, that entity is the only one that has access to both keys. Otherwise, someone else could pretend to be Fishhead and no one could tell it was a fake. If Fishhead protects its private key, it protects its identity and reputation.

When J-Signer uses a public key to verify Fishhead's identity, its main function is to make sure that the public key really belongs to the company. Because public keys can be given to anyone, Fishhead can make its public key available on its Web site. As part of its certification process, J-Signer could download this public key and compare it to the one it received. The certifying group acts as a substitute of sorts for the private key, verifying that the public key is legitimate. The certificate that is issued is linked to the public key, which can be used only with Fishhead's private key.

Anyone can issue a certificate for a public key using the `keytool` program—Fishhead Software could even certify itself. However, doing so would make it much harder for users to trust the company than if a well-established, independent certification group were used.

Working together, the public key, private key, and certificate can create a reliable digital signature for a Java archive. Sun's Java documentation for `keytool`, `jarsigner`, permissions, and other new security features are available from the following Web address:

```
http://java.sun.com/j2se/1.3/docs/guide/security/
```

Browser-Specific Signatures

At the time of this writing, the only way to digitally sign an applet is to use the procedures set up by the developers at Netscape and Microsoft for their own Web browsers. You have to use their own tools and sign an applet using both procedures if you want to reach the users of both browsers.

Signing an applet for use on Microsoft Internet Explorer requires the following:

- A Microsoft Authenticode digital ID from a company that verifies your identity, such as VeriSign or Thawte.
- Internet Explorer 4.0 or higher.
- The following tools from the Microsoft Java Software Development Kit: `cabarc.exe`, `chktrust.exe`, `signcode.exe`, and the `.DLL` files `javasign.dll` and `signer.dll`. This kit is available for download from Microsoft at `http://www.microsoft.com/java/download.htm`.

Signing an applet for Netscape Navigator browsers requires the following:

- A Netscape Object Signing software publishing digital ID, which can be acquired from one of the companies listed at the Web page with the address `https://certs.netscape.com/client.html`.
- The Netscape Signing Tool, which is available from the Web page with the address `http://developer.netscape.com/software/signedobj/jarpack.html`. The Signing Tool has a feature for using a test certificate before you have acquired a digital ID.

Note

Documentation for the use of these tools is available from the places at Microsoft and Netscape where they were downloaded from the Web. In addition, Daniel Griscom of Suitable Systems has compiled an excellent Java code signing resource at the following Web address:

`http://www.suitable.com/Doc_CodeSigning.shtml`

Security Policies

Prior to Java 2, there was a built-in assumption that all applications should be completely trusted and allowed to use all features of the language.

To make it easier to create applications that are more limited, applications now are held to the same security scrutiny as applets.

In general practice, this will not change how applications are written or run—those you have created during this book should not have encountered any security exceptions as they ran on your system. This occurs because the security policy set up during the SDK installation is the most liberal possible, allowing all the features available to applications.

The security policy is stored in a file called `java.policy`. This file can be found in the `lib\security\` subfolder of the main SDK installation folder. This file can be edited with any text editor, although you shouldn't alter it unless you're well versed in how it is established. You also can use a graphical policy-editing tool included with the SDK called policytool.

An overview of the security features implemented in Java 2 is available from Sun at the following Web page:

```
http://java.sun.com/j2se/1.3/docs/guide/security/spec/security-
spec.doc.html
```

16

Summary

Today you learned about how exceptions aid your program's design and robustness. Exceptions give you a way of managing potential errors in your programs and of alerting your programs' users that potential errors can occur. By using try, catch, and finally, you can protect code that might result in exceptions, catch and handle those exceptions if they occur, and execute code whether an exception was generated or not.

Handling exceptions is only half of the equation; the other half is generating and throwing exceptions yourself. Today you learned about the throws clause, which tells your method's users that the method might throw an exception. throws can also be used to pass on an exception from a method call in the body of your method.

In addition to the information given by the throws clause, you learned how to actually create and throw your own methods by defining new exception classes and by throwing instances of any exception classes using throw.

You also learned the basics of how Java 2's security model are being implemented, and how the different browser developers are offering a way to bypass the normal applet security with digital signatures.

Q&A

Q I'm still not sure I understand the differences between exceptions, errors, and runtime exceptions. Is there another way of looking at them?

A Errors are caused by dynamic linking or virtual machine problems, and are thus too low-level for most programs to care about—or be able to handle even if they did care about them. Runtime exceptions are generated by the normal execution of Java code, and although they occasionally reflect a condition you will want to handle explicitly, more often they reflect a coding mistake made by the programmer, and thus simply need to print an error to help flag that mistake. Exceptions that are non-runtime exceptions (IOException exceptions, for example) are conditions that, because of their nature, should be explicitly handled by any robust and well thought-out code. The Java class library has been written using only a few of these, but those few are extremely important to using the system safely and correctly. The compiler helps you handle these exceptions properly via its throws clause checks and restrictions.

Q **Is there any way to get around the strict restrictions placed on methods by the throws clause?**

A Yes. Suppose that you have thought long and hard and have decided that you need to circumvent this restriction. This is almost never the case because the right solution is to go back and redesign your methods to reflect the exceptions that you need to throw. Imagine, however, that for some reason a system class has you in a straitjacket. Your first solution is to subclass RuntimeException to make up a new, exempt exception of your own. Now you can throw it to your heart's content because the throws clause that was annoying you does not need to include this new exception. If you need a lot of such exceptions, an elegant approach is to mix in some novel exception interfaces to your new Runtime classes. You're free to choose whatever subset of these new interfaces you want to catch (none of the normal Runtime exceptions need be caught), while any leftover Runtime exceptions are allowed to go through that otherwise annoying standard method in the library.

Questions

1. What keyword is used to jump out of a try block and into a finally block?
   (a) catch
   (b) return
   (c) while

2. What class should be the superclass of any exceptions you create in Java?
   (a) Throwable
   (b) Error
   (c) Exception

3. If you want to digitally sign an applet you created, which of the following must you get from a trusted source rather than creating it yourself?
   (a) A public key
   (b) A private key
   (c) A certificate

Answers

1. b.

2. c. Throwable and Error are of use primarily by Java. The kinds of errors you'll want to note in your programs belong in the Exception hierarchy.

3. c. The certificate must be issued by a group that verifies your identity and is trusted by the audience that will use your applet.

16

Exercises

To extend your knowledge of the subjects covered today, try the following exercises:

- Create a modified version of the HexRead application that pauses for 10 seconds whenever a decimal value of 25 is read.

- Create an application that takes a command-line argument and determines if it is an integer or not, using the Integer.parseInt() method described in Day 6. This method throws a NumberFormatException.

DAY **17**

Handling Data Through Java Streams

Many of the programs you create with Java will need to interact with some kind of data source. There are countless ways in which information can be stored on a computer, including files on a hard drive or CD-ROM, pages on a Web site, and even the computer's memory itself.

You might expect there to be a different technique to handle each of the different storage devices. Fortunately, that isn't the case.

In Java, information can be stored and retrieved using a communications system called streams, which are implemented in the `java.io` package.

Today, you learn how to create input streams to read information and output streams to store information. You'll work with each of the following:

- Byte streams, which are used to handle bytes, integers, and other simple data types
- Character streams, which handle text files and other text sources

You can deal with all data the same way once you know how to work with an input stream, whether it's coming from a disk, the Internet, or even another program. The converse is true for output streams.

Streams are a powerful mechanism for handling data, but you don't pay for that power with classes that are difficult to implement.

Introduction to Streams

All data in Java is written and read using streams. Streams, like the bodies of water that share the same name, carry something from one place to another.

NEW TERM A *stream* is a path traveled by data in a program. An *input stream* sends data from a source into a program, and an *output stream* sends data out of a program to a destination.

You deal with two different types of streams today: byte streams and character streams. *Bytes* carry integers with values that range from 0 to 255. A diverse assortment of data can be expressed in byte format, including numerical data, executable programs, Internet communications, and bytecode—the class files that are run by a Java virtual machine.

In fact, every kind of data imaginable can be expressed using either individual bytes or a series of bytes combined with each other.

NEW TERM *Character streams* are a specialized type of byte stream that handles only textual data. They're distinguished from byte streams because Java's character set supports Unicode, a standard that includes many more characters than could be expressed easily using bytes.

Any kind of data that involves text should use character streams, including text files, Web pages, and other common types of text.

Using a Stream

Whether you're using a byte stream or a character stream, the procedure for using either in Java is largely the same. Before you start working with the specifics of the java.io classes, it's useful to walk through the process of creating and using streams.

For an input stream, the first step is to create an object that is associated with the data source. For example, if the source is a file on your hard drive, a FileInputStream object could be associated with this file.

After you have a stream object, you can read information from that stream by using one of the object's methods. FileInputStream includes a read() method that returns a byte read from the file.

When you're done reading information from the stream, you call the `close()` method to indicate that you're done using the stream.

For an output stream, you begin by creating an object that's associated with the data's destination. One such object can be created from the `BufferedWriter` class, which represents an efficient way to create text files.

The `write()` method is the simplest way to send information to the output stream's destination. For instance, a `BufferedWriter` `write()` method can send individual characters to an output stream.

As you do with input streams, the `close()` method is called on an output stream when you have no more information to send.

Filtering a Stream

The simplest way to use a stream is to create it and then call its methods to send or receive data, depending on whether it's an output stream or an input stream.

Many of the classes you work with today achieve more sophisticated results by associating a filter with a stream before reading or writing any data.

NEW TERM A *filter* is a type of stream that modifies the way an existing stream is handled. Think of a beaver dam on a mountain stream. The dam regulates the flow of water from the points upstream to the points downstream. The dam is a type of filter—remove it, and the water would flow in a much less-controlled fashion.

The procedure for using a filter on a stream is basically as follows:

- Create a stream associated with a data source or a data destination.
- Associate a filter with that stream.
- Read or write data from the filter rather than the original stream.

The methods you call on a filter are the same as the methods you would call on a stream: There are `read()` and `write()` methods, just as there would be on an unfiltered stream.

You can even associate a filter with another filter, so the following path for information is possible: an input stream associated with a text file, which is filtered through a Spanish-to-English translation filter, which is then filtered through a no-profanity filter, and is finally sent to its destination—a human being who wants to read it.

If this is still confusing in the abstract, you get plenty of opportunity to see it in practice in the following sections.

17

Byte Streams

All byte streams are either a subclass of InputStream or OutputStream. These classes are abstract, so you cannot create a stream by creating objects of these classes directly. Instead, you create streams through one of their subclasses, such as the following:

- FileInputStream and FileOutputStream—Byte streams stored in files on disk, CD-ROM, or other storage devices.
- DataInputStream and DataOutputStream—A filtered byte stream from which data such as integers and floating-point numbers can be read.

InputStream is the superclass of all input streams.

File Streams

The byte streams you work with most are likely to be file streams, which are used to exchange data with files on your disk drives, CD-ROMs, or other storage devices you can refer to by using a folder path and filename.

You can send bytes to a file output stream and receive bytes from a file input stream.

File Input Streams

A file input stream can be created with the FileInputStream(*String*) constructor. The *String* argument should be the name of the file. You can include a path reference with the filename, which enables the file to be in a different folder than the class loading it. The following statement creates a file input stream from the file scores.dat:

```
FileInputStream fis = new FileInputStream("scores.dat");
```

After you create a file input stream, you can read bytes from the stream by calling its read() method. This method returns an integer containing the next byte in the stream. If the method returns a -1, which is not a possible byte value, this signifies that the end of the file stream has been reached.

To read more than one byte of data from the stream, call its read(*byte[ ]*, *int*, *int*) method. The arguments to this method are as follows:

- A byte array where the data will be stored
- The element inside the array where the data's first byte should be stored
- The number of bytes to read

Unlike the other read() method, this does not return data from the stream. Instead, it returns an integer that represents the number of bytes read or -1 if no bytes were read before the end of the stream was reached.

The following statements use a while loop to read the data in a FileInputStream object called df:

```
int newByte = 0;
while (newByte != -1) {
    newByte = df.read();
    System.out.print(newByte + " ");
}
```

This loop reads the entire file referenced by df one byte at a time and displays each byte followed by a space character. It also will display a -1 when the end of the file has been reached—you could guard against this easily with an if statement.

The ReadBytes application in Listing 17.1 uses a similar technique to read a file input stream. The input stream's close() method is used to close the stream after the last byte in the file is read. This must be done to free system resources associated with the open file.

LISTING 17.1   The Full Text of ReadBytes.java

```
 1: import java.io.*;
 2:
 3: public class ReadBytes {
 4:     public static void main(String[] arguments) {
 5:         try {
 6:             FileInputStream file = new
 7:                 FileInputStream("class.dat");
 8:             boolean eof = false;
 9:             int count = 0;
10:             while (!eof) {
11:                 int input = file.read();
12:                 System.out.print(input + " ");
13:                 if (input == -1)
14:                     eof = true;
15:                 else
16:                     count++;
17:             }
18:             file.close();
19:             System.out.println("\nBytes read: " + count);
20:         } catch (IOException e) {
21:             System.out.println("Error -- " + e.toString());
22:         }
23:     }
24: }
```

If you run this program, you'll get the following error message:

```
Error -- java.io.FileNotFoundException: class.dat (The system
cannot find the file specified).
```

This error message looks like the kind of exceptions generated by the compiler, but it's actually coming from the `catch` block in lines 20–22 of the `ReadBytes` application. The exception is being thrown by lines 6–7 because the `class.dat` file cannot be found.

You need a file of bytes in which to read. This can be any file—a suitable choice is the program's class file, which contains the bytecode instructions executed by the Java virtual machine. Create this file by making a copy of `ReadBytes.class` and renaming the copy `class.dat`. Don't rename `ReadBytes.class` itself, or you won't be able to run the program.

Tip

> Windows 95 and Windows NT users can use the MS-DOS prompt to create `class.dat`. Go to the folder that contains `ReadBytes.class` and use the following DOS command:
>
> `copy ReadBytes.class class.dat`
>
> UNIX users can type the following at a command line:
>
> `cp ReadBytes.class class.dat`

When you run the program, each byte in `class.dat` will be displayed, followed by a count of the total number of bytes. If you used `ReadBytes.class` to create `class.dat`, the last several lines of output should resemble the following:

```
101 109 46 111 117 116 46 112 114 105 110 116 108 110 40 34 92 110 66 121 116
101 115 32 114 101 97 100 58 32 34 32 43 32 99 111 117 110 116 41 59 13 10 32
32 32 32 32 32 32 32 125 32 99 97 116 99 104 32 40 73 79 69 120 99 101 112 116
105 111 110 32 101 41 32 123 13 10 32 32 32 32 32 32 32 32 32 32 32 32 83 121
115 116 101 109 46 111 117 116 46 112 114 105 110 116 108 110 40 34 69 114 114
111 114 32 45 45 32 34 32 43 32 101 46 116 111 83 116 114 105 110 103 40 41 41
59 13 10 32 32 32 32 32 32 32 32 125 13 10 32 32 32 32 125 13 10 125 13 10 -1
Bytes read: 717
```

The number of bytes displayed on each line of output depends on the column width that text can occupy on your system. The bytes shown depend on the file used to create `class.dat`.

File Output Streams

A file output stream can be created with the `FileOutputStream(String)` constructor. The usage is the same as the `FileInputStream(String)` constructor, so you can specify a path along with a filename.

You have to be careful when specifying the file to which to write an output stream. If it's the same as an existing file, the original will be wiped out when you start writing data to the stream.

You can create a file output stream that appends data after the end of an existing file with the FileOutputStream(*String, boolean*) constructor. The string specifies the file and the Boolean argument should equal true to append data instead of overwriting any existing data.

The file output stream's write(*int*) method is used to write bytes to the stream. After the last byte has been written to the file, the stream's close() method closes the stream.

To write more than one byte, the write(*byte[], int, int*) method can be used. This works in a manner similar to the read(*byte[], int, int*) method described previously. The arguments to this method are the byte array containing the bytes to output, the starting point in the array, and the number of bytes to write.

The WriteBytes application in Listing 17.2 writes an integer array to a file output stream.

LISTING 17.2   The Full Text of WriteBytes.java

```
 1: import java.io.*;
 2:
 3: public class WriteBytes {
 4:     public static void main(String[] arguments) {
 5:         int[] data = { 71, 73, 70, 56, 57, 97, 15, 0, 15, 0,
 6:             128, 0, 0, 255, 255, 255, 0, 0, 0, 44, 0, 0, 0,
 7:             0, 15, 0, 15, 0, 0, 2, 33, 132, 127, 161, 200,
 8:             185, 205, 84, 128, 241, 81, 35, 175, 155, 26,
 9:             228, 254, 105, 33, 102, 121, 165, 201, 145, 169,
10:             154, 142, 172, 116, 162, 240, 90, 197, 5, 0, 59 };
11:         try {
12:             FileOutputStream file = new
13:                 FileOutputStream("pic.gif");
14:             for (int i = 0; i < data.length; i++)
15:                 file.write(data[i]);
16:             file.close();
17:         } catch (IOException e) {
18:             System.out.println("Error -- " + e.toString());
19:         }
20:     }
21: }
```

The following things are taking place in this program:

- Lines 5–10   An integer array called data is created with 66 elements.
- Lines 12 and 13   A file output stream is created with the filename pic.gif in the same folder as the WriteBytes.class file.

- Lines 14 and 15   A `for` loop is used to cycle through the `data` array and write each element to the file stream.
- Line 16   The file output stream is closed.

After you run this program, you can display the `pic.gif` file in any Web browser or graphics editing tool. It's a small image file in the GIF format, as shown in Figure 17.1.

FIGURE 17.1

The `pic.gif` file (enlarged).

Filtering a Stream

NEW TERM   *Filtered streams* are streams that modify the information sent through an existing stream. They are created using one of the subclasses `FilterInputStream` or `FilterOutputStream`.

These classes do not handle any filtering operations themselves. Instead, they have subclasses such as `BufferInputStream` and `DataOutputStream` that handle specific types of filtering.

Byte Filters

Information is delivered more quickly if it can be sent in large chunks, even if those chunks are received faster than they can be handled.

As an example of this, consider which of the following book-reading techniques is faster:

- A friend loans you a book in its entirety and you read it.
- A friend loans you a book one page at a time, and doesn't give you a new page until you finish the previous one.

Obviously, the first technique is going to be faster and more efficient. The same benefits are true of buffered streams in Java.

NEW TERM A *buffer* is a storage place where data can be kept before it is needed by a program that reads or writes that data. By using a buffer, you can get data without always going back to the original source of the data.

Buffered Streams

A buffered input stream fills a buffer with data that hasn't been handled yet, and when a program needs this data, it looks to the buffer first before going to the original stream source. This is much more efficient—using a stream without a buffer is analogous to being given a book one page at a time. Any slowdowns from that stream will slow down efforts to use it.

Buffered byte streams use the `BufferedInputStream` and `BufferedOutputStream` classes.

A buffered input stream is created using one of the following two constructors:

- `BufferedInputStream(InputStream)`—Creates a buffered input stream for the specified `InputStream` object.
- `BufferedInputStream(InputStream, int)`—Creates the specified `InputStream` buffered stream with a buffer of `int` size.

The simplest way to read data from a buffered input stream is to call its `read()` method with no arguments, which normally returns an integer from 0 to 255 representing the next byte in the stream. If the end of the stream has been reached and no byte is available, -1 is returned.

You also can use the `read(byte[], int, int)` method available for other input streams, which loads stream data into a byte array.

A buffered output stream is created using one of these two constructors:

- `BufferedOutputStream(OutputStream)`—Creates a buffered output stream for the specified `OutputStream` object.
- `BufferedOutputStream(OutputStream, int)`—Creates the specified `OutputStream` buffered stream with a buffer of `int` size.

The output stream's `write(int)` method can be used to send a single byte to the stream, and the `write(byte[], int, int)` method writes multiple bytes from the specified byte array. The arguments to this method are the byte array, array starting point, and number of bytes to write.

When data is directed to a buffered stream, it will not be output to its destination until the stream fills up or the buffered stream's `flush()` method is called.

17

Note Although the write() method takes an integer as input, the value should be from 0 to 255. If you specify a number higher than 255, it will be stored as the remainder of the number divided by 256. You can test this when running the project created later in this section.

The next project, the BufferDemo application, writes a series of bytes to a buffered output stream associated with a text file. The first and last integer in the series are specified as two command-line arguments, as in the following statement:

```
java BufferDemo 7 64
```

After writing to the textfile, BufferDemo creates a buffered input stream from the file and reads the bytes back in. Listing 17.3 contains the source code.

LISTING 17.3 The Full Text of BufferDemo.java

```
 1: import java.io.*;
 2:
 3: public class BufferDemo {
 4:     public static void main(String[] arguments) {
 5:         int start = 0;
 6:         int finish = 255;
 7:         if (arguments.length > 1) {
 8:             start = Integer.parseInt(arguments[0]);
 9:             finish = Integer.parseInt(arguments[1]);
10:         } else if (arguments.length > 0)
11:             start = Integer.parseInt(arguments[0]);
12:         ArgStream as = new ArgStream(start, finish);
13:         System.out.println("\nWriting: ");
14:         boolean success = as.writeStream();
15:         System.out.println("\nReading: ");
16:         boolean readSuccess = as.readStream();
17:     }
18: }
19:
20: class ArgStream {
21:     int start = 0;
22:     int finish = 255;
23:
24:     ArgStream(int st, int fin) {
25:         start = st;
26:         finish = fin;
27:     }
28:
29:     boolean writeStream() {
30:         try {
```

```
31:              FileOutputStream file = new
32:                  FileOutputStream("numbers.dat");
33:              BufferedOutputStream buff = new
34:                  BufferedOutputStream(file);
35:              for (int out = start; out <= finish; out++) {
36:                  buff.write(out);
37:                  System.out.print(" " + out);
38:              }
39:              buff.close();
40:              return true;
41:          } catch (IOException e) {
42:              System.out.println("Exception: " + e.getMessage());
43:              return false;
44:          }
45:      }
46:
47:      boolean readStream() {
48:          try {
49:              FileInputStream file = new
50:                  FileInputStream("numbers.dat");
51:              BufferedInputStream buff = new
52:                  BufferedInputStream(file);
53:              int in = 0;
54:              do {
55:                  in = buff.read();
56:                  if (in != -1)
57:                      System.out.print(" " + in);
58:              } while (in != -1);
59:              buff.close();
60:              return true;
61:          } catch (IOException e) {
62:              System.out.println("Exception: " + e.getMessage());
63:              return false;
64:          }
65:      }
66: }
```

This program's output depends on the two arguments specified at the command line. If you use java BufferDemo 4 13, the following output is shown:

```
Writing:
 4 5 6 7 8 9 10 11 12 13
Reading:
 4 5 6 7 8 9 10 11 12 13
```

This application consists of two classes: BufferDemo and a helper class called ArgStream. BufferDemo gets the two arguments' values, if they are provided, and uses them in the ArgStream() constructor.

The `writeStream()` method of `ArgStream` is called in line 14 to write the series of bytes to a buffered output stream, and the `readStream()` method is called in line 16 to read those bytes back.

Even though they are moving data in two different directions, the `writeStream()` and `readStream()` methods are substantially the same. They take the following format:

- The filename, `numbers.dat`, is used to create a file input or output stream.
- The file stream is used to create a buffered input or output stream.
- The buffered stream's `write()` method is used to send data, or the `read()` method is used to receive data.
- The buffered stream is closed.

Because file streams and buffered streams throw `IOException` objects if an error occurs, all operations involving the streams are enclosed in a `try...catch` block for this exception.

Tip

> The `boolean` return values in `writeStream()` and `readStream()` indicate whether the stream operation was completed successfully. They aren't used in this program, but it's good practice to let callers of these methods know if something goes wrong.

Data Streams

If you need to work with data that isn't represented as bytes or characters, you can use data input and data output streams. These streams filter an existing byte stream so that each of the following primitive types can be read or written directly from the stream: `boolean`, `byte`, `double`, `float`, `int`, `long`, and `short`.

A data input stream is created with the `DataInputStream(InputStream)` constructor. The argument should be an existing input stream such as a buffered input stream or a file input stream.

Conversely, a data output stream requires the `DataOutputStream(OutputStream)` constructor, which indicates the associated output stream.

The following list indicates the read and write methods that apply to data input and output streams, respectively:

- `readBoolean()`, `writeBoolean(boolean)`
- `readByte()`, `writeByte(integer)`

- readDouble(), writeDouble(*double*)
- readFloat(), writeFloat(*float)*
- readInt(), writeInt(*int*)
- readLong(), writeLong(*long*)
- readShort(), writeShort(*int*)

Each of the input methods returns the primitive data type indicated by the name of the method. For example, the readFloat() method returns a float value.

There also are readUnsignedByte() and readUnsignedShort() methods that read in unsigned byte and short values. These are not data types supported by Java, so they are returned as int values.

17

> **Note**
>
> Unsigned bytes have values ranging from 0 to 255. This differs from Java's byte variable type, which ranges from -128 to 127. Along the same line, an unsigned short value ranges from 0 to 65,535, instead of the -32,768 to 32,767 range supported by Java's short type.

A data input stream's different read methods do not all return a value that can be used as an indicator that the end of the stream has been reached.

As an alternative, you can wait for an EOFException (end-of-file exception) to be thrown when a read method reaches the end of a stream. The loop that reads the data can be enclosed in a try block, and the associated catch statement should only handle EOFException objects. You can call close() on the stream and take care of other cleanup tasks inside the catch block.

This is demonstrated in the next project. Listings 17.4 and 17.5 contain two programs that use data streams. The WritePrimes application writes the first 400 prime numbers as integers to a file called 400primes.dat. The ReadPrimes application reads the integers from this file and displays them.

LISTING 17.4 The Full Text of WritePrimes.java

```
1: import java.io.*;
2:
3: class WritePrimes {
4:     public static void main(String[] arguments) {
5:         int[] primes = new int[400];
6:         int numPrimes = 0;
```

LISTING 17.4   continued

```
 7:            // candidate: the number that might be prime
 8:            int candidate = 2;
 9:            while (numPrimes < 400) {
10:                if (isPrime(candidate)) {
11:                    primes[numPrimes] = candidate;
12:                    numPrimes++;
13:                }
14:                candidate++;
15:            }
16:
17:            try {
18:                // Write output to disk
19:                FileOutputStream file = new
20:                    FileOutputStream("400primes.dat");
21:                BufferedOutputStream buff = new
22:                    BufferedOutputStream(file);
23:                DataOutputStream data = new
24:                    DataOutputStream(buff);
25:
26:                for (int i = 0; i < 400; i++)
27:                    data.writeInt(primes[i]);
28:                data.close();
29:            } catch (IOException e) {
30:                System.out.println("Error -- " + e.toString());
31:            }
32:        }
33:
34:        public static boolean isPrime(int checkNumber) {
35:            double root = Math.sqrt(checkNumber);
36:            for (int i = 2; i <= root; i++) {
37:                if (checkNumber % i == 0)
38:                    return false;
39:            }
40:            return true;
41:        }
42: }
```

LISTING 17.5   The Full Text of ReadPrimes.java

```
1: import java.io.*;
2:
3: class ReadPrimes {
4:     public static void main(String[] arguments) {
5:         try {
6:             FileInputStream file = new
7:                 FileInputStream("400primes.dat");
8:             BufferedInputStream buff = new
```

```
 9:                    BufferedInputStream(file);
10:                DataInputStream data = new
11:                    DataInputStream(buff);
12:
13:            try {
14:                while (true) {
15:                    int in = data.readInt();
16:                    System.out.print(in + " ");
17:                }
18:            } catch (EOFException eof) {
19:                buff.close();
20:            }
21:        } catch (IOException e) {
22:            System.out.println("Error -- " + e.toString());
23:        }
24:    }
25: }
```

17

Most of the WritePrimes application is taken up with logic to find the first 400 prime numbers. After you have an integer array containing the first 400 primes, it is written to a data output stream in lines 17–31.

This application is an example of using more than one filter on a stream. The stream is developed in a three-step process:

- A file output stream that is associated with a file called 400primes.dat is created.
- A new buffered output stream is associated with the file stream.
- A new data output stream is associated with the buffered stream.

The writeInt() method of the data stream is used to write the primes to the file.

The ReadPrimes application is simpler because it doesn't need to do anything regarding prime numbers—it just reads integers out of a file using a data input stream.

Lines 6–11 of ReadPrimes are nearly identical to statements in the WritePrimes application, except that input classes are used instead of output classes.

The try...catch block that handles EOFException objects is in lines 13–20. The work of loading the data takes place inside the try block.

The while(true) statement creates an endless loop. This isn't a problem—an EOFException will automatically occur when the end of the stream is encountered at some point as the data stream is being read. The readInt() method in line 15 reads integers from the stream.

The last several output lines of the ReadPrimes application should resemble the following:

```
2137 2141 2143 2153 2161 2179 2203 2207 2213 2221 2237 2239 2243 22
51 2267 2269 2273 2281 2287 2293 2297 2309 2311 2333 2339 2341 2347
 2351 2357 2371 2377 2381 2383 2389 2393 2399 2411 2417 2423 2437 2
441 2447 2459 2467 2473 2477 2503 2521 2531 2539 2543 2549 2551 255
7 2579 2591 2593 2609 2617 2621 2633 2647 2657 2659 2663 2671 2677
2683 2687 2689 2693 2699 2707 2711 2713 2719 2729 2731 2741
```

Character Streams

After you know how to handle byte streams, you have most of the skills needed to handle character streams as well. Character streams are used to work with any text that is represented by the ASCII character set or Unicode, an international character set that includes ASCII.

Examples of files that you can work with through a character stream are plain text files, HTML documents, and Java source files.

The classes used to read and write these streams are all subclasses of Reader and Writer. These should be used for all text input instead of dealing directly with byte streams.

Note

The techniques for handling character streams were greatly improved after Java 1.0 with the introduction of the Reader and Writer classes and their subclasses; they enable Unicode character support and better handling of text. A Java applet that's 1.0-ready can read characters by using the byte stream classes described previously.

Reading Text Files

FileReader is the main class used when reading character streams from a file. This class inherits from InputStreamReader, which reads a byte stream and converts the bytes into integer values that represent Unicode characters.

A character input stream is associated with a file using the FileReader(String) constructor. The string indicates the file, and it can contain path folder references in addition to a filename.

The following statement creates a new FileReader called look and associates it with a text file called index.html:

```
FileReader look = new FileReader("index.html");
```

After you have a file reader, you can call the following methods on it to read characters from the file:

- read() returns the next character on the stream as an integer.
- read(*char[]*, *int*, *int*) reads characters into the specified character array with the indicated starting point and number of characters read.

The second method works like similar methods for the byte input stream classes. Instead of returning the next character, it returns either the number of characters that were read or –1 if no characters were read before the end of the stream was reached.

The following method loads a text file using the FileReader object text and displays its characters:

```
FileReader text = new
    FileReader("readme.txt");
int inByte;
do {
    inByte = text.read();
    if (inByte != -1)
        System.out.print( (char)inByte );
} while (inByte != -1);
System.out.println("");
text.close();
```

Because a character stream's read() method returns an integer, you must cast this to a character before displaying it, or storing it in an array, or using it to form a string. Every character has a numeric code that represents its position in the Unicode character set. The integer read off the stream is this numeric code.

If you want to read a line of text at a time instead of reading a file character by character, you can use the BufferedReader class in conjunction with a FileReader.

The BufferedReader class reads a character input stream and buffers it for better efficiency. You must have an existing Reader object of some kind to create a buffered version. The following constructors can be used to create a BufferedReader:

- BufferedReader(*Reader*)—Creates a buffered character stream associated with the specified Reader object, such as FileReader.
- BufferedReader(*Reader*, *int*)—Creates a buffered character stream associated with the specified Reader and with a buffer of *int* size.

A buffered character stream can be read using the read() and read(*char[]*, *int*, *int*) methods described for FileReader. You can read a line of text using the readLine() method.

The readLine() method returns a String object containing the next line of text on the stream, not including the character or characters that represent the end of a line. If the end of the stream is reached, the value of the string returned will be equal to null.

An end-of-line is indicated by any of the following:

- A newline character (`'\n'`)
- A carriage return character (`'\r'`)
- A carriage return followed by a newline

The project contained in Listing 17.6 is a Java application that reads its own source file through a buffered character stream.

LISTING 17.6   The Full Text of ReadSource.java

```
 1: import java.io.*;
 2:
 3: public class ReadSource {
 4:     public static void main(String[] arguments) {
 5:         try {
 6:             FileReader file = new
 7:                 FileReader("ReadSource.java");
 8:             BufferedReader buff = new
 9:                 BufferedReader(file);
10:             boolean eof = false;
11:             while (!eof) {
12:                 String line = buff.readLine();
13:                 if (line == null)
14:                     eof = true;
15:                 else
16:                     System.out.println(line);
17:             }
18:             buff.close();
19:         } catch (IOException e) {
20:             System.out.println("Error -- " + e.toString());
21:         }
22:     }
23: }
```

Much of this program is comparable to projects created earlier today, as illustrated:

- Lines 6 and 7—An input source is created—the FileReader object associated with the file ReadSource.java.
- Lines 8 and 9—A buffering filter is associated with that input source—the BufferedReader object buff.
- Lines 11–17—A readLine() method is used inside a while loop to read the text file one line at a time. The loop ends when the method returns the value null.

The ReadSource application's output is the text file ReadSource.java.

Writing Text Files

The `FileWriter` class is used to write a character stream to a file. It's a subclass of `OutputStreamWriter`, which has behavior to convert Unicode character codes to bytes.

There are two `FileWriter` constructors: `FileWriter(String)` and `FileWriter(String, boolean)`. The string indicates the name of the file that the character stream will be directed into, which can include a folder path. The optional Boolean argument should equal `true` if the file is to be appended to an existing text file. As with other stream-writing classes, you must take care not to accidentally overwrite an existing file when you're appending data.

Three methods of `FileWriter` can be used to write data to a stream:

- `write(int)`—Write a character.
- `write(char[], int, int)`—Write characters from the specified character array with the indicated starting point and number of characters written.
- `write(String, int, int)`—Write characters from the specified string with the indicated starting point and number of characters written.

The following example writes a character stream to a file using the `FileWriter` class and the `write(int)` method:

```
FileWriter letters = new FileWriter("alphabet.txt");
for (int i = 65; i < 91; i++)
    letters.write( (char)i );
letters.close();
```

The `close()` method is used to close the stream after all characters have been sent to the destination file. The following is the `alphabet.txt` file produced by this code:

```
ABCDEFGHIJKLMNOPQRSTUVWXYZ
```

The `BufferedWriter` class can be used to write a buffered character stream. This class's objects are created with the `BufferedWriter(Writer)` or `BufferedWriter(Writer, int)` constructors. The `Writer` argument can be any of the character output stream classes, such as `FileWriter`. The optional second argument is an integer indicating the size of the buffer to use.

`BufferedWriter` has the same three output methods as `FileWriter`: `write(int)`, `write(char[], int, int)`, and `write(String, int, int)`.

Another useful output method is `newLine()`, which sends the preferred end-of-line character (or characters) for the platform being used to run the program.

Tip

> The different end-of-line markers can create conversion hassles when trans-
> ferring files from one operating system to another, such as when a Windows
> 95 user uploads a file to a Web server that's running the Linux operating sys-
> tem. Using newLine() instead of a literal (such as '\n') makes your program
> more user-friendly across different platforms.

The close() method is called to close the buffered character stream and make sure that all buffered data is sent to the stream's destination.

Files and Filename Filters

In all of the examples thus far, a string has been used to refer to the file that's involved in a stream operation. This often is sufficient for a program that uses files and streams, but if you want to copy files, rename files, or handle other tasks, a File object can be used.

File, which also is part of the java.io package, represents a file or folder reference. The following File constructors can be used:

- File(*String*)—Creates a File object with the specified folder—no filename is indicated, so this refers only to a file folder.
- File(*String*, *String*)—Creates a File object with the specified folder path and the specified name.
- File(*File*, *String*)—Creates a File object with its path represented by the spec-ified *File* and its name indicated by the specified *String*.

You can call several useful methods on a File object.

The exists() method returns a Boolean value indicating whether the file exists under the name and folder path established when the File object was created. If the file exists, you can use the length() method to return a long integer indicating the size of the file in bytes.

The renameTo(*File*) method renames the file to the name specified by the *File* argu-ment. A Boolean value is returned, indicating whether the operation was successful.

The delete() or deleteOnExit() method should be called to delete a file or a folder. The delete() method attempts an immediate deletion (returning a Boolean value indi-cating whether it worked). The deleteOnExit() method waits to attempt deletion until the rest of the program has finished running. This method does not return a value—you couldn't do anything with the information—and the program must finish at some point for it to work.

The mkdir() method can be used to create the folder specified by the File object it is called on. It returns a Boolean value indicating success or failure. There is no comparable method to remove folders because delete() can be used on folders as well as files.

As with any file-handling operations, these methods must be handled with care to avoid deleting the wrong files and folders or wiping out data. There's no method available to undelete a file or folder.

Each of the methods will throw a SecurityException if the program does not have the security to perform the file operation in question, so these need to be dealt with through a try...catch block or a throws clause in a method declaration.

The program in Listing 17.7 converts all the text in a file to uppercase characters. The file is pulled in using a buffered input stream, and one character is read at a time. After the character is converted to uppercase, it is sent to a temporary file using a buffered output stream. File objects are used instead of strings to indicate the files involved, which makes it possible to rename and delete files as needed.

LISTING 17.7   The Full Text of AllCapsDemo.java

```
 1: import java.io.*;
 2:
 3: public class AllCapsDemo {
 4:     public static void main(String[] arguments) {
 5:         AllCaps cap = new AllCaps(arguments[0]);
 6:         cap.convert();
 7:     }
 8: }
 9:
10: class AllCaps {
11:     String sourceName;
12:
13:     AllCaps(String sourceArg) {
14:         sourceName = sourceArg;
15:     }
16:
17:     void convert() {
18:         try {
19:             // Create file objects
20:             File source = new File(sourceName);
21:             File temp = new File("cap" + sourceName + ".tmp");
22:
23:             // Create input stream
24:             FileReader fr = new
25:                 FileReader(source);
26:             BufferedReader in = new
```

LISTING **17.7** continued

```
27:                       BufferedReader(fr);
28:
29:              // Create output stream
30:              FileWriter fw = new
31:                   FileWriter(temp);
32:              BufferedWriter out = new
33:                   BufferedWriter(fw);
34:
35:              boolean eof = false;
36:              int inChar = 0;
37:              do {
38:                  inChar = in.read();
39:                  if (inChar != -1) {
40:                       char outChar = Character.toUpperCase( (char)inChar );
41:                       out.write(outChar);
42:                  } else
43:                       eof = true;
44:              } while (!eof);
45:              in.close();
46:              out.close();
47:
48:              boolean deleted = source.delete();
49:              if (deleted)
50:                   temp.renameTo(source);
51:          } catch (IOException e) {
52:              System.out.println("Error -- " + e.toString());
53:          } catch (SecurityException se) {
54:              System.out.println("Error -- " + se.toString());
55:          }
56:      }
57: }
```

After you compile the program, you need a text file that can be converted to all capital letters. One option is to make a copy of AllCapsDemo.java and give it a name like TempFile.java.

The name of the file to convert is specified at the command line when running AllCapsDemo, as in the following example:

```
java AllCapsDemo TempFile.java
```

This program does not produce any output. Load the converted file into a text editor to see the result of the application.

Summary

You learned how to work with streams today in two different directions: pulling data into a program over an input stream and sending data out of a program using an output stream.

You used byte streams for many types of nontextual data and character streams to handle text. Filters were associated with streams to alter the way information was delivered through a stream, or to alter the information itself.

Today's lesson covers most `java.io` package classes, but there are other types of streams you might want to explore. Piped streams are useful when communicating data between different threads, and byte array streams can connect programs to a computer's memory.

Because the stream classes in Java are so closely coordinated, you already possess most of the knowledge you need to use these other types of streams. The constructors, read methods, and write methods are largely identical.

Streams are a powerful way to extend the functionality of your Java programs because they offer a connection to any kind of data you might want to work with.

Tomorrow you see how streams reach the largest data source imaginable: the Internet.

17

Q&A

Q A C program that I use creates a file of integers and other data. Can I read this using a Java program?

A You can, but one thing you have to consider is whether your C program represents integers in the same manner that a Java program represents them. As you might recall, all data can be represented as an individual byte or a series of bytes. An integer is represented in Java using four bytes that are arranged in what is called big-endian order. You can determine the integer value by combining the bytes from left-to-right. A C program implemented on an Intel PC is likely to represent integers in little-endian order, which means the bytes must be arranged from right-to-left to determine the result. You might have to learn about advanced techniques, such as bit shifting, to use a data file created with a programming language other than Java.

Q The `FileWriter` class has a `write(int)` method that's used to send a character to a file. Shouldn't this be `write(char)`?

A The `char` and `int` data types are interchangeable in many ways—you can use an `int` in a method that expects a `char`, and vice versa. This is possible because each character is represented by a numeric code that is an integer value. When you call the write() method with an int, it outputs the character associated with that integer value. When calling the write() method, you can cast an int value to a char to ensure that it's being used as you intended.

Questions

1. What happens when you create a FileOutputStream using a reference to an existing file?

    (a) An exception is thrown.

    (b) The data you write to the stream is appended to the existing file.

    (c) The existing file is replaced with the data you write to the stream.

2. What two primitive types are interchangeable when you're working with streams?

    (a) byte and boolean

    (b) char and int

    (c) byte and char

3. In Java, what is the maximum value of a byte variable and the maximum value of an unsigned byte in a stream?

    (a) Both are 255

    (b) Both are 127

    (c) 127 for a byte variable and 255 for an unsigned byte

Answers

1. c. That's one of the things to look out for when using output streams—you can easily wipe out existing files.

2. b. Because a char is represented internally by Java as an integer value, you can often use the two interchangeably in method calls and other statements.

3. c. The byte primitive data type has values ranging from -128 to 127, whereas an unsigned byte can range from 0 to 255.

Exercises

To extend your knowledge of the subjects covered today, try the following exercises:

* Write a modified version of the HexRead program from Day 16, "Error Handling and Security," that reads two-digit hexadecimal sequences from a text file and displays their decimal equivalents.

- Write a program that reads a file to determine the number of bytes it contains, and then overwrites all those bytes with zeroes (0). (For obvious reasons, don't test this program on any file you intend to keep—the data in the file will be wiped out.)

Where applicable, exercise solutions are offered on the book's Web site at http://www.java21days.com.

17

DAY 18

Object Serialization and Reflection

An essential concept of object-oriented programming is the way it represents data. In an object-oriented language such as Java, an object represents two things:

- Behavior—The things an object can do.
- Attributes—The data that differentiates the object from other objects.

Combining behavior and attributes is a departure from many other programming languages. A program has typically been defined as a set of instructions that manipulate data. The data itself is a separate thing, as in the example of word-processing software. Most word processors are considered programs that are used to create and edit textual documents.

Object-oriented programming and other techniques are blurring the line between program and data. Current word processors such as Microsoft Word and Lotus WordPro might include programming instructions that affect how the document is formatted, edited, and displayed. These instructions are saved with a document, along with the text and formatting codes that compose the document's data.

Along the same lines, an object in a language such as Java encapsulates both instructions (behavior) and data (attributes).

Today you discover three ways that a Java program can take advantage of this representation:

- Object serialization—The capability to read and write an object using streams.
- Reflection—The capability of one object to learn details about another object.
- Remote method invocation—The capability to query another object to investigate its features and call its methods.

Object Serialization

Java handles access to external data via the use of a class of objects called streams. A *stream* is an object that carries data from one place to another. Some streams carry information from a source into a Java program. Others go the opposite direction and take data from a program to a destination.

A stream that reads a Web page's data into an array in a Java program is an example of the former. A stream that writes a String array to a disk file is an example of the latter.

Two types of streams were introduced during Day 17, "Handling Data Through Java Streams."

- *Byte streams*, which read and write a series of integer values ranging from 0 to 255
- *Character streams*, which read and write textual data

These streams separate the data from the Java class that works with it. To use the data at a later time, you must read it in through a stream and convert it into a form the class can use, such as a series of variables or objects.

A third type of stream, *object streams*, makes it possible for data to be represented as part of an object rather than something external to it.

Object streams, like byte and character streams, are part of the java.io package. Working with them requires many of the same techniques you used during Day 17.

For an object to be saved to a destination such as a disk file, it must be converted to serial form.

Note

> Serial data is sent one element at a time, like a line of cars on an assembly line. You might be familiar with the *serial port* on a computer, which is used to send information as a series of bits one after the other. Another way to send data is in *parallel*, where more than one element is transferred simultaneously.

An object indicates that it can be used with streams by implementing the `Serializable` interface. This interface, which is part of the `java.io` package, differs from other interfaces you have worked with—it does not contain any methods that must be included in the classes that implement it. The sole purpose of `Serializable` is to indicate that objects of that class can be stored and retrieved in serial form.

Objects can be serialized to disk on a single machine or can be serialized across a network such as the Internet, even in a case where different operating systems are involved. You can create an object on a Windows machine, serialize it to a UNIX machine, and load it back into the original Windows machine without introducing any errors. Java transparently works with the different formats for saving data on these systems when objects are serialized.

A programming concept involved in object serialization is *persistence*—the capability of an object to exist and function outside the program that created it.

Normally, an object that is not serialized is not persistent. When the program that uses the object stops running, the object ceases to exist.

Serialization enables object persistence because the stored object continues to serve a purpose even when no Java program is running. The stored object contains information that can be restored in a program so that it can resume functioning.

When an object is saved to a stream in serial form, all objects to which it contains references are saved also. This makes it easier to work with serialization; you can create one object stream that takes care of numerous objects at the same time.

You also can exclude some of an object's variables from serialization, which might be necessary to save disk space or prevent information that presents a security risk from being saved. As you see later today, this requires the use of the `transient` modifier.

18

Object Output Streams

An object is written to a stream via the `ObjectOutputStream` class.

An object output stream is created with the `ObjectOutputStream(OutputStream)` constructor. The argument to this constructor can be either of the following:

- An output stream representing the destination where the object should be stored in serial form
- A filter that is associated with the output stream leading to the destination

As with other streams, you can chain more than one filter between the output stream and the object output stream.

The following code creates an output stream and an associated object output stream:

```
FileOutputStream disk = new FileOutputStream(
    "SavedObject.dat");
ObjectOutputStream obj = new ObjectOutputStream(disk);
```

The object output stream created in this example is called `obj`. Methods of the `obj` class can be used to write serializable objects and other information to a file called `SavedObject.dat`.

After you have created an object output stream, you can write an object to it by calling the stream's `writeObject(Object)` method.

The following statement calls this method on `disk`, the stream created in the previous example:

```
disk.writeObject(userData);
```

This statement writes an object called `userData` to the `disk` object output stream. The class represented by `userData` must be serializable in order for it to work.

An object output stream also can be used to write other types of information with the following methods:

- `write(int)`—Write the specified integer to the stream.
- `write(byte[])`—Write the specified byte array.
- `write(byte[], int, int)`—Write a subset of the specified byte array. The second argument specifies the first array element to write and the last argument represents the number of subsequent elements to write.
- `writeBoolean(boolean)`—Write the specified `boolean`.
- `writeByte(int)`—Write the specified integer as a byte value.

- `writeBytes(String)`—Write the specified string as a series of bytes.
- `writeChar(int)`—Write the specified character.
- `writeChars(String)`—Write the specified string as a series of characters.
- `writeDouble(double)`—Write the specified `double`.
- `writeFloat(float)`—Write the specified `float`.
- `writeInt(int)`—Write the specified `int`.
- `writeLong(long)`—Write the specified `long`.
- `writeShort(short)`—Write the specified `short`.

The `ObjectOutputStream` constructor and all methods that write data to an object output stream throw `IOException` objects. These must be accounted for using a `try...catch` block or a `throws` clause.

Listing 18.1 contains a Java application that consists of two classes: `ObjectToDisk` and `Message`. The `Message` class represents a message that one person could send to another, perhaps as electronic mail or a short note in a private chat. This class has `from` and `to` objects that store the names of the sender and recipient, a `now` object that holds a `Date` value representing the time it was sent, and a `text` array of `String` objects that holds the message itself. There also is an `int` called `lineCount` that keeps track of the number of lines in the message.

When designing a program that transmits and receives electronic messages, it makes sense to use some kind of stream to save these messages to disk. The information that constitutes the message must be saved in some form as it is transmitted from one place to another; it also might need to be saved until the recipient is able to read it.

Messages can be preserved by saving each message element separately to a byte or character stream. In the example of the `Message` class, the `from` and `to` objects could be written to a stream as strings and the `text` object could be written as an array of strings. The `now` object is a little trickier because there isn't a way to write a `Date` object to a character stream. However, it could be converted into a series of integer values representing each part of a date: hour, minute, second, and so on. Those could be written to the stream.

Using an object output stream makes it possible to save `Message` objects without first translating them into another form.

The `ObjectToDisk` class in Listing 18.1 creates a `Message` object, sets up values for its variables, and saves it to a file called `Message.obj` via an object output stream.

LISTING 18.1   The Full Text of `ObjectToDisk.java`

```
 1: import java.io.*;
 2: import java.util.*;
 3:
 4: public class ObjectToDisk {
 5:     public static void main(String[] arguments) {
 6:         Message mess = new Message();
 7:         String author = "Sam Wainwright, London";
 8:         String recipient = "George Bailey, Bedford Falls";
 9:         String[] letter = { "Mr. Gower cabled you need cash. Stop.",
10:             "My office instructed to advance you up to twenty-five",
11:             "thousand dollars. Stop. Hee-haw and Merry Christmas." };
12:         Date now = new Date();
13:         mess.writeMessage(author, recipient, now, letter);
14:         try {
15:             FileOutputStream fo = new FileOutputStream(
16:                 "Message.obj");
17:             ObjectOutputStream oo = new ObjectOutputStream(fo);
18:             oo.writeObject(mess);
19:             oo.close();
20:             System.out.println("Object created successfully.");
21:         } catch (IOException e) {
22:             System.out.println("Error -- " + e.toString());
23:         }
24:     }
25: }
26:
27: class Message implements Serializable {
28:     int lineCount;
29:     String from, to;
30:     Date when;
31:     String[] text;
32:
33:     void writeMessage(String inFrom,
34:         String inTo,
35:         Date inWhen,
36:         String[] inText) {
37:
38:         text = new String[inText.length];
39:         for (int i = 0; i < inText.length; i++)
40:             text[i] = inText[i];
41:         lineCount = inText.length;
42:         to = inTo;
43:         from = inFrom;
44:         when = inWhen;
45:     }
46: }
```

You should see the following output after you compile and run the `ObjectToDisk` application:

```
Object created successfully.
```

Object Input Streams

An object is read from a stream using the `ObjectInputStream` class. As with other streams, working with an object input stream is very similar to working with an object output stream. The primary difference is the change in the data's direction.

An object input stream is created with the `ObjectInputStream(InputStream)` constructor. Two exceptions are thrown by this constructor: `IOException` and `StreamCorruptionException`. `IOException`, common to stream classes, occurs whenever any kind of input/output error occurs during the data transfer. `StreamCorruptionException` is specific to object streams, and it indicates that the data in the stream is not a serialized object.

An object input stream can be constructed from an input stream or a filtered stream.

The following code creates an input stream and an object input stream to go along with it:

```
try {
    FileInputStream disk = new FileInputStream(
        "SavedObject.dat");
    ObjectInputStream obj = new ObjectInputStream(disk);
} catch (IOException ie) {
    System.out.println("IO error -- " + ie.toString());
} catch (StreamCorruptionException se) {
    System.out.println("Error - data not an object.");
}
```

This object input stream is set up to read from an object that is stored in a file called `SavedObject.dat`. If the file does not exist or cannot be read from disk for some reason, an `IOException` is thrown. If the file isn't a serialized object, a thrown `StreamCorruptionException` indicates this problem.

An object can be read from an object input stream by using the `readObject()` method, which returns an `Object`. This object can be immediately cast into the class it belongs to, as in the following example:

```
WorkData dd = (WorkData)disk.readObject();
```

This statement reads an object from the `disk` object stream and casts it into an object of the class `WorkData`. In addition to `IOException`, this method throws `OptionalDataException` and `ClassNotFoundException` errors.

`OptionalDataException` indicates that the stream contains data other than serialized object data, which makes it impossible to read an object from the stream.

`ClassNotFoundException` occurs when the object retrieved from the stream belongs to a class that could not be found. When objects are serialized, the class itself is not saved to the stream. Instead, the name of the class is saved to the stream and the class is loaded by the Java interpreter when the object is loaded from a stream.

Other types of information can be read from an object input stream with the following methods:

- `read()`—Read the next byte from the stream, which is returned as an `int`.
- `read(byte[], int, int)`—Read bytes into the specified byte array. The second argument specifies the first array element where a byte should be stored. The last argument represents the number of subsequent elements to read and store in the array.
- `readBoolean()`—Read a `boolean` value from the stream.
- `readByte()`—Read a `byte` value from the stream.
- `readChar()`—Read a `char` value from the stream.
- `readDouble()`—Read a `double` value from the stream.
- `readFloat()`—Read a `float` value from the stream.
- `readInt()`—Read an `int` value from the stream.
- `readLine()`—Read a `String` from the stream.
- `readLong()`—Read a `long` value from the stream.
- `readShort()`—Read a `short` value from the stream.
- `readUnsignedByte()`—Read an unsigned byte value and return it as an `int`.
- `readUnsignedShort()`—Read an unsigned short value and return it as an `int`.

Each of these methods throws an `IOException` if an input/output error occurs as the stream is being read.

When an object is created by reading an object stream, it is created entirely from the variable and object information stored in that stream. No constructor method is called to create variables and set them up with initial values.

Listing 18.2 contains a Java application that reads an object from a stream and displays its variables to standard output. The `ObjectFromDisk` application loads the object that was serialized to the file `message.obj`.

This class must be run from the same folder that contains the file `message.obj`. In addition, the `Message` class must be either in the same folder or in a folder that is accessible from the `CLASSPATH` folders on your system.

LISTING 18.2 The Full Text of `ObjectFromDisk.java`

```
1: import java.io.*;
2: import java.util.*;
3:
4: public class ObjectFromDisk {
5:     public static void main(String[] arguments) {
6:         try {
7:             FileInputStream fi = new FileInputStream(
8:                 "message.obj");
9:             ObjectInputStream oi = new ObjectInputStream(fi);
10:            Message mess = (Message) oi.readObject();
11:            System.out.println("Message:\n");
12:            System.out.println("From: " + mess.from);
13:            System.out.println("To: " + mess.to);
14:            System.out.println("Date: " + mess.when + "\n");
15:            for (int i = 0; i < mess.lineCount; i++)
16:                System.out.println(mess.text[i]);
17:            oi.close();
18:        } catch (Exception e) {
19:            System.out.println("Error -- " + e.toString());
20:        }
21:    }
22: }
```

18

The output of this program is as follows:

```
Message:

From: Sam Wainwright, London
To: George Bailey, Bedford Falls
Date: Thu Jun 22 15:09:01 EDT 2000

Mr. Gower cabled you need cash. Stop.
My office instructed to advance you up to twenty-five
thousand dollars. Stop. Hee-haw and Merry Christmas.
```

Transient Variables

When creating an object that can be serialized, one design consideration is whether all the object's instance variables should be saved.

In some cases, an instance variable must be created from scratch each time the object is restored. A good example is an object referring to a file or input stream. Such an object must be created anew when it is part of a serialized object loaded from an object stream, so it doesn't make sense to save this information when serializing the object.

It's a good idea to exclude from serialization a variable that contains sensitive information. If an object stores the password needed to gain access to a resource, that password is more at risk if serialized into a file. The password also might be detected if it is part of an object that was restored over a stream that exists on a network.

A third reason not to serialize a variable is to save space on the storage file that holds the object. If its values can be established without serialization, you might want to omit the variable from the process.

To prevent an instance variable from being included in serialization, the `transient` modifier is used.

This modifier is included in the statement that creates the variable, preceding the class or data type of the variable. The following statement creates a transient variable called `limit`:

```
public transient int limit = 55;
```

Inspecting Classes and Methods with Reflection

On Day 4, "Working with Objects," you learned how to create `Class` objects that represent the class to which an object belongs. Every object in Java inherits the `getClass()` method, which identifies the class or interface of that object. The following statement creates a `Class` object named `keyclass` from an object referred to by the variable `key`:

```
Class keyClass = key.getClass();
```

By calling the `getName()` method of a `Class` object, you can find out the name of the class:

```
String keyName = keyClass.getName();
```

These features are part of Java's support for reflection, a technique that enables one Java class—such as a program you write—to learn details about any other class.

Through reflection, a Java program can load a class it knows nothing about, find the variables, methods, and constructors of that class, and work with them.

Inspecting and Creating Classes

The `Class` class, which is part of the `java.lang` package, is used to learn about and create classes, interfaces, and even primitive types.

In addition to using getClass(), you can create Class objects by appending .class to the name of a class, interface, array, or primitive type, as in the following examples:

```
Class keyClass = KeyClass.class;
Class thr = Throwable.class;
Class floater = float.class;
Class floatArray = float[].class;
```

You also can create Class objects by using the forName() class method with a single argument: a string containing the name of an existing class. The following statement creates a Class object representing a JLabel, one of the classes of the javax.swing package:

```
Class lab = Class.forName("javax.swing.JLabel");
```

The forName() method throws a ClassNotFoundException if the specified class cannot be found, so you must call forName() within a try-catch block or handle it in some other manner.

To retrieve a string containing the name of a class represented by a Class object, call getName() on that object. For classes and interfaces, this name will include the name of the class and a reference to the package to which it belongs. For primitive types, the name will correspond to the type's name (such as int, float, or double).

Class objects that represent arrays are handled a little differently when getName() is called on them. The name begins with one left bracket character ([) for each dimension of the array—float[] would begin with [, int[][] with [[, KeyClass[][][] with [[[, and so on.

If the array is of a primitive type, the next part of the name is a single character representing the type, as shown in Table 18.1.

TABLE 18.1 Type Identification for Primitive Types

Character	Primitive Type
B	byte
C	char
D	double
F	float
I	int
J	long
S	short
Z	boolean

For arrays of objects, the brackets are followed by an L and the name of the class. For example, if you called getName() on a String[][] array, the result would be [[Ljava.lang.String.

You also can use the Class class to create new objects. Call the newInstance() method on a Class object to create the object and cast it to the correct class. For example, if you have a Class object named thr that represents the Throwable interface, you can create a new object as follows:

```
Throwable thr2 = (Throwable)thr.newInstance();
```

The newInstance() method throws several kinds of exceptions:

- IllegalAccessException: You do not have access to the class, either because it is not public or because it belongs to a different package.
- IllegalAccessException: You cannot create a new object because the class is abstract.
- SecurityViolation: You do not have permission to create an object of this class.

When newInstance() is called and no exceptions are thrown, the new object is created by calling the constructor of the corresponding class with no arguments.

Note   You cannot use this technique to create a new object that requires arguments to its constructor method. Instead, you must use a newInstance() method of the Constructor class, as you see later today.

Working with Each Part of a Class

Although Class is part of the java.lang package, the primary support for reflection is the java.lang.reflect package, which includes the following classes:

- Field—Manage and find information about class and instance variables
- Method—Manage class and instance methods
- Constructor—Manage constructors, the special methods for creating new instances of classes
- Array—Manage arrays
- Modifier—Decode modifier information about classes, variables, and methods (which were described on Day 15, "Packages, Interfaces, and Other Class Features")

Each of these reflection classes has methods for working with an element of a class.

A Method object holds information about a single method in a class. To find out about all methods contained in a class, create a Class object for that class and call getDeclaredMethods() on that object. An array of Method[] objects will be returned that represents all methods in the class that were not inherited from a superclass. If no methods meet that description, the length of the array will be 0.

The Method class has several useful instance methods:

- getParameterTypes()—This method returns an array of Class objects representing each argument contained in the method signature.
- getReturnType()—This method returns a Class object representing the return type of the method, whether it's a class or primitive type.
- getModifiers()—This method returns an int value that represents the modifiers that apply to the method, such as whether it is public, private, and the like.

Because the getParameterTypes() and getReturnType() methods return Class objects, you can use getName() on each object to find out more about it.

The easiest way to use the int returned by getModifiers() is to call the Modifier class method toString() with that integer as an argument. For example, if you have a Method object named current, you can display its modifiers with the following code:

```
int mods = current.getModifiers();
System.out.println(Modifier.toString(mods));
```

The Constructor class has some of the same methods as the Method class, including getModifiers() and getName(). One method that's missing is getReturnType(), as you might expect—constructors do not contain return types.

To retrieve all constructors associated with a Class object, call getConstructors() on that object. An array of Constructor objects will be returned.

To retrieve a specific constructor, first create an array of Class objects that represents every argument sent to the constructor. When this is done, call getConstructors() with that Class array as an argument.

For example, if there is a KeyClass(String, int) constructor, you can create a Constructor object to represent this with the following statements:

```
Class kc = KeyClass.class;
Class[] cons = new Class[2];
cons[0] = String.class;
cons[1] = int.class;
Constructor c = kc.getConstructor(cons);
```

18

The getConstructor(*Class[]*) method throws a NoSuchMethodException if there isn't a constructor with arguments that match the Class[] array.

After you have a Constructor object, you can call its newInstance(*Object[]*) method to create a new instance using that constructor.

Inspecting a Class

To bring all this material together, Listing 18.3 is a short Java application named SeeMethods that uses reflection to inspect the methods in a class.

LISTING 18.3   The Full Text of SeeMethods.java

```
 1: import java.lang.reflect.*;
 2:
 3: public class SeeMethods {
 4:     public static void main(String[] arguments)  {
 5:         Class inspect;
 6:         try {
 7:             if (arguments.length > 0)
 8:                 inspect = Class.forName(arguments[0]);
 9:             else
10:                 inspect = Class.forName("SeeMethods");
11:             Method[] methods = inspect.getDeclaredMethods();
12:             for (int i = 0; i < methods.length; i++) {
13:                 Method methVal = methods[i];
14:                 Class returnVal = methVal.getReturnType();
15:                 int mods = methVal.getModifiers();
16:                 String modVal = Modifier.toString(mods);
17:                 Class[] paramVal = methVal.getParameterTypes();
18:                 StringBuffer params = new StringBuffer();
19:                 for (int j = 0; j < paramVal.length; j++) {
20:                     if (j > 0)
21:                         params.append(", ");
22:                     params.append(paramVal[j].getName());
23:                 }
24:                 System.out.println("Method: " + methVal.getName() + "()");
25:                 System.out.println("Modifiers: " + modVal);
26:                 System.out.println("Return Type: " + returnVal.getName());
27:                 System.out.println("Parameters: " + params + "\n");
28:             }
29:         } catch (ClassNotFoundException c) {
30:             System.out.println(c.toString());
31:         }
32:     }
33: }
```

The SeeMethods application displays information about the public methods in the class you specify at the command line (or SeeMethods itself, if you don't specify a class). To try the program, enter the following at a command line:

```
java SeeMethods java.util.Random
```

If you run the application on the java.util.Random class, the program's output is the following:

```
Method: next()
Modifiers: protected synchronized
Return Type: int
Parameters: int

Method: nextDouble()
Modifiers: public
Return Type: double
Parameters:

Method: nextInt()
Modifiers: public
Return Type: int
Parameters: int

Method: nextInt()
Modifiers: public
Return Type: int
Parameters:

Method: setSeed()
Modifiers: public synchronized
Return Type: void
Parameters: long

Method: nextBytes()
Modifiers: public
Return Type: void
Parameters: [B

Method: nextLong()
Modifiers: public
Return Type: long
Parameters:

Method: nextBoolean()
Modifiers: public
Return Type: boolean
Parameters:
```

18

```
Method: nextFloat()
Modifiers: public
Return Type: float
Parameters:

Method: nextGaussian()
Modifiers: public synchronized
Return Type: double
Parameters:
```

By using reflection, the SeeMethods application can learn every method of a class.

A Class object is created in lines 7–10 of the application. If a class name was specified as a command-line argument when SeeMethods was run, the Class.forName() method is called with that argument. Otherwise, SeeMethods is used as the argument.

After the Class object is created, its getDeclaredMethods() method is used in line 11 to find all the methods contained in the class (with the exception of methods inherited from a superclass). These methods are stored as an array of Method objects.

The for loop in lines 12–28 cycles through each method in the class, storing its return type, modifiers, and arguments and then displaying them.

Displaying the return type is straightforward: Each method's getReturnType() method is stored as a Class object in line 14, and that object's name is displayed in line 26.

When a method's getModifiers() method is called in line 15, an integer is returned that represents all modifiers used with the method. The class method Modifier.toString() takes this integer as an argument and returns the names of all modifiers associated with it.

Lines 19–23 loop through the array of Class objects that represents the arguments associated with a method. The name of each argument is added to a StringBuffer object named params in line 22.

Reflection is most commonly used by tools such as class browsers and debuggers as a way to learn more about the class of objects being browsed or debugged. It also is needed with JavaBeans, where the capability for one object to query another object about what it can do (and then ask it to do something) is useful when building larger applications. You learn more about JavaBeans during Day 20, "Working with JavaBeans."

Reflection is an advanced feature that you might not be readily using in your programs. It becomes most useful when you're working on object serialization, JavaBeans, and other programs that need runtime access to Java classes.

Remote Method Invocation

Remote method invocation (RMI) creates Java applications that can talk to other Java applications over a network. To be more specific, RMI allows an application to call methods and access variables inside another application, which might be running in a different Java environment or different operating system altogether, and to pass objects back and forth over a network connection. RMI is a more sophisticated mechanism for communicating between distributed Java objects than a simple socket connection is; the mechanisms and protocols by which you communicate between objects are defined and standardized. You can talk to another Java program by using RMI without having to know beforehand what protocol to speak to or how to speak it.

Note
Another form of communicating between objects is called RPC (*remote procedure calls*), where you can call methods or execute procedures in other programs over a network connection. Although RPC and RMI have a lot in common, the major difference is that RPC sends only procedure calls over the wire, with the arguments either passed along or described in such a way that they can be reconstructed at the other end. RMI actually passes whole objects back and forth over the Internet, and is therefore better suited for a fully object-oriented distributed object model.

18

Although the concept of RMI might bring up visions of objects all over the world merrily communicating with each other, RMI is most commonly used in a more traditional client/server situation: A single server application receives connections and requests from a number of clients. RMI is simply the mechanism by which the client and server communicate.

RMI Architecture

The goals for RMI were to integrate a distributed object model into Java without disrupting the language or the existing object model, and to make interacting with a remote object as easy as interacting with a local one. A programmer should be able to do the following:

- Use remote objects in precisely the same ways as local objects (assign them to variables, pass them as arguments to methods, and so on).
- Call methods in remote objects the same way that local calls are accomplished.

In addition, RMI includes more sophisticated mechanisms for calling methods on remote objects to pass whole objects or parts of objects either by reference or by value; it also includes additional exceptions for handling network errors that might occur while a remote operation is occurring.

RMI has several layers in order to accomplish all these goals, and a single method call crosses many of these layers to get where it's going (see Figure 18.1). There are actually three layers:

FIGURE 18.1

RMI layers.

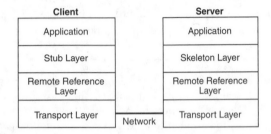

- The Stub and Skeleton Layers on the client and server, respectively. These layers behave as surrogate objects on each side, hiding the remoteness of the method call from the actual implementation classes. For example, in your client application you can call remote methods in precisely the same way that you call local methods; the stub object is a local surrogate for the remote object.

- The Remote Reference Layer, which handles packaging of a method call and its parameters and return values for transport over the network.

- The Transport Layer, which is the actual network connection from one system to another.

Having three layers for RMI allows each layer to be independently controlled or implemented. Stubs and skeletons allow the client and server classes to behave as if the objects they were dealing with were local, and to use exactly the same Java language features to access those objects. The Remote Reference Layer separates the remote object processing into its own layer, which can then be optimized or reimplemented independently of the applications that depend on it. Finally, the Network Transport Layer is used independently of the other two so that you can use different kinds of socket connections for RMI (TCP, UDP, or TCP with some other protocol, such as SSL).

When a client application makes a remote method call, the call passes to the stub and then onto the Remote Reference Layer, which packages the arguments if necessary. That layer then passes the call via the Network Layer to the server, where the Remote Reference Layer on the server side unpackages the arguments and passes them to the skeleton and then to the server implementation. The return values for the method call then take the reverse trip back to the client side.

The packaging and passing of method arguments is one of the more interesting aspects of RMI because objects have to be converted into something that can be passed over the network by using serialization. As long as an object can be serialized, RMI can use it as a method parameter or a return value.

Remote Java objects used as method parameters or return values are passed by reference, just as they would be locally. Other objects, however, are copied. Note that this behavior affects how you write your Java programs when they use remote method calls—you cannot, for example, pass an array as an argument to a remote method, have the remote object change that array, and expect the local copy to be modified. This is not how local objects behave, where all objects are passed as references.

Creating RMI Applications

To create an application that uses RMI, you use the classes and interfaces defined by the java.rmi packages, which include the following:

- java.rmi.server—For server-side classes
- java.rmi.registry—Which contains the classes for locating and registering RMI servers on a local system
- java.rmi.dgc—For garbage collection of distributed objects

The java.rmi package itself contains the general RMI interfaces, classes, and exceptions.

To implement an RMI-based client/server application, you first define an interface that contains all the methods your remote object will support. The methods in that interface must all include a throws RemoteException statement, which handles potential network problems that might prevent the client and server from communicating.

Listing 18.4 contains a simple interface that can be used with a remote object.

LISTING 18.4   The Full Text of PiRemote.java

```
1: package com.prefect.pi;
2:
3: import java.rmi.*;
4:
5: interface PiRemote extends Remote {
6:     double getPi() throws RemoteException;
7: }
```

An RMI interface like this must be part of a package for it to be accessible from a remote client program.

Caution   Using a package name causes the Java compiler and interpreter to be pickier about where a program's Java and class files are located. A package's root folder should be a folder in your system's CLASSPATH, and each part of a package name is used to create a subfolder. If the folder C:\jdk1.3 is on your system, the PiRemote.java file could be saved in a folder called C:\jdk1.3\com\prefect\pi. If you don't have a folder matching the package name, you should create it.

This interface doesn't do anything, requiring a class to implement it. For now, you can compile it by entering the following command from the folder where PiRemote is located:

```
javac PiRemote.java
```

Although the package name is required when compiling the file, it isn't needed when compiling the interface.

The next step is to implement the remote interface in a server-side application, which usually extends the UnicastRemoteObject class. You implement the methods in the remote interface inside that class, and you also create and install a security manager for that server (to prevent random clients from connecting and making unauthorized method calls). You can, of course, configure the security manager to allow or disallow various operations. The Java class library includes a class called RMISecurityManager, which can be used for this purpose.

In the server application, you also register the remote application, which binds it to a host and port.

Listing 18.5 contains a Java server application that implements the PiRemote interface:

LISTING 18.5   The Full Text of Pi.java

```
1: package com.prefect.pi;
2:
3: import java.net.*;
4: import java.rmi.*;
5: import java.rmi.registry.*;
6: import java.rmi.server.*;
7:
8: public class Pi extends UnicastRemoteObject
```

```
 9:    implements PiRemote {
10:
11:    public double getPi() throws RemoteException {
12:        return Math.PI;
13:    }
14:
15:    public Pi() throws RemoteException {
16:    }
17:
18:    public static void main(String[] arguments) {
19:        System.setSecurityManager(new
20:            RMISecurityManager());
21:        try {
22:            Pi p = new Pi();
23:            Naming.bind("//Default:1010/Pi", p);
24:        } catch (Exception e) {
25:            System.out.println("Error -- " +
26:                e.toString());
27:                e.printStackTrace();
28:        }
29:    }
30: }
```

18

In the call to the `bind()` method in line 23, the text `Default:1010` identifies the machine name and port for the RMI registry. If you were running this application from a Web server of some kind, the name `Default` would be replaced with a URL. The name `Default` should be changed to your machine's real name. On a Windows 95 or 98 system, you can find your system's name by selecting Settings, Control Panel, Network. Click the Identification tag to see the machine name, which is located in the Computer Name field.

On the client side, you implement a simple application that uses the remote interface and calls methods in that interface. A `Naming` class (in `java.rmi`) allows the client to transparently connect to the server. Listing 18.6 contains `OutputPi.java`.

LISTING 18.6   The Full Text of `OutputPi.java`

```
1: package com.prefect.pi;
2:
3: import java.rmi.*;
4: import java.rmi.registry.*;
5:
6: public class OutputPi {
7:     public static void main(String[] arguments) {
8:         System.setSecurityManager(
9:             new RMISecurityManager());
```

LISTING 18.6   continued

```
10:         try {
11:             PiRemote pr =
12:                 (PiRemote)Naming.lookup(
13:                     "//Default:1010/Pi");
14:             for (int i = 0; i < 10; i++)
15:                 System.out.println("Pi = " + pr.getPi());
16:         } catch (Exception e) {
17:             System.out.println("Error -- " + e.toString());
18:             e.printStackTrace();
19:         }
20:     }
21: }
```

At this point, you can compile these programs using the standard Java compiler. Before you can use these programs, you must use the `rmic` command-line program to generate the Stub and Skeleton Layers so that RMI can actually work between the two sides of the process.

To create the stubs and skeletons files for the current project, go to the folder that contains the file `Pi.class` and enter the following command:

```
rmic com.prefect.pi.Pi
```

Two files are created: `Pi_Stub.class` and `Pi_Skel.class`.

Finally, the `rmiregistry` program connects the server application to the network itself and binds it to a port so that remote connections can be made.

The `rmiregistry` program does not work correctly if the `Pi_Stub.class` and `Pi_Skel.class` files are located on your system's CLASSPATH. This is because the program assumes you don't need remote implementations of these files if they can be found locally.

The easiest way to avoid this problem is to run `rmiregistry` after temporarily disabling your CLASSPATH. This can be done on a Windows 95 or 98 system by opening a new MS-DOS window and entering the following command:

```
set CLASSPATH=
```

Because the client and server applications use port 1010, you should start the `rmiregistry` program with the following command:

```
start rmiregistry 1010
```

After starting the RMI registry, you should run the server program Pi. Because this application is part of a package, you must include its full package name when running the application with the Java interpreter.

You also must indicate where all the class files associated with the application can be found, including Pi_Stub.class and Pi_Skel.class. This is done by setting the java.rmi.server.codebase property.

If the application's class files were stored at http://www.naviseek.com/java21/java/, the following command could be used to run the application from the same folder that contains Pi.class:

```
java -Djava.rmi.server.codebase=http://www.naviseek.com/java21/
➥java/ com.prefect.pi.Pi
```

The last step is to run the client program OutputPi. Switch to the folder that contains OutputPi.class and enter the following:

```
java com.prefect.pi.OutputPi
```

This program produces the following output:

```
Pi = 3.141592653589793
Pi = 3.141592653589793
Pi = 3.141592653589793
Pi = 3.141592653589793
Pi = 3.141592653589793
Pi = 3.141592653589793
Pi = 3.141592653589793
Pi = 3.141592653589793
Pi = 3.141592653589793
Pi = 3.141592653589793
```

RMI and Security

RMI generates security errors when you attempt to run the Pi and OutputPi programs on some systems.

If you get AccessControlException error messages associated with calls to the Naming.bind() and Naming.lookup() methods, your system needs to be configured so that these RMI calls can execute successfully.

One way to do this is to set up a simple file that contains the most lax security policy possible for Java and use this file to set the java.security.policy property when you run Pi and OutputPi.

Listing 18.7 contains a text file that can be used for this purpose. Create this file using a text editor and save it as policy.txt in the same folder as OutputPi.class and Pi.class.

LISTING 18.7   The Full Text of `policy.txt`

```
1: grant {
2:     permission java.security.AllPermission;
3:     // Allow everything for now
4: };
```

Security policy files of this kind are used to grant and deny access to system resources. In this example, all permissions are granted, which prevents the `AccessControlException` error from occurring as you run the RMI client and server programs.

The `-Djava.security.policy=policy.txt` option can be used with the Java interpreter. The following examples show how this can be done:

```
java -Djava.rmi.server.codebase=http://www.naviseek.com/java21/
➥java/ -Djava.security.policy=policy.txt com.prefect.pi.Pi
```

```
java -Djava.security.policy=policy.txt com.prefect.pi.OutputPi
```

Summary

Although Java has always been a network-centric language, with applets running on Web browsers since version 1.0, the topics covered today show how the language is extending in two directions.

Object serialization shows how objects created with Java have a lifespan beyond that of a Java program itself. You can create objects in a program that are saved to a storage device such as a hard drive and re-created later, long after the original program has ceased to run.

RMI shows how Java's method calls have a reach beyond that of a single machine. By using RMI's techniques and command-line tools, you can create Java programs that can work with other programs no matter where they're located, whether in another room or another continent.

Although both of these features can be used to create sophisticated networked applications, object serialization is suitable for many other tasks. You might see a need for it in some of the first programs that you create; persistence is an effective way to save elements of a program for later use.

Q&A

Q Are object streams associated with the `Writer` and `Reader` classes that are used to work with character streams?

A The `ObjectInputStream` and `ObjectOutputStream` classes are independent of the byte stream and character stream superclasses in the `java.io` package, although they function similarly to many of the byte classes.

There shouldn't be a need to use `Writer` or `Reader` classes in conjunction with object streams because you can accomplish the same things via the object stream classes and their superclasses (`InputStream` and `OutputStream`).

Q Are `private` variables and objects saved when they are part of an object that's being serialized?

A They are saved. As you might recall from today's discussion, no constructor methods are called when an object is loaded into a program using serialization. Because of this, all variables and objects that are not declared `transient` are saved to prevent the object from losing something that might be necessary to its function.

Saving `private` variables and objects might present a security risk in some cases, especially when the variable is being used to store a password or some other sensitive data. Using `transient` prevents a variable or object from being serialized.

Questions

1. What is returned when you call `getName()` on a `Class` object that represents a `String[]` array?

   (a) `java.lang.String`

   (b) `[Ljava.lang.String`

   (c) `[java.lang.String`

2. What is persistence?

   (a) The ability of an object to exist after the program that created it has stopped running.

   (b) An important concept of object serialization.

   (c) The ability to work through 18 days of a programming book and still be determined enough to answer these end-of-chapter questions.

18

3. What `Class` method is used to create a new `Class` object using a string containing the name of a class?

   (a) `newInstance()`

   (b) `forName()`

   (c) `getName()`

Answers

1. b. The bracket indicates the depth of the array, the `L` indicates that it is an array of objects, and the class name that follows is self-explanatory.

2. a, b, or c.

3. b. If the class is not found, a `ClassNotFoundException` will be thrown.

Exercises

To extend your knowledge of the subjects covered today, try the following exercises:

- Use reflection to write a Java program that takes a class name as a command-line argument and checks whether it is an application—all applications have a `main()` method with `public static` as modifiers, `void` as a return type, and `String[]` as the only argument.

- Write a program that creates a new object using `Class` objects and the `newInstance()` method that serializes the object to disk.

Where applicable, exercise solutions are offered on the book's Web site at `http://www.java21days.com`.

DAY 19

Communicating Across the Internet

One of the more remarkable things about Java is how Internet-aware the language is. As you might recall from Day 1, "21st Century Java," Java was developed initially as a language that would control a network of interactive consumer devices. Connecting machines together was one of the main purposes of the language when it was designed, and that remains true today.

The java.net package makes it possible to communicate over a network with your Java programs. The package provides cross-platform abstractions for simple networking operations, including connecting and retrieving files by using common Web protocols and creating basic UNIX-like sockets.

Used in conjunction with input and output streams, reading and writing files over the network becomes almost as easy as reading or writing files on disk.

Today you will write Java programs that are Net-aware and learn why it's harder to use networking in applets than applications. You will create a program that can load a document over the World Wide Web, a program that mimics a popular Internet service, and a client/server network program.

Networking in Java

 Networking is the capability of different computers to make connections with each other and to exchange information.

In Java, networking involves classes in the `java.net` package, which offers support for many different kinds of networking operations, including connecting and retrieving files by HTTP and FTP, as well as working at a lower level with basic UNIX-like sockets.

The easiest way to use Java's network capabilities is to create applications because they aren't subject to the same default security policies as applets. Applets cannot connect to any networked machine other than the one that hosts the server they were loaded from. Even with this restriction, you can accomplish a great deal and take advantage of the Web to read and process information over the Web.

This section describes three simple ways you can communicate with systems on the Net:

- Loading a Web page and any other resource with a URL from an applet
- Using the socket classes, `Socket` and `ServerSocket`, which open standard socket connections to hosts and read to and write from those connections
- Calling `getInputStream()`, a method that opens a connection to a `URL` and can extract data from that connection

Creating Links Inside Applets

Because applets run inside Web browsers, it's often useful to direct the browser to load a new Web document.

Before you can load anything, you must create a new instance of the class `URL` that represents the address of the resource you want to load. *URL* is an acronym for *uniform resource locator*, and it refers to the unique address of any document or other resource that is accessible on the Internet.

`URL` is part of the `java.net` package, so you must import the package or refer to the class by its full name in your programs.

To create a new `URL` object, use one of four constructors:

- `URL(String)` creates a URL object from a full Web address such as `http://www.naviseek.com/java21` or `ftp://ftp.netscape.com`.
- `URL(URL, String)` creates an `URL` object with a base address provided by the specified `URL` and a relative path provided by the `String`. When specifying the address, you can call `getDocumentBase()` for the URL of the page containing your applet or `getCodeBase()` for the URL of the applet's class file. The relative path will be tacked onto the base address.

- URL(*String*, *String*, *int*, *String*) creates a new URL object from a protocol (such as "http", or "ftp"), host name (such as "www.naviseek.com" or "ftp.net-com.com"), port number (80 for HTTP), and a filename or path name.

- URL(*String*, *String*, *String*) is the same as the previous constructor minus the port number.

When you use the URL(*String*) constructor, you must deal with MalformedURLException objects. One way is by placing it in a try-catch block as shown in the following:

```
try {
    URL load = new URL("http://www.mcp.com");
} catch (MalformedURLException e) {
    System.out.println("Bad URL");
}
```

After you have a URL object, you pass it to the browser by calling the showDocument() method of the AppletContext class in your applet. AppletContext is an interface that represents the environment in which an applet runs—the Web browser, the page it is contained in, and the other applets on the same page.

Call getAppletContext() in your applet to get an AppletContext object to work with, and then call showDocument(*URL*) on that object:

```
getAppletContext().showDocument(load);
```

The browser that contains the Java applet with this code will then load and display the document at that URL.

Listing 19.1 contains two classes: WebMenu and a helper class called WebButton. The WebMenu applet displays three buttons that contain links to Web sites, as shown in Figure 19.1. Clicking the buttons causes the document to be loaded from the locations to which those buttons refer.

FIGURE 19.1

The WebMenu *applet.*

LISTING 19.1   The Full Text of `WebMenu.java`

```
 1: import java.net.*;
 2: import java.awt.event.*;
 3: import javax.swing.*;
 4:
 5: public class WebMenu extends JApplet implements ActionListener {
 6:     WebButton[] choices = new WebButton[3];
 7:
 8:     public void init() {
 9:         choices[0] = new WebButton("Obscure Store",
10:             "http://www.obscurestore.com/");
11:         choices[1] = new WebButton("Need to Know",
12:             "http://www.ntk.net/");
13:         choices[2] = new WebButton("Bleat",
14:             "http://www.lileks.com/bleats");
15:
16:         for (int i = 0; i < choices.length; i++) {
17:             choices[i].addActionListener(this);
18:             getContentPane().add(choices[i]);
19:         }
20:     }
21:
22:     public void actionPerformed(ActionEvent evt) {
23:         WebButton clicked = (WebButton)evt.getSource();
24:         try {
25:             URL load = new URL(clicked.address);
26:             getAppletContext().showDocument(load);
27:         } catch (MalformedURLException e) {
28:             showStatus("Bad URL:" + clicked.address);
29:         }
30:     }
31: }
32:
33: class WebButton extends JButton {
34:     String address;
35:
36:     WebButton(String iLabel, String iAddress) {
37:         super(iLabel);
38:         address = iAddress;
39:     }
40: }
```

This applet can be tested using the following HTML on a Web page:

```
<applet code="WebMenu.class" height="100" width="125">
</applet>
```

Note

This applet must be run from a Web browser rather than `appletviewer` for the buttons to load new pages. Because it uses event-handling techniques introduced after Java 1.0, you should use a current version of Opera, Netscape Navigator, or Microsoft Internet Explorer to run the applet.

Two classes make up this project: `WebMenu`, which implements the applet, and `WebButton`, a user-interface component that extends the `JButton` class to add an instance variable that holds a Web address.

This applet creates three `WebButton` instances (lines 9–14) and stores them in an array. Each button is assigned a name, which is used as a label, and a Web address, which is stored as a `String` rather than a `URL`. After each button is set up, an `ActionListener` is attached to it.

Because of these listeners, the `actionPerformed()` method in lines 22–30 is called when a button is pressed. This method determines which button was clicked, and then uses the `address` variable of that button to construct a new `URL` object. After you have a `URL` object, the call to `showDocument()` in line 26 tells the browser to load that Web page in the current window.

Tip

You can also load a URL in a new browser window or a specific frame. For a new window, call `showDocument(URL, String)`, using "`_blank`" as the second argument. For a frame, use its name as the second argument.

19

Because the Web page information is stored in the applet, you must recompile the class file every time you add, remove, or modify an address. A better way to implement this program would be to store the Web page names and URLs as parameters in an HTML document, which was described in Day 7, "Writing Java Applets."

Opening Web Connections

As you have seen when working with applets, it is easy to load a Web page or anything else with a `URL`. If the file you want to grab is stored on the Web and can be accessed by using the more common URL forms (HTTP, FTP, and so on), your Java program can use the `URL` class to get it.

For security reasons, applets by default can connect only to the same host from which they originally loaded. That means if you have your applets stored on a system called `www.naviseek.com`, the only machine your applet can open a connection to will be that same host—and that same hostname. If the file that the applet wants to retrieve is on that same system, using URL connections is the easiest way to get it.

This restriction will change how you write and test applets that load files through their URLs. Because you haven't been dealing with network connections, you've been able to do all your testing on the local disk simply by opening the HTML files in a browser or with the `appletviewer` tool. You cannot do this with applets that open network connections. For those applets to work correctly, you must do one of two things:

- Run your browser on the same machine on which your Web server is running. If you don't have access to your Web server, you can often install and run a Web server on your local machine.
- Upload your class and HTML files to your Web server each time you want to test them. You then run the applet off the uploaded Web page instead of running it locally.

You'll know when you're not doing things correctly in regard to making sure your applet and the connection it's opening are on the same server. If you try to load an applet or a file from a different server, you get a security exception, along with a lot of other error messages printed to your screen or to the Java console. Because of this, you might want to work with applications when you're connecting to the Internet and using its resources.

Opening a Stream over the Net

As you learned during Day 17, "Handling Data Through Java Streams," there are several ways you can pull information through a stream into your Java programs. The classes and methods you choose depend on what form the information is in and what you want to do with it.

One of the resources you can reach from your Java programs is a text document on the World Wide Web, whether it's an HTML file or some other kind of plain text document.

You can use a four-step process to load a text document off the Web and read it line by line:

1. Create a URL object that represents the resource's World Wide Web address.
2. Create a URLConnection object that can load that URL and make a connection to the site hosting it.
3. Use the getInputStream() method of that URLConnection object, create an InputStreamReader that can read a stream of data from the URL.
4. Using that input stream reader, create a BufferedReader object that can efficiently read characters from an input stream.

There's a lot of interaction going on between Point A—the Web document—and Point B—your Java program. The URL is used to set up a URL connection, which is used to set up an input stream reader, which is used to set up a buffered input stream reader. The need to catch any exceptions that occur along the way adds more complexity to the process.

This is a confusing process, so it's useful to step through a program that implements it. The GetFile application in Listing 19.2 uses the four-step technique to open a connection to a Web site and read an HTML document from it. When the document is fully loaded, it is displayed in a text area.

LISTING 19.2   The Full Text of GetFile.java

```
 1: import javax.swing.*;
 2: import java.awt.*;
 3: import java.awt.event.*;
 4: import java.net.*;
 5: import java.io.*;
 6:
 7: public class GetFile {
 8:     public static void main(String[] arguments) {
 9:         if (arguments.length == 1) {
10:             PageFrame page = new PageFrame(arguments[0]);
11:             page.show();
12:         } else
13:             System.out.println("Usage: java GetFile url");
14:     }
15: }
16:
17: class PageFrame extends JFrame {
18:     JTextArea box = new JTextArea("Getting data ...");
19:     URL page;
20:
21:     public PageFrame(String address) {
22:         super(address);
23:         setSize(600, 300);
24:         JScrollPane pane = new JScrollPane(box);
25:         getContentPane().add(pane);
26:         WindowListener l = new WindowAdapter() {
27:             public void windowClosing(WindowEvent evt) {
28:                 System.exit(0);
29:             }
30:         };
31:         addWindowListener(l);
32:
33:         try {
34:             page = new URL(address);
35:             getData(page);
```

19

LISTING **19.2**   continued

```
36:            } catch (MalformedURLException e) {
37:                System.out.println("Bad URL: " + address);
38:            }
39:      }
40:
41:      void getData(URL url) {
42:          URLConnection conn = null;
43:          InputStreamReader in;
44:          BufferedReader data;
45:          String line;
46:          StringBuffer buf = new StringBuffer();
47:          try {
48:              conn = this.page.openConnection();
49:              conn.connect();
50:              box.setText("Connection opened ...");
51:
52:              in = new InputStreamReader(conn.getInputStream());
53:              data = new BufferedReader(in);
54:
55:              box.setText("Reading data ...");
56:              while ((line = data.readLine()) != null)
57:                  buf.append(line + "\n");
58:
59:              box.setText(buf.toString());
60:          } catch (IOException e) {
61:              System.out.println("IO Error:" + e.getMessage());
62:          }
63:      }
64:
65: }
```

To run the GetFile application, specify a URL as the only command-line argument. For example:

```
java GetFile http://tycho.usno.navy.mil/cgi-bin/timer.pl
```

Any URL can be chosen—try http://www.mcp.com for Macmillan USA's Web site or http://random.yahoo.com/bin/ryl for a random link from the Yahoo! directory. The preceding example loads a page from the U.S. Naval Observatory's official timekeeping site, as shown in Figure 19.2.

Two-thirds of Listing 19.2 is devoted to running the application, creating the user interface, and creating a valid URL object. The only thing that's new in this project is the getData() method in lines 41–63, which loads data from the resource at a URL and displays it in a text area.

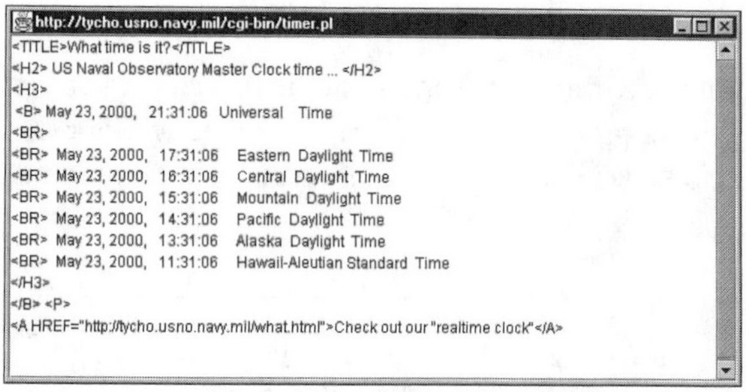

FIGURE 19.2

The GetFile
application.

```
http://tycho.usno.navy.mil/cgi-bin/timer.pl                          _ □ ×
<TITLE>What time is it?</TITLE>
<H2> US Naval Observatory Master Clock time ... </H2>
<H3>
 <B> May 23, 2000,  21:31:06  Universal  Time
<BR>
<BR>  May 23, 2000,  17:31:06    Eastern Daylight Time
<BR>  May 23, 2000,  16:31:06    Central Daylight Time
<BR>  May 23, 2000,  15:31:06    Mountain Daylight Time
<BR>  May 23, 2000,  14:31:06    Pacific Daylight Time
<BR>  May 23, 2000,  13:31:06    Alaska Daylight Time
<BR>  May 23, 2000,  11:31:06    Hawaii-Aleutian Standard Time
</H3>
</B> <P>
<A HREF="http://tycho.usno.navy.mil/what.html">Check out our "realtime clock"</A>
```

First, three objects are initialized: a URLConnection, InputStreamReader, and
BufferedReader. These will be used together to pull the data from the Internet to the
Java application. In addition, two objects are created to actually hold the data when it
arrives—a String and a StringBuffer.

Lines 48–49 open a URL connection, which is necessary to get an input stream from that
connection.

Line 52 uses the URL connection's getInputStream() method to create a new input
stream reader.

Line 53 uses that input stream reader to create a new buffered input stream reader—a
BufferedReader object called data.

After you have this buffered reader, you can use its readLine() method to read a line of
text from the input stream. The buffered reader puts characters in a buffer as they arrive,
and pulls them out of the buffer when requested.

The while loop in lines 56–57 reads the Web document line by line, appending each line
to the StringBuffer object that was created to hold the page's text. A string buffer is
used instead of a string because you can't modify a string at runtime in this manner.

After all the data has been read, line 59 converts the string buffer into a string with the
toString() method and then puts that result in the program's text area by calling the
component's append(*String*) method.

One thing to note about this example is that the part of the code that opened a network
connection, read from the file, and created a string is surrounded by a try and catch
statement. If any errors occur while you're trying to read or process the file, these statements enable you to recover from them without the entire program crashing. (In this
case, the program exits with an error because there's little else to be done if the application can't read the file.) The try and catch give you the ability to handle and recover
from errors.

19

Sockets

For networking applications beyond what the URL and URLconnection classes offer (for example, for other protocols or for more general networking applications), Java provides the Socket and ServerSocket classes as an abstraction of standard TCP socket programming techniques.

> **Note**
>
> Java also provides facilities for using datagram (UDP) sockets, which are not covered here. See the Java documentation for the java.net package if you're interested in working with datagrams.

The Socket class provides a client-side socket interface similar to standard UNIX sockets. Create a new instance of Socket to open a connection (where *hostName* is the host to connect to and *portNum* is the port number):

```
Socket connection = new Socket(hostName, portNum);
```

After you create a socket, you should set its timeout value, which determines how long the application will wait for data to arrive. This is handled by calling the socket's setSoTimeOut(*int*) method with the number of milliseconds to wait as the only argument:

```
connection.setSoTimeOut(50000);
```

By using this method, any efforts to read data from the socket represented by connection will only wait for 50,000 milliseconds (50 seconds). If the timeout is reached, an InterruptedIOException will be thrown, which gives you an opportunity in a try-catch block to either close the socket or try to read from it again.

If you don't set a timeout in a program that uses sockets, it might hang indefinitely waiting for data.

> **Tip**
>
> This problem is usually avoided by putting network operations in their own thread and running them separately from the rest of the program, a technique used with animation on Day 13, "Threads and Animation."

After the socket is open, you can use input and output streams to read and write from that socket:

```
BufferedInputStream bis = new
    BufferedInputStream(connection.getInputStream());
DataInputStream in = new DataInputStream(bis);

BufferedOutputStream bos = new
    BufferedOutputStream(connection.getOutputStream());
DataOutputStream out= new DataOutputStream(bos);
```

Because you really don't need names for all these objects—they are only used to create a stream or stream reader—an efficient shortcut is to combine several statements, as in this example using a Socket object named sock:

```
DataInputStream in = new DataInputStream(
    new BufferedInputStream(
    sock.getInputStream()));
```

In this statement, the call to sock.getInputStream() returns an input stream associated with that socket. This stream is used to create a BufferedInputStream, and the buffered input stream is used to create a DataInputStream. The only variables you are left with are sock and in, which would still be needed as you receive data from the connection and close it afterward. The intermediate objects—a BufferedInputStream and an InputStream—are needed only once.

After you're done with a socket, don't forget to close it by calling the close() method. This also closes all the input and output streams you might have set up for that socket. For example:

```
connection.close();
```

19

Socket programming can be used for a large number of services that are delivered using TCP/IP networking, including telnet, SMTP (incoming mail), NNTP (Usenet news), and finger.

The last of these, finger, is a protocol for asking a system about one of its users. By setting up a finger server, a system administrator enables an Internet-connected machine to answer requests for user information. Users can provide more information about themselves by creating .plan files, which are sent back to anyone who uses finger to find out more about them.

Although it has fallen into disuse in recent years because of security concerns, before the World Wide Web was introduced, finger was the most popular way that Internet users published facts about themselves and their activities. You could use finger on a friend's account at another college to see if that person was online and read the most current .plan file.

> **Note**
>
> Today, there's still one community that spreads personal messages by finger rather than Web site or mailing list—the game-programming community. The GameFinger Web site, which acts as a gateway between the Web and finger, has links to hundreds of these throwbacks at `http://finger.planetquake.com/`.

As an exercise in socket programming, the `Finger` application is a rudimentary finger client (see Listing 19.3).

LISTING 19.3 The Full Text of `Finger.java`

```
 1: import java.io.*;
 2: import java.net.*;
 3: import java.util.*;
 4:
 5: public class Finger {
 6:     public static void main(String[] arguments) {
 7:         String user;
 8:         String host;
 9:         if ((arguments.length == 1) && (arguments[0].indexOf("@") > -1)) {
10:             StringTokenizer split = new StringTokenizer(arguments[0],
11:                 "@");
12:             user = split.nextToken();
13:             host = split.nextToken();
14:         } else {
15:             System.out.println("Usage: java Finger user@host");
16:             return;
17:         }
18:         try {
19:             Socket digit = new Socket(host, 79);
20:             digit.setSoTimeout(20000);
21:             PrintStream out = new PrintStream(digit.getOutputStream());
22:             out.print(user + "\015\012");
23:             BufferedReader in = new BufferedReader(
24:                 new InputStreamReader(digit.getInputStream()));
25:             boolean eof = false;
26:             while (!eof) {
27:                 String line = in.readLine();
28:                 if (line != null)
29:                     System.out.println(line);
30:                 else
31:                     eof = true;
32:             }
33:             digit.close();
34:         } catch (IOException e) {
35:             System.out.println("IO Error:" + e.getMessage());
```

```
36:            }
37:      }
38: }
```

When making a finger request, you specify a username followed by an at sign ("@") and a host name, the same format as an email address. One real-life example is romero@ionstorm.com, the finger address of Quake and Daikatana designer John Romero. You can request his .plan file by running the Finger application as follows:

```
java Finger romero@ionstorm.com
```

If romero has an account on the ionstorm.com finger server, the output of this program will be his .plan file and perhaps other information. The server also will let you know if a user can't be found.

The GameFinger site includes addresses for other game designers who provide .plan updates, including Kenn Hoekstra (khoekstra@ravensoft.com), Markus Mäki (markus@remedy.fi), Chris Hargrove (chrish@finger.3drealms.com), and Chris Norden (cnorden@ionstorm.com).

The Finger application uses the StringTokenizer class to convert an address in *user@host* format into two String objects: user and host (lines 10–13).

The following socket activities are taking place:

- Lines 19–20: A new Socket is created using the host name and port 79, the port that is traditionally reserved for finger services, and a timeout of 20 seconds is set.
- Line 21: The socket is used to get an OutputStream, which feeds into a new PrintStream object.
- Line 22: The finger protocol requires that the username be sent through the socket, followed by a carriage return ('\015') and linefeed ('\012'). This is handled by calling the print() method of the new PrintStream.
- Lines 23–24: After the username has been sent, an input stream must be created on the socket to receive input from the finger server. A BufferedReader stream, in, is created by combining several stream-creation expressions together. This stream is well suited for finger input because it can read a line of text at a time.
- Lines 26–32: The program loops as lines are read from the buffered reader. The end of output from the server causes in.readLine() to return null, ending the loop.

The same techniques used to communicate with a finger server through a socket can be used to connect to other popular Internet services. You could turn it into a telnet or Web reading client with a port change in line 19 and little other modification.

19

Socket Servers

Server-side sockets work similarly to client sockets, with the exception of the `accept()` method. A server socket listens on a TCP port for a connection from a client; when a client connects to that port, the `accept()` method accepts a connection from that client. By using both client and server sockets, you can create applications that communicate with each other over the network.

Create a new instance of `ServerSocket` with the port number in order to create a server socket and bind it to a port:

```
ServerSocket servo = new ServerSocket(8888);
```

Use the `accept()` method to listen on that port (and to accept a connection from any clients if one is made):

```
servo.accept();
```

After the socket connection is made, you can use input and output streams to read from and write to the client.

In the next section, you implement a simple socket-based application.

To extend the behavior of the socket classes—for example, to allow network connections to work across a firewall or a proxy—you can use the abstract class `SocketImpl` and the interface `SocketImplFactory` to create a new transport-layer socket implementation. This design fits with the original goal of Java's socket classes: to allow those classes to be portable to other systems with different transport mechanisms. The problem with this mechanism is that although it works for simple cases, it prevents you from adding other protocols on top of TCP (for example, to implement an encryption mechanism such as SSL) and from having multiple socket implementations per Java runtime.

For these reasons, sockets were extended after Java 1.0 so that the `Socket` and `ServerSocket` classes are not final and extendable. You can create subclasses of these classes that use either the default socket implementation or one of your own making. This allows much more flexible network capabilities.

To finish up the discussion on networking in Java, here's an example of a Java program that uses the `Socket` classes to implement a simple network-based server application, `TriviaServer`.

The `TriviaServer` application presents a trivia quiz with multiple choice answers. It works like this:

1. The server program waits for a client to connect.

2. When a client connects, the server sends a question to the client and waits for a response.

3. When the client sends an answer, the server notifies the client whether it is correct or incorrect. If it is incorrect, the correct answer is provided.

4. The server then asks the client whether the quiz should continue. If any response other than N or n is received, the process repeats.

Designing a Server Application

It's usually a good idea to perform a brief preliminary design before you start churning out code. With that in mind, take a look at what is required of the `TriviaServer` and a client.

On the server side, you need a program that monitors a particular port on the host machine for client connections. Port 4413 was chosen arbitrarily for this project, but it could be any number from 1024 to 65535.

Note

> The Internet Assigned Numbers Authority controls the usage of ports 0 to 1023, but claims are staked to the higher ports on a more informal basis. When choosing port numbers for your own client/server applications, it's a good idea to do research on what ports are currently being used by others. Search the Web for references to the port you want to use and plug the terms "Registered Port Numbers" and "Well-Known Port Numbers" into search engines to find lists of in-use ports. A good guide to port usage is available on the Web at `http://www.sockets.com/services.htm`.

19

When a client is detected, the server picks a random question and sends it to the client over the specified port. This begins an exchange of information between the server and client, with the server doing almost all of the work.

The client's only responsibility in this client/server project is to establish a connection to the server, display messages received from the server, take input from a user, and send that input to the server.

Although you could develop a simple client for a project like this, you also can use any telnet application to act as the client, as long as it can connect to a port you designate. Windows includes a command-line application called telnet you can use for this purpose.

Implementing the Server

The heart of the instance variables defined in the TriviaServer class follow:

```
private static final int WAIT_FOR_CLIENT = 0;
private static final int WAIT_FOR_ANSWER = 1;
private static final int WAIT_FOR_CONFIRM = 2;
private String[] questions;
private String[] answers;
private Socket sock;
private int numQuestions;
private int num = 0;
private int state = WAIT_FOR_CLIENT;
private Random rand = new Random();
```

The WAIT_FOR_CLIENT, WAIT_FOR_ANSWER, and WAIT_FOR_CONFIRM variables are all constants that define different states that the server can be in; you see these constants in action in a moment. The questions and answers variables are string arrays used to store the questions and corresponding answers. The sock instance variable keeps up with the server-socket connection. numQuestions is used to store the total number of questions, whereas num is the number of the current question being asked. The state variable holds the current state of the server as defined by the three state constants (WAIT_FOR_CLIENT, WAIT_FOR_ANSWER, and WAIT_FOR_CONFIRM). Finally, the rand variable is used to pick questions at random.

The TriviaServer constructor doesn't do much except create a Socket rather than a DatagramSocket:

```
public TriviaServer() {
    super("TriviaServer");
    try {
        sock = new ServerSocket(4413);
        System.out.println("TriviaServer up and running ...");
    } catch (IOException e) {
        System.err.println("Error: couldn't create socket.");
        System.exit(1);
    }
}
```

Most of the action takes place in the run() method:

```
public void run() {
    Socket client = null;
```

```
// Initialize the question and answer data
if (!loadData()) {
    System.err.println("Error: couldn't initialize Q&A data.");
    return;
}

// Look for clients and ask trivia questions
while (true) {
    // Wait for a client
    if (sock == null)
        return;
    try {
        client = sock.accept();
    } catch (IOException e) {
        System.err.println("Error: couldn't connect to client.");
        System.exit(1);
    }

    // Process questions and answers
    try {
        InputStreamReader isr = new InputStreamReader(
            client.getInputStream());
        BufferedReader is = new BufferedReader(isr);
        PrintWriter os = new PrintWriter(new
            BufferedOutputStream(client.getOutputStream()), false);
        String outLine;
        // Output server request
        outLine = processInput(null);
        os.println(outLine);
        os.flush();

        // Process and output user input
        while (true) {
            String inLine = is.readLine();
            if (inLine.length() > 0)
                outLine = processInput(inLine);
            else
                outLine = processInput("");
            os.println(outLine);
            os.flush();
            if (outLine.equals("Bye."))
                break;
        }

        // Clean up
        os.close();
        is.close();
        client.close();
    } catch (Exception e) {
        System.err.println("Error: " + e);
        e.printStackTrace();
```

19

```
            }
        }
    }
```

The `run()` method first initializes the questions and answers by calling `loadData()`, which you learn about in a moment. An infinite `while` loop that waits for a client connection is then entered.

When a client connects, the appropriate input and output streams are created and the communication is handled via the `processInput()` method. This method continually processes client responses and handles asking new questions until the client user decides not to receive any more questions. The server acknowledges this by sending the string `"Bye."` and closing the streams and client socket.

The `processInput()` method keeps up with the server state and manages the logic of the question/answer process:

```
String processInput(String inStr) {
    String outStr = null;

    switch (state) {
        case WAIT_FOR_CLIENT:
            // Ask a question
            outStr = questions[num];
            state = WAIT_FOR_ANSWER;
            break;
        case WAIT_FOR_ANSWER:
            // Check the answer
            if (inStr.equalsIgnoreCase(answers[num]))
                outStr="\015\012That's correct! Want another (y/n)?";
            else
              outStr="\015\012Wrong, the correct answer is " + answers[num] +
                    ". Want another (y/n)?";
            state = WAIT_FOR_CONFIRM;
            break;
        case WAIT_FOR_CONFIRM:
            // See if they want another question
            if (!inStr.equalsIgnoreCase("N")) {
                num = Math.abs(rand.nextInt()) % questions.length;
                outStr = questions[num];
                state = WAIT_FOR_ANSWER;
            } else {
                outStr = "Bye.";
                state = WAIT_FOR_CLIENT;
            }
            break;
    }
    return outStr;
}
```

The first thing to note about the processInput() method is the outStr local variable. This string's value is sent back to the client in the run method when processInput returns, so keep an eye on how processInput uses outStr to convey information to the client.

In TriviaServer, the state WAIT_FOR_CLIENT represents the server when it is idle and waiting for a client connection. Understand that each case statement in processInput() represents the server leaving the given state. For example, the WAIT_FOR_CLIENT case statement is entered when the server has just left the WAIT_FOR_CLIENT state—a client has just connected to the server. When this occurs, the server sets the output string to the current question and sets the state to WAIT_FOR_ANSWER.

If the server is leaving the WAIT_FOR_ANSWER state, the client has responded with an answer. processInput() checks the client's answer against the correct answer and sets the output string accordingly. It then sets the state to WAIT_FOR_CONFIRM.

The WAIT_FOR_CONFIRM state represents the server waiting for a confirmation answer from the client. In processInput(), the WAIT_FOR_CONFIRM case statement indicates that the server is leaving the state because the client has returned a confirmation (yes or no). If the client gave any answer other than N or n, processInput picks a new question and sets the state back to WAIT_FOR_ANSWER. Otherwise, the server tells the client "Bye." and returns the state to WAIT_FOR_CLIENT to await a new client connection.

The questions and answers in Trivia are stored in a text file called qna.txt, which is organized into a list of questions and answers in alternating question, answer, question, answer sequence. To mark the end of a question or answer, a pound sign ("#") is used. A listing for the first two questions and answers in the qna.txt file follows:

```
Which one of the Smothers Brothers did Bill Cosby once punch out?
(a) Dick
(b) Tommy
(c) both#
b#

What's the nickname of Dallas Cowboys fullback Daryl Johnston?
(a) caribou
(b) moose
(c) elk#
b#
```

Tip

You can create your own questions and answers for this trivia quiz by following the format above, or download a full qna.txt file from the book's Web site—visit http://www.java21days.com and go to the Day 19 page.

19

The `loadData()` method handles the work of reading the questions and answers from the text file and storing them in separate string arrays, as shown here:

```
private boolean loadData() {
    try {
        File inFile = new File("qna.txt");
        FileInputStream inStream = new FileInputStream(inFile);
        byte[] data = new byte[(int)inFile.length()];

        // Read questions and answers into a byte array
        if (inStream.read(data) <= 0) {
            System.err.println("Error: couldn't read q&a.");
            return false;
        }

        // See how many question/answer pairs there are
        for (int i = 0; i < data.length; i++)
            if (data[i] == (byte)'#')
                numQuestions++;
        numQuestions /= 2;
        questions = new String[numQuestions];
        answers = new String[numQuestions];

        // Parse questions and answers into String arrays
        int start = 0, index = 0;
        boolean isQuestion = true;
        for (int i = 0; i < data.length; i++)
            if (data[i] == (byte)'#') {
                if (isQuestion) {
                    questions[index] = new String(data, start,
                        i - start);
                    isQuestion = false;
                } else {
                    answers[index] = new String(data, start,
                        i - start);
                    isQuestion = true;
                    index++;
                }
                start = i + 3;
            }
    } catch (FileNotFoundException e) {
        System.err.println("Exception: couldn't find the Q&A file.");
        return false;
    } catch (IOException e) {
        System.err.println("Exception: couldn't read the Q&A file.");
        return false;
    }
    return true;
}
```

The loadData() method uses two arrays and fills them with alternating strings from the qna.txt file: first a question, and then an answer, alternating until the end of the file is reached.

The only remaining method in TriviaServer is main(), which simply creates the server object and gets it started with a call to the start method:

```java
public static void main(String[] arguments) {
    TriviaServer server = new TriviaServer();
    server.start();
}
```

Listing 19.4 contains the full source code for the server application.

LISTING 19.4   The Full Text of TriviaServer.java

```java
 1: import java.io.*;
 2: import java.net.*;
 3: import java.util.Random;
 4:
 5: public class TriviaServer extends Thread {
 6:     private static final int WAIT_FOR_CLIENT = 0;
 7:     private static final int WAIT_FOR_ANSWER = 1;
 8:     private static final int WAIT_FOR_CONFIRM = 2;
 9:     private String[] questions;
10:     private String[] answers;
11:     private ServerSocket sock;
12:     private int numQuestions;
13:     private int num = 0;
14:     private int state = WAIT_FOR_CLIENT;
15:     private Random rand = new Random();
16:
17:     public TriviaServer() {
18:         super("TriviaServer");
19:         try {
20:             sock = new ServerSocket(4413);
21:             System.out.println("TriviaServer up and running ...");
22:         } catch (IOException e) {
23:             System.err.println("Error: couldn't create socket.");
24:             System.exit(1);
25:         }
26:     }
27:
28:     public static void main(String[] arguments) {
29:         TriviaServer server = new TriviaServer();
30:         server.start();
31:     }
32:
33:     public void run() {
34:         Socket client = null;
```

19

LISTING 19.4   continued

```
35:
36:         // Initialize the question and answer data
37:         if (!loadData()) {
38:             System.err.println("Error: couldn't initialize Q&A data.");
39:             return;
40:         }
41:
42:         // Look for clients and ask trivia questions
43:         while (true) {
44:             // Wait for a client
45:             if (sock == null)
46:                 return;
47:             try {
48:                 client = sock.accept();
49:             } catch (IOException e) {
50:                 System.err.println("Error: couldn't connect to client.");
51:                 System.exit(1);
52:             }
53:
54:             // Process questions and answers
55:             try {
56:                 InputStreamReader isr = new InputStreamReader(
57:                     client.getInputStream());
58:                 BufferedReader is = new BufferedReader(isr);
59:                 PrintWriter os = new PrintWriter(new
60:                     BufferedOutputStream(client.getOutputStream()), false);
61:                 String outLine;
62:
63:                 // Output server request
64:                 outLine = processInput(null);
65:                 os.println(outLine);
66:                 os.flush();
67:
68:                 // Process and output user input
69:                 while (true) {
70:                     String inLine = is.readLine();
71:                     if (inLine.length() > 0)
72:                         outLine = processInput(inLine);
73:                     else
74:                         outLine = processInput("");
75:                     os.println(outLine);
76:                     os.flush();
77:                     if (outLine.equals("Bye."))
78:                         break;
79:                 }
80:
81:                 // Clean up
82:                 os.close();
83:                 is.close();
```

```
84:                     client.close();
85:                 } catch (Exception e) {
86:                     System.err.println("Error: " + e);
87:                     e.printStackTrace();
88:                 }
89:         }
90:     }
91:
92:     private boolean loadData() {
93:         try {
94:             File inFile = new File("qna.txt");
95:             FileInputStream inStream = new FileInputStream(inFile);
96:             byte[] data = new byte[(int)inFile.length()];
97:
98:             // Read questions and answers into a byte array
99:             if (inStream.read(data) <= 0) {
100:                 System.err.println("Error: couldn't read q&a.");
101:                 return false;
102:             }
103:
104:             // See how many question/answer pairs there are
105:             for (int i = 0; i < data.length; i++)
106:                 if (data[i] == (byte)'#')
107:                     numQuestions++;
108:             numQuestions /= 2;
109:             questions = new String[numQuestions];
110:             answers = new String[numQuestions];
111:
112:             // Parse questions and answers into String arrays
113:             int start = 0, index = 0;
114:             boolean isQuestion = true;
115:             for (int i = 0; i < data.length; i++)
116:                 if (data[i] == (byte)'#') {
117:                     if (isQuestion) {
118:                         questions[index] = new String(data, start,
119:                             i - start);
120:                         isQuestion = false;
121:                     } else {
122:                         answers[index] = new String(data, start,
123:                             i - start);
124:                         isQuestion = true;
125:                         index++;
126:                     }
127:                     start = i + 3;
128:                 }
129:         } catch (FileNotFoundException e) {
130:             System.err.println("Exception: couldn't find the Q&A file.");
131:             return false;
132:         } catch (IOException e) {
133:             System.err.println("Exception: couldn't read the Q&A file.");
134:             return false;
```

19

LISTING **19.4**   continued

```
135:            }
136:            return true;
137:        }
138:
139:    String processInput(String inStr) {
140:        String outStr = null;
141:
142:        switch (state) {
143:            case WAIT_FOR_CLIENT:
144:                // Ask a question
145:                outStr = questions[num];
146:                state = WAIT_FOR_ANSWER;
147:                break;
148:
149:            case WAIT_FOR_ANSWER:
150:                // Check the answer
151:                if (inStr.equalsIgnoreCase(answers[num]))
152:                    outStr="\015\012That's correct! Want another (y/n)?";
153:                else
154:                    outStr="\015\012Wrong, the correct answer is "
155:                        + answers[num] +". Want another (y/n)?";
156:                state = WAIT_FOR_CONFIRM;
157:                break;
158:
159:            case WAIT_FOR_CONFIRM:
160:                // See if they want another question
161:                if (!inStr.equalsIgnoreCase("N")) {
162:                    num = Math.abs(rand.nextInt()) % questions.length;
163:                    outStr = questions[num];
164:                    state = WAIT_FOR_ANSWER;
165:                } else {
166:                    outStr = "Bye.";
167:                    state = WAIT_FOR_CLIENT;
168:                }
169:                break;
170:        }
171:        return outStr;
172:    }
173: }
```

Testing the Server

The TriviaServer application must be running in order for a client to be able to connect to it. To get things started, you must first run the server:

```
java TriviaServer
```

The server will display only one line of output if it is running successfully:

```
TriviaServer up and running ...
```

With the server running, you can connect to it using a telnet program such as the one that's included with Windows.

To run `telnet` on Windows, click Start, Run to open the Run dialog, and then type **telnet** in the Open text field and press Enter. A telnet window will open.

To make a telnet connection using this program, choose the menu command Connect, Remote System. A Connect dialog box will open, as shown in Figure 19.3. Enter **localhost** in the Host Name field, 4413 in the Port field, and leave the default value—vt100—in the TermType field.

FIGURE 19.3

Making a telnet *connection.*

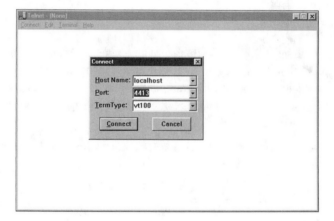

The host name `localhost` represents your own machine—the system running the application. You can use it to test server applications before deploying them permanently on the Internet.

Depending on how Internet connections have been configured on your system, you might need to log on to the Internet before a successful socket connection can be made between a telnet client and the `TriviaServer` application.

If the server was on another computer connected to the Internet, you would specify that computer's host name or IP address instead of `localhost`.

Figure 19.4 shows a Windows `telnet` session connected to the `TriviaServer` application.

```
Telnet - localhost
Connect  Edit  Terminal  Help

Which one of the Smothers Brothers did Bill Cosby once punch out?
(a) Dick
(b) Tommy
(c) both
c

Wrong, the correct answer is b. Want another (y/n)?
y

What's the nickname of Dallas Cowboys Fullback Daryl Johnston?
(a) caribou
(b) moose
(c) elk
b

That's correct! Want another? (y/n)?
y

Which person at Sun Microsystems came up with the name Java in early 1995?
(a) James Gosling
(b) Kim Polese
(c) Alan Baratz
```

Summary

Networking has many applications of which your programs can make use. You might not
have realized it, but the GetFile project was a rudimentary Web browser. It brought a
Web page's text into a Java program and displayed it. Of course, the HTML parsing is
what turns a bunch of markup tags into a real Web page. Sun wrote an entire Web browser in Java—HotJava.

Today you learned how to use URLs, URL connections, and input streams in conjunction
to pull data from the World Wide Web into your program.

You created a socket application that implements the basics of the finger protocol, a
method for retrieving user information on the Internet.

You also learned how client and server programs are written in Java and how a server
program makes connections to clients and exchanges information with them.

Q&A

Q How can I mimic an HTML form submission in a Java applet?

A Currently, applets make it difficult to do this. The best (and easiest way) is to use
GET notation to get the browser to submit the form contents for you.

HTML forms can be submitted two ways: either by using the GET request or by
using POST. If you use GET, your form information is encoded in the URL itself,
something like this:

```
http://www.blah.com/cgi-bin/myscript?foo=1&bar=2&name=Laura
```

Because the form input is encoded in the URL, you can write a Java applet to mimic a form, get input from the user, and then construct a new URL object with the form data included on the end. Then just pass that URL to the browser by using getAppletContext() and showDocument(), and the browser will submit the form results itself. For simple forms, this is all you need.

Q How can I do POST form submissions?

A You have to mimic what a browser does to send forms using POST. Create a URL object for the form-submission address such as http://www.prefect.com/cgi/mail2rogers.cgi, and then call this object's openConnection() method to create a URLConnection object. Call the connection's setDoOutput() method to indicate that you will be sending data to this URL, and then send the connection a series of name-value pairs that hold the data, separated by ampersand characters ("&").

For instance, the mail2rogers.cgi form is a CGI program that sends mail to Rogers Cadenhead, the coauthor of this book. It transmits name, subject, email, comments, who, rcode, and scode data. If you have created a PrintWriter stream called pw that is connected to this CGI program, you can post information to it using the following statement:

```
pw.print("name=YourName&subject=Your+Book&email=you@yourdomain.com&"
    + "comments=Your+POST+example+works.+I+owe+you+$1,000&"
    + "who=preadm&rcode=2java21&scode=%2Fmailsent.html");
```

Questions

1. What network action is not permitted in an applet under the default security level for Java?

(a) Loading a graphic from the server that hosts the applet

(b) Loading a graphic from a different server

(c) Loading a Web page from a different server in the browser containing the applet

2. In the finger protocol, which program makes a request for information about a user?

(a) The client

(b) The server

(c) Both can make that request

19

3. Which method is preferred for loading the data from a Web page into your Java
   application?

   (a) Creating a `Socket` and an input stream from that socket

   (b) Creating a `URL` and a `URLConnection` from that object

   (c) Loading the page using the applet method `showDocument()`

Answers

1. b. Applets cannot make network connections to any machine other than the one
   from which they were served.

2. a. The client requests information and the server sends something back in response.
   This is traditionally how client/server applications function, although some programs can act as both client and server.

3. b. Sockets are good for low-level connections, such as when you are implementing
   a new protocol. For existing protocols such as HTTP, there are classes that are better suited to that protocol—`URL` and `URLConnection`, in this case.

Exercises

To extend your knowledge of the subjects covered today, try the following exercises:

- Modify the `WebMenu` program so that it generates 10 URLs that begin with
  `http://www.`, end with `.com`, and contain three random letters or numbers in
  between (such as `http://www.mcp.com`, `http://www.cbs.com`, and
  `http://www.eod.com`). Use these URLs in 10 `WebButton` objects on an applet.

- Write a program that takes finger requests, looks for a `.plan` file matching the
  username requested, and sends it if found. Send a "user not found" message otherwise.

Where applicable, exercise solutions are offered on the book's Web site at
`http://www.java21days.com`.

DAY 20

Working with JavaBeans

As you have learned, one of the primary advantages of object-oriented programming is the capability to reuse an object in different programs. If you have created a spellchecker object that works great with your word-processing program, you should be able to use the same object with an email program also.

Sun has extended this principle with the introduction of JavaBeans. A *JavaBean*, also called a *bean*, is a software object that interacts with other objects according to a strict set of guidelines—the JavaBeans Specification. By following these guidelines, the bean can most easily be used with other objects. After you know how to work with one JavaBean according to these rules, you know how to work with them all.

Another advantage of JavaBeans occurs when you're using a programming tool that has been developed with beans in mind. These environments, including Sun's own free JavaBeans Development Kit, make it possible to develop Java programs quickly by using existing beans and establishing the relationships between them.

Today, you'll explore the following subjects:

- Creating reusable software objects in Java
- How JavaBeans relates to the Java class library
- The JavaBeans API
- JavaBeans development tools
- The JavaBeans Development Kit
- Working with JavaBeans
- Creating an applet with JavaBeans

Reusable Software Components

A growing trend in the field of software development is the use of *reusable components*—elements of a program that can be used with more than one software package.

NEW TERM   A *software component* is a piece of software isolated into a discrete, easily reusable structure.

If you develop parts of a program so that they are completely self-contained, it should be possible for these components to be assembled into programs with much greater development efficiency. This notion of reusing carefully packaged software was borrowed, to some extent, from the assembly-line approach that became so popular in the United States during the Industrial Revolution. This idea, as applied to software, is to build small, reusable components once and then reuse them as much as possible, thereby streamlining the entire development process.

Perhaps the greatest difficulty that component software has had to face is the wide range of disparate microprocessors and operating systems in use today. There have been several reasonable attempts at component software, but they've always been limited to a specific operating system. Microsoft's VBX and OCX component architectures have had great success in the Intel PC world, but they've done little to bridge the gap between PCs and other operating systems.

 Note

> Microsoft's ActiveX technology, which is based on its OCX technology, aims to provide an all-purpose component technology that's compatible across a wide range of platforms. However, considering the dependency of ActiveX on 32-bit Windows code, it remains to be seen how Microsoft will solve the platform-dependency issue.

Some existing component technologies also suffer from having been developed in a particular programming language or for a particular development environment. Just as platform-dependency cripples components at runtime, limiting component development to a particular programming language or development environment cripples components at the development end. Software developers want to decide for themselves which language is the most appropriate for a particular task. Likewise, they want to select the development environment that best fits their needs, rather than being forced to use an environment based on a component technology. Therefore, any realistic long-term component technology must deal with both platform-dependency and language-dependency.

Java has been a major factor in making platform-independent software development a reality, and it offers software component development through JavaBeans.

JavaBeans is an architecture- and platform-independent set of classes for creating and using Java software components. It takes advantage of the portable Java platform to provide a component software solution.

The Goal of JavaBeans

JavaBeans was designed to be compact because components will often be used in distributed environments where entire components are transferred across a low-bandwidth Internet connection. The second part of this goal relates to the ease with which the components are built and used. It's not such a stretch to imagine components that are easy to use, but creating a component architecture that makes it easy to build components is a different issue altogether.

The second major goal of JavaBeans is to be fully portable. As a result, developers will not need to worry about including platform-specific libraries with their Java applets.

The existing Java architecture already offers a wide range of benefits that are easily applied to components. One of the more important (but rarely mentioned) features of Java is its built-in class discovery mechanism, which allows objects to interact with each other dynamically. This results in a system where objects can be integrated with each other, independent of their respective origins or development histories. The class discovery mechanism is not just a neat Java feature; it is a necessary requirement in any component architecture.

20

NEW TERM   Another example of JavaBeans inheriting existing Java functionality is *persistence*, which is the capability of an object to store and retrieve its internal state. Persistence is handled automatically in JavaBeans by using the serialization mechanism already present in Java. *Serialization* is the process of storing or retrieving information through a standard protocol. Alternatively, developers can create customized persistence solutions whenever necessary.

Although support for distributed computing is not a core element of the JavaBeans architecture, it is provided. JavaBeans component developers can select the distributed computing approach that best fits their needs. Sun provides a distributed computing solution in its Remote Method Invocation (RMI) technology, but JavaBeans developers are in no way handcuffed to this solution. Other options include CORBA (Common Object Request Broker Architecture) and Microsoft's DCOM (Distributed Component Object Model), among others.

Distributed computing has been cleanly abstracted from JavaBeans to keep things tight while still giving a wide range of options to developers who require distributed support. JavaBeans's final design goal deals with design-time issues and how developers build applications by using JavaBeans components.

The JavaBeans architecture includes support for specifying design-time properties and editing mechanisms to better facilitate visual editing of JavaBeans components. The result is that developers will be able to use visual tools to assemble and modify JavaBeans components in a seamless fashion, much the way existing PC visual tools work with components such as VBX or OCX controls. In this way, component developers specify the way in which the components are to be used and manipulated in a development environment.

How JavaBeans Relates to Java

Although Java's object-oriented nature provides a means for objects to work in conjunction with each other, there are a few rules or standards governing how object interactions are conducted. These rules are needed for a robust component software solution, and they are provided through JavaBeans.

JavaBeans specifies a rich set of mechanisms for interaction between objects, along with common actions that most objects will need to support, such as persistence and event handling. It also provides the framework by which this component communication can take place. Even more important is the fact that JavaBeans components can be easily tweaked via a standard set of well-defined properties.

JavaBeans components aren't limited to user-interface objects such as buttons, however. You can just as easily develop nonvisual JavaBeans components that perform some background function in concert with other components. In this way, JavaBeans merges the power of visual Java applets with nonvisual Java applications under a consistent component framework.

> **Note**
>
> **NEW TERM** A *nonvisual component* is any component that doesn't have a
> visible output. If you think of components in terms of Swing
> components such as buttons and menus, this might seem a little strange.
> However, keep in mind that a component is simply a tightly packaged pro-
> gram and doesn't need to be visual. A good example is a timer component,
> which fires timing events at specified intervals and is nonvisual. Timer com-
> ponents are very popular in other component development environments,
> such as Microsoft Visual Basic.

With visual tools, you can use a variety of JavaBeans components together without necessarily writing any code. JavaBeans components expose their own interfaces visually,
providing a means to edit their properties without programming. Furthermore, by using a
visual editor, you can drop a JavaBeans component directly into an application without
writing any code. This is an entirely new level of flexibility and reusability that was
impossible in Java alone.

The JavaBeans API

JavaBeans is ultimately a programming interface, meaning that all its features are implemented as extensions to the standard Java class library. All the functionality provided by
JavaBeans is actually implemented in the JavaBeans API, a suite of smaller APIs devoted
to specific functions (services). The following is a list of the main component services in
the JavaBeans API that are necessary for all the features you're been learning about
today:

- Graphical user interface merging
- Persistence
- Event handling
- Introspection
- Application builder support

If you understand these services and how they work, you'll have much more insight into
exactly what type of technology JavaBeans is. These services are implemented as smaller
APIs contained within the larger JavaBeans API.

The user-interface–merging APIs enable a component to merge its elements with a container. Most containers have menus and toolbars that display any special features provided by the component. The interface-merging APIs allow the component to add features to
the container document's menu and toolbar. These APIs also define the mechanism that
facilitates interface layout between components and their containers.

20

The persistent APIs specify the mechanism by which components can be stored and retrieved within the context of a containing document. By default, components inherit the automatic serialization mechanism provided by Java. Developers are also free to design more elaborate persistence solutions based on the specific needs of their components.

The event-handling APIs specify an event-driven architecture that defines how components interact with each other. Java already includes a powerful event-handling model, which serves as the basis for the event-handling component APIs. These APIs are critical in giving components the freedom to interact with each other in a consistent fashion.

The introspection APIs define the techniques by which components make their internal structure readily available at design time. These APIs allow development tools to query a component for its internal state, including the interfaces, methods, and member variables of which the component is composed.

These APIs are divided into two distinct sections, based on the level at which they are being used. For example, the low-level introspection APIs give development tools direct access to component internals, which is a function you wouldn't necessarily want in the hands of component users. This brings us to the high-level APIs, which use the low-level APIs to determine which parts of a component are exported for user modification. Although development tools will undoubtedly use both APIs, they will use the high-level APIs only when providing component information to the user.

The application builder support APIs provide the overhead necessary for editing and manipulating components at design time. These APIs are used largely by visual development tools to visually lay out and edit components while constructing an application. The section of a component that provides visual editing capabilities is specifically designed to be physically separate from the component itself. This is because standalone runtime components should be as compact as possible. In a purely runtime environment, components are transferred with only the necessary runtime component. Developers who want to use only the design-time portion of the component can do so.

The JavaBeans specifications are available at the Java Web site at `http://java.sun.com/j2se/1.3/docs/guide/beans/`.

Development Tools

The best way to understand JavaBeans is to work with them in a programming environment that supports bean development.

Bean programming requires an environment with a fairly sophisticated graphical user interface because much of the development work is done visually. In an integrated development environment such as Symantec Visual Café, you can establish a relationship between two beans in an interface by dragging a line between them with your mouse.

The tools in the Software Development Kit are almost exclusively used from the command line without a graphical interface. Because of this, you need a different programming tool to develop JavaBeans when using the SDK tools. Most of the commercially available Java development tools support JavaBeans, including Visual Café, Metrowerks CodeWarrior Professional, IBM VisualAge for Java, and Borland JBuilder.

> **Caution**
>
> If you're shopping for a Java integrated development environment that supports JavaBeans, an important thing to note is whether it supports Java 1.1, Java 2 SDK 1.2, or the current edition, Java 2 SDK 1.3.

If you don't have a development tool that supports JavaBeans programming, you can use the free JavaBeans Development Kit from Sun.

JavaBeans Development Kit

Sun's JavaBeans Development Kit, also called the BDK, is a free tool that can be used if no other bean-enabled programming environment is available.

If this sounds like damning the BDK with faint praise, it is. Sun makes the following recommendation on its Java Web site: "The BDK is not intended for use by application developers, nor is it intended to be a full-fledged application development environment. Instead, application developers should consider the various Java application development environments supporting JavaBeans."

When the BDK was released, it served a similar purpose to the original Java Development Kit: enabling programmers to work with a new technology when no other alternative was available. With the arrival of numerous JavaBeans-capable programming tools, Sun has not focused its efforts on extending the functionality of the BDK and improving its performance. The BDK is now useful primarily as an introduction to JavaBeans development, and that's what it will be used for today.

The BDK is available for Windows and Solaris. It was developed using the Java language, so there also is a platform-independent version that you can use on other Java-enabled operating systems. It currently can be downloaded from

```
http://java.sun.com/beans/software/bdk_download.html
```

20

Caution
> If this page is not available, visit the main page at Sun's Java site at http://java.sun.com. The JavaBeans Development Kit and other programming tools are available in the "Products & APIs" section of the site.

The BDK is 2.4MB in size, requiring up to 20 minutes to download on a 28,800-baud Internet connection. While you're waiting for the file transfer to finish, be sure to read the installation instructions and last-minute notes on the BDK download page. You might need to make changes to your system's CLASSPATH setting for the BDK to function properly.

The BDK is transferred as a single executable file that must be run to install the software.

Caution
> At the time of this writing, on a Windows system, the BDK installation program recommends \Program Files\bdk1.1 as the place to install the program. Some Java tools have trouble with the space in the folder name, so you might want to choose a different folder, such as \bdk1.1 or \jdk1.3\bdk1.1.

During the installation, you will select the Java virtual machine that the BDK will use. Choose the Java interpreter that you've been using to run Java 2 programs as you worked through the lessons in this book.

The following things are included in the BDK:

- The BeanBox—a JavaBean container that can be used to manipulate sample beans and work with those of your own creation.
- More than a dozen sample beans, including a Juggler bean that displays a juggling animation, a Molecule bean that displays a 3D molecule, and OrangeButton, a user interface component.
- The complete Java source code of the BeanBox.
- Makefiles—configuration scripts that can be used to re-create the BDK.
- A tutorial about JavaBeans and the BeanBox from Sun.

Working with JavaBeans

As you work with JavaBeans in a development environment such as the BDK, you'll quickly discover how different they are from Java classes that weren't designed to be beans.

JavaBeans differ from other classes in a fairly major way: They can interact with a development environment, running inside it as if a user were running them. The development environment also can interact directly with the JavaBean, calling its methods and setting up values for its variables.

If you have installed the BDK, you can use it in the following sections to work with existing JavaBeans and create a new one. If not, you'll still learn more about how JavaBeans are used in conjunction with a development environment.

Bean Containers

The AWT (Abstract Windowing Toolkit) and Swing use *containers*—user interface components that hold other components.

JavaBeans development takes place within a bean container. The BDK includes the BeanBox, a rudimentary container that can be used to do the following:

- Save a bean
- Load a saved bean
- Drop beans into a window where they can be laid out
- Move and resize beans
- Edit a bean's properties
- Configure a bean
- Associate a bean that generates an event with an event handler
- Associate the properties of different beans with each other
- Convert a bean into an applet
- Add new beans from a Java archive (`jar` files)

To run the BeanBox application, go to the folder where the BDK was installed and open the `beanbox` subfolder. This subfolder contains two batch-command files that can be used to run the BeanBox: `run.bat` for Windows systems, and `run.sh` for Solaris systems.

These batch files load the BeanBox application using the Java interpreter you selected during BDK installation, which is probably the Java 2 interpreter. Four windows will open, as shown in Figure 20.1.

20

FIGURE 20.1

The windows that
make up the BeanBox
application.

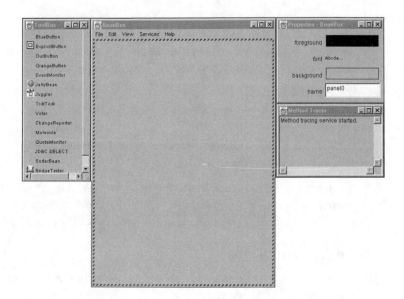

The largest window is the BeanBox composition window, which arranges beans and creates their associations with each other.

The other two windows along the top are the Toolbox window (on the left), which lists several JavaBeans that can be selected for placement in the composition window, and a Properties window (on the right), which is used to configure the bean. The fourth window in the lower-right corner is the Method Tracer window, which provides more information on how components are interacting in the BeanBox.

Most of the work will be done within the composition window, which is comparable to the main window of a drawing program such as Adobe Illustrator. All beans are placed, rearranged, lined up, and selected for editing within this window.

Placing a Bean

The first step in placing a bean in the BeanBox is to select it in the Toolbox window. When you do this, your cursor will switch to a cross-hairs symbol. With the cross hairs, you can click anywhere in the main composition window to place the selected type of bean in it. When you place a bean, it's best to choose someplace near the middle of the composition window. You can use the Edit, Cut and Edit, Paste menu commands to move the bean if needed. You also can move a bean by placing your cursor over the edge of the bean until the cursor becomes a set of compass-direction arrows, dragging the bean to a new location, and releasing the mouse.

Try this out by clicking the Juggler label in the Toolbox window and then clicking somewhere in the middle of the main composition window. An animation of a juggling bicuspid will appear in the main window (see Figure 20.2). You'll probably recognize the juggler—rather than a tooth, he's Duke, the official mascot of the Java language. Appropriately enough, the objects he's tossing around are giant beans.

FIGURE 20.2

Duke juggles some giant beans in the main BeanBox window.

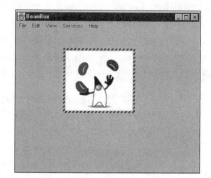

In Figure 20.2, the striped line around the Juggler bean indicates that it is currently selected for editing. You can select the BeanBox window itself by clicking anywhere other than the Juggler bean, and you can select the Juggler bean again by clicking it. You can edit, copy, cut, and paste a bean only if it has been selected for editing.

Adjusting a Bean's Properties

When a bean has been selected in the main composition window of the BeanBox, its editable properties, if any, are displayed in the Properties window. This window for the current project is shown in Figure 20.3.

FIGURE 20.3

Editable properties of a bean, shown in the Properties window.

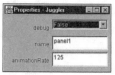

20

As shown in Figure 20.3, the Juggler bean has three editable properties: debug, animationRate, and name.

Changes to a JavaBean's properties will be reflected in the bean. If you give the Juggler bean's animationRate property a higher integer value, there'll be a longer pause between each frame of the animation. If you decrease the property, the animation will speed up.

After you change the `animationRate` property, the bean will change accordingly after you skip to a different property by either pressing the Tab key or clicking a different property's value. Try entering extreme values such as 1 and 1000 for the animation speed to see the response in the Juggler bean itself.

A JavaBean's editable properties can be established by public methods within the bean itself. Each property that can be set has a `set()` method whose full name matches the name of the property in the Properties window of the BeanBox. Likewise, each property whose value can be read has a corresponding `get()` method. A JavaBeans development environment such as the BeanBox uses reflection to find these methods, and then makes it possible for you to work with the properties at design time or as a program is running.

For example, the `animationRate` property of the Juggler bean could have two methods like the following:

```
public int getAnimationRate(){
    return animRate;
}

public void setAnimationRate(int newRate) {
    animRate = newRate;
}
```

In these two methods, `animRate` is a private variable that determines the pause between frames of the juggling animation.

By using the prefixes `set` and `get` for these method names, the Juggler bean developer indicates that the `animationRate` property can be altered from within a JavaBean development environment such as the BeanBox.

The BeanBox, like all bean development tools that follow the standards established by Sun, calls the public `get()` methods of the bean to determine which properties to include in the Properties window. When one of the properties is changed, a `set()` method is called with the changed value as an argument.

The developer of a bean can override this behavior by providing a `BeanInfo` class that indicates the methods, properties, events, and other things that should be accessible from a bean development environment.

> **Tip**
>
> Keeping a variable private and using `get()` and `set()` methods to read and change it is a good principle in all object-oriented programming, even when you're not trying to develop a JavaBean. This practice is called *encapsulation*, and it is used to control how an object can be accessed by other objects. The more encapsulated an object is, the harder it becomes for other objects to use it incorrectly.

Creating Interactions Between Beans

Another purpose of the BeanBox is to establish interactions between different beans.

To see how this works, first place two ExplicitButton beans anywhere in the main composition window of the BeanBox. If they overlap with the Juggler bean or with each other, move the beans farther away from each other.

To move a bean, first click it so that a striped line appears around it in the BeanBox window. Then, place your cursor above the lower edge of the bean until the cursor changes to a four-sided arrow. After this happens, drag the bean to a new location. Figure 20.4 shows two buttons along the bottom edge of the Juggler bean.

FIGURE 20.4

Two ExplicitButton beans and a Juggler bean in the main BeanBox window.

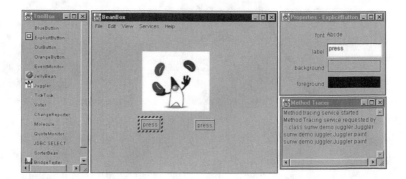

ExplicitButton beans are similar to the JButton components that you have used in graphical user interfaces. They have a background color, a foreground color, and a text label with configurable fonts.

After placing the buttons, give one the label "Stop!" and change its background color to red. Give the other the label "Go!" and change its background color to green.

To change a button's label, click the button in the BeanBox, and then edit the label textfield in the Properties window. To change the background color, click the panel next to the label Background in the Properties window. A new Color Editor dialog will open that enables you to select a color by entering numeric values for red, green, and blue or by using a list box. The changes that you make will be reflected instantly in the bean.

At this point, the purpose of these buttons should be fairly obvious: One will stop the animation, and the other will start it. For these things to take place, you must establish a relationship between the buttons and the Juggler bean.

20

The first step is to select the bean that is causing something to take place. In the current example, that bean would be either of the ExplicitButton beans. Clicking one of these should cause something to happen to the Juggler bean.

After selecting the bean, choose the menu command Edit, Events, button push, actionPerformed. A red line will connect the button and the cursor, as shown in Figure 20.5.

FIGURE 20.5

Establishing an event association between two beans.

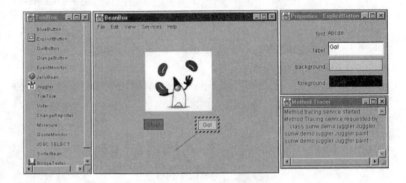

This red line should connect the ExplicitButton bean with the Juggler bean. Drag the line to the Juggler bean, and then click it to establish the association between the two beans.

When this association has been established, you'll see an EventTargetDialog window that lists different methods in the target bean, as shown in Figure 20.6. The method that is chosen will be called automatically when the specified ExplicitButton bean fires an `actionPerformed` event. (This event occurs when the button is clicked or the Enter key is pressed while the button has the input focus on the interface.)

FIGURE 20.6

Choosing a method to call in the EventTargetDialog window.

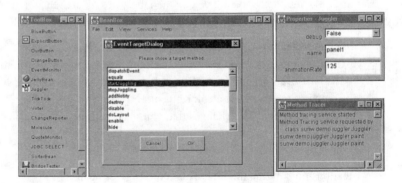

The Juggler bean contains two methods that are used to either stop or start the juggling animation. These are called `stopJuggling()` and `startJuggling()`, respectively. By separating behavior like this into its own method, the Juggler developer enables these methods to be useful in an interaction between different beans. Organizing a bean's methods in this way, offering as many different interactions as necessary, is one of the biggest tasks in JavaBeans development.

The Stop! button should be associated with the Juggler bean's `stopJuggling()` method, and the Go! button should be associated with `startJuggling()`.

By establishing this interaction between three JavaBeans, you have created a simple, functional Java program that can display, start, and stop an animation.

Creating a JavaBeans Program

After you have placed one or more JavaBeans on a shared interface, set up their properties, and established interactions between them, you have created a Java program.

To save a project in the BeanBox, use the File, Save menu command. This enables you to save the following information to a file:

- The beans as they are currently configured
- The arrangement of the beans
- The size of the window the beans occupy
- The interactions between the beans

This does not save the project as a Java program that you can run outside of the BeanBox. To save a project in a form that you can run, use the File, MakeApplet command. This command requires two things: the name to give the applet's main class file, and the name of the `jar` archive that will hold all files needed to run the applet, including class files and other data.

After you specify these items, an applet will be created with a sample HTML page that loads it. The HTML file will be placed in the same folder that contains the applet's `jar` archive. You can load this page by using appletviewer or any Web browser that supports Java 2.

These applets are distributed using `jar` archives for the applet itself and any beans in it. Listing 20.1 contains the applet tag generated by BeanBox for the applet, which was named JugglingFool.

20

LISTING 20.1   The Applet Tag Generated by BeanBox

```
 1: <html>
 2: <head>
 3: <title>Test page for JugglingFool as an APPLET</Title>
 4: </head>
 5: <body>
 6: <h1>Test for JugglingFool as an APPLET</h1>
 7: This is an example of the use of the generated
 8: JugglingFool applet.  Notice the Applet tag requires several
 9: archives, one per JAR used in building the Applet
10: <p>
11: <applet
12:     archive="./JugglingFool.jar,./support.jar
13:          ,./buttons.jar
14:          ,./juggler.jar
15:     "
16:     code="JugglingFool"
17:     width=382
18:     height=513
19: >
20: Trouble instantiating applet JugglingFool!!
21: </applet>
```

Figure 20.7 shows the Juggler animation applet running in the `appletviewer` tool.

FIGURE 20.7

A JavaBeans applet running in appletviewer.

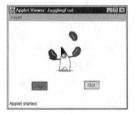

Note

The size of the applet's window will be determined by the size of the main composition window in the BeanBox. To resize the window, select it by clicking outside all JavaBeans inside the window and then resize it as you would a bean.

Working with Other JavaBeans

Developing software by using prepackaged components like this is a form of *rapid application development*. Unlike many of the terms you have learned in this book, rapid application development, also called RAD, is self-explanatory jargon. It's often used to quickly create a working version of software for demonstration or prototype purposes.

A common example of RAD is using Microsoft Visual Basic to create a prototype of a Visual C++ program. One of the strengths of Visual Basic is its speedy graphical user interface design, which makes it a more effective solution for prototyping than the more complex Visual C++.

JavaBeans make RAD development more commonplace in Java software development. A programmer can swiftly cobble together a working program by using existing JavaBeans components.

Hundreds of JavaBeans are available from Sun and other developers, including those at the following sites:

- Gamelan, Developer.Com's directory of Java-related resources:
  `http://gamelan.earthweb.com`
- *JavaWorld* Magazine's Developer Tools Guide:
  `http://www.javaworld.com/javaworld/tools/`
- Sun's JavaBeans home page: `http://java.sun.com/beans`

Beans are packaged into `jar` archives. If you have downloaded a bean and would like it to show up in the Toolbox window of the BeanBox, save the bean's `jar` archive in BDK's `jars` folder. This folder can be found in the folder where the BDK was installed on your system—if you installed the BDK in `c:\bdk1.1`, the `jar` file for beans you would like to use should be saved in `c:\bdk1.1\jars`.

Summary

When combined with an integrated development environment that supports them, JavaBeans enable rapid application development of Java programs.

Today, you learned about the underlying principles of reusable software components and how these principles are realized in Java. Putting these ideas into practice, you saw how Sun's JavaBeans Development Kit (BDK) can be used to work with existing beans, establish relationships between them, and create full Java programs.

Although you should seek a more capable development tool than the BDK for developing your own programs with JavaBeans, you can use the BDK to evaluate the applicability of beans to your own programming tasks.

You also should use the JavaBeans resources on the World Wide Web. Many of the beans that are available over the Web already accomplish tasks you'll try to handle in your own programs. By using beans, you can reduce the number of things you must create from scratch.

20

Q&A

Q Will the JavaBeans Development Kit be upgraded into a fully featured bean programming tool?

A At the time of this writing, Sun continues to state that the BDK is intended for testing beans and providing a reference version of how beans should be used inside development environments. It appears that professional programming tools, such as Visual Café and others, are going to remain the best choice for JavaBeans development.

Q In the Juggler example, the `animationRate` property has a different capitalization in the `setAnimationRate()` and `getAnimationRate()` methods. What accounts for this difference?

A The capitalization is different because of the following naming conventions for Java programs: All variables and method names begin with a lowercase letter, and all words but the first in a variable name begin with a single uppercase letter.

Questions

1. If you develop a bean that has a `getWindowHeight()` method that returns an integer and a `setWindowHeight(int)` method, what property will show up in a bean development environment?

    (a) `WindowHeight`

    (b) windowHeight

    (c) Nothing unless you also set up something in a `BeanInfo` file

2. When can you modify a bean's properties?

    (a) At design time

    (b) At runtime

    (c) Both

3. How do you change the size of an applet created using the BDK?

    (a) Edit the HTML generated by the BDK after you create the applet.

    (b) Edit a property of the BeanBox.

    (c) Resize the BeanBox before creating the applet.

Answers

1. b. Although you can also use a `BeanInfo` file to exclude `windowHeight` from showing up as a property in a bean development environment.

2. c. As you have seen with the Juggler example, beans will even run as they are being designed.

3. c. Although answer a is also true because you can edit the HTML directly, and modify the `HEIGHT` and `WEIGHT` attributes of the `APPLET` tag.

Exercises

To extend your knowledge of the subjects covered today, try the following exercises:

- Download a bean from Gamelan and make use of it in the BeanBox.
- Add a TickTock bean—a bean that causes something to happen at set intervals—to the Juggler project. Experiment with the bean and see whether you can make it restart the juggling bean every 30 seconds.

Where applicable, exercise solutions are offered on the book's Web site at `http://www.java21days.com`.

20

WEEK 3

DAY 21

Java Database Connectivity and Data Structures

Almost all Java programs deal with data in some way. You have used primitive types, objects, arrays, and linked lists to represent data up to this point, but as you develop more sophisticated programs, those might not be the best choices.

Today, you will finish the three-week trip into Java programming by working with data in more sophisticated ways.

You begin by exploring Java Database Connectivity (JDBC), a class library that connects Java programs to relational databases developed by Microsoft, Sybase, Oracle, Informix, and other sources. By using a driver as a bridge to the database source, you can store and retrieve data directly from Java.

Next, you will look at how data is represented internally in Java, working with new data structures that complement arrays and linked lists.

Today's lesson looks at data structures and database connectivity, and you are introduced to the following subjects:

- Using JDBC drivers to work with different relational databases
- Accessing a database with Structured Query Language (SQL)
- Moving through the records that result from an SQL database operation
- Setting up a JDBC data source
- Working with stacks, bit sets, hash tables, and other data structures
- Creating classes that implement the Iterator interface

By the end of today's lesson, you'll have a much larger arsenal of solutions when you are working with data in your programs.

Java Database Connectivity

Java Database Connectivity (JDBC) is a set of classes that can be used to develop client/server database applications using Java. Client/server software connects a user of information with a provider of that information, and it's one of the most commonplace forms of programming. You use it every time you surf the Web: A client program called a Web browser requests Web pages, image files, and other documents using a Uniform Resource Locator or URL. Different server programs provide the requested information, if it can be found, for the client.

One of the biggest obstacles faced by database programmers is the wide variety of database formats in use, each with its own proprietary method of accessing data. To simplify using relational database programs, a standard language called SQL (Structured Query Language) has been introduced. This language supplants the need to learn different database-querying languages for each database format.

In database programming, a request for records in a database is called a *query*. Using SQL, you can send complex queries to a database and get the records you're looking for in any order you specify.

Consider the example of a database programmer at a student loan company who has been asked to prepare a report on the most delinquent loan recipients. The programmer could use SQL to query a database for all records in which the last payment was more than 180 days ago and the amount due is more than $0.00. SQL also can be used to control the order in which records are returned, so the programmer can get the records in the order of Social Security number, recipient name, amount owed, or another field in the loan database.

All this is possible with SQL, and the programmer hasn't used any of the proprietary languages associated with popular database formats.

> **Note** SQL is strongly supported by many database formats, so in theory you should be able to use the same SQL commands for each database tool that supports the language. However, you still might need to learn some idiosyncrasies of a specific database format when accessing it through SQL.

SQL is the industry-standard approach to accessing relational databases. JDBC supports SQL, enabling developers to use a wide range of database formats without knowing the specifics of the underlying database. It also enables the use of database queries that are specific to a database format.

The JDBC class library's approach to accessing databases with SQL is comparable to existing database development techniques, so interacting with an SQL database by using JDBC isn't much different than it is by using traditional database tools. Java programmers who already have some database experience can hit the ground running with JDBC. The JDBC API has already been widely endorsed by industry leaders, including some development-tool vendors who have announced future support for JDBC in their development products.

The JDBC library includes classes for each of the tasks that are commonly associated with database usage:

- Making a connection to a database
- Creating a statement using SQL
- Executing that SQL query in the database
- Viewing the resulting records

These JDBC classes are all part of the `java.sql` package in Java 2.

Database Drivers

Java programs that use JDBC classes can follow the familiar programming model of issuing SQL statements and processing the resulting data. The format of the database and the platform it was prepared on don't matter.

This platform- and database-independence is made possible in a Java program by a driver manager. The classes of the JDBC class library are largely dependent on driver managers, which keep track of the drivers required to access database records. You'll need a different driver for each database format that's used in a program, and sometimes might need several different drivers for different versions of the same format.

21

JDBC database drivers can be either written entirely in Java or implemented using native methods to bridge Java applications to existing database access libraries.

JDBC also includes a driver that bridges JDBC and another database connectivity standard, called ODBC.

The JDBC-ODBC Bridge

ODBC, Microsoft's common interface for accessing SQL databases, is managed on a Windows system by the ODBC Data Source Administrator. This is run from the Control Panel on a Windows system by clicking the Start button and then Settings, Control Panel, ODBC Data Sources. The administrator adds ODBC drivers, configures drivers to work with specific database files, and logs SQL use. Figure 21.1 shows the ODBC Data Source Administrator on a Windows system.

FIGURE 21.1

The ODBC Data Source Administrator on a Windows system.

In Figure 21.1, the Drivers tabbed dialog box lists all the ODBC drivers that are present on the system. Some of the drivers are specific to a database company's format, including the Microsoft Access Driver. Other drivers work with a server that is centered around SQL itself, including the INTERSOLV SQLServer driver.

The JDBC-ODBC bridge allows JDBC drivers to be used as ODBC drivers by converting JDBC method calls into ODBC function calls.

Using the JDBC-ODBC bridge requires three things:

- The JDBC-ODBC bridge driver included with Java 2:
  `sun.jdbc.odbc.JdbcOdbcDriver`
- An ODBC driver
- An ODBC data source that has been associated with the driver using software such as the ODBC Data Source Administrator

ODBC data sources can be set up from within some database programs. For example, when a new database file is created in Lotus Approach, users have the option of associating it with an ODBC driver.

All ODBC data sources must be given a short descriptive name. This name will be used inside Java programs when a connection is made to the database that the source refers to.

On a Windows system, after an ODBC driver is selected and the database is created, they will show up in the ODBC Data Source Administrator. Figure 21.2 shows an example of this for a data source named World Energy.

FIGURE 21.2

A listing of data sources in the ODBC Data Sources Administrator.

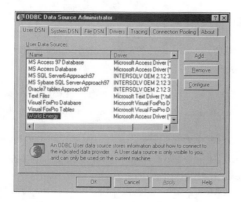

The data source World Energy is associated with a Microsoft Access driver, according to Figure 21.2.

Note

Microsoft Access includes ODBC drivers that can be used to connect to an Access database file. Most Windows database programs will include one or more ODBC drivers that correspond to the format.

Connecting to an ODBC Data Source

Your first project today is a Java application that uses a JDBC-ODBC bridge to connect to a Microsoft Access file.

21

The Access file for this project is `world20.mdb`, a database of world energy statistics published by the U.S. Energy Information Administration. The Coal table in this database includes these fields:

- Country
- Year
- Anthracite Production

The database used in this project is included on this book's official Web site at `http://www.java21days.com`.

To use this database, you must have an ODBC driver on your system that supports Microsoft Access files. Using the ODBC Data Source Administrator (or a similar program if you're on a non-Windows system), you must create a new ODBC data source that is associated with `world20.mdb`.

Other setup work might be needed depending on the ODBC drivers that are present on your system, if any. Consult the documentation included with the ODBC driver.

 Caution

> This aspect of JDBC-ODBC bridge programming often can be more difficult than using the JDBC class library in a program. You might need to install an ODBC driver and learn more about its use before you try to create a JDBC-ODBC application.

After you have downloaded `world20.mdb` to your computer or found another database that's compatible with the ODBC drivers on your system, the final step in getting the file ready for JDBC-ODBC is to create a data source associated with it. Unlike other input-output classes in Java, JDBC doesn't use a filename to identify a data file and use its contents. Instead, a tool such as the ODBC Data Source Administrator is used to name the ODBC source and indicate the file folder where it can be found.

In the ODBC Data Source Administrator, click the User DSN tab to see a list of data sources that are currently available. To add a new one associated with `world20.mdb` (or your own database), click the Add button, choose an ODBC driver, and then click the Finish button.

A Setup window will open that you can use to provide a name, short description, and other information about the database. Click the Select button to find and choose the database file.

Figure 21.3 shows the Setup window used to set up `world20.mdb` as a data source in the ODBC Data Sources Administrator.

FIGURE 21.3

The driver Setup window.

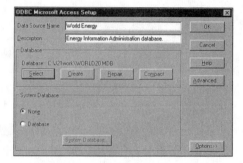

After a database has been associated with an ODBC data source, working with it in a Java program is relatively easy if you are conversant with SQL.

The first task in a JDBC program is to load the driver (or drivers) that will be used to connect to a data source. A driver is loaded with the `Class.forName(String)` method. `Class`, part of the `java.lang` package, can be used to load classes into the Java interpreter. The `forName(String)` method loads the class named by the specified string. A `ClassNotFoundException` may be thrown by this method.

All programs that use an ODBC data source will use `sun.jdbc.odbc.JdbcOdbcDriver`, the JDBC-ODBC bridge driver that is included with Java 2. Loading this class into a Java interpreter requires the following statement:

```
Class.forName("sun.jdbc.odbc.JdbcOdbcDriver");
```

After the driver has been loaded, you can establish a connection to the data source by using the `DriverManager` class in the `java.sql` package.

The `getConnection(String, String, String)` method of `DriverManager` can be used to set up the connection. It returns a reference to a `Connection` object representing an active data connection.

The three arguments of this method are as follows:

- A name identifying the data source and the type of database connectivity used to reach it
- A username
- A password

The last two items are needed only if the data source is secured with a username and a password. If not, these arguments can be null strings (`""`).

The name of the data source is preceded by the text `jdbc:odbc:` when using the JDBC-ODBC bridge, which indicates the type of database connectivity in use.

The following statement could be used to connect to a data source called `Payroll` with a username of `Doc` and a password of `Notnow`:

```
Connection payday = DriverManager.getConnection(
    "jdbc:odbc:Payroll", "Doc", "Notnow");
```

The `getConnection()` method and all others called on a data source will throw `SQLException` errors if something goes wrong as the data source is being used. SQL has its own error messages, and they will be passed along as part of `SQLException` objects.

An SQL statement is represented in Java by a `Statement` object. `Statement` is an interface, so it can't be instantiated directly. However, it is returned by the `createStatement()` method of a `Connection` object, as in the following example:

```
Statement lookSee = payday.CreateStatement();
```

After you have a `Statement` object, you can use it to conduct an SQL query by calling the object's `executeQuery(String)` method. The `String` argument should be an SQL query that follows the syntax of that language. Although you need to learn SQL to do any extensive work with it, a lot of the language is easy to pick up from any examples you can find.

The following is an example of an SQL query that could be used on the Coal table of the `world20.mdb` database:

```
SELECT Country, Year, Anthracite Production FROM Coal
    WHERE (Country Is Not Null) ORDER BY Year
```

This SQL query retrieves several fields for each record in the database where the `Country` field is not equal to null. The records that are returned are sorted according to their `Country` field, so Afghanistan would precede Burkina Faso.

If the SQL query has been phrased correctly, the `executeQuery()` method will return a `ResultSet` object holding all the records that have been retrieved from the data source.

When a `ResultSet` is returned from `executeQuery()`, it is positioned at the first record that has been retrieved. The following methods of `ResultSet` can be used to pull information out of the current record:

- `getDate(String)`—Returns the `Date` value stored in the specified field name.
- `getDouble(String)`—Returns the `double` value stored in the specified field name.
- `getFloat(String)`—Returns the `float` value stored in the specified field name.

- getInt(*String*)—Returns the int value stored in the specified field name.
- getLong(*String*)—Returns the long value stored in the specified field name.
- getString(*String*)—Returns the String stored in the specified field name.

These are just the simplest methods that are available in the ResultSet interface. The methods you should use depend on the form that the field data took when the database was created, although methods such as getString() and getInt() can be more flexible in the information they retrieve from a record.

You also can use an integer as the argument to any of these methods, such as getString(5), instead of a string. The integer indicates which field to retrieve (1 for the first field, 2 for the second field, and so on).

An SQLException will be thrown if a database error occurs as you try to retrieve information from a result set. You can call this exception's getSQLState() and getErrorCode() methods to learn more about the error.

After you have pulled the information you need from a record, you can move to the next record by calling the next() method of the ResultSet object. This method returns a false Boolean value when it tries to move past the end of a result set.

You also can move through the records in a result set with these other methods:

- afterLast()—Moves to a place immediately after the last record in the set.
- beforeFirst()—Moves to a place immediately before the first record in the set.
- first()—Moves to the first record in the set.
- last()—Moves to the last record in the set.
- previous()—Moves to the previous record in the set.

With the exception of afterLast() and beforeFirst(), these methods return a false Boolean value if no record is available at that position in the set.

When you're done using a connection to a data source, you can close it by calling the connection's close() method with no arguments.

Listing 21.1 contains the CoalTotals application, which uses the JDBC-ODBC bridge and an SQL statement to retrieve some records from a database of favorite Web sites. Four fields are retrieved from each record indicated by the SQL statement: FIPS, Country, Year, and Anthracite Production. The result set is sorted according to the Year field, and these fields are displayed to standard output.

21

LISTING 21.1 The Full Text of `CoalTotals.java`

```
 1: import java.sql.*;
 2:
 3: public class CoalTotals {
 4:     public static void main(String[] arguments) {
 5:         String data = "jdbc:odbc:World Energy";
 6:         try {
 7:             Class.forName("sun.jdbc.odbc.JdbcOdbcDriver");
 8:             Connection conn = DriverManager.getConnection(
 9:                 data, "", "");
10:             Statement st = conn.createStatement();
11:             ResultSet rec = st.executeQuery(
12:                 "SELECT * " +
13:                 "FROM Coal " +
14:                 "WHERE " +
15:                 "(Country='" + arguments[0] + "') " +
16:                 "ORDER BY Year");
17:             System.out.println("FIPS\tCOUNTRY\tYEAR\t" +
18:                 "ANTHRACITE PRODUCTION");
19:             while(rec.next()) {
20:                 System.out.println(rec.getString(1) +  "\t"
21:                     + rec.getString(2) + "\t"
22:                     + rec.getString(3) + "\t"
23:                     + rec.getString(4));
24:             }
25:             st.close();
26:         } catch (SQLException s) {
27:             System.out.println("SQL Error: " + s.toString() + " "
28:                 + s.getErrorCode() + " " + s.getSQLState());
29:         } catch (Exception e) {
30:             System.out.println("Error: " + e.toString()
31:                 + e.getMessage());
32:         }
33:     }
34: }
```

This program must be run with a single argument specifying the `Country` field in the database form which to pull records. If the application were run with an argument of `Poland`, the output from the sample database would be the following:

```
FIPS  COUNTRY  YEAR   ANTHRACITE PRODUCTION
PL    Poland   1990   0.0
PL    Poland   1991   0.0
PL    Poland   1992   0.0
PL    Poland   1993   174.165194805424
PL    Poland   1994   242.50849909616
PL    Poland   1995   304.237935229728
PL    Poland   1996   308.64718066784
```

| PL | Poland | 1997 | 319.67029426312 |
| PL | Poland | 1998 | 319.67029426312 |

Try running the program with other countries that produce anthracite, such as France, Swaziland, and New Zealand. For any country that has a space in the name, remember to put quotation marks around it when running the program.

JDBC Drivers

Creating a Java program that uses a JDBC driver is substantially similar to creating one that uses the JDBC-ODBC bridge.

The first step is to acquire and install a JDBC driver. Sun does not include a JDBC driver with Java 2, but more than a dozen companies now sell them or package them with commercial products, including Informix, Oracle, Symantec, IBM, and Sybase. A list of JDBC drivers that are currently available can be found on Sun's JDBC site at `http://java.sun.com/products/jdbc/jdbc.drivers.html`.

Some of these drivers are available to download for evaluation. You can use one of them, NetDirect's JDataConnect Server, for today's next project. The JDataConnect Server is currently available for trial download from `http://www.j-netdirect.com/`.

The steps for setting up a data source for JDBC are the same as with JDBC-ODBC:

- Create the database.
- Associate the database with a JDBC driver.
- Establish a data source, which may include selecting a database format, database server, username, and password.

NetDirect's JDataConnect Server uses the ODBC Data Source Administrator to create a new data source associated with a database.

Listing 21.2 is a Java application that uses the JDataConnect JDBC driver to access a database file called `People.mdb`. This database is a Microsoft Access file with contact information for U.S. presidents.

LISTING 21.2 The Full Text of `Presidents.java`

```
1: import java.sql.*;
2:
3: public class Presidents {
4:     public static void main(String[] arguments) {
6:         String data = "jdbc:JDataConnect://localhost:1150/Presidents";
7:         try {
8:             Class.forName("JData2_0.sql.$Driver");
```

21

LISTING 21.2   continued

```
09:                Connection conn = DriverManager.getConnection(
10:                    data, "", "");
11:                Statement st = conn.createStatement();
12:                ResultSet rec = st.executeQuery(
13:                    "SELECT NAME, ADDRESS1, ADDRESS2, PHONE, E-MAIL " +
14:                    "FROM People.mdb Contacts " +
15:                    "ORDER BY NAME");
16:                while(rec.next()) {
17:                    System.out.println(rec.getString("NAME") +   "\n"
18:                        + rec.getString("ADDRESS1") + "\n"
19:                        + rec.getString("ADDRESS2") + "\n"
20:                        + rec.getString("PHONE") + "\n"
21:                        + rec.getString("E-MAIL") + "\n");
22:                }
23:            st.close();
24:        } catch (Exception e) {
25:            System.out.println("Error -- " + e.toString());
26:        }
27:    }
28: }
```

Before this program will run successfully, the JDataConnect Server must be started. The reference to localhost:1150 in line 6 refers to this server—localhost is a substitute for the name of your own machine, and 1150 is the default port number on which the JDataConnect server runs.

The JDataConnect Server can be used to connect remotely to servers on the Internet, so localhost could be replaced with an Internet address, such as db.naviseek.com:1150, if a JDataConnect Server is running at that location and port.

Line 6 creates the database address that will be used when creating a Connection object representing the connection to the Presidents data source. This address includes more information than the one used with the JDBC-ODBC bridge driver, as shown:

```
jdbc:JDataConnect://localhost:1150/Presidents
```

Line 8 of the Presidents application loads the JDBC driver included with JDataConnect Server:

```
JData2_0.sql.$Driver
```

Configuration information for the data source and driver will be provided by the company that developed the JDBC driver. The database address can vary widely from one JDBC driver implementation to another, although there should always be a reference to a server, a database format, and the name of the data source.

If the `People.mdb` database exists and the JDBC driver has been set up correctly, the output of the `Presidents` application should be similar to the following (depending on the records in the database):

```
Gerald Ford
Box 927
Rancho Mirage, CA 92270
(734) 741-2218
library@fordlib.nara.gov

Jimmy Carter
Carter Presidential Center
1 Copenhill, Atlanta, GA 30307
(404) 727-7611
carterweb@emory.edu

Ronald Reagan
11000 Wilshire Blvd.
Los Angeles, CA 90024
library@reagan.nara.gov

George Bush
Box 79798
Houston, TX 77279
(409) 260-9552


Bill Clinton
White House, 1600 Pennsylvania Ave.
Washington, DC 20500
(202) 456-1414
president@whitehouse.gov
```

Data Structures

Many Java programs that you create will rely on some means of storing and manipulating data within a class. Up to this point, you have used two structures for storing and retrieving data: arrays and linked lists. If you don't understand the full range of programming options in terms of data structures, you'll find yourself trying to use arrays and lists when other options would be more efficient or easier to implement.

A solid understanding of data structures and when to use them will be applicable throughout your Java programming efforts.

Outside of primitive data types, arrays are the simplest data structures supported by Java. An array is simply a series of data elements of the same primitive type or objects of any class. It's treated as a single entity, just as a primitive data type is, but contains multiple

21

elements that can be accessed independently. Arrays are useful whenever you need to store and access related information.

The glaring limitation of arrays is that they can't change in size to accommodate more or fewer elements. That means you can't add new elements to an array that's already full. Because linked lists and vectors do not have this limitation, these objects can be used as an alternative.

The Java class library provides a set of data structures in the java.util package that give you more flexibility in approaching the organization and manipulation of data.

 Note

Unlike the data structures provided by the java.util package, arrays are considered such a core component of Java that they are implemented in the language itself. Therefore, you can use arrays in Java without importing any packages.

Java Data Structures

The data structures provided by the java.util package are very powerful and perform a wide range of functions. These data structures consist of the Iterator interface, the Map interface, and classes such as the following:

- BitSet
- Vector
- Stack
- Hashtable

Each of these data structures provides a way to store and retrieve information in a well-defined manner. The Iterator interface isn't itself a data structure, but it defines a means to retrieve successive elements from a data structure. For example, Iterator defines a method called next() that gets the next element in a data structure that contains multiple elements.

 Note

Iterator is an expanded and improved version of the Enumeration interface that was added in Java 2. Although Enumeration is still supported, Iterator has simpler method names and support for removing items.

The BitSet class implements a group of bits, or flags, that can be set and cleared individually. This class is very useful when you need to keep up with a set of Boolean values; you just assign a bit to each value and set or clear it as appropriate.

NEW TERM A *flag* is a Boolean value that represents one of a group of on/off type states in a program.

The Vector class is similar to a traditional Java array, except that it can grow as necessary to accommodate new elements. Like an array, elements of a Vector object can be accessed via an index into the vector. The nice thing about using the Vector class is that you don't have to worry about setting it to a specific size upon creation; it shrinks and grows automatically when necessary.

The Stack class implements a last-in-first-out stack of elements. You can think of a stack literally as a vertical stack of objects; when you add a new element, it's stacked on top of the others. When you pull an element off the stack, it comes off the top. In other words, the last element you added to the stack is the first one to come back off. That element is removed from the stack completely, unlike a structure such as an array, where the elements are always available.

The Dictionary class is an abstract class that defines a data structure for mapping keys to values. This is useful when you want to access data through a particular key rather than an integer index. Because the Dictionary class is abstract, it provides only the framework for a key-mapped data structure rather than a specific implementation.

NEW TERM A *key* is an identifier used to reference, or look up, a value in a data structure.

An actual implementation of a key-mapped data structure is provided by the Hashtable class, which organizes data based on some user-defined key structure. For example, in an address list hash table, you could store and sort data based on a key such as ZIP Code rather than on a person's name. The specific meaning of keys in a hash table is totally dependent on how the table is used and the data it contains.

The next section looks at the data structures provided by the java.util package in more detail to show how they work.

Iterator

The Iterator interface provides a standard means of iterating through a list of elements in a defined sequence, which is a common task for many data structures. Even though you can't use the interface outside a particular data structure, understanding how the Iterator interface works will help you understand other Java data structures.

21

With that in mind, take a look at the methods defined by the Iterator interface:

```
public boolean hasNext();

public Object next();

public void remove();
```

The hasNext() method determines whether the structure contains any more elements. You will typically call this method to see whether you can continue iterating through a structure. An example of this is calling hasNext() in the conditional clause of a while loop that is iterating through a list.

The next() method retrieves the next element in a structure. If there are no more elements, next() will throw a NoSuchElementException exception. To avoid generating this exception, use hasNext() in conjunction with next() to make sure there is another element to retrieve.

The following is a while loop that uses these two methods to iterate through a data structure object called users that implements the Iterator interface:

```
while (users.hasNext()) {
    Object ob = users.next();
    System.out.println(ob);
}
```

This sample code displays the contents of each list item by using the hasNext() and next() methods.

Note

> Because Iterator is an interface, you'll never use it directly as a data structure. Rather, you'll use the methods defined by Iterator within the context of other data structures. The significance of this architecture is that it provides a consistent interface for many of the standard data structures, which makes them easier to learn and use.

Bit Sets

The BitSet class is useful whenever you need to represent a group of Boolean flags. The nice thing about using the BitSet class is that you can use individual bits to store Boolean values without the mess of extracting bit values by using bitwise operations. You simply refer to each bit using an index. Another nice feature is that it automatically grows to represent the number of bits required by a program. Figure 21.4 shows the logical organization of a bit set data structure.

FIGURE 21.4

The logical organization of a bit set data structure.

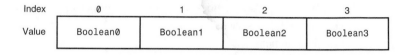

Index	0	1	2	3
Value	Boolean0	Boolean1	Boolean2	Boolean3

For example, you can use `BitSet` as an object with a number of attributes that can easily be modeled by Boolean values. Because the individual bits in a bit set are accessed via an index, you can define each attribute as a constant index value:

```
class SomeBits {
    public static final int READABLE = 0;
    public static final int WRITEABLE = 1;
    public static final int STREAMABLE = 2;
    public static final int FLEXIBLE = 3;
}
```

Notice that the attributes are assigned increasing values, beginning with 0. You can use these values to get and set the appropriate bits in a bit set. But first, you need to create a `BitSet` object:

```
BitSet bits = new BitSet();
```

This constructor creates a bit set with no specified size. You can also create a bit set with a specific size:

```
BitSet bits = new BitSet(4);
```

This creates a bit set containing four Boolean bit fields. Regardless of the constructor used, all bits in new bit sets are initially set to `false`. After you have a bit set created, you can easily set and clear the bits by using the `set` and `clear` methods along with the bit constants you defined:

```
bits.set(SomeBits.WRITEABLE);
bits.set(SomeBits.STREAMABLE);
bits.set(SomeBits.FLEXIBLE);
bits.clear(SomeBits.WRITEABLE);
```

In this code, the `WRITEABLE`, `STREAMABLE`, and `FLEXIBLE` attributes are set and then the `WRITEABLE` bit is cleared. Notice that the fully qualified name is used for each attribute because the attributes are declared as static in the `SomeBits` class.

You can get the value of individual bits in a bit set by using the `get` method:

```
boolean canIWrite = bits.get(SomeBits.WRITEABLE);
```

You can find out how many bits are being represented by a bit set by using the `size` method:

```
int numBits = bits.size();
```

21

The BitSet class also provides other methods for performing comparisons and bitwise operations on bit sets such as AND, OR, and XOR. All these methods take a BitSet object as their only argument.

Vectors

The Vector class implements an expandable array of objects. Because the Vector class is responsible for expanding as necessary to support more elements, it has to decide when and how much to grow as new elements are added. You can easily control this aspect of vectors upon creation.

Before getting into that, take a look at how to create a basic vector:

```
Vector v = new Vector();
```

This constructor creates a default vector containing no elements. Actually, all vectors are empty upon creation. One of the attributes that determines how a vector sizes itself is its initial capacity, or the number of elements it allocates memory for by default.

New Term The *size* of a vector is the number of elements currently stored in it.

New Term The *capacity* of a vector is the amount of memory allocated to hold elements, and is always greater than or equal to the size.

The following code shows how to create a vector with a specified capacity:

```
Vector v = new Vector(25);
```

This vector will allocate enough memory to support 25 elements. Once 25 elements have been added, however, the vector must decide how to expand to accept more elements. You can specify the value by which a vector grows using another Vector constructor:

```
Vector v = new Vector(25, 5);
```

This vector has an initial size of 25 elements, and will expand in increments of 5 elements when more than 25 elements are added to it. That means the vector will jump to 30 elements in size, and then 35, and so on. A smaller growth value results in greater memory management efficiency at the cost of more execution overhead because more memory allocations are taking place. A larger growth value results in fewer memory allocations, but sometimes memory might be wasted if you don't use all the extra space created.

You can't just use square brackets ([ ]) to access the elements in a vector, as you can in an array. You must use methods defined in the Vector class. Use the add() method to add an element to a vector, as in the following example:

```
v.add("Watson");
v.add("Palmer");
v.add("Nicklaus");
```

This code shows how to add some strings to a vector. To retrieve the last string added to the vector, you can use the lastElement() method:

```
String s = (String)v.lastElement();
```

Notice that you have to cast the return value of lastElement() because the Vector class is designed to work with the Object class. Although lastElement() certainly has its usefulness, you will probably find more value in the get() method, which enables you to retrieve a vector element using an index.

The following is an example of the get() method:

```
String s1 = (String)v.get(0);
String s2 = (String)v.get(2);
```

Because vectors are zero-based, the first call to get() retrieves the "Watson" string and the second call retrieves the "Palmer" string. Just as you can retrieve an element at a particular index, you can also add and remove elements at an index by using the add() and remove() methods:

```
v.add(1, "Hogan");
v.add(0, "Jones");
v.remove(3);
```

The first call to add() inserts an element at index 1, between the "Watson" and "Palmer" strings. The "Palmer" and "Nicklaus" strings are moved up an element in the vector to accommodate the inserted "Hogan" string. The second call to add() inserts an element at index 0, which is the beginning of the vector. All existing elements are moved up one space in the vector to accommodate the inserted "Jones" string. At this point, the contents of the vector look like this:

- "Jones"
- "Watson"
- "Hogan"
- "Palmer"
- "Nicklaus"

21

The call to remove() removes the element at index 3, which is the "Palmer" string. The resulting vector consists of the following strings:

- "Jones"
- "Watson"
- "Hogan"
- "Nicklaus"

You can use the set() method to change a specific element:

```
v.set(1, "Woods");
```

This method replaces the "Watson" string with the "Woods" string, resulting in the following vector:

- "Jones"
- "Woods"
- "Hogan"
- "Nicklaus"

If you want to clear out the vector completely, you can remove all the elements with the clear() method:

```
v.clear();
```

The Vector class also provides some methods for working with elements without using indexes. These methods actually search through the vector for a particular element. The first of these methods is the contains() method, which simply checks if an element is in the vector:

```
boolean isThere = v.contains("O'Meara");
```

Another method that works in this manner is the indexOf() method, which finds the index of an element based on the element itself:

```
int i = v.indexOf("Nicklaus");
```

The indexOf() method returns the index of the element in question if it is in the vector, or -1 if not. The removeElement() method works similarly, removing an element based on the element itself rather than on an index:

```
v.removeElement("Woods");
```

If you're interested in working sequentially with all the elements in a vector, you can use the `iterator()` method, which returns a list of the elements you can iterate through:

```
Iterator it = v.iterator();
```

As you learned earlier today, you can use an iterator to step through elements sequentially. In this example, you can work with the `it` list using the methods defined by the `Iterator` interface.

At some point you might want to work with the size of a vector. Fortunately, the `Vector` class provides a few methods for determining and manipulating a vector's size. First, the `size` method determines the number of elements in the vector:

```
int size = v.size();
```

If you want to explicitly set the size of the vector, you can use the `setSize()` method:

```
v.setSize(10);
```

The `setSize()` method expands or truncates the vector to the size specified. If the vector is expanded, null elements are inserted as the newly added elements. If the vector is truncated, any elements at indexes beyond the specified size are discarded.

Recall that vectors have two different attributes relating to size: size and capacity. The size is the number of elements in the vector, and the capacity is the amount of memory allocated to hold all the elements. The capacity is always greater than or equal to the size. You can force the capacity to exactly match the size by using the `trimToSize()` method:

```
v.trimToSize();
```

You can also check to see what the capacity is by using the `capacity()` method:

```
int capacity = v.capacity();
```

Stacks

Stacks are a classic data structure used to model information that is accessed in a specific order. The `Stack` class in Java is implemented as a last-in-first-out (LIFO) stack, which means that the last item added to the stack is the first one to be removed. Figure 21.5 shows the logical organization of a stack.

21

FIGURE 21.5

The logical organiza-tion of a stack data structure.

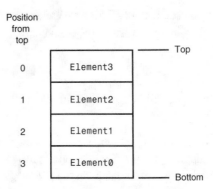

You might wonder why the numbers of the elements don't match their positions from the top of the stack. Keep in mind that elements are added to the top, so Element0, which is on the bottom, was the first element added to the stack. Likewise, Element3, which is on top, was the last element added. Also, because Element3 is at the top of the stack, it will be the first to be removed.

The Stack class defines only one constructor, which is a default constructor that creates an empty stack. You use this constructor to create a stack like this:

```
Stack s = new Stack();
```

You add new elements to a stack by using the push() method, which pushes an element onto the top of the stack:

```
s.push("One");
s.push("Two");
s.push("Three");
s.push("Four");
s.push("Five");
s.push("Six");
```

This code pushes six strings onto the stack, with the last string ("Six") remaining on top. You pop elements back off the stack by using the pop() method:

```
String s1 = (String)s.pop();
String s2 = (String)s.pop();
```

This code pops the last two strings off the stack, leaving the first four strings. This code results in the s1 variable containing the "Six" string and the s2 variable containing the "Five" string.

If you want to get the top element on the stack without actually popping it off the stack, you can use the peek() method:

```
String s3 = (String)s.peek();
```

This call to peek() returns the "Four" string but leaves the string on the stack. You can search for an element on the stack by using the search() method:

```
int i = s.search("Two");
```

The search() method returns the distance from the top of the stack of the element if it is found, or -1 if not. In this case, the "Two" string is the third element from the top, so the search() method returns 2 (zero-based).

Note
As in all Java data structures that deal with indexes or lists, the Stack class reports element position in a zero-based fashion. This means that the top element in a stack has a location of 0, and the fourth element down has a location of 3.

The only other method defined in the Stack class is empty, which determines whether a stack is empty:

```
boolean isEmpty = s.empty();
```

Although the Stack class isn't quite as useful as the Vector class, it provides the functionality for a very common and established data structure.

Map

The Map interface defines a framework for implementing a basic key-mapped data structure. You can put the key-mapped approach to work by using the Hashtable class, which implements the Map interface, or by creating your own class that uses the interface. You'll learn about the Hashtable class in the next section.

The Map interface defines a means of storing and retrieving information based on a key. This is similar in some ways to the Vector class, in which elements are accessed through an index, which is a specific type of key. However, keys in the Map interface can be just about anything. You can create your own classes to use as the keys for accessing and manipulating data in a dictionary. Figure 21.6 shows how keys map to data in a dictionary.

The Map interface declares a variety of methods for working with the data stored in a dictionary. Implementing classes will have to implement all of those methods to actually be useful. The put and get methods are used to put objects in the dictionary and get them back. Assuming look is a class that implements the Map interface, the following code shows how to use the put method to add elements:

21

```
look.put("small", new Rectangle(0, 0, 5, 5));
look.put("medium", new Rectangle(0, 0, 15, 15));
look.put("large", new Rectangle(0, 0, 25, 25));
```

FIGURE 21.6

*The logical organiza-
tion of a key-mapped
data structure.*

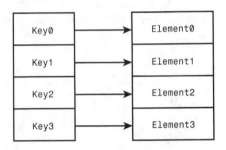

This code adds three rectangles to the dictionary, using strings as the keys. To get an element, use the get method and specify the appropriate key:

```
Rectangle r = (Rectangle)look.get("medium");
```

You also can remove an element with a key by using the remove() method:

```
look.remove("large");
```

You can find out how many elements are in the structure by using the size() method, much as you did with the Vector class:

```
int size = look.size();
```

You also can check whether the structure is empty by using the isEmpty() method:

```
boolean isEmpty = look.isEmpty();I~data structures;dictionaries>
```

Hash Tables

The Hashtable class is derived from Dictionary, implements the Map interface, and provides a complete implementation of a key-mapped data structure. Hash tables enable you to store data based on some type of key and have an efficiency defined by the load factor of the table. The *load factor* is a number between 0.0 and 1.0 that determines how and when the hash table allocates space for more elements.

Like vectors, hash tables have a capacity, or the amount of allocated memory. Hash tables allocate memory by comparing the current size of the table with the product of the capacity and the load factor. If the size of the hash table exceeds this product, the table increases its capacity by rehashing itself.

Load factors that are closer to 1.0 result in more efficient use of memory at the expense of a longer lookup time for each element. Similarly, load factors closer to 0.0 result in more efficient lookups but also tend to be more wasteful with memory. Determining the load factor for your own hash tables is dependent on how you use each hash table and whether your priority is performance or memory efficiency.

You can create hash tables in any one of three ways. The first constructor creates a default hash table:

```
Hashtable hash = new Hashtable();
```

The second constructor creates a hash table with the specified initial capacity:

```
Hashtable hash = new Hashtable(20);
```

Finally, the third constructor creates a hash table with the specified initial capacity and load factor:

```
Hashtable hash = new Hashtable(20, 0.75F);
```

All the abstract methods defined in Map are implemented in the Hashtable class. In addition, the Hashtable class implements a few others that perform functions specific to supporting hash tables. One of these is the clear() method, which clears a hash table of all its keys and elements:

```
hash.clear();
```

The contains() method checks whether an object is stored in the hash table. This method searches for an object value in the hash table rather than searching for a key. The following code shows how to use the contains() method:

```
boolean isThere = hash.contains(new Rectangle(0, 0, 5, 5));
```

Similar to contains(), the containsKey() method searches a hash table, but is based on a key rather than a value:

```
boolean isThere = hash.containsKey("Small");
```

As mentioned earlier, a hash table will rehash itself when it determines that it must increase its capacity. You can force a rehash yourself by calling the rehash() method:

```
hash.rehash();
```

The practical use of a hash table is actually in representing data that is too time-consuming to search or reference by value. In other words, hash tables often come in handy when you're working with complex data and it's much more efficient to access the data by using a key rather than comparing the data objects themselves.

21

Furthermore, hash tables typically compute a key for elements, which is called a hash code. For example, a string can have an integer hash code computed for it that uniquely represents the string. When a bunch of strings are stored in a hash table, the table can access the strings by using integer hash codes as opposed to using the contents of the strings themselves. This results in much more efficient searching and retrieving capabilities.

NEW TERM   A *hash code* is a computed key that uniquely identifies each element in a hash table.

This technique of computing and using hash codes for object storage and reference is exploited heavily throughout the Java system. The parent of all classes, `Object`, defines a `hashCode()` method that is overridden in most standard Java classes. Any class that defines a `hashCode()` method can be efficiently stored and accessed in a hash table. A class that wants to be hashed must also implement the `equals()` method, which defines a way of telling whether two objects are equal. The `equals()` method usually just performs a straight comparison of all the member variables defined in a class.

Hash tables are an extremely powerful data structure that should probably be integrated into some of your programs that manipulate large amounts of data. The fact that hash tables are so widely supported in the Java class library via the `Object` class should give you a clue as to their importance in Java programming.

Summary

In today's lesson, you learned about working with existing data stored in popular database formats such as Microsoft Access, MySQL, and xBase. Using either Java Database Connectivity (JDBC) or a combination of JDBC and ODBC, you can incorporate existing data storage solutions into your Java programs.

You also learned several ways to work with data that doesn't exist yet, by using some of the data structures that are more sophisticated than arrays and linked lists.

These standard data structures provide a range of options that cover many practical programming scenarios.

This brings us to the main event: the conclusion of your three-week trip through the Java language. Now that you've had a chance to work with the syntax and the core classes that make up Java, you're ready to tackle the really hard stuff: your own programs.

This book has an official Web site at `http://www.java21days.com`. It features answers to frequently asked questions, all the book's source code, error corrections, and supplementary material.

Q&A

Q Can the JDBC-ODBC bridge driver be used in an applet?

A The default security in place for applets does not allow the JDBC-ODBC bridge to be used because the ODBC side of the bridge driver employs native code rather than Java. Native code can't be held to the security restrictions in place for Java, so there's no way to ensure that this code is secure.

JDBC drivers that are implemented entirely in Java can be used in applets, and they have the advantage of requiring no configuration on the client computer.

Q What is the importance of using a hash table?

A Calculating a hash code for a complex piece of data is important because you can lessen the overhead involved in searching for the data. The hash code enables you to home in on a particular point in a large set of data before you begin the arduous task of searching based on the data itself. This can greatly improve performance.

Q How are linked lists different from vectors in the storage of individual elements?

A Vectors manage the memory requirements of all elements by allocating a certain amount of memory upon creation. When a vector is required to grow, it will allocate enough memory to hold the existing data and the new data and will then copy everything to it. Even if a vector holds only references to objects, it must still manage the memory that holds the references. Linked lists don't manage any of the memory for the elements contained in the list, except for references to the start and end elements.

Questions

1. What does a `Statement` object represent in a database program?

   (a) A connection to a database

   (b) A database query written in Structured Query Language

   (c) A data source

2. What kind of driver is not included with Java 2 SDK 1.3?

   (a) A JDBC driver

   (b) A JDBC-ODBC driver

   (c) Both

21

3. Which of the following data structures cannot grow in size after it is created?

   (a) Vectors

   (b) Arrays

   (c) Linked lists

Answers

1. b. The class, part of the `java.sql` package, represents an SQL statement.

2. a. Many relational database programs include a JDBC driver, but one is not shipped with the SDK at this writing.

3. b.

Exercises

To extend your knowledge of the subjects covered today, try the following exercises:

- Modify the `CoalTotals` application to pull fields from the Country Oil Totals table instead of the Coal table.

- Create an application that uses a vector to issue new license plate tags and reject requests for tags that are already taken.

Where applicable, exercise solutions are offered on the book's Web site at `http://www.java21days.com`.

APPENDIX A

Configuring the Software Development Kit

The Java 2 Software Development Kit 1.3 (SDK 1.3) is a set of command-line utilities that are used to create, compile, and run Java programs.

This appendix covers how to use the command line and fix any SDK configuration errors that might occur.

If you haven't installed the SDK yet, you should do so before reading this appendix. That topic is covered during Day 1, "21st Century Java."

Using a Command-Line Interface

The Java Software Development Kit requires the use of a command line to compile Java programs, run them, and handle other tasks.

A command line is a way to operate a computer entirely by typing commands at your keyboard, rather than by using a mouse.

Very few programs designed for Windows users require the command line today. To get to a command line on a Windows 98 or 95 system, click the Start button, choose Programs, and then click MS-DOS Prompt on the Windows taskbar, as shown in Figure A.1. On a Windows NT or 2000 system, click Start, Programs, Command Prompt. A new window opens where you can type commands.

FIGURE A.1

Finding a command line from the Windows taskbar.

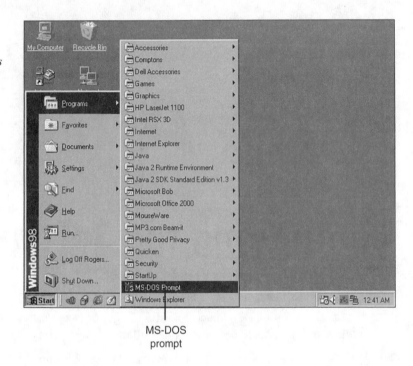

MS-DOS
prompt

The command line in Windows uses MS-DOS, the Microsoft operating system that preceded Windows. MS-DOS supports all the same functions as Windows—copying, moving, and deleting files and folders; running programs; scanning and repairing a hard drive; formatting a floppy disk; and so on.

When you click Start, Programs, MS-DOS Prompt in Windows, a new window opens where you can use MS-DOS commands, as shown in Figure A.2.

In the MS-DOS Prompt window, a cursor will blink on the command line when MS-DOS is ready for you to type in a new command with your keyboard. In Figure A.2, C:\WINDOWS> is the command line.

FIGURE A.2

An MS-DOS Prompt window.

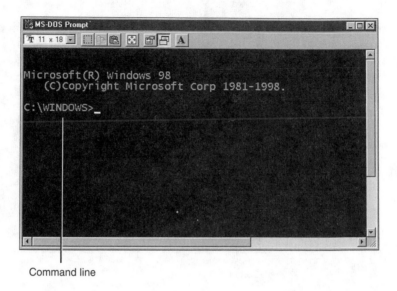

Command line

Because MS-DOS can be used to delete files and even format your hard drive, you should learn something about the operating system before experimenting with its commands. Two DOS books to consider are Dan Gookin's *DOS for Dummies* and *Special Edition Using MS-DOS 6.22, Second Edition*, published by Que.

However, you only need to know a few things about MS-DOS to use the Software Development Kit: how to create a folder, how to open a folder, and how to run a program.

Opening Folders in MS-DOS

When you are using MS-DOS on a Windows system, you will have access to all of the folders you normally use in Windows. For example, if you have a Windows folder on your C: hard drive, the same folder is accessible as C:\Windows from an MS-DOS Prompt.

To open a folder in MS-DOS, type the command CD followed by the name of the folder and press Enter, such as the following example:

```
CD C:\TEMP
```

When you enter this command, the TEMP folder on your system's C: drive will be opened, if it exists. After you open a folder, your command line will be updated with the name of that folder, as shown in Figure A.3.

FIGURE A.3

Opening a folder in an MS-DOS Prompt window.

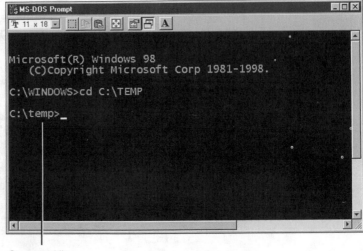

Command line

You also can use the CD command in other ways:

- CD \—Open the root folder on the current hard drive.
- CD *subfoldername*—Open a subfolder matching the name you've used in place of *subfoldername*, if that subfolder exists.
- CD ..—Open the folder that contains the current folder. For example, if you are in C:\Windows\Cookies and you use the CD .. command, C:\Windows will be opened.

One of the book's suggestions is to create a folder called J21work where you could edit, compile, and run Java programs. If you have already done this, you can switch to that folder by using the following commands:

1. CD \
2. CD J21work

If you haven't created that folder yet, you can accomplish that task within MS-DOS.

Creating Folders in MS-DOS

To create a folder from an MS-DOS Prompt, type the command MD followed by the name of the folder and press Enter, such as in the following example:

MD C:\STUFF

The STUFF folder will be created in the root folder of the system's C: drive. To open a newly created folder, use the CD command followed by that folder's name, as shown in Figure A.4.

FIGURE A.4

Creating a new folder in an MS-DOS Prompt window.

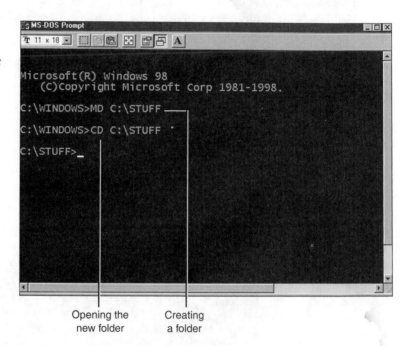

Opening the new folder   Creating a folder

This book recommends creating a J21work folder where you can do all your Java-related work. If you haven't already done this within Windows, you can do it from an MS-DOS Prompt:

- Change to the root folder (using the CD \ command).
- Type the command MD J21work and press Enter.

After J21work has been created, you can go to it at any time from an MS-DOS Prompt by using the CD \J21work command.

The last thing you need to learn about MS-DOS for the Software Development Kit is how to run programs.

Running Programs in MS-DOS

The simplest way to run a program at the MS-DOS Prompt is to type its name and press Enter. For example, type DIR and press Enter to see a list of files and subfolders in the current folder.

You also can run a program by typing its name followed by a space and some options that control how the program runs. These options are called *arguments*.

To see an example of this, change to the root folder (using CD \) and type DIR J21work. You'll see a list of files and subfolders contained in the J21work folder, if it contains any.

After you have installed the Software Development Kit, you should run the Java interpreter to see that it works. Type the following command at an MS-DOS Prompt:

```
java -version
```

In the preceding example, java is the name of the Java interpreter program and -version is an argument that tells the interpreter to display its version number.

You can see an example of this in Figure A.5, but your version number might be a little different depending on which version of the SDK you have installed.

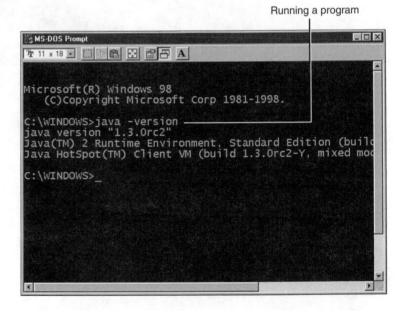

Running a program

FIGURE A.5

Running the Java interpreter in an MS-DOS Prompt window.

If java -version works and you see a version number, it should begin with a 1.3 because you are using SDK 1.3. Sun sometimes tacks on a third number, such as 1.3.1, to track maintenance and security releases, but as long as it begins with 1.3 you are using the correct version of the Software Development Kit.

If you see an incorrect version number or a Bad command or file name error after running java -version, you need to make some changes to how the Software Development Kit is configured on your system.

Configuring the Software Development Kit

When you are writing and compiling Java programs for the first time, the most likely source for problems is not typos, syntax errors, or other programming mistakes.

Most errors result from a misconfigured Software Development Kit.

If you type java -version at a command line and get a Bad command or file name error or a similar error, it indicates that your system can't find the folder that contains java.exe, the Java interpreter.

Setting Up the PATH Command

The root folder of your Windows system should contain a file called AUTOEXEC.BAT. This file is used by MS-DOS to configure how the operating system and some command-line programs function.

AUTOEXEC.BAT is a text file you can edit with Windows Notepad. Start Notepad by clicking Start, Programs, Accessories, Notepad from the Windows taskbar.

The Notepad text editor will open. Choose File, Open from Notepad's menu bar and open the file \AUTOEXEC.BAT. (The slash in front of the filename causes Notepad to look for it in the root folder.)

When you open the file, you'll see a series of MS-DOS commands, each on its own line, as shown in Figure A.6.

FIGURE A.6

Editing the
AUTOEXEC.BAT *file*
with Notepad.

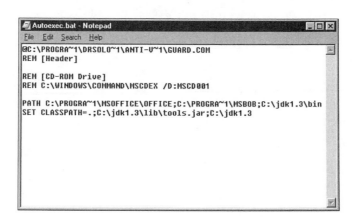

```
Autoexec.bat - Notepad
File  Edit  Search  Help
@C:\PROGRA~1\DRSOLO~1\ANTI-V~1\GUARD.COM
REM [Header]

REM [CD-ROM Drive]
REM C:\WINDOWS\COMMAND\MSCDEX /D:MSCD001

PATH C:\PROGRA~1\MSOFFICE\OFFICE;C:\PROGRA~1\MSBOB;C:\jdk1.3\bin
SET CLASSPATH=.;C:\jdk1.3\lib\tools.jar;C:\jdk1.3
```

The only commands you need to look for are any that begin with PATH or SET CLASSPATH=.

The PATH command is followed by a space and a series of folder names separated by semicolons.

PATH is used to help MS-DOS find programs when you run them at a command line. In the preceding example, the PATH command in Figure A.6 includes three folders:

- C:\PROGRA~1\MSOFFICE\OFFICE
- C:\PROGRA~1\MSBOB
- C:\jdk1.3\bin

You can see what PATH has been set to by typing the following command at an MS-DOS Prompt:

PATH

To set up the Software Development Kit correctly, the folder that contains the Java interpreter must be included in the PATH command in AUTOEXEC.BAT. The interpreter has the filename java.exe. If you installed SDK 1.3 in the C:\jdk1.3 folder on your system, java.exe is probably in C:\jdk1.3\bin.

If you can't remember where you installed the SDK, you can look for java.exe by clicking the Start button, choosing Find, and clicking Files or Folders. You might find several copies in different folders. To see which one is correct, open an MS-DOS Prompt window and do the following for each copy of the program:

1. Use the CD command to open a folder that contains java.exe.
2. Run the command java -version in that folder.

When you know the correct folder, create a blank line at the bottom of the AUTOEXEC.BAT file and add the following:

PATH rightfoldername;%PATH%

For example, if c:\javajdk\bin is the correct folder, the following line should be added at the bottom of AUTOEXEC.BAT:

PATH c:\javajdk\bin;%PATH%

The %PATH% text keeps you from wiping out any other PATH commands in AUTOEXEC.BAT.

After making changes to AUTOEXEC.BAT, save the file and reboot your computer. When this is done, try the java -version command.

If it displays the right SDK version, your system might be configured correctly and require no more adjustments.

A

Setting Up the CLASSPATH Command

When you compile a Java program with the Software Development Kit, you type a command such as the following at a command line:

```
javac Ellsworth.java
```

The Ellsworth.java argument refers to the program created during Day 1.

If you compile a program successfully, you won't see any output. If you have compiled Ellsworth.java, try to run the program with the following command:

```
java Ellsworth
```

Note

You can also download Ellsworth.class, the compiled version of Ellsworth.java, from the book's Web site. Visit http://www.java21days.com and open the Day 1 page to find links to all files from that chapter.

If programs compile and run okay, the Software Development Kit has been configured successfully. You don't need to make any more changes to AUTOEXEC.BAT.

If you see a Class not found error or NoClassDef error whenever you try to run a program, you need to adjust the SET CLASSPATH= line in your AUTOEXEC.BAT file.

When you run Notepad and open \AUTOEXEC.BAT, you'll see a series of MS-DOS commands like those shown in Figure A.6.

The SET CLASSPATH= command is followed by a series of folder and filenames separated by semicolons.

CLASSPATH is used to help the Java compiler find the Java class library and other class files that it needs. In the preceding example, the SET CLASSPATH= command in Figure A.6 included three things:

- .
- c:\jdk1.3\lib\tools.jar
- c:\jdk1.3

A CLASSPATH can contain folders (such as c:\jdk1.3 in the preceding example) and files (c:\jdk1.3\lib\tools.jar). It also can contain a period character ("."), which is another way to refer to the current folder in MS-DOS.

You can see what CLASSPATH has been set to by typing the following command at an MS-DOS Prompt:

```
ECHO %CLASSPATH%
```

If your CLASSPATH includes folders or files that you know are no longer on your computer, you should remove the references to them on the SET CLASSPATH= line in AUTOEXEC.BAT. Make sure to remove any extra semicolons also.

To set up the Software Development Kit correctly, the file containing the Java class library must be included in the SET CLASSPATH= command. The interpreter has the filename tools.jar. If you installed the SDK in the C:\jdk1.3 folder on your system, tools.jar is probably in the folder C:\jdk1.3\lib.

If you can't remember where you installed the SDK, you can look for tools.jar by clicking Start, Find, Files or Folders from the Windows taskbar. If you find several copies, you should be able to find the correct one using this method:

1. Use CD to open the folder that contains the Java interpreter (java.exe)
2. Enter the command CD ..
3. Enter the command CD lib

The lib folder normally contains the right copy of tools.jar.

When you know the correct location, create a blank line at the bottom of the AUTOEXEC.BAT file and add the following:

```
SET CLASSPATH=%CLASSPATH%;.;rightlocation
```

For example, if tools.jar file is in the c:\javajdk\lib folder, the following line should be added at the bottom of AUTOEXEC.BAT:

```
SET CLASSPATH=%CLASSPATH%;.;c:\javajdk\lib\tools.jar
```

As you might expect, the %CLASSPATH% text keeps you from removing any other CLASSPATH commands in AUTOEXEC.BAT.

After making changes to AUTOEXEC.BAT, save the file and reboot your computer. After this is done, try to compile one of the programs from the first several days of the book. You should be able to compile and run them without any SDK-related problems.

> **Tip**
>
> This book has a Web site where you can find solutions to problems, corrections, answers to reader questions, and other useful material. There's an online version of this appendix on the site and a way to contact coauthor Rogers Cadenhead if you are still having problems with the Software Development Kit. The site is available at http://www.java21days.com.

UNIX Configuration

A

To configure the SDK on a Solaris system, add the java/bin or JDK/bin directory to your execution path. You can usually do this by adding a line like the following to your .profile, .cshrc, or .login file:

```
set path= (~/java/bin/ $path)
```

This line assumes that you've installed the SDK into the directory java in your home directory. An installation elsewhere will require a change to the directory added to your execution path.

These changes will not take effect until you log out and back in again, or use the source command with the name of the file you changed. If you altered the .login file, the source command would be as follows:

```
source ~/.login
```

Fixing Class Not Found Errors on Other Platforms

To correct any Class not found errors on Solaris systems, the best thing to do is make sure that the CLASSPATH environment variable is not being set automatically at login.

To see whether CLASSPATH is being set, enter the following at a command prompt:

```
echo $CLASSPATH
```

If a CLASSPATH value has been set, you can unset it by entering the following command:

```
unsetenv CLASSPATH
```

To make this change permanent, you should remove the command that sets up CLASSPATH from your .profile, .cshrc, or .login file.

These changes will not take effect until you log out and back in again, or use the source command with the name of the file you changed. If you altered the .login file, the source command would be as follows:

```
source ~/.login
```

APPENDIX B

Using a Text Editor with the Software Development Kit

Unlike Java development tools such as Visual Café and SunSoft Java WorkShop, Java 2 Software Development Kit 1.3 (SDK 1.3) does not come with a text editor to use when you create source files.

In this appendix, you learn how to select an editor for use with the SDK and how to configure your system to work with that editor.

Choosing a Text Editor

For an editor or word processor to work with the SDK, it must be able to save text files with no formatting.

This feature has different names in different editors. Look for a format option such as one of the following when you save a document or set the properties for a document:

- Plain text
- ASCII text
- DOS text
- Text-only

If you're using Windows, there are several editors included with the operating system.

Windows Notepad, available at Programs, Accessories, Notepad from the Start button, is a no-frills text editor that only works with plain-text files. It can handle only one document at a time.

Windows WordPad (Programs, Accessories, WordPad from the Start button) is a step above Notepad. It can handle more than one document at a time and can handle both plain-text and Microsoft Word formats. It also remembers the last several documents it has worked on and makes them available from the File pull-down menu.

DOS Edit, which can be run from an MS-DOS prompt with the command `edit`, is another simple editor that handles plain-text documents. It will seem crude to a Windows user who isn't familiar with MS-DOS, but it and some other text editors do have one feature that Notepad and WordPad lack: They show you the number of the line you're currently editing. Numbering begins with `1` at the topmost line in the file and increases as you move downward. Figure B.1 shows Edit; the line number is indicated in the lower-right corner of the program window.

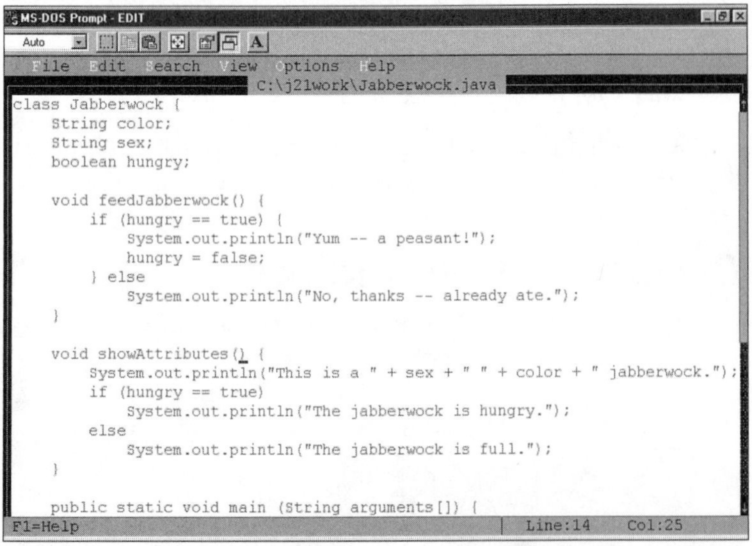
MS-DOS Prompt - EDIT
Auto
File Edit Search View Options Help
C:\j21work\Jabberwock.java
class Jabberwock {
String color;
String sex;
boolean hungry;
void feedJabberwock() {
if (hungry == true) {
System.out.println("Yum -- a peasant!");
hungry = false;
} else
System.out.println("No, thanks -- already ate.");
}
void showAttributes() {
System.out.println("This is a " + sex + " " + color + " jabberwock.");
if (hungry == true)
System.out.println("The jabberwock is hungry.");
else
System.out.println("The jabberwock is full.");
}
public static void main (String arguments[]) {
F1=Help
Line:14 Col:25

FIGURE B.1

A Java source file loaded in DOS Edit.

Seeing the line number helps in Java programming because many Java compilers indicate the line number at which an error occurred. Take a look at the following error generated by the SDK compiler:

```
Palindrome.java:2: Class Font not found in type declaration.
```

The number 2 after the name of the Java source file indicates that the line that triggered the compiler error. With a text editor that supports numbering, you can go directly to that line and start looking for the error.

Usually there are better ways to debug a program with a commercial Java programming package, but SDK users must search for compiler-generated errors using the line number indicated by the `javac` tool. Because of this, it's best to use a text editor that supports numbering.

Creating a File Association in Windows

After a text editor has been selected, Windows users should associate that editor with the `.java` file extension. This makes it possible to open a `.java` source file by double-clicking its name in a folder. It also prevents editors, such as Windows Notepad, from incorrectly adding the `.txt` file extension to `.java` source files.

To create a file association, you first must have a file to work on. Open a folder in Windows and create a new text document by selecting File, New, Text Document from the folder's menu bar (see Figure B.2).

FIGURE B.2

Creating a new text document in a Windows folder.

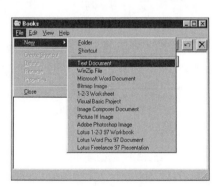

A new text document called New Text Document.txt is created, and you have a chance to immediately rename it. Change the name to Anything.java and confirm this new name when Windows asks whether you really want to change the file extension.

Double-click Anything.java. If your system does not associate the `.java` file extension with any program, you'll see an Open With window. You can use this to associate the

.java file extension with your chosen editor. Skip to "Creating a New Association" later in this appendix.

If anything else happens, you must delete the existing .java association before you can create a new one.

Deleting an Existing File Association

If your system already has something associated with the .java file extension, you can remove this association from any Windows folder. Select View, Options from a folder's menu bar; an Options window with three tabbed dialog boxes opens. Select the File Types tab to see that dialog box (see Figure B.3).

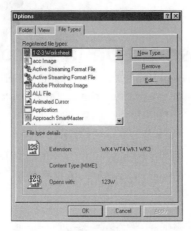

The Registered File Types list box in this window shows all the file extensions that are associated with programs on your system. Highlight a file type in the list box to see two other fields that provide information about it:

- The Extensions field displays all file extensions that work with this file type.
- The Opens With field displays the program that is used to open this file type.

The file type 1-2-3 Worksheets in Figure B.3 has four file extensions: WK4, WT4, WK1, and WK3. Any file with these extensions can be opened with the program 123W (which is the Lotus 1-2-3 spreadsheet application).

Scroll through the Registered File Types list until you find one that includes JAVA in its Extension field. The most likely place to find it is under a heading such as "Java files" or "Java programs," but that might not be the case on your system.

When you find the right file type, you must delete the existing association so that you can replace it with a new one. Select Remove to delete the existing association, and click Yes to confirm that you want to remove it. After you do this, you can create a new association for the .java file extension.

Creating a New Association

An Open With window opens when you double-click a file that has no known association for its file extension. This is shown in Figure B.4.

B

FIGURE B.4

Associating a file extension with a program.

Use the following steps to create a .java file association:

- In the Description of .java Files text box, enter **Java source file** or something similar.
- In the Choose the Program You Want to Use list box, find the text editor or word processor you want to use with Java source files. If you don't find it, click the Other button and find the program manually. If you're using DOS Edit, on most systems it can be found in the \Windows\Command folder with the filename edit or edit.exe.
- Make sure that the Always Use This Program to Open This File option is checked.

When you click OK to confirm these settings, your chosen editor opens the Anything.java file and any other files that have the .java file extension.

Associating an Icon with a File Type

After you have associated .java files with your chosen editor, an icon is assigned by default to all .java files on your system.

If you want to change this icon, select View, Options, File Types from a folder's menu bar to see the File Types dialog box. Scroll through the registered file types to find the one associated with the JAVA file extension.

When this file type is highlighted, select Edit to open an Edit File Type window, which is shown in Figure B.5.

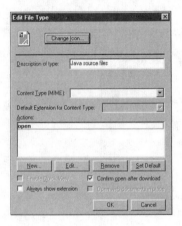

Select Change Icon from the Edit File Type window and choose a different icon to display for all .java files. If you like one of the icons displayed in the Current Icon window, highlight that icon and click OK to make the change. If you would like to look at other icons, select Browse to look inside files on your system to see the icons they contain. You can open any icon file, Windows program, or .DLL file to see what icons it contains. They are displayed in the Current Icon window after you select a file.

After you find an icon you like, highlight it and click OK to select it.

APPENDIX C

The Software Development Kit

The Software Development Kit (SDK) is used throughout this book to create, compile, and run Java programs.

The tools that make up the SDK contain numerous features that many programmers don't explore at all, and some of the tools themselves might be new to you.

This appendix covers features of the SDK you can use to create more reliable, better-tested, and faster-running Java programs.

The following topics will be covered:

- Running Java applications with the interpreter
- Compiling programs with the compiler
- Running Java applets with the `appletviewer`
- Creating documentation with the documentation tool
- Finding bugs in your program and learning more about its performance with the debugger
- Setting system properties with the interpreter and `appletviewer`

An Overview of the SDK

Although there are several dozen software packages that you can use to create Java programs, the most widely used is the Software Development Kit (SDK) from Sun Microsystems. The SDK is the set of command-line tools that are used to develop software with the Java language.

There are two main reasons for the popularity of the SDK:

- It's free. You can download a copy at no cost from Sun's official Java World Wide Web site at `http://java.sun.com`.
- It's first. Whenever Sun releases a new version of the language, the first tools that support this version are in the SDK.

The SDK uses the command line—also called the MS-DOS prompt on Windows 95 and 98 systems and the console on Windows NT and 2000 systems. Commands are entered using the keyboard, as in the following example:

```
javac VideoBook.java
```

This command compiles a Java program called `VideoBook.java` using the SDK compiler. There are two elements to the command: the name of the SDK compiler, `javac`, followed by the name of the program to compile, `VideoBook.java`. A space character separates the two elements.

Each SDK command follows the same format: the name of the tool to use, followed by one or more elements indicating what the tool should do. These elements are called *arguments*.

The following illustrates the use of command-line arguments:

```
java VideoBook add VHS "Bad Influence"
```

This command tells the Java interpreter to run a class file called `VideoBook` with three command-line arguments: the strings `add`, `VHS`, and `Bad Influence`.

 Note

> You might think there are four command-line arguments because of the space between the words `Bad` and `Influence`. The quotation marks around `"Bad Influence"` cause it to be considered one command-line argument rather than two. This makes it possible to include a space character.

Some arguments used with the SDK modify how a tool will function. These arguments are preceded by a hyphen character and are called *options*.

The following command shows the use of an option:

```
java -version
```

This command tells the Java interpreter to display its version number rather than trying to run a class file. It's a good way to find out whether the SDK is correctly configured to run Java programs on your system. Here's an example of the output run on a system equipped with SDK 1.3.0:

```
java version "1.3.0"
Java(TM) 2 Runtime Environment, Standard Edition (build1.3.0)
Java HotSpot(TM) Client VM (build 1.3.0, mixed mode)
```

In some instances, you can combine options with other arguments. If you compile a Java class that uses deprecated methods, you can see more information on these methods by compiling the class with a -deprecation option, as in the following:

```
javac -deprecation OldVideoBook.java
```

The java Interpreter

java, the Java interpreter, is used to run Java applications from the command line. It takes as an argument the name of a class file to run, as in the following example:

```
java BidMonitor
```

Although Java class files end with the .class extension, this extension is not specified when using the interpreter.

The class loaded by the Java interpreter must contain a main() method that takes the following form:

```
public static void main(String[] arguments) {
    // Method here
}
```

Some simple Java programs might use only one class—the one containing the main() method. In other cases, the interpreter automatically loads any other classes that are needed.

The Java interpreter runs bytecode—the compiled instructions that are executed by a Java virtual machine. After a Java program is in bytecode form as a .class file, it can be run by different interpreters without modification. If you have compiled a Java 2 program, it should be compatible with any interpreter that fully supports Java 2.

Note

Interestingly enough, Java is no longer the only language that you can use to create Java bytecode. NetRexx, JPython, and several other languages will compile into .class files of executable bytecode through the use of compilers specific to those languages. A list of these languages is currently available from the Web page at http://grunge.cs.tu-berlin.de/~tolk/vmlanguages.html.

There are two different ways to specify the class file that should be run by the Java interpreter. If the class is not part of any package, you can run it by specifying the name of the class, as in the preceding java BidMonitor example and all the examples in prior chapters of this book. If the class is part of a package, you must specify the class by using its full package and class name.

For example, consider a SellItem class that is part of the com.prefect.auction package. To run this application, the following command would be used:

```
java com.prefect.auction.SellItem
```

Each element of the package name corresponds to its own subfolder The Java interpreter will look for the SellItem.class file in several different places:

- The com\prefect\auction subfolder of the folder where the java command was entered. (If the command was made from the C:\J21work folder, for example, the SellItem.class file could be run successfully if it was in the C:\J21work\com\prefect\auction folder.)

- The com\prefect\auction subfolder of any folder in your CLASSPATH setting.

If you're creating your own packages, an easy way to manage them is to add a folder to your CLASSPATH that's the root folder for any packages you create, such as C:\javapackages or something similar. After creating subfolders that correspond to the name of a package, place the package's class files in the correct subfolder.

The javac Compiler

javac, the Java compiler, converts Java source code into one or more class files of bytecode that can be run by a Java interpreter.

Java source code is stored in a file with the .java file extension. This file can be created with any text editor or word processor that can save a document without any special formatting codes. The terminology varies depending on the text-editing software being used, but these files are often called plain text, ASCII text, DOS text, or something similar.

A Java source code file can contain more than one class, but only one of the classes can be declared to be public. A class can contain no public classes at all if desired, although this isn't possible with applets because of the rules of inheritance.

If a source code file contains a class that has been declared to be public, the name of the file must match the name of that class. For example, the source code for a public class called BuyItem must be stored in a file called BuyItem.java.

To compile a file, the javac tool is run with the name of the file as an argument, as in the following:

```
javac BidMonitor.java
```

You can compile more than one source file by including each separate filename as a command-line argument, such as this command:

```
javac BidMonitor.java SellItem.java
```

You also can use wildcard characters such as * and ?. Use the following command to compile all .java files in a folder:

```
javac *.java
```

When you compile one or more Java source code files, a separate .class file will be created for each Java class that compiles successfully.

> **Caution**
>
> An easy mistake to make when you're putting a Java applet on the Web is to forget some of the .class files that make up the applet. You can combine several files into a single archive using the jar tool, which you learned about on Day 7, "Writing Java Applets." jar enables all files associated with an applet to be grouped together into a single file.

One of the javac tool's options is -deprecation, which you can use to find out more about the deprecated methods being employed in a Java program. Normally, the compiler will issue a single warning if it finds any deprecated methods in a program. The -deprecation option causes the compiler to list each method that has been deprecated, as in the following command:

```
javac -deprecation SellItem.java
```

If you're more concerned with the speed of a Java program than the size of its class files, you can compile its source code with the -O option. This creates class files that have been optimized for faster performance. Methods that are static, final, or private might be compiled *inline*, a technique that makes the class file larger but causes the methods to be executed more quickly.

Normally, the Java compiler doesn't provide a lot of information. In fact, if all the source code compiles successfully and no deprecated methods are employed, you won't see any output from the compiler at all. No news is good news in this case.

If you'd like to see more information on what the javac tool is doing as it compiles source code, use the -verbose option. The more verbose compiler will describe the time it takes to complete different functions, the classes that are being loaded, and the overall time required.

The appletviewer Browser

appletviewer, the Java applet viewer, is used to run Java programs that require a Web browser and are presented as part of an HTML document.

appletviewer takes an HTML document as a command-line argument, as in the following example:

```
appletviewer NewAuctions.html
```

When an HTML document is loaded by appletviewer, every applet on that document will begin running in its own window. The size of these windows depends on the HEIGHT and WIDTH attributes that were set in the applet's HTML tag.

Unlike a Web browser, appletviewer cannot be used to view the HTML document itself. If you want to see how the applet is laid out in relation to the other contents of the document, you must use a Java-capable Web browser such as Netscape Navigator or Microsoft Internet Explorer.

> **Note**
>
> At the time of this writing, neither Navigator nor Internet Explorer offers built-in support for Java 2 applets. The Java Plug-in from Sun can be used to run a Java 2 applet with either browser, as long as the HTML document containing the applet has been designed to work with the Plug-in. You can download it from Sun's Web site at http://java.sun.com/products/plugin. SDK's appletviewer is the only tool that runs Java 2 applets on HTML documents that aren't configured to use the Plug-in.

Using appletviewer is reasonably straightforward, but you may not be familiar with some of the menu options that are available as the viewer runs an applet. Figure C.1 shows the options on the appletviewer tool's Applet pull-down menu.

FIGURE C.1

The Applet pull-down menu of appletviewer.

The following menu options are available:

- The Restart and Reload options are used to restart the execution of the applet. The difference between these two options is that Restart does not unload the applet before restarting it, whereas Reload does. The Reload option is equivalent to closing the applet viewer and opening it up again on the same Web page.

- The Start and Stop options are used to directly call the start() and stop() methods of the applet.

- The Clone option creates a second copy of the same applet running in its own window.

- The Tag option displays the program's <APPLET> tag, along with the HTML for any <PARAM> tags that configure the applet.

Another option on the Applet pull-down menu is Info, which calls the getAppletInfo() and getParameterInfo() methods of the applet. A programmer can implement these methods to provide more information about the applet and the parameters that it can handle. The getAppletInfo() method should return a string that describes the applet. The getParameterInfo() method should return an array of string arrays that specify the name, type, and description of each parameter.

Listing C.1 contains an applet that demonstrates the use of these methods.

C

LISTING C.1 The Full Text of `AppInfo.java`

```
1: import java.awt.Graphics;
2:
3: public class AppInfo extends java.applet.Applet {
4:     String name, date;
5:     int version;
6:
7:     public String getAppletInfo() {
8:         String response = "This applet demonstrates the "
9:             + "use of the Applet's Info feature.";
10:        return response;
11:    }
12:
13:    public String[][] getParameterInfo() {
14:        String[] p1 = { "Name", "String", "Programmer's name" };
15:        String[] p2 = { "Date", "String", "Today's date" };
16:        String[] p3 = { "Version", "int", "Version number" };
17:        String[][] response = { p1, p2, p3 };
18:        return response;
19:    }
20:
21:    public void init() {
22:        name = getParameter("Name");
23:        date = getParameter("Date");
24:        String versText = getParameter("Version");
25:        if (versText != null)
26:            version = Integer.parseInt(versText);
28:    }
29:
30:    public void paint(Graphics screen) {
31:        screen.drawString("Name: " + name, 5, 50);
32:        screen.drawString("Date: " + date, 5, 100);
33:        screen.drawString("Version: " + version, 5, 150);
34:    }
35: }
```

The main function of this applet is to display the value of three parameters: Name, Date, and Version. The getAppletInfo() method returns the following string:

```
This applet demonstrates the use of the Applet's Info feature.
```

The getParameterInfo() method is a bit more complicated if you haven't worked with multidimensional arrays. The following things are taking place:

- Line 13 defines the return type of the method as a two-dimensional array of String objects.

- Line 14 creates an array of String objects with three elements: "Name", "String", and "Programmer's Name". These elements describe one of the parameters that can be defined for the AppInfo applet. They describe the name of the parameter (Name in this case), the type of data that the parameter should hold (a string), and a description of the parameter ("Programmer's Name"). The three-element array is stored in the p1 object.
- Lines 15–16 define two more String arrays for the Date and Version parameters.
- Line 17 uses the response object to store an array that contains three string arrays: p1, p2, and p3.
- Line 18 uses the response object as the method's return value.

Listing C.2 contains a Web page that can be used to load the AppInfo applet.

C

LISTING C.2   The Full Text of AppInfo.html

```
1: <applet code="AppInfo.class" height=200 width=170>
2: <param name="Name" value="Rogers Cadenhead">
3: <param name="Date" value="04/07/00">
4: <param name="Version" value="2">
5: </applet>
```

Figure C.2 shows the applet running with the applet viewer, and Figure C.3 is a screen capture of the dialog box that opens when the viewer's Info menu option is selected.

FIGURE C.2

The AppInfo *applet running in* appletviewer.

These features require a browser that makes this information available to users. The appletviewer handles this through the Info menu option, but browsers such as Internet Explorer do not offer anything like it at this time.

FIGURE C.3

*The Info dialog box of
the* AppInfo *applet.*

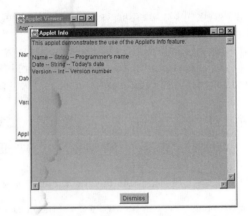

The javadoc Documentation Tool

javadoc, the Java documentation creator, takes a .java source code file or package name as input and generates detailed documentation in HTML format.

For javadoc to create full documentation for a program, a special type of comment statement must be used in the program's source code. Tutorial programs in this book use //, /*, and */ in source code to create *comments*—information for people who are trying to make sense of the program.

Java also has a more structured type of comment that can be read by the javadoc tool. This comment is used to describe program elements such as classes, variables, objects, and methods. It takes the following format:

```
/** A descriptive sentence or paragraph.
 * @tag1 Description of this tag.
 * @tag2 Description of this tag.
 */
```

A Java documentation comment should be placed immediately above the program element it is documenting and should succinctly explain what the program element is. For example, if the comment precedes a class statement, it should describe the purpose of the class.

In addition to the descriptive text, different items can be used to further document the program element. These items, called *tags,* are preceded by an @ sign and are followed by a space and a descriptive sentence or paragraph.

Listing C.3 contains a thoroughly documented version of the AppInfo applet called AppInfo2. The following tags are used in this program:

- @author—The program's author. This tag can be used only when documenting a class, and it will be ignored unless the -author option is used when javadoc is run.

- @version *text*—The program's version number. This also is restricted to class documentation, and it requires the -version option when you're running javadoc or the tag will be ignored.

- @return *text*—The variable or object returned by the method being documented.

- @serial *text*—A description of the data type and possible values for a variable or object that can be serialized. More information about serialization is available during Day 18, "Object Serialization and Reflection."

C

LISTING C.3   The Full Text of AppInfo2.java

```
 1: import java.awt.Graphics;
 2:
 3: /** This class creates displays the values of three parameters:
 4:    * Name, Date and Version.
 5:    * @author <a href="http://www.naviseek.com/java21">
        ➥Rogers Cadenhead</a>
 6:    * @version 2.0
 7:    */
 8: public class AppInfo2 extends java.applet.Applet {
 9:     /**
10:      * @serial The programmer's name.
11:      */
12:     String name;
13:     /**
14:      * @serial The current date.
15:      */
16:     String date;
17:     /**
18:      * @serial The program's version number.
19:      */
20:     int version;
21:
22:     /**
23:      * This method describes the applet for any browsing tool that
24:      * request information out the program.
25:      * @return A String describing the applet.
26:      */
27:     public String getAppletInfo() {
28:         String response = "This applet demonstrates the "
```

Listing C.3   continued

```
29:                      + "use of the Applet's Info feature.";
30:          return response;
31:     }
32:
33:     /**
34:      * This method describes the parameters that the applet can take
35:      * for any browsing tool that requests this information.
36:      * @return An array of String[] objects for each parameter.
37:      */
38:     public String[][] getParameterInfo() {
39:         String[] p1 = { "Name", "String", "Programmer's name" };
40:         String[] p2 = { "Date", "String", "Today's date" };
41:         String[] p3 = { "Version", "int", "Version number" };
42:         String[][] response = { p1, p2, p3 };
43:         return response;
44:     }
45:
46:     /**
47:      * This method is called when the applet is first initialized.
48:      */
49:     public void init() {
50:         name = getParameter("Name");
51:         date = getParameter("Date");
52:         String versText = getParameter("Version");
53:         if (versText != null)
54:             version = Integer.parseInt(versText);
55:     }
56:
57:     /**
58:      * This method is called when the applet's display window is
59:      * being repainted.
60:      */
61:     public void paint(Graphics screen) {
62:         screen.drawString("Name: " + name, 5, 50);
63:         screen.drawString("Date: " + date, 5, 100);
64:         screen.drawString("Version: " + version, 5, 150);
65:     }
66: }
```

The following command would be used to create HTML documentation from the source code file AppInfo2.java:

```
javadoc -author -version AppInfo2.java
```

The Java documentation tool will create several different Web pages in the same folder as AppInfo2.java. These pages will document the program in the same manner as Sun's official documentation for the Java language.

Tip

To see the official documentation for Java 2, SDK 1.3, and the Java class libraries, visit http://java.sun.com/products/JDK/1.3/docs/.

To see the documentation that javadoc has created for AppInfo2, load the newly created Web page index.html on your Web browser. Figure C.4 shows this page loaded with Internet Explorer 4.72.

FIGURE C.4

Java documentation for the AppInfo2 *program.*

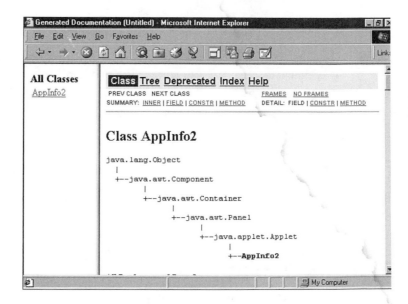

The javadoc tool produces extensively hyperlinked Web pages. Navigate through the pages to see where the information in your documentation comments and tags shows up.

If you're familiar with HTML programming, you can use HTML tags such as <A>, <TT>, and <B> within your documentation comments. Line 5 of the AppInfo2 program uses an <A> tag to turn the text "Rogers Cadenhead" into a hyperlink to this book's Web site.

The javadoc tool also can be used to document an entire package by specifying the package name as a command-line argument. HTML files will be created for each .java file in the package, along with an HTML file indexing the package.

If you would like the Java documentation to be produced in a different folder than the default, use the -d option followed by a space and the folder name.

The following command creates Java documentation for `AppInfo2` in a folder called `C:\JavaDocs\`:

```
javadoc -author -version -d C:\JavaDocs\ AppInfo2.java
```

The following list details the other tags you can use in Java documentation comments:

- `@deprecated` *text*—A note that this class, method, object, or variable has been deprecated. This causes the `javac` compiler to issue a deprecation warning when the feature is used in a program that's being compiled.

- `@exception` *class description*—Used with methods that throw exceptions, this tag documents the exception's class name and its description.

- `@param` *name description*—Used with methods, this tag documents the name of an argument and a description of the values the argument can hold.

- `@see` *class*—The name of another class, which will be turned into a hyperlink to the Java documentation of that class. This can be used without restriction in comments.

- `@see` *class#method*—The name of a method of another class, which will be used for a hyperlink directly to the documentation of that method. This is usable without restriction.

- `@since` *text*—A note describing when a method or feature was added to its class library.

The `jdb` Debugger

`jdb`, the Java debugger, is a sophisticated tool that helps you find and fix bugs in Java programs. You can also use it to better understand what is taking place behind the scenes in the Java interpreter as a program is running. It has a large number of features, including some that might be beyond the expertise of a Java programmer who is new to the language.

You don't need to use the debugger to debug Java programs. This is fairly obvious, especially if you've been creating your own Java programs as you read this book. After the Java compiler generates an error, the most common response is to load the source code into an editor, find the line cited in the error message, and try to spot the problem. This dreaded compile-curse-find-fix cycle is repeated until the program compiles without complaint.

After using this debugging method for a while, you might think that the debugger isn't necessary to the programming process because it's such a complicated tool to master.

This reasoning makes sense when you're fixing problems that cause compiler errors. Many of these problems are simple things such as a misplaced semicolon, unmatched { and } brackets, or the use of the wrong type of data as a method argument. However, when you start looking for logic errors—more subtle bugs that don't stop the program from compiling and running—a debugger is an invaluable tool.

The Java debugger has two features that are extremely useful when you're searching for a bug that can't be found by other means: single-step execution and breakpoints. *Single-step execution* pauses a Java program after every line of code is executed. *Breakpoints* are points where execution of the program will pause. Using the Java debugger, these breakpoints can be triggered by specific lines of code, method calls, or caught exceptions.

The Java debugger works by running a program using a version of the Java interpreter that it has complete control over.

Before you use the Java debugger, you should compile the program with the -g option, which causes extra information to be included in the class file. This information greatly aids in debugging. Also, you shouldn't use the -O option because its optimization techniques might produce a class file that does not directly correspond with the program's source code.

Debugging Applications

If you're debugging an application, the `jdb` tool can be run with a Java class as an argument. This is shown in the following:

```
jdb WriteBytes
```

This example runs the debugger with `WriteBytes.class`, an application that's available from the book's Web site at `http://www.java21days.com`. Visit the site and select the Appendix C page, and then save the files `WriteBytes.class` and `WriteBytes.java` in the same folder that you run the debugger from.

The `WriteBytes` application writes a series of bytes to disk to produce the file `pic.gif`.

The debugger loads this program but does not begin running it, displaying the following output:

```
Initializing jdb...
>
```

The debugger is controlled by typing commands at the > prompt.

To set a breakpoint in a program, the `stop in` or `stop at` commands are used. The `stop in` command sets a breakpoint at the first line of a specific method in a class. You specify the class and method name as an argument to the command, as in the following example:

```
stop in SellItem.SetPrice
```

This command sets a breakpoint at the first line of the `SetPrice` method. Note that no arguments or parentheses are needed after the method name.

The `stop at` command sets a breakpoint at a specific line number within a class. You specify the class and number as an argument to the command, as in the following example:

```
stop at WriteBytes:14
```

If you're trying this with the `WriteBytes` class, you'll see the following output after entering this command:

```
breakpoint set at WriteBytes:14
```

You can set as many breakpoints as desired within a class. To see the breakpoints that are currently set, use the `clear` command without any arguments. The `clear` command lists all current breakpoints by line number rather than method name, even if they were set using the `stop in` command.

By using `clear` with a class name and line number as an argument, you can remove a breakpoint. If the hypothetical `SellItem.SetPrice` method was located at line 215 of `SellItem`, you could clear this breakpoint with the following command:

```
clear SellItem:215
```

Within the debugger, you can begin executing a program with the `run` command. The following output shows what the debugger displays after you begin running the `WriteBytes` class:

```
run WriteBytes
running...
main[1]
Breakpoint hit: WriteBytes.main(WriteBytes:14)
```

After you have reached a breakpoint in the `WriteBytes` class, experiment with the following commands:

- `list`—At the point where execution stopped, this displays the source code of the line and several lines around it. This requires access to the `.java` file of the class where the breakpoint has been hit, so you must have `WriteBytes.java` in either the current folder or one of the folders in your `CLASSPATH`.

- `locals`—Lists the values for local variables that are currently in use or will soon be defined.
- `print` *text*—Displays the value of the variable, object, or array element specified by *text*.
- `step`—Executes the next line and stops again.
- `cont`—Continues running the program at the point it was halted.
- `!!`—Repeats the previous debugger command.

After trying out these commands within the application, you can resume running the program by clearing the breakpoint and using the `cont` command. Use the `exit` command to end the debugging session.

The `WriteBytes` application creates a file called `pic.gif`. You can verify that this file ran successfully by loading it with a Web browser or image editing software. You'll see a small letter *J* in black and white.

After you have finished debugging a program, you should remember to recompile it without the `-g` option.

Debugging Applets

You can't debug an applet by loading it using the `jdb` tool. Instead, use the `-debug` option of the `appletviewer`, as in the following example:

```
appletviewer -debug AppInfo.html
```

This will load the Java debugger, and when you use a command such as `run`, the `appletviewer` will begin running also. Try out this example to see how these tools interact with each other.

Before you use the `run` command to execute the applet, set a breakpoint in the program at the first line of the `getAppletInfo` method. Use the following command:

```
stop in AppInfo.getAppletInfo
```

After you begin running the applet, the breakpoint won't be hit until you cause the `getAppletInfo()` method to be called. This is accomplished by selecting Applet, Info from the `appletviewer`'s menu.

Advanced Debugging Commands

With the features you have learned about so far, you can use the debugger to stop execution of a program and learn more about what's taking place. This might be sufficient for many of your debugging tasks, but the debugger also offers many other commands. These include the following:

- up—Moves up the stack frame so that you can use `locals` and `print` to examine the program at the point before the current method was called.
- down—Moves down the stack frame to examine the program after the method call.

In a Java program, often there are places where a chain of methods is called. One method calls another method, which calls another method, and so on. At each point where a method is being called, Java keeps track of all the objects and variables within that scope by grouping them together. This grouping is called a *stack*, as if you were stacking these objects like a deck of cards. The various stacks in existence as a program runs are called the *stack frame*.

By using `up` and `down` along with commands such as `locals`, you can better understand how the code that calls a method interacts with that method.

You can also use the following commands within a debugging session:

- classes—Lists the classes currently loaded into memory.
- methods—Lists the methods of a class.
- memory—Lists the total memory and the amount that isn't currently in use.
- threads—Lists the threads that are executing.

The `threads` command numbers all the threads, which enables you to use the `suspend` command followed by that number to pause the thread, as in `suspend 1`. You can resume a thread by using the `resume` command followed by its number.

Another convenient way to set a breakpoint in a Java program is to use the `catch text` command, which pauses execution when the Exception class named by `text` is caught.

You can also cause an exception to be ignored by using the `ignore text` command with the Exception class named by `text`.

Using System Properties

One obscure feature of the SDK is that the command-line option `-D` can modify the performance of the Java class library.

If you have used other programming languages prior to learning Java, you might be familiar with environment variables, which provide information about the operating system in which a program is running. An example is the CLASSPATH setting, which indicates the folders in which the Java interpreter should look for a class file.

Because different operating systems have different names for their environment variables, they cannot be read directly by a Java program. Instead, Java includes a number of different system properties that are available on any platform with a Java implementation.

Some properties are used only to get information. The following system properties are among those that should be available on any Java implementation:

- `java.version`   The version number of the Java interpreter.
- `java.vendor`   A string identifying the vendor associated with the Java interpreter.
- `os.name`   The operating system in use.
- `os.version`   The version number of that operating system.

Other properties can affect how the Java class library performs when being used inside a Java program. An example of this is the `java2d.font.usePlatformFont` property. If this property has a value of `true`, a Java program will use the Java 1.1 style of font rendering rather than the system used in subsequent versions of the language. This property became useful with a beta version of Java 1.2 that had some bugs in how the `appletviewer` tool handled fonts.

A property can be set at the command line by using the `-D` option followed by the property name, an equal sign, and the new value of the property, as in this command:

```
java -Djava2d.font.usePlatformFont=true Auctioneer
```

The use of the system property in this example will cause the `Auctioneer` application to use 1.1-style fonts.

You also can create your own properties and read them using the `getProperty()` method of the `System` class, which is part of the `java.lang` package.

Listing C.4 contains the source code of a simple program that displays the value of a user-created property.

Listing C.4   The Full Text of `ItemProp.java`

```
1: class ItemProp {
2:     public static void main(String[] arguments) {
3:         String n = System.getProperty("item.name");
4:         System.out.println("The item is named " + n);
5:     }
6: }
```

If this program is run without setting the item.name property on the command line, the output is the following:

```
The item is named null
```

The item.name property can be set using the -D option, as in this command:

```
java -Ditem.name="Microsoft Bob" ItemProp
```

The output is the following:

```
The item is named Microsoft Bob
```

The -D option is used with the Java interpreter. To use it with the appletviewer as well, all you have to do differently is precede the -D with -J. The following command shows how this can be done:

```
appletviewer -J-Djava2d.font.usePlatformFont=true AuctionSite.html
```

This example causes appletviewer to use Java 1.1-style fonts with all applets on the Web page AuctionSite.html.

Summary

This appendix explores several features of the SDK that are increasingly helpful as you develop more experience with Java:

- Using the Java debugger with applets and applications
- Creating an optimized version of a compiled class
- Writing applet methods that provide information to a browser upon request
- Using the Java documentation creation tool to fully describe a class, its methods, and other aspects of the program

These SDK features weren't required during the 21 days of this book because of the relative simplicity of the tutorial programs. Although it can be complicated to develop a Swing application or to work with threads and streams for the first time, your biggest challenge lies ahead: integrating concepts like these into more sophisticated Java programs.

Tools such as javadoc and the debugger really come into their own on complex projects.

When a bug occurs because of how two classes interact with each other, or similar subtle logic errors creep into your code, a debugger is the best way to identify and repair the problems.

As you create an entire library of classes, javadoc can easily document these classes and show how they are interrelated.

Q&A

Q **The official Java documentation is filled with long paragraphs that describe classes and methods. How can these be produced using javadoc?**

A In the Java documentation creator, there's no limit to the length of a description. Although they're often as brief as a sentence or two, they can be longer if necessary. End the description with a period, immediately followed by a new line with a tag of some kind or the end of the comment.

Q **Do I have to document everything in my Java classes if I'm planning to use the javadoc tool?**

A The Java documentation creator will work fine no matter how many or how few comments you use. Deciding which elements of the program need to be documented is up to you. You probably should describe the class and all methods, variables, and objects that aren't hidden from other classes.

The javadoc tool will display a warning each time a serializable object or variable is defined in a program without a corresponding Java documentation comment.

C

INDEX

Symbols

2D graphics, 298, 301
  arcs, 307-309
    drawing, 306, 322
    filling, 307
  coordinate spaces,
    317-318
  coordinate system, 301
  copy/paste functions,
    310-311
  ellipses, 321
  Graphics2D objects, 171,
    299
  lines, 302, 321
  Map2D applet, 323-326
  ovals, 306
  polygons, 304, 322-323
  rectangles
    drawing, 302, 321
    filling, 303
    rounded corners, 303
  rendering attributes,
    318-320

& (ampersand), AND
  operators, 78
* (asterisk), 171, 395
[ ] (brackets), 108, 114
^ (caret), XOR operator, 78
/**...*/ comment notation,
  68
/*...*/ comment notation, 67
// comment notation, 67
{ } (curly braces), 61
> (greater than), 77
<= (greater than or equal
  to), 77
! (exclamation point), NOT
  operator, 78
!! command (jdb), 605
== (equal), 77, 102
= (equal sign), assignment
  operator, 62, 66
- (hyphen), decrement
  operator (—), 76
!= (inequality operator), 102
!= (not equal), 77
< (less than), 77

<= (less than or equal to),
  77
- (minus signs), 69
. (period), dot notation, 89
| (pipe character), OR
  operators, 78
+ (plus sign)
  concatenation operator
    (+), 81
  increment operator (++),
    76
; (semicolon), statement
  termination character, 60

A

abstract classes, 392-393
abstract methods, 392-393
abstract modifier, 393
access control, 383, 386-387
  accessor methods,
    387-388
  default access, 383

inheritance, 387
packages, 398
    default access, 399
    public access, 399
private access, 384-385
protected access, 385-386
public access, 385
accessing
    array elements, 110-111
    class methods, 389
    command-line prompts, 20
    databases, JDBC, 545
    elements
        Map interfaces, 565
        vector, 561
    MS-DOS, 572
    Notepad, 577
    variables
        class, 91, 389
        instance, 89
accessor methods, 387-388, 415
action events, event handling, 274-275
ActionListener event listener, 270, 275
actionPerformed() method, 271, 275, 499
ActiveX, 524
acyclic gradients, 318
add() method, 205, 561
addActionListener() method, 275
adding
    applets to Web pages, 174-176
    classes to packages, 398
    components to
        applets, 207
        containers, 197, 205-207
        panels, 251
        toolbars, 235

elements to vectors, 561
files
    to Java archives, 181
    JavaBeans, 539
    MIDI, 368
addItem() method, 218
addPoint() method, 304
adjustment events, event handling, 275-277
AdjustmentListener event listener, 270, 276-277
adjustmentValueChanged() method, 276
afterLast() method, 551
ALIGN attribute (<APPLET> tag), 177
aligning
    applets, 177
    components, 244-245
        border layouts, 249-250
        card layouts, 251-252
        flow layouts, 245, 247
        grid bag layouts, 253-264
        grid layouts, 247-249
        insets, 264
        panels, 251
    labels, 211
AllCapsDemo.java application, 463-464
allocating memory to objects, 88
ampersand (&), AND operators, 78
anchor constraint, 261
AND operators, 78
animated applets, 329
animated applications, pausing, 333
animating
    components, 331-335
    images, 349-352

animations
    controlling, 335
    creating
        with images, 346
        in Java, 330
        Pixel Pete, 346-356
APIs, 527-528
AppInfo.html, 597
AppInfo.java, 596
AppInfo2.java, 599-600
Apple Macintosh, 11
Applet class, 167
Applet menu options, 595
<APPLET> tag, 174-180
    ALIGN, 177
    ARCHIVE, 181
    CODE, 175, 179
    CODEBASE, 179
    HEIGHT, 175
    HSPACE, 178
    VSPACE, 178
    WIDTH, 175
applet windows, 169-171
applets, 11, 207-208. See also programs
    adding
        components, 207
        to Web pages, 174-176
    animated, 329
    Applet class, 167
    archival formats, JAR files, 180-181
    background color, setting, 316
    background windows, colors, 168
    creating, 167-172, 174
    debugging, 190, 605
    destroying, 170
    digital signatures, 434-437
        browser-specific, 437-438
        certificate authorities, 435
        certificates, 435

displaying on-screen, 170
downloading, 12
Every icon, 12
hostile, 165
HTML tags
    <APPLET>, 174-176,
        178-179

, 177
    <OBJECT>, 179-180
HTML markup, 177
initializing, 168
JApplet class, 167
Java
    choosing versions,
        165-167
    developing Java 2,
        185-187, 189
    running Java Plug-in,
        186-187
    troubleshooting, 166
limitations, 164-165
linking, 496-499
Map2D, 323-326
methods, 168
    getCodeBase(), 344
    getDocumentBase(),
        344
    run(), 349
NewWatch.html, 183-184
painting, 170
passing parameters to, 182
    getParameter() method,
        182
    null values, 182
    <PARAM> tag, 181
prohibited features, 434
running, 164
searching, 179
security, 164-167, 438-439
starting, 169
stopping, 169
testing, 175-176
threads, 336
triggering, 167

uploading to Web servers,
    176
versus applications, 164
Watch.java, 174
appletview browser, 595-597
**appletviewer browser,
595-597**
appletviewer tool, 165
**appletviewing browser,
594-597**
applications, 13, 143. *See
also* **programs**
    AllCapsDemo, 463-464
    animated, pausing, 333
    arguments
        handling, 145-146
        passing to, 144
    BufferDemo.java, 452-453
    Buttons.java, 206-207
    ChangeTitle.java, 273-274
    Checkers.java, 340-343
    ChooseTeam.java, 217,
        219
    constructing, 528
    CopyArrayWhile.java,
        125-126
    creating, 196-197
    DayCounter.java, 119-120
    debugging, 603-605
    DigitalClock.java, 337-339
    DOS Edit, 584
    ExitFrame.java, 204
    ExitWindow.java, 203
    Finger.java, 506-507
    Form.java, 213-214
    GetFile.java, 501-502
    Giftshop, 411
    HalfDollars, 111-113
    HalfLoop.java, 123
    Headlines.java, 333-334
    helper classes, 144
    HexRead.java, 425
    HTMLConverter, 187
    Icons.java, 209-210

Info (dialog box), 229-231
Inner.java, 413
JavaBeans, 538
Looper.java, 361-362
main() method, 143
Map.java, 299-300,
    308-309
Map2D.java, 324-325
MidiApplet.html, 370
MidiApplet.java, 371-373
multitasking, 335
NotePad, 584
ObjectFromDisk.java, 477
ObjectToDisk.java, 474
OutputPi.java, 489-490
Pete.java, 352-355
Pi.java, 488-489
PiRemote.java, 487
PlayMidi.java, 366-368
policy.txt, 492
Progress.java, 238-239
RAD (rapid application
    development), 538-539
RangeClass.java, 137
ReadBytes.java, 447
ReadPrimes.java, 456-457
ReadSource.java, 460
RMI, 487
running, 164, 591
security policies, 438-439
SeeMethods.java, 482
SelectItem.java, 279
SimpleFrame.java, 200
SimpleWindow.java, 201
Slider.java, 233
SoLong.html, 313
SoLong.java, 313
Storefront, 407-408, 410
SumAverage.java, 145-146
Swing, 198
SwingColorTest, 282-292
SwingColorText.java,
    292-294

threaded
    clock, 337, 339
    writing, 336-337
Toolbar.java, 236
TriviaServer client/server,
    508
    designing, 510
    running, 518-519
    server implementation,
        509-515
TriviaServer.java, 515-518
versus applets, 164
VolcanoRobot.java, 45-46,
    135
WellAdjusted.java,
    276-277
WordPad, 584
WriteBytes.java, 449
Arc2D.Float class, 322
architecture, RMI (Remote
Method Invocation),
485-487
archival formats, JAR,
180-181
ARCHIVE attribute
(<APPLET> tag), 181
archives, 180
arcs
    drawing
        Arc2D.Float class, 322
        drawArc() method, 306
    example, 307-309
    filling, 307
ArgStream() method, 453
arguments
    applications
        handling in, 145-146
        passing to, 144
    command line, 590
    grouping, 145
    objects, 86
    passing to methods,
        140-141
    quotation marks in, 145

arithmetic, string, 80-81
arithmetic operators, 72-74
arranging. See aligning
array elements, 113
ArrayIndexOutofBounds
    exception, 420
arrays, 17, 107-108, 555
    boundaries, 110
    creating, 111
    declaring variables, 108
    elements
        accessing, 110-111
        changing, 111, 113
        data types, 110
    HalfDollars.java
        application, 111-112
    Image objects, 347
    implementing, 108
    limitations, 556
    modifying, 111
    multidimensional, 113
    objects, 109-110
    primitive types, 479-480
    references, 111
    subscripts, 110
    troubleshooting, 111
ASCII text, 26
assigning
    constraints to components,
        257
    variable values, 62, 66, 83
assignment operators, 62,
    74-75
associating
    components with event
        listeners, 270-271
    filters, 445
    icons with file types,
        587-588
associations
    file type icons, 587-588
    files, 585-587
asterisk (*), 171, 395

attributes, 181. See also
    parameters
    <APPLET> tag
        ALIGN, 177
        ARCHIVE, 181
        CODE, 175, 179
        CODEBASE, 179
        HEIGHT, 175
        HSPACE, 178
        VSPACE, 178
        WIDTH, 175
    classes, 40-41
    objects, 40
    <PARAM> tag, 182
audio, 360-362
    exceptions, 364-365
    files
        MIDI, 363-369
        modifying, 369-371,
            373-375
    loading, 360
    looping, 360
    playing, 360
    retrieving, 360-362
    terminating, 361, 371
    troubleshooting, 361
@author tag (javadoc), 599
AUTOEXEC.BAT, 577
avoiding exceptions, 433
AWT, 195

B

background color, setting,
316
background windows
(applets), 168
Bad command or file name
error, 577
base-8 numbering system,
69
base-16 numbering system,
69

BDK (Bean Development Kit), 528-529
downloading, 529-530
features, 530
BeanBox, 531-532
composition window, 532
Method Tracer window, 532
Properties window, 533
Toolbox window, 532
BeanInfo class, 534
beans. *See* JavaBeans
beforeFirst() method, 551
behavior
classes, 41, 47-54
shared, 53
bits, 557-560
BitSet class, 557-560
blank images, loading, 355
block statements, 61
BLOCK_DECREMENT return value (getAdjustmentType() method), 276
BLOCK_INCREMENT return value (getAdjustmentType() method), 276
blocks, 114-115
try and catch, 422
try...catch, 423-424
Boolean data type, 65
Boolean literals, 69-70
Boolean values, 65
border layout manager, 249-250
BorderLayout() method, 249
Borland JBuilder, 15
boundaries, arrays, 110
**
 tag, 177**
brackets ([ ]), 108, 114
break keyword, 127
breaking loops, 127

breakpoints
deleting, 604
listing, 604
searching, 603
setting, 604
bridges, JDBC-ODBC bridge, 546-547
browsers
appletviewer, 594-597
browser-specific signatures, 437-438
Java Plug-in plug-in, 166, 185-189
support, 185
BufferDemo.java application, 452-453
buffered streams, 451-454
BufferedInputStream() method, 451
BufferedOutputStream() method, 451
BufferedReader() method, 459
BufferedWriter() method, 461
buffers, 451
bugs, searching, 603
buildConstraints() method, 255-256, 258-259
buildRect() method, 148
built-in fonts, 311
ButtonApplet.java, 207
ButtonGroup object, 217
buttons
event handling
action events, 275
item events, 278-280
modifying labels, 535
Buttons.java, 206-207
byte data type, 64
byte filters, 450
byte streams, 444-446, 470. *See also* **streams**
file input streams, 446-448
file output streams, 448-450

bytecode (machine codes), 18, 19
bytes, writing multiple, 449

C

c option (jar command), 180
Cadenhead, Rogers, 17
calling
constructor methods, 151
constructors from another constructor, 152
methods, 41, 92-93
class methods, 95
constructors, 157
finalize(), 158
of objects, 94
start(), 595
stop(), 595
in superclasses, 156
calls method, nesting, 93-94
capabilities, Java, 11
capacity of vectors, 560, 563
capacity() method, 563
card layout manager, 251-252
CardLayout() method, 252
caret (^), XOR operator, 78
case-sensitivity, 63
casting, 97. *See also* **converting**
Boolean values, 98
datatypes, 97-99
destinations, 98
objects, 97-98
to classes, 99-100
Graphics2D, 171, 299
to interfaces, 100, 403-404
primitive types, 97-99
sources, 98
superclasses, 99
variables, 97-99

casts, explicit, 98-99
catch blocks, Exception classes in, 424
catch clauses, empty, 434
catching exceptions, 420, 422
    finally statement, 424-426
    try...catch blocks, 423-424
cd command, 29
CD command (MS-DOS), 573-574
cell padding, 264
certificate authorities, 435
certificates (digital signatures), 435
ChangeTitle application, 273-274
ChangeTitle.java application, 273-274
changing array elements, 111, 113
char data type, 65
character literals. *See also* Unicode character set, 70-71
character sets, Unicode, 63, 70
character streams, 458, 470. *See also* streams
    reading text files, 458-460
    writing text files, 461-462
charAt() method, 93
charWidth() method, 313
check boxes, 216-218
    event handling
        action events, 275
        item events, 278, 280
    exclusive, 216
    nonexclusive, 216
Checkers.java application, 340-343
checkTemperature() method, 47
choice lists, 218

ChooseTeam.java, 217, 219
choosing
    Java versions, 165-167
    text editors, 583-585
circles, drawing, 306
Claris Home Page, 174
.class extensions, 591
class keyword, 134
Class not found error, 397, 579-581
class.dat file
    creating, 448
classes, 133, 393, 508. *See also* packages
    abstract, 392-393
    adding to packages, 398
    Applet, 167
    Arc2D.Float, 322
    attributes, 40-41
    BeanInfo, 534
    behavior, 41, 47-54
    BitSet, 557-560
    CLASSPATH variable, 397
    Color, 314
    ColorSpace, 314
    constants, 66-67
    Constructor, 480
    CountInstances, 389-390
    creating, 42-44, 478-480
    defining, 37-38, 134
    definition of, 54
    Dictionary, 557, 566
    Dimension, 198
    efficiency, increasing, 391
    Ellipse2D.Float, 321
    Error, 420
    exceptions, 420-424, 431
    Field, 480
    files, specifying, 592
    FilterInputStream, 450
    FilterOutputStream, 450
    final, 391-392
    final classes, 392

FlowLayout, 244-245
FontMetrics, 312
functionality, 47
Graphics, 298
GridBagConstraints, 260
grouping, 53-54
Hashtable, 557, 566-568
helper classes, 144
hierarchies, 48-51
    identifying, 394
Image, 343
importing, 171, 395
inheritance, 51-52
    multiple, 53, 400
    overview, 49
    single, 53, 400
inner classes, 413-414
InputStream, 446
inspecting, 478-484
instances of, 39
IOException, 421
JApplet, 167, 344
Java 2 Class Library, 39
javax.sound.midi, 363
javax.sound.sampled, 363
javax.swing.JButton, 39
javax.swing.JComponent, 208
JCheckBox, 216
JComboBox, 218
JOptionPane, 225-229
JProgressBar, 237-240
JRadioButton, 216
JScrollPane, 233-235
JSlider, 232-233
JToolBar, 235-237
Line2D.Float, 321
loading multiple, 171
Method, 480
methods, 41, 94-95, 141
    accessing, 389
    availability, 142
    calling, 95
    defining, 142

main(), 44-45
Thread.sleep(), 333
Modifier, 480
modifying, 336
MyRect, 147-150
MyRect2, 153-154
name conflicts, 396
NamedPoint, 157
Object, 48
object-oriented program-
ming, 38, 47-48
ObjectInputStream,
475-477
ObjectOutputStream,
472-473
objects
casting to, 99-100
determining, 103
organization, 47-54, 382,
393
packages, 53-54, 592
PassByReference, 140-141
permissions, 435
PrintClass, 154-155
protecting, 394
Random(), 88
reflection, 478, 482-484
ScrollPaneConstants, 214
Socket, 504
SocketImpl, 508
Stack, 557, 563-565
StringTokenizer, 87
as subclasses, 48
subclasses, 47-49, 55
superclasses, 47, 55
indicating, 134
modifying, 49
Swing, 195
SwingConstants, 211, 232
Thread, 329, 336
Throwable, 420
Toolkit, 343
top-level, 413-415
types, 65

UIManager. *See* Swing
utility, 155
variables, 40, 55, 61, 89,
135
accessing, 389
class variables, 135
defining, 63, 91
instance variables,
134-135
troubleshooting, 92
values, 63, 91
versus instance
variables, 91
Vector, 557, 560-563
versus interfaces, 400-401
WindowAdapter, 203
wrapper classes, 142
**classes (object-oriented
programming), 37**
classes command (jdb), 606
classesRectangle.Float, 321
**CLASSPATH command
(MS-DOS), 579-580**
**CLASSPATH variable, 25,
397**
clauses, catch, 434
cleanup code, executing, 425
clear command (jdb), 604
clear() method, 567
clearing windows, 310
clearRect() method, 310
client-side sockets
closing, 505
instantiating, 504
opening, 504
**clients, TriviaServer
application, 518-519**
**clock, threaded application,
337, 339**
**Clone option (Applet menu),
595**
close() method, 445
closePath() method, 323

closing
ODBC data source
connections, 551
socket connections, 505
streams, 445
CMYK color system, 314
CoalTotals.java, 552
code
cleanup, 425
Java, complexity, 433
**CODE attribute
(<APPLET> tag), 175, 179**
code signing, 438. *See also*
digital signatures
**CODEBASE attribute
(<APPLET> tag), 179**
codes
machine. *See* machine
codes
source. *See* source code
collection, garbage, 89
Color class, 314
color spaces, 314
colors
background colors, 316
background windows,
applets, 168
CMYK color system, 314
dithering, 315
finding current color, 317
as rendering attribute, 318
setting drawing colors,
315-316
sRGB color system, 314
ColorSpace class, 314
**com.sun.java.swing package
UIManager class, 224**
combining
layout managers, 250-251
nested methods, 94
combo boxes, 218-219
action events, 275
item events, 278, 280

command line, 590. *See also*
MS-DOS Prompt
  arguments, 590
  options, 590-591
command-line interfaces,
571, 573-576
command-line programs, 19
command-line prompts,
  accessing, 20
command-line tools, javac,
29
commands
  appletviewer, 595
  arguments, 590
  File menu, MakeApplet,
    537
  jar, 180
  java, 46
  jdb (debugger)
    !!, 605
    classes, 606
    clear, 604
    cont, 605
    down, 606
    exit, 605
    ignore, 606
    list, 604
    locals, 605
    memory, 606
    methods, 606
    print, 605
    run, 604
    step, 605
    stop at, 604
    stop in, 604
    suspend, 606
    threads, 606
    up, 606
  MS-DOS, 26
    cd, 29, 573-574
    CLASSPATH, 579-580
    MD, 574
    PATH, 577-578
    SET CLASSPATH=,
      579

SDK 1.3, 590
Start menu
  Find, 578
  Programs, MS-DOS
    Prompt, 20
  Run, 21
  Settings, Control Panel,
    ODBC Data Sources,
    546
comments, 67
  notation, 68
    /**...*/, 68
    /*...*/, 67
    //, 67
    computer-readable, 68
  source code, 598
commercial development
tools, 15
comparing
  instances, 102
  objects, 101-103
comparison operators, 77
compilation errors, 110
compilers, 19, 592-594
compiling
  files, 593
  Java programs, 18, 28-31
  programs, 571, 579
  troubleshooting, 579
complexity, code (Java), 433
complications, multiple
  interfaces, 402-403
components, 208-209, 524
  ActiveX, 524
  adding to
    applets, 207
    containers, 197,
      205-207
    panels, 251
    toolbars, 235
  advantages, 524
  aligning, 244-245
    border layouts,
      249-250
    card layouts, 251-252

flow layouts, 245, 247
grid bag layouts,
  253-262, 264
grid layouts, 247-249
insets, 264
panels, 251
animating, 331-333, 335
associating with event
  listeners, 270-271
check boxes, 216-218
combo boxes, 218-219
constraints
  anchor, 261
  assigning, 257
  fill, 260-261
  gridheight, 256
  gridwidth, 256
  gridx, 256
  gridy, 256
  setting, 255
  weightx, 258
  weighty, 258
creating, 204-205
cross-platform issues,
  524-525
dialog boxes, 225
  confirm, 225-226
  Info sample
    application, 229, 231
  input, 226-227
  message, 227-228
  option, 228-229
disabled, 208
displaying, 208
drop-down lists, 218-219
getImage() method, 343
grid bag layout manager,
  arranging, 260
hiding, 208
icons, 209-210
JavaBeans, 525-527
  architecture, 525
  BDK (Bean
    Development Kit),
    528-530

BeanBox, 531-533
class discovery
    mechanism, 525
compared to Java,
    526-527
design-time issues, 526
distributed computing
    support, 526
event-handling API,
    528
ExplicitButton, 535
interactions between
    beans, 535-537
introspection API, 528
persistence, 525
persistent API, 528
placing, 532-533
portability, 525
programs, creating,
    537-538
properties, 533-534
serialization, 525
user interface/merging
    API, 527
Web site, 528, 539
labels, 210-211
manipulating, 528
methods
    createImage(), 343
    drawImage(), 345
    getImage(), 355
    paintComponent(), 345
    repaint(), 330
    scroll(), 335
    stop(), 339
modifying, 528
nonvisual, 527
painting, 330-331
progress bars, 237-238
Progress.java sample
    application, 238-240
radio buttons, 216-218
repaint() method, delays,
    331

repainting, 330-331
resizing, 209
scroll panes, 233
    creating, 234
    scrollbars, 234-235
    sizing, 234
scrollbars, 214-215
scrolling panes, 214-215
SDK 1.3, 23
sliders, 232-233
Swing, 196-197
text areas, 212-214
text fields, 211-212
toolbars, 235
    dockable toolbars,
        235-237
    orientation, 235
user-interface manager,
    224-225
windows, frames, 198
composition window
    (Beanbox), 532
compound statements. See
    blocks
computer-readable
    comment notation, 68
concatenating strings, 80-81
concatenation operator (+),
    81
conditional operators,
    128-129
    if, 115-116
    switch, 117-118
conditionals, 115-117, 121
configuring
    JDBC (Java Database
        Connectivity) drivers,
        553
    scrollbars, 214
    SDK 1.3, 24-25, 577-581
        troubleshooting, 22
        for Windows 2000, 25
        for Windows 95, 24-25

for Windows 98, 24-25
for Windows NT, 25
ConfirmDialog dialog box,
    225-226
conflicts, names, 393
connections, telnet, 519
consistency checking
    (exceptions), 421-422
constant local variables, 66
constant variables. See final
    variables
constants, 66-67
constraints
    anchor, 261
    assigning to components,
        257
    fill, 260-261
    gridheight, 256
    gridwidth, 256
    gridx, 256
    gridy, 256
    setting, buildConstraints()
        method, 255
    weightx, 258
    weighty, 258
constructing applications,
    528
Constructor class, 480
constructor methods,
    150-151, 154
    calling, 151-152, 157
    naming, 151
    overloading, 152-153
    overriding, 156-158
constructors, 86-88
    Dimension(), 198
    exception classes, 431
    JCheckBox(), 216
    JComboBox(), 218
    JFrame(), 198
    methods
        isSelected(), 216
        JScrollBar(), 215

setSelected(), 216
SimpleFrame(), 200
URL(), 496
cont command (jdb), 605
containers
applets, 207-208
components, adding, 197,
205-207
content panes, 205
panels, 205
windows, 197
contains() method, 562, 567
containsKey() method, 567
content panes (containers),
205
contents, labels, 211
continue keyword, 127
controlling
access. *See* access control
animation with threads,
335
conventions, naming, 397
converting, 97. *See also*
casting
objects, 97-98
primitive types, 97-98
primitive types and
objects, 100
primitive types to objects,
101
between sRGB and HSB,
287-290
source code, 592
text to uppercase, 463-464
coordinate spaces
(graphics), 317-318
coordinate system
(graphics), 301
coordinates
graphics, specifying, 304
images, 345
strings, 330
copyArea() method, 310
CopyArrayWhile.java,
125-126

CopyArrayWhile.java
application, 125
CountInstances class,
389-390
createImage() method, 343
createStatement() method,
550
creating
animation
with images, 346
in Java, 330
applets, 167-172, 174
applications, 196-197, 487
arrays, 109-111
class.dat files, 448
classes, 42-44, 478-480,
592
components, 197, 204-205
drawing surfaces,
298-299, 301
exceptions, 431
file associations, 585
folders in MS-DOS,
574-575
grids, 255-257
instances of classes, 39
interfaces, 197-199,
404-405
Java applications, 143-144
JavaBeans programs,
537-538
labels, 211
layout managers, 244, 253
layouts, 253
methods
finalizer, 158
overloaded, 147-148
objects, 85, 87
arguments, 86
Font, 311
Image, 343
ImageIcon, 209
MediaTracker, 355-356
with new operator,
86-88

String, 43
StringTokenizer, 87-88
URL, 496
online storefronts,
407-413
output streams, 472
source files, 26-31
streams, 444
threads, 336
variables, 61
vectors, 560
windows, 200
Cringely, Robert X., 9
cross-platform languages,
11
curly braces ({}), 61
current objects, references,
138
custom packages
access control, 398-399
adding classes, 398
folder structure, 398
naming, 397-398
cyclic gradients, 318

D

data, storing, 451
data sources (ODBC),
connections
closing, 551
naming, 547
opening, 547-551, 553
data streams, 454
creating, 454
reading, 454-455
ReadPrimes, 456-457
WritePrimes, 455-456
data structures, 543-544,
555-556
arrays, 555-556
bits, 557-560

dictionaries, 557, 565
Enumeration interface, 556
hash tables, 557, 566-568
Iterator interface, 556-558
Java, 556
key-mapped, 565-566
stacks, 557, 563-565
  adding elements, 564
  logical organization, 563
  popping off elements, 564
  searching, 565
vectors, 557, 560-563
  accessing, 561
  adding elements, 561
  capacity, 560, 563
  changing elements, 562
  creating, 560
  removing elements, 562
  size, 560, 563
data types, 64-65
Boolean, 65
char, 65
double, 64
float, 64
integers, 64
primitive, 64-65
databases
JDBC (Java Database Connectivity), 544-545
  accessing, 545
  drivers, 545-546, 553-554
  JDBC-ODBC bridge, 546-547
  ODBC data source connections, 547-553
navigating records, 551
queries, 544
DataInputStream() method, 454

DataOutputStream() method, 454
datatypes, 104
casting, 97-99
converting to objects, 101
DayCounter.java application, 119
deallocating memory, 89
debugger (jdb) commands, 602-606
!!, 605
classes, 606
clear, 604
cont, 605
down, 606
exit, 605
ignore, 606
list, 604
locals, 605
memory, 606
methods, 606
print, 605
run, 604
step, 605
stop at, 604
stop in, 604
suspend, 606
threads, 606
up, 606
debugging
applets, 190, 605
applications, 603-605
programs, 585, 602
declarations
import, 395-396
package, 384, 398
declaring
array variables, 108
arrays of arrays, 113
constants, 66-67
interfaces, 401, 404-405
methods, buildRect(), 148
variables, 61-62

decrement operator (—), 75-76
decrementing variables, 76
default access, 383
defining
attributes, 40
class variables, 63
classes, 37-38, 134
  as subclasses, 48
  top-level, 415
hierarchies, 392
methods, 136
  class methods, 142
  parameter lists, 136
  this keyword, 138
shared values, 66
subpanels, 285-287
variables
  class variables, 91
  instance variables, 134-135
delete() method, 462
deleteOnExit() method, 462
deleting
breakpoints, 604
file associations, 586-587
files, 462
vector elements, 562
Demos component (SDK 1.3), 23
@deprecated tag (javadoc), 602
–deprecation option (javac), 593
designing
class hierarchies, 50-51
grids, 254-255
socket application, 509
socket client/server application, 510
Swing projects layout, 283-285
destinations (casting), 98
destroy() method, 170

destroying applets, 170
determining classes of
  objects, 103
developing
  applets, Java 2, 185-187,
    189
  frameworks, 199-200, 202
  Java programs, 19
development history of
  Java, 13-14
development kits, 15
development tools, selecting,
  19-20
dialog boxes, 225
  confirm dialog boxes,
    225-226
  ConfirmDialog, 225
  File Type, 586-587
  Info sample application,
    229, 231
  input, 226-227
  InputDialog, 225
  message, 227-228
  MessageDialog, 225
  ODBC dBase Driver
    Setup, 549
  option, 228-229
  OptionDialog, 225
Dictionary class, 557, 566
digital signatures, 434-437
  browser-specific, 437-438
  certificates, 435
DigitalClock.java
  application, 337-339
Dimension class, 198
Dimension() constructor,
  198
disabled components, 208
disappearing images, 355
displaying
  applets, 170
  components, 208
  errors, 29
  frames, 198

distributed computing,
  JavaBeans support for,
  526
dithering, 315
division operators, 73
do...while loops, 126
dockable toolbars, 235-237
documentation tools
  (javadoc), 598-602
documents, HTML, 594
DOS Edit, 584
DOS for Dummies, 573
DOS text, 26
dot notation, 89, 92
double data type, 64
down command (jdb), 606
downloading
  applets, 12
  BDK (Bean Development
    Kit), 529-530
  SDK 1.3, 20, 590
drawArc() method, 306
drawImage() method, 345
drawing
  arcs, 306-309, 322
  circles, 306
  coordinate spaces,
    317-318
  coordinate system, 301
  images, 344-345
  lines, 302, 321
  ovals, 306, 321
  polygons, 304, 322-323
  rectangles, 302-303, 321
  rendering attributes, 318
    color, 318
    drawing strokes, 320
    fill patterns, 318-320
  text, 299-301
drawing colors, setting,
  315-316
drawing surfaces, creating,
  298-299, 301
drawLine() method, 302

drawOval() method, 306
drawPolygon() method,
  304-305
drawRect() method, 302
drawRoundRect() method,
  303
drawString() method, 299,
  312
drivers
  JDBC (Java Database
    Connectivity), 545-546,
    553-554
drop-down lists, 218-219
duplicating variables, 140

E

Edit File Type window, 588
editing. See modifying
editors (text). See text
  editors
efficiency, classes, 391
elements
  array, 110-113
  Map interfaces, accessing,
    565
  stack, 564-565
  vectors, 561-562
Ellipse2D.Float class, 321
ellipses. See ovals
Ellsworth, Henry, 26
else keyword, 115
empty catch clauses, 434
empty statements, 122
enabling classes, 88
encapsulating objects, 385
encapsulation, 383, 534
end-of-file exception
  (EOFException), 455
end-of-line characters, 460,
  462

endcap styles (drawing strokes), 320
enumerating linked lists, 407, 413
Enumeration interface, 556
environment variables, 606
EOFException (end-of-file exception), 455
EOFException exception, 420
equal sign (=)
    assignment operator, 62, 66
    equality operator (==), 102
equal symbol (==), 77
equality operator (==), 102
equals() method, 102, 568
Error class, 420
error-handling, 418-419, 427
errors, 417, 439. *See also* **exceptions**
    Bad command or file name, 577
    class not found, 397, 579-581
    compilation, 110, 434
    displaying, 29
    Error class, 420
    error-handling, traditional method, 418-419
    Exception class, 420
    managing. *See* error-handling
    NoClassDef, 579
    troubleshooting fatal, 422
escape codes, 70
establishing
    interfaces, 529
    security, 435
evaluating dot notation, 89
event listeners, 269
    ActionListener, 270, 275
    AdjustmentListener, 270, 276-277

    associating components with, 270-271
    FocusListener, 270, 278
    importing, 270
    ItemListener, 270, 278
    KeyListener, 270, 280
    MouseListener, 270, 280
    MouseMotionListener, 270, 281
    WindowListener, 270
event-handling, 202, 269
    action events, 274-275
    adjustment events, 275-277
    ChangeTitle.java application, 273-274
    event listeners
        ActionListener, 270
        AdjustmentListener, 270
        associating components with, 270-271
        FocusListener, 270
        importing, 270
        ItemListener, 270
        KeyListener, 270
        MouseListener, 270
        MouseMotionListener, 270
        WindowListener, 270
    events
        focus, 278
        item, 278-279
        key, 280
        mouse, 280-281
        mouse-movement, 281
    JavaBeans, 528
    methods, 271
        actionPerformed(), 271
        getSource(), 272
        instanceof keyword, 272
    SwingColorTest, 282-294

    WellAdjusted application, 276-277
    window events, 282
Every Icon applet Web site, 12
Exception class, 420-421, 424
exception classes, constructors, 431
@exception tag (javadoc), 602
exceptions, 417, 421. *See also* **errors**
    ArrayIndexOutofBounds, 420
    audio, 364-365
    avoiding, 433
    catching, 420, 422
        finally statement, 424-426
        try and catch blocks, 422
        try...catch blocks, 423-424
    class hierarchy, 420
    classes, 423
    compiler errors, 434
    consistency checking, 421-422
    creating, 431
    EOFException (end-of-file exception), 420, 455
    Error class, 420
    Exception class, 420-421
    floating, 432
    handling nested handlers, 431-432
    hierarchy, 432
    indicating potential, 427
    inheritance, 431
    InvalidMidiDataException, 365
    IOException, 421, 475
    limitations, 433

MalformedURLException, 421

managing. *See* error-handling

methods, 427

MidiUnavailableException, 364

multiple, 433

NullPointerException, 365, 420

overview, 439

passing, 428-429

runtime, 420

StreamCorruption Exception, 475

Throwable class, 420

throwing, 420, 426-427, 430-431

  explicit exceptions, 428

  implicit exceptions, 428

  inheritance issues, 429-430

  throws keyword, 427-428

when to use, 432-433

exclamation point (!), NOT operator, 78

exclusive check boxes, 216

exclusive radio buttons, 216

executeQuery() method, 550

executing

bytecode, 19

cleanup code, 425

exists() method, 462

exit command (jdb), 605

ExitFrame.java, 204

exiting

frames, 199

loops, 127

windows, 202-204

ExitWindow.java application, 203

explicit casts, 98-99

explicit exceptions, 428

ExplicitButton Java Beans, 535

exponential notation, literals, 69

expressions, 60, 72

dot notation, 89

grouping, 79

improving readability, 80

return values, 60, 72

extending interfaces, 406

extends keyword, 134, 406

extensions (.class), 591

F

f option (jar command), 180

false value (Boolean), 69

fatal errors, troubleshooting, 422

features, prohibited in applets, 434

Field class, 480

file input streams

creating, 446

reading, 446-448

File menu commands, MakeApplet, 537

File objects, 462

file output streams

creating, 448

writing to, 449-450

File Types dialog box, 586-587

File() method, 462

FileInputStream() method, 446

FileOutputStream() method, 448-449

FileReader() method, 458

files

adding to Java archives, 181

associations, 585-587

audio, modifying, 369-371, 373-375

compiling, 593

deleting, 462

File objects, 462

file type icons, 587-588

JAR formats, 180-181

HTML, 175

installation (SDK 1.3), 21

renaming, 462

returning size of, 462

saving unformatted, 584

FileWriter() method, 461

fill constraint, 260-261

fillArc() method, 306

fillOval() method, 306

fillPolygon() method, 304-305

fillRect() method, 302

fillRoundRect() method, 303

fills

arcs, 307

Java2D, 318-320

rectangles, 303

filtering streams, 445, 450

FilterInputStream class, 450

FilterOutputStream class, 450

filters, associating, 445

final classes, 391-392

final keyword, 66

final methods, 391-392

final modifier, 390

final variables, 391

finalize() method, 158

calling, 158

versus destroy() method, 170

finalizer methods, 158

finally statement, 424-426

Find command (Start menu), 578
Finger.java application, 506-507
first() method, 551
flags, 557-560
float data type, 64
floating exceptions, 432
floating-point numbers, 64, 69
flow layout manager, 245-247
FlowLayout class, 244-245
flowLayout() method, 245-247
focus, object-oriented programming, 36
focus events, event handling, 278
focusGained() method, 278
FocusListener event listener, 270, 278
focusLost() method, 278
folder structure (packages), 398
folders
    creating, 463
    deleting, 462
    in MS-DOS, 573-575
Font objects, creating, 311-312
Font styles, selecting, 312
Font() method, 312
FontMetrics class, 312-313
fonts
    built-in, 311
    Font objects, creating, 311-312
    returning information about, 312-314
    setting, 312
for loops, 121-124
    empty statements, 122
    troubleshooting, 123

Form.java, 213-214
format commands (SDK 1.3), 590
forms, submitting
    GET method, 520
    POST method, 521
forName() method, 479
forward slash (/), comment notation, 67
frames, 197
    displaying, 198
    exiting, 199
    hiding, 198
    locations, 199
    sizing, 198
    user interfaces, 200
    visible, 198
frameworks, developing, 199-200, 202
functionality, classes, 47
functions (tools), modifying, 590
functions. See methods
future of Java, 15

G

–g option (debugger), 603
GameFinder Web site, 506
Gamelan Web site, 539
games, Iceblox, 346
garbage collection, 89
general utility methods, 94
GeneralPath objects, 323
GET method, 520
get() method, 561
getActionCommand() method, 275
getAdjustmentType() method, 276
getAppletInfo() method, 595-596

getAudioClip() method, 360
getClass() method, 103
getClickCount() method, 281
getCodeBase() method, 344
getColor() method, 317
getConnection() method, 549-550
getConstructors() method, 481
getCrossPlatformLookAndFeelClassName() method, 224
getDate() method, 550
getDefaultToolkit() method, 343
getDocumentBase() method, 344
getDouble() method, 550
GetFile sample application
    BufferedReader object, 503
    error handling, 503
    getInputStream() method, 503
    readLine() method, 503
    source code listing, 501
GetFile.java application, 501-502
getFloat() method, 550
getFontMetrics() method, 312
getHeight() method, 313
getImage() method, 343, 355
getInputStream() method, 500
getInsets() method, 264
getInt() method, 551
getItemAt() method, 218
getItemCount() method, 218
getKeyChar() method, 280
getLong() method, 551
getMessage() method, 423
getMicrosecondLength() method, 368

getMicrosecondPosition() method, 369
getModifiers() method, 481
getName() method, 479
getNumberOfFiles() method, 238
getParameter() method, 182
getParameterInfo() method, 595
getParameterTypes() method, 481
getPoint() method, 281
getReturnType() method, 481
getSelectedItem() method, 219
getSelectedIndex() method, 219
getSequencer() method, 364
getSize() method, 209
getSource() method, 272, 274
getStateChange() method, 278
getString() method, 551
getSystemLookAndFeelClass Name() method, 224-225
getX() method, 281
getY() method, 281
Giftshop application, 411
global variables, 61
goals, Java, 18
Google Web site, 368
Gookin, Dan, 573
Gosling, James, 13
gradient fills, 318
graphical Swing applications, 198
graphics, 297-298. *See also*
AWT
  arcs, 306-309, 322
  coordinate spaces, 317-318
  coordinate system, 301

coordinates, specifying, 304
copy/paste functions, 310-311
ellipses, 321
Graphics objects, 299
Graphics2D objects, 171, 299
icons. *See* icons
lines, 302, 321
Map2D example, 323-326
ovals, 306
polygons, 304, 322-323
rectangles, 302-303, 321
rendering attributes, 318
  color, 318
  drawing strokes, 320
  fill patterns, 318-320
text, drawing, 299, 301
Graphics class, 298
graphics operations, Java 2D, 100
Graphics2D objects, casting, 171, 299
greater than or equal to symbol (=>), 77
greater than symbol (>), 77
Green project, 13
grid bag layout manager
  arranging components, 260-262
  cell padding, 264
  creating, 253-254
  grids
    creating, 255-257
    designing, 254-255
    proportions, 258-260
  overview, 253
  versus grid layout manager, 253
grid bag layouts
  aligning components, 258
  creating, 253

grid layout manager, 247
  creating, 247
  example, 247-249
  versus grid bag layout manager, 253
GridBagConstraints class, 260
gridheight constraint, 256
GridLayout() method, 247
grids
  cell padding, 264
  creating
    grid bag layout manager, 255-257
    grid layout manager, 247-248
  designing, 254-255
  element arrays, 113
  row/column proportions, 258-260
gridwidth constraint, 256
gridx constraint, 256
gridy constraint, 256
grouping
  arguments, 145
  classes, 53-54
  expressions, 79
  interfaces, 53-54
  methods, 95
Grunge Web site, 592
Guggenheim Museum, 12
GUI
  look and feel, 196
  resizing windows, 244
  Swing, 195
GUIs
  dialog boxes, 225
    confirm, 225-226
    Info sample application, 229-231
    input, 226-227
    message, 227-228
    option, 228-229

event handling
  action events, 274-275
  adjustment events, 275-277
  ChangeTitle sample application, 273-274
  component setup, 270-271
  event listeners, 270
  focus events, 278
  item events, 278-280
  key events, 280
  methods, 271-272
  mouse events, 280-281
  mouse-movement events, 281
  SwingColorTest sample application, 282, 292
  window events, 282
layout managers, 244
  border layout, 249-250
  card layout, 251-252
  combining, 250-251
  creating, 244
  flow layout, 245-247
  grid bag layout, 253-264
  grid layout, 247-249
  insets, 264
  specifying, 244-245
progress bars, 237-238
scroll panes, 233
  creating, 234
  scrollbars, 234-235
  sizing, 234
  toolbars, 235-237
sliders, 232-233
user-interface manager, 224-225

H

HalfDollars application
  arrays, 111-112
  main() method, 112-113
  output, 112
  source code, 111
HalfLoop.java application, 123
handlers, nested, 432
handling
  arguments in applications, 145-146
  strings, 97
hash tables, 557, 566-568
  clearing, 567
  creating, 567
  hash codes, 568
  load factor, 566-567
  searching, 567
hashCode() method, 568
Hashtable class, 557, 566-568
hasNext() method, 558
Headlines.java application, 333-334
HEIGHT attribute (<APPLET> tag), 175
helper classes, 144
hexadecimal numbers, 69
HexRead.java application, 425
hiding
  components, 208
  frames, 198
hierarchies
  classes, 48-50
  defining, 392
  designing, 50-51
  exceptions, 432
  interface, 400, 406
  methods, 51
high-level APIs, 528
history of Java, 13-14

Hornell, Karl, 18, 346
hostile applets, 165
HotJava, 14
HotSpot, 15
HSB, converting to sRGB, 287-290
HSPACE attribute (<APPLET> tag), 178
HTML
  files, Watch.html, 175
  submitting forms, 520-521
  tags
    <APPLET>, 174–180

, 177
    <OBJECT>, 179-180
    <PARAM>, 182
  viewing documents, 594
HTMLConverter application, 187

I

I/O (input/output) streams, 443-444
  buffered, 451-454
  byte streams, 444, 446
  character streams, 444, 458-462
  closing, 445
  creating, 444
  data streams, 454-457
  file input streams, 446-448
  file output streams, 448-450
  filtering, 445, 450
  filters, 445
  reading, 444
  writing to, 445
IBM Visual Age for Java, 15
Iceblox, 346
icons, 209-210, 587-588

**Icons.java application,
209-210**
identifying classes, 394
if keyword, 115
if statements, 115
   else keyword, 115
   examples, 116
   nested, 117
ignore command (jdb), 606
Image class, 343
image handling, 343
**image loading, tracking,
355-356**
Image objects
   arrays, 347
   creating, 343
ImageIcon objects, 209
images
   animating, 349-352
   coordinates, 345
   creating with animation,
      346
   disappearing, 355
   drawing, 344-345
   loading, 343, 355
   observers, 345
   retrieving, 343-344
   tracking
      multiple, 356
      progress, 345
implementations, stub, 403
implementing
   arrays, 108
   interfaces, 400-401
      example, 407, 413
      multiple, 402-403
      single, 402
**implements keyword, 336,
401**
implicit exceptions, 428
import declaration, 395-396
import statement, 196, 399

importing
   classes, 171, 395
   event listeners, 270
   packages, 395-396
improving readability
   expressions, 80
   programs, 67
**increasing efficiency of
classes, 391**
increment operations, 75
increment operator (++), 76
incrementing variables, 76
increments, loops, 122
indexOf() method, 93, 562
**indicating potential
exceptions, 427**
Indigo Web site, 332
inequality operator (!=), 102
infinite loops, 333
**Info application (dialog box
example), 229, 231**
**Info option (Applet menu),
595**
**Info.java application,
229-231**
inheritance, 47
   access control, 387
   class hierarchies, 49-50
   classes, 47-48, 51-52
   exceptions, 429-431
   multiple, 53, 400
   object-oriented
      programming, 49
   overview, 49
   single, 53, 400
**init() method, overriding,
168**
initialization, loops, 122
initializing
   applets, 168
   objects, 88
inner classes, 413-414
Inner.java application, 413
input dialog boxes, 226-227

input streams, 475
   creating, 475
   ObjectFromDisk, 476-477
   reading, 475-476
   transient variables,
      477-478
input streams. *See* streams
input/output. *See* I/O
InputDialog dialog box, 225
InputStream class, 446
insets, 264
insets() method, 264
**inspecting classes, 478-480,
482-484**
**installation files (SDK 1.3),
21**
installing SDK 1.3, 20-25
   troubleshooting, 21
   on Windows, 21-23
**instance methods. *See*
methods**
**instance variables, 40, 55,
61, 89**
   defining, 134-135
   length, 111
   modifying, 90
   testing, 90
   values
      accessing, 89
      initial values, 63
      modifying, 90-91
   versus class variables, 91
instanceof keyword, 272
instanceof operator, 79, 103
**instances, 37, 86. *See also*
objects**
   of classes, 39
   comparing, 102
   passing, 99
int data type, 64
integer literals, 68-69
integers, data types, 64
interactions, JavaBeans, 535
**interactive Web
programming, 11-13**

interface hierarchy, 400, 406
interfaces, 53
    casting objects to, 100,
        403-404
    command-line, 571-576
    creating, 197-199,
        404-405
    declaring, 401, 404-405
    definition of, 55
    Enumeration, 556
    establishing JavaBeans,
        529
    event listeners. *See* event
        listeners
    extending, 406
    grouping, 53-54
    implementing, 400-402,
        407, 413
    Iterator, 556-558
    Map, 565
    methods, 405-406
    multiple, 402-403
    overview, 53, 399-400
    protection, 405
    Runnable, 336
    Serializable, 471
    variables, 403-405
    versus classes, 400-401
    WindowListener, 202
Internet Explorer, browser-
    specific signatures, 438
interpreters
    Java, 164, 576, 591-592
    SDK 1.3, 30
InterruptedException
    exceptions, 422
INTERSOLV driver, 547
introspection. *See* reflection
introspection API
    (JavaBeans), 528
InvalidMidiDataException,
    365
invoking, 92-93. *See also*
    calling

IOException, 475
IOException class, 421
isEmpty() method, 566
isSelected() method, 216
issues
    event handling, 278
    performance, 19
ItemListener event listener,
    270
itemStateChanged()
    method, 278
Iterator interface, 556-558

J

J2SE 1.3. *See* SDK 1.3
JApplet class, 167, 344
JAR files (Java archive),
    180-181
jar tool (JDK), 180-181
Java
    advantages, 14, 16
    animation, 330
    applets, troubleshooting,
        166
    applications, 144
        creating, 143-144
        HTMLConverter, 187
        running, 591
    archives, 180-181
    arrays, 17
    data structures, 556
    developing applets,
        185-187, 189
    browser support, 185
    built-in fonts, 311
    capabilities, 11
    case-sensitivity, 63
    casting Graphics objects,
        299
    code complexity, 433
    compilers, 19

exceptions. *See* exceptions
exiting frames, 199
future, 15
goals, 18
history, 13-14
interpreter, 18-19, 164,
    591-592. *See also* virtual
    machine
licensing, 14
managing memory, 17,
    170
portability, 14
programs
    comiling, 18, 28-31
    developing, 19
    running in Windows,
        28-31
    speed, 593
running on various
    platforms, 18-19
security, 14
selecting development
    tools, 19-20
simplicity, 17
size, 14
source level neutrality, 18
strings, 17
testing, 18
versions, choosing,
    165-167
Java 2 Class Library, 39
Java 2 SDK 1.3. *See*
    SDK 1.3
Java 2 Software
    Development Kit 1.3.
    See SDK 1.3
Java 2D graphics
    operations, 100
Java on the Brain Web site,
    346
java command, 46
Java Database Connectivity.
    See JDBC
java package, 53

Java Plug-in, 186-187, 594
Java Plug-in plug-in, 166,
    185-189
Java Sources component
    (SDK 1.3), 23
Java Web site, 14, 590
java.awt package, 298, 383
java.io package, 443. *See
    also* streams
java.lang package, 100
java.lang.reflect package,
    480
java.net package. *See*
    networking
java.policy, 438
java.rmi packages. *See* RMI
    (Remote Method
    Invocation)
java.sql package, 545. *See
    also* JDBC (Java Database
    Connectivity)
java.util package, 556. *See
    also* data structures
Java2D, 317
    arcs, 322
    coordinate spaces,
        317-318
    ellipses, 321
    Graphics2Dobjects, 171,
        299
    lines, 321
    polygons, 322-323
    rectangles, 321
    rendering attributes, 318
        color, 318
        drawing strokes, 320
        fill patterns, 318-320
    sample applet, 323-326
JavaBeans, 527
    advantages, 525-526
    APIs, 527-528
    application, 538
    archives, 539
    BDK (Bean Development
        Kit), 528-529

downloading, 529-530
features, 530
BeanBox, 531-532
    composition window,
        532
    Properties window, 533
    Toolbox window, 532
compared to Java, 526-527
creating programs,
    537-538
establishing interfaces,
    529
ExplicitButton, 535
interactions between
    beans, 535-537
Juggler, 533-534
placing, 532-533
properties, 533-534
Web site, 528, 539
javac
    options
        -depreciation, 593
        -verbose, 594
    running Windows
        platforms, 29
javac command-line tool, 29
javac compiler, 592-594
javadoc documentation tool,
    598-602
javadoc tags, 598-599, 602
    @author, 599
    @deprecated, 602
    @exception, 602
    @param, 602
    @return, 599
    @see, 602
    @serial, 599
    @since, 602
    @version, 599
JavaSound, 15, 359, 363,
    369
JavaWorld Magazine, 9
JavaWorld Web site, 539
javax.sound.midi class, 363

javax.sound.sampled class,
    363
javax.swing.JButton class,
    39
javax.swing.JComponent
    class, 208
jbd tools, 603
JCheckBox class, 216
JCheckBox() constructor,
    216
JComboBox class, 218
JComboBox() constructor,
    218
JDataConnect Server,
    553-554
jdb commands
    !!, 605
    classes, 606
    clear, 604
    cont, 605
    down, 606
    exit, 605
    ignore, 606
    list, 604
    locals, 605
    memory, 606
    methods, 606
    print, 605
    run, 604
    step, 605
    stop at, 604
    stop in, 604
    suspend, 606
    threads, 606
    up, 606
jdb debugger, 602-606
JDBC (Java Database
    Connectivity), 544-545
    accessing databases, 545
    drivers, 545-546, 553-554
        configuring, 553
        JDataConnect Server,
            553-554
        sample application,
            553

ODBC data source
connections
closing, 551
opening, 547-551, 553
**JDBC-ODBC bridge,
546-547**
JDK 1.3. *See* **SDK 1.3**
JFC
JOptionPane, 225
confirm dialog boxes,
225-226
input dialog boxes,
226-227
message dialog boxes,
227-228
option dialog boxes,
228-229
JProgressBar, 237
constructors, 237
methods, 238
Progress.java sample
application, 240
JScrollPane, 233-235
JSlider, 232
constructors, 232
methods, 232
Slider.java sample
application, 233
JToolBar, 235
constructors, 235
dockable toolbars,
235-237
JFrame() constructor, 198
Jini, 16
JLabel() methods, 211
JOptionPane class, 225
confirm dialog boxes,
225-226
input dialog boxes,
226-227
message dialog boxes,
227-228
option dialog boxes,
228-229

JProgressBar class, 237
constructors, 237
methods, 238
JPython language, 592
JRadioButton class, 216
JScrollBar() method, 215
JScrollPane class, 233-235
JScrollPane() method, 214
JSlider class, 232
JTextArea() method, 212
JTextField() method, 211
JToolBar class, 235
constructors, 235
dockable toolbars,
235-237
Juggler JavaBean, 533-534
**juncture styles (drawing
strokes), 320**

K

key-mapped data structures
Dictionary class, 557, 566
Hashtable class, 557,
566-568
Map interface, 565
**keyboard, event handling,
280**
KeyListener, 280
**KeyListener event listener,
270**
keyPressed() method, 280
keyReleased() method, 280
keys
private, 437
public, 437
keytool utility, 436
keyTyped() method, 280
keywords
abstract, 393
break, 127
class, 134

continue, 127
else, 115
extends, 134, 406
final, 66, 390
if, 115
implements, 336, 401
instanceof, 272
modifiers. *See* modifiers
null, 109
private, 384-385
protected, 386
public, 385
return, 137
static, 91, 134-135, 142,
388
super, 156
this, 138, 152
throws, 427-428
kits, development, 15
KPCB Web site, 16

L

labeled loops, 127
labels, 210-211
aligning, 211
buttons, modifying, 535
progress bars, 238
sliders, 232
languages
cross-platform, 11
JPython, 592
NetRexx, 592
programming
Oak, 13
object-oriented, 11
SQL (Structured Query
Language), 544-545
last() method, 551
lastElement() method, 561
**layout, Swing projects,
283-285**

layout managers, 244
    border layout, 249-250
    card layout, 251-252
    combining, 250-251
    creating, 244
    flow layout, 245-247
    grid bag layout, 253,
        262-263
        arranging components,
            260-262
        cell padding, 264
        creating, 253-254
        determining
            proportions, 258-260
        example, 262
        grids, 254-257
        overview, 253
    grid layout, 247-249
    insets, 264
    specifying, 244-245
Lemay, Laura, 174
length instance variable, 111
length() method, 93
less than or equal to symbol
    (<=), 77
less than symbol (<), 77
lexical scope, 129
licensing, Java, 14
line breaks, HTML
    markup, 177
Line2D.Float class, 321
lines, drawing
    drawLine() method, 302
    Line2D.Float class, 321
lineTo() method, 323
linked lists, enumerating,
    407, 413
linking
    applets, 496, 498-499
        URL objects, 496-497
        WebMenu example,
            497
    node objects, 105

Linux, 11
list command (jdb), 604
listeners, 269
    ActionListener, 270, 275
    AdjustmentListener, 270,
        276-277
    associating components
        with, 270-271
    FocusListener, 270, 278
    importing, 270
    ItemListener, 270, 278
    KeyListener, 270, 280
    MouseListener, 270, 280
    MouseMotionListener,
        270, 281
    WindowListener, 270
listings
    AllCapsDemo.java
        application, 463-464
    Alphabet.java, 245-246
    AppInfo.html, 597
    AppInfo.java, 596
    AppInfo2.java, 599-600
    arrays, HalfDollars.java
        application, 111-112
    Bunch.java, 247-248
    ButtonApplet.java, 207
    Buttons.java, 206
    calling methods, 92-93
    Checkers.java, 340-342
    ChooseTeam.java, 217,
        219
    CoalTotals.java, 552
    comparing objects, 102
    CountInstances class, 389
    creating objects, 87
    defining instance
        variables, 135
    defining methods, 137
    DigitalClock.java, 337-338
    Ellsworth example source
        code, 27

event handling
    ChangeTitle.java
        application, 273-274
    SelectItem application,
        278
    SwingColorTest
        application, 292
ExitFrame.java, 204
ExitWindow.java, 203
Finger.java application,
    506-507
for loops, 123
Form.java, 213-214
GetFile.java application,
    501-502
Giftshop application, 411
Headlines.java application,
    333-334
Icons.java, 209-210
Info.java application,
    229-231
inner classes, 413
instance variables,
    testing/modifying, 90
ItemProp.java, 607
JavaBeans application,
    538
layout managers, border
    layout, 250
Looper.java, 361-362
loops, while, 125
Map.java application,
    299-300, 308-309
Map2D applet, Java
    source code, 324-325
Map2D.html applet, 325
Map2D.java, 324-325
MidiApplet.html, 370
MidiApplet.java, 371-373
MyRect class definition,
    149-150
MyRect2 class, 153-154
NamedPoint class, 157
NamePass.java, 262-263

NewWatch.html, 184
NewWatch.java source
code, 183
ObjectFromDisk.java, 477
ObjectToDisk.java, 474
OutputPi.java, 489-490
PassbyReference class,
140-141
Pete.java, 352-355
Pi.java, 488-489
PiRemote.java, 487
PlayMidi.java, 366-368
policy.txt, 492
Presidents.java, 553-554
PrintClass class, 154-155
Progress.java application,
238-239
references, 96
ReferencesTest.java
application, 95
reflection, 484
SeeMethods.java, 482
SelectItem.java
application, 279
simple arithmetic example,
73
SimpleFrame.java, 200
SimpleWindow.java, 201
Slider.java application,
233
SoLong.html, 313
SoLong.java, 313
statements
switch, 119
Storefront application,
407-408, 410
streams
BufferDemo.java
application, 452-453
ReadBytes.java
application, 447
ReadPrimes.java
application, 456-457
ReadSource
application, 460

WriteBytes application,
449
WritePrimes.java
application, 455-456
SumAverage.java
application, 145-146
SwingColorText.java
application, 292-294
ToolBar.java application,
236
TriviaServer.java
application, 515-518
try...finally blocks, 425
VolcanoRobot class
example, 42
VolcanoRobot.java
application, 45-46
Watch.html, 175
Watch.java, 172
WebMenu.java, 498
WellAdjusted.java
application, 276-277
literals, 68
Boolean, 69-70
characters, 70
integers, 68-69
strings, 71
**load factor (hash tables),
566-567**
loadData() method, 514-515
loading
audio, 360
images, 343
tracking, 355-356
blank, 355
MIDI sequences, 365
multiple classes, 171
local variables, 61
assigning values, 63
constant, 66
declaring, 62
locals command (jdb), 605
locations, frames, 199
logical operators, 78-79

long data type, 64
look and feel, 196, 224-225
Looper.java, 361-362
looping audio, 360
loops
breaking, 127
do...while, 126
for, 121-122
empty statements, 122
example, 123-124
troubleshooting, 123
increments, 122
index values, 122
infinite, 333
initialization, 122
labeling, 127
restarting, 127
run() methods, 339-340
tests, 122
while, 124-126
low-level APIs, 528
**lowercase, converting to
uppercase, 463-464**

M

machine codes, 18
machines, virtual, 18
**Macromedia Dreamweaver,
174**
main() class method, 44-45
**main() method, 46, 143, 385,
591**
signature, 143
TriviaServer application,
515
**MakeApplet command (File
menu), 537**
makeRange() method, 137
**MalformedURLException
exception, 421**

managing
errors. *See* error-handling
exceptions. *See* error-
handling
Java, 170
memory, 17, 88-89
**manipulating components,
528**
Map interface, 565
**Map.java application,
299-300, 308-309**
Map2D applet, 323-326
**Map2D.java application,
324-325**
math operators, 72-74
McCarthy, Ciaran P., 332
**MD command (MS-DOS),
574**
**MediaTracker object,
355-356**
member functions. *See*
methods
memory
allocating to objects, 88
deallocating from objects,
89
managing, 17, 88-89, 170
reclaiming, 89
**memory command (jdb),
606**
message dialog box, 227-228
**MessageDialog dialog box,
225**
method calls, nesting, 93-94
Method class, 480
method overloading, 136
**Method Tracer window
(Beanbox), 532**
methods. *See also* **RMI
(Remote Method
Invocation)**
abstract methods, 392-393
access control, 383,
386-387

default access, 383
inheritance, 387
private access, 384-385
protected access,
385-386
public access, 385
accessor methods,
387-388
actionPerformed(), 271,
275, 499
add(), 205, 561
addActionListener(), 275
addItem(), 218
addPoint(), 304
adjustmentValueChanged(),
276
afterLast(), 551
applets, 168
ArgStream(), 453
beforeFirst(), 551
BorderLayout(), 249
BufferedInputStream(),
451
BufferedOutputStream(),
451
BufferedReader(), 459
BufferedWriter(), 461
buildConstraints(),
255-256, 258-259
buildRect(), 148
calling, 41, 92-93, 156
capacity(), 563
CardLayout(), 252
charAt(), 93
charWidth(), 313
checkTemperature(), 47
class, 41
accessing, 389
main(), 44-45
class methods, 94-95, 141
availability, 142
calling, 95
defining, 142
of classes, 41

clear(), 567
clearRect(), 310
close(), 445
closePath(), 323
constructors, 86, 150-151,
154
calling, 151-152, 157
definition of, 88
naming, 151
overloading, 152-153
overriding, 156-158
contains
contains(), 562, 567
containsKey(), 567
copyArea(), 310
createImage(), 343
createStatement(), 550
DataInputStream(), 454
DataOutputStream(), 454
defining, 136
multiple, 147
parameter lists, 136
this keyword, 138
delete(), 462
deleteOnExit(), 462
destroy(), 170
drawArc(), 306
drawImage(), 345
drawLine(), 302
drawOval(), 306
drawPolygon(), 304-305
drawRect(), 302
drawRoundRect(), 303
drawString(), 312
equals(), 102, 568
event handling, 271
exceptions, 427
executeQuery(), 550
exists(), 462
File(), 462
FileInputStream(), 446
FileOutputStream(),
448-449
FileReader(), 458

FileWriter(), 461
fillArc(), 306
fillOval(), 306
fillPolygon(), 304-305
fillRect(), 302
fillRoundRect(), 303
final, 391
final methods, 391-392
finalize(), 158
    calling, 158
    versus destroy()
        method, 170
finalizers, 158
first(), 551
flowLayout(), 245-247
focusGained(), 278
focusLost(), 278
Font(), 312
forName(), 479
general utility, 94
GET, form submission,
    520
get(), 561
getActionCommand(), 275
getAdjustmentType(), 276
getAppletInfo(), 595-596
getAudioClip(), 360
getClass(), 103
getClickCount(), 281
getCodeBase(), 344
getColor(), 317
getConnection(), 549-550
getConstructors(), 481
getCrossPlatformLookAnd
    FeelClassName(), 224
getDate(), 550
getDefaultToolkit(), 343
getDocumentBase(), 344
getDouble(), 550
getFloat(), 550
getFontMetrics(), 312
getHeight(), 313
getImage(), 343, 355
getInputStream(), 500

getInsets(), 264
getInt(), 551
getItemAt(), 218
getItemCount(), 218
getKeyChar(), 280
getLong(), 551
getMessage(), 423
getMicrosecondLength(),
    368
getMicrosecondPosition(),
    369
getModifiers(), 481
getName(), 479
getNumberOfFiles(), 238
getParameter(), 182
getParameterInfo(), 595
getParameterTypes(), 481
getPoint(), 281
getReturnType(), 481
getSelectedIndex(), 219
getSelectedItem(), 219
getSequencer(), 364
getSize(), 209
getSource(), 272, 274
getStateChange(), 278
getString(), 551
getSystemLookAndFeelCl
    assName(), 224-225
getX(), 281
getY(), 281
GridLayout(), 247
grouping, 95
hashCode(), 568
hasNext(), 558
hierarchies, 51
in interfaces, 405-406
indexOf(), 93, 562
init(), overriding, 168
insets(), 264
instance methods, 142
interfaces, 53
isEmpty(), 566
isSelected(), 216
itemStateChanged(), 278

JLabel(), 211
JScrollBar(), 215
JScrollPane(), 214
JTextArea(), 212
JTextField(), 211
keyPressed(), 280
keyReleased(), 280
keyTyped(), 280
last(), 551
lastElement(), 561
length(), 93
lineTo(), 323
loadData(), 514-515
main(), 46, 143, 385, 591
    signature, 143
    TriviaServer
        application, 515
makeRange(), 137
mkdir(), 463
mouseClicked(), 281
mouseDragged(), 281
mouseEntered(), 281
mouseExited(), 281
mouseMoved(), 281
mousePressed(), 281
mouseReleased(), 280-281
moveTo(), 323
naming conventions, 540
nested, combining, 94
newAudioClip(), 361
newInstance(), 480
newLine(), 461-462
next(), 558
onetoZero(), 141
overloaded, 147-150
overriding, 51, 154-156
paint(), 168-170, 173, 331
paintComponent(), 345
parseInt(), 142
passing to arguments,
    140-141
peek(), 565
play(), 360
pop(), 564

POST, form submission, 521
previous(), 551
println(), 74
processInput(), 512-513
protecting, 394
push(), 564
read(), 444-445, 459, 476
readBoolean(), 476
readByte(), 476
readChar(), 476
readDouble(), 476
readFloat(), 455, 476
readInt(), 476
readLine(), 459, 476, 503
readLong(), 476
readObject(), 475
readShort(), 476
readStream(), 454
readUnsignedByte(), 455, 476
readUnsignedShort(), 455, 476
rehash(), 567
remove(), 561, 566
removeAllElements(), 562
renameTo(), 462
repaint(), 171, 173, 330-331
return types, 136-137
RGBtoHSB(), 289
run(), 337-340, 349, 510, 512
scroll(), 335
search(), 565
set(), 562
setActionCommand(), 275
setBackground(), 168, 316
setBounds(), 199
setColor(), 316, 318
setConstraints(), 257
setContentPane(), 206
setDefaultCloseOperation(), 199

setEchoChar(), 212
setEnabled(), 208
setFont(), 312
setForeground(), 316-317
setLayout(), 244, 251-252
setLineWrap(), 213
setLookAndFeel(), 224
setMajorTickSpacing(), 232
setMaximum(), 238
setMaximumRowCount(), 219
setMinimum(), 238
setMinorTickSpacing(), 232
setPaint(), 318
setPaintLabels(), 232
setPaintTicks(), 232
setSelected(), 216
setSelectedIndex(), 219
setSize(), 198, 209, 563
setSoTimeOut(), 504
setStringPainted(), 238
setStroke(), 320
setTempoFactor(), 369
setText(), 277
setValue(), 238
setVisible(), 198, 208
setWrapStyleWord(), 213
show(), 252
showAttributes(), 47
showConfirmDialog(), 225-226
showInputDialog(), 227
showMessageDialog(), 227
showOptionDialog(), 228
signatures, 136, 147
SimpleFrame(), 200
size(), 311, 566
start()
    calling, 595
    overriding, 169
startJuggling(), 537

static, 388-390
stop(), 339, 361
    calling, 595
    overriding, 169
stopJuggling(), 537
stringWidth(), 313
substring(), 93
System.out.println(), 74
testBlock(), 114
testing, 137
toUpperCase(), 93
trimToSize(), 563
URL(), 496
valueOf(), 94
waitForID, 356
windowActivated(), 203, 282
windowClosed(), 203, 282
windowClosing(), 203, 282
windowDeactivated(), 203, 282
windowDeiconified(), 203, 282
windowIconified(), 203, 282
windowOpened(), 203, 282
write(), 445, 451, 461, 472
writeBoolean(), 472
writeByte(), 472
writeBytes(), 473
writeChar(), 473
writeChars(), 473
writeDouble(), 473
writeFloat(), 473
writeInt(), 457, 473
writeLong(), 473
writeObject(), 472
writeShort(), 473
writeStream(), 454
methods command (jdb), 606
microseconds, 369

Microsoft Windows, 11
MIDI (Musical Instrument
  Digital Interface), 363-365
  archives, 368
  files, 363-364
    playing, 364-366,
      368-369
    tempo, 369, 373-374
  loading sequences, 365
MidiApplet.html, 370
MidiApplet.java, 371-373
MidiUnavailableException,
  364
minus sign (-), 69
mkdir() method, 463
models, security (applets),
  165
Modifier class, 480
modifiers, 382
  abstract, 393
  final, 390
  multiple, 382
  private, 384-385
  protected, 386
  public, 385
  static, 388
modifying
  arrays, 111
  audio files, 369-375
  AUTOEXEC.BAT, 577
  class variable values, 91
  classes, 336
  components, 528
  functions, 590
  instance variable values,
    90-91
  instance variables, 90
  labels, buttons, 535
  precedence, operators, 80
  superclasses, 49
  system properties,
    606-608
  vector elements, 562
modulus operators, 73

monitoring windows,
  202-203
mouse, event handling,
  280-281
mouseClicked() method, 281
mouseDragged() method,
  281
mouseEntered() method,
  281
mouseExited() method, 281
MouseListener, 280-281
MouseListener event
  listener, 270
MouseMotionListener event
  listener, 270
mouseMoved() method, 281
mousePressed() method, 281
mouseReleased() method,
  280-281
moveTo() method, 323
MS-DOS
  accessing, 572
  commands, 26
    cd, 29
    CD, 573-574
    CLASSPATH, 579-580
    MD, 574
    PATH, 577-578
    SET CLASSPATH=,
      579
  folders in, 573-575
  running programs in,
    575-576
MS-DOS Prompt, 590. See
  also command line
MS-DOS Prompt window,
  572
multidimensional arrays,
  113
multiple method definitions,
  147
multiple bytes, writing, 449
multiple classes, 171

multiple constructor
  definitions, 88
multiple exceptions, 433
multiple files, compiling,
  593
multiple images, tracking,
  356
multiple inheritance, 53, 400
multiple interfaces, 402-403
multiple modifiers, 382
multiple variables, 62, 108
multitasking, 335
Musical Instrument Digital
  Interface. See MIDI
MyRect class, 147-150
MyRect2 class, 153-154

N

NAME attribute
  (<PARAM> tag), 182
name conflicts (classes), 396
NamedPoint class, 157
naming
  constructor methods, 151
  conventions, 397, 540
  inner classes, 414
  ODBC data sources, 547
  reducing conflicts, 393
  packages, 397-398
  variables, 63
Native Interface Header
  Files component (SDK
  1.3), 23
Navigator, browser-specific
  signatures, 438
navingating records, 551
Naviseek Web site, 45,
  579-580
negative numbers,
  representing as literals, 69
nested if statements, 117

nested methods, combining, 94
nesting
    exception handlers, 431-432
    method calls, 93-94
NetDirect Web site, 553
NetRexx language, 592
Netscape, 14, 438
Netscape Navigator, browser-specific signatures, 438
networking, 496
    Finger.java application, 506-507
    GetFile.java application, 501-502
    opening Web connections, 499-500
    sockets, 504
        client-side, 504-505
        server-side, 508
        transport-layer implementation, 508
    streams, 500-503
    TriviaServer application, 508
        designing, 509-510
        running, 518-519
        server implementation, 510-515, 518
new operator, 79, 86, 88
    instantiating arrays, 109
    creating objects with, 86-88
newAudioClip() method, 361
newInstance() method, 480
newLine() method, 461-462
NewWatch sample applet, HTML file, 184
NewWatch.html, 184
NewWatch.java source code, 183

next() method, 558
NoClassDef error, 579
node objects, linking, 105
nonexclusive check boxes, 216
nonexclusive radio buttons, 216
nonvisual components, 527
not equal symbol (!=), 77
NOT operator, 78
notation, dot, 89, 92
NotePad, 577, 584
null keyword, 109
null strings, 277
null values, parameters, 182
NullPointerException, 365, 420
number literals, 68-69
numbering systems, 69
numbers
    floating-point, 64
    octal, 69

O

–O option (javac), 593
Oak programming language, 13
Object class, 48
object streams, 470. *See also* **streams**
<OBJECT> tag, 179-180
object variables. *See* **instance variables**
object-oriented programming (OOP), 16, 35-36
    classes, 37-38, 47-48
    focus, 36
    inheritance, 49
        class hierarchies, 49-50
        multiple, 53
        single, 53

    languages, 11
    objects, 37
ObjectFromDisk.java application, 477
ObjectInputStream class, 475-477
ObjectOutputStream class, 472-473
objects, 36-37, 86. *See also* **instances**
    arrays, 109-110
    attributes, 40
    ButtonGroup, 217
    casting, 97-98, 403-404
        casting to classes, 99-100
        casting to interfaces, 100
    classes
        attributes, 40-41
        behavior, 41
        determining, 103
    comparing, 101, 103
    converting, 97-101
    creating, 85-88
    encapsulating, 385
    File, 462
    Font, 311-312
    GeneralPath, 323
    Graphics2D, casting, 171, 299
    Image, 343, 347
    ImageIcon, 209
    initializing, 88
    linking nodes, 105
    MediaTracker, 355-356
    memory
        allocating to, 88
        deallocating from, 89
    methods of, 94
    references, 95-96, 102
    referring to current, 138
    reusing, 38-39
    Sequencer, 364

serialization, 470-471
 advantages, 471
 input streams, 475-477
 output streams,
  472-474
 persistence, 471
 transient variables,
  477-478
 String, 43
 strings, 71
 StringTokenizer, 87-88
 URL
  creating, 496-497
  retrieving, 344
ObjectToDisk.java
 application, 474
obscuring password fields,
 212
observers, images, 345
octal numbering systems, 69
ODBC
 data source connections
  closing, 551
  opening, 547-551, 553
 JDBC-ODBC bridge,
  546-547
ODBC data sources, 547
ODBC dBase Driver Setup
 dialog box, 549
Old Native Interface
 Header Files component
 (SDK 1.3), 23
onetoZero() method, 141
online storefronts, 407-413
OOP. See object-oriented
 programming
opening
 folders in MS-DOS,
  573-574
 socket connections, 504
 streams over Internet, 500
  BufferedReader
   objects, 500
  GetFile sample
   application, 501, 503

getInputStream()
 method, 500
 URLConnection
  objects, 500
 Web connections, 499-500
operating systems, Star 7,
 13
operators, 72
 arithmetic, 72-74
 assignment, 62, 74-75
 comparison, 77
 concatenation (+), 81
 conditional, 128-129
 decrement (--), 76
 division, 73
 equality (==), 102
 increment (++), 76
 inequality (!=), 102
 instanceof, 79, 103
 logical, 78-79
 modulus, 73
 new, 79, 86-88
  creating objects with,
   86-88
  instantiating arrays,
   109
 postfix, 76
 precedence, 79-80
 prefix, 76
 subtraction, 72
option dialog boxes, 228-229
OptionDialog dialog boxes,
 225
options
 Applet menu, 595
 appletviewer, 595
 command line, 590-591
 javac
  -depreciation, 593
  -verbose, 594
OR operators, 78
order of precedence,
 operators, 79-80

organizing
 behavior, 47-54
 classes, 47-54, 382, 393
 panels, 283-284
 stacks, 563
output streams. See streams
OutputPi.java application,
 489-490
ovals, drawing
 drawOval() method, 306
 Ellipse2D.Float class, 321
overflow (variable
 assignment), 83
overloaded methods, 136,
 147
 buildRect(), 148
 constructors, 152-153
 creating, 147-148, 150
 troubleshooting, 147
overriding
 methods, 51, 154-155
  advantages, 156
  constructors, 156-158
  destroy(), 170
  init(), 168
  start(), 169
  stop(), 169
  super keyword, 156
 scrollbars, 234

P

package declaration, 384,
 398
packages, 53-54, 393
 access control, 398-399
 advantages, 393-394
 classes, 398, 592
 folder structure, 398
 importing, 395-396
 java, 53
 java.awt, 298, 383

java.lang, 100
  names, 397-398
  overview, 54
  referencing, 394-395
padding, 264
paint() method, 168, 170
  versus repaint() method, 331
  Watch.java, 173
paintComponent() method, 345
painting
  applets, 170
  components, 330-331
panels, 205, 251
  adding components, 251
  creating, 251
  defining subpanels, 285-287
  insets, 264
  organizing, 283-284
  panes, 205
panes
  panels, 205
  scrolling, 214-215
@param tag (javadoc), 602
<PARAM> tag, 182
parameters, 181-184, 190. See also attributes
Pardon My Icons Web site, 210
parseInt() method, 142
PassByReference class, 140-141
passing
  arguments
    to applications, 144
    to methods, 140-141
  exceptions, 428-429
  instances, 99
  parameters to applets, 181-182
password fields, 212

PATH command (MS-DOS), 577-578
PATH variable, 24-25
pausing animated applications, 333
peek() method, 565
performance issues, Java interpreter, 19
period (.), dot notation, 89
permissions (classes), 435
persistence, 471, 525
Pete.java application, 352-355
Pi.java application, 488-489
pipe character (|), OR operators, 78
PiRemote.java application, 487
Pixel Pete, 346-356
placing JavaBeans, 532
platforms, running Java on various, 18-19
play() method, 360
playing
  audio, 360-369
  sequences, 366
PlayMidi.java, 366-368
plug-ins, Java Plug-in, 166, 185-189
pluggable look and feel, setting, 224-225
plus sign (+)
  concatenation operator (+), 81
  increment operator (++), 76
pointers, 96, 105. See also arrays; references
policy.txt applications, 492
policytool utility, 439
polygons
  adding points to, 304
  drawing
    drawPolygon() method, 304
    Java2D, 322-323

pop() method, 564
portability, Java, 14
POST method, form submission, 521
postfix operators, 76
potential exceptions, indicating, 427
precedence of operators, 79-80
prefix operators, 76
Presidents.java, 553-554
previous() method, 551
primitive type arrays, 479-480
primitive types, 104
  casting, 97-99
  converting, 97-101
primitive types (data), 64-65
print command (jdb), 605
PrintClass class, 154-155
println() method, 74
private access, 384-385
private keys, 437
private modifier, 384-385
procedural programming, 36
processInput() method, 512-513
Program Files component (SDK 1.3), 23
programming
  Oak, 13
  object-oriented. See object oriented programming
  procedural, 36
  Web, 11-13
programs. See also applets; applications
  command-line, 19
  compiling, 571, 579
  debugging, 585, 602
  improving readability, 67
  Java. See Java programs
  JavaBeans, 537-538

running, 44-47, 571, 575-576
searching, 578
Programs, MS-DOS Prompt command (Start menu), 20
progress of images, tracking, 345
progress bars, 237
labels, 238
orientation, 238
Progress.java sample application, 240
updating, 238
Progress.java application, 238-239
prohibited features, applets, 434
projects, Swing, 283-285
prompts, command-line, 20
properties
JavaBeans, 533-534
system properties, 606-608
Properties window (Beanbox), 533
protected access, 385-386
protected modifier, 386
protecting
classes, 394
interfaces, 405
methods, 394
variables, 394
protocols, RMI (Remote Method Invocation), 485
applications, 487-491
architecture, 485-487
security, 491-492
public access, 385
public keys, 437
public modifier, 385
publishing applets, 176
push() method, 564

Q-R

qna.txt file (TriviaServer application), 513
queries, databases, 544
quotation marks in arguments, 145

RAD (rapid application development), 538-539
radio buttons, 216-218
event handling
action events, 275
item events, 278-280
exclusive, 216
nonexclusive, 216
Random() class, enabling, 88
RangeClass.java application, 137
rapid application development (RAD), 538-539
read() method, 444-445, 459, 476
readability, improving, 67, 80
readBoolean() method, 476
readByte() method, 476
ReadBytes.java application, 447
readChar() method, 476
readDouble() method, 476
readFloat() method, 455, 476
reading streams, 444
buffered streams, 451
character streams, 458-460
data streams, 454-455
file input streams, 446-448
input streams, 475-476
readInt() method, 476
readLine() method, 459, 476, 503
readLong() method, 476

readObject() method, 475
ReadPrimes.java application, 456-457
readShort() method, 476
ReadSource.java application, 460
readStream() method, 454
readUnsignedByte() method, 455, 476
readUnsignedShort() method, 455, 476
reclaiming memory, 89
records, navigating, 551
Rectangle2D.Float class, 321
rectangles
drawing
drawRect() method, 302
Rectangle2D.Float class, 321
filling, 303
rounded corners, 303
redrawing windows, 171
reducing conflicts, names, 393
references, 95-96
arrays, 111
objects, 102
passing by, 140
ReferencesTest.java application, 95-96
referencing packages, 394-395
referring to current objects, 138
reflection, 478-484
rehash() method, 567
Reload option (Applet menu), 595
Remote Method Invocation. See RMI
remote procedure calls (RPC), 485
Remote Reference layer (RMI), 486

remove () method, 561, 566
removeAllElements()
    method, 562
removing vector elements,
    562
renameTo() method, 462
renaming files, 462
rendering attributes
    (Java2D), 318
    color, 318
    drawing strokes, 320
    fill patterns, 318-320
repaint() method, 171-173,
    330-331
repainting components,
    330-331
reserved words, 382. See
    also modifiers
resizing
    components, 209
    windows, 244
Restart option (Applet
    menu), 595
restarting loops, 127
retrieving
    audio, 360-362
    images, 343-344
    URL objects, 344
return keyword, 137
@return tag (javadoc), 599
return types, 136-137
return values, 60, 72
reusable components. See
    components
reusing objects, 38-39
RGB-to-HSB converter, 289
RGBtoHSB() method, 289
RMI (Remote Method
    Invocation), 485
    applications, 488-491
        creating, 487
        OutputPi.java, 489-490
        Pi.java, 488-489
        policy.txt, 492

architecture, 485-487
    layers, 486
    security, 491-492
RPC (remote procedure
    calls), 485
run command (jdb), 604
Run command (Start
    menu), 21
run() method, 337, 349, 510,
    512
run() methods, loops,
    339-340
Runnable interface, 336
runner (Thread variable),
    347
running
    applets, 164, 186-187
    applications, 164, 187,
        591
    interpreter, 576
    Java on various platforms,
        18-19
    Java Plug-in plug-in, 187,
        189
    Java programs in
        Windows, 28-31
    jdb tools, 603
    programs, 44-47, 571,
        575-576
    threads, 337
runtime exceptions, 420, 439

S

Sams Teach Yourself Java 2
    in 24 Hours, 17
Sams Teach Yourself Web
    Publishing with HTML 4
    in 21 Days, 174
San Francisco Museum of
    Modern Art, 12

saving
    source code, 28
    unformatted files, 584
School of Visual Arts in
    Manhattan, 12
scope
    inner classes, 414
    lexical scope, 129
    variables, 114, 138-140
scroll panes, 233-235
scroll() method, 335
scrollbars, 215
    configuring, 214
    event handling, 275-277
    overriding, 234
scrolling panes, 214-215
scrolling windows, 331-333,
    335
ScrollPaneConstants class,
    214
SDK 1.3, 9-10, 589-590
    appletviewer, 595
    command line, arguments,
        590
    commands, 590
    components, 23
    configuring, 24-25
        for Windows 2000, 25
        for Windows 95, 24-25
        for Windows 98, 24-25
        for Windows NT, 25
        troubleshooting, 22
    downloading, 20
    installation files, 21
    installing, 20-25
    interpreter, 30
    keytool utility, 436
    modifying system
        properties, 606-608
    tools, 589
    UNIX configuration, 581
    utilities
        AppInfo.java sample
            application, 597
        Applet menu
            commands, 595

appletviewer browser,
594-597
command line, 590
commands, 604-606
downloading, 590
java interpreter,
591-592
javac compiler,
592-594
javadoc documentation
tool, 598-602
jdb debugger, 602-606
options, 590-591
policytool, 439
SDK Setup Wizard, 22
search() method, 565
searching
applets, 179
breakpoints, 603
bugs, 603
hash tables, 567
Java interpreters, 19
programs, 578
stack, 565
security
applets, 164-167
digital signatures, 434-437
browser-specific,
437-438
certificate authorities,
435
certificates, 435
establishing, 435
Java, 14
policies, 438-439
RMI (Remote Method
Invocation), 491-492
security models, applets,
165
@see tag (javadoc), 602
SeeMethods.java
application, 482

selecting
development tools, 19-20
Font styles, 312
SelectItem.java application,
279
semicolon (;), statement
termination character, 60
Sequencer objects, 364
sequences
loading MIDI, 365
playing, 366
@serial tag (javadoc), 599
Serializable interface, 471
serialization, 470-471, 525
advantages, 471
input streams, 475
creating, 475
ObjectFromDisk,
476-477
reading, 475-476
output streams, 472
creating, 472
ObjectToDisk, 474
writing to, 472-473
persistence, 471
transient variables,
477-478
server-side sockets, 508
servers, TriviaServer
application, 510
constructor, 510
instance variables, 510
loadData() method,
514-515
main() method, 515
processInput() method,
512-513
qna.txt file, 513
run() method, 510, 512
running, 518-519
source code listing, 515
WAIT_FOR_ANSWER
state, 513

WAIT_FOR_CLIENT
state, 513
WAIT_FOR_CONFIRM
state, 513
ServerSocket class, 508
SET CLASSPATH=, 24
SET CLASSPATH=
command (MS-DOS), 579
set() method, 562
setActionCommand()
method, 275
setBackground() method,
168, 316
setBounds() method, 199
setColor() method, 316, 318
setConstraints() method,
257
setContentPane() method,
206
setDefaultCloseOperation()
method, 199
setEchoChar() method, 212
setEnabled() method, 208
setFont() method, 312
setForeground() method,
316-317
setLayout() method, 244,
251-252
setLineWrap() method, 213
setLookAndFeel() method,
224
setMajorTickSpacing()
method, 232
setMaximum() method, 238
setMaximumRowCount()
method, 219
setMinimum() method, 238
setMinorTickSpacing()
method, 232
setPaint() method, 318
setPaintLabels() method,
232
setPaintTicks() method, 232
setSelected() method, 216

setSelectedIndex() method, 219
setSize() method, 198, 209, 563
setSoTimeOut() method, 504
setStringPainted() method, 238
setStroke() method, 320
setTempoFactor() method, 369
setText() method, 277
setting
    breakpoints, 604
    drawing colors, 315-316
    fonts, 312
    PATH variables, 24-25
Settings, Control Panel, ODBC Data Sources command (Start menu), 546
setValue() method, 238
setVisible() method, 198, 208
setWrapStyleWord() method, 213
shapes
    arcs, 306-309
    coordinate system, 301
    lines, 302
    ovals, 306
    polygons, 304
    rectangles, 302-303
shared behavior, 53
shared values, defining, 66
short data type, 64
show() method, 252
showAttributes() method, 47
showConfirmDialog() method, 225-226
showInputDialog() method, 227
showMessageDialog() method, 227
showOptionDialog() method, 228

ShowTokens.java, 87
signatures
    digital, 434-437
        browser-specific, 437-438
        certificate authorities, 435
        certificates, 435
    methods, 136, 147
Signing Tool (Netscape), 438
Simon, John F., Jr., 12
SimpleFrame() method, 200
SimpleFrame.java, 200
SimpleWindow.java application, 201
simplicity of Java, 17
@since tag (javadoc), 602
single inheritance, 53, 400
size
    Java, 14
    vectors, 560
size() method, 311, 566
sizing
    components, 209
    frames, 198
    scroll panes, 234
Skeletons layer (RMI), 486
sliders, 232-233
Socket class, 504
SocketImpl class, 508
sockets, 504
    client-side
        closing, 505
        instantiating, 504
        opening, 504
    server-side, 508
    timeout values, 504
    transport-layer implementation, 508
    TriviaServer application, 508
        designing, 509-510
        running, 518-519
        server implementation, 510-515, 518

Sockets Web site, 509
software
    components. See components
    Java Plug-in plug-in, 166, 185-189
Solaris, 11
sounds. See audio
source code
    comments, 598
    converting, 592
    Ellsworth example, 27
    saving, 28
    Watch.java, 172
source files, creating, 26-31
sources (casting), 98
Special Edition Using MS-DOS 6.22, 573
specifying
    class files, 592
    coordinates, graphics, 304
    layout managers, 244
speed, Java programs, 593
SQL (Structured Query Language), 544-545
sRGB color system, 287-290, 314
Stack class, 557, 563-565
stacks, 557, 563-565
    elements, 564
    logical organization, 563
    searching, 565
Star 7 operating system, 13
Start menu, commands
    Find, 578
    Programs, MS-DOS Prompt, 20
    Run, 21
    Settings, Control Panel, ODBC Data Sources, 546
Start option (Applet menu), 595

start() method
  calling, 595
  overriding, 169
starting applets, 169
startJuggling() method, 537
statements, 60-61, 382. *See
  also* modifiers
  block statements, 61
  blocks, 114-115, 423-424
  conditionals, 115
    conditional operator,
      128-129
    if, 115-116
    switch, 116-118, 121
  empty for loops, 122
  expressions, 60, 72
  finally, 424-426
  if, 117
  import, 196, 395, 399
  loops
    breaking, 127
    do, 126
    for, 121-124
    index values, 122
    labeling, 127
    restarting, 127
    while, 124-126
  switch, 117
  termination character, 60
static keyword, 91, 134-135,
  142
static methods, 388-390
static modifier, 388
static variables, 91, 388-390
step command (jdb), 605
stop at command (jdb), 604
stop in command (jdb), 604
Stop option (Applet menu),
  595
stop() method, 339, 361
  calling, 595
  overriding, 169
stopJuggling() method, 537
stopping applets, 169

Storefront application,
  407-408, 410
storefronts, creating online,
  407-413
storing data, 451
StreamCorruption
  Exception exceptions, 475
streams, 443-444, 470
  buffered, 451-454
  byte streams, 444-446
    file input streams,
      446-448
    file output streams,
      448-450
  character streams, 444,
    458
    reading text files,
      458-460
    writing text files,
      461-462
  closing, 445
  creating, 444
  data streams, 454-457
  filtering, 445, 450
  filters, 445
  input streams, 475
    creating, 475
    ObjectFromDisk,
      476-477
    reading, 475-476
    transient variables,
      477-478
  opening over Internet, 500
    BufferedReader
      objects, 500
    GetFile sample
      application, 501, 503
    getInputStream()
      method, 500
    URL connection
      objects, 500
  output streams, 472
    creating, 472
    ObjectToDisk, 474
    writing to, 472-473

    reading, 444
    writing to, 445
string arithmetic, 80-81
string literals, 71
String objects, 43
strings, 17, 71
  concatenating, 80-81
  coordinates, 330
  handling, 97
  null, 277
StringTokenizer class, 87
StringTokenizer objects,
  87-88
stringWidth() method, 313
Stroustrup, Bjarne, 13
Structured Query Language
  (SQL), 544-545
structures. *See* data
  structures
stub implementations, 403
Stubs layer (RMI), 486
subclasses, 47-49, 55, 392
submitting forms
  GET method, 520
  POST method, 521
subpanels, defining, 285-287
subscripts (arrays), 110
substring() method, 93
subtraction operator, 72
SumAverage.java
  application, 145-146
Sun Forte for Java, 15
Sun Microsystems, 590
Sun Web site, 20, 437
super keyword, 156
superclasses, 47, 55
  casting, 99
  indicating, 134
  calling methods in, 156
  modifying, 49
support, Java, 185
surfaces, drawing, 298-301
suspend command (jdb),
  606

Swing, 15
applications
  creating, 196-197
  graphical, 198
  Slider.java, 233
components, 196, 208-209
  check boxes, 216-218
  combo boxes, 218-219
  creating, 197, 204-205
  disabled, 208
  displaying, 208
  drop-down lists,
    218-219
  hiding, 208
  icons, 209-210
  labels, 210-211
  radio buttons, 216-218
  resizing, 209
  scrollbars, 215
  scrolling panes,
    214-215
  text areas, 212-214
  text fields, 211-212
containers
  applets, 207-208
  panels, 205
dialog boxes
  confirm dialog box,
    225-226
  creating, 225
  input dialog box,
    226-227
  message dialog box,
    227-228
  option dialog box,
    228-229
  sample application,
    229, 231
event-handling, 269
  action events, 274-275
  adjustment events,
    275-277
  ChangeTitle.java, 274
  ChangeTitle.java
    example, 273

component setup,
    270-271
  event listeners, 270
  focus events, 278
  instanceof keyword,
    272
  item events, 278
  key events, 280
  methods, 271
  mouse events, 280-281
  mouse-movement
    events, 281
  SwingColorTest,
    282-291
  SwingColorTest
    sample application,
    282, 292
  window events, 282
Info application, 229-231
layout managers, 244
  border layout, 249-250
  card layout, 251-252
  combining, 250-251
  creating, 244
  flow layout, 245-247
  grid bag layout,
    253-264
  grid layout, 247-249
  insets, 264
  specifying, 244-245
look and feel, 196,
    224-225
progress bars, 237
  labels, 238
  orientation, 238
  updating, 238
Progress.java application,
    238-239
projects, designing layout,
    283-285
resizing windows, 244
scroll panes, 233
  creating, 234
  scrollbars, 234-235
  sizing, 234

sliders, 232-233
ToolBar.java application,
    236
toolbars, 235
  dockable toolbars,
    235-237
  orientation, 235
  user-interface manager,
    224-225
Swing classes, 195
SwingColorTest, 282-294
**SwingConstants class, 211,
232**
**switch statements, 116-118,
121**
Symantec Visual Cafe, 15
system properties, 606-608
**System.out.println()
method, 74**

T

**tables, hash tables, 557,
566-568**
**Tag option (Applet menu),
595**
tags
  <APPLET>, 174-180
    ALIGN, 177
    ARCHIVE, 181
    CODE, 175, 179
    CODEBASE, 179
    HEIGHT, 175
    HSPACE, 178
    VSPACE, 178
    WIDTH, 175

, 177
  javadoc, 598-599, 602
    @author, 599
    @deprecated, 602
    @exception, 602
    @param, 602

@return, 599
@see, 602
@serial, 599
@since, 602
@version, 599
<OBJECT>, 179-180
<PARAM>, 182
    NAME, 182
    VALUE, 182
tasks, 60-61
TCP sockets, 504
    client-side, 504-505
    server-side, 508
    transport-layer
        implementation, 508
    TriviaServer application,
        508
        designing, 509-510
        running, 518-519
        server implementation,
            510, 512-515, 518
telnet connections, 519
**tempo, MIDI files, 369,
    373-374**
terminating
    audio, 361, 371
    threads, 339-343
ternary operators. *See*
    conditional operator
testBlock() method, 114
testing
    applets, 175-176
    instance variables, 90
    Java, 18
    loops, 122
    methods, 137
    Watch.html, 175-176
text
    ASCII, 26
    converting to uppercase,
        463-464
    DOS, 26
    drawing, 299-301
    unformatted, 26

text areas, 212-214
text editors
    choosing, 583-585
    DOS Edit, 584
    NotePad, 584
    WordPad, 584
text fields, 211-212
    event handling
        action events, 275
        item events, 278-280
    password fields, 212
Thawte Web site, 435
**third-party development
    tools, 15**
this keyword, 138, 152
Thread class, 329, 336
Thread variables, 347
**Thread.sleep() class method,
    333**
threaded applications
    clock, 337-339
    writing, 336-337
threads
    applets, 336
    controlling animation, 335
    creating, 336
    run() methods, 337-340
    running, 337
    terminating, 339-343
threads command (jdb), 606
Throwable class, 420
**throwing exceptions, 420,
    426-427, 430-431**
    explicit, 428
    implicit, 428
    inheritance issues,
        429-430
    throws keyword, 427-428
throws keyword, 427-428
timeout values, sockets, 504
**Toolbar.java application,
    236**

toolbars, 235
    adding components, 235
    dockable toolbars,
        235-237
    orientation, 235
Toolbox (Beanbox), 532
**Toolbox window (Beanbox),
    532**
Toolkit class, 343
tools
    appletviewer, 165
    development, 19-20
    functions, 590
    jar, 180
    jdb, 603
    keytool, 436
    SDK 1.3, 589
top-level classes, 413-415
toUpperCase() method, 93
**TRACK return value
    (getAdjustmentType()
    method), 276**
**tracking images, 345,
    355-356**
transient variables, 477-478
Transport layer (RMI), 486
**transport-layer socket
    implementation, 508**
triggering applets, 167
trimToSize() method, 563
**TriviaServer application
    (socket client/server), 508**
    client, running, 518-519
    designing, 509-510
    server, 510
        constructor, 510
        instance variables, 510
        loadData() method,
            514-515
        main() method, 515
        processInput() method,
            512-513
        qna.txt file, 513
        run() method, 510, 512

running, 518-519
source code listing,
515
WAIT_FOR_ANSWER
state, 513
WAIT_FOR_CLIENT
state, 513
WAIT_FOR_
CONFIRM state, 513
**TriviaServer.java
application, 515-518**
troubleshooting. *See also*
debugging
arrays, 111
audio, 361
Class Not Found errors
(UNIX platforms), 581
compiling, 579
fatal errors, 422
for loops, 123
Java applets, 166
MIDI, 365
overloaded methods, 147
SDK 1.3
configuring, 22
installing, 21
variables
class, 92
scope, 139
true value (Boolean), 69
try and catch blocks, 422
try...catch blocks, 423-426
try...finally blocks, 425
Tyler, Denise, 174
types
primitive. *See* primitive
types
variables, 64

U

UIManager class, 224
**unformatted files, saving,
584**
unformatted text, 26
Unicode, 444
**Unicode character set, 63,
70**
**Unicode Consortium Web
site, 71**
**uniform resource locator
(URL), 496**
**UNIT_DECREMENT
return value
(getAdjustmentType()
method), 276**
**UNIT_INCREMENT
return value
(getAdjustmentType()
method), 276**
**UNIX, JDK configuration,
581**
up command (jdb), 606
updating progress bars, 238
**uploading applets to Web
servers, 176**
**uppercase, converting text
to, 463-464**
**URL (uniform resource
locator), 496**
URL objects
creating, 496-497
linking applets, 496
retrieving, 344
URL() method, 496
user coordinate space, 317
**user interface/merging API
(JavaBeans), 527**
user interfaces, frames, 200
**user persistent API
(JavaBeans), 528**

utilities
appletviewer
AppInfo.java sample
application, 597
Applet menu
commands, 595
command line, 590-591
jdb commands, 604-606
policytool, 439
utilities. *See* **tools**
utility classes, 155

V

**VALUE attribute
(<PARAM> tag), 182**
valueOf() method, 94
values
assigning to variables, 66
Boolean, 65, 98
class variables, 91
instance variables, 90-91
shared, 66
variables, 61
access control, 383,
386-387
default access, 383
private access, 384-385
protected access,
385-386
public access, 385
array variables, 108
assigning
values to, 62
to values, 66
casting, 97-99
class, 40, 55, 61, 89
accessing, 389
accessing values, 91
defining, 63, 91
modifying values, 91
troubleshooting, 92
versus instance, 91

class types, 65
class variables, 135
CLASSPATH, 25, 397
constant variables, 66-67
creating, 61
data types, 64-65
datatypes, converting to
   objects, 100-101
declaring, 61
decrementing, 76
duplicating, 140
encapsulation, 383
environment, 606
final, 391
global, 61
incrementing, 76
instance, 40, 55, 61, 89
   accessing values, 89
   length, 111
   modifying, 90-91
   testing, 90
instance variables,
   134-135
interface type, 403
in interfaces, 405
local, 61
   constant, 66
   declaring, 62
multiple, 62, 108
naming, 63
naming conventions, 540
overflow, 83
PATH, 24-25
protecting, 394
scope, 114, 138-140
   lexical scope, 129
   troubleshooting, 139
static, 388-390
Thread, 347
transient variables,
   477-478
types, 64
various platforms, running
Java on, 18-19

Vector class, 557, 560-563
vectors, 557, 560-563
   capacity, 560, 563
   creating, 560
   elements, 561-562
   size, 560, 563
–verbose option (javac), 594
VeriSign Web site, 435
@version tag (javadoc), 599
viewing HTML documents,
   594
virtual machine, 18. See also
   Java interpreter
visible frames, 198
void return type (methods),
   137
VolcanoRobot class
   example, 43
VolcanoRobot.java
   application, 45-46, 135
VSPACE attribute
   (<APPLET> tag), 178

W-Z

waitForID method, 356
WAIT_FOR_ANSWER
   state (TriviaServer), 513
WAIT_FOR_CLIENT state
   (TriviaServer), 513
WAIT_FOR_CONFIRM
   state (TriviaServer), 513
Watch sample applet,
   172-176
Watch.html, 175-176
Watch.java, 173
Web connections, opening,
   499-500
Web pages adding applets
   to, 174-176
Web programming,
   interactive, 11-13

Web sites
   BDK (Bean Development
      Kit), 529
   certificate authorities, 435
   Code Signing resource
      page, 438
   Every Icon applet, 12
   GameFinger, 506
   Gamelan, 539
   Google, 368
   Grunge, 592
   Indigo, 332
   Java, 14, 590
   Java 2 documentation, 68
   JavaBeans, 528, 539
   JavaWorld magazine, 539
   Jave on the Brain, 346
   KPCB, 16
   Naviseek, 45, 579-580
   NetDirect, 553
   Netscape Signing Tool,
      438
   Pardon My Icons, 210
   Sockets, 509
   Sun, 20, 437
   Thawte, 435
   Unicode Consortium, 71
   VeriSign, 435
WebMenu sample applet,
   497
WebMenu.java, 498
weightx constraint, 258
weighty constraint, 258
WellAdjusted.java
   application, 276-277
while loops, 124-126
WIDTH attribute
   (<APPLET> tag), 175
wildcard character (*), 171
windowActivated() method,
   203, 282
WindowAdapter class, 203
windowClosed() method,
   203, 282

windowClosing() method,
  203, 282
windowDeactivated()
  method, 203, 282
windowDeiconified()
  method, 203, 282
windowIconified() method,
  203, 282
WindowListener event
  listener, 270
WindowListener interface,
  202
windowOpened() method,
  203, 282
windows, 197
  applet, 169-171
  background, 168
  BeanBox, 532-533
  clearing, 310
  creating, 200
  Edit File Type, 588
  event handling, 282
  exiting, 202-204
  frames, 197
    displaying, 198
    exiting, 199
    hiding, 198
    locations, 199
    sizing, 198
    user interfaces, 200
    visible, 198
  GUI, resizing, 244
  monitoring, 202-203
  MS-DOS Prompt, 572
  scrolling, 331-333, 335
  Swing, 244
Windows
  installing SDK 1.3 on,
    21-23
  Java programs, 28-31
Windows 95, 24-25
Windows 98, 24-25
Windows 2000, 25
Windows NT, 25

wizards, SDK Setup, 22
word processors. See text
  editors
WordPad, 584
world20.mdb, 548
wrapper classes, 142
write() method, 445, 451,
  461, 472
writeBoolean() method, 472
writeByte() method, 472
writeBytes() method, 473
WriteBytes.java application,
  449
writeChar() method, 473
writeChars() method, 473
writeDouble() method, 473
writeFloat() method, 473
writeInt() method, 457, 473
writeLong() method, 473
writeObject() method, 472
WritePrimes.java
  application, 455-456
writeShort() method, 473
writeStream() method, 454
writing
  multiple bytes, 449
  to streams, 445
    buffered, 451-454
    character, 461-462
    output, 449-450,
      472-473
  text files, 461
  threaded applications,
    336-337

XOR operator, 78

Zeldman, Jeffrey, 210

Other Related Titles

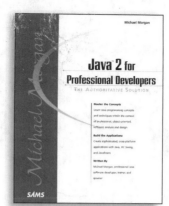

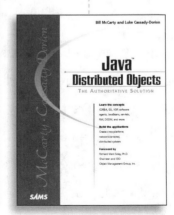